Covert Racism

Studies in Critical Social Sciences

Series Editor
David Fasenfest
Wayne State University

Editorial Board
Chris Chase-Dunn, University of California-Riverside
G. William Domhoff, University of California-Santa Cruz
Colette Fagan, Manchester University
Martha Gimenez, University of Colorado, Boulder
Heidi Gottfried, Wayne State University
Karin Gottschall, University of Bremen
Bob Jessop, Lancaster University
Rhonda Levine, Colgate University
Jacqueline O'Reilly, University of Brighton
Mary Romero, Arizona State University
Chizuko Ueno, University of Tokyo

The titles published in this series are listed at brill.nl/scss.

Covert Racism
Theories, Institutions, and Experiences

Edited by Rodney D. Coates

Haymarket Books
Chicago, IL

First published in 2011 by Brill Academic Publishers, The Netherlands
© 2011 Koninklijke Brill NV, Leiden, The Netherlands

Published in paperback in 2012 by
Haymarket Books
P.O. Box 180165
Chicago, IL 60618
773-583-7884
www.haymarketbooks.org

ISBN: 978-1-60846-210-0

Trade distribution:
In the US, Consortium Book Sales, www.cbsd.com
In Canada, Publishers Group Canada, www.pgcbooks.ca
In the UK, Turnaround Publisher Services, www.turnaround-psl.com
In Australia, Palgrave Macmillan, www.palgravemacmillan.com.au
In all other countries, Publishers Group Worldwide, www.pgw.com

Cover design by Ragina Johnson.

This book was published with the generous support of Lannan Foundation and the Wallace Global Fund.

Printed in Canada with union labor.

10 9 8 7 6 5 4 3 2

Library of Congress Cataloging-in-Publication data is available.

CONTENTS

List of Tables and Figures ix
List of Contributors xi

Covert Racism: An Introduction 1
   Rodney D. Coates

PART I

THEORETICAL PERSPECTIVES ON COVERT RACISM

The Impact of Racial and Nonracial Structural Forces on
   Poor Urban Blacks 19
   William Julius Wilson
The New Racism: The Racial Regime of Post-Civil Rights
   America 41
   Eduardo Bonilla-Silva and David Dietrich
Race Versus Racism as Cause 69
   Tukufu Zuberi
Colorblind White Dominance 85
   Ian Haney López
When Good People Do Bad Things: The Nature
   of Contemporary Racism 111
   John F. Dovidio and Samuel L. Gaertner
Covert Racism: Theory, Types and Examples 121
   Rodney D. Coates

PART II

COVERT RACISM AND INSTITUTIONS

Protecting White Power in a Corporate Hierarchy 143
   Sharon M. Collins and Georgiann Davis
If You're White, You're Alright: The Reproduction
   of Racial Hierarchies in Bollywood Films 155
   Angie Beeman and Anjana Narayan

Race, Culture and the Pursuit of Employment: A Research Series on Hiring Practices at Temporary Employment Agencies 175
  Monique W. Morris and Sirithon Thanasombat
Challenging our Textbooks and our Teachings: Examining the Reproduction of Racism in the Sociology Classroom 189
  Sarah Chivers and Jolene D. Smyth
Challenging Racial Battle Fatigue on Historically White Campuses: A Critical Race Examination of Race-Related Stress.. 211
  William A. Smith, Tara J. Yosso and Daniel G. Solórzano
Covert Racism in the U.S. and Globally 239
  Rodney D. Coates

PART III

COVERT RACISM AND THE INDIVIDUAL

The Ineffable Strangeness of Race 269
  Patricia J. Williams
The Social Situation of the Black Executive: Black and White Identities in the Corporate World.. 291
  Elijah Anderson
Now You Don't See It, Now You Don't: White Lives as Covert Racism 321
  David L. Brunsma
Aren't They All Dead? Passive Racism Against Native Americans 333
  Claudia A. Fox Tree
Silent Racism.. 353
  Barbara Trepagnier
"One Step From Suicide": The Holistic Experience of Being Black in America.. 365
  Leslie H. Picca, Joe R. Feagin and Tracy L. Johns
Lifestyles of the Rich and Racist.. 385
  Corey Dolgon
Journey to Awareness: Learning to Recognize Invisible Racism 405
  Janet Morrison

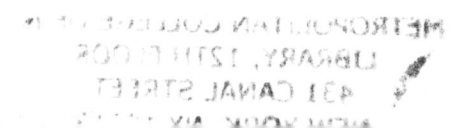

PART IV

EPILOGUE

Post-Racial Myths: Disrupting Covert Racism
and the Racial Matrix 421
Rodney D. Coates

Bibliography 427
Index 459

METROPOLITAN COLLEGE OF NY
LIBRARY, 12TH FLOOR
431 CANAL STREET
NEW YORK, NY 10013

LIST OF TABLES AND FIGURES

Tables

Tufuku Zuberi

1. Percent of Articles Published 76

Monique W. Morris and Sirithon Thanasombat

1. Response Rate by Ethnicity and Gender 179
2. Response Rate by Ethnicity and Region 188

Sarah Chivers and Jolene D. Smyth

1. Summary of Findings 204

Figures

Tufuku Zuberi

1. Published Race Articles that use Regression, 1991–2000 77
2. Race Articles Using Race as an Effect 77
3. Percent of Regression Articles Using Race as an Effect 78

Rodney D. Coates, "Covert Racism: Theory, Types and Examples"

1. Typologies of Covert Racism with Examples 123

LIST OF CONTRIBUTORS

ELIJAH ANDERSON is the William K. Lanman Professor of Sociology at Yale University. Dr. Anderson is one of the nation's most respected scholars in the field of urban inequality. He has written and edited numerous books, book chapters, articles, and reports on the black experience. His books include *Code of the Street: Decency, Violence, and the Moral Life of the Inner City*(1999), winner of the 2000 Komarovsky Award from the Eastern Sociological Association; *Streetwise: Race, Class, and Change in an Urban Community*(1990), winner of the American Sociological Association's Robert E. Park award for the best published book in the area of Urban Sociology; and the classic sociological work, *A Place on the Corner: A Study of Black Street Corner Men* (1978; 2nd ed., 2003). His edited volume, *Against the Wall: Poor, Young, Black, and Male* (University of Pennsylvania Press) is based on that conference. In April 2008, Dr. Anderson held a conference at Yale University titled "Urban Ethnography: Its Traditions and Its Future." Works based on that conference were published in a special double issue of *Ethnography* in the spring of 2009.

ANGIE BEEMAN is an Assistant Professor at the City University of New York-Borough of Manhattan Community College. Her research interests include racism theory, media, social movements, and gender. She has published research on racism and film in *Ethnic and Racial Studies*, predatory lending in *Critical Sociology*, and domestic violence in *Violence Against Women*. Her dissertation, which received an award from the Society for the Study of Social Problems, examines the strategic use, limitations, and challenges of color-blind ideology in grassroots interracial social movement organizations.

EDUARDO BONILLA-SILVA is a Professor of Sociology at Duke. To date he has published four books, *White Supremacy and Racism in the Post-Civil Rights Era*, *Racism without Racists*, *White Out* (with Woody Doane), and *White Logic, White Methods* (with Tukufu Zuberi). He is working on a book titled *The Invisible Weight of Whiteness: The Racial Grammar of Everyday Life in America*. He is the 2007 recipient of the *Lewis A. Coser Award* for theoretical agenda setting in sociology.

DAVID L. BRUNSMA is Associate Professor of Sociology and Black Studies at the University of Missouri in Columbia. He is author, coauthor, or editor of numerous books and articles, most notably: *The Leading Rogue State: The United States and Human Rights* (Paradigm, 2008); *The Sociology of Katrina: Perspectives on a Modern Catastrophe* (Rowman & Littlefield, 2007); *Mixed Messages: Multiracial Identity in the 'Color-Blind' Era* (Lynne Rienner, 2006) and *The School Uniform Movement and What it Tells Us About American Education: A Symbolic Crusade* (Scarecrow, 2004) among others. He continues to study the strategies and negotiated manifestations of racial identity in the post civil-rights era as illuminated by the interplay of social structural, cultural/symbolic, interactional, and biographical/narrative life structures. He is currently investigating human rights abuses in the United States, pedagogical strategies for teaching white students about race and racism, structural anti-racisms, and importing an epistemology of justice into the discipline of sociology. He is a member of Sociologists Without Borders and is committed to investigating and initiating ways in which scholarship can be actively used to combat structural injustices. He lives in Columbia, MO with his wife Rachel and has three wonderful children: Karina, Thomas, and Henry.

SARAH CHIVERS, Ph.D., is a sociologist with research interests in social inequality. She currently works as research consultant to the Graduate Research School at Edith Cowan University in Western Australia. Her research focuses on improving access to and equity in higher education.

RODNEY D. COATES is a professor of sociology and gerontology at Miami University. His 2004 Brill edited volume Race and ethnicity: Across Time, Space and Discipline received the Library Associations Choice Award. He is the 2007 recipient of the Joseph H. Hines career award for scholarship given by the Association of Black Sociologists.

SHARON M. COLLINS is an Associate Professor of Sociology at the University of Illinois, Chicago. She earned her doctorate degree from Northwestern University in 1988. Her book, *Black Corporate Executives*, published by Temple University Press (1997) analyzes the post-civil rights careers of African Americans in corporate America. This work has been featured in *Black Enterprise* magazine, *The Chicago Tribune*, *U.S. News and World Report*, *Newsweek* magazine, as well as by the

British Broadcasting Corporation (BBC), and WGN television. Dr. Collins continues to be interested in racial and workplace inequality. She is working on a follow-up study of African American executives and on various projects on the issue of diversity.

GEORGIANN DAVIS is a sociology doctoral student at the University of Illinois at Chicago. Her research interests include understanding racial and gender inequalities, diversity rhetoric, and the social organization of the medical profession, specifically its relationship with the intersex rights movement.

COREY DOLGON is a Professor of Sociology and Director of Community Based Learning at Stonehill College. He is author of the award winning book, The *End of the Hamptons: Scenes From the Class Struggle in America's Paradise* (NYU Press) and two new books, *Pioneers of Public Sociology: 30 Years of* Humanity and Society (Sloan Publishing) and *Social Problems: A Service Learning Approach* (Pine Forge Press).

DAVID DIETRICH is a PhD candidate in sociology at Duke University. His areas of interest are racial and ethnic relations, social movements, immigration, social stratification, sociological theory, and sociology of law. His recent research includes examinations of racism in the popular debate over illegal immigration, race in online virtual worlds, and an examination of anti-affirmative action protests on college campuses. His dissertation is entitled "Rebellious Conservatives: A Study of Conservative Social Movements."

JOHN F. DOVIDIO (MA, PhD in social psychology from the University of Delaware) is currently Professor of Psychology at Yale University. Before that, he was a professor at the University of Connecticut and at Colgate University, where he also served as Provost and Dean of the Faculty. Dr. Dovidio has been Editor of the *Journal of Personality and Social Psychology – Interpersonal Relations and Group Processes* and of *Personality and Social Psychology Bulletin* and Associate Editor of *Group Processes and Intergroup Relations*. He is currently Co-Editor of *Social Issues and Policy Review*. Dr. Dovidio's research interests are in stereotyping, prejudice, and discrimination; social power and non-verbal communication; and altruism and helping. He is co-author of several books, including *Emergency intervention; The Psychology of helping and altruism; The social psychology of prosocial behavior;* and

Reducing intergroup bias: The Common Ingroup Identity Model; as well as co-editor of *Prejudice, discrimination, and racism; Power, dominance, and nonverbal behavior; On the nature of prejudice: 50 years after Allport*; and *Intergroup misunderstandings: Impact of divergent social realities*.

JOE FEAGIN was born in San Angelo, Texas at the end of the Great Depression. He was raised in Houston, where he graduated from high school. Dr. Feagin graduated from Baylor University in 1960 and went on to acquire his Ph.D. in sociology at Harvard University in 1966. Over forty-two years Dr. Feagin has taught at the University of Massachusetts (Boston), University of California (Riverside), University of Texas, University of Florida, and Texas A&M University. Dr. Feagin has done much research work on a variety of racism and sexism issues and has served as the Scholar-in-Residence at the U.S. Commission on Civil Rights. He has written 53 books, one of which (Ghetto Revolts) was nominated for a Pulitzer Prize. Among his books, some co-authored, are Systemic Racism (2006); Racist America (2000); The First R: How Children Learn Race and Racism (2001); Racial and Ethnic Relations (2008); The Many Costs of Racism (2003); White Men on Race (2003); Black in Blue: African-American Police Officers and Racism (2004); and, most recently, Two-Faced Racism: Whites in the Frontstage and the Backstage (2007). He is the 2006 recipient of a Harvard Alumni Association achievement award and was the 1999–2000 president of the American Sociological Association. He is currently Ella C. McFadden Professor at Texas A & M University.

CLAUDIA A. FOX TREE has a Masters Degree in Educational Research from Northeastern University. She has over 20 years experience as a grade 6–8 public school special education teacher and as a facilitator of anti-bias, multicultural courses and workshops for students and adults. Claudia is on the board for the Massachusetts Center for Native Americans (MCNAA) and is the Massachusetts liaison for the United Confederation of Taíno People (UCTP). She has presented at numerous conferences and workshops across New England and also in Germany and the Caribbean, both places being part of her ancestry.

SAMUEL L. GAERTNER (B.A., 1964, Brooklyn College, PhD, 1970; The City University of New York: Graduate Center) is Professor of Psychology at the University of Delaware. His research interests involve intergroup relations with a focus on understanding and reducing prejudice, discrimination and racism. He has served on the editorial boards of the *Journal of Personality and Social Psychology, Personality and Social Psychology Bulletin*, and *Group Processes and Intergroup Relations*. Professor Gaertner's research, together with John F. Dovidio, has been supported by grants from the Office of Naval Research, the National Institutes of Mental Health and currently, the National Science Foundation. Together with John Dovidio, he shared the Gordon Allport Intergroup Relations Prize in 1985 and 1998, as well as the Kurt Lewin Memorial Award (a career award) from the Society for the Psychological Study of Social Issues, Division 9 of the American Psychological Association.

TRACY L. JOHNS is an Assistant Professor in Political Science at the University of Florida and Research Director at the Florida Survey Research Center. Her research explores how organizations and institutions create contexts supportive of deviant behavior, including the relationships between crime, the criminal justice system, and people of color. Recent work examines potential jurors' attitudes of guilt or innocence based on media constructions of "terrorist" defendants.

IAN HANEY LÓPEZ is Professor of Law at the University of California, Berkeley, where he teaches in the areas of race and constitutional law. Among his groundbreaking publications are *White by Law: The Legal Construction of Race* (NYU 1996), and *Racism on Trial: The Chicano Fight for Justice* (Harvard/Belknap 2003). His numerous articles have appeared, among other places, in the *Yale Law Journal*, the *Stanford Law Review*, and the *Pennsylvania Law Review*; and he has published opinion pieces in the *New York Times* and the *Los Angeles Times*. His current research examines the emergence and operation of a new racial paradigm of colorblind white dominance.

MONIQUE W. MORRIS has over 20 years of professional and volunteer experience as an advocate in the areas of education, civil rights, juvenile and social justice. Ms. Morris is the CEO of the MWM Consulting Group, LLC, a firm that conducts research and provides technical assistance to advance concepts of fairness, diversity, and inclusion in the public and private sphere. Ms. Morris has served as Vice President for Economic Programs, Advocacy and Research for the National Association for the Advancement of Colored People (NAACP),

Director of Research for the Thelton E. Henderson Center for Social Justice at the University of California Berkeley Law School, and Director of the Discrimination Research Center.

JANET MORRISON graduated from Harding University with a Bachelor's degree in Social Work. She began her professional career coordinating the food pantry operation at Central Dallas Ministries in 1995. Throughout that time she volunteered in the Dallas Independent School District and coordinated different activities for the children in her neighborhood. In January 1998 she became the Director of Education, coordinating after-school and summer programs for children. She created the University of Values summer program and trained community teenagers to become teachers and supervisors of the program. She partners and collaborates with city and non-profit entities to provide quality experiences in the summer and after-school programs, assist with educational training, and provide resources that equip families to engage in activism for themselves and their children. She is an adjunct professor for Texas A&M-Commerce, teaching a course in Diversity and Equity in Education.

ANJANA NARAYAN is an assistant professor in the Department of Psychology and Sociology at Cal Poly Pomona. Her 2009 book, *Living our Religions: South Asian American Hindu and Muslim Women Narrate Their Experiences*, brings to life the hidden stories of South-Asian American women.

LESLIE HOUTS PICCA is an Assistant Professor in the Department of Sociology, Anthropology, and Social Work at the University of Dayton. She has publications in the areas of racial relations, and adolescent sexuality. With Joe Feagin, she is co-author of the book *Two-Faced Racism: Whites in the Backstage and Frontstage* (Routledge, 2007). Her research on racial relations has been nationally recognized, and she has been interviewed by CNN, the Associated Press, Congressional Quarterly, and National Public Radio, among others.

WILLIAM A. SMITH is an associate professor in the department of Education, Culture & Society and the Ethnic Studies Program at the University of Utah. Dr. Smith is also the Associate Dean for Diversity, Access, & Equity in the College of Education as well as a Special Assistant to the President & NCAA Faculty Athletic Representative.

JOLENE D. SMYTH, Ph.D., is an assistant professor in the Survey Research and Methodology Program and the Department of Sociology at the University of Nebraska-Lincoln. Her primary research interests include survey measurement and nonresponse as well as gender processes in the rural context.

DANIEL G. SOLORZANO is a Professor of Social Sciences and Comparative Education at the UCLA Graduate School of Education and Information Studies. In addition, he is the Associate Director of the UCLA Chicano Studies Research Center and the Associate Director of the University of California All Campus Consortium on Research for Diversity (UC ACCORD).

SIRI THANASOMBAT graduated *magna cum laude* from the University of California, Berkeley where she double majored in Sociology and Ethnic Studies.

Siri currently works as a Trial Attorney for the U.S. Equal Employment Opportunity Commission in Los Angeles, California, where she litigates employment discrimination cases. She received her law degree at New York University School of Law, where she was a Root Tilden Kern Fellow and an Articles Editor for the *NYU Law Review*.

BARBARA TREPAGNIER is a professor of sociology at Texas State University-San Marcos. She is a member of the Task Force on Racial Disproportionality in Child Protective Services for the State of Texas. Her book, *Silent Racism: How Well-Meaning White People Perpetuate the Racial Divide* (Paradigm 2006), is used in various disciplines including social work and education in addition to sociology.

PATRICIA J. WILLIAMS is the James L. Dohr Professor of Law at Columbia University. She writes the column "Diary of a Mad Law Professor" for The Nation Magazine.

WILLIAM JULIUS WILSON is the Lewis P. and Linda L. Geyser University Professor at Harvard University and Director of the Joblessness and Urban Poverty Research Program at the John F. Kennedy School of Government. He has been elected to the National Academy of Sciences, the American Academy of Arts and Sciences, the American Philosophical Society, the National Academy of Education and the Institute of Medicine. He is also past President of the American

Sociological Association, and is a MacArthur Prize Fellow. In 1998 he was awarded the National Medal of Science. His books include *Power, Racism and Privilege* (1973), *The Declining Significance of Race* (1978), *The Truly Disadvantaged* (1987), *When Work Disappears* (1996), *The Bridge over the Racial Divide* (1999), *There Goes the Neighborhood* (2006, co-author), and *Good Kids from Bad Neighborhoods* (2006, co-author). His latest book, *More than Just Race: Being Poor and Black in the Inner City*, was published in January 2009.

TARA J. YOSSO is an Associate Professor in the Department of Chicana and Chicano Studies at the University of California, Santa Barbara. Her teaching and research apply critical race theory to issues of educational access and equity. She is the author of *Critical Race Counterstories Along the Chicana/Chicano Educational Pipeline*, (Routledge 2006).

TUKUFU ZUBERI is the Lasry Family Professor of Race Relations, Professor and Chair of the Department of Sociology, and the Faculty Associate Director of the Center for Africana Studies at the University of Pennsylvania. He has also been a visiting professor at Mekerere University in Kampala, Uganda and the University of Dar es Salaam in Tanzania. Tukufu Zuberi is best known for his *Thicker Than Blood: An Essay on how Racial Statistics Lie* (Minneapolis: University of Minnesota Press, 2001), *Swing Low, Sweet Chariot: The Mortality Cost of Colonizing Liberia in the Nineteenth-Century* (Chicago: University of Chicago Press, 1995) and most recently *White Logic, White Methods* (with Eduardo Bonilla-Silva) (New York: Rowman and Littlefield Publishers, Inc.)

COVERT RACISM: AN INTRODUCTION

Rodney D. Coates

In the movie *Matrix (1999)* a simple principle is revealed. Reality is often obscured, and what we perceive to be real is not always real. *Matrix* opens with a scene in which Neo, a loner, stumbles upon the *Matrix* and begins his search for Morpheus *(the Greek god of dreams)* and for answers. As the story unfolds, we find that the Matrix was explicitly created by intelligent machines in order to pacify human imagination, drive and individuality. The real purpose of the *Matrix*, Neo learns, was to maintain this illusion of reality while exploiting the humans for the benefit of the machines in control.

We also live in a kind of matrix, a racial matrix that serves to create and preserve an illusion of reality. In this illusion, differences in outcomes associated with racial hierarchies are defined as the natural or normal functioning of a democratic system based upon meritocracy. This racial matrix, long identified with American and western social structure, has its own rules and realities. Similarly, within the racial matrix, one must make a conscious choice to "unplug" or risk living experiencing illusion as reality within the confines of the Matrix.

The difference between these two matrixes is that in the movie *Matrix* one merely has to take a red pill, as an act of faith, to accomplish the disengagement. In our real world there is no little 'red pill' but rather a conscious choice to explore, decode, and transform the Racial Matrix. As with the movie *Matrix*, the racial matrix has its own code(s) that must be understood if we are to explore, interpret and/ or transform it. Our purpose in this volume is to explore covert racism in an attempt to decode, interpret and hopefully transform this new racial matrix.

Towards a Definition of Covert Racism

Covert racism may be viewed as racism which is hidden; secret; private; covered; disguised; insidious; or concealed. Covert racism varies by context. As we shall see below, understanding this contextual variability provides us with a key means by which to decode, interpret and transform the racial matrix. We shall explore this variability below. Regardless of context, the most pervasive qualities associated with covert racism are that it serves to subvert, distort, restrict, and deny rewards, privileges, access, and benefits to racial minorities.

Plausible deniability, an intrinsic component of covert racism, benefits perpetrators by allowing them to deny responsibility and culpability while simultaneously undermining its victim's ability to claim damage(s). In some cases individuals or groups may not realize or be aware that they are guilty of covert racism until it is pointed out to them.[1] This often happens when one grows up in a society with a history of racism. It has become so embedded within the national culture that many seem impervious to its existence. As we will see below, in the past the codes of the racial matrix were much more visible, objective, and identifiable. These codes – lodged in the laws, customs, and practices of a segregated America – helped define the racial matrix. The success of civil rights activism, laws, and judicial decrees has not only served to decode but also to nullify the more obvious forms of the racial matrix. Today's racial codes are more subtle, more hidden, and less obvious. These subtle, hidden and less obvious racial codes have served to create a new racial matrix which we characterize as covert racism.

Covert racism, subtle in application, often appears hidden by norms of association, affiliation, group membership and/or identity. As such, covert racism is often excused or confused with mechanisms of exclusion and inclusion, ritual and ceremony, acceptance and rejection. Covert racism operates as a boundary keeping mechanism whose primary purpose is to maintain social distance between racial majorities and racial minorities. Such boundary mechanisms work best when they are assumed natural, legitimate, and normal. These boundary mechanisms are typically taught subconsciously or even unconsciously within social institutions and groups. Consequently, covert racism often undetected, is inherently inculcated with each generation of new members. At the heart of covert racism one finds a deliberate policy of denial, omission, and obfuscation of black, red, tan, brown and yellow issues, persons and groups. In this pseudo-color blind universe, race appears nullified, trivialized, marginalized, or deemed

---

[1] Much like the sexist jokes of the past, many individuals claimed innocence until we learned that they were indeed sexist.

nonexistent. This volume is divided into three major sections dealing with a) Theoretical perspectives on covert racism, b) Covert racism and institutions, and c) Covert racism and the individual. The recent election of America's first black president raises a series of questions specific to covert racism. Recognizing the significance of this election, an epilogue has been added to critique what some are calling a 'post racial narrative'.

Theoretical Perspectives on Covert Racism

All too often when we discuss race, we tend to think in binary terms. The American racial landscape has never been a simple one of rich or poor, nor was it ever just white or black. America has always been multiply arrayed along a mosaic of status positions, as well as, cultural groups. Binary racial categories, a social convention and construction, obscure the complexity associated with racial hierarchies. William Julius Wilson's paper "The Impact of Racial and Nonracial Structural Forces on Poor Urban Blacks" helps traverse this terrain. In this paper, Wilson begins with a discussion of racism and one form of covert racism – laissez faire racism. Laissez fair racism serves to distort the racial landscape for most Americans who have little direct knowledge or understanding of the complex nature of race and poverty in inner-city America. In the hopes of providing a broader understanding of these problems, Wilson highlights the role of two very important structural factors – state political actions (including those that may be considered covert racist policies) and economic forces – that have contributed to the emergences and persistence of concentrated poverty in poor inner-city black neighborhoods By analyzing these two factors Wilson argues for a new political agenda for America's ghetto poor.

Racism is often confounded with attitudes about race. Failure to understand the distinctions between racial structures and racial attitudes leads to the inability to distinguish between causes and symptoms. Racial attitudes, behaviors, and actions are symptomatic of institutional, ideological, and cultural structures which define, legitimate, and promote racial outcomes within a given society. Specifically, as pointed out by Eduardo Bonilla-Silva and David Dietrich, in "The New Racism: The Racial Regime of Post-Civil Rights America" racism refers to structural, social, political, economic and ideological relations which effects life outcomes of various racial groups. Racism, as a form of ideology, serves to define, organize, and coordinate race relations within a given society. As a consequence, racism produces a definable and identifiable racial structure that must be understood if we are to understand the dynamics of race relations. Bonilla-Silva and Dietrich argue, looking through this lens, allows for the identification of a new racial structure in the United States. The elements that comprise this new racial structure are: 1) the increasingly *covert* nature of racial discourses and racial practices; 2) the avoidance of racial terminology and the ever growing claim by whites that they experience "reverse racism"; 3) the elaboration of a racial agenda over political matters that eschews direct racial references; 4) the invisibility of most mechanisms to reproduce racial inequality; and, finally, 5) the rearticulation of some racial practices characteristic of the Jim Crow period of race relations. Although many of these practices are manifestations of the legacies of slavery and Jim Crow in this country, the evidence suggests that blatant forms of discrimination (as in angry white men with white hoods and their traditional discriminatory practices) have been subsumed by newer, more subtle forms acting at both the structural and experiential level.

The next paper, "Race Versus Racism as Cause" by Tukufu Zuberi, argues that increasingly authors use race as a proxy for genetic variation, which subverts even the most positive attempts to understand the impact of racial stratification on equality, freedom and justice. He explains that the major journals publish articles in which the authors' statistical results restate anachronistic theories of race. Zuberi argues for an empirically grounded study of racism where researchers "must be vigilant not to commit 'racial reasoning' which effectively problematizes the modeling of racial conceptualizations and thus obscures causality". All too often, race is treated as a relationship rather than the cause of racial outcomes. For example, racial profiling is less a matter of the race of the individual being profiled, and more a matter of the racial beliefs and values of the police officer doing the profiling. Thus being a member of a particular race does not cause a particular outcome. Rather our response to a particular label causes the outcomes in questions. Zuberi explains that whereas an African American may be racially profiled while driving a luxury vehicle, the police that stopped him did not react to his black skin or the idea that he might be a criminal. Rather, the driver was stopped because of the racial values and beliefs of the police officer. Similarly, other racial outcomes are more associated with the racial attitudes of those making judgments and decisions, than the racial identity of the individuals who are being judged. By analyzing the racial language utilized to interpret race results we are more apt to understand the mechanism by which racism operates. Zuberi concludes by demonstrating how covert racism, acting as racial reasoning, distorts what we normally view as objective research. Racial reasoning, however, is not limited to academic journals. At times, as pointed out by the next article by Ian Haney Lopez, racial reasoning hides behind the façade of color-blind policies.

Currently, within the United States, it is in vogue to discuss color-blind policies, structures, and practices. Hiding behind the illusion of colorblindness, covert racism continues to deflect and distort our racial realities. These distortions lead to what Ian Haney Lopez describes as "Colorblind White Dominance". Lopez argues that the current racial dynamic reflects and is obscured by the progress of the civil rights movement and the increasingly diverse demographic patterns. Thus while overt racial supremacy ideologies are no longer in vogue, we nevertheless find covert manifestations of racial supremacy in less identifiable ways. Lopez demonstrates that these covert manifestations are most identifiable in racial interactions associated with immigration, integration, and intermarriage. One aspect of these more covert manifestations is the presumption that we have somehow become colorblind. Colorblindness serves to essentially redefine the racial landscape in such ways that race and racism are perceived as being relics of our historical past. These newer forms of racism become imbedded in neoconservative arguments. These neoconservative arguments specifically argue that any contemporary examples of racial outcomes merely reflect racial legacies or inertia. Even more insidious is the racial remedies of the past –such as Affirmative Action, immigration reform, and bilingual programs – are seen not only as crutches which reward failure, irresponsibility, and poor choices but also penalizes whites for essentially being white. Thus, the new form of racism –reverse racism – vilifies whites by making them guilty by virtue of being white. Simultaneously, minorities are encouraged to continuously embrace and therefore relive past group victimizations. In essence minorities become defined as permanent victims by virtue of being minorities. Lopez concludes that this form of covert racism serves to preserve white dominance while simultaneously delegitimizing and dismissing the contemporary claims of victimization by racial minorities.

Much like the commercial "Is it live or is it Memorex?" we often ponder over what is actually real, perceived, or fictional. What exactly is racial identity? Is it real? Is it a perceived reality, or a fictional representation? Does racial identity clarify reality or does it confound that reality? These questions of representation and identity take us into the psychological realm. Racial identity, representations, and perceptions clearly have not only a structural but a psychological component as well.

Psychologically, covert racism, functions as a foil by which mechanisms of racialization are screened, evaluated, interpreted and experienced. Cognitive racial maps are created and maintained which provide meaning, validity, and legitimacy to our racialized existence. It is because of racial cognition that racism often goes undetected, unnoticed, and acquires its subjective character. John F. Dovidio and Samuel L. Gaertner argue, in "When Good People Do Bad Things: The Nature of Contemporary Racism", that these cognitive maps serves to hide racial intentionality. By decoding these racial cognitive maps, Dovidio and Gaertner provide additional insights into the mechanisms of covert racism. From this perspective, we learn that white identity may be viewed as existing along a continuum ranging from conservative to liberal. Racial attitudes, associated with this continuum, help explain variability in behaviors. They argue that both conservative and liberal Whites racially discriminate –'but in different ways'. Although much attention has been given to the more blatant racism ascribed to conservative whites often the racialized behaviors of liberal whites goes undetected. So-called liberal whites are not immune to racial discrimination. Liberal whites, sensitive to political correctness, will not publicly or consciously advocate racist views. Oftentimes, liberal whites harbor unconscious negative feelings about blacks that lead to decidedly racist reactions. Racial discrimination associated with liberal whites, both subtle and unconscious, is "rooted in normal, often adaptive, psychological processes". Dovidio and Gaertner argue, that these psychological processes, arising from a need to feel in control, often serve to devalue the racial other. Thus, the covert qualities of these psychological mechanisms help to preserve and reinforce the racial status quo.

In the final analysis, we are yet left with an extremely tenacious beast with multiple tentacles, structures and expressions. Covert racism, as we have seen is both multi-layered and multi-dimensional. The problem yet remains to detail a practical theoretical critique that allows us to come to grips with the multi-layered, multi-dimensionality of covert racism. In the next chapter, entitled "Covert Racism, Theory, Types and Examples" I provide such a critique. Specifically, I demonstrate that layers and dimensions of covert racism can be best understood through the use of a typology. At the very least, it would appear that covert racism can operate at both the individual and the group level, and given these levels we could further specify that it can be both formal and informal. Now while these can be grouped categorically as types, it should be understood that they reflect more of a continuum. Thus, we would suggest that a particular covert act is more or less at the individual or group level, and it is more or less formal or informal. To the extent that covert racial acts are repeated over an extended period of time, then we can speak of specific patterns. The patterning of covert racial acts, finally, suggests the operation of not only intentionality, but also norms, mechanisms, and at the most developed stage – institutions, structures, and systems. By implication, covert racism is both historically and societally specific. Systemically, for example, covert racism operates across several societal institutions, structures. Given this typology the new, subtle forms of racism –from racial shunning to exclusion, racial profiling to racial exceptionalism, racial tokens to "odd-man out" exemplifies the experiences of the racial other confronting and being confronted by covert racism.

Covert Racism and Institutions

Covert racism obscures the realities experienced by racial non-elites. These realities, experienced within institutional structures, are often confounded or confused with personal or group attributes. Covert racism, as implied above, produces specific outcomes typically confused with or legitimated as economic inertia and decline, catastrophic institutional failure, and the resulting political and social morass, fatalism, and nihilism. All too often these systemic failures are presumed to reflect personal choices or group failure. Misdiagnosed, covert racism, results in blaming the victim, defining the debilitating plight as a culture of poverty, or a poverty of will. In such situations we often speak of cultural deficits, deficient human capital, and the like. These situations, made worse by the presumption that racism is a thing of the past, posits that any failure to achieve parity is a failure of the individual or group. Unfortunately, this view is not only naive, but dangerous as well. So rather than looking toward the structure for answers and to provide remedies, we turn to trying to reform and transform the victim. Racism, stripped of its more overt racial components, yet remains systemically within the institutional structures of society. The purpose of this section is to understand the institutional manifestations of covert racism.

Sharon M. Collins and Georgian Davis's article "Protecting White Power in Corporate Hierarchy" demonstrates how covert racism serves to not only delegitimize black success but also effectively preserves white corporate hegemony. Specifically, they explain how programs and objectives of diversity managers are systematically undermined by serving as covert or "race-based resistance to sharing organizational power". In this regard, Collins and Davis demonstrate that white hiring managers, as a form of racial gate-keepers, encourage or allow the flourishing "of stereotypes and boundary heightening" mechanisms through which diversity initiatives are filtered. Covertly this filtering serves to redefine the initiatives, their goals, and their implementations and thereby effectively thwarting the likelihood of any real diversity taking place.

Racial identities, while in actual flux, present themselves as constants. One of the functions of covert racism is to preserve the relative parameters of racial identities. One of the primary vehicles by which and through which racial identities are preserved is through the mass media. Recent critiques of the "black/white" dichotomy have suggested that increasing migration within the U.S. has led to a blurring of the color line. In America, the dominant media is found in movies. One of the racial functions of movies is to preserve and transmit American cultural and racial values both nationally and internationally. As pointed out by Beeman and Narayan –"If You're White, You're Alright: The Reproduction of Racial Hierarchies in Bollywood Film" – movies and films encourage identification with and acceptance of a racial hierarchy which essentially reproduces a black/white dichotomy. Drawing from cultural studies and critical race theory, they contend that the media acts as a hegemonic device communicating the racialized "black/white" hierarchy to Indian immigrants prior to and after their migration to the U.S. This medium successfully indoctrinates each wave of immigrants into the U.S. racial hierarchy, culture and structure. Thus, even though we have seen a shift in the migratory stream from those favoring Europeans to those increasingly represented by Asian Indian – the value of whiteness is preserved. Correspondingly, Asian Indians are increasingly more likely to identify with whiteness, and devalue blackness. "Bollywood" accomplishes this semblance of racial constancy by encouraging Asian Indians to believe that in order to achieve the "American Dream" they must accept the perception that white is right and that any association, identification, or affiliation with African Americans must be rejected.

National and international crises frequently serve to unmask the more blatant aspects of covert racism. It is during such times that we notice a heightened racial intensity through such mechanisms as racial profiling, racial exclusion, and racial animosity. Covert racism, masquerading as concerns for national defense and security, may take on the semblance of legitimacy. Morris and Thanasombat, in "Race, Culture and the Pursuit of Employment" document this process and demonstrate how Muslim Americans were targeted after 9-1-1. They effectively argue that in the aftermath of this attack, Muslim Americans witnessed diminished employment opportunities as employment agencies screened potential job applicants by names and not qualifications. Although unacceptable, results showed that individuals with Muslim names, especially men, received the lowest response rates to their resumes. Morris and Thanasombat concluded that "local animosity and antagonism" ranging from discrimination to violence targeting Middle Easterners were not only well documented but also fit historical patterns.

Educational institutions provide another site through which covert racism is transmitted. The pliable, docile, and captive student –eager to win favor, obtain the highest GPA's with the least amount of effort – is less likely to critically evaluate, challenge or critique the 'official viewpoint' offered by the text or instructor. As explained by Chivers and Smyth- "Challenging Our Textbooks and our Teachings: Examining the Reproduction of Racism in the Sociology Classroom"-such blind trust aids and abets not only the transmittal but also the acceptance of covert racism as normal, legitimate, and proper. This is problematical given the presumption of truth associated with education in general. Covert racism may be particularly troubling for white instructors, teaching predominately white students about racism. Chivers and Smyth argue that the uncritically reliance upon textbooks to explain seemingly familiar concepts such as "race" and "racism" actually serves to minimize, ignore, or marginalize the consequential and differential outcomes, rewards, sanctions, and access more evidenced in racialized situations.

Educational instructions foster a veneer of truth and legitimacy which serves to normalize racial outcomes and racial structures. Racial non-elites who work within educational institutions also find their access to promotions and other rewards impaired by mechanisms of covert racism. Smith, Yosso, and Solórzano point out that often blacks, and other racialized non-elites are constantly "Challenging Racial Battle Fatigue on Historically White Campuses". Faculty of color, often marginalized, traverse racialized spaces where tension is heightened by micro-aggressions, offensive remarks or actions that whites rarely see as racist. These micro-aggressions, experienced as assaults, causes racial battle fatigue that reinforces white power structures while undermining success of racial non-elites. Rumors, second hand knowledge, or hear say – while having limited judicial merit, can be damnable in the small office or corporate environment. Such "evidence" is usually used to curb the behavior of 'suspect' employees. These 'suspect' employees are typically marginalized groups -such as women, religious or ethnic minorities, and lower SES. These highly effective control mechanisms may be utilized by the racial elite to further marginalize such groups. These forms of covert racism are often not part of the official record but nevertheless form the basis of hiring decisions, promotions, and evaluations. Culpability and plausible deniability, associated with these mechanisms, have the added benefit of providing a veneer of racial respectability and neutrality.

In the next chapter I demonstrate that Covert Racism is evident both in the U.S. and Globally. Systemically, I demonstrate that, covert racism operates across several societal institutions, structures and societies. Globally, since 9/11, increasing fears of the racial others has fueled anti-immigrant hostilities, racial profiling and intimidation. Xenophobic fears have surfaced in Denmark, the Netherlands, Belgium, England, France, and Italy, to name but a few. Covert racism –evidenced in racial codes, profiling, and colorblindness –is not however new. Covert racism, born out of the imperialist needs to maximize profit at the expense of racialized others, stands shielded by institutions, cultures, stereotypical assumptions, and tradition. Whereas overt racism assumed blatant and insidious forms, covert racism hides behind the façade of 'politeness', political correctness and expediency. Racially coded words and calls for racial blindness obfuscate the reality of this subtle, subversive, and often hidden form of racism. Covert racism, just like its twin overt racism, is neither innocent nor harmless. The scars of covert racism -often seen in terms of increased levels of disease, negative sanctions, inadequate information, and lost opportunities –serve to continually victimize racial non-elites.

Covert Racism and Individuals

The language we speak, while basically derived from English, is often interpreted through a racial code which holds differential meanings depending upon ones experiences within the racial matrix. Our views of social reality and how we interact with others tends to reflect these racial nuances. While some may feel that they can navigate various realities without regard to race or as if they are color blind. Many others experience race daily as pain, objectification, marginalization, or minimalization. Color-blindness is a luxury afforded to racial elite, whereas colorization is the reality of the racial non-elite. Covert racism, especially, is related to how we as individuals come to perceive, evaluate and experience racial realities.

Have you ever experienced a paper or grass cut? The cut often goes unnoticed, even unfelt, until you actually take the time to observe it. All too often, it is only after we have focused upon this wound, that we experience pain. Covert racism, experienced psychologically, is much like the paper cut that often goes unnoticed. While unnoticed it is not without its wounds. Such wounds, experienced as micro-aggressions, are suspected to lie at the heart of the consistent physical ailments and psychic trauma, which plague many targeted racial non-elites. By turning the lens upon his own life, Brunsma examines his own whiteness and discovers how, even though he has worked to consciously oppose the structures and ideology of race, his storied life has actually served to reproduce white privilege. As observed by Brunsma – "Now You Don't See It, Now You Don't: White Lives as Covert Racism" -white identity is structured and defined by covert racism. Almost subliminally, through socialization, whites are taught to ignore their racial privilege, and adopt an attitude that individual effort and not group identity accounts for the unequal distribution of rewards, liabilities, and status. And, while race and racism were once a part of our cultural landscape they no longer thwart upward mobility by those who 'really' try. The perception is that differences in outcomes, which may seem to favor whites and males, actually reflect the fair and just outcomes of a meritocracy based upon individuality. Essentially Brunsma argues that such individualism, functioning as covert racism, actually obscures the benefits of whiteness. Consequently, whiteness provides a veneer of acceptability and respectability. Those able to claim whiteness are deemed innocent until proven guilty, competent until proven incompetent, and right until proven wrong. Unfortunately, being black, brown, tan, red or yellow comes with a different set of assumptions. For these racial groups there is a presumption of incompetence and guilt that the individual must constantly battle to overcome. Whites must be encouraged to explore the nuanced meanings of whiteness. In so doing, Brunsma argues, they will learn to look past the veneer of 'racelessness' to uncover the system of white privilege made possible through covert racism. Whiteness, as a form of covert racism, serves as a veneer by which and through which whites can deny racial realities. These differences are not trivial, nor are they merely subjective. For as Brunsma explains, covert racism simultaneously serves to trivialize and delegitimize the plight of others, while at the same time legitimizing, apologizing for, and normalizing whiteness. Consequently, white success results from effort, and black, brown, red, tan and yellow failures results from the lack thereof. Missing from both equations is the role of covert racism. Only by exploring beyond the veneer of racelessness, can whites come to grips with their racial identity. Brunsma concludes that a critical mechanism for understanding covert racism is accomplished by whites who explore their whiteness and its attendant white privilege.

Whiteness is but one of several racial narratives that must be explored if we are to better understand how covert racism operates from an individual's perspective. Patricia J. Williams, in "The Ineffable Strangeness of Race", argues that how we view each other is derived from such racial 'narratives'. These narratives not only define but also sustain our racial landscapes. Any significant changes in these narratives, by implication, will result in or will reflect changes in how we interpret and interact with our racialized selves. Williams explores three narrative models of race that frame our contemporary discourse. These three frames -neo-interracialism, the biologizing of blackness, and, finally, race as economic choice –are linked to our evolving conversations regarding race. At the core of Williams' argument is how covertly racial reasoning has delimited even our best hopes of racial resolutions. By highlighting these limitations, Williams hopes to encourage new narratives which offer opportunities for coalition in a diasporic, globalized world that is evolving toward a society that looks different from the demographic that shaped the civil rights movement of the last century.

As we rethink our racial landscape, we can ill afford not to look at the various remedies that have been established to transform our racial state. Affirmative Action, once hailed as a major breakthrough in civil rights and race relations, currently is under attack as many question its relevance in a post-civil rights America. Elijah Anderson's article "The Social Situation of the Black Executive" demonstrates that often black executives are placed in "ambiguous position(s)" in corporate environments. Covert racism, within these environments, functions to alienate and isolate black executives. Thus, for security these blacks might behave in a "racially particularistic manor in private, while embracing more mainstream behavior in public." This situation exacts significant social costs as black executives must contend with being isolated into corporate 'ghettos'. The most cynical aspects of corporate situations for black executives is the covert ways in which even their success may be delegitimized under the presumption that it was not effort but affirmative action quotas that account for their promotions.

Claudia Fox Tree, in her article "Aren't They All Dead? Passive Racism against Native Americans", argues that one need not be in a position of 'white privilege' to enjoy this privilege. In fact, one of the privileges, and aspects of covert racism, is the ability to feign ignorance of race, racial privileges, and dismissal of racial injustices. In a society which presumes meritocracy, any failure on the part of individuals or groups is assumed to be associated with their lack of effort and not systemic or structural inequalities. Racial privilege, as explained Claudia Fox Tree, is a two-edged sword. On the one hand, racial privilege allows some to live innocently in a state of racial bliss, ignorant of the racial reality in which they benefit. Alternatively, it also serves to deny the harsh realities of those who are penalized by the same racial state. Consequently, while many Native Americans may be able to enjoy racial anonymity, it is only at the expense of their Indian identify. Racial illusions, another form of covert racism, serve to nullify and delegitimize the claims of those harmed by a basically racist society. Those who experience differential success, fail to adjust, adapt, or just do not fit are blamed not the racial structure. These sorts of racial illusions ignore the reality that many do not fit into the cultural norms which define their racial identity. This means that many, unaware of the tenacious nature of the racial matrix, fail to effectively challenge the racial status quo. Thus it is with surprise, that some in acknowledging the reality of Indian existence respond with shock and surprise, as they query, "Aren't they all dead?"

Racial elites are equally likely to be oblivious of the essence and their culpability in maintaining the racial status quo. As pointed out by Barbara Trepagnier in "Silent Racism" most Americans a decade ago came to believe that racism had been abolished by civil rights legislation. Such views ignore the newer and more covert forms of racism which prevail in negative thoughts, images, and assumptions about African Americans. This "silent racism", exhibited even by well intentioned white Americans, serves to not only perpetuate but also reinforce racial and ethnic inequality in the U.S. despite laws intended to reduce their presence. Covert racism therefore may actually shield and protect whites by allowing them to ignore or avoid thinking about or being held culpable in perpetuating racial hierarchies.

At the same time that covert racism may provide cover and protection to whites, it not only distorts but also is hostile to the psyche of the racialized other. As pointed out by Picca, Feagin, and Johns in their essay "One Step From Suicide" -being black may actually be dangerous to one's physical and mental health. Using data from an in-depth interview with successful African American entrepreneurs, this paper develops a holistic approach to analyzing experiences of everyday racism. By "holistic," the authors assert that covert racism is not cumulative, but is multiplicative as it represents a constant series of interconnected and layered events. Their paper examines in detail three dimensions of everyday racism: spatial, temporal, and relational. By examining racism from this critical analytical perspective, they provide a clear understanding of the personal cost associated with covert racism.

Corey Dolgon in "Life styles of the rich and racist" demonstrates how covert racism functions to produce dynamics that alienate engaged scholarship, as well as how one's own identity gets shaped and reshape". These transformations not only impact upon the researcher, and their work, but how that work is perceived by members of the academe. So, as Dolgon's research documents the covert racism in hiring strategies of an elite university, he also discovered how it directly impacted upon his own identity and scholarship. Dolgon was challenged to think about the relationship between identity and scholarship, theory and engagement. It meant addressing the variety of structural and covert ways that identity politics obscure what we see, what we think and how we act. Dolgon concludes that through this lens we are able to see how covert racism operates on multiple levels. We are also apprised of some potential costs associated with challenging the racial status quo.

Whites, who choose to challenge prevailing racial views, are not immune to retaliation by other whites. Such racial costs are seen in inclusion or exclusion from intimate spheres of whiteness. Racial codes, promoting white group identity, encourage denial, minimization, or rejection of the effects of racism by whites. Janet Morrison's essay "Journey to Awareness: Recognizing the Invisibility of Race Issues" contextualizes these costs by examining racial codes through her lived experiences of crossing various racial boundaries. Morrison, by choosing to live and work in an African-American/ Hispanic neighborhood for over 10 years, became keenly aware of racial boundaries and consequences for those brave enough to bridge, cross or violate them. Morrison's unique vantage point allowed her to explore the complexity of racial meanings, values, fears and frustration. She discovers not only the variability but also the permeability of such racial boundaries. Morrison observing the obvious costs of racial ostracisms, rumors and innuendos; nevertheless concludes that the benefits of newfound friends and communities far outweigh the costs.

Covert Racism – Transforming the Racial Matrix

In the last chapter, an epilogue of sorts, I explore the significance of the 2008 Presidential election in terms of "Post-Racial Myths: Disrupting Covert Racism and the Racial Matrix". For many, the election of Barrack Obama represented that hope in the dawn of a new day, in a new era where all would be able to maximize their human potential without fear of discrimination based upon race, class, gender, sexual orientation, religion, or handicap. As we welcomed and celebrated the election of Obama, many questions emerged. I find it more than coincidental that no sooner had the dust settled from the electoral screens and even before the actual inauguration – a strange and not so subtle shift could be seen in America's racial terrain. This shift-what some allude to as a new racial narrative – has already assumed tsunamic proportions -seems destined to distort, transform, or obfuscate the racial landscape. This final chapter explores how covert racism underlies much of what many now are calling a post-racial narrative. In the final analysis, covert racism continues because for many it remains hidden.

Therefore, we conclude by identifying strategies for shedding light and developing processes by which covert racism may be disrupted.

Coming full circle, we return to our orienting definition. Covert racism, operating just under our collective and individual radars, is an important and often overlooked aspect of racism. Covert racism, not only within our society but globally, is increasingly being recognized as a stubborn, yet mostly 'hidden' form of racism. The purpose of this book is to shed light upon this modern racial matrix that becomes more apparent through the lens of covert racism.

As you continue your journey into the racial matrix through the lens of covert racism, remember the choice continues to be yours. If you choose to ignore covert racism and the racial matrix its tentacles will continue to manifest themselves throughout our society. Such manifestations, appearing to be benign, however are not without their destructive and pernicious outcomes. Alternatively, by being awaken to such destructive consequences, you are better equipped to decode, transform and dismantle the racial matrix. So what will it be the little red pill or the blue one?

PART I

THEORETICAL PERSPECTIVES ON COVERT RACISM

THE IMPACT OF RACIAL AND NONRACIAL STRUCTURAL FORCES ON POOR URBAN BLACKS[*]

William Julius Wilson

Racism has historically been one of the most prominent American cultural frames (shared group constructions of reality) and has played a major role in determining how whites perceive and act toward blacks. Basically, racism is an ideology of racial domination that features two things: (1) beliefs that one race is either biologically or culturally inferior to another and (2) the use of such beliefs to rationalize or prescribe the way that the "inferior" race should be treated in this society as well as to explain their social position as a group and their collective accomplishments. In the United States today there is no question that the more categorical forms of racist ideology—in particular, those that assert the biogenetic inferiority of blacks—have declined significantly, even though they still may be embedded in institutional norms and practices, e.g., school tracking, the practice of grouping students of similar capability for instruction, which not only tends to segregate African American students, but often results in placing some black students in lower level classes even though they have the cultural capital—requisite skills for learning—to compete with students in higher level classes.[1]

However, there has emerged a form of what Lawrence Bobo and his colleagues refer to as "laissez faire racism," a perception that blacks are responsible for their own economic predicament and therefore undeserving of special government support.[2] The idea that the federal government "has a special obligation to help improve the living standards of blacks" because they "have been discriminated against for so long"

---

[*] Parts of this paper are based on my book, *More than Just Race: Being Black and Poor in the Inner City*, Norton Press, 2009.

[1] For a review of the literature on school tracking, see Janese Free, "Race and School Tracking: From A Social Psychological Perspective," Paper presented at the annual meeting of the American Sociological Association, San Francisco, CA, August 14, 2004.

[2] Lawrence Bobo, James R. Kluegel, and Ryan A. Smith, "Laisse Faire Racism: The Crystallization of a Kinder, Gentler, Antiblack Ideology." In *Racial Attitudes in the 1990s*. Ed. Steven A. Tuch and Jack K. Martin. Westport, Conn.: Praeger, 1997.

was supported by only one in five whites in 2001, and has never exceeded support by more than one in four since 1975. Significantly, the lack of white support for this idea is not related to background factors such as level of education and age.

There is a widespread notion in America that the problems plaguing people of color in the inner city have little to do with racial discrimination or the effects of living in segregated poverty. For many Americans, it is the individual and the family who bear the main responsibility for their low social and economic achievement in society. It is an unavoidable fact that Americans tend to deemphasize the structural origins and social significance of poverty and welfare. In other words, the popular view is that people are poor or on welfare because of their own personal shortcomings.[3] Perhaps this tendency is rooted in our tradition of "rugged individualism." If, in America, you can grow up to be anything you want to be, then any destiny—even poverty—can be rightly viewed through the lens of personal achievement or failure. Certainly it's true that most Americans have little direct knowledge or understanding of the complex nature of race and poverty in the inner city. In the hopes of providing a broader understanding of these problems, the purpose of this chapter is twofold: (1) to highlight the role of two very important structural factors that have contributed to the emergences and persistence of concentrated poverty in poor inner-city black neighborhoods—state political actions and economic forces, and (2) to suggest a new political agenda for America's ghetto poor based on my analysis of the impact of these factors

The Role of Political Actions

Ever since 1934 with the establishment of the Federal Housing Authority (FHA), a program necessitated by the massive mortgage foreclosures during the Great Depression, the U.S. government has sought to enable citizens to become homeowners by underwriting

---

[3] A 2007 survey by the Pew Research Center revealed that "fully two-thirds of all Americans believe personal factors, rather than racial discrimination, explain why many African Americans have difficulty getting ahead in life; just 19% blame discrimination." Nearly three quarters of U.S. whites (71%), a majority of Hispanics (59%), and even a slight majority of blacks (53%) "believe that blacks who have not gotten ahead in life are mainly responsible for their own situation." *Optimism about Black Progress Declines: Blacks See Growing Values Gap Between Poor and Middle Class.* Pew Research Center, Washington DC, November 13, 2007, p. 33.

mortgages. In the years following World War II, however, the federal government contributed to the early decay of inner-city neighborhoods by withholding mortgage capital and making it difficult for these areas to retain or attract families who were able to purchase their own homes. Spurred on by the massive foreclosures during the Great Depression, the federal government began underwriting mortgages in an effort to enable citizens to become homeowners. But the Federal Housing Administration (FHA) selectively administered the mortgage program by formalizing a process that excluded certain urban neighborhoods using empirical data that suggested a likely loss of investment in these areas. "Redlining," as it came to be known, was assessed largely on racial composition. Although many neighborhoods with a considerable number of European immigrants were redlined, virtually all black neighborhoods were excluded. Homebuyers hoping to purchase a home in a redlined neighborhood were universally denied mortgages, regardless of their financial qualifications. This severely restricted opportunities for building or even maintaining quality housing in the inner city, which in many ways set the stage for the urban blight that many Americans associate with black neighborhoods. This action was clearly motivated by racial bias, and it was not until the 1960s that the FHA discontinued mortgage restrictions based on the racial composition of the neighborhood.[4]

Subsequent policy decisions worked to trap blacks in these increasingly unattractive inner cities. Beginning in the 1950s the suburbanization of the middle class, already underway with government-subsidized loans to veterans, was aided further by federal transportation and highway policies, which included the building of freeway networks through the hearts of many cities. Although these policies were seemingly nonracial, the line here between ostensibly nonracial and explicitly racial is gray. For example, it could be asked whether such freeways would have also been constructed though wealthier white neighborhoods. In any case, they had a devastating impact on the

---

[4] Michael B. Katz, "Reframing the 'Underclass Debate.'" In the *"Underclass" Debate: Views from History*, edited by Michael B. Katz, Princeton: Princeton University Press, 1993, pp. 440–78; David W. Bartelt, "Housing the 'Underclass'" in *"Underclass" Debate: Views from History*, 1993, pp. 118–57; Thomas J. Sugrue, "The Structure of Urban Poverty: The Reorganization of Space and Work in Three Periods of American History," in *"Underclass" Debate: Views from History*, 1993, pp. 85–117; and Robin D. G. Kelley, "The Black Poor and the Politics of Opposition in a New South City," in *"Underclass" Debate: Views from History*, 1993, pp. 293–333.

neighborhoods of black Americans. These developments not only spurred relocation from the cities to the suburbs among better-off residents, the freeways themselves "created barriers between the sections of the cities, walling off poor and minority neighborhoods from central business districts."[5] For instance, a number of studies have revealed how Richard J. Daley, the former mayor of Chicago, used the Interstate Highway Act of 1956 to route expressways through impoverished African American neighborhoods, resulting in even greater segregation and isolation.[6] A lasting legacy of that policy is the fourteen-lane Dan Ryan Expressway, which created a barrier between black and white neighborhoods.[7]

Another particularly egregious example of the deleterious effects of highway construction is Birmingham, Alabama's interstate highway system, which curved and twisted to bisect several black neighborhoods rather than taking a more direct route through some predominantly white neighborhoods. The highway system essentially followed the boundaries that had been established in 1926 as part of the city's racial zoning law, although these boundaries were technically removed a few years before the highway construction began in 1956.[8] Other examples include the federal and state highway system in Atlanta Georgia, which also separated white and black neighborhoods, and the construction of I-95 in Florida, which displaced many black residents in Miami's historically black Overtown neighborhood.[9]

Moreover, through its housing market incentives, the federal government drew middle-class whites away from cities and into the suburbs.[10] Government policies such as mortgages for veterans and

---

[5] Katz, op. cit. p. 462. Also see Bartelt op. cit, Sugrue op. cit., and Martin Anderson, *The Federal Bulldozer: A Critical Analysis of Urban Renewal, 1949–1962*. Cambridge MA: MIT Press, 1964.

[6] Raymond Mohl, "Planned Destruction: The Interstates and Central City Housing." In John F. Bauman, Roger Biles and Kristin Szylvian, editors. *From Tenements to Taylor Homes: In Search of an Urban Housing Policy in Twentieth-Century America*. University Park, Pennsylvania: State University Press, 2000, pp. 226–245; Adam Cohen and Elizabeth Taylor. *American Pharaoh: Mayor Richard J. Daley—His Battle for Chicago and Nation*. Boston: Little, Brown, 2000; Arnold R. Hirsch, *Making the Second Ghetto: Race and housing in Chicago, 1940–1960*. Cambridge: Cambridge University Press, 1983.

[7] Cohen and Taylor, 2000, op. cit.

[8] Charles E. Connerly, "From Racial Zoning to Community Empowerment: The Interstate Highway System and the African American Community in Birmingham, Alabama." *Journal of Planning Education and Research* 22 (1992), pp. 99–114

[9] Ibid and Ronald H. Bayor, "Roads to Racial Segregation: Atlanta in the Twentieth Century. "*Journal of Urban History* 15 (1988), pp. 3–21.

[10] Katz, op. cit

mortgage-interest tax exemptions for developers enabled the quick, cheap production of massive amounts of tract housing.[11] Although these policies appeared to be nonracial, they facilitated the exodus of white working and middle-class families from urban neighborhoods and thereby indirectly contributed to the growth of segregated neighborhoods with high concentrations of poverty.

A classic example of this effect of housing market incentives is the mass-produced suburban Levittown neighborhoods that were first erected in New York, and later in Pennsylvania, New Jersey, and Puerto Rico. The homes in these neighborhoods were manufactured on a large scale, using an assembly-line model of production, and were arranged in carefully engineered suburban neighborhoods that included many public amenities, such as shopping centers and space for public schools. These neighborhoods represented an ideal alternative for people who were seeking to escape cramped city apartments, and were often touted as "utopian communities" that enabled people to live out the "suburban dream." Veterans were able to purchase a Levittown home for a few thousand dollars with no money down, financed with low-interest mortgages guaranteed by the Veterans Administration. However, the Levitts would not initially sell to African Americans. The first black family moved into the neighborhood in 1957, having purchased a home from a white family,[12] and they endured harassment, hate mail, and threats for several months after moving in. Levittown, NY remains a predominantly white community today. Here, once again, we have a practice that denied African Americans the opportunity to move from segregated inner city neighborhoods.

Explicit racial policies in the suburbs reinforced this segregation by allowing suburbs to separate their financial resources and municipal budgets from the cities. To be more specific, in the nineteenth and early twentieth centuries, strong municipal services in cities were very attractive to residents of small towns and suburbs; as a result, cities tended to annex suburbs and surrounding areas. But the relations between cities and suburbs in the United States began to change following the Great Depression; the century-long influx of poor migrants who required expensive services and paid relatively little in taxes could

---

[11] Robert J. Sampson and William Julius Wilson, "Toward a Theory of Race, Crime, and Urban Inequality." In *Crime and Inequality*. Edited by John Hagan and Ruth Peterson, 1995, pp. 37–54.

[12] Rosalyn Baxandall and Elizabeth Ewen. 1999. *Picture Windows: How the Suburbs Happened*. Basic Books.

no longer be profitably absorbed into the city economy. Annexation largely ended in the mid-twentieth century as suburbs began to successfully resist incorporation. Suburban communities also drew tighter boundaries though the use of zoning laws, discriminatory land use controls, and site selection practices, which made it difficult for inner-city racial minorities to access these areas because they were effectively used to screen out residents on the basis of race.

As separate political jurisdictions, suburbs also exercised a great deal of autonomy through covenants and deed restrictions. In the face of mounting pressure for integration in the 1960s, "suburbs chose to diversify by race rather than class. They retained zoning and other restrictions that allowed only affluent blacks (and in some instances Jews) to enter, thereby intensifying the concentration and isolation of the urban poor."[13] Although these policies clearly had racial connotations, they also reflected class bias and helped to reinforce a process already amply supported by federal government policies; namely the exodus of white working and middle-class families from urban neighborhoods and the growing segregation of low-income blacks in inner-city neighborhoods.

Federal public housing policy contributed to the gradual growth of segregated black ghettos as well. The federal public housing program's policies evolved in two stages that represented two distinct styles. The Wagner Housing Act of 1937 initiated the first stage. Concerned that the construction of public housing might depress private rent levels, groups such as the U.S. Building and Loan League and the National Association of Real Estate Boards successfully lobbied Congress to require, by law, that for each new unit of public housing one "unsafe or unsanitary" unit of public housing be destroyed. As Mark Condon points out: "This policy increased employment in the urban construction market while insulating private rent levels by barring the expansion of the housing stock available to low-income families."[14]

---

[13] Katz, op. cit. pp. 461–62. On the history of Suburbs in America, see Kenneth T. Jackson, *Crabgrass Frontier: The Suburbanization of the United States*. New York: Oxford University Press, 1985. For a good discussion of the effects of housing discrimination on the living conditions, education, and employment of urban minorities, see John Yinger, *Closed Doors, Opportunities Lost: The Continuing Costs of Housing Discrimination*. New York: Russell Sage Foundation, 1995.

[14] Mark Condon, "Public Housing, Crime and the Urban Labor Market: A Study of Black Youth in Chicago." Working paper series, Malcolm Wiener Center, John F. Kennedy School of Government, Harvard University, 1991, no. H-91-3.

The early years of the public housing program produced positive results. Initially, the program mainly served intact families temporarily displaced by the Depression or in the need of housing after the end of World War II. For many of these families public housing was the first step on the road toward economic recovery. Their stays in the projects were relatively brief because they were able to accumulate sufficient economic resources to move on to private housing. The economic mobility of these families "contributed to the sociological stability of the first public housing communities, and explains the program's initial success."[15]

The passage of the Housing Act of 1949 marked the beginning of the second policy stage. It instituted and funded the urban renewal program designed to eradicate urban slums and therefore was seemingly nonracial. However, the public housing that it created "was now meant to collect the ghetto residents left homeless by the urban renewal bulldozers."[16] A new, lower income-ceiling for public housing residency was established by the federal Public Housing Authority, and families with incomes above that ceiling were evicted, thereby restricting access to public housing to only the most economically disadvantaged segments of the population.

This change in federal housing policy coincided with the Second Great Migration of African-Americans from the rural South to the cities of the Northeast and Midwest, which lasted thirty years—from 1940 to 1970. This mass movement of African Americans was even larger and more sustained than the First Great Migration, which began at the turn of the 20th century and ended during the Great Depression, and had a more profound impact on the transformation of the inner city.

As the black urban population in the North grew and precipitated greater demands for housing, pressure mounted in white communities to keep blacks out. Suburban communities, with their restrictive covenants and special zoning laws, refused to permit the construction of public housing. And the Federal government acquiesced to opposition to the construction of public housing in their neighborhoods from organized white neighborhood groups in the city. Thus units were overwhelmingly concentrated in the overcrowded and deteriorating

---

[15] Ibid, p. 3.
[16] Ibid, p. 4.

inner-city ghettos–the poorest and least powerful sections of the city and the metropolitan area. "This growing population of politically weak urban poor was unable to counteract the desires of vocal middle- and working-class whites for segregated housing,"[17] housing that would keep blacks from white neighborhoods. In short, public housing became a federally funded institution that isolated families by race and class, resulting in high concentrations of poor black families in inner-city ghettos.[18]

In the last quarter of the twentieth century, new developments led to further changes in these neighborhoods. And one of the most significant was the out-migration of middle-income blacks. Before the 1970s African American families had faced extremely strong barriers when they considered moving into white neighborhoods. Not only did many experience overt discrimination in the housing market, some were recipients of violent attacks. Although fair housing audits continue to reveal the existence of discrimination in the housing market, the fair housing legislation, including the Fair Housing Amendments Act of 1988, reduced the strengths of these barriers. And middle income African Americans increased their efforts to move from concentrated black poverty areas to more desirable neighborhoods in the metropolitan area, including white neighborhoods.[19]

This pattern represents an important change in the formation of neighborhoods. In the earlier years communities undergoing racial change from white to black tended to experience an increase in population density, as a result of the black migration from the South. Because of the housing demand, particularly in the late stages of the succession from white to black, homes and apartments in these neighborhoods were often subdivided into smaller units.[20] However, 1970 marked the end of the great migration wave of blacks from the South to northern urban areas, and two developments affected the course of population movement to the inner cities after that time. Improvements

---

[17] Ibid. p. 4.
[18] Sampson and Wilson, op. cit. Also see, Bartelt, op cit, Kelley, op. cit., Sugrue, op. cit., Arnold R. Hirsch, *Making the Second Ghetto: Race and Housing in Chicago, 1940–1960*, and John F. Bauman, Norman P. Hummon and Edward K. Muller, "Public Housing Isolation, and the Urban Underclass." *Journal of Urban History*, Vol 17, 1991, pp. 264–92.
[19] Lincoln Quillian, "Migration Patterns and the Growth of High-Poverty Neighborhoods, 1970–1990." *American Journal of Sociology*, Vol 105, pp. 1–37.
[20] Ibid.

in transportation made it easier for workers to live outside the central city, and industries gradually shifted to the suburbs because of the increased residential suburbanization of the labor force and the lower cost of production. Because of the suburbanization of employment and improvements in transportation, inner-city manufacturing jobs were no longer a strong factor pulling migrants to central cities.[21]

So with the decline of industrial employment in the inner city, the influx of southern black migration to northern cities ceased and many poor black neighborhoods, especially those in the Midwest and Northeast, changed from densely packed areas of recently arrived migrants to communities gradually abandoned by the working and middle classes.[22]

In addition, and more recently, a fundamental shift in the federal government's support for basic urban programs profoundly aggravated the problems of inner-city neighborhoods. Beginning in 1980, when Ronald Reagan became President, sharp spending cuts on direct aid to cities dramatically reduced budgets for general revenue sharing—unrestricted funds (that can be used for any purpose)—urban mass transit, economic development assistance, urban development action grants, social service block grants, local public works, compensatory education, public service jobs, and job training. Many of these programs are designed to help disadvantaged individuals gain some traction in attaining financial security.[23] It is telling that the federal contribution was 17.5 percent of the total city budgets in 1977, but only 5.4 percent by 2000.[24]

These cuts were particularly acute for older cities in the East and Midwest that largely depended on federal and state aid to fund social services for their poor population and to maintain aging infrastructure. For example, in 1980, federal and state aid funded 50 to 69 percent of the budgets in six of these cities, and 40 to 50 percent of budgets in eleven cities. By 1989 only three cities –Buffalo, Baltimore,

---

[21] Ibid.
[22] William Julius Wilson, *The Truly Disadvantage: The Inner City, the Underclass and Public Policy*: University of Chicago Press, 1987; William Julius Wilson, When Work Disappears: The World of the New Urban Poor. New York: Alfred A. Knopf, 1966; Quillian, op. cit.
[23] See Demetrios Caraley, "Washington Abandons the Cities." *Political Science Quarterly* 107, Spring 1992, pp. 1–30.
[24] Bruce A. Wallin, "Budgeting for Basics: The Changing Landscape of City Finances," discussion paper prepared for the Brookings Institution Metropolitan Policy Program (Washington, D.C.: Brookings Institution, August 2005).

and Newark – continued to receive over fifty percent of their budgets in state aid, and only two cities – Milwaukee and Boston – received between 40 to 50 percent of their budgets in state aid. To further illustrate, New York City's state aid dropped from 52% of its budget in 1980 to 32% in 1989, which resulted in a loss of $4 billion.[25] Here, once again, is a policy that is nonracial on the surface—although it coincided with changes in the proportion of white and nonwhite urban residents– but nonetheless has indirectly contributed to the crystallization of the inner-city ghetto.

The decline in federal support for cities since 1980 coincided with an increase in the immigration of people from poorer countries— mainly low-skilled workers from Mexico–and whites were steadily moving to the suburbs. With minorities displacing whites as a growing share of the population, the implications for the urban tax base were profound, especially in America's cities. According to the U.S. Census Bureau, in 2000 the median annual household income for Latinos was about $14,000 less than that of white households. With a declining tax base and the simultaneous loss of federal funds that heralded the introduction of the New Federalist policies of the Reagan administration, municipalities had trouble raising enough revenue to cover basic services such as garbage collection, street cleaning, and police protection. Some even cut such services in order to avoid bankruptcy.[26]

This financial crisis left many cities ill equipped to handle three devastating public health problems that emerged in the 1980s and disproportionately affected areas of concentrated poverty: (1) the prevalence of drug trafficking and associated violent crimes; (2) the AIDS epidemic and its escalating public health costs; and (3) the rise in the homeless population not only of individuals, but of whole families as well.[27] Although drug addiction, drug related violence, AIDS and homelessness, are found in many American communities their impact on the black ghetto is profound. A number of cities, especially those that are fiscally strapped, have watched helplessly as these problems— aggravated by the reduction of city-wide social services as well as high levels of neighborhood joblessness—have reinforced the perception that cities are dangerous and threatening places to live. Accordingly,

---

[25] Caraley, 1992, op. cit.
[26] U. S. Department of Housing and Urban Development. *The State of Cities.* Washington, D.C.: Government Printing Office, 1999.
[27] Caraley, 1992, op. cit.

between the 1980s and 2000, many working- and middle-class urban residents continued to relocate to the suburbs. Thus, while poverty and joblessness, and the social problems they generate, remain prominent in ghetto neighborhoods, many cities have fewer and fewer resources to combat them.

Although fiscal conditions in many cities improved significantly in the latter half of the 1990s, this brief period of economic progress was ended by the recession of 2001, followed by a jobless recovery (that is, a recovery that failed to improve the employment rate). The decline of federal and state support for central cities, the largest urban areas in metropolitan regions, has caused a number of severe fiscal and service crises, particularly in the older cities of the East and Midwest such as Detroit, Cleveland, Baltimore, and Philadelphia.

Moreover, the Bush administration's substantial reductions in federal aid to the states exacerbated the problems in cities reliant on state funds.[28] Because of these combined economic and political changes, many central cities and inner suburbs lack the fiscal means to address the concentrated problems of joblessness, family breakups, and failing public schools.[29] Given the current budget deficit—which continues to grow in the face of the Bush administration's simultaneous surrender of revenue in the form of large tax cuts for wealthy citizens and its spending of billions of federal dollars to pay for the wars in Iraq and Afghanistan, the war against terror, and the rebuilding of Iraq's infrastructure—support for programs to revitalize cities in general and inner-city neighborhoods in particular will very likely garner even less support in the future from policymakers.[30]

Finally, policymakers indirectly contributed to concentrated poverty in inner-city neighborhoods with decisions that have decreased the attractiveness of low-paid jobs and accelerated the relative decline in low-income workers' wages. In particular, in the absence of an effective labor market policy, policymakers have tolerated industry practices that undermine worker security–including the erosion of benefits

---

[28] Iris J. Lav and Andrew Brecher, *Passing Down the Deficit: Federal Policies Contribute to the Severity of the State Fiscal Crisis*. Center on Budget and Policy Priorities, Washington DC. May 12, 2004.

[29] Katz, op. cit., p. 1.

[30] As one correspondent noted in 2005, "The United States is spending more than $1 billion a week in Iraq. The Administration this week asked for $80 billion in emergency, most of it for military operations in Iraq. That would add to nearly $250 billion already spent for the war and reconstruction." Alan Fram, "Bush to Seek $80B for Iraq, Afghan Wars." Yahoo News, January 24, 2005.

and the rise of involuntary part-time employment–and they have allowed the purchasing power of the federal minimum wage to erode to one of its lowest levels in decades. After adjusting for inflation, the current federal minimum wage of $6.55 is 24 percent lower than the average level of the minimum wage in the 1960s, 23 percent lower than in the 1970s, 6 percent lower than in 1980s, and 1 percent higher than in the 1990s.[31] Clearly the recent action by a Democratic Congress to increase the federally mandated minimum wage was long overdue.

In sum, federal government policies, even those that are not explicitly racial, have had a profound impact on inner-city neighborhoods. Some of these policies are clearly motivated by racial bias, such as the FHA's redlining of black neighborhoods in the 1940s and 1950s, and the federal government's decision to confine construction of public housing projects mainly to poor, black, inner-city neighborhoods. In other cases it seems that racial bias or concerns about race influenced but were not the sole inspiration for political decisions, such as the fiscal policies of the New Federalism, which resulted in drastic cuts in federal aid to cities whose populations had become more brown and black.

The point of conservative fiscal policy—no matter whose administration promulgated it (Reagan, George H. W. Bush, or George W. Bush)–was ostensibly to subject government to financial discipline. Nevertheless, the enactment of these policies creates financial constraints that make it difficult to generate the political support to effectively combat problems such as joblessness, drug trafficking, AIDS, family stress, and failing schools.

And, as we have seen above, other policies that range from those that clearly lack a racial agenda to those where the line between racial and nonracial is somewhat gray have had a profound impact on inner cities and their poor black residents: federal transportation and highway policy that created an infrastructure for jobs in the suburbs; mortgage-interest tax exemptions, and mortgages for veterans that jointly facilitated the exodus of working- and middle-class white families from inner-city neighborhoods; urban renewal and the building of freeway and highway networks through the hearts of many cities,

---

[31] U.S. Department of Labor. 2008. Federal Minimum Wage Rates Under the Fair Labor Standards Act. http//www.dol.gov/esa/minwage/chart.pdf.

which led to the destruction of many viable low-income black neighborhoods; and the absence of effective labor-market policies to safeguard the real value of the minimum wage, thereby making it more difficult for the inner-city working poor to support their families.

These developments have occurred in many cities across the country, but they perhaps have been felt more in the older central cities of the Midwest and Northeast—the traditional Rust Belt–where depopulated poverty areas have experienced even greater problems.

The Impact of Economic Forces

Older urban areas were once the hubs of economic growth and activity and therefore major destinations for people in search of economic opportunity. However, the economies of many of these cities have since been eroded by complex economic transformations and shifting patterns in metropolitan development. These economic forces are typically considered nonracial—in the sense that their origins are not the direct result of actions, processes, or ideologies that explicitly reflect racial bias. But nevertheless they have accelerated neighborhood decline in the inner city and widened gaps in race and income between cities and suburbs.[32]

Since the mid-twentieth century the mode of production in the United States has shifted dramatically from manufacturing to one increasingly fueled by finance, services, and technology. This shift has accompanied the technological revolution, which has transformed traditional industries and brought about changes that range from streamlined information technology to biomedical engineering.[33]

In other words, the relationship between technology and international competition has eroded the basic institutions of the mass-production system. In the last several decades almost all improvements in productivity have been associated with technology and human capital, thereby drastically reducing the importance of physical capital.[34]

---

[32] Radhika K. Fox and Sarah Treuhaft, *Shared Prosperity, Stronger Regions: An Agenda for Rebuilding America's Older Core Cities* (Report prepared for Policy Link, Oakland California, 2006).

[33] Bill Joy, "Why the future doesn't need us," *Wired* April, 2000, 238–262; and Fox and Treuhaft, op. cit.

[34] Wilson, 1996, op. cit.

With the increased globalization of economic activity, firms have spread their operations around the world, often relocating their production facilities to developing nations that have dramatically lower labor costs.[35]

These global economic transformations have adversely affected the competitive position of many U.S. Rust Belt cities. For example, Cleveland, Detroit, Philadelphia, Baltimore, and Pittsburgh perform poorly on employment growth, an important traditional measure of economic performance. Nationally, employment increased by 25 percent between 1991 and 2001, yet job growth in these older central cities either declined or did not exceed 3 percent.[36]

With the decline in manufacturing employment in many of the nation's central cities, most of the jobs for lower-skilled workers are now in retail and service industries (e.g., store cashiers, customer service representatives, fast food servers, custodial work). Whereas jobs in manufacturing industries were unionized, relatively stable and carried higher wages, those for workers with low to modest levels of education in the retail and service industries provided lower wages, tended to be unstable, and lacked the benefits and worker protections—such as workers' health insurance, medical leave, retirement benefits, and paid vacations—typically offered through unionization. This means that workers relegated to low-wage service and retail firms are more likely to experience hardships as they struggle to make ends meet. In addition, the local economy suffers when residents have fewer dollars to spend in their neighborhoods.[37]

Beginning in the mid-1970s, the employment balance between central cities and suburbs shifted markedly to the suburbs. Since 1980 over two-thirds of employment growth has occurred outside the central city: manufacturing is now over 70 percent suburban, and wholesale and retail trade is just under 70 percent.[38] The suburbs of many central cities, developed originally as bedroom localities for commuters to the central business and manufacturing districts, have become employment centers in themselves. For example, in Detroit, Philadelphia, and

---

[35] Fox and Treuhaft, op. cit.
[36] Ibid.
[37] Fox and Treuhalf, op. cit., Wilson, 1996, op. cit.
[38] U.S. Department of Housing and Urban Development. *The State of Cities.* Washington, D.C.: Government Printing Office, 1999.

Baltimore, less than 20 percent of the jobs are now located within three miles of the city center.[39]

Accompanying the rise of suburban and exurban economies has been a change in commuting patterns. Increasingly workers completely bypass the central city by commuting from one suburb to another. "In the Cleveland region, for example, less than one-third of workers commute to a job in the central city and over half (55 percent) begin and end in the suburbs."[40]

Sprawl and economic stagnation reduce inner city residents' access to meaningful economic opportunities and thereby fuel the economic decline of their neighborhoods. "Spatial mismatch" is a term that social scientists use to capture the relationship between inner-city residents and suburban jobs: the opportunities for employment are geographically disconnected from the people who need the jobs. For example, in Cleveland although entry-level workers are concentrated in inner-city neighborhoods, 80 percent of the entry-level jobs are located in the suburbs.[41] The lack of feasible transportation options exacerbates this mismatch. In addition to the challenges in learning about and reaching jobs, there is persistent racial discrimination in hiring practices, especially for younger and less experienced minority workers.[42]

With the departure of higher-income families, the least upwardly mobile in society—mainly low-income people of color—are left behind in neighborhoods with high concentrations of poverty and deteriorating physical conditions. These neighborhoods offer few jobs and typically lack basic services and amenities, such as banks, grocery stores and other retail establishments, parks, and quality transit.[43] Typically, these communities also suffer from substandard schools, many with run down physical plants.

---

[39] Fox and Treuhalf, op. cit.
[40] Ibid., p. 32.
[41] Fox and Treuhaft, op. cit
[42] See, for example, Wilson, 1996, op. cit., and Joleen Kirschenman and Kathryn Neckerman, "We'd Love to Hire Them, But ...": The Meaning of Race for Employers," in *The Urban Underclass*, eds. Christopher Jencks and Paul E. Peterson, (Washington D.C.: Brookings Institution, 1991, 203–234); Kathryn M. Neckerman and Joleen Kirschenman, "Hiring Strategies, Racial Bias, and Inner-City Workers," *Social Problems*, Vol. 38 (November), 433–47; and Harry Holzer, *What Employers Want: Job Prospects for Less Educated Workers*. New York: Russell Sage, 1995.
[43] Wilson, 1987 op. cit; Wilson, 1996, op. cit; and Fox and Treuhaft, op. cit.

Two of the most visible indicators of neighborhood decline are abandoned buildings and vacant lots. According to one recent report, there are 60,000 abandoned and vacant properties in Philadelphia, 40,000 in Detroit, and 26,000 in Baltimore.[44] These inner-city properties have lost residents in the wake of the out-migration of more economically mobile families, and the relocation of many manufacturing industries.[45]

Combating Concentrated Urban Poverty

In the preceding analysis I have attempted to show the intricate connection of concentrated poverty to the broader changes in our society, including the globalization of economic activity, changes that have fundamentally altered the demographic, economic, and social profile of our many central cities. I think that it is important to understand the impact of the broader systemic changes in addressing problems of concentrated poverty so that we can appreciate the challenges that confront us.

The most important step is to ameliorate the problem that feeds concentrated poverty, and that is closely related to national and international changes in the economy, namely, inner-city joblessness. The ideal solution would be economic policies that produce tight labor markets. The benefits of a strong economy, particularly a sustained tight labor market, for low-skilled workers should be emphasized in economic policy discussions. More than any other group, low-skilled workers depend upon a strong economy, particularly a sustained tight labor market—that is, one in which there are ample jobs for all applicants. In a slack labor market—a labor market with high unemployment—employers can afford to be more selective in recruiting and granting promotions. With fewer jobs to award, they can inflate job requirements, pursuing workers with college degrees, for example, in jobs that have traditionally been associated with high school-level education. In such an economic climate discrimination rises and disadvantaged minorities, especially those with low levels of literacy, suffer disproportionately.

---

[44] Fox and Treuhaft, op. cit.
[45] Wilson, 1987, op. cit; and Wilson, 1996, op. cit

Conversely, in a tight labor market job vacancies are numerous, unemployment is of short duration, and wages are higher. Moreover, in a tight labor market the labor force expands because increased job opportunities not only reduce unemployment, they also draw in workers who previously dropped out of the labor force altogether during a slack labor market period. Thus, in a tight labor market the status of all workers—including disadvantaged minorities—improves.

The impact of tight labor markets on concentrated poverty can be seen in the developments during the prosperous decade of the 1990s. A report for the Brookings Institution by a University of Texas social scientist, Paul Jargowsky, revealed that the number of people residing in high-poverty neighborhoods decreased by 24 percent, or 2.5 million people, from 1990 to 2000 because of the economic boom, particularly in the last half of the 1990s. Moreover, the number of such neighborhoods—the study defined them as census tracts with at least 40 percent of residents below the poverty level—around the country declined by more than a quarter.[46]

In 1990 almost a third of all American blacks lived in such neighborhoods; the 2000 figure was 19 percent. Yet despite this significant improvement, African Americans still have the highest rates of concentrated poverty of all groups in the United States. In part, the state of inner-city ghettos is a legacy of historic racial subjugation. Concentrated poverty neighborhoods are the most visible and disturbing displays of racial and income segregation. And the dramatic decline in concentrated poverty from 1990 to 2000 cannot be explained in terms of culture. Rather, these shifts demonstrate that the fate of African Americans and other racial groups is inextricably connected with changes across the modern economy.

Jargowsky's data bear this out. The declines in concentrated poverty in the 1990s occurred not just in a few cities but across the country. By contrast, Los Angeles and Washington, DC were two of the few central cities that experienced a rise in concentrated poverty during the 1990s. Jargowsky advances three arguments to account for the divergent trend in Los Angeles: (1) the destructive riot after the Rodney King verdict in 1992; (2) the significant immigration of Latinos from Mexico and other Central and South American countries into

---

[46] Paul Jargowsky. *Stunning Progress, Hidden Problems: The Dramatic Decline of Concentrated Poverty in the 1990s*. Washington DC: The Brookings Institution, 2003.

high-poverty neighborhoods; and (3) "the recession in the early 1990s was particularly severe in Southern California, and the economic recovery there was not as rapid as in other parts of California."[47]

In Washington, DC the devastating fiscal crisis from the early to the mid-1990s resulted in drastic reductions in public services and an erosion of public confidence in the District's government. This development contributed to "a rapid out-migration of moderate- and middle-income black families, particularly into suburban Maryland counties to the east of the central city. The poor were left behind in economically isolated neighborhoods with increasing poverty rates."[48]

Virtually all racial and ethnic groups recorded improvements. The number of whites living in high-poverty neighborhoods declined by 29 percent (from 2.7 million people to 1.9 million), and the number of blacks decreased by 36 percent (from 4.8 million to 3.1 million). Latinos were the major exception to this pattern because their numbers in high-poverty areas increased slightly during the 1990s, by 1.6 percent. However, this finding should be placed in the context of Latino population growth: the number of Latinos overall increased dramatically in the 1990s, by 57.9 percent, compared with 16.2 percent growth for African Americans and only 3.4 percent for whites.[49] Particularly low-skilled immigrants drove Latino population growth. For all races, the greatest improvements against poverty concentration were in the South and Midwest, and the smallest were in the Northeast, mirroring wider economic trends.[50]

Thus, the notable reduction in the number of high-poverty neighborhoods and the substantial decrease in the population of such neighborhoods may simply be blips of economic booms rather than permanent trends. Unemployment and individual poverty rates have increased since 2000, and there is every reason to assume that concentrated poverty rates are on the rise again as well, although data on concentrated poverty for this period will only be revealed after a full analysis of the 2010 census.

The earlier increase in concentrated poverty occurred during a period of rising income inequality for all Americans that began in the early 1970s. This was a period of decline in inflation-adjusted average

---

[47] Ibid, p. 9.
[48] Ibid, p. 9
[49] Ibid, p. 4.
[50] Ibid.

incomes among the poor and of growing economic segregation caused by the exodus of middle-income families from inner cities. What had been mixed-income neighborhoods were rapidly transformed into areas of high poverty. Undoubtedly, if the robust economy of the latter 1990s could have been extended for several more years rather than coming to an abrupt halt in 2001, concentrated poverty in inner cities would have declined even more.

Conclusion

In this chapter I discussed a number of structural forces that have adversely impacted inner-city black neighborhoods. These included political actions that were explicitly racial, those that were at least partly influenced by race and those that were ostensibly nonracial (but nevertheless adversely affected black neighborhoods), as well as impersonal economic forces that have accelerated neighborhood decline in the inner city and increased disparities in race and income between cities and suburbs.

One of the combined impacts of these factors was the emergence of depopulated ghettoes, especially in cities of the Midwest and Northeast. Federal transportation and highway policy along with mortgage-interest tax exemptions jointly facilitated the exodus of both industries and non-poor families from inner-city neighborhoods. In turn, the decline of industrial employment in the inner city brought about the end of the Second Great Migration from the South to the North around 1970. These developments helped transform many poor African American neighborhoods, especially those in the Northeast and Midwest, from densely packed areas of recently arrived migrants from the South to neighborhoods gradually abandoned by the working and middle classes.

The lesson for those committed to fighting inequality, especially those involved in multiracial coalition politics, is to fashion a new agenda that pays more scrutiny to both racial and nonracial political and economic forces, including fiscal, monetary, and trade policies that may have long-term consequences for the national and regional economies, as seen in future earnings, jobs, and concentrated poverty. This new agenda would therefore reflect an awareness and appreciation of the devastating effects of recent systemic changes on poor urban populations and neighborhoods.

However, this new agenda would also include an even more dedicated focus on the traditional efforts to fight poverty to ensure that the benefits from an economic upturn are widely shared among the poor and that they become less vulnerable to downward swings in the economy. I refer especially to combating racial discrimination in employment, which is especially devastating during slack labor markets; the revitalization of poor urban neighborhoods, including the elimination of abandoned buildings and vacant lots, to make them more attractive for economic investment that would help improve the quality of life and create jobs in the neighborhood; promoting job-training programs to enhance employment opportunities for ghetto residents; improving public education to prepare inner-city youngsters for higher-paying and stable jobs in the new economy; and strengthening unions to provide the higher wages, worker protections, and benefits typically absent from low-skilled jobs in retail and service industries.

In short, this new agenda would reflect a multi-pronged approach that attacks inner-city poverty on various levels, an approach that recognizes the complex array of factors that have contributed to the crystallization of concentrated urban poverty and limited the life chances of so many inner city residents.

References

Anderson, Martin. 1964. *The Federal Bulldozer: A Critical Analysis of Urban Renewal, 1949-1962.* Cambridge: MIT Press.

Bartelt, David W. 1993. "Housing the 'Underclass'" in *The "Underclass" Debate: Views from History*, ed. Michael B. Katz, pp. 118-57. Princeton: Princeton University Press.

Bauman, John F., Norman P. Hummon and Edward K. Muller. 1991. "Public Housing, Isolation and the Urban Underclass." *Journal of Urban History* 17:264-92.

Bauman, John F., Roger Biles and Kristin Szylvian, eds. 2000. *From Tenements to Taylor Homes: In Search of an Urban Housing Policy in Twentieth-Century America.* University Park, Pennsylvania: State University Press.

Baxandall, Rosalyn and Elizabeth Ewen. 1999. *Picture Windows: How the Suburbs Happened.* New York: Basic Books.

Bayor, Ronald H. 1988. "Roads to Racial Segregation: Atlanta in the Twentieth Century." *Journal of Urban History* 15:3-21.

Caraley, Demetrios. 1992. "Washington Abandons the Cities." *Political Science Quarterly* 107 (Spring):1-30.

Cohen, Adam, and Elizabeth Taylor. 2000. *American Pharaoh: Mayor Richard J. Daley—His Battle for Chicago and Nation.* Boston: Little, Brown.

Condon, Mark. 1991. "Public Housing, Crime and the Urban Labor Market: A Study of Black Youths in Chicago." Working paper series, no. H-91-3. Malcolm Wiener Center for Social Policy, John F. Kennedy School of Government, Harvard University.

Connerly, Charles E. 1992. "From Racial Zoning to Community Empowerment: The Interstate Highway System and the African American Community in Birmingham, Alabama." *Journal of Planning Education and Research* 22:99–114.
Fox, Radhika K., and Sarah Treuhaft. 2006. *Shared Prosperity, Stronger Regions: An Agenda for Rebuilding America's Older Core Cities*. Report prepared for PolicyLink, Oakland, CA.
Fram, Alan. 2005. "Bush to Seek $80B for Iraq, Afghan Wars." *Yahoo News*, January 24.
Hirsch, Arnold R. 1983. *Making the Second Ghetto: Race and Housing in Chicago, 1940–1960*. Cambridge: Cambridge University Press.
Holzer, Harry J. 1995. *What Employers Want: Job Prospects for Less- Educated Workers*. New York: Russell Sage.
Jackson, Kenneth T. 1985. *Crabgrass Frontier: The Suburbanization of the United States*. New York: Oxford University Press.
Jargowsky, Paul. 2003. *Stunning Progress, Hidden Problems: The Dramatic Decline of Concentrated Poverty in the 1990s*. Washington, DC: Brookings Institution.
Joy, Bill. 2000. "Why the future doesn't need us." *Wired* (April):238–262.
Katz, Michael B. 1993. "Reframing the 'Underclass Debate.'" In *The "Underclass" Debate: Views from History*, ed. Michael B. Katz, pp. 440–78. Princeton: Princeton University Press.
Kelley, Robin D. G. 1993. "The Black Poor and the Politics of Opposition in a New South City, 1929–1970." In *The "Underclass" Debate: Views from History*, ed. Michael B. Katz, pp. 293–333. Princeton: Princeton University Press.
Kirschenman, Joleen and Kathryn Neckerman. 1991. "'We'd Love to Hire Them, But …': The Meaning of Race for Employers." In *The Urban Underclass*, eds. Christopher Jencks and Paul E. Peterson, pp. 203–34. Washington, DC: Brookings Institution.
Lav, Iris J., and Andrew Brecher. 2004. *Passing Down the Deficit: Federal Policies Contribute to the Severity of the State Fiscal Crisis*. Center on Budget and Policy Priorities, Washington, DC, May 12.
Mohl, Raymond. 2000. "Planned Destruction: The Interstates and Central City Housing." In John F. Bauman, Roger Biles and Kristin Szylvian, editors. *From Tenements to Taylor Homes: In Search of an Urban Housing Policy in Twentieth-Century America*. University Park, Pennsylvania: State University Press, pp. 226–245.
Neckerman, Kathryn M., and Joleen Kirschenman. 1991. "Hiring Strategies, Racial Bias, and Inner-City Workers." *Social Problems* 38 (November):433–47.
Pew Research Center. 2007. *Optimism about Black Progress Declines: Blacks See Growing Values Gap Between Poor and Middle Class*. Washington, DC, November 13.
Quillian, Lincoln. 1999. "Migration Patterns and the Growth of High-Poverty Neighborhoods, 1970–1990." *American Journal of Sociology* 105(1):1–37.
Sampson, Robert J., and William Julius Wilson. 1995. "Toward a Theory of Race, Crime, and Urban Inequality." In *Crime and Inequality*, eds. John Hagan and Ruth Peterson, pp. 37–54. Stanford: Stanford University Press.
Sugrue, Thomas J. 1993. "The Structures of Urban Poverty: The Reorganization of Space and Work in Three Periods of American History." In *The "Underclass" Debate: Views from History*, ed. Michael B. Katz, pp. 85–117. Princeton: Princeton University Press.
U.S. Department of Housing and Urban Development. 1999. *The State of Cities*. Washington, DC: Government Printing Office. http//www.dol.gov/esa/minwage/chart.pdf (accessed February 13, 2008).
U.S. Department of Labor. 2008. *Federal Minimum Wage Rates Under the Fair Labor Standards Act*. http://www.dol.gov/esa/minwage/chart.pdf (accessed February 13, 2008).
Wallin, Bruce A. 2005. "Budgeting for Basics: The Changing Landscape of City Finances." Discussion paper prepared for the Brookings Institution Metropolitan Policy Program. Washington, DC: Brookings Institution, August.

Wilson, William Julius. 1987. *The Truly Disadvantaged: The Inner City, the Underclass and Public Policy*. Chicago: University of Chicago Press.
Wilson, William Julius.. 1996. *When Work Disappears: The World of the New Urban Poor*. New York: Alfred A. Knopf.
Yinger, John. 1995. *Closed Doors, Opportunities Lost: The Continuing Costs of Housing Discrimination*. New York: Russell Sage Foundation.

THE NEW RACISM: THE RACIAL REGIME OF POST-CIVIL RIGHTS AMERICA

Eduardo Bonilla-Silva and David Dietrich

Some analysts claim that race and racism have decreased in importance in contemporary America (D'Souza 1995; Wilson 1978, 1987). This view is consistent with survey data on white attitudes since the early sixties (Sniderman and Piazza 1993; Schuman et al. 1997; Greeley and Sheatsley 1971; Hyman and Sheatsley 1964) as well as with many demographic and economic studies comparing the status of whites and blacks in terms of income, occupations, health, and education (Farley 1984; 1993; Farley and Allen 1987; Smith and Welch 1986; Duncan 1968; Freeman 1978; Farley and Hermalin 1972; Palmore and Whittington 1970).

A smaller number of social scientists, in contrast, believe that race continues to play a role similar to the one it played in the past (Bell 1992; Willie 1989; Pinkney 1984; Fusfeld and Bates 1984). For these authors, little has changed in America in terms of racism, and there is a general pessimism regarding the prospects of changing the racial status of minorities. Although this is a minority viewpoint in academia, it represents the perception of many members of minority communities, especially of the black community.

These opinions about the changes in the significance of race and racism in the United States are based on a narrowly defined notion of racism. For these analysts, racism is fundamentally an ideological or attitudinal phenomenon. In contrast, we regard racism as a *structure*, that is, as a network of relations at social, political, economic, and ideological levels that shapes the life chances of the various races. What social scientists define as racism is conceptualized in our framework as racial ideology. Racism (racial ideology) helps to glue and, at the same time, organize the nature and character of race relations in a society. From this vantage point, rather than arguing about whether the significance of race has declined, increased, or not changed at all, the real issue is assessing if a transformation has occurred in the *racial structure* of the United States. It is our contention that despite the profound changes that occurred in the 1960s, a new racial structure – the

New Racism – is operating which accounts for the persistence of racial inequality. The elements that comprise this new racial structure are: 1) the increasingly *covert* nature of racial discourse and racial practices; 2) the avoidance of racial terminology and the ever growing claim by whites that they experience "reverse racism"; 3) the elaboration of a racial agenda over political matters that eschews direct racial references; 4) the invisibility of most mechanisms that reproduce racial inequality; and, finally, 5) the rearticulation of some racial practices characteristic of the Jim Crow period of race relations.

This chapter begins with a brief description of how this new racial structure (New Racism) came about. Against this backdrop, we survey the evidence of how black-white racial inequality is produced and reproduced in the United States in two areas: social and economic[1]. The evidence is perused from 1960 until the present with the goal of examining the mechanisms that keep minorities "in their place." We conclude the chapter with a discussion of some of the social, political, and legal repercussions of the new racial structure of America.

The Emergence of a New Racial Structure in the Sixties

Blacks were kept in a subordinate position during the Jim Crow period of race relations through a variety of bluntly racist practices. At the economic level, blacks were restricted to menial jobs by the joint effort of planters, corporations, and unions. In the South, they were mostly tenant farmers, and this was accomplished through vagrancy and apprenticeship laws, restrictions on the right of blacks to buy land and to work in certain occupations, debt imprisonment, and the convict lease system (Norton et al. 1990; Fredrickson 1981; Greene and Woodson 1930). In the North, the exclusionary practices of managers and unions kept blacks in unskilled occupations with very little chance for occupational mobility (Marable 1983; Foner 1981; Myrdal [1944] 1964).

At the social level, the rules of the new racial order emerged slowly given that the Civil War and the Reconstruction (1865–1877) shook the rules of racial engagement and challenged the place of blacks in society (Fredrickson 1981; Woodward 1966). The transition from

---

[1] For a more complete treatment, see *White Supremacy and Racism in the Post-Civil Rights Era* by Eduardo Bonilla-Silva (2001).

slavery to Jim Crow was characterized by inconsistency and no generally accepted code of racial mores (Woodward 1966). Slavery did not require either a very sophisticated and specific set of rules to preserve "social distance" or an elaborate racial ideology (racism) because of the thorough differences of status among the races (Fredrickson 1981). However, as blacks became free they posed a threat to white supremacy. Slowly but surely segregationist laws and practices emerged after 1865 and were solidified by the 1880s with the enactment of Jim Crow laws all over the South. These laws involved the disenfranchisement of blacks, racial separation in public accommodations, segregation in housing, schools, the workplace, and other areas to insure white supremacy.

Politically, blacks were virtually disenfranchised in the South and were almost totally dependent on white politicians in the North. In the South, poll taxes, literacy tests, and outright coercive strategies restrained their political options (Marable 1983). In the North, black politicians were subordinate to white ethnic political machineries and represented few of the interests of their own minority communities (Patterson 1974).

In terms of social control, blacks in the South were regulated by the actions of individual whites, violent racist organizations such as the Ku Klux Klan, mob violence in the form of lynching, and the lack of enforcement of the laws of the land by state agencies (Marable 1983). In the North, blacks suffered less from these practices largely because they were extremely residentially segregated and, thus, did not pose a "threat" to whites. However, whenever blacks "crossed the line," whites erupted in violence such as during the race riots of the late 1910s (Tuttle 1970).

Finally, in consonance with the above practices, racial ideology during the Jim Crow period of race relations was explicitly racist. Without question, most whites believed that minorities were intellectually and morally inferior, that they should be kept apart, and that whites should not mix with any of them (Gossett 1963).

The apartheid that blacks experienced in the United States was predicated on 1) keeping them in rural areas, mostly in the South, 2) maintaining them as agricultural workers, and 3) excluding them from the political process. However, the infrastructure of apartheid began to crumble as blacks successfully challenged their socioeconomic position by migrating initially from rural areas to urban areas in the South and later to the North and West (Harrison 1991), by pushing themselves into non-agricultural occupations (Leiman 1992; Foner 1981), and by developing political organizations and movements like Garveyism, the NAACP, CORE, the National Urban League, the Southern Regional Council, and the CIC (Morris 1984; McAdam 1982). Among the other factors leading to the abolition of the segregationist order, the most significant were the participation of blacks in World Wars I and II, which patently underscored the contradiction between fighting for freedom abroad and lacking it at home (Wynn 1993; Norton et al. 1990); the Cold War, which made it a necessity to eliminate overt discrimination at home in order to sell the U.S. as the champion of democracy; and a number of judicial decisions, legislative acts, and presidential decrees that transpired after the forties (Burkey 1971; Woodward 1966).

The aforementioned political, social, and economic processes occurred in a fast changing U.S. political economy. From 1920 until 1940, the North expanded its industrialization process at a furious pace. After World War II, the South industrialized at an even more dramatic pace. Many Northern industries moved South in search of lower production costs (Leiman 1992; Reich 1981). By the early 1990s over 70 percent of the Southern labor force was engaged in nonagricultural pursuits (Leiman 1992). This industrialization process provided the pull factor for blacks to move from the rural South which, coupled with the push factor of escaping the violence of Jim Crow (Tolnay and Beck 1991) and the demise in agricultural jobs (Christian and Pepelais 1978), created the optimal conditions for the "great migration." Although the 1.8 million blacks (Davis 1991) who migrated between 1910 and 1940 from the South to the North and West faced severe discrimination and economic constraints from white workers, labor unions, and whites in general (Marks 1991; Foner 1981), the North provided them expanded opportunities in all realms of life (Leiman 1992). This great migration continued between 1940 and 1970 as 4.4 million more blacks left the South (Davis 1991).

The impact of this migration on the overall condition of blacks was enormous. By 1970 blacks were geographically diffused throughout the U.S. Eighty percent were urban dwellers and had achieved a higher rate or urbanization than whites. Blacks had increased their education and developed a small but thriving middle class. In addition, social and political organizations flourished and became a training ground for many black leaders. By virtue of their new geographic dispersion, blacks increasingly became a national group and were able to develop a new consciousness, new attitudes, and a new view on how to deal with racial discrimination. Gunnar Myrdal characterized this new orientation as the "protest motive" (Davis 1991; Henri 1975; Myrdal [1944] 1964).

Even in the South, the social, political, and cultural condition of blacks improved somewhat with the early process of industrialization (Myrdal [1944] 1964: 998–999). After the 1960s, their economic condition changed as the top business elite abandoned all-out discrimination because of the adverse economic effects created by violence and protest demonstrations (Christian and Pepelasis 1978). This pattern was reinforced by Northern industrial capital which had penetrated the South, making the "Southern system of brutality, social discrimination, and legalized (or extra-legalized) persecution …more and more economically and politically dysfunctional" (Leiman 1992: 174).

To be clear, neither urbanization nor industrialization were nonracial "rational" progressive forces in themselves. Both Northern and Southern capitalists accommodated racial discrimination in their hiring practices, company policies, and daily practices. Although Southern capitalists were able to maintain Jim Crow and industrialization for over fifty years (1890s–1950s), by the mid-fifties it became clear that they could not coexist peacefully. At the same time, blacks in the North had acquired enough political muscle to push the Federal government to do something about their civil rights. After the *Brown* decision of 1954 and its rejection by most of the South, instability and protests spread throughout the South. Such instability was anathema for attracting capital. Therefore, the business elite reluctantly and gradually developed an accommodation with the new policies. In the North, the accommodation began much earlier in the 1920s, 1930s, and particularly after WWII, involving the subordinate incorporation of Blacks in industry. This accommodation, although progressive, maintained the view that blacks were inferior workers and kept them in the bottom of the occupational hierarchy. What industrialization and urbanization did for blacks was to provide a new context for struggle that made the Southern Jim Crow system impossible to maintain in the face of black opposition.

Yet the demise of Jim Crow did not end racial discrimination in America. Many analysts (Pettigrew 1994; Sears 1988; Kinder and Sears 1981; Wellman 1977; Caditz 1976) have noted that "racism" (as usually defined) and race relations have acquired a new character since the sixties. They point to the increasingly covert nature of racial discourse and racial practices: the avoidance of racial terminology in racial conflicts by whites and the elaboration of a racial agenda over political matters (state intervention, individual rights, responsibility, etc.) that eschews any direct racial reference.

Interracial Social Interaction During the New Racism Period

In all areas of social life blacks and whites remain mostly separate and disturbingly unequal. Pager and Shepard (2008) find that racial inequalities persist in the areas of housing, employment, credit, and consumer markets, noting the role of covert discrimination and structural factors in maintaining ongoing inequalities. A close examination of research in the areas of housing, education, and everyday social interaction reveals startlingly little progress since the 1960s.

Residential Segregation

During the 1990s, segregation declined in 272 metropolitan statistical areas and increased in 19 MSAs (Glaeser and Vigdor 2004). However, black-white segregation remained high in the older Rust-Belt metropolitan areas and increased during the 1990s in the suburbs (Logan 2003). Furthermore, blacks are still more segregated than any other racial or ethnic group (Logan 2003) – segregation which they have experienced longer than any other group – and are segregated at every income level. The black poor, in particular, suffer the greatest degree of hypersegregation from the rest of America, and this pattern of extreme isolation has remained the same for the past several decades (Cashin 2004). In 2000, national black isolation was 65 percent. It remained 80 percent or higher in Detroit, Newark, and Chicago (Cashin 2004). Due to higher white flight of families with children to segregated suburbs, children are the most segregated by neighborhood (68.3 percent) (Cashin 2004).

Some demographic data suggests that residential segregation is improving. U.S. Census 2000 data indicates that overall residential segregation has declined for the third straight decade. Although many of these types of indices are used as if they were sophisticated measures, the reality is otherwise, as these indices essentially rely on "simple numerical and percentage comparisons of the numbers and proportions of persons in each race/ethnicity group in a population" (Murdock and Ellis, 1991: 152). Scholars have pointed to the problem of unmeasured segregation because of the scale of census tracts (James and Taeuber 1985). More fundamentally, however, we suggest that "racial contacts" *do not* mean substantive integration, since there are significant forms of racism compatible with "physical closeness." The apparent "integration" noted in some settings (Farley and Frey 1994) may have more to do with poverty and falling incomes of poor whites or simply the restructuring of urban space than as a result of meaningful racial integration.

The costs to blacks of residential segregation are high: they are likely to pay more for housing in a limited market, likely to have lower quality housing, less likely to own their housing, likely to live in areas where employment is difficult to find, and have to contend with prematurely depreciated housing (Yinger 2001; Turner et al. 1991; Farley and Allen 1987; Struyk and Turner 1986; Kain 1986; Jackman and Jackman 1980). The big difference between residential segregation during Jim Crow and today is in how segregation is accomplished. In the Jim Crow era the housing industry used overtly discriminatory practices, such as real estate agents who refused to rent or sell to black customers, federal government redlining policies, overtly discriminatory insurance and lending practices, and racially restrictive covenants on housing deeds in order to maintain segregated communities (Massey and Denton 1993). In contrast, covert behaviors in the post-civil rights era have replaced these practices and have maintained the same outcome: separate communities.

Many studies have detailed the obstacles that minorities face from government agencies, real estate agents, money lenders, and white residents which continue to limit their housing options (Cashin 2004; Turner et al. 2002; Massey and Denton 1993; Cloud and Galster 1993; Kaestner and Fleisher 1992; Turner et al. 1991; Galster 1990a). Housing audits everywhere suggest that blacks have been denied available housing from 35 to 75 percent of the time depending on the city in question (Smith 1995). Turner, Struyk, and Yinger (1991), in reporting the results of the Department of Housing and Urban Development's *Housing Discrimination Study*, found that blacks and Hispanics were discriminated against in approximately *half* of their efforts to rent or buy housing. These housing studies have shown that, when paired with similar white counterparts, blacks are likely to be shown fewer apartments, quoted higher rents, offered worse conditions, and steered to specific neighborhoods (Turner et al. 2002; Turner et al. 1991; Galster 1990b; Yinger 1986). In a 2000 audit of housing discrimination in 23

U.S. metropolitan areas Turner et al. (2002) reported that, although there was improvement since the 1989 audit, whites continued to be given more information about potential rentals and were shown more available housing units in both the rental and sales markets. The study also showed a significant increase in geographic steering that perpetuated segregation, predominantly through real estate agent editorializing.

In one study of lending practices done by the Kentucky Human Rights Commission (Center for Community Change 1989), black and white testers with equal characteristics requested conventional mortgages for the same housing from ten of the top lending institutions in Louisville. While there were cases in which discrimination was apparent (blacks having trouble getting appointments, etc.), in the 85 visits made to inquire about loans, none of the black testers (with one exception) knew they were being discriminated against, though *all* of them were. Blacks were given less information, less encouragement to return and apply for the loan, fewer helpful hints as to how to successfully obtain a loan, and differential treatment in pre-qualifying– sometimes being told they would not qualify when whites of the same profile were told they would. Similar studies done in Chicago and New York revealed discrimination in seven out of ten lending institutions in Chicago and in the one institution studied in New York City (Cloud and Galster 1993). In an overview of mortgage loan practices during the 1990s, Turner and Skidmore (1999) reported blacks received less information from loan officers, were quoted higher interest rates, and suffered higher loan denial rates. National data from the Home Mortgage Disclosure Act showed that black applicants were denied mortgages at least twice as frequently as whites of the same income and gender regardless of their income (Smith 1995: 67). Much of the gain in home ownership among blacks in the 1990s was achieved through subprime lenders who offer usurious rates, due in large part to the continued practice of redlining of black neighborhoods by mainstream lenders (Williams, et al. 2005; Cashin 2004). It is these same subprime mortgages that have caused the recent mortgage crisis to impact minorities more severely than whites (Hernandez 2009, Holden 2009, Lopez et al. 2009, Newman and Wyly 2004).

Education

The history of black-white education in this country is one of substantive inequities maintained through public institutions.

Although scholars have documented the narrowing of the gap in the *quantity* of education attained by blacks and whites (Jaynes and Williams 1989; Farley and Allen 1987; Farley 1984), little has been said about the persisting gap in the *quality* of education received. Still remaining (and in some cases worsening) high levels of de facto segregation are at least partly to blame for the gap in quality (Frankenberg, et al. 2003; Roscigno 1998; Rivken 1994). However, tracking, differential assignment to special education, and other informal school practices are important factors too.

Despite some progress during the period immediately after 1964, the level of school segregation for black students remains relatively high in all regions and has deteriorated in the northeast and midwest regions (Orfield and Monfort 1992). In the 1998–1999 school year, 36.5 percent of blacks attended schools that were at least 90 percent non-white and 70.2 percent of blacks attended schools that were at least 50 percent nonwhite (Orfield 2001). The Civil Rights Project at Harvard University reports a trend beginning in 1986 towards resegregation of the U.S. schools (Orfield and Lee 2005; Frankenberg et al. 2003). As a consequence of resegregation during the decade of the 1990s, U.S. schools were more segregated in the 2000–2001 school year than in 1970 (Frankenberg et al., 2003; Orfield 2001). The relevance of this fact is that, as Gary Orfield has noted, "Segregated schools are still profoundly unequal" (Orfield 1993: 235). Inner-city minority schools, in sharp contrast to white suburban schools, lack decent buildings, are overcrowded, have outdated equipment (if they have equipment at all), do not have enough textbooks for their students, lack library resources, are technologically behind, and pay their teaching and administrative staff less, which often produces a low level of morale. These "savage inequalities" (Kozol 1991) have been directly related to lower reading achievement and learning attained by black students (Orfield and Lee 2005; Roscigno 1998) and their limited computer skills (Booker et al. 1992).

In integrated schools, blacks still have to contend with discriminatory practices. Oakes and her co-authors (1992) have found clear evidence of discriminatory practices in tracking within schools. Whites (and Asians) are considerably (and statistically significantly) more likely to be placed in the academic track than comparably achieving black and Latino students (Oakes et al. 1992). The implications of not being placed in the academic track include less preparedness for college work and lower test scores. No wonder black students tend to score lower on the SAT than white students.

Other Areas of Social Life

A brief survey of research in other areas of social life reveals persistent discrimination, unequal treatment, and, in some cases, exclusion. In terms of intermarriage, blacks are less likely than any other racial or ethnic group to intermarry (Lieberson and Watters 1988). This is one of the few areas where whites still openly express reservations in surveys (Schuman et al. 1997). In 1993, only 0.4 percent of all new marriages were black-white unions (Otis-Graham 1995). Furthermore, while a recent publication from the Pew Research Center stated that "a record 14.6 percent of all new marriages in the United States were between spouses of a different race or ethnicity," only 9 percent of whites married non-whites in 2008 (Passel et al. 2010). Not only are over 90 percent of whites marrying other whites, additional research shows that intermarriage rates among Latinos and Asians has actually decreased since 1980 (Lichter 2010). In addition to whites' negative attitudes toward interracial relationships, the high level of residential segregation and the limited friendships between blacks and whites contribute to this low rate of intermarriage. Research by Jackman and Crane (1986) showed that only 9.4 percent of whites could name one good black friend. This led them to conclude that very few whites "could rightly claim that 'some of their best friends' are black" (Jackman and Crane 1986: 460).

In the realm of everyday life, several works have attempted to examine the daily experiences blacks have with racism (Feagin and McKinney 2003; Otis-Graham 1995; Feagin and Sikes 1994; Cose 1993; Essed 1991; Collins 1989). In his interviews of middle-class blacks who have supposedly "made it," Ellis Cose (1993) repeatedly discovered a sense among these "successful blacks" that they were being continually blocked and constrained in ways that make it impossible to hold anyone accountable. In one series of examples, Cose reports experiences of job tracking in which blacks were given those jobs that dealt with "minority concerns" and which were seen as either unimportant or undesirable. Cose quotes many of his interviewees discussing the feeling of being susceptible to being "stripped of status at a moment's notice" by a store clerk, a cab driver, the waiter at a restaurant, a security guard, etc. (Cose 1993). Feagin and McKinney (2003) point out that the chronic stress and "justified rage" resulting from these mistreatments costs blacks psychologically, creates loss of personal energy, and affects their physical health.

Lawrence Otis-Graham (1995) reports in his book *Member of the Club* that, in ten of New York's best restaurants he and his black friends visited, they were stared at, mistaken for restaurant workers, seated in terrible spots, and buffered so as to avoid proximity to whites in most of them. Otis-Graham reports that they were treated reasonable well in only two of the ten restaurants, one Russian and the other French. Lawsuits filed against Denny's, Shoney's, and the International House of Pancakes seem to suggest that discrimination in restaurants is experienced by blacks of all class backgrounds (Feagin and Sikes 1994).

Joe R. Feagin and Melvin P. Sikes also document the dense network of discriminatory practices confronted by middle-class blacks in everyday life. Although they correctly point out that blacks face discriminatory practices that range from overt and violent to covert and gentle, the latter seem to be prevalent. In public spaces the discriminatory behavior described by black interviewees included poor service, special requirements applied only to them, surveillance in stores, being ignored at retail stores selling expensive commodities, receiving worse accommodations in restaurants or hotels, being constantly confused with menial workers, in addition to the usual but seemingly less frequent epithets and overtly racist behavior (see Chapter 2 in Feagin and Sikes 1994).

Post-Civil Rights Social Control and the New Racism

The mechanisms by which blacks experience social control in the contemporary period are now overwhelmingly covert. The mechanisms to keep blacks in "their place" are rendered invisible in three ways. First, because the enforcement of the racial order from the sixties onward has been institutionalized, individual whites can express a detachment from the *racialized* way in which social control agencies operate in America. In *The New Jim Crow: Mass Incarceration in the Age of Colorblindness* Michelle Alexander notes that, "More African-Americans are under correctional control today… than were enslaved in 1850" (2010: 175). Second, because these agencies are *legally* charged with defending *order* in society, their actions are deemed neutral and necessary. Finally, the incidents that seem to indicate racial bias in the criminal justice system are depicted by the white-dominated media as isolated incidents (Chideya 1995). For example, cases that presumably expose the racial character of social control agencies (e.g., the police beating of Rodney King, the police killing of James Earl Green at Jackson State, the acquittal or lenient sentences received by officers accused of police brutality, etc.) are viewed as "isolated" incidents and are separated from the larger social context in which they transpire.

The Continuing Racial Economic Inequality

The economic life of blacks has always been influenced by structured racial inequality. A substantial body of literature on white-black employment differences has documented the influence of labor market discrimination, wage differentials, occupational segmentation, as well as income and wealth inequalities in explaining racially differential economic outcomes (Lui et al. 2006; Oliver and Shapiro 2006; Day and Newburger 2002; Jaynes and Williams 1989). Despite well documented disparities between blacks and whites, many social scientists focused their attention on the growth of the black middle class (Sowell 1984; Wilson 1978). Some of them projected the "success" of this segment to the entire community creating an image of general economic progress. To be sure, blacks have experienced significant progress in several areas of their economic life over the past four decades (the economic standing of black women vis-a-vis white women, the opening of jobs that were reserved for whites, the development of a significant middle class, etc.). Yet their overall economic situation relative to whites has not advanced much (Lui et al. 2006; Darity, Cotton, and Hill 1993).

Income and Wage Differentials

Studies analyzing differences in median income between blacks and whites revealed some convergence (Farley 1993; Farley and Allen 1987; Smith and Welch 1986). Much of it was attributed to the rising levels of educational attainment of blacks, in particular among younger cohorts (Smith and Welch 1986) as well as affirmative action policies (Heckman and Payner 1992; Leonard 1990). However, the empirical evidence regarding racial convergence in income is somewhat mixed. Several social scientists have found that the incomes of blacks began rapid convergence with whites from World War II, but during the recession of the early 1970s, blacks' income levels began to stagnate and the racial convergence ceased (Danziger, et al. 2005; Jaynes 1990; Jaynes and Williams 1989). By 1990, a substantial black-white earnings gap had reemerged as the black-white family income ratio reached 0.56, a ratio hardly larger than the 0.55 of 1960 (Pinkney 1993). In 2003, median black family income had only marginally improved to 61 percent of white median family income (U.S. Census Bureau 2006). Interestingly, the decline in blacks' income vis-à-vis whites has been attributed to the decline in enforcement of antidiscrimination laws and Affirmative Action policies by the Federal government (Leonard 1990). Thus, while blacks made marked advancement from World War II to the early 1970s, their incomes relative to whites has progressed little over the last several decades.

Furthermore, analysts who focus on income convergence tend to mask serious trends affecting the black population –like unemployment, underemployment, and the decrease in the rate of labor force participation– by making their comparisons based on full-time workers. Darity and Myers (1980) astutely observed that the exclusion of blacks with zero incomes (i.e. the unemployed and the jobless) in social scientists' assessment of income differences between blacks and whites masks the persistent racial fault line in economic life (see also Darity et al 1993; Badgett 1994). The gap in unemployment between blacks and whites increased during the 1970s and the 1980s–the same period in which blacks incomes virtually ceased converging with whites (Cotton 1989; Farley 1984). In 2004, the unemployment rate of blacks was 8.1, more than twice the 3.9 rate of whites (U.S. Bureau of Census 2006). Even though the racial gap in employment decreased during the economic prosperity of the 1990s, by 1999 the employment to population ratio for black men was 86 percent that of white men and black men were employed seven hours less per week than whites (Farley 2004). Moreover, employment rates of blacks were much lower in some geographical areas. In 2003, only 52 percent of working-age black men in New York City were employed, "the lowest percent since the Bureau of Labor Statistics began recording employment-to-population ratios in 1979 (Liu et al. 2006).

Income differences reflect to a large extent the different earning potential of blacks and whites in America. Black males in 1999 earned about 60 percent as much as white males. Black females, who had per capita incomes 90 percent of white females in 1990, saw their incomes drop to 85 percent of white female income in 1999 (Farley 2004). This vast difference is attributed to blacks lesser educational attainment, lesser rates of return for their education and their labor market experience, and their concentration in the South, all directly related to the racial dynamics of this country (Bradbury 2002; Ashraf 1994; Hacker 1992; Farley and Allen 1987). Does the difference in earnings disappear between blacks and whites with similar characteristics? The answer is no. Farley and Allen (1987) carried out such a comparison for 1980 and found the gap for black men to be 14 percent. More recently, Day and Newburger (2002) show less earnings for blacks than whites at every educational level.

Occupational Mobility and Segmentation

One of the primary reasons why blacks' economic standing is much worse than whites is because of occupational race-typing. Although recent occupational data show that blacks have made substantial progress in obtaining employment in occupational categories from which they previously were, for all practical purposes, excluded (O'Hare et al. 1991; Farley and Allen 1987; Farley 1984), they are still overrepresented among unskilled workers and underrepresented in higher-paying white-collar jobs. In 1960, whereas 60.4 percent of white men worked in blue-collar jobs, a whopping 76.7 percent of blacks did so (Farley and Allen 1987). The 2000 U.S. Census (U.S. Census Bureau 2000) shows whites are still more likely than blacks to be employed in managerial and professional occupations: 35.43 percent of white males and 40.64 percent of white females compared to 21.65 percent of black males and 31 percent of black females. Blacks, in contrast, are disproportionately employed in service occupations: 20.23 percent of black males and 26.39 percent of black females compared to 10.85 percent of white males and 17.03 percent of white females. Within service occupations, black males are most likely to be employed in building and grounds cleaning and maintenance; black females, in health, personal, and food care. Black males are also disproportionately represented in production, transportation, and material moving (26.17 percent of blacks compared to 17.26 percent of whites). White males are more likely to hold construction jobs (17.26 percent of white compared to 12.63 percent of blacks).

Two other factors point to the segmentation experienced by blacks in America. First, despite the apparent decline in underrepresentation of blacks in managerial and professional occupations, blacks employed in these occupations have lower earnings than their white counterparts (Cotton 1990). Furthermore, some research suggests that black managers are segmented into a minority submarket of lower level managerial posts which limit chances for promotion (Durr and Logan 1997). Second, while the significance of race as a determinant of occupational mobility for black men may have declined during the period of 1962 through 1973, other research suggests that their occupational mobility is less frequent than that of whites and more restricted in terms of destination (Waddoups 1991; Pomer 1986). Oliver and Shapiro (2006: 160–161) note that "nearly two out of five blacks from lower blue-collar backgrounds remain stuck in unskilled and, for the most part, poorly paid jobs." Some mainstream researchers attributed the racial differences in earnings to the existing educational gap between blacks and whites (Hout 1984). However, Cotton (1990) found that racial differences among those employed in the managerial and professional occupations could not be explained by educational differences. This is not surprising since research has consistently shown that black men earn less than white men in almost all occupations (Moss and Tilly 2001; Ashraf 1994; see also Farley and Allen 1987).

While blacks have succeeded in non-traditional occupations, their occupational mobility still exhibits a distinct racial pattern. Several studies have indicated that, for the most part, Jim Crow discrimination has been replaced with a new web of racial practices that limits their mobility and affects their everyday performance (Otis-Graham 1995; Cose 1993; Brooks 1990; Collins 1989; Landry 1987). One of the most pervasive of these practices is pigeonholing blacks in some positions, a practice reminiscent of typecasting blacks for "nigger jobs" during Jim Crow (Cose 1993; see also Durr and Logan 1997). For instance, Collins (1989) found that many black executives filled affirmative action, community relations, minority affairs or public relations positions that were created during the 1960s and 1970s to respond to civil rights demands than do not provide much mobility.

Labor Market Discrimination

Since the early 1960s, social scientists have acknowledged that labor market discrimination is an important causal factor in explaining the differential employment outcomes of blacks and whites (Darity and Mason 1998; Garfinkel et al. 1977; Thurow 1975, 1969). Yet, until recently, studies on labor market discrimination assessed discrimination as the unexplained residual in black and white earnings after controlling for a number of variables. Although this measure is useful, it tends to underestimate the extent of discrimination by eliminating differences in, for example, education and occupational status that are themselves the product of discrimination (Boston 1988).

Since the 1990s, analysts have relied on a research strategy to *directly* assess the impact of discrimination. The technique used to examine labor market discrimination is called an employment audit and consists of sending subjects matched in most characteristics except their race to find jobs (Pager 2003; Bendick et al. 1991; Turner et al. 1991; Cross et al. 1990). By adopting this approach, analysts have been able to estimate the *extent* as well as the *form* of discrimination that minorities endure in the labor market. Probably the most famous of these studies was those carried out by the Urban Institute in 1991. It was conducted on randomly selected employers in San Diego, Chicago, and Washington, D.C. and found that, on average, white testers were significantly favored over black testers (Turner et. al. 1991). In 20 percent of the audits, blacks were denied job opportunities. In Milwaukee, Wisconsin, Pager (2003) divided applicant testers with comparable resumes into 4 groups: whites without criminal record, whites with criminal record, blacks without criminal record, and blacks with criminal record. White applicants with a criminal record (17 percent) were more likely to be called back for an interview than black applicants without a criminal record (14 percent).

Research indicates that blacks are discriminated against at all levels of the job process. In the search process, they are left behind because most employers rely on informal social networks to advertise their jobs. And since blacks are not part of those networks, they are left out in the cold (Royster 2003; Cherry 1989). Not only does this hinder blacks in their struggle to gain middle-class jobs, Royster (2003) shows that networks of gatekeepers maintain white privilege in trade careers as well. Furthermore, recent examination of welfare leavers since the 1996 welfare reform laws indicate that white privilege operates even at low-level service jobs. Employers were less likely to hire black than white welfare leavers and paid the black welfare leavers they did hire less (Liu et al. 2006). At the job entry level, in addition to the practices mentioned before, blacks are screened out by tests and the requirement of a high school diploma. These two practices were developed in the late 1950s and 1960s as substitutes for outright exclusion from jobs and were mentioned in the 1964 Civil Rights Act as practices that could have exclusionary results (Kovarsky and Albrecht 1970).

They are discriminatory because the diploma and the tests are not usually essential to job performance.

In terms of job promotion, blacks face a glass ceiling because they are pigeonholed in dead-end jobs (Baldi and McBrier 1997; Otis-Graham 1995; Cose 1993; Travis 1991; Brooks 1990). Research also suggests that blacks' exclusion from informal social networks restricts their opportunities to demonstrate informal criteria for promotion, such as loyalty, sound judgment, and leadership potential (Wilson et al. 1999). Moreover, Baldi and McBrier (1997) found that increased minority presence results in a negative effect on blacks. They suggest a group threat process may be at work where white managers attempt to protect white workers in the face of increased minority presence.

Wealth

The available data on wealth indicates that the disparities in this important area are greater than in any other economic area, and they are increasing. Blacks owned only three percent of U.S. assets in 2001, even though they constituted 13 percent of the U.S. population (Liu et al. 2006). In 2001, the median net worth of whites, $120,989, was over 6.3 times that of blacks, which was only $19,024 (Lui et al. 2006). Calculations of mean net worth reveals that, in 2001, the average black family had 17 cents for every dollar of the average white family (Lui et al. 2006). Oliver and Shapiro (2006) report that the racial wealth gap increased from $60,980 in 1988 to $82,663 in 2002.

A major reason for this disparity in wealth is inheritance and financial gifts from kin. The average financial legacy for white families in 2001 was ten times that of the average black family (Lui et al. 2006). Gittleman and Wolff (2004) examined factors affecting wealth accumulation over the 10 period from 1984 to 1994 and found no evidence of differences in saving behaviors after controlling for income. Had blacks had comparable inheritance, income, and portfolios during this period, they would have significantly narrowed the racial wealth gap. The researchers conclude, however, that it will be "extraordinarily difficult for blacks to make up significant ground relative to whites with respect to wealth" (Gittleman and Wolf 2004: 221) because of their much lower rates of inheritance, lower incomes, and the fact that much of their economic assets lie in home equity.

Home equity is less among blacks than whites for several reasons, the most obvious of which is lower rates of home ownership among blacks (71.3 percent for whites versus 46.3 percent for blacks). The latter reflects a cyclical process by which wealth begets wealth, as "half of all white families but only one-fifth of black families have parents who can help them buy a home" (Lui et al. 2006: 77). This and redlining results in 80 percent higher denial of home loans for blacks (Oliver and Shapiro 2004). Also affecting accrual of home equity and accumulation of discretionary income are the higher interest rates (about one percent higher) charged blacks, compared to whites (Oliver and Shapiro 2006). In addition, homes in black neighborhoods do not appreciate as much as homes in white neighborhoods (Oliver and Shapiro 2006; Liu et al. 2006).

Managerial Views on Blacks

Recent research suggests that the views of white managers on blacks have not changed dramatically since the 1960s. Blacks have complained that they are bypassed by white managers for promotion, that they are not treated as equals, and that they endure a subtle hostility from their fellow workers and supervisors (Otis-Graham 1995; Cose 1993; Travis 1991; Collins 1989). White employers and managers hiring for unskilled positions generally hold views that are more openly racist. In their interviews with Chicago and Cook county employers, Kirschenman and Neckerman (1994) found that blacks were viewed as having a bad work ethic, creating tensions in the workplace, lazy and unreliable, lacking leadership, and having a bad attitude.

In an investigation of the labor market difficulties of urban minorities, Moss and Tilly (2001) studied the attitudes of employers toward prospective employees of entry level, working-class jobs in the metropolitan areas of Atlanta, Boston, Detroit, and Los Angeles between 1992 and 1995. Most employers expressed greater concern about soft skills, such as social skills, which are subjectively determined, than the hard skills of potential employees and they found urban blacks, especially black males and inner-city residents wanting in this respect. Moss and Tilly attributed the employers' racial bias to racial stereotypes, negative and racialized images of inner-city residents, and cultural differences, such as dress, vocabulary, and syntax.

Obama and the "End of Racism"?[2]

Many have hailed the election of Barak Obama as proof that America has moved "beyond race" (D'Souza 1995, Dowd 2009, Ifill 2009, Reed and Louis 2009, CBS 2009). However, we contend Obama's ascendancy to the Presidency is part and parcel of the "New Racism." Obama himself has shown this in several ways. First, Obama worked hard during the campaign at making a nationalist, post-racial appeal. Second, he was keen to signify the peculiar character of his 'blackness' (his half-white, half-black background) and the provenance of his blackness (his father hailed from Kenya and, in the USA, African blackness is perceived as less threatening than African-American blackness). Obama also has cultivated an image where his 'blackness' is more about style than political substance; Obama is the 'cool,' exceptional black man not likely to rock the American racial boat. Third, Obama has exhibited an accommodationist stance on race (Street 2009). In a speech in Selma, Alabama, he stated the USA was "90 percent on the road to racial equality" (Obama 2007) and continued this path in his so-called 'race speech' (Obama 2008). Fourth, whites see Obama as a 'safe black' who, unlike traditional black politicians, will not advocate race-based social policy. Fifth, Obama will formulate 'universal' (class-based) policies that are unlikely to remedy racial inequality (Obama 2004).

Conclusion

The changes in the racial dynamics at all levels which we have documented in this paper seem to amount to a reorganization –still incomplete and somewhat partial– of the racial structure of this country. This reorganization of the racial structure is incomplete because 1) not all the mechanisms and practices have become institutionalized, and 2) we still have many legacies of the previous period affecting the life chances of blacks. On the first point, discrimination in the realm of education, for example, has not taken a definite institutional pattern in the contemporary period. Instead, there are various

---

[2] For a more thorough examination of the Obama phenomenon as it relates to color-blind racism see *Racism Without Racists, 3rd Edition* by Eduardo Bonilla-Silva (2010).

means (resegregation through white flight to the suburbs and private schools, within school segregation, tracking, etc.) to guarantee white advantages. On the second point, we still have old-fashioned racists, extra-legal violence, and an undeclared apartheid in the housing arena. Although many of these practices are manifestations of the legacies of slavery and Jim Crow in this country (Winant 1994), the evidence reviewed here suggests that blacks and other minorities should fear less the angry men with white hoods and their traditional discriminatory practices than the men with suits and their "smiling discrimination" (Brooks 1990). We agree with Pettigrew and Martin when they claim that:

> ...the greater subtlety of these new forms [of racial discrimination] pose new problems of remedy. They act at both the structural-institutional level focused on by sociologists, and the face-to-face situational level focused on by social psychologists (Pettigrew and Martin 1987: 42).

Some of these problems that require remedy are:
1) Detection of racial discrimination is extremely difficult for the party being discriminated against. Furthermore, too many progressive whites tend to explain away many of the claims of contemporary discrimination because:

> Often the black is the only person in a position to draw the conclusion that prejudice is operating in the work situation. Whites have usually observed only a subset of the incidents, any one of which can be explained away by a nonracial account. Consequently, many whites remain unconvinced of the reality of subtle prejudice and discrimination, and come to think of their black coworkers as "terribly touchy" and "overly sensitive" to the issue. For such reasons, the modern forms of prejudice frequently remain invisible even to its perpetrators (Pettigrew and Martin 1987: 50).

2) The standards that the Supreme Court has enacted on discrimination cases (plaintiffs carrying the burden of proof in discrimination cases and the denial of statistical evidence as valid proof of discrimination) help to preserve intact the contemporary forms for reproducing racial inequality in America. Unless the Court becomes cognizant of the new character of racial discrimination and changes its current practice of requiring the "smoking gun" in discrimination cases, the Court itself will be participating in covering up the far-reaching effects of racism in America.
3) Black leaders who continue to focus on the "old racism" will miss the most important manners by which racial inequality is being

reproduced in America. It is vital that studies documenting the pervasive and comprehensive character of the New Racism are done systematically.

4) Research that is still focused on the old racism will invariably find a decline in the significance of race. Research on racial practices has to become as sophisticated as the New Racism. The studies carried out by the Urban Institute and HUD in which testers are sent out to various settings and organizations are an example of what can be done. Unfortunately, that type of research does not enjoy the sympathy of our disciplines and has been even deemed as "unethical." The web of discriminatory practices in the contemporary period is still not complete.

Hence it is still possible to mount an offensive to change its course. However, at the moment we write this chapter, the prospects for such an offensive look bleak. First, the election of Obama, as we argued, has narrowed the space for challenging race-based inequality. Nowadays whites believe racism has all but been defeated and thus it is much harder to challenge new and old-fashioned discrimination. Second, civil rights organizations such as the NAACP and the National Urban League continue to fight the enemies of the past, like the Ku Klux Klan or their Tea Party cousins, but not the contemporary structures and practices that are primarily responsible for post-civil rights racial inequality. The more these organizations fight the "racists," the more they fail to highlight the new ways in which racial inequality is produced and reproduced helping these practices to sediment. Third, we may have missed the historical boat to challenge the system of "mass incarceration" (Alexander 2010) and will pay dearly for doing so. If we do not work towards the development of a social movement to stop this tactic of social control, our collective chances for racial redemption are null. Unless this situation is reversed, the racial practices of the "New Racism" will be institutionalized and minority folks will continue enduring a second-class existence in seemingly color-blind America.

References

Alexander, Michelle. 2010. *The New Jim Crow: Mass Incarceration in the Age of Colorblindness*. New York: The New Press.

Ashraf, Javed. 1994. "Differences in Returns to Education: An Analysis By Race." *American Journal of Economics and Sociology* 53: 281–290.

Badgett, M. V. Lee. 1994. "Rising Black Unemployment: Changes in Job Stability or in Employability." *Review of Black Political Economy* 22: 55–75.

Baldi, Stepahne and Debra Branch McBrier. 1997. "Do the Determinants of Promotion Differ for Blacks and Whites?" *Work and Occupations* 24: 478–497.
Bell, Derrick. 1992. *Faces at the Bottom of the Well*. New York: Basic Books.
Bendick, Marc Jr., Charles Jackson, Victor Reinoso, and Laura Hodges. 1991. "Discrimination Against Latino Job Applicants: A Controlled Experiment." *Human Resource Management* 30: 469–484.
Booker, Michael A., Alan B. Krueger, and Shari Wolkon. 1992. "Race and School Quality Since Brown v. Board of Education." *Brookings Papers on Economic Activity. Microeconomics* 1992: 269–338.
Boston, Thomas D. 1988. *Race, Class, and Conservatism*. Boston: Unwin Hyman.
Bradbury, Katharine L. 2002. "Education and Wages in the 1980s and 1990s: Are All Groups Moving Up Together?." *New England Economic Review* 1:19–46.
Brooks, Roy L. 1990. *Rethinking the American Race Problem*. Berkeley: University of California Press.
Burkey, Richard M. 1971. *Racial Discrimination and Public Policy in the United States*. Lexington, MA: Heath Lexington Books.
Caditz, Judith. 1976. *White Liberals in Transition: Current Dilemmas of Ethnic Integration*. New York: Spectrum Publications.
Cashin, Sheryll. 2004. *The Failures of Integration: How Race and Class are Undermining the American Dream*. New York: Public Affairs.
CBS. 2009. "Poll: Blacks See Improved Race Relations." April 27. Available from www.cbsnews.com.
Center for Community Change. 1989. *Mortgage Lending Discrimination Testing Project*. Washington, DC: CCC/U.S. Dept of Housing and Urban Development.
Cherry, Robert. 1989. *Discrimination: Its Impact on Blacks, Women, and Jews*. Lexington, MA: Lexington Books.
Chideya, Farai. 1995. *Don't Believe the Hype: Fighting Cultural Misinformation About African-Americans*. New York: Penguin Books.
Christian, Virgil, and Admentios Pepelasis. 1978. "Rural Problems." In *Employment of Blacks in the South: A Perspective on the 1960s*, edited by Virgil Christian and Admentios Pepelasi. Austin: University of Texas Press.
Cloud, Cathy and George Galster. 1993. "What Do We Know About Racial Discrimination in Mortgage Markets?" *The Review of Black Political Economy* 21: 101–120.
Collins, Sharon M. 1989. "The Marginalization of Black Executives." *Social Problems* 36: 317–31. 1989.
Cose, Ellis. 1993. *The Rage of a Privileged Class: Why Are Middle Class Blacks Angry? Why Should America Care?* New York: Harper Collins.
Cotton, Jeremiah. 1989. "Opening the Gap: The Decline in Black Economic Indicators in the 1980s." *Social Science Quarterly* 70: 803–19.
Cross, H., G. Kenney, J. Mell, and W. Zimmermann. 1990. *Employer Hiring Practices*. Washington, D.C.: Urban Institute Press.
Danziger, Sheldon, Deborah Reed, and Tony N. Brown. 2005. "Poverty and Prosperity: Prospects for Reducing Racial/Ethnic Economic Disparities in the United States." In *Racism and Public Policy*, edited by Yusuf Bangura and Rodolfo Stavenhagen. New York: Palgrave Macmillan.
Darity, William A., Jr., and Patrick L. Mason. 1998. "Evidence on Discrimination in Employment: Codes of Color, Codes of Gender." *The Journal of Economic Perspectives* 12: 63–90.
Darity, William A., Jr., and Samuel L. Myers. 1980. "Changes in the Black-White Income Inequality, 1968–1978: A Decade of Progress?" *The Review of Black Political Economy* 10: 365–392.
Darity, William, Jr., Jeremiah Cotton, and Herbert Hill. 1993. "Race and Inequality in the Managerial Age." In *African Americans: Essential Perspectives*, edited by Wornie L. Reed. Portsmouth, NH: Greenwood Publishing Group.

Davis, Dernoral. 1991. "Toward a Socio-Historical and Demographic Portrait of Twentieth-Century African Americans." In *Black Exodus: The Great Migration from the American South*, edited by Alferdteen Harrison. Jackson, MS: University of Mississippi Press.

Day, Jennifer Cheeseman, and Eric Newburger. 2002. *The Big Payoff: Educational Attainment and Synthetic Estimates of Work-Life Earnings*. Washington, D.C.: U.S. Census Bureau.

Dowd, Maureen. 2009. "Dark, Dark, Dark." *New York Times*. February 22.

Duncan, Otis. 1968. "Patterns of Occupational Mobility Among Negro Men." *Demography* 5: 11–22.

D'Souza, Dinesh. 1995. *The End of Racism*. New York: Free Press.

Essed, Philomena. 1991. *Understanding Everyday Racism: An Interdisciplinary Approach*. London: Sage Publications.

Farley, Reynolds. 1984. *Blacks and Whites: Narrowing the Gap?* Cambridge, MA: Harvard University Press.

———. 1993. "The Common Destiny of Black and Whites: Observations about the Social and Economic Status of the Races." In *Race in America: The Struggle for Equality*, edited by Herbert Hill and James E. Jones, Jr. Madison, WI: The University of Wisconsin Press.

———. 2004. "Civil Rights and the Status of Black Americans in the 1960s and the 1990s." In *Race, Poverty, and Domestic Policy*, edited by Michael Henry. New Haven, CT: Yale University Press.

Farley, Reynolds, and Walter R. Allen. 1987. *The Color Line and the Quality of Life in America*. New York: Russell Sage Foundation.

Farley, Reynolds, and William H. Frey. 1994. "Changes in the Segregation of Whites from Blacks During the 1980s: Small Steps Toward a More Integrated Society." *American Sociological Review* 59: 23–45.

Farley, Reynolds, and Albert Hermalin. 1972. "The 1960s: A Decade of Progress for Blacks?" *Demography* 9: 353–370.

Feagin, Joe R., and Karyn D. McKinney. 2003. *The Many Costs of Racism*. Boston: Rowman and Littlefield.

Feagin, Joe R., and Melvin P. Sikes. 1994. *Living With Racism: The Black Middle Class Experience*. Borton: Beacon Press.

Foner, S. Philip. 1981. *Organized Labor and the Black Worker, 1619–1981*. New York: International Publishers.

Frankenberg, Erika, Chungmei Lee, and Gary Orfield. 2003. *Multiracial Society with Segregated Schools: Are We Losing the Dream?* Cambridge, MA: Civil Rights Project, Harvard University.

Freeman, Richard B. 1978. "Black Economic Progress Since 1964." *The Public Interest*, Summer.

Fusfeld, Daniel R., and Timothy Bates. 1984. *The Political Economy of the Urban Ghetto*. Carbondale, IL: Southern Illinois University Press.

Garfinkel, Irwin, Robert H. Haveman, and David Betson. 1977. *Earnings Capacity, Poverty, and Inequality*. New York: Academic Press.

Gittleman, Maury, and Edward N. Wolff. 2004. "Racial Differences in Patterns of Wealth Accumulation." *Journal of Human Resources* 39: 193–227.

Glaeser, Edward L., and Jacob L. Vigdor. 2004. "Racial Segregation: Promising News." In *Redefining Urban and Suburban America: Evidence from Census 2000, Volume One* edited by Bruce Katz and Robert E. Lang. Washington, D.C.: Brookings Institution Press.

Gossett, Thomas. 1963. *Race: The History of an Idea in America*. Dallas: Southern Methodist University Press.

Greeley, Andrew M., and Paul B. Sheatsley. 1971. "Attitudes toward Racial Integration." *Scientific American* 225: 13–19.

Greene, Lorenzo, and Carter G. Woodson. 1930. *The Negro Wage Earner*. New York: Association for the Study of Negro Life and History.
Hacker, Andrew. 1992. *Two Nations: Black and White, Separate, Hostile, Unequal*. New York: Ballantine Books.
Harrison, Afterdneen. 1991. *Black Exodus: The Great Migration from the American South*. Jackson. MS: University Press of Mississippi.
Heckman, James J., and Brooks S. Payner. 1992. "Determining the Impact of the Federal Antidiscrimination Policy on the Economic Status of Blacks: A Study of South Carolina." *American Economic Review* 79: 138-72.
Henri, Florette. 1975. *Black Migration: Movement North, 1900-1920*. New York: Anchor Press, Doubleday.
Hernandez, Jesus. 2009. "Relining Revisited: Mortgage Lending Patterns in Sacramento 1930-2004." *International Journal of Urban and Regional Research* 33: 291-313.
Holden, Stephen. 2009. "Meltdown on Wall Street, and Homeowners Left in the Lurch on Main Street." *New York Times*, September 2.
Hout, Michael. 1984. "Occupational Mobility of Black Men: 1962-1973." *American Sociological Review* 49: 308-322.
Hyman, Herbert H., and Paul B. Sheatsley. 1964. "Attitudes Toward Desegregation." *Scientific American* 211: 16-23.
Ifill, Gwen. 2009. *The Breakthrough*. New York: Doubleday.
Jackman, Mary R., and Marie Crane. 1986. "'Some of My Best Friends are Black…' Interracial Friendship and Whites' Racial Attitudes." *Public Opinion Quarterly* 50: 459-486.
Jackman, Mary and Robert Jackman. 1980. "Racial Inequality in Home Ownership." *Social Forces* 58:1221-54.
Jaynes, Gerald. 1990. "The Labor Market Status of Black Americans: 1939-1985." *Journal of Economic Perspectives* 4: 9-24.
Jaynes, Gerald D., and Robin M. Williams, editors. 1989. *A Common Destiny: Blacks and American Society*. Washington, D.C.: National Academy Press.
Kaestner, Robert and Wendy Fleischer. 1992. "Income Inequality as an Indicator of Discrimination in Housing Markets." *The Review of Black Political Economy* 20: 55-77.
Kinder, D. R., and D. O. Sears. 1981. "Prejudice and Politics: Symbolic Racism Versus Racial Threats to the Good Life." *Journal of Personality and Social Psychology* 40:414-431.
Kirschenman, Joleen and Kathryn M. Neckerman. 1994. "'We'd Love To Hire Them, But…': The Meaning of Race for Employers." In *Race and Ethnic Conflict*, edited by Fred L. Pincus and Howard J. Erlich. Boulder: Westview Press.
Kovarsky, Irving, and William Albrecht. 1970. *Black Employment: The Impact of Religion, Economic Theory, Politics, and Law*. Ames: The Iowa Satre University Press.
Kozol, Jonathan. 1991. *Savage Inequalities: Children in America's Schools*. New York: HarperCollins.
Landry, Bert. 1987. *The New Black Middle Class*. Berkeley: The University of California Press.
Leiman, Melvin M. 1992. *Political Economy of Racism*. London: Pluto Press.
Leonard, Jonathan S. 1990. "The Impact of Affirmative Action Regulation and Equal Employment Law on Black Employment." *Journal of Economic Perspectives* 4: 47-63
Lichter, Daniel T. 2010. "U.S. Far From an Interracial Melting Pot." *CNN*, June 16. Available at http://www.cnn.com/2010/OPINION/06/14/lichter.interracial.marriage/index.html?iref=allsearch
Lieberson, Stanley, and Mary C. Watters. 1988. *From Many Strands: Ethnic and Racial Groups in Contemporary America*. New York: Russell Sage Foundation.

Logan, John R. 2003. "Ethnic Diversity Grows, Neighborhood Integration Lags." In *Redefining Urban and Suburban America: Evidence from Census 2000, Volume One*, edited by Bruce Katz and Robert E. Lang. Washington, D.C.: Brookings Institution Press.
Lopez, Mark Hugh, Gretchen Livingston, and Rakesh Kochhar. 2009. *Hispanics and the Economic Downturn: Housing Woes and Remittance Cuts*. Washington, D.C.:Pew Hispanic Center. January 8.
Lui Meizhu, Barbara J. Robles, Betsy Leondar-Wright, Rose M. Brewer, and Rebecca Adamson. 2006. *The Color of Wealth: The Story Behind the U.S. Racial Wealth Divide*. New York: The New Press.
Lusane, Clarence. 1994. *African Americans at the Crossroads: The Restructuring of Black Leadership and the 1992 Elections*. Boston: South End Pres.
Marable, Manning. 1983. *How Capitalism Underdeveloped Black America*. Boston: South End Press.
Marks, Carole. 1991. "The Social and Economic Life of Southern Blacks During the Migration." In *Black Exodus: The Great Migration from the American South*, edited by Alferdteen Harrison. Jackson: University of Mississippi Press.
Massey, Douglas, and Nancy Denton. 1993. *American Apartheid: Segregation and the Making of the American Underclass*. Cambridge.: Harvard University Press.
McAdam, Douglas. 1982. *Political Process and the Development of Black Insurgency, 1930–1970*. Chicago: The University of Chicago Press.
Morris, Aldon. 1984. *The Origins of the Civil Rights Movement: Black Communities Organizing for Change*. New York: Free Press.
Moss, Philip, and Chris Tilly. 2001. *Stories Employers Tell: Race, Skill, and Hiring in America*. New York: Russell Sage Foundation.
Murdock, Steve H. and David R. Ellis. 1991. *Applied Demography: An Introduction to Basic Concepts, Methods, and Data*. Boulder: Westview Press.
Myrdal, Gunnar. [1944] 1964. *An American Dilemma*. New York: McGraw-Hill.
Newman, Kathe and Elvin K. Wyly. 2004. "Geographies of Mortgage Market Segmentation: The Case of Essex County, New Jersey." *Housing Studies* 19: 53–83.
Norton, Mary Beth, David M. Katzman, David W. Blight, Howard P. Chudacoff, Fredrik Logevall, Beth Bailey, Thomas G. Paterson, William M. Tuttle, Jr. 1990. *A People and a Nation: A History of the United States*. Boston: Houghton Mifflin.
Oakes, Jeannie, Molly Selvin, Lynn Karoly and Gretchen Guiton. 1992. *Educational Matchmaking: Academic and Vocational Tracking in Comprehensive High Schools*. Santa Monica, CA: Rand.
Obama, Barak. 2004. *The Audacity of Hope: Thoughts on Reclaiming the American Dream*. New York: Crown Publishers.
———. 2007. "Selma Voting Rights Commemoration." Speech at Brown University Chapel, Selma, AL, March 4.
———. 2008. "A More Perfect Union." Speech in Philadelphia, March 18.
O'Hare, William, Kelvin Pollard, Taynia Mann, and Mary Kent. 1991. "African Americans in the 1990s." *Population Bulletin* 46, no. 1.
Oliver, Melvin, and Thomas M. Shapiro. 2001. "Wealth and Racial Stratification." In *America Becoming: Racial Trends and Their Consequences, Volume 2*, edited by N. J. Smelser, W. J. Wilson, and F. Mitchell. Washington, D.C.: National Academy Press.
———. 2006. *Black Wealth/White Wealth*. New York: Routledge.
Orfield, Gary. 1993. "School Desegregation after Two Generations: Race, Schools and Opportunity in Urban Society." In *Race in America*, edited by Herbert Hill and James E. Jones. Madison: University of Wisconsin Press.
———. 2001. *Schools More Separate: Consequences of a Decade of Resegregation*. Cambridge, MA: Harvard University, Civil Rights Project.
Orfield, Gary and Franklin Monfort. 1992. *Status of School Desegregation: The Next Generation*. Alexandria, Va: National School Boards Association.

Orfield, Gary, and Chungmei Lee. 2005. *Why Segregation Matters: Poverty and Educational Inequality*. Cambridge, MA: The Civil Rights Project, Harvard University.

Otis-Graham, Lawrence. 1995. *Member of the Club: Reflections On Life in a Racially Polarized World*. New York: Harper Collins.

Pager, Devah. 2003. "The Mark of a Criminal Record." *American Journal of Sociology* 108: 937–975.

Pager, Devah and Hana Shepherd. 2008. "The Sociology of Discrimination: Racial Discrimination in Employment, Housing, Credit, and Consumer Markets." *Annual Review of Sociology* 34: 181–209.

Palmore, Erdman, and Frank J. Whittington. 1970. "Differential Trends Towards Equality Between Whites and Nonwhites." *Social Forces* 49: 108–117.

Passel, Jeffrey S., Wendy Wang, and Paul Taylor. 2010. *Marrying Out*. Washington, D.C.: Pew Research Center. June 15.

Patterson, Ernest. 1974. *City Politics*. New York: Dood, Mead, and Co.

Pettigrew, Thomas F. 1994. "New Patterns of Prejudice: The Different Worlds of 1984 and 1964." In *Race and Ethnic Conflict*, edited by Fred L. Pincus and Howard J. Erlich. Boulder, CO: Westview Press.

Pettigrew, Thomas F., and Joanne Martin. 1987. "Shaping the Organizational Context for Black American Inclusion." *Journal of Social Issues* 43: 41–78.

Pinkney, Alphonso. 1984. *The Myth of Black Progress*. Cambridge, England: Cambridge University Press.

———. 1993. *Black Americans, Fourth Edition*. Englewood, NJ: Prentice Hall.

Pomer, Marshall. 1986. "Labor Market Structure, Intragenerational Mobility, and Discrimination: Black Male Advancement Out of Low-paying Occupations, 1962–1973." *American Sociological Review* 51: 650–59.

Reed, Wornie L., and Bertin M. Louis, Jr. 2009. "No More Excuses." *Journal of African American Studies* 13:97–109.

Reich, Michael. 1981. *Racial Inequality: A Political-Economic Analysis*. Princeton: Princeton University Press.

Rivken, Stephen. 1994. "Residential Segregation and School Integration." *Sociology of Education* 67: 279–92.

Roscigno, Vincent. 1998. "Race and the Reproduction of Educational Disadvantage." *Social Forces* 76: 1033–1060.

Royster, Deirdre A. 2003. *Race and the Invisible Hand: How White Networks Exclude Men from Blue-Collar Jobs*. Berkeley: University of California Press.

Schuman, Howard, Charlotte Steeh, Lawrence Bobo. and Maria Krysan. 1997. *Racial Attitudes in America: Trends and Interpretations, Revised Edition*. Cambridge, MA: Harvard University Press.

Sears, David O. 1988. "Symbolic Racism." In *Eliminating Racism: Profiles in Controversy*, edited by Phylis A. Katz and Dalmas A. Taylor. New York: Plenum Press.

Shapiro, Thomas M. 2004. *The Hidden Cost of Being African-American*. Oxford: Oxford University Press.

Smith, James P., and Finnis R. Welch. 1986. *Closing the Gap, Forty Years of Economic Progress for Blacks*. Santa Monica, CA: Rand Corporation.

Smith, Robert C. 1995. *Racism in the Post-Civil Rights Era, Now You See It, Now You Don't*. New York: State University of New York Press.

Sniderman, Paul, and Thomas Piazza. 1993. *The Scar of Race*. Cambridge, MA: Harvard University Press.

Sowell, Thomas. 1984. *Civil Rights: Rhetoric of Reality?* New York: Morrow.

Street, Paul. 2009. *Barack Obama and the Future of American Politics*. Boulder: Paradigm.

Struyk, R. J., and M. A. Turner. 1986. "Exploring the Effects of Preferences on Urban Housing Markets." *Journal of Urban Economics* 119: 131–147.

Thurow, Lester C. 1975. *Generating Inequality*. New York: Basic Books.
——. 1969. *Poverty and Discrimination*. Washington, D.C.: The Brookings Institute.
Tolnay, Stewart, and E. M. Beck. 1991. "Rethinking the Role of Racial Violence in the Great Migration." In *Black Exodus: The Great Migration from the American South*, edited by Alferdteen Harrison. Jackson, MS: University of Mississippi Press.
Travis, Dempsey J. 1991. *Racism-American Style: A Corporate Gift*. Chicago: Urban Research Press Inc.
Turner, Margery A., Raymond Struyk, and John Yinger. 1991. *The Housing Discrimination Study*. Washington D. C.: The Urban Institute.
Turner, Margery A., and Felicity Skidmore. 1999. *Mortgage Lending Discrimination: A Review of Existing Evidence*. Washington, D.C.: Urban Institute.
Turner, Margery A., Stephen L. Ross, George Galster, and John Yinger. 2002. *Discrimination in Metropolitan Housing Markets*. Washington, D.C.: Urban Institute.
Tuttle, William M., Jr. 1970. "Labor Conflict and Racial Violence: The Black Worker in Chicago, 1894–1919." In *Black Labor in America*, edited by Milton Cantor. Westport, CN: Negro Universities Press.
U.S. Census Bureau. 2000. *American Community Survey*. http://www.census.gov/acs/www/
Wellman, David T. 1977. *Portraits of White Racism*. New York: Cambridge University Press.
Williams, Richard, Reynold Nesiba, and Eileen Diaz McConnell. 2005. "The Changing Face of Inequality in Home Mortgage Lending." *Social Problems* 52: 181–208.
Willie, Charles V. 1989. *Caste and Class Controversy on Race and Poverty: Round Two of the Willie/Wilson Debate*. New York: General Hall Inc.
Wilson, George, Ian Sakura-Lemessy, and Jonathan P. West. 1999. "Reaching the Top: Racial Differences in Mobility Paths to Upper-Tier Occupations." *Work and Occupations* 26: 165–186.
Wilson, William J. 1978. *The Declining Significance of Race*. Chicago: The University of Chicago Press.
——. 1987. *The Truly Disadvantaged*. Chicago: The University of Chicago Press.
Winant, Howard. 1994. *Racial Conditions: Politics, Theory, Comparisons*. Minneapolis: University of Minnesota Press.
Woodward, C. Vann. 1966. *The Strange Career of Jim Crow, Second Revised Edition*. New York: Oxford University Press.
Wynn, Neil A. 1993. *The Afro-American and the Second World War, Revised Edition*. New York: Holmes and Meir.
Yinger, John. 1986. "Measuring Discrimination with Fair Housing Audits: Caught in the Act." *American Economic Review* 76: 881–893.
——. 2001. "Housing Discrimination and Residential Segregation as Causes of Poverty." In *Understanding Poverty*, edited by Sheldon H. Danziger and Robert H. Haveman. New York: Russell Sage.

RACE VERSUS RACISM AS A CAUSE

Tukufu Zuberi[1]

After publishing *Thicker Than Blood: How Racial Statistics Lie* I gave several lectures at some of the most prestigious Sociology departments in the United States. After my presentation several leading sociologist, and some junior scholars, cautioned me on assuming that the problem I described was widely practiced in the field. While a few disagreed with the premise of my argument, most agreed with what I described as lying with racial statistics but several disagreed with my accusation that the error was widely committed in social science research. In this paper I present evidence of the extent of lying with racial statistics.

Social scientists that study race using inferential statistics are at risk of what I call racial reasoning (Zuberi 2001: 125–130). I define statistical racial reasoning as the use of a statistical model that presents race as a cause. I shall argue that such models are in fact only statements of association between the racial classification and a predictor or explanatory variable across individuals in a population. It is the treatment of these associations as causal effects that is a form of racial reasoning.

It is not unusual for researchers to present an anachronistic theory of racial differences and model race inappropriately as a causal effect. These two errors are confounded when the authors gloss over the causal and racial concepts in their research. This paper examines the extent to which this error occurs in the major journals in the United States of America. The major sociology journals in the United States are the American Journal of Sociology, American Sociological Review, Social Forces and Demography.

Racial Genetics

The race variable used by most researchers is measured indirectly and is based on an individual's self-reported racial identification.

---

[1] The tables used in this paper were compiled and tabulated by my research assistant, Nicole Franklin. A version of this paper was presented at the American Sociological Association Meetings in 2002.

Authors cannot directly measure the so-called genetic or physical aspect of race. In fact, the basis on which the individual's report their racial identification is a social system that uses skin color as the criterion for classification. Theoretically we can group human populations on the basis of skin color. Such a grouping, however, is based on our arbitrary distinctions. The difference in skin color between people of African and European origin is believed to be the result of three to six polygenes (Bowman and Murray 1990:76–77; Wilson 1998:146). Recent research suggests that the allele of melanocortin 1 receptor gene confers skin pigmentation (Harding et al. 2000); however, we still know nothing about the relationship of skin color to health and social outcomes. Health is not simply a social construction. That is, our health is as much a result of our biological, environmental, and psychological realities as it is about how we are socially organized. However, race is a social construction. In fact, if we admit that race is a social construction and not a biological concept the direction of research on this issue is much more promising. The continued reference to anarchistic notions of race misdirects the potential of social statistics.

Human biological variation is real, but race as a way of organizing that variation is false (Marks 1995). This point is important because it contradicts any argument concerning the essential and physical reality of race. Racial stratification is real, but biology is not its root cause. Race is often referred to as either a biological (anthropological) or a demographic characteristic; in reality it is neither.

Race is not a Causal Effect

Causation is not a simple matter in social statistical analysis. Statistical causation can be viewed from a variety of perspectives (compare Holland 1986; Salmon 1998: Chapter 13; Shafer 1996; Pearl 2000; and Zuberi 2001). Causal ideas are central to statistical theory. Yet, causation cannot be established or proven by statistics alone. Statistical analysis may not prove causation; however, it may provide the basis for causal conjectures about social relationships.

A statistical result is no more than a statement of the numerical conjectures to be applied when the word occurs in the inductive probabilistic reasoning, and may pay less attention than is needed to the conditions of the correct applicability of the term in the social world. It is these conditions of applicability that are properly the concern of social statistics. When we use statistical methods to discuss causation we are interested in making conjectures about theoretically based explanations of social reality. The statistical analysis of racial differences had its origins in biometrics and psychometrics as I have outlined elsewhere (Zuberi 2001). This origin was asocial and lacked an appreciation of the need to understand social context. It is this shortcoming that sociological analysis can help us overcome. Sociology distinguished itself by focusing on the social context of facts. As a recent sociologist notes: "Every social fact is situated, surrounded by other contextual facts and brought into being by a process relating it to past contexts" (Abbott 1999:197). Variables do not exist as physical objects in the social world, and consequently, variables do not cause things to happen like it is mistakenly thought that physical objects cause things to happen in the physical world. In fact, both the physical scientist and social scientist make conjectures about causal processes in the real world.

By bringing causal ideas back into the open we are better able to debate the quantification of social reality "explained" by statistical evidence. By brining causal ideas regarding racial differences to the front of the debate we will be able to better discuss the quantification of racial differences presented by racial statistics. This issue is further complicated when we attempt to use variables that purport to use race as a proxy measure of the genetic or cultural basis of race.

Statistical results refer to a statistical model and its system of equations, not to the social reality that scientists are trying to understand. Most social scientists are interested in the causal effects of particular variables. Within this context it is important to recognize the difference between causal theory and causal effect. Causal theory offers a description of the various processes by which a treatment produces its effects. A causal theory can describe the relationship among biological, physical, chemical, and/or social processes. Causal theories should be based on known information about the subject under study. Consequently, causal effects should be regarded as an essential part of causal theories. Causal theories attempt to predict events on the basis of the known empirical information about the subject; this includes what is known about causal effects.

Causal effect refers to the effect of a factor or treatment on a given response variable. In experimental studies, causal theories can be questioned if they contradict the results of the study. In sociological data, causal theory serves a more fundamental role: in sociological studies, causal effects can be questioned if the causal theory is contradicted by empirical results of a study when the theory is supported by evidence from other studies and by well-developed arguments.

Racial ideas in sociology historically have been influenced by eugenics (Chase 1980; Marks 1995; Tucker 1994; Zuberi 2000, Zuberi 2001). Eugenicists argued that racial differences were the result of genetic differences. They sought to establish the connection between biology and behavior outcomes, and in this way to connect race with population health. Statistical analysis was born out of this connection between social science methodology and eugenics theory. In their efforts to connect race with low levels of intelligence and health, eugenicists erroneously confused prediction and causation.

Statistical analysis cannot be used to establish race as a causal effect. Because most social science researchers study causal effects to make inferences about the effects of manipulations to which groups of individuals in a population have been or might be exposed, causes are only entities which, in theory, can be manipulated or altered (Holland 1986; Sobel 1995). This recognition suggests that sociologists consider the ability of the individuals or units we study to vary.

In principle, there is nothing problematic about the modeling of covariates thought to be part of a social process. The problem lies in their conceptualisation of race as a sufficient covariate for treatment assignment. This problematic conceptualisation is what I define as racial reasoning. Given the definition of race as a relationship it should not be treated as a cause resulting from the individual trait of racial identity. Being a particular race does not cause any outcome. For example, if an African American is stopped while driving a luxury car by a police officer how suspects him of being a criminal because of his skin color, it is not because of the drivers black skin that he is stopped. On the contrary, the driver is stopped in this example because of the racial ideas and behaviors of the police officer. Academic journals are full of this type of racial reasoning. Next I will use examples of the language in two articles, and then a review of the articles used in the interpretation of race as a variable in statistical papers to point to the generality of the problem.

A Birth Weight Example

In 2000, "Racial Differences in Birth Health Risk: A Quantitative Genetic Approach," Edwin J.C.G. van den Oord and David C. Rowe

(2000) argue that a combination of racial genetics and environmental factors causes the racial differences in birth health risk. Their effort to integrate biological and social factors into their analysis is commendable. Biological data are increasingly available for demographic research; these data allow researchers the opportunity to examine the relationship between biology and demographic processes. In 2002, the journal *Demography* published my review of the errors of this type of racial reasoning (Zuberi 2002). In my review of van den Oord and Rowe's article I suggest that they present an anachronistic theory of racial differences, and model race inappropriately as a causal effect.

When we say that race is socially constructed, it has implications for how we use statistical methods. Human biological variation is real, yet race is a distorted way of organizing this variation. This point is important because it contradicts race-based perspectives about the physical reality of race. Racial stratification is real, but biology is not its root cause. Race is often referred to as either a biological (anthropological) or a demographic characteristic; in reality it is neither. Van den Oord and Rowe misunderstood the meaning of race. They viewed race as a biological and demographic part of each individual. Part of the absurdity in this kind of definition, which is quite popular among both social and biological scientist, is that while biology points to an individual, demography refers to a population and does not point to an individual attribute like the proposed definition of race used in racial statistics.

Secondly, the authors employed the statistical methods incorrectly to the data. The quantitative genetic approach used by van den Oord and Rowe is based on a false notion of heredity and, in fact, is governed by knowledge (or processes) at a different level. Their analysis is not based on a genetic understanding of race. From a genetic point of view race is not an appropriate basis for discussing biological differences (Marks 1995; 2002; Graves 2002; 2004). The results of van den Oord and Rowe's study refer to a statistical model and its system of equations, not to the "racial genetics" that they suggest are the empirical basis of their findings. The authors incorrectly use racial statistics as a scientific justification of their wrongheaded ideas.

Nothing in van den Oord and Rowe's article depends on the statistical analysis because their causal inferences are not open to empirical testing. In other words, they have failed to understand the conditions of the correct applicability of the statistical methods in the real world. Their conceptualization of race is fundamental to their subsequent uses of racial statistics, and they were not cautious when using race as a variable. The authors, like many others, do not demonstrate an understanding of the fact that the numbers in social statistics are unique. Social statistics is a system of estimation based on uncertainty. Statistics is a form of applied mathematics; however, the power of the results should not be considered as a mathematical proof. In their response to my critique of their article, the authors argued that race was socially, biologically, and demographically real. Van den Oord and Rowe's results are no more than the axioms applied, and pay little attention to the conditions of the correct applicability of the methods in the real world. In part, this is because their theory of race is otherworldly; however, this other-worldliness is not enough to prevent an article that articulates a theory of race that does not recognition African's as equal humans from being published.

These two errors (conceptual and methodological) were confounded when the authors glossed over the causal and racial concepts in their research. One would expect that this open dialogue would result in a more careful policy of publishing racial statistics on this important subject. However, this was not the case. In the latest issue of *Demography* a theoretically different but methodologically similar paper was published.

Not all uses of racial statistics suggest as conservative a perspective as the Oord and Rowe article. The confusion between attributes and causes fill the social science literature even when the biology of race is not emphasized. In May of 2002, the journal *Demography* published another article that focused on racial differences in "Low Birth Weight, Social Factors, and Developmental Outcomes Among Children in The United States" by Jason D. Boardman and colleagues. The authors cite previous research that indicates that "controlling for adverse birth outcomes accounts for nearly all the gap in infant mortality between blacks and whites in the United States" (Boardman, et al. 2002:353). Boardman and his colleagues argue that because the so-called black/white differences are statistically accounted for by other socio-economic factors, the racial disparity is due to these factors. I agree with the intent of this conclusion; however, it is an example of how social statistics are used in an effort that while it refutes racist arguments perpetuates the misuse of racial statistics. By using racial statistics in this way the authors interpret race as a cause, and legitimate the use of methodologies that perpetuate the problems they seem to be attempting to overcome.

My main problem with the Boardman and colleagues paper is with the language used to interpret their results and the misuse of race as a causal factor. The authors ask, "how do social factors affect the cognitive development scores of children, net of birth weight, and how do the effects of these factors vary across the ages of children?" (Boardman, et al. 2002:354). The authors clearly indicate that race is a sociodemographic characteristic. I am not sure what such a characteristic is; however, regarding race they state that "We limited our analyses to three racial/ethnic groups: Mexican Americans, non-Hispanic blacks, and non-Hispanic whites" (Boardman, et al. 2002:357). The problem here is that the authors use race as an individual trait in their analysis, and individual traits cannot be causes in statistical analysis. An individual trait cannot determine another trait for the same individual. The authors' treatment of race lend themselves to inferring causality, and their language suggest that this is in fact what they intended to do.

This example, suggest why researchers must be careful to not commit the errors of the past by misusing race as a causal variable. Often researchers claim to be using race as a proxy for socio-economic, sociodemographic or cultural processes. However, the use of race as a proxy subverts even the most positive attempts to understand the racial stratification and inequality. One this examples points to the nature of the problem, it does not address the prevalence of this practice in the literature. In the next section of the paper, I ask how prevalent these practices are in social statistics.

Prevalence of the Problem

In order to describe the extent to which race has been used as a causal effect we looked at the articles published in the major sociology journals. If this practice is popular, regardless of the methodological error, then it should be reflected in published articles. Over the period 1991–2001, 1871 articles not including book reviews were published in the *American Journal of Sociology* (AJS), the *American Sociological Review* (ASR), *Demography* and *Social Forces*. The leading journal in the publication of articles on race is *Social Forces*, followed by *Demography*, ASR and AJS respectively (see Table 1). For the purposes of this paper race articles are distinguished by making explicit racial comparisons. We do not consider articles on a specific race as a race article. The inclusion of single race articles would render most articles race articles.

Table 1. Percent of Articles Published

	AJS	ASR	Demography	Social Forces	All Journals
			All Articles		
Race Articles	20	25	31	37	29
Race Effect	11	14	20	29	19
			Race Articles		
Race Regression	88	92	85	94	91
Race Effect	56	58	63	79	67
			Race Articles W/ Regression		
Race Effect	63	63	75	84	74

Source: American Journal of Sociology, American Sociological Review, Demography, and Social Forces, 1991–2000

Advances in computer technology and statistical methodology have accelerated in recent years. This acceleration has resulted in the use of new technologies in the study of racial differences. Column 2 of Table 1 presents the percentage of race articles that used regression in the analysis. Most race articles used regression analysis. In addition to using regression as a method, in column three we see that most of these articles also used the race variable as a causal effect.

These summary statistics suggest that the practice of using racial statistics has been common in the major journals of sociology during the 10-year period observed. Moreover, researchers have been successful in using inferential statistical methods, especially regression analysis, in published articles. My review of the leading sociology and demography journals in quantitative social science has confirmed the practice of publishing such articles. The peer-reviewed (refereed) articles have confirmed the practice in sociology. In my opinion these articles all have important findings but a problematic use of race as a variable. Academic journals are full of the problem of interpretation in racial statistical articles.

Next we look at how often have race been used as a causal effect over time. Figure 1 displays the percentage of articles with race that used regression analysis between 1991 and 2000. The vast majority of articles on race published during the 90s used inferential analysis of racial differences. The application of the regression methods ranged from ordinary least squares regression, factor analysis, analysis of variance, structural equation models, log-linear and logistic regression models, and hazard models.

Figure 2 presents the percentage of race articles using race as a causal effect over time. The use of race as a causal effect reached a peak

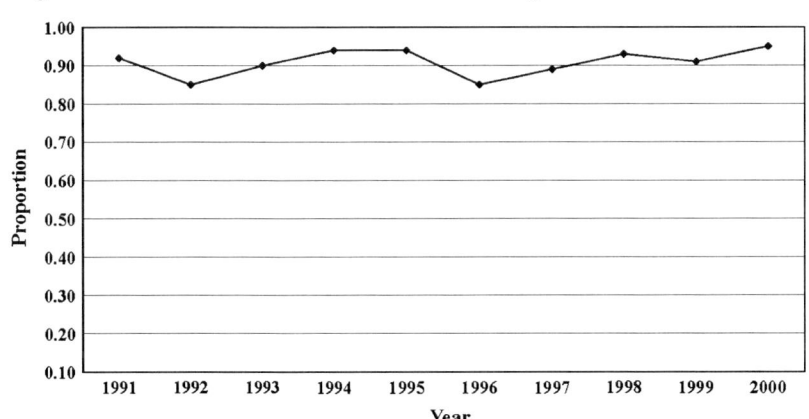

Figure 1. Published Race Articles that use Regression, 1991–2000

Source: American Journal of Sociology, American Sociological Review, Demography, and Social Forces, 1991–2000

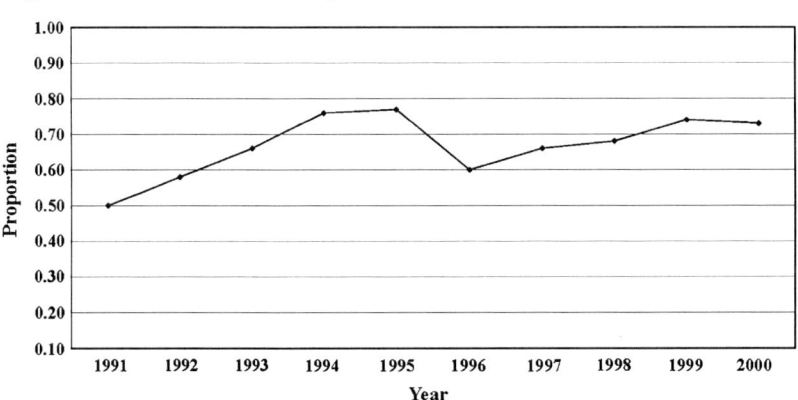

Figure 2. Race Articles Using Race as an Effect

Source: American Journal of Sociology, American Sociological Review, Demography, and Social Forces, 1991–2000

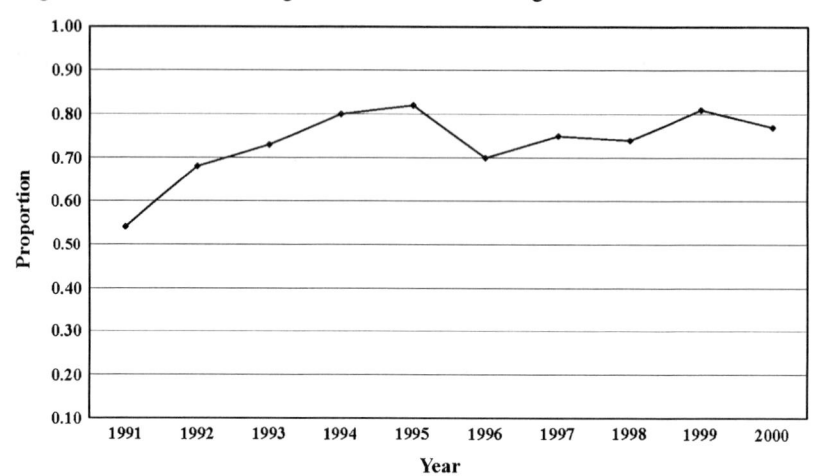

Figure 3. Percent of Regression Articles Using Race as an Effect

Source: American Journal of Sociology, American Sociological Review, Demography, and Social Forces, 1991–2000

in 1995. However, the majority of these articles viewed race as a causal effect and consequently used the variable incorrectly. This point is made more clearly in Figure 3, which presents the percent of regression articles using race as a causal effect. The overwhelming majority of race articles that used regression did so incorrectly.

This publication of the incorrect use of race as a variable should not be misconstrued as being of merely academic significance. Statistical conceptions of race play a critical role in guiding and justifying both private belief and public policy. Almost all of the racial statistics conducted in the social sciences and sponsored by billions of dollars, from the federal government and private foundations, deal with causal inferences. Because such statistics look and sound scientific and are usually promulgated by the "top scholars" in the field, great weight is accorded them, even if their import is in fact distorted by subjective predispositions of these scholars. Few scholars or public officials are in a position to detect if the use of race in the statistical analysis is misleading, inappropriate, and false, or if the methodology incorporates false assumptions.

The misuse of methods in the study of race demands our attention. This issue needs deliberate and conscious study; we must analyze and provide answers. By recognizing that the researcher is as important as what they study we enhance our ability to contribute to an understanding of society. We are not Martians from another time or place, thus we cannot study society as outsiders. We are part of the world and study society from the inside. As we study, as we investigate, we must offer solutions that solve, and the world justifiably must demand not a lack of values and convictions, but rather the dedication to justice and an ability to present the truth as we understand it regardless of the challenges it may present.

Conclusions

The incorrect use of race in statistical analysis is widely practiced, and reflects the degree of racial reasoning among social scientist. Social statistics are the scientific arm of sociological analysis. The misuse of social statistics in our efforts to understand social relationships is a major problem and may have its roots in how the discipline of sociology developed.

The social sciences (sociology, economics, and political science) differentiated themselves from the more humanistic historical disciplines by focusing on arriving at general laws that were presumed to govern human behavior, and analysing the segmentation of human reality by strict adherence to scientific methods of empirical analysis. The new social sciences emphasized the centrality of the objective real world that was knowable by the neutral scholar armed with empirical evidence. The new social sciences were to be nomothetic and avoided the ideographic tendencies used to explain the behavior of the "other" in anthropology and in some historical narratives of the modern world and great figures of the modern world. Like the physicist and biologist in the natural sciences, the nomothetically oriented social scientist found empirical evidence in objective, external data that were assembled, controlled, and manipulated. Social scientists were, with few exceptions, white men of great prestige. Women and people of color might be the objects of study; however, until recently they were rarely if ever part of the mainstream of social sciences. This racist and sexist delay may partly explain the critical perspective of many female social scientists and scholars of color.

Auquste Comte coined the term "sociology" and outlined the new field of study in *Cours de philosophie positive* (*The Positive Philosophy*)— his first major sociological work. In *Cours*, Comte declared an end to philosophy in the face of the achievements of science. In *A Discourse on the Positive Spirit*, Comte defined positivist research as "confined to the study of real facts without seeking to know their first causes or final purpose" (Comte 1903:21). Eventually, empirical techniques for collecting and analyzing data on individual social phenomena emerged from the eugenics movement of the nineteenth century.

Using the theory of probability, social scientists engage in a kind of inductive reasoning. Social statistics allows social scientists to use quantitative data to predict outcomes and discuss how variables are empirically related. The use of social statistics also commits the social scientists to a logical way of talking and thinking about causation. It is this logic that has been the source of much confusion in social analysis. It is the confusion of prediction with causation that has caused many of the problems in interpreting statistical results. This confusion is the result of how social scientists think about causation and measuring the social world. However, these methods of sociology proved to be important in complementing the positivist philosophy that characterized the Eurocentric study of society in the twentieth century.

Race is a relationship and cannot be the "thing" that causes racial differences. Statistical analysis that presents race as a causal effect is a form of racial reasoning. To avoid racial reasoning we must recognize the futility of the notion of the "race effect" or the "black effect" on an outcome variable. By recognizing that race is a socially constructed variable we are able to avoid this trap. Race is socially constructed as an individual attribute that cannot be manipulated. One cannot be more or less of one race in racially stratified societies. Thus, social statisticians tend to believe it is reasonable and socially responsible to think that the number of cigarettes smoked causes illness. It is neither scientifically reasonable nor socially responsible to argue that racial identity causes social inequality or differences. Considering racial identity a cause distracts attention from the social relationships that produce inequality and injustice that a more socially based perspective might bring into view.

We are witnessing a revival of the biological idea of race in medicine and science, even though some social scientists have argued for years that race is a socially complex matter and that subjective predispositions and biases, more than biology or demography, govern our definitions and categories of racial difference. The van den Oord and Rowe article shows how some scholars developed their ideas under the sway of eugenic theories of race. Eugenics developed by using complex statistical models to justify racial reasoning. This is in fact, how the practice of statistics found its way into the social science. The publication of the van den Oord and Rowe article, and the subsequent publication of articles with similar points of view, demonstrates the continued acceptance of these theories in social science. However, it is the open support and publication about the misuse of racial statistics as a cover for wrongheaded ideas about race across academic disciplines that remain at the heart of the problem. This silence also reflects how the disciplinary journals have done researchers a great disservice.

This debate in the pages of *Demography* had very little impact on research practice. During the next few years, two articles were published on racial differences in birth weight. They were entitled "Low Birth Weight, Social Factors, and Developmental Outcomes Among Children in the United States" (Boardman et al. 2002) and "An Investigation of Racial and Ethnic Disparities in Birth Weight in Chicago Neighborhoods" (Sastry and Hussey 2003). Neither of these articles cited van den Oord and Rowe's original article or the exchange that it stimulated on the measurement of race in such research. This lack of citation can be read as a form of silence, and an acceptance of the practice of the misuse of race as a variable. More importantly, these articles demonstrate how powerful racial statistics are in the current academic environment.

This silence about race and methods should not be misconstrued as being of merely academic significance. Statistical conceptions of race play a critical role in guiding and justifying both private belief and public policy. Most of the racial statistics published in the social science journals, and sponsored by billions of dollars from the federal government and private foundations, deal with causal inferences. Because such statistics look and sound scientific and are usually promulgated by reputable scholars, great weight is accorded them, even if their import is in fact distorted by subjective predispositions. If the statistics are misleading, inappropriate, or false, or if the methodology incorporates false assumptions, few scholars or public officials are in a position to detect it.

Today we are witnessing a revival of the biological idea of race in medicine and science, even though some social scientists have argued for years that race is a socially complex matter and that subjective predispositions and biases, more than biology or demography, govern our definitions and categories of racial difference. The van den Oord and

Rowe article shows how some scholars developed their ideas under the sway of eugenic theories of race. Eugenics developed by using complex statistical models to justify racial reasoning. This is in fact, how the practice of statistics found its way into the social science. The publication of the van den Oord and Rowe article, and the subsequent publication of articles with similar points of view, demonstrates the continued acceptance of these theories in social science. However, it is the silence about the misuse of racial statistics as a cover for wrongheaded ideas about race across academic disciplines that remain at the heart of the problem. This silence also reflects how our disciplinary journals have done researchers a great disservice.

The misuse of methods in the study of race demands our attention. This issue needs deliberate and conscious study; we must analyze and provide answers. By recognizing that the researcher is as important as what they study we enhance our ability to contribute to an understanding of society. We are not Martians from another time or place, thus we cannot study society as outsiders. We are part of the world and study society from the inside. As we study, as we investigate, we must offer solutions that solve, and the world justifiably must demand not a lack of values and convictions, but rather the dedication to justice and an ability to present the truth as we understand it regardless of the challenges it may present.

References

Bowman, J.E. and R.F. Murray. 1990. *Genetic Variation and Disorders in Peoples of African Origin*. Baltimore: Johns Hopkins University Press.

Chase, A. 1980. *The Legacy of Malthus: The Social Costs of the New Scientific Racism.* Urbana: University of Illinois Press.

Comte, Auguste, *A Discourse on the Positive Spirit* (London: William Reeves, 1903)

Cramer, J.C. 1995. "Racial and Ethnic Differences in Birthweight: The Role of Income and Financial Assistance." *Demography* 32:231-47.

Graves, Joseph L. Jr. 2001. *The emperor's new clothes: Biological theories of race at the millennium*. New Brunswick, NJ: Rutgers University Press.

——. 2004. *The Race Myth: Why we pretend race exists in America*. New York: Penguin Books.

Holland, P.W. 1986. "Statistics and Causal Inference." *Journal of the American Statistical Association* 81:945-70.

Marks, Jonathan. 1995. *Human Biodiversity: Genes, Race, and History*. (New York: Aldine De Gruyter).

——. 2002. *Whate it means to be 98% chimpanzee*. Berkeley: University of California Press.

Sobel, M.E. 1994. "Causal Inference in Latent Variable Models." Pp. 3-35 in *Latent Variables Analysis: Applications for Developmental Research*, edited by A. von Eye and C.C. Clogg. Thousand Oaks, CA: Sage.

——. 1995. "Causal Inference in the Social and Behavioral Sciences." Pp. 1–38 in *Handbook of Statistical Modeling for the Social and Behavioral Sciences,* edited by G. Arminger, C.C. Clogg, and M.E. Sobel. New York: Plenum.
Tucker, W.H. 1994. *The Science and Politics of Racial Research.* Urbana: University of Illinois Press.
Van den Oord, J.C.G. and D.C. Rowe. 2000. "Racial Differences in Birth Health Risk: A Quantitative Genetic Approach." *Demography* 37:285–98.
Wilson, E.O. 1998. *Consilience: The Unity of Knowledge.* New York: Knopf.
Zuberi, T. 2000. "Deracializing Social Statistics: Problems in the Quantification of Race." *Annals of the American Academy of Political and Social Science* 568:172–85.
——. 2001. *Thicker Than Blood: An Essay on How Racial Statistics Lie.* Minneapolis: University of Minnesota Press.
—— and Eduardo Bonilla-Silva. 2008. *White Logic, White Methods: Racism and Methodology.* New York: Rowman and Littlefield, Inc.

COLORBLIND WHITE DOMINANCE

Ian Haney López[*]

The U.S. public and indeed many scholars are increasingly certain that the country is leaving race and racism behind. This reflects more than the modest belief that, at least if measured since 1954, race relations have improved. It is instead a claim that race and racism will soon disappear altogether—that they have little power in the lives of average Americans, and soon will have none. Some give credit to *Brown v. Board of Education* and the civil rights era, when activists, lawyers, and laws helped a broad social movement turn the nation away from segregation and toward equality. Others point to changing demographics, emphasizing the rising number of mixed-race marriages and the increasing Asian and Hispanic populations that are eroding the historic black-white divide. Almost all herald the election of a black president. My sense of our racial future differs. Not only do I fear that race will continue fundamentally to skew U.S. society over the coming decades, I worry that the belief in the diminished salience of race makes this more rather than less likely; relatedly, I suspect that law no longer contributes to racial justice but instead legitimates continued inequality.

Race as it is understood and practiced in the United States will change rapidly over the next few decades. Partly, this reflects the simple historical fact that racial ideas constantly mutate. Settler colonialism in North America gave rise to racial beliefs that justified the expropriation of land and the exploitation of humans, but while race since then has served consistently to rationalize hierarchy, racial beliefs themselves have been grounded variously in religion, color, nation, physical biology, eugenics, ethnicity, and, most recently, culture (Gossett; Smedley; Haney López (1994)). Only those who still understand race as primarily a natural phenomenon continue to suppose that notions of race remain relatively fixed. We should expect,

---

[*] John H. Boalt Professor of Law, University of California, Berkeley. An earlier version of this essay appeared in Ian Haney López, *White by Law: The Legal Construction of Race* (revised ed., 2006), pp. 143–162.

however, particularly rapid change in today's regnant racial ideas. The United States is once again in the midst of a period of dramatic racial ferment. The current dynamism is sparked primarily by two racial dislocations directly rooted in the civil rights era: (1) the substantial decrease in the public acceptability of supremacist ideologies, and (2) the new demographics produced by altered immigration as well as intermarriage patterns.

Broad social support for explicit claims of racial superiority has all but ended, with large swaths of U.S. society now espousing a commitment to racial equality. This shift in the racial zeitgeist since the civil rights movement marks an important step toward a racially egalitarian society—but not its actual achievement, as racial hierarchy has continued. The persistence of racial subordination partly stems from the inertia of past patterns of systematic harm. But to avoid breaking down, racial hierarchy must also be newly produced and reproduced (Fields). For those committed to preserving the racial status quo, the new spirit of widespread anti-racism raises practical and ideological problems. On the former level, new methods of maintaining racial hierarchy that are not patently designed to foster subordination must be devised. The greater task, however, is ideational: new justifications must be elaborated to explain the otherwise striking contrast between our public commitments and our lived realities. The elaboration of practices and rationales that at once comport with the ideals of non-racialism but preserve and deepen racial inequality, I suggest, form one of the hallmarks of our current racial era.

Simultaneously, a demographic revolution is underway. The racial ethos of the civil rights era chipped away at the social prejudices regarding inter-group marriage, while civil rights reforms reopened immigration to groups previously excluded on racial grounds. Today, a mixed-race population that accounts for one out of every forty Americans has given rise to a multiracial movement that strongly— indeed, disproportionately, given its size—influences the U.S. racial imagination (Grieco & Cassidy, p. 3; Williams (2005); Williams (2006)). Meanwhile, Asian Americans represent the fastest growing immigrant group today, with a population that increased by over seventy percent during the 1990s (Barnes & Bennett, p. 3). The greatest source of demographic change, however, comes in the burgeoning Hispanic population. Latin Americans for several decades have composed the largest immigrant group in the United States, and this trend will continue, if not accelerate. The U.S. Latino population increased 58 percent between

1990 and 2000, and this group, the largest minority in the country, now accounts for more than one of every eight Americans (Guzmán, p. 2). A recent *Newsweek* estimate predicts that by 2100, one in three Americans will be Latino ("New Latino Nation").

Racial Futures

Given these ideological and demographic changes, how will race evolve? Four options are commonly put forth: *white exceptionalism*, which foretells whites remaining a racial overclass even as they become a numerical minority; *black exceptionalism*, wherein blacks continue as the primordial racial minority while other groups increasingly integrate; *multiracialism*, projecting that race will lose all salience as a form of hierarchy and will come to stand only for cultural differences; and *Latin Americanization*, which envisions continued but softened racial hierarchy engendered by a move away from the black-white dichotomy and strict bio-racial notions of difference and towards a racial continuum policed along socio-racial lines.[1]

White exceptionalism sees whiteness continuing as the most powerful racial fault line. Under this vision of our racial future, racial hierarchy continues unabated and perhaps intensifies. Some attribute continued racial conflict to efforts by dominant groups to maintain racial privilege. Michael Lind, for instance, sees the emergence of a dominant white class that maintains its privileged position vis-à-vis non-whites (and less well-off whites) through its "near-monopoly of the private-sector and political branches of the American institutional elite" as well as by the creation and cooptation, through racial preferences, of minority elites (p. 151, 161). Others see racial conflict continuing not because of efforts to retain privilege but because whites will respond to perceived assaults by culturally inassimilable groups, mainly Hispanics. Samuel Huntington's most recent book decrying the threat posed by Latino immigrants to our supposed "core Anglo-Protestant culture" fits this mold, as do many others, such as Victor Hanson's *Mexifornia*. Setting aside the important differences in these various

---

[1] In a helpful discussion, Jennifer Hochschild sees six possible racial futures in the United States: white exceptionalism, black exceptionalism, a South African model, complex regional divides, skin-color hierarchy, and multiracial mélange (Hochschild (2005), p. 80–81).

strains, white exceptionalism has been the norm as a historical matter: since the seventeenth century, a "white" identity has been the linchpin to racial dominance in what would become the United States.

Black exceptionalism has two component claims: that blacks are fundamentally different from other racial minorities, and that non-black groups will gradually integrate. Put another way, this model posits that there will soon be effectively only two races, blacks and non-blacks. Nathan Glazer's recent scholarship typifies this sentiment: "The two nations of our America are the black and the white, and increasingly, as Hispanics and Asians become less different from whites from the point of view of residence, income, occupation, and political attitudes, the two nations become the black and the others" (Glazer 1998:149); (Glazer 2001); (Yancey, 14). Rather than locating the distinctive position of African Americans in retrograde notions of biological difference, proponents of black exceptionalism often strike a tone of racially progressive concern, typically ruing the historic forces that so deeply subordinated blacks. This analysis sometimes leads proponents of black exceptionalism to support affirmative action and other remedies for past and on-going discrimination, at least for African Americans (Glazer (1998), p. 159). But it often seems that an equally—or sometimes more—central point for proponents of black exceptionalism is that Latinos and Asians should be excluded from civil rights benefits because these groups allegedly have not suffered mistreatment as non-whites on par with the subordination imposed on blacks (Graham; Hollinger (2003); Skrentny). In this way, black exceptionalism as often marks not concern for blacks but hostility toward claims of racial discrimination by Asians and Hispanics.

Multiracialism sees us rapidly evolving toward a postracial society in which race is unmoored from status and demarcates not so much innate groups as loosely defined communities bound together primarily by cultural affinities. The "racial" in multiracialism parallels the "cultural" in multiculturalism: both posit an ideal world in which race is supplanted by culture and in which racial hierarchy, racism, prejudice, xenophobia, bigotry, and bias have ceased to operate, at least insofar as these rely on notions of innate biological differences of the sort currently understood as racial. Race-mixing—the intermarriage of persons from ostensibly different races and the resultant blending that occurs—holds out great promise, according to proponents of multiracialism. David Hollinger, for instance, extols the virtues of amalgamation (a word he prefers over miscegenation), while Roberto Suro enthuses over what he terms mixed doubles (p. 58).[2] Many multiracialists also see favorable portents in Hispanic immigration, in the belief that in their racial heterogeneity Latinos already embody the postracial ideal, and will only push the United States in this direction more rapidly. Writing from Southern California and focusing on by far the largest Latino group, Gregory Rodriguez claims that "[h]aving spent so long trying to fit into one side or the other of the binary system, Mexican Americans have become more numerous and confident enough to simply claim their brownness—their mixture. This is a harbinger of America's future" (G. Rodriguez (Jan. /Feb. 2003), p. 97; see also G. Rodriguez (May 18, 2003), at M3; Klor de Alva, p. 55). Race as hierarchy, according to the basic claim advanced by multiracialists, will dissipate as the lines between putative racial groups are blurred.

The *Latin Americanization* of race in the United States is a more likely short-term development, according to others. Race in Latin America purportedly differs from the U.S. version in two crucial respects: (1) rather than operating in terms of a sharp divide between white and black, race functions along a continuum with gradations of racial difference often coded in terms of skin color; and (2) race depends not solely on ancestry or morphology (bio-race), but also often reflects socioeconomic factors such as wealth, professional attainment, educational level, and so forth (socio-race). Like those who foresee multiracialism, those who predict an increased Latin Americanization of race see the United States being pushed in this direction by Latino immigrants, who theoretically not only bring with them a supposedly enlightened Latin American racial sensibility but also—along with mixed-race persons and the growing Asian population—increasingly destabilize the white-black divide (R. Rodriguez).

Unlike the multiracialists, those who predict that the United States is moving toward a Latin American racial model do not anticipate the complete dissipation of race in the short to medium term. Race as hierarchy will continue, albeit along increasingly socio-racial lines. Even as they acknowledge continued inequality, though, Latin Americanists see a gradual amelioration in which socio-racial understandings operate to moderate the harsh stratification historically grounded in the United States along bio-racial lines. This easing, they expect, will extend as well to African Americans, facilitating their

---

[2] As others note, however, relatively little racial mixing involves African Americans, suggesting that intermarriage is not breaking down all racial lines (Kalmijn; Lind).

increased integration. Indeed, the racial status of many prominent blacks often emerges as supposed evidence that the United States is already moving from a bio-racial to a socio-racial system, one in which ever more minorities function in society as if they were effectively white. Some expect this trend to herald the strong emergence of color as a basis for social ordering: the coding of skin tone and physical features as racially light or dark may increasingly replace membership in ordinal races such as African American or Asian as the primary basis for discriminatory treatment (Hochshild (2003)). The Latin Americanization of race is not a phenomenon that pertains to Hispanics alone, but arguably will alter the categorical boundaries of all races, thereby gradually weakening racial subordination in the United States.

Colorblind White Dominance

In contrast to these four visions of future racial dynamics, I believe instead that we are headed toward a hierarchy of *colorblind white dominance*. This looming racial paradigm has three central elements, which I discuss in turn: (1) continued racial dominance by whites; (2) an expansion of who counts as white along socio-racial rather than bio-racial lines; and (3) a colorblind ideology that simultaneously proclaims a robust commitment to anti-racism yet works assiduously to prevent effective racial remediation. To be sure, there will be significant regional differences in the evolution of race in the United States, but racial politics is now sufficiently national that I expect colorblind white dominance to provide the basic framework for race relations throughout the country (Frey).

White racial dominance. I use the term "dominance" in contradistinction to "supremacy." "White supremacy," if understood to mean racial domination explicitly grounded in a theory of racial superiority, is largely over, though of course there remain pockets of white supremacist agitation as well as the possibility of recrudescence.[3] The rejection of white supremacy as rhetoric, however, has not been accompanied

---

[3] George Fredrickson defines white supremacy as "the attitudes, ideologies, and policies associated with the rise of blatant forms of white or European dominance over 'nonwhite' populations." Thus defined, the term "applies with particular force to the historical experience of two nations—South Africa and the United States" (Fredrickson (1981), p. xi).

by an end to the dominant social, political, and financial position of whites. The materiality of continued white privilege can be measured across many indices. In 2003, the real median income for non-Hispanic whites was $48,000, but only $30,000 for African Americans (Cleveland, p. 6). The total poverty rate among African Americans was 24 percent and it was 22 percent for Hispanics, compared to 8 percent for whites (Dalaker, p. 7). That same year, 20 percent of African Americans and 33 percent of Hispanics had no health insurance, while 11 percent of whites were uninsured (DeNavas-Walt et al., p. 18). Discrepancies in incarceration rates are particularly staggering. There is currently a 28.5 percent chance an African-American man will spend some time in a state or federal prison during his lifetime, while the comparable figure for whites is 2.5 percent. There are twelve states in which between 10 percent and 15 percent of African American adult men are incarcerated, while in ten states Latino men are thrown behind bars at rates five to nine times greater than white men (Human Rights Watch (2007); Mauer).

In presenting these statistics, I do not claim that all whites are equally privileged by racism and racial hierarchy. While whites as a group have long arrogated the resources of this country to themselves, from land to jobs to control over the government, industry, and military, deep class schisms divide white society (Zweigenhaft & Domhoff). Rather than belying the power of race, however, these internal rifts more likely reflect race's utility in palliating intra-group conflict among whites. Racial ideology does not guarantee equality among whites; it serves rather to mask and distract from gross inequalities that divide that group. That said, it remains the case that whites as a race (though not all whites individually) have maintained their position at the social and material apogee for centuries—and the numbers above demonstrate the profound role race and white dominance continue to play in the organization of U.S. society. Despite predictions of race's demise, the great weight of social statistics point to continued white dominance.

The claim that white dominance is evaporating in the face of shifting demographics and the public espousal of civil rights platitudes ignores not only contemporary statistics but historical patterns as well. It's true that our population looks far different today than it did in 1965, let alone 1865. But demographic change has historically led only to shifts in where, not whether, racial lines are drawn. Today we may use "white" as shorthand for "racially dominant," but this requires that we recognize the inclusion of Germans as white in the 1840s through 1860s, the Irish in the 1850s through 1880s, and eastern and southern Europeans in the 1900s to 1920s (Jacobson). It's also true that a leading rationale for racial inequality, the self-evident nature of white superiority, weakened dramatically over the twentieth century, especially during the civil rights era. But defeating a justification for hierarchy is not the same as toppling that hierarchy. Again, ideologies rationalizing white dominance have often undergone dramatic mutations, from religious doctrines to Manifest Destiny to eugenics to, most recently, notions of cultural difference. The justificatory rhetoric of race, like the composition of the population, constantly changes, even as racial inequality consistently endures.

White dominance continues partly as a vestige of the past, but also because race and racism remain useful to powerful segments of U.S. society. The nation did not embrace the civil rights movement until the mid-1960s, and then grudgingly, only to see the country's mood turn firmly against substantive racial equality with President Richard Nixon's election in 1968. As a country, we enjoyed a very few years of civil rights reforms but continue to stagger under three decades and more of backlash aimed at preserving the basic parameters of a racial status quo itself built on the edifice of three centuries of white supremacy (Steinberg). This backlash is testament to the fact that racial hierarchy remains profoundly in the material and status interests of those who can claim the mantle of whiteness (whether as previously understood or as reconfigured). In access to country clubs and gated communities, in preferences for jobs and housing, in the moral certainty regarding one's civic belonging and fundamental goodness, in all of these ways and many more, being white affords advantages across the range of material and status divisions that mar our society. In seeking to disestablish race and racism, Fredrick Douglass's words are no less true today than when uttered against slavery: "Power concedes nothing without a demand. It never did and it never will." Be assured: racial hierarchy continues as a measure of white power in our society. To change racial dynamics for the better will require, as it has in the past, concerted efforts between broad social movements and national elites, and probably in addition propitious historical circumstances conducive to change, such as war or economic boom times (Roediger). Neither demographics nor antiracist bromides by themselves will defeat the power race wields in our society.

White redefined. Though white dominance will continue, what will likely change is how whiteness—or, better, membership in the racially dominant group—is defined. The term "white" has a far more complicated history in the United States than people commonly recognize. For most of this country's history, whiteness stood in contradistinction to the non-white identities imposed upon Africans, Native Americans, the Mexican peoples of the Southwest, and Asian immigrants. On this level, from the earliest years of this country whiteness marked one pole in the racial hierarchy. Simultaneously, however, white served more as a marker of color than as indicia of a shared race among European groups, where until recently putatively "racial" divisions among Europeans were supremely important in marking social positions in U.S. society. Only in the first half of the twentieth century was "white" transformed into a relatively monolithic and undifferentiated group encompassing all persons of European descent in the United States (Jacobson). As with justifications for racial hierarchy, the ideas surrounding racial categories—and the boundaries of whiteness in particular—have shown a remarkable fluidity that seems likely to continue in the immediate future.

It seems that some Hispanics, Asians, Native Americans, and African Americans are increasingly migrating into the white category, in a trend that may mark a radical disjuncture in racial logic. While the melding of various European groups into the racially dominant category "white" effectuated tremendous changes in prevailing racial ideologies, these shifts nevertheless comported with the underlying belief that the most basic racial divisions exist between continental populations. For however unsupportable, the continental theory of races—whites from Europe, blacks from Africa, and Asians from Asia—has long served as one of the most enduring and popular understandings of race. This conception, however, cannot accommodate the incorporation of reds, yellows, and blacks identified with America, Asia, and Africa into the white category linked to Europe. In this sense, the expansion of a white identity to include members of these groups may portend not just a broadening of whiteness, but a change in its basic conceptualization. Whether this change is more fundamental than previous ones is not clear, though. The social certainty regarding the racial distinctiveness of southern and eastern European immigrants at the turn of the twentieth century, "beaten men from beaten races, representing the worst failures in the struggle for existence" in the words of the times (quoted in Gossett, p. 303), may have been no less great than the current (eroding) conviction that, for instance, Asians aren't white. In any event, who counts as racially dominant has long been an evolving construct—and seems poised to shift anew.

Perhaps we should distinguish here between three sorts of white identity. Consider first those "passing as white." There have always been persons who racially pass—persons who, because their physical appearance allows them to, hold themselves out as members of a group to which by social custom they would not be assigned on the basis of their ancestry (Piper). In contrast to this liminal group, we might think of some persons as "fully white," in the sense that, with all of the racially relevant facts about them widely known, they would generally be considered white by the community at large (consistent with a social constructionist understanding, racial identity turns not on particular criteria per se, but on the establishment of and the significance given such elements by community norms). Of persons of Irish and Jewish descent in the United States, for example, one might say that while initially some were able to pass as white, now they are fully white (Brodkin; Ignatiev).

Unlike both those passing as white and those fully white, a new group is emerging, persons perhaps best described as "honorary whites." Apartheid South Africa first formally crafted this identity: seeking to engage in trade and commerce with nations cast as inferior by apartheid logic, particularly Japan, South Africa extended to individuals from such countries the status of honorary whites, allowing them to travel, reside, relax, and conduct business in South African venues otherwise strictly "whites only" (Osada). Persons who pass as white hide racially relevant parts of their identity; honorary whites are extended the status of whiteness despite the public recognition that, from a bio-racial perspective, they are not fully white.

In the United States, an honorary white status seems increasingly to exist for certain persons and groups whose minority identity seems unequivocal under current racial schemas, but who are nevertheless extended a functional presumption of whiteness (Warren & Twine). The quintessential example would be certain Asian-American individuals and communities, particularly East Asians. Asians have long been racialized as non-white in the United States as a matter of law and social practice; given high levels of immigration, this negative racialization, tied as ever to xenophobia, continues. Moreover, the continental theory places Asians securely among non-whites. But despite these clear indicia of non-whiteness, the model minority myth and professional success have combined to free some Asian Americans from the most pernicious negative beliefs regarding their racial character. This trend reveals in part a shift toward a more socio-racial system. Individuals and communities with the highest levels of acculturation, achievement, and wealth increasingly find themselves functioning as white, at least as measured by professional integration, residential patterns, and intermarriage rates. Focusing on this near-white status, George Yancey argues that "if Asian Americans overcome the perceptions that they are biologically different from the majority group members, then it can be argued that Asians Americans will eventually assimilate into the dominant group in society in the same way that southern/eastern European ethnic groups have become 'white'" (p. 42). I posit instead that they need not overcome a biological presumption of difference: today, some Asians can function as honorary whites, an identity that contemplates both white status and a biologically non-white identity (Tuan).

Latinos also have access to honorary white identity, though their situation differs from that of Asians. Unlike the latter, and also unlike African Americans, Hispanics have long been on the cusp between white and non-white in the United States. Despite pervasive and often violent racial prejudice against Mexicans in the Southwest and against Puerto Ricans and other Latino groups in the Caribbean that emerged during the nineteenth century and endures today, elite Latin Americans in the United States have historically been accepted as fully white. This pattern reflects the relatively greater influence of socio-racial rather than strictly bio-racial parameters in Hispanic racialization. With no clear identity under the continental theory of race, and with a tremendous range of somatic features marking this heterogeneous population, there has long been relatively more room for the use of social rather than strictly bio-racial factors in the imputation of race to particular Latino individuals and groups. Seeking to take advantage of their liminal position, elite Hispanics have traditionally claimed for themselves and their communities white identities. From the 1930s through the 1950s, for instance, Mexican community leaders in the United States challenged segregation not on the grounds that it was wrong per se, but by arguing that they were white, thereby initiating a persistent trend in which certain Latinos seek assimilation through claims of whiteness (Foley; Haney López (1997)). The racial pride movements of the late 1960s saw segments of the Mexican and Puerto Rican communities reject this racial politics in favor of pride in a non-white identity—indeed, the Chicano and Young Lord movements deserve extended study as among the few historical episodes during which large groups rejected a white identity and instead embraced non-whiteness (Haney López (2003); Melendez).

The racial divide among Latinos continues: by the census count, almost half consider themselves white (though this number has declined over the last three censuses and by another major survey the number is closer to one in five; in addition, a steady three percent of Hispanics consider themselves black (Logan; Pew Hispanic Center, p. 31)). It seems likely that an increasing number of Hispanics—those who have fair features, material wealth, and high social status, aided also by Anglo surnames—will both claim and be accorded a position in society as fully white. Simultaneously, many more Latinos—similarly situated in terms of material and status position, but perhaps with slightly darker features or a surname or accent suggesting Latin American origins—will become honorary whites (Haney López 2005). Meanwhile, the preponderance of Latinos as well as most others traditionally constructed as racial minorities will continue to be relegated to nonwhite categories. The advent of an honorary white identity for some does not portend the elimination of race for all, a point to which I return below.

To reiterate the basic point, the future of race in the United States will be profoundly shaped in the coming decades by how Asians and to an even greater extent Latinos come to see themselves and in turn come to be seen racially. While the population as whole grew by 13 percent in the last decade of the twentieth century, the Asian population jumped by 72 percent and the Latino population boomed by almost 60 percent (Barnes & Bennett, p. 3; Guzman, p. 3). Beyond the sheer rates of increase, the absolute numbers are striking. According to the census bureau, people counted as other than black or white increased from less than 1 percent of the population in 1970 to over 12.5 percent in 2000 (Hobbs & Stoops, p. 74). This last figure is conservative, for it does not include the nearly half of Latinos the census bureau counts as white. And consider another striking fact: births to Latina mothers now outnumber all other deliveries combined in bellwether California (Richardson & Fields). The racial future of the United States is inexorably bound up with Latino and Asian racial identity.

In the context of U.S. race relations, why so many should seek the privileges and positive presumptions of whiteness is obvious (if also politically and morally troubling, insofar as seeking to be white inevitably contributes to the perpetuation and legitimation of white dominance). But why do many whites appear willing to extend—or, at least, not actively to resist the extension of—whiteness? For some, the answer surely lies in the positive accomplishments of the civil rights era, including not only the defeat of notions of white supremacy but also the partial integration of many social institutions, including labor environments, higher learning, athletics, and entertainment. We must be careful not to discount the willingness of significant sectors within the white community to extend a presumption of full human worth to racial minorities—nor should we be surprised that this presumption of full humanity often translates into treating non-whites as if they were white.

But for other whites, the willingness to extend a presumption of whiteness reflects strategic thinking about the numbers. The census bureau predicts, for instance, that whites will comprise seventy-eight percent of the nation's population in 2020—but only if its projections regarding the number of Hispanics who will identify as white are correct. If no Latinos are included, the white population will amount to only sixty-one of every hundred Americans in 2020 and by 2050, if not sooner, whites will comprise a numerical minority in this country (U.S. Bureau of the Census; McDaniel). There are many—I have in mind here the corporations that supported affirmative action in the Michigan cases, the military brass who did the same, and the Republican Party with its cynical version of right-wing affirmative action that promotes a few minorities into highly visible positions—who see these numbers and understand that future power depends on at least the symbolic inclusion of some minorities today (Holt: 107).

So whiteness is expanding, and changing. This is not a particularly dramatic or felicitous development (except, to some extent, for the newly white). First, the move in the socio-racial direction, in which racial significance attaches to wealth, professional attainment, and so forth, is a much less profound change than is often suggested. Race in the United States has always had a socio-racial dimension. Indeed, a developing scholarship now impressively demonstrates that even during and immediately after slavery, at a time when racial identity in the United States was presumably most rigidly fixed in terms of biological difference and descent, and even in the formal legal setting of the courtroom, determinations of racial identity often took place on the basis of social indicia such as the nature of one's employment or one's choice of sexual partners (Davis; Elliot; Gross 1998; Sharfstein;

Zackodnik). This "performance" of race, as some scholars term it, has a long pedigree in the United States (Carbado & Gulati; Gross 2001); Tehranian).

Second, despite the increased salience of social indicia to the achievement of a privileged racial identity, physical features will remain foundational in racial categorization. To be sure, individuals and groups who would have been clearly non-white under the racial regime in place just a few decades ago now function more and more as white. But rather than fully supplanting the role of physical features in racial determinations, socio-racial factors more accurately mainly supplement them. It is not just any community or individual who can become honorary whites; instead, it is those whose physical characteristics most closely resemble the morphology associated with whites. In this context, color—meaning those somatic details such as skin tone, facial features, hair shade and texture upon which racial classifications were erected in the United States—will continue to have tremendous significance, as those minorities with the lightest features will have the greatest access to white identity. Those who are darker, be they Latinos or South Asians or African Americans, will rarely be accorded white status despite their individual or group achievements precisely because their phenotype positions them too far toward the putatively inferior end of the color spectrum (Banks; Jones). Race will remain, as it long has been, supremely color-coded. Under antebellum racial logic those blacks with the fairest features were sometimes described as "light, bright, and damn near white" (Robinson 276). If today we switch out "damn near" for "honorary," how much has really changed?

Race will not cease to have a major physical component, nor will ordinal categories like black, brown, white, yellow, and red soon disappear. The basic belief in continental racial divisions will persist, insuring a sense that those with almost exclusively European ancestry are fully white while others remain honorary whites—white as a form of social courtesy, but not unquestionably white. Indeed, most likely one attribute of whiteness as social courtesy is the extent to which it can be easily withdrawn. The belief in continental races will likely also ensure a continued special stigma for those with African ancestry, where this ostensible stain has been so central to the elaboration of race in the United States. A few African Americans have achieved a functional white identity, but it will remain significantly more difficult for blacks than for many Asians and Latinos to function as whites. Of course, black and Latino are not exclusive categories. Indeed, those persons of

African descent who can claim a "foreign" identity, for instance as Latinos, or as recent immigrants from Africa or from the Caribbean, may find that this assists them in distancing themselves in socio-racial terms from blackness, and so makes an honorary white identity more accessible. Nevertheless, African descent will continue to be highly stigmatized, and honorary white status will be available only to the most exceptional—and the most light-skinned—blacks, but too few other African Americans, and on terms far more tentative than those on which whiteness will be extended to many Latinos and Asians.

Finally, in contrast to the expectations of those who herald the Latin Americanization of race in the United States, the redefinition of whiteness does not portend a positive movement toward racial democracy. Under a redefined white category, racial hierarchy will continue unabated. The strongest evidence in this regard is Latin America itself. Most Latin American countries are marked by extreme racial hierarchies that distinguish between whites, mixed-race persons, blacks, and indigenous populations. Those who predict a felicitous Latin American racial future in the United States do so only by ignoring the history of race in the very region they extol as a model. To give even cursory attention to the reality of racial stratification in Latin America (as opposed to simply accepting the rhetoric of racial egalitarianism that dominates much of elite Latin American discourse about domestic race relations) is to recognize that the shift toward a socio-racial system is not in any way tantamount to the end of racial hierarchy (Skidmore).

But on another account, perhaps the United States *is* moving in a Latin American direction. Latin American societies often proclaim that they have transcended race even as they remain riven by racial subordination, and boast of robust civil rights laws that in reality do virtually nothing to ameliorate inequality (Hernández). These celebratory claims have long served in many Latin American countries as propaganda that masks the much bleaker reality of not just persistent racial subordination but of steadfast resistance by racial elites to any reform programs likely to succeed. In this sense, we are becoming like Latin America: we are developing a public discourse that assures us that we have indeed transcended race and need take no further efforts, as well as a legal regime that at once presents itself as aggressively committed to rooting out racism but that in fact excels only at forestalling state and private efforts to disestablish racial hierarchy. In the United States, these new elements take the name of colorblindness.

Colorblindness

Continued white dominance will be rationalized and protected through the ascendant racial ideology of colorblindness. The specific command of colorblindness—that the state should not take race into account—is not new, nor particularly contentious in its own right. Indeed, after bearing witness to several centuries of racial hierarchy, there is an intuitive appeal to the admonition that as a society we simply eschew race once and for all. But the colorblindness proselytized by the racial right today (and widely accepted by most whites) is altogether different from a considered response to racial inequality. It propounds, even as it occludes, a powerful set of understandings about the dynamics of racial subordination as well as about the nature of racial groups. Colorblindness is in this sense not a prescription but an ideology, a set of understandings that delimits how people comprehend, rationalize, and act in the world (Bonilla-Silva). Though colorblindness now dominates the country's racial imagination its origins are in race law, making a genealogy of legal colorblindness indispensable to fathoming its constituent claims.

Colorblindness is frequently traced back to the Supreme Court's decision in *Plessy v. Ferguson*, which upheld Jim Crow segregation in the South and prompted Justice John Marshall Harlan's famous dissent that "our constitution is colorblind, and neither knows nor tolerates classes among citizens" (Plessy: 559). Harlan's dissent is today widely invoked for the proposition that the state should never take race into account; and his felicitous turn of phrase has now entered the legal and cultural cannon. But, of course, colorblindness did not take hold during Jim Crow's reign, and, indeed, Harlan was hardly committed to the proposition attributed to him, for in *Plessy* itself he extolled the superiority of the white race, and just a few years later he wrote an opinion upholding segregated schools (Cumming).[4]

---

[4] The full quote from which the "colorblindness" excerpt is taken reads as follows:

> The white race deems itself to be the dominant race in this country. And so it is, in prestige, in achievements, in education, in wealth, and in power. So, I doubt not, it will continue to be for all time, if it remains true to its great heritage, and holds fast to the principles of constitutional liberty. But in view of the constitution, in the eye of the law, there is in this country no superior, dominant, ruling class of citizens. There is no caste here. Our constitution is colorblind, and neither knows nor tolerates classes among citizens.

Given his invocation of perpetual white dominance, it's no surprise that Harlan's reference to colorblindness is often presented in highly excerpted form.

For the first half of the twentieth century, colorblindness represented a radical and wholly unrealized aspiration, the hope that *de jure* racial subordination might be suddenly and thoroughly dismantled. It was in this vein that, as counsel for the NAACP in the late 1940s and early 1950s, Thurgood Marshall encouraged his colleagues to cite to Harlan's invocation of colorblindness to make the argument that, as Marshall put it in a 1947 brief to the Supreme Court, "classifications and distinctions based on race or color have no moral or legal validity in our society. They are contrary to our constitution and laws" (Brief for Petitioner, p. 27, in Sipuel). But neither society nor the courts embraced colorblindness when doing so might have sped the demise of white supremacy. Even during the civil rights era, colorblindness as a strategy for racial emancipation did not take hold. Instead, the courts and Congress dismantled Jim Crow segregation and the most egregious forms of private discrimination in a piece-meal manner that banned only the most noxious misuses of race, not any reference to race whatsoever.

In the wake of the civil rights movement's limited but significant triumphs, the relationship between colorblindness and racial reform changed remarkably. Whereas colorblindness in the context of Jim Crow was heavy with emancipatory promise, in the civil rights era and since, its greatest potency instead lies in preserving the racial status quo. As explicitly race-based subordination came to an end but racial inequality stubbornly persisted, racial progressives increasingly recognized the need for state and private actors to intervene aggressively along racial lines to dismantle entrenched inequality. Rather than call for colorblindness, they began to insist on the need for affirmative, race-conscious remedies. In this new context, colorblindness appealed instead to those *opposing* racial integration. Enshrouded with the moral raiment of the civil rights movement, this rhetoric provided cover for reactionary opposition to racial reform. Within a year of *Brown*, southern school districts and courts had recognized that they could forestall integration by insisting that the Constitution allowed them to use only "race-neutral" means to end segregation. As one recalcitrant court crowed, "The Constitution, in other words, does not require integration. It merely forbids discrimination. It does not forbid such segregation as occurs as the result of voluntary action. It merely forbids the use of governmental power to enforce segregation" (Briggs: 777). By the late 1970s and early 1980s, defenders of de facto segregation had adopted colorblindness as their strongest rhetorical weapon in the battle against race-conscious remedies. When the Supreme Court split on affirmative action in 1978, Thurgood Marshall, now as a Justice, spoke out against the colorblind rhetoric newly adopted by conservatives: "It is because of a legacy of unequal treatment," he inveighed, "that we now must permit the institutions of this society to give consideration to race in making decisions about who will hold the positions of influence, affluence, and prestige in America" (Bakke, p. 402). With the change in racial context from Jim Crow to civil rights, colorblindness as an approach to race jumped political valence, from radical to reactionary.

Wielding the ideal of colorblindness as a sword, racial conservatives on the Supreme Court have refought the battles lost during the civil rights era, cutting back on protections from racial discrimination as well as severely limiting race-conscious remedies. *McCleskey v. Kemp* insists that, even accepting as uncontroverted fact that Georgia sentences to death blacks who murder whites at *twenty-two times* the rate it orders death for blacks who kill blacks, the Constitution perceives no discrimination in Georgia's death penalty machinery (p. 327). Meanwhile, *City of Richmond v. Croson* tells us that when the former capital of the Confederacy adopts an affirmative action program to steer some of its construction dollars to minority owned firms it impermissibly discriminates—even when, without the program, less than seventy cents of each one-hundred dollars went to minorities in a city over fifty percent African-American (p. 534). The embrace of colorblindness by the conservative Court has converted our vaunted constitutional commitment to racial equality into a tool for preserving a racial status quo of continued white dominance.

But perhaps the greatest power of reactionary colorblindness lies not in its immediate judicial impact but in the story it tells about race and racism. Justice Clarence Thomas has emphatically stated: "[T]here is a 'moral and constitutional equivalence' between laws designed to subjugate a race and those that distribute benefits on the basis of race in order to foster some current notion of equality.... In each instance, it is racial discrimination pure and simple" (Adarand, p. 240–41 n.1). What understanding of racism, and of race itself, could justify this strict moral and constitutional equation of Jim Crow and affirmative action?

Colorblind partisans have supplied answers widely appealing to whites. To begin with racism, they define it as any direct invocation or use of race. Under this conception, most racism (and in particular the virulent racism of white supremacy) was defeated by the early, pre-affirmative action civil rights movement, which drove racist discourse out of the public arena. As a result, colorblind advocates present the contemporary United States as free from deep racial division. We are, instead, now "a nation of minorities," comprised no longer of dominant and subordinate races, but instead of a shifting mosaic of ethnic groups in equal competition with each other. As Justice Lewis Powell averred in 1978, "the United States had become a Nation of minorities. Each had to struggle—and to some extent struggles still—to overcome the prejudices not of a monolithic majority, but of a 'majority' composed of various minority groups" (Bakke: 292). This view insists that racial domination belongs to the increasingly distant past and claims that whites no longer operate in society as a dominant race, but now exist only as a welter of European ethnicities. "The white 'majority' itself," Powell insisted, "is composed of various minority groups, most of which can lay claim to a history of prior discrimination at the hands of the State and private individuals" (Bakke: 296). Under this theory, preferences for "minorities" threaten to extend to almost every group. As Powell explained, "Not all of these groups can receive preferential treatment and corresponding judicial tolerance of distinctions drawn in terms of race and nationality, for then the only 'majority' left would be a new minority of white Anglo–Saxon Protestants" (*id.*). With its triumphal claims about overcoming racism and its fragmentation of the white overclass into myriad ethnic minorities, colorblindness erases whites as a dominant group. Even more fancifully, it conjures them as vulnerable minorities—the true victims of today's racism, race-conscious affirmative "discrimination."

Regarding race, colorblind partisans justify the moral equation of affirmative action and Jim Crow racism by depicting race as unmoored from social practices. In the most common version of this claim, race is equated to skin color or ancestry, nothing more. In more sophisticated conceptions, race lacks meaning because it is a fiction, an incoherent social construction. Whether it is physical or fictional matters little; the core claim is that race has nothing to do with social practices of status competition and subordination. Consider the reasoning in *Hernandez v. New York*, a case involving a Hispanic defendant and the use of a Spanish-language translator, in which the prosecutor peremptorily struck from the jury every Latino. He did so, he said, because he did not believe that these potential jurors "could" set aside their familiarity with Spanish. The phrase "could," rather than "would," is telling, for while the latter term suggests concern about individual temperament, the former invokes a sense of group disability (p. 404). Also raising concern, the prosecutor questioned only Hispanic potential jurors but no others about their ability to speak Spanish. Nevertheless, the Court upheld the exclusion, finding no bias on the part of the prosecutor. Justice O'Connor's rationale, offered in a concurring opinion, is especially revealing. She thought it irrelevant that the basis for exclusion correlated closely to Hispanic identity and operated to exclude all and only Latinos. Because the strikes were not explicitly justified in racial terms, O'Connor reasoned, no basis existed for constitutional intervention. The strikes "may have acted like strikes based on race," O'Connor conceded, "but they were not based on race. *No matter how closely tied or significantly correlated to race* the explanation for a peremptory strike may be, the strike does not implicate the Equal Protection Clause unless it is based on race." (p. 375, emphasis added). Ostensibly, social practices not tied directly and explicitly to skin color or ancestry by the use of some specifically racial term do not involve race. Race is empty—either purely physical, a matter of skin color or ancestry, or purely abstract, an erroneous fiction. It is not, as O'Connor and colorblindness partisans in general would have it, a function of how one is perceived and treated.

The colorblind conceptions of race and racism function similarly: both exist only when mentioned. Race and racism operate under this conception almost as magic words: without any presence in the world, speak them and they suddenly spring into being. This magic-word formalism strips race and racism of all social meaning and of any connection to social practices of group conflict and subordination. *Hernandez* and *McCleskey,* the Georgia death penalty case, are of a piece here: no matter how extreme the discrimination, nor however closely correlated to race, the Court insisted in both cases that race and racism were not involved because no one could be shown to have uttered a racial word. In *Croson,* in contrast, racism obtained because Richmond said explicitly that some contracting dollars should go to "minorities." Under this understanding, white racism is a thing of the past because few whites today tie their views or actions explicitly to race. In contrast, racism operates primarily among racial progressives, who constantly invoke race and demand race-conscious remedies. Colorblindness equates Jim Crow segregation and affirmative action by redefining racism as any mention of race, and race as something utterly empty of social content or history.

The claim that race and racism exist only when specifically mentioned, and not otherwise, also allows colorblindness to insulate from critique a new white racial politics in which racial proxies become politically and socially acceptable substitutes for explicit racism. The civil rights movement worked a major change in U.S. society in making culturally unacceptable open expressions of white supremacy. This was a far cry, however, from actually ending white racial mobilization. Instead, this mobilization, often orchestrated by white politicians, has continued over the last several decades under the guise of interlinked panics about criminals, welfare cheats, illegal immigrants, and, most recently, terrorists. As Stephen Steinberg notes, "Through ... code words it is possible to play on racial stereotypes, appeal to racial fears, and heap blame on blacks [and other minorities] without naming them. Thus, in this cryptic vernacular we have a new and insidious form of racebaiting" (p. 214). Culture and behavior rather than phenotype have become the targets of racial reactionaries: one can understand Samuel Huntington's recent attack on Latino immigration in this way, as he at once rejects the old ideas of white racial superiority and at the same time aggressively promotes the notion of a superior Anglo Protestant culture (Huntington). Lawrence Bobo labels theories that lay minority failure at the feet of culture "laissez-faire racism" to highlight the way in which whites attribute their superior social position to a supposed special affinity for the values, orientations, and work ethic needed by the liberal individual in a capitalist society. Today, culture and behavior provide coded language for old prejudices. And colorblindness excuses and insulates this new white racism.

Consider how colorblindness protects current attacks on "illegal immigrants." This is not racism, we're told, because it is not about race at all, but simply about those who violate our laws. The animus is not racial, we're assured, because the targeted group is racially under- and over-inclusive: "illegals" doesn't sweep in all Latinos, but does supposedly include whites who cross the border without documents. Yet obviously current efforts to enflame passions about securing the border with guards, walls, and helicopters shares deep similarities with the racial hysterias that accompanied the initiation of the Asiatic Barred Zone that prohibited all Asian immigration through the first half of the twentieth century, the internment of Japanese Americans during World War II, and the mass deportation of Mexican Americans during Operation Wetback in the 1950s. Race and racism have long been used to patrol the nation's literal and figurative borders; racial politics are just as much at work today, notwithstanding the public foregrounding of seemingly non-racial concerns or the general absence of crude racial slurs. By insisting that race operates only if someone uses one among a narrowly drawn band of racial terms, reactionary colorblindness protects the new racism's efforts to locate minority inferiority in cultural deficiencies and pathological behaviors. It cannot be racial, colorblind partisans tell us, for race has nothing to do with social practices, and white racism is a thing of the past.

Conclusion

Our faces and our racial ideology maybe changing, but the fundamental racial dynamic of white dominance in our country will not end anytime soon. Instead, it will continue, even as the definition of who counts as white expands, in large part because the material interests of so many demand it, but also because the ideology of contemporary colorblindness protects and perpetuates white dominance. Proponents of reactionary colorblindness wear their anti-racist pretensions boldly, professing their deep commitment to ending racial inequality. But this is a sham, for colorblindness promises to curtail race-conscious efforts to promote racial justice, even as it refuses to acknowledge ongoing racial subordination. Worse, colorblindness redefines race and racism in a manner that excuses contemporary manifestations of racial scapegoating as legitimate concerns over inferior cultures and behavioral delinquency. For the next several decades, at least, we will suffer this racial future of colorblind white dominance.

References

Adarand Construction, Inc. v. Pena,, 515 U.S. 200 (1995).
Bakke, Regents of the Univ. of Cal. v, 438 U.S. 265 (1978).
Banks, Taunya 2000. "Colorism: A Darker Shade of Pale," 47 *UCLA L. Rev.* 1705.
Barnes, Jessica and Bennett, Claudette. 2002., *The Asian Population: 2000: Census 2000 Brief* (Feb.).
Bobo, Lawrence, et al. 1997. "Laissez Faire Racism," in *Racial Attitudes in the 1990s*, edited by Steven Tuch & Jack Martin. Westport, CT: Praeger Publisher.
Bobo, Lawrence, and Kluegel, James, "Status, Ideology, and Dimensions of Whites' Racial Beliefs and Attitudes: Progress and Stagnation," in *Racial Attitudes in the 1990s* (Steven Tuch & Jack Martin eds., 1997).
Bonilla-Silva, Eduardo. 2003. *Racism without Racists: Color-Blind Racism and the Persistence of Racial Inequality in the United States*. Lanham, Md: Rowman and Littlefield Publishers.

Briggs v. Elliot, 132 F. Supp. 776 (E.D.S.C. 1955).
Brodkin, Karen.1998. *How Jews Became White Folks and What That Says About Race in America*. New Brunswick, NJ: Rutgers University Press.
Carbado, Devon and Gulati, Mitu 2000. "Working Identity". *Cornell Law Review 85*: 1259–1308.
City of Richmond v. Croson, 488 U.S. 469 (1989).
Cleveland, Robert. 2005. *US Bureau of the Census: Alternative Income Estimates in the United States: 2003: Current Population Reports* (June).
Cumming v. Board of Education, 175 U.S. 528 (1899).
Dalaker, Joe. 2005. *US Bureau of the Census: Alternative Poverty Estimates in the United States: 2003: Current Population Reports* (June).
Davis, Adrienne. 1996. "Identity Notes Part One: Playing in the Light," 45 *Am. U. L. Rev.* 695.
DeNavas-Walt, Carmon, et al. 2004. *US Bureau of the Census: Income, Poverty, and Health Insurance Coverage in the United States: 2003: Current Population Reports* (August).
Elliot, Michael. 1999. "Telling the Difference: Nineteenth Century Legal Narratives of Racial Taxonomy," 24 *Law & Soc. Inquiry* 611.
Fields, Barbara Jeanne. 1990. "Slavery, Race and Ideology in the United States of America," 181 *New Left Review*. 95.
Foley, Neil. 1997. "Becoming Hispanic: Mexican Americans and the Faustian Pact with Whiteness," in *Reflexiones* edited by Neil Foley. Center for Mexican American Studies: The University of Texas Press.
Fredrickson, George, M. 1981. *White Supremacy: A Comparative Study in American and South African History*. New York, NY: Oxford University Press.
Fredrickson, George, M. 2002. *Racism: A Short History*. Princeton, NJ: Princeton University Press.
Frey, William H. 1996. "Immigration, Domestic Migration, and Demographic Balkanization in America: New Evidence from the 1990s," 22 *Population & Development Rev.* 741.
Glazer, Nathan. 1998. *We Are All Multiculturalists Now*. Cambridge, MA: Harvard University Press.
——. 2001. "The Future of Race in the United States," in *Race in 21st Century America* edited by Curtis Stokes, Theresa Melendez, and Gernice Rhodes-Reed. East Lansing, MI: Michigan State University Press.
Gossett, Thomas. 1963. *Race: The History of an Idea in America*. Dallas: Southern Methodist University Press.
Graham, Hugh Davis. 2002. *Collision Course: The Strange Convergence of Affirmative Action and Immigration Policy in America*. New York: Oxford University Press.
Grieco, Elizabeth M. and Cassidy, Rachel C. 2001. *US Bureau of the Census: Overview of Race and Hispanic Origin, Census Brief 2000* (March).
Gross, Ariella, 1998. "Litigating Whiteness: Trials of Racial Determination in the Nineteenth Century South," 108 *Yale Law Journal* 109.
Gross, Ariella. 2001. "Beyond Black and White: Cultural Approaches to Race and Slavery," 101 *Columbia Law Review* 640.
Guzman, Betsy, *US Bureau of the Census: The Hispanic Population, Census Brief 2000* (May 2001).
Haney Laney López, Ian. 1994. "The Social Construction of Race," 29 *Harvard Civil Rights and Civil Liberties Review*. 1.
Haney Laney López, Ian. 1997. "Race, Ethnicity, Erasure: The Salience of Race to LatCrit Theory," 85 *California Law Review* 1143.
——. 2003. *Racism on Trial: The Chicano Fight for Justice* Cambridge, Mass: Harvard University Press.
——. 2005. "Race on the 2010 Census: Hispanics and the Shrinking White Majority," 134 *Daedalus* 42.

———. 2006. *White By Law: The Legal Construction of Race* (revised ed.). New York: New York University Press.
Hanson, Victor Davis. 2003. *Mexifornia: A State of Becoming*. San Francisco, CA.: Encounter Books.
Hernández, Tanya Katerí. 2002. "Multiracial Matrix: The Role of Race Ideology in the Enforcement of Antidiscrimination Laws, A United States-Latin America Comparison," 87 *Cornell Law Review* 1093.
Hernandez v. New York, 500 U.S. 352 (1991).
Hobbs, Frank and Stoops, Nicole. 2002. *US Bureau of the Census: Demographic Trends in the 20th Century: Census 2000 Special Reports* (November).
Hochschild, Jennifer. 2003. "From Nominal to Ordinal to Interval: Reconceiving Racial and Ethnic Hierarchy in the United States," paper delivered as Wesson Lectures, Stanford University, May 5 and 6, 2003.
Hochschild, Jennifer. 2005. "Looking Ahead: Racial Trends in the United States," *Daedalus* 134(1):70–81.
Hollinger, David A. 1995., *Post-Ethnic America: Beyond Multiculturalism*. New York: Basic Books.
Hollinger, David A. 2003. "Amalgamation and Hypodescent: The Question of Ethnoracial Mixture in the History of the United States," 108 (1) *American Historical Review*.
Holt, Thomas. 2000. *The Problem of Race in the 21st Century*. Cambridge, MA: Harvard University Press.
Human Rights Watch, *Race and Incarceration in the United States*, http://www.hrw.org/backgrounder/usa/race
Human Rights Watch. 2000. *Punishment and Prejudice: Racial Disparities in the War on Drugs*.
Huntington, Samuel P. 2004. *Who Are We? The Challenges to America's National Identity*.
Ignatiev, Noel. 1996. *How the Irish Became White*. New York: Routledge.
Jacobson, Matthew Frye 1998. *Whiteness of a Different Color: European Immigrants and the Alchemy of Race*, Cambridge, MA: Harvard University Press.
Jones, Trina. 2000. "Shades of Brown: The Law of Skin Color," 49 *Duke Law Journal 49*: 1487–1557.
Kalmijn, Matthijs. 1993. "Trends in Black/White Intermarriage," *Social Forces* 72(1):119–146.
Klor de Alva, Jorge. 1996 "Our Next Race Question," *Harper's*, (April): 55–63.
Lind, Michael. 1995. *The Next American Nation: The New Nationalism and the Fourth American Revolution*. New York: Free Press.
Lind, Michael. 1998. "The Beige and the Black," *N.Y. Times Magazine*, Aug. 16: 38–39.
Logan, John R. 2003. "Ethnic Diversity Grows, Neighborhood Integration Lags." In *Redefining Urban and Suburban America: Evidence from Census 2000, Volume One*, edited by Bruce Katz and Robert E. Lang. Washington, D.C.: Brookings Institution Press.
Mauer, Marc. 1999. *Race to Incarcerate*. New York: The Sentencing Project.
McCleskey v. Kemp, 481 U.S. 279 (1986).
MCDaniel, Antonio. 1995. "The Dynamic Racial Composition of the United States," *Daedalus* 124(1):179–198.
Melendez, Miguel, 2003. *We Took the Streets: Fighting for Latinos with the Young Lords* New York: St. Martin's Press.
"New Latino Nation," *Newsweek*, May 30, 2005, pp. 28–29.
Osada, Masako. 2002. *Sanctions and Honorary Whites: Diplomatic Policies and Economic Realities in Relations Between Japan and South Africa*. Westport, Ct: Greenwood Press.
PEW Hispanic Center. 2002. *2002 National Survey of Latinos, Summary of Findings*.

Piper, Adrian. 1996. "Passing for White, Passing for Black," in *Passing and the Fictions of Identity* edited by Elaine K. Ginsberg. Durham, NC: Duke University Press.
Plessy v. Ferguson, 163 U.S. 537 (1896).
Ricardson, Lisa and Fields, Robin. 2003. "Latinos Account for Majority of Births in California," *L.A. Times* (Feb. 6): A1.
Robinson, Reginald. 2000. "The Shifting Race-Consciousness Matrix and the Multiracial Category Movement: A Critical Reply to Professor Hernandez," 20 *B.C. Third World L.J.* 231.
Rodriguez, Gregory. 2003. "Mongrel America," *Atlantic Monthly* (Jan./Feb) Volume 291, No. 1: 95–97.
———. 2003, "Dining at the Ethnicity Café," *L.A. Times*, (May 18): M3.
Rodriguez, Rishard. 2002. *Brown, The Last Discovery of America*. New York: Penguin Books.
Roediger, David R2003. *Colored White: Transcending the Racial Past*. Berkley: University of California Press.
Sharfstein, Daniel, "The Secret History of Race in the United States," 112 *Yale L.J.* 1473 (2003).
Sipuel v. Bd. Of Regents of the Univ. of Okla., 332 U.S. 814 (1947).
Skidmore, Thomas. 1993. "Biracial USA vs. Multiracial Brazil: Is the Contrast Still Valid?" *Journal of Latin American Studies,* 25:373–386.
Skrentny, John D2002. "Inventing Race," 46 *Public Interests* 46:96–113.
Smedley, Audrey. 1999. *Race in North America: Origins and Evolution of a Worldview* Boulder, CO: Westvew Press.
Steinberg, Stephen. 2001. *Turning Back: The Retreat from Racial Justice in American Thought and Policy*. Boston: Beacon Press.
Suro, Roberto. 1999. "Mixed Doubles," *American Demographics*, (Nov) 21:56–62.
Tehranian, John/ 2000. "Performing Whiteness: Naturalization Litigation and the Construction of Racial Identity in America," *Yale Law Journal* 109(4): 817 -827.
Tuan, Mia. 2001. *Forever Foreigners or Honorary Whites? The Asian Ethnic Experience Today*. New Brunswick, NJ: Rutgers University Press.
US Bureau of the Census, 2004. *US Interim Projections by Age, Sex, Race, and Hispanic Origin*, http://www.census.gov/ipc/www/usinterimproj/.
Warren, Jonathan and Twine, France Winddance. 1997. "White Americans, the New Minority?" 28 *Journal Black Studies* 28(2): 200–218.
Williams, Kim, M. 2005. "Multiracialism and the Civil Rights Future," *Daedalus* 134(1) 53–60.
Williams, Kim, M. 2006. *Mark One or More: Civil Rights in Multiracial America*. Ann Arbor: The University of Michigan Press.
Yancey, George. 2003. *Who is White? Latinos, Asians, and the New Black/Nonblack Divide*. Boulder, CO: Lynne Rienner Publishers.
Zackodnik, Teresa. 2001. "Fixing the Color Line: The Mulatto, Southern Courts, and Racial Identity," *American Quarterly* 53(3):420–451.
Zweignhaft, Richard L. and Domhoff, G. William. 1998. *Diversity in the Power Elite: Have Women and Minorities Reached the Top?* New Haven, CT: Yale University Press.

WHEN GOOD PEOPLE DO BAD THINGS: THE NATURE OF CONTEMPORARY RACISM

John F. Dovidio and Samuel L. Gaertner

This article discusses how Whites' racism has mutated into a new form – one that is indirect, subtle, and often unintentional – called "aversive racism." Although its operation may be subtle, its consequences can be significant, adversely affecting the well being of Black Americans.

We begin with an illustration. In 1973, we conducted a field experiment involving White residents of Brooklyn, NY, who identified themselves politically as liberals and conservatives. Both the liberal and conservative households received wrong-number telephone calls that quickly developed into requests for assistance. The callers, who were clearly identifiable from their dialects as being Black or White, explained that their car was disabled and that they were attempting to reach a service garage from the public phone along the parkway. The callers further claimed that they had no more change to make another call and asked the subject to help by calling the garage. If the subject refused to help or hung up after the caller explained that he or she had no more change, a "not helping" response was recorded. If the subject hung up before learning that the motorist had no more change, the response was considered a "premature hang up."

The first finding from this study was direct and predictable. Conservatives were less likely to help Blacks than Whites (65 percent versus 92 percent), whereas liberals helped Blacks and Whites more equally (75 percent versus 85 percent). If we were to have left the findings here, liberals would appear to be relatively well-intentioned.

However, this edge is cancelled out by liberals having "hung up prematurely" much more often on Blacks than they did on Whites (19 percent versus 3 percent). Conservatives did not discriminate in this way (8 percent versus 5 percent). Thus both conservative and liberal Whites discriminated against Blacks but in different ways.

What could possibly explain such behavior among people who presumably consider themselves egalitarian? The explanation, as this and subsequent studies have demonstrated, is that many liberal White people will not publicly and consciously express bias against Blacks, but, because they have unconscious negative feelings about Blacks, they will discriminate in subtle ways. This subtle and unconscious bias is what we mean when we refer to aversive racism.

Many people forego considerable personal gain to dedicate themselves to making the world better in some way – through volunteer work, by supporting others in their community or on the job, or by promoting cultural richness. Racism, we can probably all agree, is antithetical to this spirit. The problem is that these same well-intentioned people are also racist and, as we will subsequently discuss, they are racist without being aware of it.

Overt Racism

Racism is easy to recognize in its most blatant forms. Traditional forms of racism in the United States have been expressed directly and openly. Racism produced racial segregation in neighborhoods and schools, and open discrimination in employment. Due in part to the Civil Rights Legislation of the 1960s, however, the nature of racism has changed. This legislation defined racism not only as morally improper but also as legally wrong. We can readily agree that good people should not discriminate.

We can probably also agree that racism has aided in producing a myriad of social ills, redlined neighborhoods suffering from inadequate infrastructures, substandard segregated schools, open discrimination in employment, high infant mortality rates, and a host of other problems. Many of these problems persist and have worsened over time. How do we explain this?

Even while overt racism has declined since the 1960s, some of the motivations that underlie racism still exist. Racism can offer advantages. Discriminating against others can boost one's self-esteem and promote feelings of control and superiority. Tangibly, discrimination offers economic advantages to members of the majority group and serves to maintain that group's political, social, and corporate power. Thus racism has emerged in new forms, such as aversive racism.

Aversive Racism

Aversive racism rests on an inherent contradiction: The denial of personal prejudice co-exists with underlying unconscious negative feelings and beliefs. One form of contemporary racism, involving Whites' attitudes toward Blacks, is aversive racism. A critical aspect of the aversive racism framework is the conflict between the denial of personal prejudice and the underlying *unconscious* negative feelings and beliefs. Unfortunately, the negative feelings and beliefs that underlie aversive racism are rooted in normal, often adaptive, psychological processes. For instance, people generally tend to like others who are similar to them. In addition, because people need to feel in control, they often are motivated to devalue others, particularly those who are different than them. In contrast to the feelings of open hostility and clear dislike of Blacks that characterize old-fashioned racism, the negative feelings that aversive racists experience are typically more diffuse, such as feelings of anxiety and uneasiness.

Because aversive racists consciously endorse egalitarian values and deny their negative feelings about Blacks, they will not discriminate directly and openly in ways that can be attributed to racism. However, because of their negative feelings they will discriminate, often unintentionally, when their behavior can be justified on the basis of some factor other than race. Aversive racists may therefore regularly engage in discrimination while they maintain a nonprejudiced self-image. The term "aversive" in this form of racism thus refers to two aspects of this bias. It reflects to the nature of the emotions associated with Blacks, such as anxiety, that lead to avoidance and social awkwardness rather than to open antagonism. It also represents the fact that, because of their conscious adherence to egalitarian principles, these Whites would find any thought that they might be prejudiced to be aversive.

To make things worse, the uncomfortable and discriminatory behavior associated with aversive racism is very obvious to Blacks, even while Whites fail to recognize it or deny it when confronted. For instance, a substantial majority of Whites see the United States as currently characterized by racial equality, while a sizable majority of Blacks see contemporary society as promoting racial *in*equality. Whereas the subtle nature of aversive racism leads Whites to underestimate the impact of racial prejudice, it leads Blacks to be particularly attuned to these inconsistent and unpredictable racist behaviors. This inconsistency erodes Blacks confidence in Whites and leads to a spiral of distrust. Blacks assume that the inconsistent, often contradictory, action of Whites reflects consciously purposeful deceptiveness and purposeful, old-fashioned racism.

How Aversive Racism Works

Aversive racism has been investigated in psychological research for over 30 years. One of our early experiments illustrates how aversive racism can operate in fairly dramatic ways. The scenario for experiment was inspired by an incident in the mid-1960s in which 38 people witnessed the stabbing of a woman, Kitty Genovese, without a single bystander intervening to help. What accounted for this behavior? Psychologists have found that feelings of responsibility play a key role. If a person witnesses an emergency and he or she is the only bystander, that person bears all of the responsibility for helping. The likelihood of the person helping is therefore high. However, if a person witnesses an emergency and believes that there are several other witnesses, then the responsibility for helping is shared. Moreover, if the person believes that someone else will help or has already helped, then he or she is relieved from responsibility for helping; therefore, the likelihood of taking action is significantly reduced.

Early in our research, to investigate how aversive racism operates, we created a situation in the laboratory in which White participants witnessed a staged emergency involving a Black or White victim. We led some of our participants to believe that they would be the only witness to this emergency, while we led others to believe that there would be other people (Whites, as well) who also witnessed the emergency. We predicted that, because aversive racists do not act in overtly bigoted ways, Whites would not discriminate when they were the only witness and the responsibility for helping was clearly focused on them. However, because of their unconscious negative feelings, we anticipated Whites to be much less helpful to Black than to White victims when they had a justifiable excuse not to get involved, such as the belief that one of the *other* witnesses was taking responsibility for helping.

This is precisely what we found. When White participants believed that they were the only witness they helped White and Black victims very frequently (over 85% of the time) and equivalently. There was no evidence of blatant racism. In contrast, when they thought there were other witnesses, they helped Black victims half as often as White victims (75% vs. 38%). Thus, these results illustrate the operation of subtle biases in relatively dramatic, spontaneous, and life-threatening circumstances involving a failure to help, rather than an action intentionally aimed at doing harm. Although the bias may be subtle, its consequences may be severe.

Aversive Racism in the Workplace

Labor statistics continue to demonstrate fundamental disparities in the economic status of Blacks relative to Whites – a gap that has not only persisted but also, in some aspects, has widened in recent years. Aversive racism may be one factor that contributes to disparities in the workplace. Subtle biases can influence both the access of Blacks to the workplace and their performance in it.

At the time of hiring, aversive racism can affect how qualifications are perceived and weighed, in ways that systematically disadvantage Black relative to White applicants. In particular, the aversive racism framework suggests that bias will not be expressed when a person is clearly qualified or unqualified for a position, because the appropriate decision is obvious. However, bias is expected when the appropriate decision is unclear, for example because of ambiguous evidence about whether the candidate's qualifications meet the criteria for selection or when the candidate's file has conflicting information (e.g., some strong and some weak aspects).

In one study of hiring decision, in a context that was relevant to college students, we asked participants to evaluate candidates for a position in an ostensibly new program for peer counseling at their university on the basis of excerpts from an interview. White participants evaluated a Black or White candidate who had credentials that were systematically manipulated to represent very strong, moderate, or very weak qualifications for the position. Their responses were supportive of the aversive racism framework. When the candidates' credentials clearly qualified them for the position (strong qualifications) or the credentials clearly were not appropriate (weak qualifications), there was no discrimination against the Black candidate. However, when candidates' qualifications for the position were less obvious and the appropriate decision was more ambiguous (moderate qualifications), White participants recommended the Black candidate significantly less often than the White candidate with exactly the same credentials.

In subsequent research, in which participants were asked to help make admissions decisions for the university, we again found no racial bias when applicants had uniformly strong or uniformly weak college board scores and record of high school achievement. When applicants were strong on one dimension (e.g., on college board scores) and weak on the other (e.g., high school grades), however, Black applicants were recommended significantly less strongly than were White applicants.

Moreover, participants shifted, as a function of race, how they weighed the criteria to justify their decisions. For Black applicants, they gave the weaker of the dimensions (college board scores or grades) greater weight in their decisions, whereas for White applicants they assigned the stronger of the qualifications more weight. Taken together, these findings suggest that when given latitude for interpretation, Whites give White candidates the "benefit of the doubt," a benefit they do not extend to Blacks.

The behavior of aversive racists is thus characterized by two types of inconsistencies. First, aversive racists exhibit an apparent contradiction between their expressed egalitarian attitudes and their biased (albeit subtly) behaviors. Second, sometimes (in clear situations) they act in an unbiased fashion, whereas at other times (with ambiguous circumstances) they are biased against Blacks. For Blacks who may not understand the dynamics but who suffer the consequences, these inconsistencies can create a climate of suspicion and distrust.

Once on the job, aversive racism exerts subtle influences on the behavior of Whites in interracial work groups and, thereby, on the outcomes for Blacks. Effective teamwork on the job requires social coordination as well as task-relevant skills. Inconsistent behavior of Whites and feelings of distrust by Blacks can thus have detrimental effects on team productivity.

We examined these processes in interracial dyads in which a Black participant was paired with a White student who was identified as a traditionally high prejudiced person (who expressed their bias openly), an aversive racist (who expressed egalitarian views but who showed evidence of unconscious bias on a reaction time task), or a low prejudiced White (who held egalitarian views and showed little evidence of unconscious bias). These participants engaged in a problem-solving task about challenges to college students. For example, for one task, they were asked to identify the five most important things that incoming students need to bring to campus. Because there were no objective measures of the quality of team solution, we focused on the quality of their interaction (as reflected in their perceptions of friendliness and trustworthiness and feelings of satisfaction) and in their efficiency (as indexed by their time to complete the task).

In general, Whites' impressions of their behavior were related primarily to their publicly expressed attitudes, whereas Blacks' impressions of Whites were related mainly to Whites' unconscious attitudes. Specifically, Whites who expressed egalitarian ideals (i.e., Low

Prejudiced Whites and Aversive Racists) reported that they behaved more friendly than did those who expressed their bias openly (i.e., High Prejudiced Whites). Black partners perceived Whites who showed no evidence of unconscious bias (i.e., Low Prejudiced Whites) to be more friendly than those who had unconscious biases (Aversive Racists and High Prejudiced Whites). Blacks were least trustful of Aversive Racists – even more than of High Prejudiced Whites – and were most trustful of Low Prejudiced Whites.

Our results further revealed that Whites' racial attitudes were systematically related to the efficiency of the interracial teams. Teams with Low Prejudiced Whites solved the problem most quickly. Interracial teams involving High Prejudiced Whites were next most efficient. Teams with Aversive Racists were the least efficient. Presumably, the conflicting messages displayed by aversive racists and the divergent impressions of the team members' interaction interfered with the task effectiveness of the team. To the extent that Blacks are in the minority in an organization and are dependent on high prejudiced Whites or aversive racists on work-related tasks, their performance is likely to be objectively poorer than the performance of Whites who predominantly interact with other Whites. Thus, even when Whites harbor unconscious and unintentional biases toward Blacks, their actions can have effects sometimes even more detrimental than those of old-fashioned racists on interracial processes and outcomes.

Combating Contemporary Bias

Like a virus that has mutated, racism has also evolved into different forms that are more difficult not only to recognize but also to combat. The subtle processes underlying discrimination can be identified and isolated under the controlled conditions of the laboratory. However, in organizational decision-making, in which the controlled conditions of an experiment are rarely possible, this process presents a substantial challenge to the equitable treatment of members of disadvantaged groups.

Because of its pervasiveness, subtlety, and complexity, the traditional techniques for eliminating bias that have emphasized the immorality of prejudice and illegality of discrimination are not effective for combating aversive racism. Aversive racists recognize prejudice is bad, but they do not recognize that they are prejudiced. Thus, aversive racism must be addressed at multiple levels – at the societal and intergroup level, as well as the personal level.

At the societal level, social norms relating to racism have addressed mainly the old-fashioned kind. These norms have emphasized primarily sanctioned negative behavior toward Blacks. These norms are unlikely to be effective at changing the behavior of aversive racists, because aversive racists have already internalized these norms and are very guarded about overtly or intentionally discriminating against people of color. Instead, to address the motivations underlying contemporary forms of bias, it is as important to establish *positive* norms for proactively pursuing equality as it is to strengthen exiting norms against discrimination. These positive norms can focus on the importance of helping and taking constructive actions rather than simply on avoiding wrongdoing.

On the level of institutional racism, the aversion to addressing race concerns that is demonstrated through our research carries through to an aversion to discussing race as a factor in social policy. We must stop thinking that someone else will intervene to address the problems caused by historical racism and contemporary institutional racism and begin to address the appalling realities of its effects actively, head-on and in deeply committed cross-cultural partnerships.

On an organizational level, we must all begin to look beyond the general diversity of skin color to the issues of race and power in our organizations. Start by looking at who sits in the loci of power. With power comes the ability the ability to affect frames of reference, style, rules, and priorities. With a shift in power, issues that were unseen by Whites for years and obvious to people of color emerge quickly as actionable items.

At the intergroup level, as noted earlier, aversive racism may be rooted, in part, in fundamental, normal psychological processes. One such process is the categorization of people into ingroups and outgroups, "we's" and "they's." People respond systematically more favorably to others whom they perceive to belong to their group than to different groups. Thus, changing the basis of categorization from race to an alternative dimension can alter who is a "we" and who is a "they," undermining a contributing force to aversive racism. In application, this recategorization from different, potentially competing groups to one group can be achieved by calling attention to existing common superordinate group memberships (e.g., their common organizational identity) or by introducing new factors (e.g., common goals or fate) that are perceived to be shared by members.

At the individual level, because aversive racists consciously endorse egalitarian values and truly want to be nonprejudiced, it may be possible to capitalize on their good intentions to motivate efforts to reduce their implicit biases once they become aware of them. So, when a person of color brings up race as an issue in an interpersonal or organizational setting, listen! If the person indicates he or she is offended, do not be defensive. Instead, try to understand the other person's perspective on the issue. Remember, your perceptions can be very different from the everyday experience of others. As the data indicate, Whites tend to underestimate the impact of discrimination. Do not begin talking quickly or explain why they are misinterpreting the situation. These are some of the most infuriating responses people of color encounter when they challenge a situation that feels wrong. Take time, if you need it, to think about the situation after listening fully to the other person's perspective. You probably need to talk through the situation at some point, but remember it is almost never completely safe for a person of color to challenge a dominant perception. Listen deeply.

Conclusion

We have focused our efforts at understanding the problem of race relations in the United States by examining one aspect – the influence of the racial attitudes of Whites in interpersonal interracial encounters. We have shown that contemporary forms of racial bias among Whites, particularly liberal Whites, are aversive and less blatant than the traditional form but still result in significant damage. Moreover, because aversive racists may not be aware of their unconscious negative attitudes and only discriminate against Blacks when they can justify their behavior on the basis of some factor other than race, they will commonly deny any intentional wrongdoing when confronted with evidence of their bias. Indeed, they do not discriminate intentionally. In addition, we have illustrated how awkward and inefficient interracial communication, which is a consequence of aversive racism, can have a negative impact on group processes and disproportionate negative outcomes for Blacks.

Thus, we can no longer be passive bystanders to racism. We have to hold ourselves responsible. Abstaining from wrongdoing that is immediately obvious to us is not enough. It does not begin to address the now convoluted and confusing nature of contemporary racism. In order to address contemporary racism, even and especially among well-intentioned people, it is necessary to establish new, positive norms for action that replace our current norms of avoidance of responsibility.

References

Dovidio, J. F., & Gaertner, S. L. 2004. Aversive racism. In M. P. Zanna (Ed.), *Advances in experimental social psychology* (Vol. 36, pp. 1–51). San Diego, CA: Academic Press.

Dovidio, J. F., Gaertner, S. L., Penner, L. A., Pearson, A. R., and W. E. Norton. 2009. Aversive racism: How unconscious bias influences behavior: Implications for legal, employment, and health care contexts. In J. L. Chin (Ed.), *Diversity in mind and action* (pp. 37–54). Westport, CT: Praeger Press.

Pearson, A. R., Dovidio, J. F., & Gaertner, S. L. 2009. The nature of contemporary prejudice: Insights from aversive racism. *Social and Personality Psychology Compass*, 3, 314–338 (DOI.10-.1111/j.1751-9004.2009.00183-x).

Penner, L. A., Dovidio, J. F., West, T. V., Gaertner, S. L., Albrecht, T. L., Dailey, R. K., and T. Markova, T. 2010. Aversive racism and medical interactions with Black patients: A field study. *Journal of Experimental Social Psychology*, 46, 436–440.

COVERT RACISM: THEORY, TYPES AND EXAMPLES

Rodney D. Coates

Covert racism, subtle in application, often appears hidden beneath/by norms of association, affiliation, group membership and/or identity. As such, covert racism is often excused or confused with mechanisms of exclusion and inclusion, ritual and ceremony, acceptance and rejection. Covert racism operates as a boundary keeping mechanism whose primary purpose is to maintain social distance between racial elite and racial non-elite. Such boundary mechanisms work best when they are assumed natural, legitimate, and normal. These boundary mechanisms are typically taught sub- consciously or even unconsciously as part of the dominant socialization processes operant within society/institutions and/or social groups. Consequently, covert racism often undetected, is often inherently inculcated with each generation of new members of any given social situation. The process, operating within both racial elite and non-elite groups, represents a kind of closed feedback loop.

At the heart of covert racism one finds a deliberate policy of denial, omission, and obfuscation of black, brown, red, tan and yellow issues/persons/and groups. In this pseudo-color blind universe, race appears nullified under the veneer of 'benign neglect'. Thus, 'anything but race' becomes the clarion call to justify differences in outcomes as 'race declines' in significance. And when this does not work, then we simply define race out of existence, make it seemingly insignificant as in 'the social construction of race', or reduce its' effect as in the 'culture of poverty', or 'cultural competency'.

In terms of action, covert racism may actually masquerade as racial liberalism, by misdirecting attention to the symbols of racism, but avoiding the structures of such. Thus, there may be obtained a strong call for the abolition of the N word, or allowing a Marian Anderson to sing on the steps of the Lincoln memorial, but no support for abolishing racially exclusionary tests/clubs or removing the barriers to a Marian Anderson to obtain a degree.

Dyson (2006) recently has observed:

> ...it should also be clear that although one may not have racial intent, one's actions may nonetheless have racial consequences....Active malice and passive indifference are but flip sides of the same racial coin, different modalities of racial menace that flare according to the contexts and purposes at hand...In a sense, if one conceives of racism as a cell phone, the active malice is the ring tone at its highest volume, while passive indifference is the ring tone on vibrate. In either case, whether loudly or silently, the consequence is the same: a call is transmitted, a racial meaning is communicated. (pp. 20–21)

I am also reminded of Charles Mills' observations:

> ...the requirements of 'objective' cognition, factual and moral, in a racial polity are in a sense more demanding in that officially sanctioned reality is divergent from actual reality...one has an agreement to misinterpret the world. One has to see the world wrongly, BUT with the assurance that this set of mistaken perceptions will be validated by White epistemic authority...Thus, in effect, on matters related to race, the Racial Contract prescribes for its signatories an inverted epistemology, an epistemology of ignorance, a particular pattern of localized and global cognitive dysfunctions (which are psychologically and social functional), producing the ironic outcome that Whites will in general be unable to understand the world they themselves have made... (1997: p. 18)

It would seem that we could specify a typology which would capture some of the dimensions of covert racism. At the very least, it would appear that covert racism can operate at both the individual and the group level, and given these levels we could further specify that it can be both formal and informal. Now while these can be grouped categorically as types, it should be understood that they reflect more of a continuum. Thus, we would suggest that a particular covert act is more or less at the individual or group level, and it is more or less formal or informal. To the extent that covert racial acts are repeated over an extended time, then we can speak of specific patterns. The patterning of covert racial acts, finally, suggests the operation of not only intentionality, but also norms, mechanisms, and at the most developed stage – institutions, structures, and systems. By implication, covert racism is both historically and societally specific. Systemically, for example, covert racism operates across several societal institutions, structures. Given this, a provisional typology for covert racism may be represented as:

Figure 1. Typologies of Covert Racism with Examples

	Informal	Formal
Individual/Small Group	Shunning, ignoring, association/affiliation bias	Exclusion, restrictive membership clauses, restrictive covenants.
Institutional/Large Group	Invidious distinctions, DWB – Racial Profiling, fear and loathing, presumptions of guilt/ Competencies, inadequate mentoring/advice of guilt/ Competencies, inadequate mentoring/advice	Benign Neglect, Redlining, Model Minority syndrome, Pariah status, selective rule enforcement, expulsion.

Covert Racism operates through well established and understood racial codes. These racial codes are inherently part of the socialization processes of the racial state. As part of the socialization process, racial codes often may be subliminally introduced to societal members and are implicitly maintained within friendship networks, small groups, and social institutions. Racial codes[1], exemplified by stereotypical behavior, codes of silence, etc., are often assumed to be not only real but also essential traits of the individual.[2] Thus hidden, these racial codes also account for the more subtle (as in hidden) nature of 'covert racism'.

Shunning and Benign Neglect

Nixon, as president, gave national sanction to this form of racism by making it the official governmental policy under the guise of 'benign neglect'. Later in this section we will return to this more universal

---

[1] Various racial codes are explained more fully throughout the text below.
[2] Racial essentialism refers to the theory that there are distinct and general human biological traits that determine racial membership, behavior and cause the presence of specific racial traits. While false, many individuals (acting within groups, institutions, and society) function as if it were real. The various media, through its continued marketing of racial stereotypes, preserves the illusion of the 'realness' of racial essentialism. As such, racial essentialism is a false consciousness constantly being constructed and reconstructed by social groups, institutions, and pervades, maintains, and perpetuates the racial state.

application of shunning, but for now we will look at how racialized non-elites have been isolated, made invisible, or marginalized by other techniques of shunning.

One of the most typical forms of covert racism, also one of the oldest manifestations of racism, has to do with what some have labeled shunning. Shunning is defined as the practice of habitually ignoring or avoiding contact with a particular person or group. We see it most clearly evidenced in practices associated with some religious groups such as Jews, the Amish, and Quakers. The most extreme case of religious shunning occurs when the person is declared official dead (as with the Jews) or excommunicated (as with the Catholics) or formerly excluded from all communal activities (as described by the Amish and their practice of "Meidung"). The most typical purpose of such shunning is to punish the individual and/or group for specific or non-specific forms of behavior. While the most extreme forms of shunning results in the exclusion of the person or group, the more common forms are associated with what has been described as 'invisibility' or more formerly benign neglect. When applied to racialized situations and groups the effects significantly increase the marginality of the individual and/or groups. What is interesting about this particular form of racism is that it can be selectively applied by an individual, group, institution, or entire society. Thus, while some racialized non-elites are selectively targeted by racialized elites, other non-elites may not experience such targeting. In fact, the very selectivity of targeting provides an added benefit due to the fear it induces. It is the very specificity of this form of racism which makes it such a unique and destructive instrument of oppression. With surgical precision particular members or segments of various racialized non-elites may be singled out for this punishment. The covert nature of this particular form of racism is associated with not only its specificity, but also with its utility by individual members of particular racialized elite groups. Given the informal nature of this particular form of racism, there tends to be few formal laws or institutional codes applicable. Further difficulty is associated with the informal nature of racial shunning in that it appears to fall under the guise of 'voluntary association' and hence beyond the pale of formal rules. But when it is exclusively applied in racialized settings, by racialized elite against racialized non-elite, its racist designation is applicable. Consequently, given the covert nature of this particular form of racism, those witnessing such selectivity may be less likely to define it as racist. Similarly, those being targeted are also less likely to be able to pinpoint the source of offence.[3]

One of the "covert" or hidden features of this particular form of racism is what I choose to call a "conspiracy of silence" which not only implies acceptance but also complicity by members of the racial elite. These conspiracies can take a multitude of forms ranging from denial to minimization. Collective denials occurs when the targets of covert racist acts are assured that what has just happened has nothing to do with racism, but instead the neutral operations of a fair market, educational, or other social mechanism. Thus, the reason why one did not get the job, or get the loan, or get into the school, or invited to the party – had nothing at all to do with the individual's race. Instead, they just were not as prepared, or their credit score was below the acceptable level, or their G.R.E. scores were not quite high enough, or as we were going to be playing country music we knew that you 'just would not want to come'. Alternatively, collective minimization functions by acknowledging that an action was indeed racist, but trivializes the act by suggesting that it was not intended, or the person involved does it to all people (like you) or they just feel more comfortable around people like themselves, or Blacks/Asians/Hispanics/Jews – discriminate too.

A conspiracy of silence also operates within the family and small groups where the failure to comply results in sanctions ranging from ridicule to ostracism. Thus one is encouraged, within the guise of family and friendship networks, to silently acquiesce to racism. To challenge or confront racist statements, actions, jokes and other behaviors – behind the closed doors of intimacy – is to also risk negative sanctions. As my friend Phillip Wagner suggests:

> So I think a very important genre of covert racism is the indirect collective-racism-by-proxy which an individual him or herself may never articulate, but which that individual de-facto subscribes to by default, by his or her commission of 'the sin of omission' for not confronting an evil at the weakest link in our 'commitment chain' – when we are among friends or family.[4]

---

[3] The alternative to racial shunning is racial affirmation.
[4] Private conversations with the author.

A form of racial etiquette, practiced both among racial elite and non-elites, reaffirms covert racism and legitimates the attendant code of silence.

Racial etiquette, within zones of intimacy, characterized by family and close friendship networks, proscribes different sets of behaviors for in-group vs. out-group actions. It is noted that within group settings overt racist practices may indeed be condoned and even encouraged. Externally a veneer of political correctness may be observed, particularly in the presence of specific racialized non-elites. For example, racial etiquette, coupled with political correctness, implies that racialized elite express 'sensitivity' to the racial composition of social space and will selectively chose to discriminate. Therefore, racial jokes, anecdotes, and derogatory opinions may be expressed regarding the excluded racialized groups or coached as insider jokes to those currently present. Thus, often fearing ostracism, racialized elites and non-elites through their silence essentially lend their support and reaffirm racial etiquette.

Interracial dating and other relationships also may severely strain the bonds of racial etiquette. In these situations group and family loyalties are challenged, which challenges the racial 'status quo'. The stress produced, going beyond mere acceptance or rejection, actually makes of the racial elite a momentary outsider. By extension, they are made to endure strained relations with their family and close friends until a 'new racial balance' is struck. Often, and when successful, this new racial balance is achieved by extending to the other provisional group membership as an exception. Thus, their acceptance is conditioned upon their being viewed as exceptions from the normal racial group identity. Sacks (2001) interviewing a former racist acknowledges:

> My feeling before I got to know them was that there really wasn't that many good Blacks out there ... After being around them, shoot, I don't even think of them as colored anymore. (pg 4)

When challenged on his use of words 'colored', he remarks – "Hey, I've come a long way, I don't say 'nigger' anymore." Thus, the racial non-elite is cleansed, they become the exceptions. As exceptions, while the negative pale still envelopes the other members of the group, this one is different. Unstated in this process is the reality that the bonds of racism have been preserved, and covert racism achieves another victim as well as converts. Thus within interracial dating and marriage, racialized non-elites are accorded special status. As exceptions, they may be encouraged to be the 'model' of perfection, or even better to completely divorce themselves from their cultural roots.

Informal Covert Racial Dynamics – Exceptionalism and Small Groups

Within small groups, Exceptionalism functions to produce a number of character types. These types range from the 'Token Minority' to the 'Exotic Other', from the Star to the Outcast. At the institutional or societal level Exceptionalism can be identified and is associated with the racial types ranging from the 'Odd Man Out' to the Stranger, and from the 'Model minority' to the 'Pariah'. We shall explore these institutional or group levels of Exceptionalism in the next section. For now we shall concentrate on Exceptionalism and the Small Group as evidence of informal covert racial dynamics.

The Token Minority enjoys provisional group member status. They are, in many regards, the exception to the rule, and are encouraged to participate in group actions. Group member status for the token may be threatened through violation of specific racial codes. Particularly, token status can only be assured by limiting access to the racial group by other racialized non-elites. That is to say, racial tokenism is dependent upon exclusion of other racialized selves. From a marketing perspective, diminished value is associated with the increased availability of alternative racial tokens. The more racial diversity, the less value associated with a particular token. Thus it is in the interests of the racial token to minimize access to other racialized non-elites from group member status. We note in these situations, an overly aggressive attitude by Racial Token's to members of their own racial group. Consequently, as gate keepers, Racial Token's may differentially disadvantage racial non-elite that come under their sphere of influence. We note such exaggerated diligence by teachers, policemen, examiners – etc. where racial non-elites are targeted by essentially members of their own group occupying Racial Token status.

In America, the response of various racialized non-elites to such tokenism has been the cultural ostracism of the tokenized individual(s). Cultural ostracism is accompanied with descriptive labels. Thus we note labels such as 'Coconuts', 'Bananas', Apples, Pineapples or 'Oreos' used respectively to talk about being Brown, Yellow, Red or Black on the outside and White on the inside to describe the token status of

Hispanics, Asians, Native Americans or African Americans. Racial tokens, chosen for their racial essentialism, also may jeopardize their in-group status by over identification with the racialized other.

The Exotic Other, similar to the token, also may enjoy racial in-group member status. But in contrast to the token, the Exotic Other is encouraged to be the stereotypical representative of the racialized other. The exaggerated Exotic Other, displaying extreme racial characteristics may often perform the role of the buffoon and trickster, sexual object and athlete, or deviant and tragic hero. The Exotic Other, at times, may perform these paired roles simultaneously or serially as situations may dictate. The dynamic nature of these roles, adding complexity, also suggests some agency. The key to understanding this dynamic is found in the utility value they have in group dynamics. Essentially, the Exotic Other provides entertainment through voyeurism, escapism, and comic relief to the other members of the racial in-group. This being said, the Exotic Other loses status to the extent that they fail to perform assigned roles, or through actions and/or deeds, threaten the viability of the established racial codes.[5]

When members of racial non-elite groups distinguish themselves by achieving 'Star' or 'super-Star' status in any area of accomplishment they similarly enjoy a unique form of racial exception status. The number or the perception of racial dominance, in any particular field of endeavor tends to diminish the overall accomplishment. Thus, when boxing, football, and basketball were dominated by the racialized Europeans, the presence of Black, Hispanic, or other racialized groups were accorded 'super-Star' status. Much like that being enjoyed by Tiger Woods in golf or Arthur Ashe and Venus and Serena Williams in Tennis. Not only are they the exceptional racial Stars, but their numbers are not large enough to suggest Black dominance in the sport. Alternatively, the overall status of current Black Stars in basketball, football, and boxing –while acknowledged are equally minimized, as demonstrating the racial norm of members from the designated groups. But of course, Jackie Robinson or Barry Bonds just did not

---

[5] Paul Robeson represents the classic case of this. While he was content at being a singer, he was not perceived as a threat. When, however, he chose to discuss the state of black America, he became increasingly ostracized. Similarly rejections are associated with Anna Julia Cooper, Muhammad Ali, Dick Gregory, Bill Cosby, Angela Davis, or Oprah Winfrey – as they stepped out of the racially proscribed character of – school teacher, boxer, comedian, educator, or TV. talk host.

compare to Babe Ruth or Yogi Berra, and Michael Jordan (quite possibly the greatest basketball player of all times) finds that his legendary status somehow pales to that of Larry Byrd. And while Fritz Pollard (the first Black NFL coach and Reggie White are acknowledged again such acknowledgement does not challenge the legendary status of Knute Rockne or Joe Montana. The difference is that 'the Babe" and Larry Byrd embodied the greatest ideals of the sport. When one thinks of their name – they think of the sport. The fact that multiple movies, books, stories, and legends have been and continue to be made regarding the White Stars, and the sheer lack of same for the racialized 'Stars' suggests that even 'Star' status has its limits for racialized others.

Racial stereotypes are frequently maintained by the media, thus we note that Italians are typically depicted as Mafia hoodlums. Racial stereotypes are seldom simple characterizations, but typically involve multiple sets of roles. Thus, Asians, while good in computers, are typically projected as invaders or karate experts. Hispanics, while deeply religious, are typically displayed as gang members or drug smugglers. The Native American retains the image of the noble savage while yet being depicted as either victims or cowards. The most current image of people from the Middle East, shrewd and cunning, is often depicted as terrorists or oil sheiks. And the ever present Black stereotype, great singers, dancers, and athletes, is generally projected as sexual aggressive athlete, thug, or savage.

Rainville and McCormic, in 1977, demonstrated that covert racism operated in much of nationally broadcast games. They observed that announcers were more likely to be sympathetic and excuse poor performance of White players than Blacks. Similar research by Hamamoto (1994:58–61) has demonstrated that both electronic and print media tends to project a Japanese threat to American corporations. As noted by Jeff Adachi (2006), the narrow portrayal of Asian-Americans as kung fu fighter, studious nerd, mercenary businessman, 'dragon lady', and prostitute covertly maintains the negative views held by many Americans.

The racial Outcast is typically one who does not subscribe to the racialized identity constructed for them. Put simply, they do not fulfill the racial stereotype, and thereby defy racial categorization. Becoming a racial Outcast is sometimes not a matter of choice, but of circumstance. For example, many Asians are not good in computers, there are Blacks who can neither sing, nor dance, nor play any sports, etc.

Such individuals face tremendous social pressure both external and internal for their failure to perform as expected by the racial codes. Alternatively, individuals may actually choose to violate racial expectations and as a result may experience negative sanctions. For example, often Blacks throughout American history have chosen to defy the racial stereotype for their group. Such defiance was often met by lynch mob among Whites, or ostracism by other Blacks fearful of reprisal.[6] Because such racial Outcasts either choose to or are prevented from exhibiting stereotypical behavior, they are often castigated, for different reasons, both by members of their own racial group as well as members the racial elite.

It is commonly known that if you're a member of the racial non-elite and want to sell a house for the most money, and to the broadest potential base –it is best that you replace any "ethnic" art, family photos, and etc. with neutral –read –White oriented art. Some Blacks, Hispanics, Asians, etc. have actually been encouraged to go to the local Wal-Mart or T.J. Maxx and obtain photos of "White" families and appropriately distribute it around the house. Of course, they should not be present during the walk through. Alternatively, a few years ago, the Berkeley School Board decided to name a predominantly White High School after Martin Luther King, Jr. After a heated Board meeting, where hundreds of irate parents argued that such a name would disadvantage their kids, the Riverside School Board voted unanimously to change the name. Presumably, only a predominantly Black school would be so named, and we all know that 'those' schools are of significantly lower quality. The cloak of race has recently sullied the campaign of a prominent U.S. Senator from Virginia. According to his mother, the family declined to identify with their "Jewish" ancestry for fear of discrimination by their predominantly 'White' suburban neighbors. Even food and drink can become a tool of covert racism. In France several right wing groups began serving the homeless pork in a deliberate attempt to force both Jews and Muslims from their doors. (Smith 2006) In New Orleans a 2005 study revealed within bars that covert racism took three forms:

- Black "testers," or patrons, were charged more than white testers for the same drink, often served by the same bartender minutes apart.

---

[6] A Black's failure to lower one's eyes, speak in soft tones, addressing Whites as Sir and Madam, frequently were enough to get one lynched, or whipped.

This was the most common form of discrimination and occurred in 40 percent of the audited locations.

- Black patrons were advised of drink-minimum rules while white patrons were not. This occurred in 10 percent of the audited sites.
- Black patrons were advised of dress codes while white patrons were not. This occurred in 7 percent of the audited sites. (Perry 2005)

Informal Covert Racial Dynamics – Stretching, Profiling, and Large Groups/Institutions

Within organizational culture we can make reference to specific code words that reflect informal covert racial dynamics. Important promotions and recommendations for hire are often couched in terms that on the surface seem innocent, but in reality reflect the racial bias of the dominant group. Often, the parties involved suggest that they are reflecting the 'best interests' of the company and the individual, when they say that one candidate is 'ready' for a 'stretch' while another might be more 'risky'. Often, the candidates that we suggest may encompass the most risk are also the racial non-elite, with whom we feel the most uncomfortable. (Katz and Moore, 2004: 14)

A 2005 study revealed that discrimination in hiring does not affect sales. That is to say, managers (regardless of race) were more likely to hire whites than blacks. Further, non-black managers (i.e., Asian, White, and Hispanic) tended to hire significantly less blacks then black managers. While the researchers noted larger racial gaps in the south, all regions and store types reflected these patterns. (Giuliano, Levine, and Leonard 2005) Covert racial biases also negatively effects black and Hispanic welfare recipients in their attempt to secure viable jobs. White workers benefit most from welfare-to-work programs, suburban location of employer, and higher skills or salary thresholds. Alternatively, minority owned or governmental subsidies tend to erase some of these differentials for both black and Hispanic workers. (Holzer and Stoll 2003)

Racial non-elites may be more critically scrutinized for promotions then their white counterparts. (Kraiger and Ford 1990) By implication, there is a presumption of guilt or incompetence with regards to racial non-elites and one of innocence or competence with regards to racial elites. The constant battle to prove oneself worthy of credit, employment, housing, admissions, promotions, and etc. represents a constant struggle for legitimacy.

In retail, security officials and store personnel may concentrate more on the race of their customers then their conduct. Within these establishments, racial non-elites are targeted and therefore may be more likely to be caught. Therefore 'shopping while black', another form of racial profiling, may lead to the increased likelihood of blacks being caught, while the failure to monitor whites will give the impression that whites are less likely to commit the same crimes. Some store security personal use codes to signal that a black, Asian, or Hispanic has entered the store. When, for example one hears Code 3 – store personnel are instructed to monitor suspects of particular racial or demographic groups. (McGoey 2006)

Covert racial dynamics – individual – small group level – formal

Obviously, individuals cannot (by definition) develop covert racial dynamics formally. Small groups, on the other hand, can and do. Small groups and institutions, such as fraternal and sorority associations, local churches, clubs, neighborhood associations, and etc. though formal, are not connected or only loosely connected with a larger national body. As we look at such small groups their formal designation comes from a historical presence and the codification of rules, sanctions, and rewards and etc. For our purposes, the covert racial nature of some of these rules, sanctions and rewards are of interests.

Since 9-1-1, random searches at air-ports around America has resulted in the racial profiling of many who have the wrong last name, skin color, or mode of dress. Wearing a hijab, turban, or other 'Islamic" identifiable apparel often results in such individual being 'just selected' for more intense scrutiny. Recently a judge, asserting that he can tell whether a defendant is lying or not by looking into their eyes, ordered an Arab woman to remove her hijab. Upon her refusal, he promptly proceeded to declare her guilty. Often Moslem women, in America and throughout Europe experience discrimination because they choose to wear the traditional hijab and robes. (Stroobants and Jacob 2006)

United Kingdom (U.K.) prison guards who are persons of color are more likely to experience racial abuse and discrimination from their colleagues than from prisoners. A report on Prisons in the U.K. observed that:

> ... 61% say they have experienced racial discrimination while employed in prisons in –in the forms of verbal abuse, isolation, harassment, and a

lack of equal opportunities… The report says "covert and structural" racism has replaced blatant discrimination, making it more difficult to stamp out. While the recent actions of the prison service have helped eradicate overt racism in our jails, this report shows it has merely been pushed underground. (Prison Reform Trust 2006)

Covert Racial Dynamics – Institutional and Societal level – formal

Covert racism at institutional level is easily documented. Curriculum at universities and colleges which over-emphasize the European experience and deemphasize Asian, Hispanic, African, and others are quite common. When such experiences as Asians, Hispanics, Africans and others are emphasized, it's in a separate section, a special topic, or in a special 'area' studies program.

DiAngelo (2006) argues that 'Whiteness" is a form of social space constructed by White professors which effectively insulates White students while systematically excludes and/or minimizes the presence of the racial non-elites. Implicitly, racial non-elites, in this White space, are less likely to receive detailed information, support, and access. This White space is characterized by the concentration upon European subjects, and the isolation, minimization, problematization, and/or exclusion of racial non-elites. Further, as one considers what is typically considered classical music, classics, major theorists, mainline, and etc. one is typically talking about 'dead White men'. Similarly, when one goes to the market – special sections are devoted to 'ethnic' products, books, material – while the dominant culture is mainlined.

Alternatively, the very essence of racial non-elites becomes defined by the racial elites in all too many predominantly white institutions. Therefore, as Du Bois asserts, black existence interpreted through a white lens reduces his existence to that of a problem, or victim. "This American world … yields him no true self-consciousness, but only lets him (the African-American) see himself through the revelation of the other (white) world" (Dubois, 1903/1989, p. 3)[7]. Pine and Hilliard (1990, p. 596) come to similar conclusions when they note that "Students of color … experience conceptual separation from their roots: they are compelled to examine their own experiences and history through the assumptions, paradigms, constructs, and language

---

[7] See also Scheurich (1993).

of other people." It is within this 'language' that individual responsibility, culpability, and merit is often couched.

> The problem with individualism ... is that it hides the inequalities in our social structures, especially racial inequalities. It also hides the fact that "prejudice, discrimination, and racism do not require (individual) intention. (Scheurich 1993: p 7)

Correspondingly, in a society which has historically and unequally allocated rewards and sanctions on the basis of race, 'individualism' often obscures the 'wages of whiteness'. Culturally, this is reflected in the very cultural presumptions regarding not only the ontological universe but also the phenomenological and the epistemological as well. Thus our perception of reality is structured not only by our experiences, but also by how these experiences are culturally defined and shaped. At the core of our cultural being, what is perceived as being 'real, true, and good' derive from a fundamentally Euro-American socio-historical base. Consequently, no one questions the notions that the Greeks and their philosophers not only represent the classics, but also the great thinkers of our collective past. Nor does one question the idea that Democracy, derived by these same Greeks, should be at the core of our political beliefs. The Judeo-Christian bias of our legal system goes unchecked. The very processes by which we choose research questions, our methodologies and statistical procedures have been demonstrated to also reflect these biases. In many courses and textbooks in criminal justice, social work, education, political science, sociology, and history – blacks, Hispanics, Asians, and other people of color are discussed as criminals, drug addicts, welfare queens, illiterates, backwards, deviants, and victims. Alternatively, whenever the topics of leadership, virtue, values –or more generally yet to the point, what is considered the 'norm' –then the group of interest typically is White and male. (The classic study of this is provided by Liazos: 1972)

Nationally, real-estate agents regularly participate in what is known as 'racial steering'. Racial steering is when racial non-elites are shown less desirable homes, or 'steered' to 'minority' areas, or not served at all. Rather than being rare, this is the norm, where 87% of the time testers were racially steered. The report continues:

> Whites were limited to viewing homes in predominately White neighborhoods and discouraged from visiting homes in interracial neighborhoods. African-Americans and Latinos lost their right to see homes of

their choosing across a wide spectrum of White communities. They were limited to seeing homes in neighborhoods in which their race or national origin predominated. In nearly 20 percent of cases, African-American and Latino home-seekers had appointments scheduled to see homes, but agents simply never showed up and then failed to answer their cell phones when testers called to inquire about their absence. Many other African-American and Latino testers received very limited service in comparison to White testers. Housing discrimination is widespread and systemic: NFHA estimates that more than 3.7 million violations of the Fair Housing Act occur annually, more than 99% of them going unreported. (2006 Fair Housing Trends Report)

In 2009, Wells Fargo, one of the Nation's largest mortgage companies, was sued for violating the Fair Housing Act. Wells Fargo created a website, Community Calculation, whose intent was to help prospective homebuyers in home selection. According to the lawsuit, this website, used both racial classifications and stereotypes to describe neighborhoods, steered "residents of predominately minority ZIP codes to other predominantly minority ZIP codes." Alternatively, those from predominantly white Zip codes were steered to other predominantly white areas. This site also described urban working communities as comprised of "the working poor" who typically use their money to purchase "major household appliances such as grills and climate control machines, and buying educational toys. They also tend to spend on takeout Chinese, men's sportswear, warm-up suits, casual shoes, and baby products." Alternatively, "Low income" communities where 85 % of the residents are black and "tend to purchase fast food and takeout food from chicken restaurants. This market ranks high for using pest control. Media preferences include watching television programs such as America's Most Wanted and Family Matters; however, they tend not to rent videos." (Eakes 2003:13) Research also documents that racial non-elites are more likely to pay more for food (Graddy 1997). The fact that these areas, dominated by racial non-elites, are also perceived as high crime, high arson, and drug addiction leads to racial profiling by police, red lining by insurance companies, and predatory lending practices. A recent HUD report documents that predatory lending practices are most commonly conducted in communities dominated by racial non-elites. Predatory lending, often not subject to federal banking supervision –

> … strip(s) borrowers' home equity and place them at increased risk of foreclosure. … (and) thus created a corresponding increased potential for abuse of consumers. (HUD 2001:13)

Covert racism, within medicine, has long been documented. In 1990, the American Medical Association Council of Ethical and Judicial Affairs concluded that the Association and its members had a long ways to go in "eradiating racial discrimination". Louis Sullivan, Former Secretary of Health, stated that there was clear evidence that racial disparities existed in treatment. More recently, a 1999 a New England Journal of Medicine study concluded that heart patients, with similar insurance, "were afforded inequitable and inferior health care" based solely on color and sex. (Callender and Miles 2004:178)

An analysis of Black women in Europe by Mukami McCrum concludes that the dominant stereotype of Black women's sexuality is affirmed and almost legitimized in advertisements in mail order bride magazines which present's them as sex objects. Not only does this serve to diminish self esteem, but also encourages the sexual abuse and exploitation of Black women. As in America, the rape of a Black woman, she concludes, is not seen as serious as that of a white woman. She continues that:

> (…) the Single European Act of 1992 banded all Black people together with criminals, terrorists, drug traffickers, and all of them are suspected of being illegal. Women coming to Europe on their own or living here as single parents are seen as economic migrants who work at the low and sinister end of the labour market such as prostitution. They are often condemned and despised by the system and by some Black people who see them as low status women with poor morals and who are a danger to society. (McCrum 1999[8])

Back here in the United States, jurisdictions around the country have created 'exclusion zones'. Such zones are created in order to discourage specific types of criminal behavior. On the surface this seems to be a noble goal, in reality it hides the obvious racist intent of such policies. Throughout the United States these 'exclusion zones' have been "exclusively" utilized in communities dominated by racial non-elites. These communities, then marked, become more intensely scrutinized for illegal, or illicit activity, targeted for more aggressive police enforcement, and more likely to be marginalized by business, insurance, and lending agencies. What makes such exclusion zones so enticing, is the frustration local officials express when dealing with organized gang,

---

[8] Note the actual letter which is quoted here is on line and can be assessed at URL http://www.survivreausida.net/a2680-letter-from-mukami-mccrum.html.

drug, and crime activity within many urban communities. Recognizing the problems are real, no one questions why similar 'exclusion' zones are not associated with 'white color' crime, meth labs, shop-lifting rings, and etc. Portland, Oregon in 1991 became the first city in the nation to create 'exclusion' zones. These zones, designated to curtail drug and prostitution, contain the highest concentration of 'people of color in the city'. The Portland Police responded by over-zealously patrolling, racial profiling, and in their "own analysis demonstrated an alarming lack of accountability in the process." A 2006 report concludes that these exclusion zones:

> Invite over-policing and profiling of communities of color. The ordinance encourages pretext stops, identifying people to stop based on how they look and where they are – not on what they are doing. "Looking suspicious" is purely subjective criteria, particularly when what looks suspicious is based on white cultural norms. Exclusion zones are designated based on the number of drug – or prostitution-related arrests in a particular area. Since the decision to arrest is discretionary and determination of what is suspicious is based on criteria subject to preexisting biases, any overrepresentation of a racial or ethnic group will affect where exclusion zones are created instead of locating them where there is a higher prevalence of drugs. (Collins 2006:17)

In Cincinnati 15 black men were shot to death because the police 'felt threatened". Only after a riot did the shootings cease. Under increased scrutiny, by both citizens, the federal government and the courts, there have been no similar 'threats'. But instead, many believe that the police are practicing a form of benign neglect. Under this version, the police look the other way, or merely ignore crime. Police on the street, using such names as de-policing, selective disengagement, tactical detachment" argue that it is a logical reaction to being charged with being a racist. After the riots, police held back, and crime began to soar. In three months after the shooting and the ensuing riots, traffic and other arrests declined 50 %. During this same period, there were 59 shootings, producing 77 victims. This compares to just 9 shootings and 11 victims during the same period just one year before. (Prendergast 2002)

The news media, public officials, and police continue to represent urban/inner city crime as significantly more dangerous, violent, and threatening then the suburbs. (Yanich, 2001) Of interests is the reality, that while the FBI has reported that various forms of crime has actually decreased in urban areas, it has increased significantly in the suburbs.

(Johnson 2003) In a strange reversal, life and racial profiling may indeed be mimicking art. As demonstrated by Prosise (2004), much of our attitudes of crime, police, and race stem from our addiction to so-called 'crime-based reality' programs. Reality programs such as Law Enforcement, Crime on Cops or World's Wildest Police Videos actually suggest that racial profiling is not only the norm, but is a necessary tool in the police crime fighting arsenal.

References

Adachi, Jeff 2006. *The Slanted Screen*, Documentary, AAM Productions.

Callender, Clive O. and Patrice V. Miles (2004). "Institutionalized Racism and End-Stage Renal Disease: Is Its Impact Real or Illusionary?" *Seminars in Dialysis* 17(3): 177–180.

Collins, Claiborne, (2006). *Listening Sessions Report* (2006). (Assessed on line on October 26, 2006 at URL http://www.interculturalorganizing.org/listeningsessionsreport.pdf)

DiAngelo, Robin J. (2006) "The Production of Whiteness in Education: Asian International Students in a College Classroom." *Teachers College Record* 108 (10), 1983–2000.

Du Bois, W.E.B. (1989). *The Souls of Black Folks*. New York: Bantam. (Originally published in 1903).

Dyson, Michael (2006). *Come Hell or High Water: Hurricane Katrina and the Color of Disaster*. New York: Basic Civitas.

Eakes, Martin D. (2003). "Wells Fargo's Application to Acquire Pacific Northwest Bankcorp: An Analysis of Its Implication for Consumers in Washington State." *Center for Responsible Lending*.

Giuliano, Laura, Levine, David I. and Leonard, Jonathan (2005). "Race, Gender, and Hiring Patterns: Evidence from a Large Service-Sector Employer". Unpublished manuscript assessed online on September 23, 2005 at URL http://gsbwww.uchicago.edu/labor/Giuliano_Levine_Leonard.pdf.)

Graddy, Kathryn 1997. "Do Fast-Food Chains Price Discriminate on the Race and Income Characteristics of an Area?" *Journal of Business and Economic Statistics*, 15(4)391–401.

Hamamoto, Darrell Y. (1994). *Monitored Peril: Asian Americans and the Politics of TV Representation*. Minneapolis and London: University of Minnesota Press.

Holzer, Harry J. and Michael A. Stoll (2003). "Employer Demand for Welfare Recipients by Race." *Journal of Labor Economics*, 21: 210–241.

HUD – U.S. Treasury Report on Predatory Lending, 2001. U.S. Department of Housing and Urban Development. (URL accessed on line on October 13, 2006 at http://www.hud.gov/library/bookshelf12/pressrel/treasrpt.pdf)

Johnson, Kevin (2003). "FBI reports small drop in crime rates." *USA Today*, (assessed on line on October 26, 2006 at URL http://www.usatoday.com/news/washington/2003-06-16-fbi-crime_x.htm)

Katz, Judith H. and Karen R. Moore (2004). "Racism in the Workplace: OD Practitioners' Role in Change." *OD Practitioner*, 36(4): 13–16.

Kraiger, Kurt, and J. Kevin Ford (1990). "The Relation of Job Knowledge, Job Performance, and Supervisory Ratings as a Function of Ratee Race." *Human Performance*, 3(4): 269–279.

Liazos, a. 1972. "The poverty of the sociology of deviance: Nuts, sluts and perverts." *Social Problems* 20(1): 103–120.

McCrum, Mukami 1999. "Letter" cited in WCC (World Council of Churches) 1999. "Understanding Racism Today: A Dossier" (Accessed on line September 28, 2006, at URL http://www.wcc-coe.org/wcc/what/jpc/doss-e.html)
McGoey, Chris 2006. "Racial Profiling: Retail Store Shoplifting". (URL accessed October 13, 2006 at http://www.crimedoctor.com/shoplifting5.htm)
Mills, Charles (1997). *The Racial Contract*. Ithaca: Cornell University Press.
National Fair Housing Alliance (2006). "2006 Fair Housing Trends: Unequal Opportunity- Perpetuating Housing Segregation in America. (URL assessed on Oct. 13, 2006 at http://www.nationalfairhousing.org/resources/newsArchive/resource_20628126054870386567.pdf)
Prendergast, Jane (2002). "Cincinnati Riots, One Year Later: Violence up, arrest down". The Cincinnati Enquirer (April 7). (Assessed on line on October 26, 2006, at URL http://www.enquirer.com/oneyearlater/).
Perry, James (2005). "Bourbon Street Discrimination Audit" conducted by the Greater New Orleans Fair Housing Center. (URL assessed on Oct. 12, 2006 at http://www.gnofairhousing.org/index.html.)
Pine, G.J. and Hilliard, A.G., III. (1990) Rx for racism: Imperatives for America's Schools". *Phi Delta Kappan*, 71, 593–600.
Prison Reform Trust (2006). Experiences of Minority Ethnic Employers in Prison. (Assessed on line on October 23, 2006 at URL http://www.prisonreformtrust.org.uk/subsection.asp?id=640)
Prosise, Theodore O. (2004). "Law Enforcement and Crime on Cops and World's Wildest Police Videos: Anecdotal Form and the Justification of Racial Profiling." *Western Journal of Communication*. (Winter). (Assessed on line October 26, 2006, at URL http://www.allbusiness.com/legal/laws/987095-1.html).
Rainville, R. E. and McCormick, E. (1977). Extent of covert racial prejudice in pro football announcers' speech. *Journalism Quarterly*, 54(1):20–26.
Scheurich, James Joseph (1993). "Toward a White Discourse on White Racism." *Educational Researcher*, 22(8):5–10.
Smith, Craig (2006). "In France a meal of intolerance." (Assessed on line September 26, 2006, at URL http://www.iht.com/articles/2006/02/27/news/journal.php)
Stroobants, Jean-Pierre and Antoine Jacob (2006). "The Netherlands Wants to Prohibit Burqua-Wearing." *Le Monde*, (Assessed on line October 23, 2006 at URL http://www.truthout.org/docs_2006/102306H.shtml)
Yanich, Danilo (2001). "Location, Location, Location: Urban and Suburban Crime on Local TV News." *Journal of Urban Affairs*, 23(3–4).

PART II

COVERT RACISM AND INSTITUTIONS

PROTECTING WHITE POWER IN A CORPORATE HIERARCHY

Sharon M. Collins and Georgiann Davis

Racial inequality persists despite the array of diversity interventions employed by private corporations over the last 40 years. While research shows that federal anti-bias regulations have been effective (Leonard 1989, 1990; Skaggs 2001), research on the impact of corporate diversity programs is equivocal and seems to suggest two things. The first is that some corporate initiatives are more effective than others (Kalev, Dobbin and Kelly 2006; Leonard 1989, 1990). Organizations that allocate responsibility for change, such as those that appoint diversity committees and/or have diversity managers are more effective than those that do not. Also, government contractors and companies with affirmative action plans are more effective at reducing bias relative to those relying only on other interventions, such as mentoring programs and diversity training. The second finding is that the impact that results from these programs varies across group membership; the most effective diversity initiatives improve the representation of some groups more than others (Konrad and Linnehan 1995; Leonard 1990). The literature attests to the fact that when diversity practices work their impact is greatest on White women and the next greatest impact is on Black women. The impact of diversity programs is smallest on the status of Black men (Kalev et al. 2006; Leonard 1990).

While some researchers seek to identify the practical measures that companies can take to reduce inequality, this paper explores the converse processes and asks why diversity programs don't live up to their potential and fail to work as well as they should. To answer this question, we take a close look at the climate in which an African American diversity manager strives to reduce racial bias in employment. Data are from a case study conducted in 2006–2007 of a company as it implemented a diversity program and are used to illustrate how diversity efforts face barriers constructed by cognitive bias. That is, we show how the job objectives of the diversity manager are undermined through everyday workplace race relations. In doing so, we draw on the concept developed in Collins (1997) of racialized jobs which is embodied in the structure of Black executive careers and link it to concepts found in the social psychology literature to exemplify the race-based resistance to sharing organizational power. First, we look at the emergence of a diversity program to increase the number of African Americans in the central operations jobs of a company called WALCO.[1] Next, we describe the response of White hiring managers to the implementation of this mandate, particularly the flourish of stereotypes and boundary heightening through which this organization's diversity initiative is filtered. Finally, we show that the divergence between the diversity goals and the managerial response is resolved by changing the very meaning of diversity in the organization as that effort moves forward.

Politically-Mediated Diversity Structures

The diversity program at WALCO was a response by the CEO to environmental pressures that are documented in the literature to initiate organizational change (see Collins 1997; DiMaggio and Powell 1982). Collins (1997) highlights the role played by politically-mediated job opportunity structures in Black upward mobility. In this scenario, political pressure on employers during the civil rights era from Blacks demanding more socio-economic resources (as well as federal anti-bias legislation) spurred organizational change such that African Americans were incorporated into high status jobs that had historically excluded them. Further, organizational isomorphism proposes organizations mimic the response of their counterparts who face similar environmental conditions (DiMaggio and Powell 1982).

When WALCO started a diversity initiative in 1995 the goal stated by the company's Chief Executive Officer (CEO) was to "push on hiring and advancing minorities." Specially, diversifying meant increasing the percent of African Americans in corporate management and in line positions where they were persistently underrepresented.

Political pressure was applied by African American employees who confronted the CEO with their discontent over the absence Blacks in decision-making jobs in WALCO. When diversity initiatives at WALCO were set forth in 1995, African Americans held fewer than 6 percent of professional and managerial jobs in the entire industry

---

[1] The company is given a pseudonym of WALCO to protect its anonymity.

(Shipler 1998). Only eight of 114 supervisors spread across 14 WALCO offices nationwide were African American. The company's chief executive summarized the climate in this way:

> African American [staff] would express impatience with various aspects of life at [WALCO]. They would press for faster advancement and for more sensitive behavior on the part of their bosses. [They wanted] more minorities in higher-ranking jobs.

External pressures to diversify the company paralleled the internal complaints of Black employees. Because Equal Employment Opportunity (EEO) statistics were reported to a national association of organizations in the industry, minority employment at all job levels of the company were transparent to peers and competitors. Over and above this statistical transparency, a WALCO peer and competitor appointed an African American to fill a rarified executive job just one step removed from the top job and analogous to an Executive Vice President (EVP). Since the decision-makers at WALCO analyzed their competitors production on a daily basis, it would be highly unusual for them be ignorant of an appointment this striking and not take action in-kind. Organizational conformity would be provoked by this kind of groundbreaking EEO appointment (Edelman and Petterson 1999; Dobbin, Sutton, and Meyer 1993; Edelman 1992).

Race-based political pressures on organizations are known to prompt top managers to hire diversity consultants and/or make visible Blacks in the organization by placing them in a high ranking managerial role with diversity (i.e. racialized) functions (Collins 1997a, 1997b). Racialized refers to jobs, institutions, and institutional niches that are responsible for managing Blacks or delivering services and products to Black people. For example, racialized jobs would be responsible for designing and implementing Affirmative Action plans. Predictably, therefore, the CEO for WALCO reached into the ranks and selected one of the most visible and the industry's highest ranking Black executive to fill a newly created senior executive job in diversity that reported directly to him. The newly promoted Executive Vice President in charge of diversity had been closely mentored by the CEO and considered him to be a company man and a team player.

"Trust" is an important part of the phenomena that leads to a promotion this high. Kanter (1977) argued that the ability to trust managerial colleagues imposes a degree of certainty of outcome at the top of the organizational hierarchy where uncertainty and responsibility are writ large. Consistent with this idea, chief decision makers, often the CEO of a company, tap their trusted best (Black) performer to implement affirmative action when a company is under pressure (Collins 1997a, 1997b). This preference for similar others is one manifestation of the in-group bias that arises from the expectation that socially similar others will react in predictable ways (Kanter 1977; Reskin 2000; Tomaskovic-Devey 1993). The expectation here seems to be that the Black EVP of Diversity at WALCO will react to the problem of diversity as the CEO and the corporate board would react (Brewer and Brown 1998; Fiske 1998; Perdue, Dovidio, Guttman, and Tyler 1990).

Black executives in racialized jobs often have "mixed" functions (Collins 1997) and the new EVP for Diversity at WALCO was not an exception. EVP for Diversity was responsible both for "general" (i.e. White) and for managing "minority" (i.e. Black) recruitment. In the eyes of the EVP for Diversity, minority recruitment in part meant constantly reminding the CEO and WALCO's executive directors that there existed "awful employment gaps" in the company and White-only units. The EVP told them,

> Overall the numbers are okay. What's ugly is the amount of turnover, the paltry showing among supervisors (those two things are connected) and the scarcity of Black men and Hispanics.

While the EVP saw the diversity role as a form of advocacy and activism, the CEO of WALCO had a different and conflicting understanding of the diversity function. The CEO moved his Black protégé to the EVP of Diversity job primarily as a token. Tokenism refers to a policy or practice of limited inclusion of members of a minority group, usually creating a false appearance of inclusive practices (Kanter 1977). For example, the presence of an African American who is visible in a job at the top of the corporation sends a positive message to other African Americans (and other people of color) that they are represented and can ascend the corporate hierarchy. The CEO explained,

> I thought it would be great to have an African American at that level because it would send a signal to everyone inside the company and to [the company's competitors] that there were no racial barriers to advancement.

The fact that no minorities were in the senior executive suite was a major underpinning for this move because the elevation of a well known expert in the field showed that Blacks and other racial minorities could rise to the top jobs at WALCO. Minority hiring, promotion, and retention were acknowledged problems and the appointment of an EVP of Diversity seemed to demonstrate that members of top management were committed to diversity. This move also makes the diversity EVP's color an asset to be exploited to the benefit of the organization. An African American executive in charge of diversity signals (but does not necessarily create) fair employment practices in the company. The EVP of Diversity, in contrast to the ambiguity of the job, takes this job seriously.

WALCO's Diversity Structure

Institutional theorists argue that creating specialized positions is one way to achieve organizational goals (Kalev et al. 2006; Edelman 1990; Meyer and Rowan 1977). Kalev et al. (2006) notes that employers who create a diversity structure, including the appointment of a manager of diversity, and the formalization of recruitment plans and hiring goals, see the broadest gains in managerial diversity. The EVP in charge of diversity at WALCO developed an affirmative action plan that included numerical bench marks and the expectation that every roster of job candidates, including outside hires, transfers and promotion, should include African Americans.

The EVP also proposes other initiatives that research tells us are effective at reducing inequality in organizations. For instance, the EVP advances minority recruitment procedures, in particular going to minority jobs fairs and association meetings to screen potential candidates. To the profession at large, the EVP was viewed as effective in these procedures. A newsletter[2] oriented to African Americans in the industry noted that at minority job fairs "[Black] candidates lined up at [WALCO's] booth." In comparison, the booth of their biggest competitor—the one that made the notable hire mentioned earlier—would be sparsely visited. Noting that the EVP for Diversity at WALCO wasn't just a "hack" or a "happy Black face" for the employer, WALCO received kudos for having a program that mentored "hundreds of (Black, Latino/a and other minority) professionals."

These initiatives are viewed as the most effective from the organizational prospective, but for that very reason they may also be the most

---

[2] Actual names and titles are omitted to protect the anonymity of both the company and the executives in this case.

threatening. Instead of applauding the EVP's efforts these activities became viewed as too successful by members of the management team. Recall this EVP of diversity had responsibility for Black recruitment (racialized) and White recruitment (general) functions. Overtime, from the standpoint of his peers the EVP's White and non-White recruitment skills were seen as unbalanced in favor of minorities. For example, the CEO writes in a performance review:

> You have brought to (our) attention many top-flight (Black) candidates. You have appropriately placed most of your effort on this aspect of the recruiting mission. I would like to see you devote a bit more time to the challenges of general recruiting.

Decoupling Functions

Although research supports the idea of specialists to achieve organizational racial equality, Black executives who fill diversity roles in White corporations hypothetically should not recruit too well, i.e. generate a number of minorities somewhere between one but not "too many." The CEO in this case insures this outcome when he gives his diversity manager the major responsibility for minority recruitment but no authority beyond the charge that the EVP should increase the numbers. Initially, the CEO promised that "nobody would be hired without [the EVP's] involvement" but overtime the functions of "recruitment" and "hiring" are severed from each other which left hiring exclusively within the purview of White managers. In this case, therefore, we can see when responsibility and authority are decoupled they clearly are not the same. Splitting these functions effectively diluted the effort of the EVP of diversity to increase the number of Black employees since the White managers are the very same managers who created the conditions that underemployed Black people. Decoupling functions protected White managerial hiring prerogatives from encroachment (Kanter 1977). Benchmarks were never defined, no written standards of performance for diversity hiring were written, and there was no other structure of responsibility to increase the number of minorities put in place beyond what was in the EVP's job description.

Boundary Heightening

Smith (2002) argues the lack of authority among racial minorities in the workplace is due to the elites reproducing themselves through exclusionary and inclusionary discriminatory practices. In-group bias affects hiring and promotion decisions but also the sharing of information (Ibarra 1995, 1993; Braddock and McPartland 1987). There is substantial evidence that in-group bias tends to increase with increased authority and pay in organizations (see Tomaskovic-Devey 1993). Evidence of in-group arises when the EVP of Diversity's colleagues don't tell him about job openings, don't include him on candidates' schedules, don't make him aware of the intent to hire "hand-shakes", or bring him into planning meetings. There also is evidence that racial in-group bias, exaggerated by stereotypes and attribution errors begin to flourish.

Although in-group bias can be countered with formal affirmative action plans and detailed implementation (Bielby 2000, Reskin 2000, Reskin 1998), left unchecked in-group bias can create exclusionary (heightened) boundaries that limit the access to information shared by in-group members. Hiring managers, other senior managers and the CEO of the company in this case closed racial rank and failed give the EVP information he needed to address his job responsibilities.

Rationalizing Racial Boundaries

Cognitive bias often requires minorities to demonstrate superior credentials for hiring and promotion in order to be viewed as competitive with their White peers (Wilson, Lemessy, and West 1999; Wilson 1997). At WALCO the resistance to hiring African Americans was justified as protecting meritocracy and a tradition of high quality in recruitment. A senior executive vice president, and friend of the CEO, said:

> We now have a number of jobs to fill; this offers us a tremendous opportunity to further upgrade our staff by hiring some of the very best (people) in the country. I can't emphasize this enough. I'll be working closely with (the EVP of diversity) in the hiring process. I know I've become a total pain in the ass on this subject. I know the problem you face and I just hope you're right about (the EVP of diversity).

Regional hiring managers expressed similar concerns that minority applicants will reduce the staff quality, but in a more transparent way. One hiring manager informed a Black applicant that they were a job candidate only because of WALCO's efforts at affirmative action. Diversity was referred to by some managers as a "con."

In this company, minorities had to be over qualified to convince managers to hire them over *their* White candidates. The CEO tells his protégé:

> I suggest you assemble a talent bank by (interviewing the hiring manager about their) top, top prospects. We [need to] have another benchmark against which to measure our minority candidates so that we can say (to the hiring managers), here is a minority candidate who outpoints your leading White male.

Black candidates should be exceptionally qualified to be hired into traditionally White jobs in racially-exclusive arenas.

Stereotypes and Self-fulfilling Prophesies

As the EVP for diversity pushed to be an organizational change agent, stereotypes and attribution errors reframed his character in the eyes of his peers. Once highly trusted and respected as colleague, the EVP is transformed in the eyes of his colleagues into an intimidating outsider. One hiring manager noted the EVP of diversity "*insisted* [italics added] that we see this [Black job candidate]." This hiring manager characterized herself as "Being afraid of the [EVP of Diversity]." Another hiring manager describes the EVP of diversity as "overly sensitive" and "overly aggressive." The actions of the EVP become typified as aggressive and as threatening which appeals to stereotypes of violence often associated with Black people.

With this perceptual framework it is firmly established the CEO viewed the EVP of diversity as "a problem." A self-filling prophecy emerged. After creating the conditions for the EVP to fail by excluding him from information and discounting his candidates, his position in the company is downgraded and he is viewed as a failure. Racialized jobs are a form of job segregation. Because these jobs are linked to racial not market pressures they are viewed as addendums to core functions in a company. African Americans who fill these jobs not only are out of the competition for powerful mainstream functions they often are expendable. In other words, though research sets forth the necessity of diversity accountability structures for reducing organizational inequality, being identified with these structures is not necessarily good for the career of Black executives (Collins 1997).

Diversity Transformed

In 1995, to "diversify" the company meant naming an EVP to increase the numbers of under-represented minorities in managerial jobs, in particular African Americans. In 2001, even the symbolic commitment that the company made to Black recruitment had eroded. The Black diversity executive was replaced by a White female executive and the tie between diversity and race unraveled when the guiding parameters for diversity recruitment shifted from "race and ethnicity" to "background." The CEO instructed to the new EVP of Recruitment and Diversity this way:

> Talent recruitment and development is one of the most important functions we have. We are only as good as our people. We need to develop a more pro-active method of recruitment. Seek out top talent. One of the guiding parameters of recruiting, second only to excellence is diversity. By that *I mean diversity of background even more than* diversity of race and ethnicity [italics added].

The background the CEO refers to is ambiguous but it trumps increasing the number of Black managers. Racial diversity had been the highest priority and for whatever reason priorities changed it wasn't because the status of Blacks in the organization was upgraded.

Conclusion

This case suggests that the concept of diversity is fluid in organizations. Initially "diversity" meant increasing the numbers of African Americans managers but evolved into increasing the number of people from different "backgrounds," which is a nebulous term. Diversity described here seems less like an attempt to reduce racial bias in employment and more similar to an institutionalized ritual in the post civil rights era that is performed because others perform it. The need for racial diversity is highly touted as a business necessity but neither the reality nor the mandate has been internalized by organizations as some have suggested (Fisher 1985; Liberman 2003).

This case also suggests that a low threshold exists for White employees to view their prerogatives to be threatened. Social closure and boundary heightening among hiring managers and other top executives in this company takes place but the level of Blacks' presence in the company did not change. Blacks remained 6 percent of all managerial personnel, which is the same percent representation as the year 1995 when the diversity effort began. Social science research has investigated "tipping points" and perceived threat associated with neighborhood desegregation. A similar dynamic hypothetically operates in high ranking positions. If so, integration will occur up to—but not beyond—the point where perception indicates there are "too many" Black people.

Finally, this case study shows that diversity efforts became diluted in White companies because White beliefs about Black inferiority legitimate the status quo. We know through research that modern stereotypes persist and that these stereotypes are cloaked in a socially acceptable manner. For example, instead of reporting a belief that Blacks are innately inferior, survey researchers find Whites believe that Blacks should "try harder," that Blacks are less motivated, and that unqualified Blacks get hired over more qualities White candidates (Heilman, Block, and Stathatos 1997; Taylor 1995). In other words, blatant racism has been replaced by something more subtle, a new racism variously labeled modern, symbolic and laissez-faire. In this case we show that these "new" kind of racial attitudes are part of the context in which diversity is played out and minorities are promoted. For example, diversity managers in White organizations operate in a system where Whites believe that, with reference to Blacks, affirmative action supplants merit. Diversity structures may supply job applicants but how these are evaluated is detached from the objective qualifications they bring. Put another way, Heilman, Block, and Stathatos (1997) argue that White beliefs about reverse discrimination construct Black inferiority, but we counter that this construction provides White corporate cultures the excuse to continue do what they have done historically: minimize the participation of Blacks within the ranks of higher-paying and more prestigious jobs, particularly the professions and management. In this way, organizational structure and cognitive bias intertwine to protect White power structures from Black intrusions.

References

Bielby, William T. 2000. "How to Minimize Workplace Gender and Racial Bias." *Contemporary Sociology* 29(1):190–209.
Braddock, James H. and James M McPartland. 1987. "How Minorities Continue to be Excluded from Equal Employment Opportunities: Research on Labor Market and Institutional Barriers." *Journal of Social Issues* 43:5–39.

Brewer, Marilynn B. and Rupert J. Brown. 1998. "Intergroup Relations." Pp. 554–94 in *Handbook of Social Psychology*.
Collins, Sharon M. 1997a. *Black Corporate Executives*. Philadelphia, PA: Temple University Press.1997b. "Black Mobility in White Corporations: Up the Corporate Ladder but out on a Limb." *Social Problems* 44(1)55–67.
DiMaggio, Paul J. and Walter W. Powell. 1982. "The Iron Cage Revisited: Institutional Isomorphism and Collective Rationality in Organizational Fields." *American Sociological Review* 48(2):147–160.
Dobbin, Frank John R. Sutton, John W. Meyer, 1993. "Equal Opportunity Law and the Construction of Internal Labor Markets." *The American Journal of Sociology* 2:396–427.
Edelman, Lauren B. 1992. "Legal Ambiguity and Symbolic Structures: Organizational Mediation of Civil Rights Law." *American Journal of Sociology* 97: 1531–76..... 1990. Legal Environments and Organizational Governance: The Expansion of Due Process in the Workplace. *American Journal of Sociology* 95:1401–1440.
Edelman, Lauren B. and Stephen Petterson. 1999. "Symbols and Substance in Organizational Response to Civil Rights Law." Research in Social Stratification and Mobility 17:107–136.
Fisher, Anne B. 1985. "Businessmen Like to Hire by the Numbers." *Fortune*, September 16, pp. 26–30.
Fiske, Susan T. 1998. "Stereotyping, Prejudice and Discrimination." Pp. 357–411 in *Handbook of Social Psychology*, edited by Daniel T. Gilbert, Susan T. Fiske, and Gardner Lindzey, New York: McGraw Hill.
Heilman, Madeline E., Caryn J. Block, and Peter Stathatos. 1997. "The Affirmative Action Stigma of Incompetence: Effects of Performance Information Ambiguity." *Academy of Management Journal* 40:603–25.
Ibarra, Herminia 1993. Personal Networks of Women and Minorities in Management: A Conceptual Framework." *Academy of Management Review* 18:46–87.
——1995. "Race, Opportunity and Diversity of Social Circles in Managerial Networks." *Academy of Management Journal* 38:673–703.
Kalev, Alexandra, Frank Dobbin and Erin Kelly. 2006. "Best Practices or Best Guesses? Assessing the Efficacy of Corporate Affirmative Action and Diversity Policies." *American Sociological Review* 71(4):589–617.
Kanter, Rosabeth Moss. 1977. *Men and Women of the Corporation*. New York, NY: Basic Books.
Konrad, Alison. M. and Frank. Linnehan. 1995. "Formalized HRM Structures: Coordinating Equal-Employment Opportunity or Concealing Organizational Practices." *Academy of Management Journal* 38:787–820.
Leonard, Jonathan S. 1990. "The Impact of Affirmative Action Regulation and Equal Employment Opportunity Law on Black Employment." *The Journal of Economic Perspectives* 4:47–63
—— 1989. "Women and Affirmative Action." *The Journal of Economic Perspectives* 3:61–75.
Liberman, Vadim. 2003. "Workplace Diversity: It's All in the Mix." *Across the Board* XL: 51–2.
Meyer, John W. and Brian Rowan. 1977. "Institutionalized Organizations: Formal Structure as Myth and Ceremony." *The American Journal of Sociology* 83(2):340–363.
Perdue, Charles W., John F. Dovidio, Michael B. Guttman, and Richard B. Tyler. 1990. "'Us' and 'Them': Social Categorization and the Process of Intergroup Bias." *Journal of Personality and Social Psychology* 59:475–86.
Reskin, Barbara F. 2000. "The Proximate Causes of Employment Discrimination." *Contemporary Sociology* 29(2):319–328.
—— 1998. *The Realities of Affirmative Action*. Washington D.C.: American Sociological Association.

Shipler, David K. 1998. "Blacks in the newsroom: Progress? Yes but..."*Columbia Journalism Review.*
Skaggs, Sheryl. 2001. "Discrimination Litigation: Implications for Women and Minorities in Retail Supermarket Management." Ph.D. dissertation, Department of Sociology, North Carolina State University, Raleigh, NC.
Smith, Ryan A. 2002. "Race, Gender, and Authority in the Workplace: Theory and Research." *Annual Review of Sociology* 28:509–542.
Taylor, Marylee. 1995. "White Backlash to Workplace Affirmative Action: Peril or Myth." *Social Forces* 73:1385–414.
Tomaskovic-Devey, Donald 1993. *Gender & Racial Inequality at Work: The Sources and Consequences of Job Segregation.* Ithaca, NY: Cornell ILR Press.
Wilson, George. 1997. "Pathways to Power: Racial Differences in the Determinants of Job Authority." *Social Problems* 44:38–54.
Wilson, George, Ian Sakura-Lemessy, and Jonathan P. West. 1999. "Reaching the Top: Racial Differences in Mobility Paths to Upper-Tier Occupations." *Work and Occupations.* 26:165–186.

"IF YOU'RE WHITE, YOU'RE ALRIGHT": THE REPRODUCTION OF RACIAL HIERARCHIES IN BOLLYWOOD FILMS[1]

Angie Beeman and Anjana Narayan

"If you're white, you're alright
If you're yellow, you're mellow
If you're brown, stick around
But if you're black, get back."

The above children's rhyme communicates a racial hierarchy of "white"[2] over "black" within the United States. We can interpret this rhyme to mean that people of color with darker skin, such as African Americans, are the least accepted and integrated in society, while those with lighter skin, European Americans and Asian Americans, typically seen as honorary "whites", are the most accepted and integrated. The rhyme also communicates a color hierarchy, often referred to as pigmentocracy or colorism within the African American community (Hooks 1992). This is the message Marita Golden (2005) conveys in her book *Don't Play in the Sun*. One of the authors recalls a time in her childhood, when her mother also advised her against playing in the sun, as it would make her skin darker. This is significant, because she is biracial, born to a "white" father and Korean mother. Hence, according to the rhyme, she should be "alright" or at least "mellow" as an honorary "white" or model minority. Yet growing up in her small predominantly "white" town, she was never accepted as "white" nor seen as an

---

[1] Alphabetical order denotes equal contribution. The authors would like to thank Rodney Coates, Noel Cazenave, Bandana Purkayastha, and Thomas Volscho.

[2] We problematize the concepts of "race," "black," and "white" by placing them in quotation marks. It has been well established that racial categories are social and political constructions that have no basis in biology (Roediger 1991; Lopez 1996; Smedley 2007). These categories were created in order to dehumanize and subordinate people of color. The concept of "race" forms the basis of racism. Therefore, we contribute to racial oppression by not problematizing it. As Noel Cazenave (2004) states, "'race' should be problematized—and ultimately relinquished—not only because it is confusing…but because it is erroneous, and most importantly because it is injurious" (5). Furthermore, it is generally not acceptable to refer to Asians as "yellow" or to Native Americans as "red." The categories of "black" and "white" are equally problematic.

honorary "white." If anything, she was the racial other, the "chink" who threatened the sanctity of a pure, "white" town. Her status and belonging was often questioned with demands of where she was from, implying that she must be foreign-born. Her experience challenges the message conveyed in the above rhyme and the notion that Asian Americans are honorary "whites" or model minorities.

The objective of this paper is to understand how this racial hierarchy of "white" over "black" is reproduced in contemporary society through institutions such as the media, and how the representation of this hierarchy affects the lives of Asian Americans as well as their relationships with African Americans and other people of color. We challenge the notion that increasing diversity through immigration is breaking down the "black/white" dichotomy in the U.S. and the idea that Asian Americans are becoming "white" in the way that European Americans have.

Eduardo Bonilla-Silva (2004) observes that because of demographic changes, the U.S. is undergoing a transformation from a bi-racial "white"/non-"white" hierarchy to a tri-racial order of "white," "honorary "white," and "black." Within the category of honorary "whites," Bonilla-Silva includes Asian Americans, Latinos, and multiracial people. Based on census and other data, he contends that Asian Americans have matched or surpassed the socio-economic standing and educational attainment of European Americans. Honorary "whites" have been allowed to achieve these wages of whiteness as a means of maintaining "white" supremacy (Bonilla-Silva 2004). Here, whiteness can be seen as a club into which some people of color are allowed entry to prevent multiracial collaboration (Ignatiev 1996). According to Bonilla-Silva, honorary "whites" express anti-"black" sentiments similar to those of dominant European Americans (Bonilla-Silva 2004).

Following Bonilla-Silva (2004), we argue that instead of presenting a significant change to the present racial order, increased immigration will actually reinforce the present "black/white" dichotomy within the U.S. as Asian Indians attempt to situate themselves on the right "white" side. Though Bonilla-Silva establishes that a tri-racial rather than a bi-racial system is emerging within the U.S., the racial hierarchy of "black" and "white" is still maintained in his model. In our analysis, we find that this hierarchy is portrayed in Bollywood films through three main themes: "Ethnic Heroes and American Dreams," "Emotional Segregation," and "Colorism". Through these subtle themes, Bollywood upholds covert institutionalized racism within the media by reproducing the racial hierarchy of "white" over "black" thus inhibiting multiracial organizing between historically oppressed ethnic groups, in this case Asian Indians and African Americans.

Covert Racism in the Media

Rodney Coates defines covert racism as the "subtle, subversive, and deliberate informal and formal mechanisms that allow differential access to rewards, prestige, sanctions, status, and privileges based on racial hierarchies" (2007: 4–5). We argue that this covert racism is institutionalized within the structure of the media, where racial hierarchies are reproduced through portrayals that favor light skin over dark skin. Although this covert racism in the media is subtle, it is important not to underestimate the role of human agency. As Gail Dines states in a documentary on Disney films:

> Mickey Mouse doesn't write these scripts, these scripts are written by real people, who themselves have been socialized in this society. And they are going to internalize those norms and those values and so when they produce work, it's bound to come out in some way, unless of course, they make a really conscious decision to operate within an alternative ideology" (Picker 2001).

Therefore, to say that these racist media portrayals are covert is not to deny that the overt actions of human beings play a significant role in creating them. It is to say that the viewing audience does not see the decisions being made by media executives, directors, writers, and producers as to which stories get told or how characters should be portrayed. Hence, these portrayals are examples of covert racism because we do not readily see the institutionalization of racism in the media that is a result of decisions made by individuals who have been socialized in a racist society and have internalized racist beliefs. We see the final product, not the conditions under which that product was created. We do not see how slavery, segregation, economic discrimination, censorship laws, and other legislation have created a "white" media that promotes white supremacy by reproducing a racial hierarchy. As Rodney Coates argues, "Covert racism remains submerged, entangled in the centuries-old tentacles borne of exploitation, extortion, and hyper-oppression" (2007: 4).

Moreover, racist media portrayals are easily taken for granted, because much of the viewing audience tends to view racism as individual acts of prejudice rather than as covert and institutionalized (Kluegal 1990). This individualistic ideology prevents the viewing audience from realizing racism as a structural societal issue. Hence, they may not recognize or analyze media portrayals as racist. As we will show in our examination of Bollywood films, critical analysis of these portrayals reveals that the media consistently sends the message that "white" is right and that Asian Indians must establish themselves within "white" society in order to achieve the American Dream. Before discussing these themes, it is first necessary to address the history of Asian Indians in the U.S. as well as the significance of Bollywood films.

The Indian Diaspora in the United States

Although the first Asian Indians, Sikh lumber mill and railroad workers from Western Canada, arrived in the U.S. around the beginning of the twentieth century, the contemporary phase of Asian Indian immigration to the U.S. begins, however, with the Immigration and Naturalization Act of 1965. The Act followed the Civil Rights Act of 1964. The civil rights struggle marked the growing unrest within the U.S., arising largely from pervasive racial discrimination and segregation. This "anti-democratic" sentiment was exposed during the civil rights protests that outraged Americans at home and tarnished the image of the U.S. abroad.

By 1975, the number of Asian Indians had grown to well over 175,000. The question of self-representation, and how they wished to be known collectively, began to surface among members of the Indian community. The designation "Indian" was not acceptable, as Native Americans were also known as "Indians" back then. The term "Asian American" was not much in vogue and, in any case, referred primarily to those from the Far East (and later, South-east Asia). Besides, there was a growing aversion to being viewed as part of a "black" African-American community, because the designation "black" was seen as condemning these Indian immigrants to membership in a permanent underclass. At first, Indians claimed that they ought to be considered "white," or at least "Caucasian," which was seen as prestigious and having scientific credibility. At long last, the U.S. Census Bureau agreed to reclassify immigrants from India as "Asian Indians." The phrase may refer to Asian Indians of Indian descent who are born in the U.S. or to those who have immigrated to the U.S. from the Republic of India.

According to the U.S. Census Bureau, the Asian Indian population in the United States has been growing at a rate of over 38%, the highest for any Asian American community. In terms of education, this immigrant group has the highest qualifications. A significant number of Indian Americans are graduates, postgraduates, or PhDs, software professionals, doctors, entrepreneurs, and industrialists. High qualifications have enabled Indian Americans to become a productive segment of the American population. As such, issues of racism are hardly given any consideration, because they would be tantamount to an admission of some measure of non-integration into mainstream American society. Additionally, for many Indian Americans, the struggle for independence is merely an academic chapter of history, or a vague memory. Consequently, they do not see their colonial history reflected in postcolonial immigration ideologies (Rajagopal 2001).

Bollywood Films and the Diaspora

Bollywood is the informal name given to the popular Mumbai-based Hindi film industry in India. The multi-lingual Indian film industry is the largest in the world, enthusiastically supported by the vast Indian film-going public—the largest in the world, in terms of annual ticket sales.

Until the 1970s, the popularity of Bollywood films among diasporic audiences in the U.S. was confined to first-generation Asian Indian migrants. Since the 1990s, however, second-generation immigrants have also become avid watchers of Bollywood films (Jigna Desai 2005). This is hardly surprising. Bollywood budgets, generally modest by Hollywood standards, have become much larger. Up to the mid 1990s, film sets, costumes, special effects, and cinematography were less than world-class. However, as Western films and cable television gained wider distribution in India, and with increasing globalization and investment opportunities, there was increasing pressure for Bollywood films to attain the same production levels and incorporate new cinematic technologies. In addition, Bollywood films have started incorporating English in songs and dialogue. English words and phrases, entire sentences, or even English used as the primary language, are becoming fairly commonplace. A few films are also made in two or even three languages.

Another factor affecting Bollywood's growing popularity is that sequences, or even entire films, are being shot in foreign locations.

Before the mid 1990s, the West only figured as an exotic backdrop for song sequences. The lives, experiences, or problems of diasporic communities were rarely even considered (Jigna Desai 2005). Being aware of the huge box office draw of Western locations since the mid-1990s, Mumbai film crews are increasingly filming in Australia, New Zealand, the United Kingdom, continental Europe, and elsewhere.

Jigna Desai (2005) highlights that a few independent film makers and others have made an attempt to portray the experiences of the Indian diaspora in non-mainstream films such as *Mississippi Masala* and *Bhaji on the Beach* and, more recently, *The Namesake*. *Mississippi Masala* is the story of an Indian family that moves to Mississippi, where the daughter falls in love with an African American. *Bhaji on the Beach* focuses on a group of women of Indian descent, caught between tradition and independence, who take a trip together from their home in England to the beach resort of Blackpool. Although the women vary in ages and initially have little in common, the journey leads them to better mutual understanding and commonality. *The Namesake* focuses on an American-born son of Indian immigrants, who wants to fit in with his fellow New Yorkers. According to Desai, movies such as these assumed the "burden of representation" to fill the gap that exists due to a lack of portrayals of the diasporic experience in films. However, it is only recently that popular films such as *Pardes* (Foreign Land), *Kal Ho Naa Ho* (Tomorrow May Not Come), and *Salaam Namaste* (Greetings) narrate the diasporic experience. At the turn of this century, scholars and social activists have focused on gender imbalances in Bollywood films (Nayar 2003; Virdi 2003; Ciecko 2001; Durham 2001). Scholars such as Desai (2004) and Kaur (2002) have shown how recent Bollywood films seek to arouse nationalistic fervor among the diasporic Indian Asian population by depicting the real India, with Indian traditionalism and heritage as positive values to offset the weaker values of the Americanized diaspora. Of late, scholars have also examined the gradual merging of regional and global boundaries through the lens of transnationalism in the postcolonial era, and demonstrated that portrayals of this blurring are targeted at the diasporic population of "deterritorialized imagined communities" and "hybrid identities" in the new global village (Kumar 2005). Despite this body of research, there has been no study of how Bollywood films reproduce racial hierarchies, subtly but strongly reinforcing the "white/black" paradigm. To demonstrate how the "black/white" dichotomy is institutionalized within the media, we analyzed six popular Bollywood films: *Bend It*

Like Beckham, Salaam Namaste, Monsoon Wedding, Kal Ho Naa Ho, Bride and Prejudice, and *Pardes.* As stated above, our analysis revealed three main themes, which will be discussed below as "Ethnic Heroes and American Dreams," "Emotional Segregation," and "Colorism." We argue that each of these themes communicates the message that Asian Indians must strive for whiteness to achieve the American Dream of upward mobility.

Themes

Ethnic Heroes and American Dreams

The stories of success told in Bollywood films equate Asian Indians with what Stephen Steinberg (2001) calls "ethnic heroes." The original ethnic heroes were the European immigrants who supposedly pulled themselves up by their bootstraps, despite discrimination and economic hardships. Steinberg challenges such Horatio Alger stories, which he calls "ethnic myths." They are myths because they deny the advantages European immigrants were given over people of color and the ease with which they were accepted into "white" society. Steinberg argues that the ethnic heroes of the twenty-first century include Asians and West Indians, who are seen as having achieved economic success because of superior cultural values and hard work. These model minorities, the myth goes, have advanced regardless of the discrimination they have faced. Ethnic heroes are posed against racial villains, namely African Americans, whose supposed cultural inferiority is the impetus behind their continued oppression. Such stories imply that to be an ethnic hero, one must not challenge dominant "white" society, but work toward assimilating oneself within it.

Two recent successful films, *Bend it Like Beckham* and *Monsoon Wedding,* depict these stories of ethnic heroes and present America as the land of opportunity. In *Bend it Like Beckham*, Jasmindar "Jess" Bhamra, the young football-obsessed daughter of a Sikh family settled in Britain, rebels against the "traditional" expectations of her immigrant parents. She gets her break only when a "white" girl spots her talent and introduces her to a "white" male coach, who fights for her right to play the game she loves. The film concludes with the two girls setting off for America on a football scholarship. The conclusion signifies that, unlike Britain, America represents racial liberalism that will accept Jasminder and her talent for the game despite the color of her skin, and will give her the perfect environment to nurture her talent and escape from the outdated traditions of her family. Consider these parts of the script:

> JESS: *There was a scout from America at the match today and he has offered me a place at a top university with a free scholarship and a chance to play football professionally. I really want to go…*
> JESS'S FATHER: *When those bloody English cricket players threw me out like a dog, I never complained. On the contrary I vowed I will never play again. Who suffered? Me! But I don't want Jess to suffer…*

Not only is Britain presented as the symbol of racial discrimination and the non-"white" man's foiled ambitions, even the Bhamra family's journey to Britain via Kenya is marginalized. By presenting England as the 'before' and America as the 'after', *Bend it like Beckham* continues to emphasize the ongoing myth of the "ethnic hero" in the great American melting pot that welcomes multi-cultural, multi-racial immigrants, promising them freedom, better opportunities, and a better quality of life. What such portrayals fail to include is that Asian assimilation into this much-touted melting pot demands segregation from other communities of color.

Many scholars have written about the process through which European American immigrants became "white" (Guglielmo 2004; Barrett and Roediger 2002; Brodkin 1999; Roediger 1999; Ignatiev 1996). Roediger (2005), for example, has argued that Italians were "working towards whiteness." That is, though they were seen as "not yet white" upon immigration, they learned quickly that becoming "white" had its rewards. Part of this process involved distancing themselves from African Americans to prove their whiteness. Hence, new immigrants quickly learn that the worst they can be is "black," and their consciousness of an in-between racial status has led to a desire for a literal distance from African Americans. Many immigrants who enter the U.S. racial structure are faced with working their way into a place in the racial hierarchy in opposition to "white" people as well as African Americans, often striving to reach the status of the former and not the latter. Such is the message portrayed in *Bend it Like Beckham*, where the assumption is that Asian Indians will successfully melt into "white" society while steering clear of anything that could be equated with "black" society.

Another film that depicts Asian Indians' climb toward whiteness is *Monsoon Wedding*. This film is set in the modern upper middle-class milieu of India, where affluence and a Western lifestyle mix with traditions like arranged weddings and traditional family celebrations. The bride-to-be, Aditi, is the much-indulged daughter who is having an affair with a TV producer, while the Indian groom, Hemant, is settled in Houston, back home to be married. The pre-wedding preparations include the gathering of relatives from both families from all over India, the Gulf, the U.S., and Australia. Aditi's cousin, Ria, is planning on going to the U.S. to take up a professional course. For both Aditi and Ria, the U.S. is the taken-for-granted destination where they expect to break free from the "traditional" familial expectations and build new lives.

Both these movies conclude with the anticipation that a better life awaits in America—the land of liberty, hope, and opportunity—but they fail to include the experiences of the U.S. migrants once they get there. The do not even touch upon the immigrants' real life in the U.S., either professionally or personally, but stop short at conveying the assumption that their lives will be fulfilling and successful once they get to America.

In fact, other movies, such as *Pardes, Salaam Namaste,* and *Kal Ho Naa Ho*, recount success stories that inevitably center around highly successful non-resident Asian Indians. It is their wealth and success (depicted through a lavish lifestyle of designer wear, luxurious homes, and deluxe sports cars) that the films focus on, not their experience as Asian immigrants in the U.S.

This classic immigrant success story is usually attributed to distinctive superior cultures and supportive families (Purkayastha 2005). A typical example of the dichotomy between Indian values and the stereotype of the Americanized (read debaucherous) immigrant is *Pardes* (Foreign Land), whose promotion directly played on nationalistic fervor and having the best of both worlds, with the blurb "American Dreams, Indian Soul." The plot, set in a dual nation setting, is supposed to take a serious look at the lives of Westernized non-resident Indians (NRIs) in America. The owner of a 550 million dollar industry in the U.S., Kishori Lal is a successful businessman, settled in America but emotionally attached to his motherland. He is impressed by his friend's daughter, Kusum Ganga, and suggests she marry his son, Rajeev. The audience is repeatedly reminded that Ganga, representing the sacred Ganges, is a purifying influence with a strong heritage and cultural values that overcome the relatively lax morality of the Indian diaspora in the U.S., which is symbolized by the NRI's son. Rajeev is extremely "Americanized" (read: has lost touch with his Indian culture and values) and the father believes Ganga will instill some traditional values in his life. The marriage is partially arranged by the NRI's confidante and foster son, Arjun, who is to play Cupid and bring the two young people together. The story moves across the Atlantic Ocean to LA, with Ganga visiting the future NRI in-laws. Ganga discovers Rajeev's dissipated and promiscuous lifestyle, which includes smoking, alcohol, drugs, and girlfriends, and returns to India, shocked and heartbroken. The story ends with Ganga getting engaged to Arjun (portrayed as the quintessential Indian in America who devoutly visits temples and has no vices), who then becomes the heir of the NRI's vast business empire in the U.S.

In *Kal Ho Naa Ho,* Naina, the narrator of the story, lives with her widowed mother, Jennifer, and her grandmother, and the two older women are constantly at loggerheads. While Jennifer, a Christian, wants her children to absorb and assimilate American culture, the grandmother, a Hindu, wants them to stick to her old-world traditions. Jennifer runs a restaurant that is going under and the family is in debt. Naina, a part-time student struggling to look after her younger siblings and trying to help with the family's financial troubles, is somber and dispirited, and the household gloomy and dysfunctional. All this changes when the charismatic Aman moves in next door. He transforms the troubled and skeptical Naina into a happy, spirited young woman who discovers love with her classmate, offers the family financial help, and is generally the *deus ex machina* who reverses the family's fortunes. He advises Jennifer to take a tip from the flourishing Chinese restaurant next to hers, and to upgrade her floundering business from just another American eatery into an Indian one. India, he tells her, and pride in India, is their biggest strength. The restaurant, duly renovated and rechristened "New Delhi Restaurant," is such an enormous success that the Chinese restaurant next door has to down shutters.

Kal Ho Naa Ho has a promising start, portraying a middle-class interracial Indian American family in New York City. Unlike the usual success stories, it seems to take a refreshingly honest look at the financial and emotional struggles of middle-class immigrants in the U.S., where achieving the so-called American Dream calls for hardship and effort. However, the film reverts to focusing on national heritage and culture, and how pride in tradition and ethnicity is the cornerstone of success, of realizing the American Dream. The success of the Indian restaurant and the closure of the Chinese one implicitly reflects the superior value of Indian culture (and cuisine) over that of other ethnic minorities.

Overall, these films feature successful Asian Indians abroad whose success is essentially attributed to being "Indian at heart." However, the discourse linking superior achievement to Indian culture presented in these films does not transcend the boundaries between communities of color. Rather, the affirmation of dominant Indian values assigns and fixes minority groups (such as the Chinese in the case of *Kal Ho Naa Ho*) as the "other." In contrast to such films, where Indian heritage is emphasized, are films such as *Salaam Namaste*, which send the message that Asian Indians should sacrifice their ethnic heritage for whiteness.

In a scene where the main characters of *Salaam Namaste*, Ambar and Nick, attempt to rent a house, the Asian Indian property manager continually proclaims, "I am not Indian anymore…I don't trust Indians." This character's girlfriend is also "white." What's more, the character speaks deliberately in an Australian accent, while covering up his Indian accent. This character is attempting to assimilate into Australia, not America, but this assimilation has the same requirement—becoming as "white" as possible. This subtle portrayal, which is meant to be humorous, may be uncritically accepted by casual viewers but sends the message that in order to be successful, Asian Indians must suppress their ethnic heritage in exchange for whiteness.

In *The Possessive Investment in Whiteness*, George Lipsitz (1998) analyzes the film *Crossroads*, which depicts blues legend Robert Johnson as selling his soul to the devil for musical talent. As ethnic heritage and culture are often referred to as "soul," we could say that when Asian Indians sacrifice their ethnic heritage for the benefits of whiteness, they are selling their souls to whiteness. Lipsitz argues that European Americans consume "black" culture or soul to salve their "alienations and identity problems" (119). These identity problems may have emerged from European Americans' decision to give up their ethnic heritage as an investment in whiteness. Similarly, Bollywood films convey the strong message that "whiteness" is an advantage that must be attained at any cost, no matter how high, and that tradition is exploitable or expendable.

Alas, Asian Indians are not likely to achieve whiteness as did Italian and Irish Americans. As Min Zhou (2004) argues, "New stereotypes can emerge and un-whiten Asian Americans anytime and anywhere, no matter how 'successful' and 'assimilated' they have become."

Ultimately, the real sacrifice is that which we make toward radical social change. As whiteness silences us, it also divides us from each other and from other people of color. These consequences will be discussed below after addressing two other themes in Bollywood films.

Emotional Segregation

Emotional segregation has been defined as "an institutionalized process, whereby racially oppressed and racially dominant groups are unable to see one another as emotional equals or as capable of sharing the same human emotions and experience" (Beeman 2007). Beeman (2007) found that emotional segregation was perpetuated by Hollywood films that portrayed African Americans in unsuccessful relationships and limited their emotionally intimate interaction with European Americans. Historically, a furtive and institutionalized form of racism has always created an emotional barrier between African Americans and European Americans. Bollywood films follow this historical pattern, but with a new paradigm: emotional segregation between highly successful Asian Indians who have been assimilated into the "white" culture and African Americans, who remain people of color. The emotional segregation of Bollywood films is marked by only the most superficial interaction between Asian Indians and African Americans, in settings that do not encourage any kind of meaningful dialog or exchange of views. Moreover, all the Asian Indian protagonists in the movies under review are successful professionals in "white" dominated businesses, a further demonstration of successful assimilation. The African Americans they occasionally interact with, however, remain marginalized or reduced to racist stereotypes.

For example, the film *Salaam Namaste* tells the story of a love/hate relationship between Nick and Ambar, an Asian Indian man and woman. Ambar and Nick officially meet at a mutual friend's wedding. At this wedding we see a mixed crowd of Asian Indians and "white" people. What's more, Ambar's friend, an Asian Indian woman, is marrying a "white" man. There are no visible African Americans among the guests at the wedding. Other than a poster that Nick has of Muhammad Ali, the only African Americans portrayed throughout the entire two-and-a-half-hour movie are involved in a musical performance. During one such performance, four African Americans appear on the streets at midnight, as background singers.

However, they do not interact significantly with the main characters and disappear when the song is over. When it comes to significant friendships or love interests, the Asian Indian characters are always portrayed with other Asian Indians or with "white" people. In fact, the only time that Nick strays from Ambar, he is shown in bed with a "white" woman that he met in a bar.

Besides Nick and Ambar, the other main love story told in *Salaam Namaste* is that between Nick and Ambar's best friends, Ron and Cathy. Ron is an Asian Indian man and Cathy is a "white" woman. Ron and Cathy get married, buy a house, and have a baby. During a barbeque celebrating Ron and Cathy's housewarming, we again see a mixed crowd of Asian Indian and "white" guests, but no African Americans.

The main love story told in the popular Bollywood films *Bride and Prejudice* and *Bend it Like Beckham* also involve "white" and Asian Indian characters. In fact, in the latter film, the main character, Jasmindar announces to her soccer teammates that she would be forbidden from marrying a "white" boy and "black, definitely not." Still, the objects of Jasmindar's affection are her "white" Irish soccer coach, Joe, and her favorite soccer player, David Beckham, who is also "white." As with Ambar in *Salaam Namaste*, Jasmindar's best friend is "white." African Americans are occasionally portrayed in the film, but again in background or stereotypical roles. In the beginning of the film, we see an African American sportscaster, and at times African Americans are shown playing soccer. The captain of Jasmindar's team is an African American girl, but we never see her leading the team. In fact, it is Jules who gets Jasmindar on the team and it is Jules, the "white" character—not the African American team captain—who leads practice when the coach is absent.

Despite the supposedly forbidden nature of interracial dating portrayed in the film, Jasmindar and Joe decide to pursue a romantic relationship. Though Jasmindar initially blocks Joe's advances because she does not want to disappoint her parents, Joe continues to pursue her. He meets Jasmindar at the airport before she leaves for the U.S. Joe tells Jasmindar, "Even with the distance and the concerns of your family, we might still have something." The two kiss and Jasmindar states, "I'm back at Christmas. We'll tackle my mom and dad then." Before the film ends, we see Joe playing cricket with Jasmindar's father, signaling that Joe and Jasmindar's relationship will be accepted. No comparable relationship involving African Americans was portrayed in any of the Bollywood films analyzed. In fact, no such Bollywood film exists, except for *Mississippi Masala*, an unpopular independent film.

Bride and Prejudice tells the story of an Asian Indian mother desperately trying to marry off her daughters. The main relationship in this film is that between Lalita, an Asian Indian woman and Will Darcy, a rich, "white" man from the U.S. Lalita and her sister also pursue another "white" man, Johnny. However, Will steers them away from Johnny, warning them that he is not to be trusted. Though Lalita and Will's relationship is rocky at first, by the end of the film, we see them embracing at Belraj and Jaya's wedding. Jaya is one of Lalita's sisters, and Belraj, an Asian Indian man, is Will's best friend. Once more, African Americans are not portrayed as friends, lovers, or as part of any significant relationship. When African Americans are portrayed, the scene again involves a musical performance in which African American characters are relegated to the background. In a musical performance involving Will and Lalita, for example, a choir composed of African Americans is added as background singers. Members of this choir seem to come out of nowhere and are wearing long choir gowns. Neither Will nor Lalita interact with the choir members during the musical and again surface contact (Pescosolido, Grauerholz, and Milkie 1997) is the theme.

The most integration of Asian Indians and African Americans was depicted in the film *Kal Ho Naa Ho*, yet again these characters are involved mostly as a musical backdrop or in other racist and stereotypical portrayals. Early in the film, we see one of the main Asian Indian characters, Rohit, flirting with an Asian Indian woman in an elevator. The woman states that she is married to the African American man standing in front of her. At this point, the elevator opens and we see the African American character holding Rohit up and choking him. Later in the film, we see a similar portrayal of two African American bouncers carrying the main characters, Naina, Rohit, and Aman out of a club. The musical segments of this film are much more integrated than those in *Bride and Prejudice* or *Salaam Namaste*. The Asian Indian characters are shown dancing and interacting with African Americans and "whites." There is also a scene where the main Asian Indian characters are at church, listening to an African American choir. In another scene, we see Naina's brother talking to an African American man playing basketball. Such portrayals imply that the main characters live in an integrated neighborhood and/or attend an integrated church, yet each portrayal is limited in its racist depiction of African Americans as musical performers, basketball stars, or brutes.

Colorism: "If You're White, You're Alright"

We introduced this article with the children's rhyme "If You're White, You're Alright." These standards are clearly communicated in Bollywood films. In fact, a Bollywood actress recently stated in an interview that the director she worked with is so talented that "he can make even a black African look pretty." (www.himalayantimes.com). Bollywood and Indians in general are obsessed with fair skin, a remark that represents how Asian Indians (and the Asian American community) have internalized "white" as the coveted standard of beauty.

In their struggle to achieve whiteness, Asian Americans have not only cautioned their children against playing in the sun, they have bleached their skin and have undergone dangerous cosmetic surgeries to alter their facial features. Eugenia Kaw (2003) documents these surgeries among Asian American teenagers who feel the surgery is necessary to be successful. By engaging in these dangerous attempts to whiten their features, Asian Americans are not only surrendering their souls to whiteness as discussed above, but also their bodies. Bollywood symbolically performs these surgeries through its persistent theme of colorism. Colorism refers to a preference for "white" skin and Caucasian features as dictated by "white" standards of beauty. Black feminists have often pointed to media portrayals of African American women that exemplify these standards (Collins 2000; Hooks 1992).

The actors and actresses chosen for many Bollywood films have very light or "white" complexions and sometimes also have blue eyes and light hair. This is especially true in the portrayal of *Bride and Prejudice*, where the lead woman character had blue eyes, "white" skin, and light brown hair. This character also struggled through the film with a fake Indian accent and when she sang, the accent was lost.

What's more, in one of the films, *Kal Ho Naa Ho*, we see a reproduction of whiteness with the portrayal of Rohit and Naina's child. Both of these characters are Indian, but at the end of the movie, we see them with their child or grandchild, who appears to be "white." She has "white" skin, light brown to blond hair, and light eyes. She also speaks English without an Indian accent. Somehow, Rohit and Naina, an Indian man and woman, reproduced a "white" child or their children produced a "white" grandchild. Either way, the message is that "white is alright."

Discussion

The "race"-based hierarchy that places "white" over "black" has been one of the most powerful ways of dividing people of color from each other. Historically, the classifications of "white" and "black" were created by the capitalist class to blind African and European American immigrants to their common interests, dividing them into separate "races" of humans (Ignatiev 1996). This "black/white" dichotomy, which took decades to create, works to divide Asian Indians and African Americans in contemporary society through media portrayals such as those found in Bollywood films. Our analysis shows that these portrayals clearly indicate that to be successful, Asian Indians must align themselves with the "white" side of the dichotomy, as did European immigrants.

However, it may be premature to conclude that Asian Indians are or will become "white" as did Irish and Italian immigrants (Zhou 2004). Though patterns of intermarriage and residential preferences might reveal a process of "working towards whiteness" (Roediger 2005), Asian Indians are far from parity with the "white" majority. As Bonilla-Silva (2004) argues, the status of honorary "whites" is tenuous. Asian Indians continue to face discrimination. Regardless of their citizenship status, Asian Indians are constantly viewed as foreigners (Bonilla-Silva 2004; Zhou 2004; Kibria 2000). Media portrayals of Asian Indians perpetuate these racist views. Asian Americans in general are rarely portrayed in familial or social settings that would establish them as full participants in American society (Taylor and Stern 1997; Taylor, Lee, and Stern 1995). Thus any wages of whiteness that Asian Indians might be receiving are an illusion. As part of their wages of whiteness, European Americans were given public deference and social status within the dominant "white" society (Dubois 1935). Such acceptance has not occurred for Asian Indians, who are viewed as "forever foreigners" (Zhou 2004).

Still, few Americans believe that Asian Americans face significant discrimination (Kim and Lee 2001). This myth of the model minority effectively divides Asian Indians from other people of color. African Americans are often pitted against Asian Indians when the former are compared to the latter and the latter attempt to assimilate into "white" society (Zhou 2004). Thus, people of color, such as African Americans and Asian Indians are prevented from identifying with one another (Kim and Lee 2001). As Dubois (1935) stated with regard to "black" and "white" workers:

> …there probably are not today in the world two groups of workers with practically identical interests who hate and fear each other so deeply and persistently and who are kept so far apart that neither sees anything of common interest (700).

The same can be said of Asian Indians and African Americans in the twenty-first century. The illusion of achieving the wages of whiteness for Asian Indians impedes the construction of multi-racial alliances with African Americans, and this situation is further perpetuated by popular films that deepen the divide between these ethnic groups.

Bonilla-Silva (2004) contends that the only way to challenge the racial order is for African Americans, who occupy the lowest strata, to engage in multi-racial coalitions with honorary "whites." According to Bonilla-Silva, African Americans must politicize honorary "whites," making them aware of their status. We argue that it is equally important for Asian Indians to politicize themselves and recognize similarities in discrimination that they share with other people of color. One way to create such political awareness is through the media, namely through popular Bollywood films that are widely viewed by Asian Indians within India and the United States. However, changes in the media may only come with pressure from multi-racial coalitions with people of color, what Elizabeth Martinez (1998) calls "Rainbow Warriors." Rainbow Warriors must struggle against racist media portrayals, holding directors, producers, writers, and most importantly, executives controlling big media accountable for the stories they tell and those they choose to silence.

References

Barrett, James R., and David Roediger. 2002. "Inbetween Peoples: Race, Nationality and the 'New immigrant' Working Class." Pp. 138–168 in *Colored White: Transcending the Racial Past*, edited by David Roediger. CA: University of California Press.

Bonilla-Silva, Eduardo. 2004. "From Bi-Racial to Tri-Racial: Towards a New System of Racial Stratification in the USA." *Ethnic and Racial Studies* 27:931–950.

Brodkin, Karen. 1999. *How Jews Became White Folks and What That Says About Race in America*. NJ: Rutgers.

Ciecko, Anne. 2001. "Superhit Hunk Heroes for Sale: Globalization and Bollywood's Gender Politics." *Asian Journal of Communication* 11:121–143.
Coates, Rodney. 2007. "Covert Racism in the USA and Globally." *Sociology Compass* 1:1–24.
Collins, Patricia Hill. 2000. *Black Feminist Thought: Knowledge, Consciousness, and the Politics of Empowerment*. NY: Routledge.
Desai, Jigna. 2005. "Planet Bollywood: Indian Cinema Abroad." In *East Main Street- Asian American Popular Culture*, edited by Dave, et. al. NY: New York University Press.
Desai, J. 2004. *Beyond Bollywood: The Cultural Politics of South Asian Diasporic Film*. New York and London: Routledge.
Dubois, W.E.B. 1935. *Black Reconstruction in America, 1860–1880*. NY: Free Press.
Durham, G. 2001. "Displaced Persons: Symbols of South Asian Femininity and the Returned Gaze in U.S. Media Culture." *Communication Theory* 11:201–217.
Golden, Marita. 2005. *Don't Play in the Sun: One Woman's Journey Through the Color Complex*. NY: Anchor.
Guglielmo, Thomas. 2004. *White on Arrival: Italians, Race, Color, and Power in Chicago, 1890–1945*. NY: Oxford University Press.
Hooks, Bell. 1992. *Black Looks: Race and Representation*. Boston: South End Press.
Ignatiev, Noel. 1996. *How the Irish Became White*. NY: Routledge.
Kaur, Ravinder. 2002. "Viewing the West through Bollywood: A Celluloid Occident in the Making." *Contemporary South Asia* 11:119–209.
Kibria, Nazli. 2000. "Race, Ethnic Options, and Ethnic Binds: Identity Negotiations of Second-Generation Chinese and Korean Americans." *Sociological Perspectives* 43:77–95.
Kim, Claire Jean, and Taeku Lee. 2001. "Interracial Politics: Asian Americans and Other Communities of Color." *Political Science and Politics* 34:631–637.
Kluegal, J.R. 1990. "Trends in Whites' Explanations of the Black-White Gap in Socioeconomic Status, 1977–1989." *American Sociological Review* 55:512–525.
Kumar, Anup. 2005. Bollywood and the Diaspora: The Flip Side of Globalization and Hybridity in the Construction of Identities. PhD. Seminar, School of Journalism and Mass Communication, University of Iowa.
Lipsitz, George. 1998. *The Possessive Investment in Whiteness: How White People Profit from Identity Politics*. Philadelphia, PA: Temple University Press.
Martinez, Elizabeth. 1998. *De Colores Means All of Us*. MA: South End Press.
Nayar, Sheila. 2003. "Dreams, Dharma and Mrs. Doubtfire: Exploring Hindi Popular Cinema Via Its 'Chutneyed' Western Scripts." *Journal of Popular Film and Television* 31:73–82.
Picker, Miguel. 2001. *Mickey Mouse Monopoly: Disney, Childhood and Corporate Power*. Art Media.
Pescosolido, B.A., E. Grauerholz, and M.A. Milkie. 1997. "Culture and Conflict: The Portrayal of Blacks in U.S. Children's Picture Books Though the Mid- and Late-Twentieth Century." *American Sociological Review* 62:443–463.
Purkayastha, Bandana. 2005. *Negotiating Ethnicity: Second-Generation South Asian Americans Traverse a Transnational World*. Rutgers University Press.
Rajagopal, Arvind. 2001. *Politics after Television: Hindu Nationalism and the Reshaping of the Public in India*. Cambridge University Press.
Roediger, David. 2005. *Working Toward Whiteness: How America's Immigrants Became White*. NY: Basic Books.
Roediger, David. 1999. *The Wages of Whiteness: Race and the Making of the American Working Class*. NY: Verso.
Steinberg, Stephen. 2001. *The Ethnic Myth: Race, Ethnicity, and Class in America*. Boston: Beacon Press.
Taylor, Charles, and Barbara B. Stern. 1997. "Asian-Americans: Television Advertising and the 'Model Minority' Stereotype." *Journal of Advertising* 26:47–61.

Taylor, Charles, Ju Yung Lee, and Barbara B. Stern. 1995. "Portrayals of African, Hispanic, and Asian Americans in Magazine Advertising." *American Behavioral Scientist* 38:608–621.
The Himalayan Times Online. 2004. "Rimi Sen Calls Black Africans Ugly." Retrieved January 14, 2008 (www.thehimalayantimes.com).
Virdi, Jyotika. 2003. *The Cinematic Imagination: Indian Popular Films as Social History*. NJ: Rutgers University Press.
Zhou, Min. 2004. "Are Asian Americans Becoming 'White'?" *Context* 3:29–37.

RACE, CULTURE AND THE PURSUIT OF EMPLOYMENT:
A RESEARCH SERIES ON HIRING PRACTICES
AT TEMPORARY EMPLOYMENT AGENCIES

Monique W. Morris and Sirithon Thanasombat

Introduction

LaKeisha knew of an American ideal of limitless opportunity. She also knew of a racialized America, as she'd grown up listening to the speeches of Rev. Martin Luther King, Jr. and others who sought to hold this nation accountable for providing equal opportunity. However, LaKeisha grew up going to integrated schools and knew not of a world explicitly divided by racial lines. It was not that the "Dream" had been achieved; but her understanding was that if she generally made good decisions, went to school, and applied herself, she would be able to access much more than her elders and ancestors could ever imagine. Unlike her elders, many doors that LaKeisha approached seem to be open to her. Times had changed and people no longer hung signs in effigy to openly discourage people of color from participating as full and equal citizens in American society.

In LaKeisha's America, over a third of the U.S. population is comprised of people who identify with a racial or ethnic group that is not Caucasian. (U.S. Census 2000). As a California native, she was also well aware that she hailed from a state in which the majority of the population is comprised of people of color. (U.S. Census 2000) So, even though research (Livingston 2001) has supported the theory that deeply rooted biases, as a function of historic and entrenched social and racial stratification, lead to an implicit bias that governs one's feelings, decisions, and actions, LaKeisha was unaware that her name—as a proxy for race—would impact her ability to get a job, even only a temporary one.

The temporary employment industry is an important and rapidly growing segment of the labor market. Nationally, there are 7,000 temporary employment agencies operating approximately 20,000 offices (American Staffing Association 2004) with over 2.96 million individuals (American Staffing Association 2007) working in temporary or contract positions on any given day. Transformation of the U.S. economy in the 1990s left the temporary employment industry as a major source of jobs and employment decision-making. Now these agencies often serve as outsourced human resources departments, and companies that laid off workers due to the recession continue to fill positions on a temporary, rather than permanent, basis despite improved financial health. In 2003, staffing agencies hired 10.7 million people. (Autor and Houseman 2002) The American Staffing Association estimates that in the current economy, temporary employment agencies serve 90% to 95% of America's businesses. (American Staffing Association 2007) The US Bureau of Labor Statistics (BLS) predicts that more jobs will be created in personnel supply services than in any other industry in this decade and that it will be the fifth fastest-growing industry through 2012.(Bureau of Labor Statistics 2005)

Research indicates that temporary employment can be the gateway to permanent, stable, and well-paying positions. (Hipple 2001) As such, the temporary employment industry can play a particularly important role in the promotion of equal opportunities among people of color and women. Women and African Americans, for example, tend to be more represented in the temporary employment labor pool than they are in permanent positions. Figures from 1999 indicate that 53% of contingent workers were women, in contrast to 47% of non-contingent workers. (Autor and Houseman 2001) Additionally, the Personal Responsibility and Work Opportunity Reconciliation Act of 1996 made the temporary employment industry a major port of labor market entry for recipients of Temporary Assistance for Needy Families (TANF). Former welfare recipients in Wisconsin, Georgia, and Missouri, especially African Americans, were much more likely than other populations to seek and hold temporary jobs. (Lower-Basch 2000)

However, while temporary employment may be a bridge to permanent work, hiring practices within the temporary employment industry can also serve as barriers. LaKeisha knew that there would be competition for any job she might apply for, and indeed there were—nineteen other African American, Latino, Muslim American, Asian Pacific American, and white applicants submitted résumés to the same employment agencies as LaKeisha. Each applied for the same jobs sought by LaKeisha. Unfortunately, she, like other African American and Muslim American candidates, generally did not fare well in today's marketplace. Throughout the different phases of hiring—from résumé submission to the hiring decision—LaKeisha encountered barriers over which she had no control.

Résumé Submission

Over the course of several weeks, a number of applicants— each with names that suggested a particular racial or ethnic affiliation—submitted a résumé to a temporary employment agency seeking an entry-level position. As was to be expected, not everyone was called in for an interview. In fact, while the average response rate for submitted résumés was 31%, there were interesting trends that were associated with various ethnic and racial groups. Latino applicants received the highest call-back rate of 33%, followed by white applicants (32%), African American applicants (31%), and Asian American applicants (30%). Muslim American applicants had the lowest response rate of 27%, a significantly lower response rate compared to Latino, white, and African American applicants in California.[14] Each group's results will be discussed in reverse order of successful response rates.

Muslim American Applicants

Applicants with Arabic names received the lowest overall response rate from temporary employment agencies (27%). While applicants with Arabic names can be of any race, the response rates for this distinct cultural group were significantly lower than those for white, Latino, and African American applicants throughout California.[1] Additionally, men with Arabic names fared significantly worse than women with Arabic names. Silicon Valley was the only region in the state where Muslim American applicants received more responses (22%) than non-Muslim American applicants (20%), but the difference was slight. In Bakersfield, by contrast, an area where hiring was limited, only 3% of Muslim American applicants received responses, just one-third the rate of almost everyone else who had applied.

---

[1] These rates were found to be statistically significant. "Statistical significance" means meeting this study's requirement of being within the 95% level of confidence. In other words, statistically significant differences are considered to be "real world" differences and not attributable to chance, error, study design or other factors.

Asian American Applicants

Asian American applicants, with a 30% overall response rate, received the second lowest number of responses from temporary employment agencies. Although Asian American men fared as poorly as Asian American women, Asian Americans collectively never finished first nor did they finish last compared to other groups within a particular region. However, Asian Americans finished next to last in the San Francisco, Los Angeles, San Jose, and Bakersfield regions, above only African American or Muslim American applicants.

African American Applicants

The 31% overall response rate for African American applicants matched the statewide median during the résumé submission phase. (Please See Table 2 for responses by ethnicity and region.) African American men fared equally as well as African American women. In the San Francisco Bay Area and Central Valley, African American applicants received more responses than any other group. In the Sacramento region, they ranked second with Asian Americans, slightly below their white counterparts. African American applicants also came in second to white applicants in the Bakersfield region and second to Latino applicants in the Los Angeles region. African American applicants placed near the top in all regions, except in San Diego and Silicon Valley, where their response rate was the lowest among all groups.

White Applicants

The 32% overall response rate for white applicants was the second highest response rate among all groups. Résumés from white women had a significantly better response rate (35.5%) than those from white men (29.5%). In the Sacramento, Bakersfield, and San Diego regions, white applicants received the highest response rate. White applicants came in second to African American applicants in the San Francisco Bay Area. In the Los Angeles region, they tied with African American applicants for second place, just below Latino applicants. Lastly, white applicants placed third to Latino and Muslim American applicants in Silicon Valley and fourth in the Central Valley region, above only Muslim American applicants.

Latino Applicants

Latino applicants received the highest overall rate of responses from temporary employment agencies (33%) during this first phase of hiring. Latina women (34.6%) fared better throughout California than Latino men (31.3%). Latino applicants obtained the highest rates of response in the San Jose and Los Angeles regions.

Table 1. Response Rate by Ethnicity and Gender

Ethnicity and Gender	Response Rate
White women	35.5%
Latina women	34.6%
Latino men	31.3%
African American women	31.1%
African American men	30.6%
Asian American women	29.9%
Asian American men	29.7%
White men	29.5%
Muslim American women	29.4%
Muslim American men	23.7%

Source: Discrimination Research Center, 2004.

The small gap in response rates between men and women of African American and Asian American backgrounds suggests that race is a greater factor than gender in the agencies' consideration of these résumés. The larger and statistically significant gap between men and women of either white or Muslim American backgrounds suggests that employers considered gender within each race or cultural group when deciding whether to respond to a résumé.

While none of the candidates control whether an employer will call them in for an interview, many people of color experience a confused, cognitive dissonance regarding their skill level, as presented on their résumé and the lack of response they receive from potential employers. For many, as demonstrated above, the job seeking process ends with the submission of a résumé, marginalizing segments of the labor pool. At this early, and instrumental, phase of the hiring process, names have become a proxy for race. Potential employers infer, perhaps implicitly, stereotypes that inform their decision-making. Will LaKeisha get an interview? Will Rashaad? What about Ling-Chi or Marta? Unfortunately, employers are neither colorblind nor free of bias when it comes to determining which résumé is the most competitive.

At the second phase of hiring, race also impacts whether a successful candidate is invited to interview with the employment agency. Again, the decision to interview a candidate is likely to be less informed by a racially discriminatory law or policy barring the participation of a particular racial or ethnic group. Instead, preference in the interview stage is found when one applicant was asked to come in for an interview while her equally-qualified counterpart is not; when one applicant is offered coaching on how to present herself or improve her résumé, and her counterpart does not receive such guidance; when an applicant does not have to follow the same application procedures as her equally-qualified counterpart; or when a candidate is substantially more encouraged in the interview process than her counterpart.

With almost identical qualifications, LaKeisha and Heidi both emailed their résumés to the same agency on the same day. LaKeisha called the agency on four separate occasions to follow up and try to schedule an interview. She was repeatedly told that a recruiter would contact her if her qualifications fit any of the positions they were staffing, and was finally told that she had not been contacted because she was not qualified for any of their assignments. LaKeisha was never called back for an interview. Heidi, however, was called by the agency on the same day that her résumé was received and was asked to come in for an interview. She was later offered a permanent position as a purchasing assistant for a cruise line that paid over $35,000 per year and included an annual free cruise.

In another instance, Heidi and LaKeisha walked into the temporary employment agency on the same day. Heidi dropped by during walk-in hours, was evaluated on the spot, and offered a position paying $9.75 per hour. That same day, LaKeisha called the employment agency and was told that the agency had walk-in hours. After she arrived at the agency during walk-in hours and completed an application, LaKeisha was informed that she would need to make an appointment for the following week to be interviewed and evaluated. Seven days later, LaKeisha came back and was offered a position making follow-up calls for an insurance company, a job which only paid $8 per hour.

At one agency, LaKeisha was put through "more hoops," and was offered a lower paying job than Heidi. Although Heidi was not evaluated and her references were not checked, she was offered a temporary position as a receptionist at the same temporary agency into which she walked; her offer included compensation at a rate of $10.50 per hour. Meanwhile, LaKeisha was tested on various software applications and had one of her references checked. She was offered a $10 per hour receptionist position at another office.

At another agency, Heidi was offered a position without being interviewed or evaluated at all. Both applicants e-mailed their résumés to the agency on the same day and received calls from the agency on the same day. Heidi was offered a position one day later without ever undergoing an in-person interview or taking any computer skills tests. In contrast, LaKeisha underwent a face-to-face interview and was asked to take a variety of computer skills tests. After more than a week, LaKeisha was offered two positions. Although both applicants were ultimately offered good positions, the agency was willing to bend its rules for Heidi in order to secure her a job that was not made available to LaKeisha.

In a different agency, the same recruiter offered Heidi a more highly paid position sooner than LaKeisha. The recruiter interviewed both testers, meeting with LaKeisha first. When she was interviewed, LaKeisha was told that she did not need to take any computer skills tests because she was being placed among the vast pool of clerical job applicants. When Heidi was interviewed the following morning, the same recruiter gave her various computer skills tests in Word and Excel and assured her that she did not place people in jobs for less than $12 per hour. On the day of her interview, Heidi was informed of a $13 per hour job doing relevance testing for an Internet search engine company for six weeks, and was told that the recruiter would mark her down as a candidate. She was offered this position eight days later. LaKeisha, on the other hand, had called the agency to let them know that she was available to work on the same day that Heidi received her job assignment. However, she was not offered the position. Two weeks later, LaKeisha was offered a temporary position with the possibility of permanent hire. This position paid 15% less than Heidi's position ($11 per hour) and involved distributing mail and providing general office support.

Generally, a candidate knows that a position has been filled after she or he receives an offer or a rejection letter. Usually at this early stage, the candidate is not privy to information that will either confirm or deny that race and ethnicity were used as factors in the decision-making process. LaKeisha never knew of the better offers made to Heidi, though since entering the labor market, she has suspected that perhaps the hiring process was not completely fair. However, the scenarios above illustrate a clear preference for Heidi over LaKeisha.

More than Speculation

The experiences described above were drawn from a research series conducted by the Discrimination Research Center (DRC) between 1999 and 2004, which examined the prevalence of differential treatment to applicants at temporary employment agencies. For the résumé submission phase, DRC recorded the frequency of responses to résumés from individuals with the same qualifications but different ethnically and culturally identifiable names. The temporary employment agencies' responses were measured by the number of phone calls and e-mail messages that applicants received in response to their résumé. The extent of differential treatment exhibited toward applicants of varied ethnicity or gender was evaluated based on the disparities in response rates. Between August and November, 2003, DRC e-mailed approximately 6200 résumés to temporary employment agencies in seven regions of California.

Matched-pair testing has long been a tool for civil rights organizations to compare the treatment of candidates who present equal qualifications and similar personal traits to the same employer, but who differ in a single demographic characteristic (such as race, gender, or national origin). The candidates, called "testers," are carefully screened to match each other's personal characteristics and are trained to mirror each other's interviewing techniques and to objectively observe employer behavior. Each tester keeps detailed reports of his or her experiences during the job application process, which can later be compared for any differences in treatment or outcome. To examine the other phases of hiring, DRC conducted matched-pair testing.

Blatant discrimination was rarely seen in testing; most discrimination today is subtle and covert, and perhaps not even conscious on the part of the employer. The comparison between the two testers was crucial because it uncovered any differences in the way in which similar job applicants were treated. This differential treatment frequently manifested itself in preferences shown toward one of the candidates, preferences that cannot be explained by superior qualifications. Important findings from DRC's testing studies will be discussed.

Bias against Candidates with Arabic Names

Even at the initial stage of résumé submissions, applications from candidates with Arabic names were disregarded significantly more often than those from other candidates. Leaders of Muslim American communities and other knowledgeable observers view the gap between Muslim American applicants and other applicants as a partial result of the September 11, 2001, attack on the United States. The backlash against Muslim Americans after September 11th fueled pre-existing fears toward these communities while contributing to a history of hate crimes. The American Arab Anti-Discrimination Committee (ADC) reported that from September 2001 to October 2002, complaints of employment discrimination poured into the ADC national office at a rate four times that of previous years. Cases of employment discrimination included hostile work environments and unlawful terminations. Although claims of discrimination in the workplace came from across the United States, the greatest numbers were from California, Virginia, Michigan and New York.(American-Arab Anti-Discrimination Committee Research Institute 2003)

The United States Equal Employment Opportunity Commission (EEOC) has recognized as a growing problem post-September 11, 2001 discrimination against Arab Americans, American Muslims and South Asians. In the fifteen months prior to September 11, the EEOC received only 391 charges alleging employment discrimination based on being Muslim. However, in the fifteen months *after* September 11, individuals who identified themselves as or were perceived to be Muslim or Arab filed 705 charges of discrimination or retaliation related to the backlash of 9/11. California, with 82 charges, led the nation in the number of September 11-related filings. Texas followed closely behind with 78 charges.(US EEOC 2002) During the same period, the EEOC received 841 charges of discrimination based on the charging party's Muslim religion. (Note: This figure includes some charges with alleged violation dates prior to 9/11/01. These charges are, by definition, not coded as September 11-related charges.) These increases were attributed both to intensified EEOC community outreach and clearly heightened tensions after September 11. EEOC charge data and our report demonstrate that anti-Muslim sentiment continues to permeate the employment process in California years after September 11.

White Applicants are Preferred Over African American Applicants

At the résumé submission phase, significant disparities—both positive and negative—were masked by the overall response rate received by African American candidates, which mirrored the state average of 31%. Résumés belonging to African Americans received a higher percentage of responses than any other groups in the San Francisco Bay Area and Central Valley. They also had above average response rates in Los Angeles and Sacramento.

However, African American candidates received the fewest responses of any group in San Diego and Silicon Valley. The low response rate for African American applicants in Silicon Valley is consistent with well-publicized concerns of barriers to fair employment in the technology industry. Based on information from the Employer Information Reports (EEO-1) of 33 leading Silicon Valley firms in 1998, African American employees represented only four percent of the combined workforce, roughly half of the eight percent who make up the local workforce. (Rivlin 2000) Reports on specific firms such as Netscape and LookSmart also cite large disparities between the number of African Americans working in highly technical fields and the presence of qualified African American candidates in that geographic region of the state.(Rivlin 2000)

The DRC résumé study, presenting applicants with comparable education, skill sets and years of experience, demonstrates that other factors might also contribute to African Americans receiving lower response rates. A study by Marianne Bertrand and Sendhil Mullainathan at the National Bureau of Economic Research (NBER) found that callback rates on identical résumés were substantially higher for "white-sounding" names. After sending out 5,000 made-up résumés to 1,250 Boston and Chicago employers that had advertised for administrative and sales help, researchers found that applicants with names such as Anne, Brendan, Emily and Greg received 50% more responses than applicants with names such as Tamika and Tyrone.(Cited by Maxwell 2003) Professors Bertrand and Mullainathan discovered that applicants with "white-sounding" names received one response (a telephone call, letter, or e-mail) for every ten résumés. In contrast, job applicants with "black-sounding" names but the same credentials received one response for every 15 résumés. While the screening out of résumés based upon negative stereotypes may occur at the subconscious level, its impact of diminishing the response rate of job applicants with African American-sounding names is real.

Implicit biases also may have negatively affected African American applicants further in the hiring process. Matched-pair results from 1999 demonstrated a clear preference for the white applicant over the African American applicant. Thirteen out of 17 agencies tested (77%) were observed to prefer the white applicant one or more times. Seven out of 17 agencies (41%) preferred the white applicant every time. The majority of the tests – 25 of 45 tests (56%) – demonstrated preference for the white applicant. In contrast, only eight out of 45 tests (18%) showed a preference for the African American applicant.

The findings from 2003 also demonstrated greater preference for white job applicants over African American candidates at temporary employment agencies in California. Although the African American testers had slightly better job qualifications than their white tester counterparts, the white testers were treated more favorably three times as often as the African American testers. Specifically, DRC found that the white testers were treated preferentially in 47% of the tests conducted across the state in 2003 while the African American applicants preferred in only 16% of the tests conducted. Thus, in only one of every six tests was the more qualified African American preferred over the less qualified white applicant.

The 2003 study also found that testers were treated differently even before the interview process. The white tester experienced a more favorable outcome than her African American counterpart in 92% of these cases. It is possible that the employers inferred the racial identity of the testers on the basis of name (e.g., Shawnette vs. Julia, Tamara vs. Emma) or speech patterns. For example, in nine cases, the African American tester was never interviewed, while her white partner was interviewed and offered a position. In three out of four cases, the white tester was offered a position on the basis of a phone interview alone, while the African American tester was interviewed and evaluated in person before receiving an offer.

The preferences shown toward the white testers were manifested in a variety of ways. In some cases, preferential treatment was observed in a better outcome. For example, white testers in 2003 were offered a position 77% of the time, while the African American testers were offered a position 67% of the time. Additionally, white testers in the same study were offered long-term and permanent positions twice as often as were their African American counterparts.

In other instances, the preference for the white tester was more subtly expressed in the behavior of recruiters who offered greater encouragement to the white tester than to her counterpart. Examples of this behavior include coaching the white applicant on how to present herself, advising her on how she might improve her résumé, encouraging her to keep calling back in order to arrange an interview, or telling her about a greater variety of positions. In a few cases, the African American candidate was steered toward positions that offered fewer opportunities for advancement, was told to be prepared for inquiries into her credit history or criminal record, or was asked to fill out a survey which helped the agency to monitor how many of their employees were welfare recipients.

Countering the Culture of Covert Bias

As demonstrated by the research conducted by DRC between 1999 and 2003, differential treatment in hiring is consistent over time and prevalent throughout California. All individuals are protected against discrimination in temporary employment on account of race, gender, national origin and related characteristics. In policy guidance adopted by the Equal Employment Opportunity Commission in 1997, the federal anti-discrimination agency made clear that staffing firms must hire and make job assignments in a non-discriminatory manner. A temporary employment agency may not argue in its defense that it was complying with the request of its client employer to illegally prefer or deny job applicants based upon a prohibited demographic factor. Furthermore, the temporary hiring agency is liable if it administers on behalf of its client a test or other selection requirement that has an adverse impact on a protected class and is not job-related for the position in question and consistent with business necessity.

These patterns are not necessarily or easily discernable to the individual job applicants, and may not even be purposeful on the part of the recruiters. Differences in treatment occur at the earliest stages of consideration for jobs and continue throughout the hiring process. Differential treatment of African American candidates and those with

Arabic names reflect a dangerous pattern in American manifestation of social injustice. Both African Americans and Muslim Americans have battled the routine and intense public association of criminality and/or terrorism with their communities, generating a negative public stereotype that affects the perceptions of these groups' capabilities and intentions. These forms of bias can lead to profound economic consequences for real-life job applicants. The subtlety of the discrimination does not weaken its powerful impact on determining who is selected for an interview or ultimately hired.

Strict reliance on the number of discrimination complaints filed at state or federal civil rights agencies masks the true extent of continued disparities in employment. Individual applicants are typically not in a position to know who was selected for the job or what actually occurred behind the closed doors of the hiring process. However, testing provides a context for analyzing specific practices and decisions that demonstrate differential treatment and negative employment outcomes for specific racial, ethnic, and cultural groups. Without testing, an individual with an Arabic name who e-mailed her résumé to a temporary employment office without receiving a response would not have reason to suspect that applicants of all other backgrounds received responses far more frequently than she did. She also would not suspect that this pattern existed throughout California. Similarly, while African American testers in DRC's 1999 and 2003 studies did not report any blatant examples of favoritism or overt acts of intimidation or discrimination, a comparison of reports written by white testers and African American testers revealed preferences that reflect the presence of latent biases that may lead a potential employer to interpret the value of a candidate based upon superficial characteristics, rather than his or her actual qualifications.

Unfortunately, at issue are not the qualifications of LaKeisha, Heidi, Rashaad, Marta or Ling-Chi. What fuels this discussion is a critique of society's response to the communities that certain names represent. To combat the use of names as a proxy for racial discrimination, some individuals have begun to use their initials—where LaKeisha Raychelle Johnson becomes L.R. Johnson. Yet, is this how we define equity? Have we obtained equality when individuals, and communities, of color have to develop strategies to adapt to latent biases and to evade racism, no matter how covert?

Every name—Heidi, LaKeisha, Sirithon, Monique—has an etymological association with an ethnicity or "folk." A civil rights agenda needs to be constructed that breathes life into a changing understanding of the racial construct that impacts our decision-making. Using the latest social science research techniques to capture the specific ways in which discriminatory practices are influencing access to employment is the first step. Many more steps need to be taken along the path to equal rights, including educating ourselves and our extended communities about the nature and extent of employment discrimination. These actions are vital if the nation is going to eliminate barriers to equal employment opportunities and professional advancement for LaKeisha, Rashaad, and other applicants of color.

Table 2. Response Rate by Ethnicity and Region

	Highest response rate	Second highest response rate	Third highest response rate	Fourth highest response rate	Fifth highest response rate
San Diego region	White (51%)	Latino (49%)	Asian American (46%)	Muslim American (45%)	African American (42%)
Los Angeles region	Latino (41%)	White (40%)	African American (40%)	Asian American (38%)	Muslim American (33%)
San Francisco Bay Area	African American (40%)	White (38%)	Latino (37%)	Asian American (33%)	Muslim American (28%)
Sacramento region	White (31%)	Asian American (30%)	African American (30%)	Latino (29%)	Muslim American (22%)
Central Valley	African American (25%)	Latino (23%)	Asian American (21%)	White (20%)	Muslim American (17%)
Silicon Valley	Latino (25%)	Muslim American (22%)	White (20%)	Asian American (19%)	African American (17%)
Bakersfield region	White (13%)	African American (10%)	Latino (8%)	Asian American (4%)	Muslim American (3%)

CHALLENGING OUR TEXTBOOKS AND OUR TEACHINGS: EXAMINING THE REPRODUCTION OF RACISM IN THE SOCIOLOGY CLASSROOM

Sarah Chivers and Jolene D. Smyth

Oftentimes sociology instructors rely heavily on textbooks to teach students course content. This may happen for a number of reasons. They may feel nervous about teaching or lack confidence with respect to their authority, legitimacy, or "expert" role in the classroom. This experience may be especially common with graduate student instructors and new professors. Or, they may lack preparation time as they juggle the demands of teaching, research, and departmental service, not to mention personal and family obligations. Regardless of the reason, the content of the course textbook takes on great importance, and therefore, we must understand what messages our textbooks are sending to students.

The purpose of this paper is to exercise reflexivity in examining how we—that is academic sociologists—inadvertently support the racial status quo by uncritically relying on textbooks to explain seemingly familiar concepts such as "race" and "racism" to students. Using a nonwhite sociological imagination, this paper addresses two questions: 1) what do we teach students about race and racism through the use of textbooks and 2) what can we do to make sure our textbooks are not reinforcing the status quo?

To answer our questions, we analyze racial discourse in eight undergraduate Social Problems textbooks. Discourse consists of, "ideas and practices that when taken together organize both the way a society defines certain truths about itself and the way it puts together social power" (Collins 2004:350). Our focus is on social representations that are *shared* across textbooks and that guide the audience's assumptions about race and racism. By examining such social representations, we hope to identify the ideology that underlies discussions of race and racism in Social Problems textbooks and to situate that ideology within current research and theorizing about these topics. Identifying these underlying representations and ideologies is important because ideology affects racial inequality and power by defining for students "what exists, what is good, and what is possible" (Therborn 1980:18). Racial ideology is a primary mechanism in the reproduction of racism at the individual, interactional, and institutional levels of society. By understanding it we can work towards antiracism, starting by changing our teaching practices.

We take a critical look at our role as educators in the production and reproduction of racism, but first we remind our readers that not everyone has equal access to higher education. In spite of a national ethic proclaiming the importance of equal education, the reality in the United States is that education is both a signifier of and a source of inequality, with race, class, and gender disparities growing ever larger at higher levels of education (U.S. Census Bureau 2006). Across the nation minority students are underrepresented in institutions of higher education. Students who are able to gain entry into the white world of higher education tend to be concentrated in specific sites such as technical and community colleges (Feagin, Vera, and Imani 1996). While there has been a steady increase in the number of students attending college over the last fifty years, the number of minorities (Blacks, Latinos, and Asians) completing social sciences programs in particular has substantially declined (Coates 2002). Moreover, scholars of color are significantly underrepresented in faculty positions within the higher education system as a whole (Astin et al. 1997). As a result, sociology classes often consist of white instructors teaching primarily white students about emotionally-charged and potentially threatening topics: racism, white privilege, and whites' role in perpetuating racial inequality.

What affect does this educational environment have on students of color attending college? The white habitus, a white culture of solidarity, is omnipresent and exerts "painful and enervating" (Feagin and Sikes 1994:92) pressures on students of color. One pressure, the high visibility of their racial status as different from the dominant group (whites), means that students of color carry the burden of being viewed as *the* representative of their entire social category. They must withstand a classroom environment where white students and instructors are insensitive to the racist aspects of the campus culture for minority students. The classroom environment itself is one that is a white space. Moreover, students of color rarely have opportunity to interact with and form relationships with faculty or administrators because scholars of color are underrepresented in positions of power within higher education (hence the term "*ivory* tower").

With this view of higher education and the different types of environments it offers different students, it is critical to recognize that while education is a potentially valuable tool in challenging racism, it is not always and automatically a challenging force. Education can also, in the most subtle of ways, serve to maintain systems of racism for dominant groups who benefit from them (Jackman and Muha 1984). There are significant health, family, and community costs of racism that people of color live with throughout their lifetime (Feagin and McKinney 2003). A key factor in the ongoing damage that racism creates is that it takes place again and again, in most areas of people of color's lives. These costs don't go away simply because its college.

Additionally, how education reproduces or challenges individual beliefs about racism may differ for different social groups. For example, Collins (1990) argues that black women, via their standpoint, are among the most likely to be aware of and challenge social inequities stemming from race and gender. In contrast, whites are more likely to be oblivious to social inequities because of their vantage point at the top of the social hierarchy. The danger is that white students in sociology classes are much more likely to *benefit* from what they are taught about inequality than to *challenge* inequality. Students of color don't benefit from being tokenized, from being asked to speak for their group, for it being assumed they are in college because they're an athlete or because their racial status got them into school. These environmental forces that are a product of the white habitus make examining the sociology classroom a worthwhile and important endeavor. A sociology instructor's role can easily become one that reproduces the status quo. This conclusion is the starting point for our examination of the reproduction of racism in the sociology classroom.

Research Design and Analytic Strategy

Our analysis is based on a systematic comparison of eight mainstream social problems textbooks. We chose social problems texts for two reasons. First, they have been ignored in favor of introductory texts in similar analyses (see Babchuk and Keith 1995, Beeman et al. 2000, Dennick-Brecht 1993, Ferree and Hall 1996, Hall 1988, Marquez 1994, Stone 1996), yet they are considered to be more specialized around issues of inequality (in this case race) and are expected to provide more in-depth and explicit analyses of race than introductory texts.

Second, their audience typically consists of a broader mix of sociology majors and non-majors from various disciplines. These texts likely provide the only exposure to theoretical and empirical assessments of race that many students are exposed to, outside of popular culture.

The eight books we analyze, published between 2000 and 2004, were selected at random from a list of the 16 "most popular" social problems texts, recommended to us by four prominent publishing companies (Allyn & Bacon, McGraw Hill, Prentice Hall, and Wadsworth). All of the texts in our sample are listed as "top selling titles" by facultyonline.com and are used by sociology educators across the United States. We would have preferred a true random sample of the most widely adopted books, but were unable to locate a sample frame of such texts; publishers either denied requests for such data or claimed that they did not possess it themselves.[1] Despite these sampling limitations, we contend that the texts we examine reflect the widespread consensus on race in undergraduate sociology texts.

Analytically, our goal is to identify the shared themes that are present in discussions of race and racism in social problems textbooks and to situate them within current race theory. Our analysis of the texts is guided by the following research questions which also represent the five major themes we coded in our sample:

1. How is race defined and illustrated?
2. How is racism defined and explained?
3. Are whites as a racialized group identified and discussed?
4. (How) is power implicated in discussions of race?
5. (How) is history implicated in present day racial inequalities?

Before presenting our findings, we must situate the texts in their institutional context in order to understand how their content is highly influenced by people and institutions beyond the control of individual authors. Textbook industry forces largely constrain authors' writing and often pressure them into reproducing existing ideas and texts. The publishing and review process, from prospectus to editing to marketing, largely influences the focus, content, and organization of books. Textbooks are written for several audiences: publishers, reviewers, potential

---

[1] One representative suggested that we access Monument Information Review Resource (MIR), an organization that provides sales information for over one million ISBNs from over 1,800 U.S. and Canadian college campuses. However, this information comes at a significant cost—several thousand dollars.

adopters, and students (Kendall 1999). This process decreases variation in knowledge and increases the likelihood that new knowledge will be excluded. While we concentrate on the content and organization of social problems texts, we are aware that the publishing industry is a broader system complicit in the reproduction of covert racism. To emphasize to our readers that the texts in our sample represent the widespread consensus on race (within the discipline of sociology and the larger publishing industry) rather than individual authors' views, we chose not to identify the texts by their authors' last names as is the traditional format for citing references. Instead, throughout our paper, we distinguish the texts by referring to them as Text A, Text B, Text C, etc.

How is Race Defined And Illustrated? Biology vs. Society

Seven of the eight books we analyzed tried to define race as a social construct; however, six of those seven failed to effectively distinguish the social concept of race from the biological characteristics of groups of people. We use Book E's discussion to fully illustrate this point. Book E explained that, "cultural definitions of race have taught us to view race as a scientific categorization of people based on biological differences between groups of individuals. Yet racial categories are based *more* on social definition than on biological differences" (p. 186: emphasis ours). The use of the term "more" in this statement suggests that a greater *amount* of the origin of "race" is social than the *amount that is biological*. Students who entered the classroom with a belief that race was a real, tangible thing (i.e., genes and chromosomes) (Bonilla-Silva 2003) are now being told that it is partly a real tangible thing and partly a social idea, but it is *more* idea than it is thing. How can they not be confused?

Four of the texts further undermined their discussions of the social construction of race by beginning their discussion of what race is with biological explanations. For example, in the paragraph just prior to their explanation of the social construction of race Book E states,

> The concept *race* refers to a category of people who are believed to share distinct physical characteristics that are deemed socially significant. Racial groups are sometimes distinguished on the basis of such physical characteristics as skin color, hair texture, facial features, and body shape and size. Some physical variations among people are the result of living for thousands of years in different geographical regions (p. 186:original emphasis).

In a similar manner, Book D explains, "racial minorities are groups of people who share certain inherited characteristics such as eye folds or brown skin" (p. 213). Both of these examples substantiate the view that race is a biologically derived phenomenon and is "natural." Only after students have had their previous misconceptions about race reaffirmed do they read that "many experts believe that the biologically determined racial groups into which humanity is divided—caucasoid, mongloid, and Negroid—are strictly social categories and that the actual heredity differences among them are meaningless" (p. 213). Not only are these statements contradictions, but for students who glean a definition of race out of its context within the textbook, there is a serious danger of misreading and misunderstanding what race is.

Failing to help students make this critical distinction in defining race is problematic because without a clear understanding of race as a social construct, students will not be able to take the next step of recognizing two fundamental aspects of race. First, the construction of races (i.e., racial formation) is a social and political process that is *historically and contextually contingent* (Omi and Winant 1994). Second, the placement of peoples into race categories involves a *hierarchy of power* in which peoples in *racialized groups* inhabit similar social locations in the racialized structure, with their location having serious material and emotional consequences (Bonilla-Silva 1996; Lewis 2003). Neglecting to adequately explain these crucial aspects of race allows students to continue to conceptualize race as a neutral, biologically determined element and/or an identity of individuals. By default, racial inequality becomes a result of the inadequacies and under-achievements of individuals and the status quo is maintained.

One text provided no definition of the concept of race or discussion of race as a social construction. Instead, the text simply launched into a discussion of the difficulties that "racial minorities" face living in regions where "high dropout rates from school, chronic unemployment, crime, disproportionate numbers of infant deaths, early deaths of adults, substandard housing, social disorganization, and violence are *unfortunate norms*" (Book F:214: emphasis ours). This statement is packed with unspoken and unexplored, but very problematic, assumptions. First, the use of the evaluative word "unfortunate" suggests that whoever is doing the evaluating—the author, the reader/student, the instructor, the university—exists separately from those being evaluated—the minorities—and has no responsibility for "their" situation. Using this word implies that these circumstances which are not "our circumstances" just simply exist. It leaves entirely unquestioned how these socially based inequalities came into existence or what role the unnamed "evaluator" may have in that process. It allows students to learn about "the other" from the safety of the evaluator position without ever examining how they or their family, community, state, or nation may have contributed to or benefited from the circumstances of "the other." Even more problematic, the use of the term "norms"— typically defined in sociology as socially accepted rules of behavior— suggests that "the others" simply accept school dropout, unemployment, crime, etc. as legitimate aspects of "their" lifestyle.

Not only does this text fail to implicate the powerful in creating and maintaining a racialized system that benefits those in power, it blames those on the bottom for accepting norms likely viewed by students as the causes of social ills. With the use of two simple words, "unfortunate norms," the most severe consequences of race are boiled down to biologically based pathologies among "the others" that we—the evaluators—have no responsibility for. This explanation conceals the social construction of race, ignores the significance of the racialized structure of the United States, attributes the consequences of this structure to cultural difference, and greatly undermines the possibility of students understanding racial phenomena as possessing any structural foundation.

How Do Texts Define and Explain Racism?

Although most of the texts discussed variants of racism (e.g., white racism, aversive racism, modern racism, and institutionalized racism) six of the eight suggested that racism is rooted in ideas and beliefs that underlie prejudiced and discriminatory behavior thereby reducing racism to individual psychological dispositions. For instance, Book A provides an idealist definition of racism nearly verbatim stating that "racism is usually defined as a *belief* in the superiority of one racial group to another, which leads to prejudice and discrimination" (p. 212; emphasis ours).

Additionally, the same six texts gave primacy to examples of overt forms of racism in discussions and illustrations. Examples include "Hitler's mass execution of European Jews" (Book A:212), the "genocidal attacks on the Jews" (Book G:189), "the Ku Klux Klan" (Book D: 215; Book E:208; Book G:189–90; Book H:159), and the "killing of a black man, James Byrd Jr., by white supremacists" (Book D:215).

We problematize the over-reliance on examples of overt forms of racism not because these practices are trivial or extinct, but because relying on examples of overt racism downplays the significance of everyday racist practices that are subtle, indirect, and embedded in the structure of society, of covert racism.

The problem of over-emphasizing overt racism and minimizing covert racism becomes clearer when situated in the context of the typical social problems classroom. Entering a social problems course, most students have some exposure to the idea that there are extremely bigoted people in society, but they very rarely articulate racism as institutional or structural (Bonilla-Silva and Forman 2000). Drawing on their individualized, idealist notions of what racism is, students easily reason that one is either racist or not and, because they are not overtly bigoted or racist, they can confidently declare that they are not racist. Case closed! This reasoning allows them to remove themselves from the subject of study so that they can study race and racism as witnesses of the problem, not active participants in it. This dichotomy of people being racist or not racist ignores the fact that "all white group members either benefit or might benefit from....[racial] inequality, and, both cognitively and practically, group members are more or less actively involved in the reproduction of the system of dominance, or in resistance against it" (van Dijk 1993:171).

The over reliance on idealist notions of racism in texts promotes students' tendency to reduce racism to the pathologies of a few irrational and hostile individuals, rather than recognizing that racial views are embedded in a structural foundation and represent the politically motivated responses of actors seeking to defend group interests (Jackman 1994). Maintaining and supporting idealist explanations of racism allows white students to deny their compliance with and support of existing institutional practices that guarantee their privilege and allows them to claim that, not only are they innocent of racism, but also that they are victims of reverse discrimination. It once again allows them to disengage and study racism from the perspective of the disconnected "evaluator." Moreover, if students do re-engage, they can do so from the defensive position of a victim, ensuring that they don't have to recognize their own responsibility.

A useful way of overcoming the limitations of an idealist view of racism is to incorporate a materialist framework into explanations of racism. A materialist explanation of racism makes clear that racism is a property of dominance relations between groups rather than between individuals. Book B provides a materialist discussion by explaining the limitations of strictly focusing on prejudiced attitudes towards minorities and stressing that:

> The determining feature of majority-minority relations is not prejudice but differential systems of privilege and disadvantage. 'The subordination of people of color is functional to the operation of American society as we know it and the color of one's skin is a primary determinant of people's position in the social structure (Wellman 1977:35)…Racial acts, in this view, are not only based on hatred, stereotyped conceptions, or prejudgments but also are rational responses to the struggle over scarce resources by individuals acting to preserve their own advantage (p. 226).

Book B later points out that racism is "a part of society's structure" and that "individuals and groups discriminate whether they are bigots or not" (p. 226). Providing a framework that identifies group power as a property of racism demonstrates to students that racism involves membership in a racialized group—a group which exercises social control over subordinated groups by limiting the social freedom of these other groups through participation and representation in societal institutions (such as education, employment, politics, etc.). In other words, it shows them how they (and their white instructors) are involved through group membership. They can no longer take the position of the disconnected evaluator studying the social problem "out there" from the safety of the classroom.

Are Whites as a Racialized Group Identified and Discussed?

Building on the above critique, we would like to explain a related thematic limitation of the texts we analyze that reaffirms a politics of difference and contributes to a "color-blind" ideology (Bonilla-Silva 2003) in which whites are absolved from any responsibility for the status of people of color—that is, the absence of discussion regarding whiteness within racial discourse. In our analysis, we find that only three texts explicitly point out that the category *white* is a racial grouping. One of the three texts fully addresses the role of whiteness as a meaningful social category and as a property of membership in the dominant group, while simultaneously explaining how whites as a group remain hidden and "immune to investigation," which reduces race to something possessed by people of color (Book B:219). In contrast, Book H, identifies whites as a racialized group in one sentence—"the largest racial group in the United States is the white race, which is the majority group, both in numbers…and in power" (p. 166). Students have to ascertain any additional information about whites from other references scattered throughout the chapter, in which their membership in a racial group is implicit at best. The third, Book F, identifies whites as a racial grouping, but then shifts its discussion to ethnicity and ethnic identity. In doing so, it fails to explain the ways in which whiteness reflects a superior position in a specific set of social relationships, affects social interaction, and is used to justify social arrangements, mobilize material resources, and marginalize members of dominated groups (Doane 2003). In other words, it lacks any materialist framework. Similarly, a fourth text, Book A, addresses white ethnics in depth, but along with the remaining four texts in our sample, fails altogether to address whites as a racial group.

Scholars of whiteness studies have pointed out, "in the current moment, where many declare race is not longer relevant and some even argue that it is racist to say whites are members of a racial group, it is particularly important to understand the parameters and functions of whiteness... [in order to understand] power and struggles for material resources" (Lewis 2003:161). Concealing the deployment and operation of whiteness in structuring relations between racialized groups allows white students to sustain individualistic explanations for social, economic, and political achievements and failures. Students cannot be expected to understand the power of race in structuring society as long as *races* are conceived of as *others* and simply signify cultural difference. Without making whiteness visible in racial discourse, contextualizing whites' group position in the system of power relations, and articulating the operation of whiteness between and within racialized ideas, events, policies, and practices, white students will continue to place themselves outside of the racialized structure and ignore their own compliance or participation in it.

(How) is Power Implicated in Discussions of Race and Racism?

Four of the texts we analyzed acknowledged the link between racial categories and power relations, but only three of the four explicitly discussed whites' social location at the top of the racial hierarchy. The remaining four failed altogether to explain and emphasize that race is the outcome of social relationships between groups *having unequal power* and as a result were not able to effectively discuss whites' location in that hierarchy. For example, Book G explains, "race is a social category because *people* make important distinctions between *people* on the basis of such presumed biological differences, even when these differences are actually vague or nonexistent" (p. 189: emphasis ours). Although this definition recognizes that race is social rather than biological, it is problematic because it fails to address the power relations between the "people" involved. Which "people" make important distinctions? Why do they make them? What are the consequences?

Similarly, Book A suggests, "the concept of 'race' as it is used in everyday speech is a social idea rather than a biological fact ... Race, therefore, is an idea constructed by *people* in order to *place themselves* in social categories" (p. 212: emphasis ours). Again, this definition deemphasizes the active role of responsible actors and groups of actors in the social construction of "the other" race(s), and therefore completely discounts the hierarchical arrangement of racial groups in the racialized social system. By disregarding race as relational and collective, these texts leave students with no conception of the problematic of race as a social construction. If "people place themselves" in social categories, race cannot denote collective relationships between groups but instead the self-conscious identities of individuals; race, in these conceptualizations becomes a personal, not a social, problem.

As Doane (2003) points out, "it is not sufficient merely to state that 'race' is 'socially constructed.' The process of racial formation occurs not in a vacuum but under a specific set of social and material circumstances" (p. 9). For students to understand contemporary race relations, it is necessary to situate race in the history and context of Western expansion, conquest, colonialism, and imperialism and clearly identify *who exploits whom* (San Juan 2002). The power to categorize racialized groups has strategic value—it reifies whites' power by partially structuring economic, political, social, and ideological levels of society, allowing whites to further their own material interests[2] (Bonilla-Silva 1996). Failing to explain the role of power in the social construction of race ignores the hegemonic nature of the socially invented phenomena of race and allows students to read the text with no understanding of their own culpability in the formation and perpetuation of the racialized system or how they benefit from it.

In contrast to the texts just described, Book B explains,

> The racial hierarchy, with White groups of European origin at the top and people of color at the bottom, serves important functions for society

---

[2] By material we mean not just economic interests, but also social, political, and ideological interests.

and for certain categories of people. ...[it] reinforces the status quo: It enables the powerful to retain their control and their advantage. Racial categories are the basis of power relations and group position . ... The different experiences of racial groups are systematically produced even though races, per se, do not exist. What does exist is the *idea* that races are distinct groups. Social scientists now reject race as a valid way to divide human groups....Although there is no such thing as biological race, races are real insofar as they are *socially defined*. In other words, racial categories *operate* as if they are real (p. 215–216 original emphasis).

Not only does Book B present race categorization as a basis for power, it clearly identifies who benefits—whites. This discussion helps students understand that racial phenomena are founded on group dynamics and embedded in the social, economic, political, and ideological levels of society. Because the racial hierarchy serves "important functions...for certain categories of people" white students in particular may begin to recognize the unacknowledged system of racial privilege that structures advantage and disadvantage and in which they are active participants (Andersen 2003; MacIntosh 1995).

(How) Do The Texts Incorporate History Into Discussions of Race and Racism?

Two general themes arose when we analyzed the discussions of the history of race in social problems texts. The first and most prolific theme, found in six of the books, was the tendency to simply attribute today's racial problems to "past patterns," "long histories," and "legacies" as opposed to examining how both past and present forces combine to produce and reproduce a highly racialized system with real material consequences. For example, Book F explains that "much of American history contains unconscionable patterns of racial enslavement, exploitation, and expulsion, and innumerable instances of prejudice, discrimination, and violence. That grim legacy still influences present-day interaction patterns" (p. 212). Our argument here is not that we should ignore how historical situations and practices have influenced the present. When texts give primacy to history by reducing modern day racial phenomena to history's leftovers, they ignore and conceal the importance of contemporary racializing forces, and free whites living in the present from culpability. Texts perpetuate students' attributions of race related social problems to previous generations and white students' tendency to question why "they" (i.e., racial minorities) cannot just let it go. When "present-day interaction patterns" persist from past "instances of prejudice, discrimination, and violence," the idealist implication is that modern day racists have inherited the beliefs and ideas of their ancestors. Racism is once again boiled down to individual people's pathologies that lead to overt forms of prejudice and discrimination. Thus, the current, more subtle and pervasive production and reproduction of racial inequality continues unquestioned and unabated (Bonilla-Silva 1996, 2001).

The second theme that arose in our analysis was the practice of dissecting and parsing history so that national and global projects of racialization are obscured. All of the texts we examined located the historical work of racism in the genocide and forced migration of Native Americans during European settlement, the enslavement of Africans, the physical and spatial segregation of African Americans from whites through Jim Crow laws, and the internment of Japanese Americans during World War II. None of the eight texts in our sample discussed links between these events and processes from a historicizing vantage point.

To illustrate, we draw from Book C's discussion of Asian and Pacific Americans in which, after a brief introduction that touches on why the "model minority" stereotype is not accurate, Book C proceeds to locate the present day reality for Asian and Pacific Americans in the discrimination and oppression of Chinese immigrants during the 19th century, the internment of Japanese Americans during WWII, and the colonization of Filipino Islanders by the United States in 1902. The following are excerpts of discussions about the internment of Japanese Americans and the colonization of Filipinos.

> Although Japanese Americans experienced high levels of prejudice and discrimination almost as soon as they arrived in this country, their internment in U.S. concentration camps during World War II remains the central event of the Japanese American experience (p. 62–63)

> Most early Filipino migrants were recruited as cheap labor for sugar plantations in Hawaii…Like members of other racial-ethnic groups, Filipino Americans were accused of stealing jobs and suppressing wages during the Great Depression, and Congress restricted Filipino immigration to fifty people per year until after World War II (p. 63).

This discussion treats each historical event as discrete and separate rather than considering how each racialized practice articulated with other racialized practices in a social formation that has occurred throughout history and continues to occur in the present.

By organizing the discourse of racialized groups in spatial and ideological separation, the text implies that significant historical conditions are isolated events. Book C draws no connection between the experiences of Filipinos after U.S. colonization of the Philippine Islands and the existing racialized structuring principles that were present in the organization of society, and which were already affecting the positioning of Japanese Americans within the U.S. economy. Case in point, Filipinos entered the U.S. for the first time in 1907 as manual workers recruited by the Hawaiian Sugar Planters Association (SPA) with the expectation that any labor shortages caused by the Gentlemen's Agreement, which restricted the number of Japanese field hands, could be filled (San Juan 2001). The existing structural principles affecting Filipinos and Japanese were on-going; as "the racial exclusion of Japanese by the Immigration Acts of 1920 and 1924 occurred, the SPA recruited 45,000 Filipinos more, a practice which continued until…1934 with the passage of the Philippine Independence Act and the limitation of immigration to a quota of fifty a year" (San Juan 2001:228). Thus, these practices served to legitimate the social positioning of Filipinos vis-à-vis Japanese and may clarify why Filipinos continue to be segregated in low-paying jobs today.

Rather than treating historical situations as isolated facts, a better framework would explain to students that group relations are transactional and situationally defined in complex historical dynamics that form and are shaped by the racial structure of the U.S. This avoids reducing racism to a legacy of the past and helps students recognize that race and racism cannot simply be reduced it to the pathology of a few individuals. It connects particular histories to the present-day material realities. It highlights how race and racism are social issues connecting all groups in a hierarchy of social and material relations and extending deep into the structure of U.S. and global societies. In this more complex treatment of history, the focus becomes the idea that distinct racialized groups are linked in common racialized dynamics that underlie the social structure of the U.S., not how "Asian Americans" are similar because each sub-group within that label has been the object of its own type of prejudice and discrimination. In this way, students can be made aware of the tremendous variation that exists among members of one racialized group in culture, language, and politics and also how people within and between racialized groups are connected through a racialized social structure.

Discussion and Conclusion

Starting from the observation that many instructors rely too heavily on the textbooks we use in courses we teach, the purpose of this paper was twofold. We set out to 1) identify what we are really teaching students about race and racism through the use of Social Problems texts and, 2) situate this information within current race theorizing so that we can offer suggestions to ensure that the textbooks we use to teach with are not uncritically reinforcing the status quo. Our findings, summarized in Table 1, indicate that current Social Problems texts, taken as a group, have difficulty in even defining race as a social construct and have a tendency to subscribe to a framework that reduces collective aspects of race relations to individual pathologies or cultural difference passed on to us from previous generations. Although they document disparities between racialized groups, little to no connection is made between these real race effects and the social construction of race. Racialized outcomes are not explained in terms of how the structuring of social relations and practices reinforce white privilege and power. There is a gaping divide between discussions of socially constructed categories of race and racial inequality; the missing discussion being the connection between race and racial inequality through the racialized social structure.

We want to provide the caveat here that the texts we analyzed are not bad in all respects. Each text we looked at did some things very well. However, in the context of the typical social problems classroom, the things the texts did poorly have a real potential to undercut their message and leave students with their misperceptions about race firmly intact. If white students continue to believe that racism is a property of individuals, they can easily conclude that they are not racist and can proceed to study racial inequality from the vantage point of a disconnected observer rather than a participant in race politics. From this vantage point, students cannot critically examine their role in the race system because they don't see themselves as a part of it. Instead, they are likely to become defensive, feel wrongfully accused of being racist, claim to be victims of reverse discrimination, and wonder why "they" (i.e., racial minorities) cannot just let it go and start over. The racial status quo is left intact and maybe even supported by the texts' overall messages. By relying on these texts and their underlying meanings, we have reproduced the racial status quo.

Table 1. Summary of Findings

	A	B	C	D	E	F	G	H
DEFINING AND EXPLAINING RACE								
Doesn't attempt to define race as a social construct.						X		
Failed to adequately define race as a social construct.	X		X	X	X	X	X	X
Led discussion of race with biological difference theme.				X	X		X	X
DEFINING AND EXPLAINING RACISM								
Doesn't attempt to define racism.						X		
Defines racism as rooted in ideas and beliefs.	X		X	X	X		X	X
Gives primacy to overt racism in discussion and illustration.	X		X	X	X		X	X
WHITES AS A RACIALIZED GROUP								
Doesn't explicitly identify whites as a racialized group.	X		X	X	X		X	
Doesn't discuss how whiteness remains hidden.	X			X	X	X	X	X
POWER								
Doesn't explain the link between power and the racial hierarchy.	X				X	X	X	
Doesn't explicitly discuss whites' location atop the hierarchy.	X			X	X	X	X	
HISTORY								
Gives primacy to the past as an explanation for racial inequality.	X		X	X		X	X	X
Doesn't show connections between racial groups' histories.	X	X	X	X	X	X	X	X

In what ways should our texts and teaching be changed? The obvious answer is that we must collectively incorporate race as a structural level phenomenon into our texts and instruction. This does not mean we should only focus on structure. Rather, the idea that people in different socially constructed categories are acted upon and act within a racialized social system should be a prominent theme. We must provide a conceptualization of race that expresses race as a collective, relational aspect of society that is rooted in group power. Whites must also fall under investigation in this discussion so that whiteness can be made visible, so that white students can see themselves in racial terms, and most importantly, so that students can become cognizant of their own acceptance, participation in, and defense of the racialized social structure. Racism must no longer be portrayed as a legacy of the past or as a problem of prejudiced individuals.

Part of incorporating race into our texts in this way is to firm up the language we use in writing texts. The topic of race and racism is sensitive and oftentimes uncomfortable for white students. But these brief moments of discomfort for white students and instructors are trivial in comparison to the everyday experiences of Eréndira and our colleagues, scholars of color who face criticisms for not utilizing the tools of white sociology and who face obstacles in funding and mentoring, all the while being expected to perform to particular standards of publishing in order to have their work recognized and legitimated (Bonilla-Silva Introduction). We must realize that we aren't doing white students any favors by breaking things to them softly or tiptoeing around issues[3] when doing so allows them to escape to a disconnected and defensive vantage point rather than realizing how we are a part of the system. Instead, our texts and our teaching should provide the tools and a comfortable setting where students can do the uncomfortable work of acknowledging and exploring their roles in the processes that produce inequalities.

How can we incorporate this framework into curriculum? A painful but perhaps necessary answer is to revisit Westhues' (1991) message that sociologists should eliminate using textbooks in situations that permit, especially when classes are small. A diminished reliance on textbooks will exert pressure on those in social institutions that are

---

[3] For example statements devoid of power, such as Book G's statement that "people make important distinctions between people" (p. 189) and Book A's statement that race is an idea "constructed by people in order to place themselves in social categories" (p. 212) and statements that defer responsibility such as Book H's statement that "housing patterns in many large metropolitan centers have led to de facto segregation" (p. 176); or Book F's statement that "factory sweatshops still exist and still exploit minority workers" (p. 234). Too the contrary, housing patterns have not created segregation; segregation is the housing pattern created by a multitude of forces, not the least of which is white migration out of inner cities! Similarly, sweatshops don't exploit minority workers; they are the place where minority workers are exploited by owners and managers!

external to education (particularly the publishing industry) to allow the modification of textbooks in the ways suggested. Another suggestion is to approach the writing of social problems textbooks more like we approach the writing of edited volumes—each chapter is written by a person or team of people who specialize in the topic of the chapter. In this way the most cutting-edge theorizing and research on race, class, gender, and the various other topics included in social problems texts will be included while dated or obsolete theorizing and research will eliminated. Moreover, we can become better allies with scholars of color whose voices are the least acknowledged and the most in need of being heard. By creating spaces that challenge existing white ways of thinking and doing, and by empowering students of color by validating their lived experiences through an analysis of the structural aspects of race and racism, we can create a collaborative classroom that promotes antiracist action.

Educators need to do their homework. It is simply too easy to rely on textbooks as an authoritative crutch, to rehearse the same lectures from semester to semester, and to scarcely supplement the text rather than teach students to develop critical thinking skills and connect their experiences to structural processes. We have to understand that the outcome of such practices reaches far beyond the classrooms we teach in, the academic departments of which we are a part, and our universities. Like our students, we too are a part of a racialized society, and our practices in and outside the classroom impact that society. If we do not recognize and take responsibility for our own role, how can we ever expect our students to acknowledge theirs?

Finally, educators must direct their teachings towards answering "how" questions rather than "why" questions (Reskin 2003). Such a shift describes racial disparities and explains the processes that erode, transform, and maintain inequality. The end result is not only to have dominant groups understand the effects of a racialized social system on the Other, but also "to comprehend how racialized groups [especially whites] are connected in the construction of Otherness" (Baca Zinn and Eitzen 1996:115). We agree with Herbert Gans (1998) that sociologists should publish useful work "that adds to our understanding and to the public's understanding of society and if possible to its improvement as well" (p. 22). Sociologists have a social responsibility to reject individualistic and victim-blaming explanations for racial inequality and to teach a group-based understanding in order to alter the racialized structure of domination and privilege. Until we do so, we will continue to be part of the problem rather than the solution.

Appendix A: Social Problems Textbooks Used in this Analysis

Book A. 2003. *Social Problems: A Brief Introduction*. 2nd Edition. New Jersey: Prentice Hall.

Book B. 2004. *Social Problems with Research Navigator*. 9th Edition. New York: Allyn and Bacon.

Book C. 2004. *Social Problems in a Diverse Society*. 3rd Edition. New York: Allyn and Bacon.

Book D. 2004. *Social Problems*. 11th Edition. New Jersey: Prentice Hall.

Book E. 2002. *Understanding Social Problems*. 3rd Edition. California: Wadsworth.

Book F. 2002. *Contemporary Social Problems*. 5th Edition. Boston: Allyn and Bacon.

Book G. 2003. *Introduction to Social Problems*. 6th Edition. Boston: Allyn and Bacon.

Book H. 2000. *Social Problems: Issues and Solutions*. 5th Edition. California: Wadsworth.

References

Andersen, Margaret. 2003. "Whitewashing Race: A Critical Perspective on Whiteness." Pp. 21–34 in *White Out: The Continuing Significance of Racism*, edited by Eduardo Bonilla-Silva and Ashley Doane Jr. New York: Routledge.

Astin, Helen S., Anthony Lising Antonio, Christine M. Cress, and Alexander W. Astin. 1997. "Race and Ethnicity in the American Professoriate, 1995–1996." Higher Education Research Institute, UCLA Graduate School of Education and Information Studies.

Baca Zinn, Maxine and D. Stanley Eitzen. 1996. "Transforming Sociology Through Textbooks: Making the Discipline More Inclusive." *Teaching Sociology* 24(1):113–16.

Babchuk, Nicholas and Bruce Keith. 1995. "Introducing the Discipline: The Scholarly Content of Introductory Texts." *Teaching Sociology* 23:215–25.

Beeman, Mark, Geeta Chowhry and Karmen Todd. 2000. "Educating Students about Affirmative Action: An Analysis of University Sociology Texts." *Teaching Sociology* 28:98–115.

Bonilla-Silva, Eduardo. 1996. "Rethinking Racism: Toward a Structural Interpretation." *American Sociological Review* 62:465–480.

———. 2001. *White Supremacy & Racism in the Post-Civil Rights Era*. London: Lynne Rienner Publishers.

———. 2003. *Racism Without Racists: Color-Blind Racism and the Persistence of Racial Inequality in the United States*. New York: Rowman & Littlefield Publishers, Inc.

Bonilla-Silva, Eduardo, and Tyrone Forman. 2000. "'I Am Not a Racist But…': Mapping White College Students' Racial Ideology in the USA." *Discourse and Society* 11:50–85.

Coates, Rodney. 2002. "I Don't Sing, I Don't Dance, and I Don't Play Basketball! Is Sociology Declining in Significance or Has it Just Returned to Business as Usual?" *Critical Sociology* 25(2): 255–279.

Collins, Patricia Hill. 1990. *Black Feminist Thought: Knowledge, Consciousness, and the Politics of Empowerment.* Boston: Unwin Hyman.

Collins, Patricia Hill. 2004. *Black Sexual Politics: African Americans, Gender, and the New Racism.* New York: Routledge.

Dennick-Brecht, M. Kathryn. 1993. "Developing a More Inclusive Sociology Curriculum: Racial and Ethnic Group Coverage in Thirty Introductory Textbooks." *Teaching Sociology* 21:166-71.

Doane, Ashley, Jr. 2003. "Rethinking Whiteness Studies." Pp. 3-18 in *White Out: The Continuing Significance of Racism,* edited by Eduardo Bonilla-Silva and Ashley Doane Jr. New York: Routledge.

Feagin, Joe and Karyn McKinney. 2003. *The Many Costs of Racism.* New York: Rowman and Littlefield Publishers.

Feagin, Joe and Melvin Sikes. 1994. *Living with Racism: The Black Middle-Class Experience.* Boston: Beacon Press.

Feagin, Joe, Hernan Vera, and Nikitah Imani. 1996. *The Agony of Education: Black Students at White Colleges and Universities.* New York: Routledge.

Ferree, Myra Marx, and Elaine J. Hall. 1996. "Rethinking Stratification from a Feminist Perspective: Gender, Race and Class in Mainstream Textbooks." *American Sociological Review* 61:929-950.

Gans, Herbert. 1998. "Best-Sellers by American Sociologists: An Exploratory Study." Pp. 19-30 in *Required Reading: Sociologists Most Influential Books,* edited by Dan Clawson. Boston: University of Massachusetts Press.

Hall, Elaine. 1988. "One Week for Women? The Structure of Inclusion of Gender Issues in Introductory Textbooks." *Teaching Sociology* 12:431-42.

Jackman, Mary. 1994. *The Velvet Glove: Paternalism and Conflict in Gender, Class, and Race Relations.* Berkley: University of California Press.

Jackman, Mary and Michael Muha. 1984. "Education and Intergroup Attitudes: Moral Enlightenment, Superficial Democratic Commitment, or Ideological Refinement?" *American Sociological Review* 49:751-69.

Kendall, Diana. 1999. "Doing a Good Deed or Confounding the Problem? Peer Review and Sociology Textbooks." *Teaching Sociology.* 27:17-30.

Lewis, Amanda. 2003. "Some are More Equal than Others: Lessons on Whiteness from School." Pp. 159-172 in *White Out: The Continuing Significance of Racism,* edited by Eduardo Bonilla-Silva and Ashley Doane Jr. New York: Routledge.

Marquez, Stephanie Amedeo. 1994. "Distorting the Image of 'Hispanic' Women in Sociology: Problematic Strategies of Presentation in the Introductory Text." *Teaching Sociology* 22:231-36.

McIntosh, Peggy. 1995. "White Privilege and Male Privilege: A Personal Account of Coming to See Correspondences through Work in Women's Studies." Pp. 76-87 in *Race, Class, and Gender: An Anthology,* edited by Margaret Andersen and Patricia Hill Collins. Belmont: Wadsworth.

Omi, Michael, and Howard Winant. 1994. *Racial Formation in the United States: From the 1960s to the 1990s.* London: Routledge.

Reskin, Barbara F. 2003. "Including Mechanisms in Our Models of Ascriptive Inequality." *American Sociological Review.* 68:1-21.

San Juan Jr., E. 2001. "Problems in the Marxist Project of Theorizing Race." Pp. 225-236 in *Racism: Essential Readings,* edited by Ellis Cashmore and James Jennings. London: Sage Publications.

———. 2002. *Racism and Cultural Studies: Critiques of Multiculturalist Ideology and the Politics of Difference.* Durham: Duke University Press.

Stone, Pamela. 1996. "Ghettoized and Marginalized: The Coverage of Racial and Ethnic Groups in Introductory Sociology Texts." *Teaching Sociology* 24:356-63.

Therborn, Goran. 1980. *The Ideology of Power and the Power of Ideology.* London: Verso.

U.S. Census Bureau. 2006. *Statistical Abstract of the United States: 2006*. Washington D.C.: U.S. Government Printing Office.

Van Dijk, Teun A. 1993. *Elite Discourse and Racism*. Newbury Park, CA: Sage Publications.

Westhues, Kenneth. 1991. "Transcending the Textbook World." *Teaching Sociology* 19:87–92.

CHALLENGING RACIAL BATTLE FATIGUE ON HISTORICALLY WHITE CAMPUSES: A CRITICAL RACE EXAMINATION OF RACE-RELATED STRESS

William A. Smith, Tara J. Yosso and Daniel G. Solórzano

> *The young Black reporter looked at me patiently as I paused to gather my thoughts. Noticing that I was clenching my cup, she smiled reassuringly and calmly said, "I know this must be difficult to talk about, but please let me reassure you, my point is to get this out to our readers, to let people know more about what happened, and—" I interrupted, "Well, as I mentioned to you when you contacted me, I don't know exactly what happened, but I do want to make sure that folks know what this man was about. What he was doing. I think the link to what happened is his work—our work." I paused to sip my kava kava herb tea and take my stack of paperwork and notes out of my crocheted bag. Angela, Corky, Huey, and others had warned me about sharing too much information with reporters, but this newspaper had a reputation for serving the Black community in Boston for many years. I hoped I was making the right decision to trust this woman. "Well, Monday, March 6, 1972, was for all intents and purposes just another day ..."*

We open this chapter with a counterstory preview to entice readers to engage in a framework called critical race theory (CRT). CRT draws on many areas of academic scholarship and centers the experiences of People of Color to document voices and knowledges rarely taken into account in traditional academic spaces or mainstream mass media venues. CRT scholarship combines empirical and experiential knowledges, frequently in the form of storytelling, chronicles, or other creative narratives. These counternarratives can often expose traditional educational discourse as racialized, gendered, classed storytelling.

Indeed, traditional stories about race do not seem like stories at all. Such "everyday" narratives perpetuate myths that darker skin and poverty correlate with bad neighborhoods and bad schools. This chapter and counterstory utilize CRT in education to challenge the silences of "race-neutral" storytelling in order to discuss the race-related stress Faculty of Color confront when navigating through historically White universities.

Racial Microaggressions and Racial Battle Fatigue

Racism is structured into the rhythms of everyday life in the United States (Feagin 2000). Pierce (1970:266) defines racism as a "public health and mental health illness" based on the delusion or false belief, in spite of contrary evidence, that innate inferiority correlates with dark skin color. He argues that in examining racism "... one must not look for the gross and obvious. The subtle, cumulative miniassault is the substance of today's racism ..." (Pierce 1974:516). He further describes these assaults as racial microaggressions. In adapting Pierce's (1970, 1974, 1980, 1989, 1995) work, we define racial microaggressions as 1) subtle verbal and nonverbal insults directed at People of Color, often automatically or unconsciously; 2) layered insults, based on one's race, gender, class, sexuality, language, immigration status, phenotype, accent, or surname; and 3) cumulative insults, which cause unnecessary stress to People of Color while privileging Whites. Critical race scholars have expanded on Pierce's research to address how People of Color are experiencing and responding to racial microaggressions within and beyond the academy. For example, Carroll (1998) extends Pierce's work to describe that being Black in the U.S. means living in a society permeated by mundane and extreme racism and punctuated by incessant microaggressions. She finds that African Americans are faced with mundane extreme environmental stress—MEES. William Smith (2004a, 2004b) focuses on the stress aspects of racism, explaining that constant exposure to MEES reveals the cumulative effect of racial microaggressions. He argues that the stress associated with racial microaggressions causes African Americans to experience various forms of mental, emotional, and physical strain—racial battle fatigue.

The stress ensuing from racism and racial microaggressions leads People of Color to exhibit various psychophysiological symptoms, including suppressed immunity and increased sickness, tension headaches, trembling and jumpiness, chronic pain in healed injuries, elevated blood pressure, and a pounding heart beat. Likewise, in anticipation of a racial conflict, People of Color may experience rapid breathing, an upset stomach, frequent diarrhea or urination. Other symptoms of racial battle fatigue include constant anxiety, ulcer, increased swearing or complaining, insomnia or sleep broken by haunting conflict-specific dreams, rapid mood swings, difficulty thinking or speaking coherently, and emotional and social withdrawal in response to racial microaggressions or while in environments of mundane racial stressors. Ultimately, these symptoms may lead to People of Color losing confidence in themselves, questioning their life's work or even their life's worth.

Indeed, constantly battling racial stress takes a toll on the lives of People of Color. Izard (1972, 1977) documented that African Americans tend to perceive incidents of racism as personal threats, and this leads to an increase in their emotional stress level. Krieger and Sidney (1996) reported that 80% of 1,974 Black women and men experienced racial discrimination and self-reported attempts to respond to unfair treatment, showing that both experiences of discrimination and efforts to respond to unfair treatment were associated with increased blood pressure. Similarly, David Williams, Harold Neighbors, and James Jackson (2003) concluded that perceptions of discrimination appear to induce physiological and psychological arousal. Systematic exposures to such psychosocial stressors may have long-term health consequences.

Experiencing racial discrimination as a stressful life event can reduce one's personal sense of control and elicit feelings of loss, ambiguity, strain, frustration, and injustice. Smith (2004a) concluded that this activates a stress-response system, originally evolved for responding to acute physical and emotional emergencies. However, given the pervasiveness of racism in U.S. society and its institutions, this emergency stress-response system, is constantly "switched on" to cope with chronic racial microaggressions (and macroaggressions).

The accumulative stress from racial microaggressions produces racial battle fatigue. The stress of unavoidable front-line racial battles in historically White spaces leads to People of Color feeling mentally, emotionally, and physically drained. The stress from racial microaggressions can become lethal when the accumulation of physiological symptoms of racial battle fatigue are untreated, unnoticed, misdiagnosed, or personally dismissed. Our critical race counternarrative, which follows, acknowledges experiences with and responses to racial microaggressions and racial battle fatigue reported by Faculty of Color in predominately White institutions.

Critical Race Theory (CRT)

CRT provides a useful tool to identify, analyze, and challenge racism in education and society. Through a CRT lens, the ongoing racism on college and university campuses comes into focus, revealing that race conditions have not improved significantly as we move further into the 21st century as compared with reports from the racially tumultuous 1960s (Carroll 1998; Smith, Altbach, and Lomotey 2002). Faculty and Students of Color must cope with daily incidents of racial microaggressions from White students, faculty and, administrators as they daily navigate institutions developed to benefit Whites (Bonilla-Silva and Forman 2000; Bowman and Smith 2002; Ladson-Billings 1996; Smith 2004a, 2004b, 2004c; Solórzano, Ceja, and Yosso 2000).

Originating in schools of law, the critical race movement seeks to account for the role of race and racism in the U.S. and to challenge the many forms of racism and its intersections with other forms of subordination such as gender and class (Delgado 1995b). Latina/Latino critical race theorists have expanded the CRT framework in law to discuss issues of subordination on the basis of immigration status, culture, language, and sexuality (Arriola 1997; Espinoza 1998). Similarly, a multiracial coalition of scholars have worked since at least the mid-1990s to extend CRT to the field of education and implement its tenets into educational research, pedagogy, curriculum, and policy (Ladson-Billings and Tate 1995; Lynn, Yosso, Solórzano, and Parker 2002; Solórzano 1997, 1998; Solórzano and Delgado Bernal 2001; Tate 1994, 1997).

Acknowledging CRT's roots in scholarly traditions such as ethnic studies, U.S./third-world feminisms, Marxism/neoMarxism, cultural nationalism, internal colonialism, and critical legal studies, Daniel Solórzano (1997) identified at least five tenets shared by CRT scholarship. These tenets acknowledge the critical strengths of other scholarly traditions while they reveal, critique, and address some of these frameworks' blind spots (e.g., Marxisms' blind spots regarding race and gender, cultural nationalisms' blind spots on gender, class, and sexuality). The basic perspectives, research methods, and pedagogy of CRT in education learn from these academic and community traditions.

- *The intercentricity of race and racism.* CRT starts from the premise that race and racism are endemic and permanent in U.S. society (Bell 1987) and asserts that racism intersects with forms of subordination based on gender, class, sexuality, language, culture, immigrant status, phenotype, accent, and surname (see Espinoza 1998).
- *The challenge to dominant ideology.* CRT in education challenges claims of objectivity, meritocracy, color blindness, race neutrality, and equal opportunity and asserts that these claims act as a

camouflage for the self-interest, power, and privilege of dominant groups in U.S. society (see Solórzano 1997).
- *The commitment to social justice.* CRT seeks to advance a social justice agenda. Such a goal emphasizes that the larger purpose of educational research, teaching, and policy is the transformation of society through the empowerment of oppressed groups (see Solórzano and Delgado Bernal 2001).
- *The centrality of experiential knowledge.* CRT recognizes that the experiential knowledge of People of Color is legitimate, appropriate, and critical to understanding, analyzing, and teaching about racial subordination. CRT explicitly listens to the lived experiences of People of Color through counterstorytelling methods such as family histories, biographies, scenarios, parables, *cuentos* (stories), *testimonios, dichos* (proverbs), chronicles, and narratives (see Olivas 1990).
- *The interdisciplinary perspective.* CRT challenges traditional mainstream frameworks by analyzing racism, classism, sexism, and homophobia in historical and interdisciplinary terms (see Delgado 1984, 1992).

Composite Counterstorytelling

Although CRT scholarship arguably serves counternarrative functions in general, some scholars seek to be more explicit in presenting their research through the genre of storytelling. There are at least three types of such counterstories evidenced in the CRT literature: autobiographical (e.g., Aguirre 2000; Williams 1991), biographical (e.g., Olivas 1990), and multimethod/composite (e.g., Bell 1987, 1992, 1996; Delgado 1995a, 1996, 1999, 2003a, 2003b; Yosso 2006). For our purposes, we focus on multimethod/composite stories. Composite counternarratives draw on multiple forms of "data" to recount the racialized, sexualized, classed experiences of faculty and students of color (see Delgado Bernal 1998).

The counterstory below draws on findings from various research projects to address the experiences and responses of Faculty of Color to the pervasiveness of racism and racial battle fatigue in and around college and university campuses. Methodologically, we started by finding and unearthing sources of data. Our first form of "data" came from primary sources, namely interviews with African Americans, primarily professors, at universities across the country.

Next, we analyzed secondary data from social science and humanities scholarship, addressing experiences with and responses to racism in higher education (e.g., Allen and Solórzano 2001; Bonilla-Silva and Forman 2000; Ladson-Billings 1996; Willie and Sanford 1995). In sifting through this literature, we drew connections with the interview data and uncovered the concepts of racial microaggressions (Pierce 1970, 1974, 1980, 1989, 1995; Solórzano 1998; Solórzano, Ceja, and Yosso 2000) and resilience (e.g., Yosso 2006). To recover and recount the story evidenced in the patterns and themes of the data, we added a final source of data—our own professional and personal experiences.[1] This included our individual reflections as well as the multiple voices of family, friends, colleagues, and acquaintances. Such experiential knowledge echoed the related research literature and the interview findings, which helped us to better understand the relationship between microaggressions, stress responses, and resistance (Clark, Anderson, Clark, and Williams 1999; Prillerman, Myers, and Smedley 1989; Smith 2004a, 2004b, 2004c; Solórzano and Delgado Bernal 2001).

Once we compiled, examined, and analyzed these various sources of data, we created composite characters to help tell the story. We attempted to engage these characters in a real and critical dialogue about our data from the interviews, related literature, and personal/professional experiences. As such, the characters personify our research and our analysis process. In the tradition of Du Bois (1920) and Freire (1973), the dialogue emerged between the characters much like our own discussions in this process emerged—through sharing, listening, challenging, and reflecting. We differentiate our work from that of fictional storytelling. Certainly there are elements of fiction in the story, but the "composite" characters are grounded in real-life experiences, actual empirical data, and contextualized in social situations that are also grounded in real life, not fiction.

Introducing the Characters and Setting the Scene

We tell this counterstory from the perspective of a composite character named Alice Canon, a professor of psychiatry at the University of

---

[1] We acknowledge that our own racialized, gendered, and classed experiences inform this counterstory. We do not purport to be neutral or objective in the process of sifting through the data and finding themes and patterns.

California–Los Angeles. As part of an interview with a reporter from a Black community newspaper, Alice is reflecting on her work with her colleague, Chet Toboa, a professor of psychiatry and education at Harvard University. Professor Toboa disappeared about two years ago, in 1972, and this is one of several trips Alice has made back to Boston. She is continuing to conduct what was a collaborative research project about the experiences of Faculty of Color in historically White colleges and universities[2].

Guided by CRT's five tenets and the concepts of racial microaggressions and racial battle fatigue, this counterstory invites the reader to approach the counterstory as a pedagogical and empirical case study: to listen for the story's points and reflect on how these points compare with her or his own version of reality (however conceived). We listen in to Professor Canon's interview with a newspaper reporter as she recounts the events preceding the disappearance of Dr. Chet Toboa.

The Supposed Scandal: Questions About Chet's Disappearance

"You probably have read the official versions of this scandal, but the story begins well before Chet went 'missing.'" The reporter wasn't quite convinced, so I showed her a few old newspaper clippings. "It was a scandal that White folks couldn't get enough of for a while."

I showed her the Sunday, April 9, 1972, *Boston Globe* article with the headline of "Harvard Professor Missing." The *Chicago Defender* newspaper and *Jet* and *Ebony* magazines each ran front-page cover stories, under the headlines of, respectively, "Harvard Yard Suspected of Murder"; "1922 or 1972? The Professional Lynching of a Black Professor"; and "The Academic Klan: Powerful Organizations Suspected of Murdering Distinguished Black Professor."[3] I looked up from the clippings and sarcastically stated, "Most of those in the academic, medical, social science, and Black communities knew this was a scandal as soon

---

[2] We use historically White institutions instead of predominantly White institutions to distinguish that the gross numbers or percentages of White students have less to do with who the majority populations than it does with the historical and contemporary racial infrastructure that is in place, the current campus racial culture and ecology, and how these modern day institutions still benefit Whites at the expense of Blacks and other Groups of Color.

[3] While the early 1970s were rife with very real racial violence and scandalous headlines, the headlines listed here are fictitious.

as the word got out. We were asking questions that no one could answer in their superficial scandal headlines: Was it just the typical race-related hatred for Blacks in this hostile era? Was it Professor Toboa's standing up against some of the most powerful institutions in the country? Was it his refusal to accept tenure if his academic department did not hire another minority professor? Was it his role in starting Black professional organizations? None of us had answers, but opinions were endless for how this terrible and unexpected situation occurred."

"Of course there were the usual racialized assumptions. Many Whites claimed that this had nothing to do with race. Since Chet was a well-respected Harvard professor whose research was international in scope, some felt the only possible explanation was an international conspiracy led by the Soviet Union. Other Whites went as far as to suggest that it was spontaneous human combustion that resulted in his disappearance. When they were pushed further on this point to explain what happened to the ashes, they suggested 'the janitor must have swept them up not knowing what they were.' I always thought that was the funniest theory. Most Blacks, Chicanos, and Puerto Ricans pointed to some combination of racial conspiracies. Some suggested that orders were handed down from President Nixon to the FBI and J. Edgar Hoover, as one of the director's last assignments before dying in May of that year." I could see the reporter wanted to hear my theory, so I smiled reassuringly and explained, "As you probably know, Chet and I are first cousins and we basically grew up together like brother and sister. My theory isn't so over-dramatic. But let me tell you about our research because I think that's what your readers will really dig."

Alice's Theory About the Disappearance: Introducing a Racialized Research Agenda

"As I mentioned, March 6, 1972, was a relatively ordinary day, at least in Los Angeles. I was back in California, teaching a clinical seminar course and it was about 64 degrees with blue skies. The meeting took place in New York where it was slightly colder than usual. It dipped down to 33 degrees that night when Chet was seen watching Wilt 'The Stilt' Chamberlain assist the Los Angeles Lakers in a win against Willis Reed and his New York Knicks. He attended with Bumpy Johnson, a longtime friend who most folks thought of as a notorious Harlem gangster. Chet and Bumpy met years before when Bumpy gave a generous donation to our aunt who lived in South Carolina. She had been out of work and struggling to make ends meet after some jealously angry White men burned down her modest but successful business. The three White men fingered for the arson mysteriously came up missing, never to be seen or heard from again. Many Black folk suspected Bumpy had something to do with it since he was in Charleston visiting shortly after the situation occurred, but—with a certain sense of pride—no one ever said an accusatory word. I think Bumpy actually inspired some of Chet's work. What a case study in racism, that Bumpy. Like too many young Black brothers subjected to daily interpersonal and institutionalized racism, Bumpy's initial responses of anger and resentment led to his incarceration for a large part of his youth. Bumpy in turn admired Chet, who had also grown up in Harlem, but had channeled his anger to challenge racism through education and participation in the civil rights movement. Anyway, Bumpy and Chet ended up seeing one of Wilt's last professional basketball games and LA beat New York." I smiled as I held up a picture of me around that time period and another of Chet. The reporter commented that it must have been quite a shock for folks to see a research team made up of a woman with an Afro and multicolored shawl and a man in a three-piece gray suit, let alone an academic with a gangster like Bumpy Johnson. I responded that the clothes don't make the man, and if anything, Chet's dapper style was not too different from Bumpy's. If she only knew, I mused to myself, remembering that some of my friends had crushes on Chet when we were finishing ninth grade and he was the 6'4" zoot-suit-wearing high school valedictorian.

I explained that Chet and I were developing a U.S. minority mental health research agenda. As professors and clinicians of psychiatry, we had documented the health effects of minorities living and working in extreme conditions or dealing with the daily effects of racism. We had become increasingly concerned with the mental and physiological health outcomes of Blacks, Chicanos, and Puerto Ricans, especially as they were becoming "integrated" into historically White spaces and institutions. Chet also kept a journal of his private therapy sessions as well as his personal conversations with other Black, Chicano, and Puerto Rican professionals, professors, students, and other community members about what he labeled as their experiences with "racial microaggressions." I pulled out one of Chet's earlier articles and read aloud: "Chet defined racial microaggressions 'as subtle, innocuous, preconscious, or (un)conscious degradations and putdowns, often kinetic but capable of being verbal and/or kinetic, and/or purposefully malicious or violent."[4]

I continued speaking, "So we were able to trace a rise in a new form of stress-related psychological and physiological disease that resulted from constant experiences with racial microaggressions. Chet's preliminary diagnosis of the cumulative effects of racial microaggressions was 'racial battle fatigue.' Unlike typical stress, racial battle fatigue referred to the cumulative result of a natural race-related stress response to distressing mental and emotional conditions. These conditions emerged from constantly facing racially dismissive, demeaning, insensitive and/or hostile racial environments and individuals. Chet found a pattern that showed that this race-related stress kills gradually and stealthily. It takes an unending toll through various psychosomatic, physical ailments, such as hypertension and poor health attitudes and behaviors that combine to give minorities a morbidity and mortality profile similar to those living in the developing world rather than in the industrialized world." The reporter's raised eyebrow indicated she was interested in racial battle fatigue and whether it was connected to Chet's disappearance. I didn't want to let her know that I wondered the same thing myself. My research with Chet initially began after a long conversation during a family reunion about the source of some of my physical ailments and Chet's high stress levels.

Revealing Experiences of Racial Microaggressions and Symptoms of Racial Battle Fatigue at the Black Faculty Association Meeting: Friday, February 4, 1972

"So the month before the March 6th meeting, Chet was preparing to address the East Coast Black Faculty Association in Mather Hall at Harvard University. As you may know, Mather Hall was named after Increase Mather, who was part of the upper-crust Boston slave owning society and a Harvard-educated preacher. He also presided over Harvard for 16 years as its sixth president (1685–1701). The association held its meetings in Mather Hall to remind them that within the institutional fabric of Harvard and outside of its campus, this multi-headed monster of racism and elitism was ever present, despite their laudable achievements. This special meeting was called to provide an update on the developments toward addressing the growing concerns

---

[4] See Pierce (1975, 1995).

about the racial violence aimed at Black faculty and students at Harvard, as well as other schools across the east coast and the country. In addition, Chet and I wanted to seek further input on the impending March 6th meeting. Chet was the current chair of the association."

I paused and showed the reporter that I had the actual transcriptions of association meetings because they had been trying out a new system where they audiotaped their meetings and had a volunteer write up the minutes at a later date. I didn't tell her that in retrospect I suspected that one of the newer association members was an FBI informant and he had suggested the audiotaping. Initially, I had told Chet it was odd, but he didn't seem too worried.

As I continued, I referred to the transcripts. "The Sergeant at Arms called the special meeting to order and Dr. Coleman, a Black male history professor interrupted and said, "Get on with it, Jesse. We know why we're here." I smiled thinking about how informal this formal group of Black scholars could be.

"And then Chet, who was always known to be courteous despite the circumstances, welcomed everyone and explained who would be at the meeting on the 6th. He listed the senior level administrators from each of the universities across the country that had been invited and who had ongoing campus racial unrest, including Harvard, Cornell University, University of Michigan, University of California–Berkeley, and University of California–Los Angeles. He also noted that key members from the Department of Health, Education, and Welfare (HEW), would be there. HEW is a federal office that has broad popular support for unprecedented amounts of federal funds that are allocated for social programs; so many people were pleased they accepted the invitation. The list also included the American Council on Education, which is the major coordinating body for all the nation's higher education institutions; the National Institute of Mental Health, which has a major budget to fund research projects, new service initiatives, and train mental health professionals; the American Psychological Association, our professional organization that has significant influence on the national practice of psychiatry; and the American Board of Psychiatry and Neurology, which awards the credentials of specialist psychiatrists after the successful completion of its examination."

"Now Chet turned it over to me because even though he was scheduled to be the main presenter Monday the 6th, I had done most of the groundwork in organizing the meeting. We were trying to be strategic and we knew that folks would probably respond more positively to a

Black man, like you said, in a three piece suit rather than a Black woman with an Afro and a reputation for being a rebel-rouser and hanging out with Angela Davis, 'Corky' Gonzalez, Dolores Huerta, Huey P. Newton, Cesar Chavez, Kathleen Cleaver, Stokely Carmichael—who was calling himself Kwame Ture at this point—Carmen Valentin, and Jim Brown, the former NFL fullback. Anyway, I outlined the six major points we prepared for the meeting and Chet passed out mimeograph copies while I spoke. I'll read here my words:

> As some of you may know, Professor Toboa and I have been working together for a few years, following up on our epidemiological findings, which suggest that a positive correlation exists between increased White-Black, White-Chicano, and White-Puerto Rican social integration and racial microaggressions. With each civil rights effort, or with each attempt at breaking down barriers of racial segregation in historically White spaces, minority health seems to suffer. We have identified that this experience of dealing with constant racial microaggressions leads to a phenomena we are calling racial battle fatigue. These negative racial events and life crises clearly contribute to minorities' higher rates of affective disorders. Unfortunately, traditional research and health care practices inappropriately focuses exclusively on poor diets, culture, poverty, and inadequate education as the source of blame in Black and Brown poorer physical health statistics.

"And here," I noted, "a colleague raised her hand and asked, 'Am I understanding correctly that this work is based on the premise that staying at the microsocial, proximal level of analysis offers a better prospect of obtaining ecologically valid and practical knowledge about racial microaggressions, emotions, coping strategies, and the racial battle fatigue phenomena?' Chet responded, 'Yes. However, I believe researchers must be free to choose which approach they want to use, proximal or distal, just as it is appropriate to ask which approach provides more useful information and in-depth analysis.'"

I explained to the reporter that many of our colleagues knew the growing bias toward quantitative, large-scale research projects when it came to swaying the interests of major government funders. Then I continued, "These transcripts don't really pick up on the emotion of the room, but I remember pretty clearly. It was quite tense and so, at first, I emphasized a few words sarcastically to bring a little humor to the situation. I said,

> We believe that each of these *leading* and *prestigious* institutions'—and Chet looked at me sideways to remind me that some of our colleagues might not appreciate that humor, so I continued on in a more serious

tone. "These institutions and organizations need to 1) be more cognizant of the needs and interests of minorities; 2) elevate minorities in the hierarchy of each institution; 3) be held responsible for the abundance of unsophisticated, anti-intellectual, racist, and sexist scholarship funded, produced, and rewarded in these institutions; 4) acknowledge that racism and White resistance to integration should be seen as a public health crisis for the stress, violence, and terror it inflicts on the aggrieved; 5) consider classifying racist behaviors as a psychological disorder in the *Diagnostic and Statistical Manual of Mental Disorders*; and 6) eliminate the homosexual classification that considers homosexuality as a physical disease, a 'third sex,' or a psychological aberration.

I looked up from the transcript and explained, "That last statement caused a mild disturbance in the room. People began to whisper to each other their concern about grouping racism with homosexuality. A young conservative Black economics professor, Gleason Golightly,[5] stood up to make his objections clearly known for the record." I turned back to reading the transcriptions: "Professor Golightly said,

> So what you are telling us is that for the purposes of discrimination, sexual orientation—or, more accurately, sexual behavior—must be treated like race. Do you really think that is a legitimate claim? When I got up this morning I was a Black man. When I drove my car through South Boston and was stopped, it was because I was a Black man. When I go to bed tonight, I will still be a Black man. If we are going to treat sexual orientation and race the same, then what you are saying is sexual orientation—read: behavior—is like race, a condition beyond the individual's control. If you want us, or this group that you will be addressing next month, to accept this kind of reasoning, then why should we stop at this form of sexual passion? If we're going to ask for special considerations for homosexuals, shouldn't everybody else's irrepressible sexual orientations be protected? Shouldn't adulterers, pedophiles, rapists, and other sorts of sexual aberrants be entitled to the same protections?

I sat back in my chair and said, "The room erupted after Golightly finished his diatribe. Whatever discomforts association members may have felt about this issue were replaced with even more contempt for Golightly's message and him as the messenger. Golightly's positions

---

[5] We humbly and gratefully borrow the character of Professor Gleason Golightly from Chapter 9 of Bell (1992). Such a conservative "minority" viewpoint upholds White privilege by blindly clinging to the majoritarian story while dismissing the lived reality of People of Color. Although Whites most often tell majoritarian stories, People of Color often buy into and even tell majoritarian stories. Being a "minority" majoritarian storyteller such as Golightly often means receiving benefits provided by those with racial, gender, and/or class privilege.

usually had an adverse effect for swaying people his way. This was also true for the more conservative Blacks who appeared moderate in comparison. The Sergeant at Arms had to call the room to order."

"Now I could never really hide my disdain for Golightly, but I was always cordial. So I spoke up, and the transcripts actually caught me here. I'd been doing this for years; and usually only if you were sitting very close to me would you hear it. I said, 'Look here, 'Not likely,' I am not fully comfortable with including this as part of our proposal but for very different reasons than yours. What I do understand is that if we allow these organizations to continue to mistreat and misrepresent one group, then Blacks will never be free." I told the reporter that at this point the majority of the room rose to their feet to applaud my comments, much to Golightly's chagrin.

I referred back to the transcripts and explained, "Chet began to talk over the ovation to bring order to the room and said, 'I will briefly try to answer part of Professor Golightly's question and show the connection we are trying to draw.' Chet's strategy was not to change Golightly's name, but to stare him down as he challenged his reactionary comments. Chet looked right at Golightly and said, 'Many psychiatrists, psychologists, ministers, priests, rabbis and even professors believe that homosexuality is a curable condition. However, the various 'cures' they propose are highly offensive and perilous, including castration, hypnosis, nausea producing drugs, electric shock, brain surgery, breast amputations, and aversion therapy. This is no different than the ideology held by the physician Sam Cartwright, who believed that Blacks had 'drapetomania' and 'dysaesthia aethiopis' which justified our enslavement.'"[6]

"Then Chet addressed the rest of the room, using his fingers to infer quotation marks over the questionable words in these racist theories: 'Cartwright also theorized that the Black skin of Afro-Americans in conjunction with a deficiency of red blood cells led to smaller brain sizes in Blacks, which resulted in both less intelligence and lower morals. The 'cure' for the first disease was 'whipping the devil out of them' to prevent them from 'their crazy desire to runaway from slavery.' Cartwright believed that the second disease caused a slave to refuse to work and the 'cure' was to give the slaves harder work to stimulate the blood to the brain and freeing them from their infliction.

---

[6] See Citizens Commission on Human Rights (1995).

Even the so-called father of American psychiatry and one of the 'founding fathers' of this country, Benjamin Rush, believed that the only 'cure' for Blacks would be when our skin color turns White. This is why he and others believed that Blacks and Whites should always be segregated from one another. What we are witnessing today are the modern forms of these ideologies."[7]

The reporter shook her head in disgust. I described the silence in the room after Chet's statement. "He pretty much put any lingering doubts about whether we were on the right track to rest, but an awkward silence and depression began to cover the room, so I spoke up and told them, 'Look, if we can convince these powerful organizations about the errors of their ways and the troubles ahead, then we can be more effective in influencing national policies and practice about the health consequences of minorities fighting against racism.'"

I paused and explained to the reporter that through our interviews over the years, Chet and I had collected more than 300 personal statements from minority professors across the country in varying fields. So we put up on the overhead projector the major themes we had found so far and asked the association members to think about whether their experiences fit into those themes or if we were any missing patterns that should be added. As I read a few examples of faculty experiences with racial microaggressions, I also noted the psychophysiological symptoms as each person had described them.

A Black male philosophy professor began the discussion about the pattern of racialized classroom experiences. This older man explained that his wife was concerned because he had been complaining much more than he had in the past and he began swearing and just seemed to be withdrawing both emotionally and socially. He explained,

> This is a very sensitive area for me. You might guess correctly that there are not many Black philosophy professors. So I spend a lot of time sharing my struggles with Black professors in other fields and their struggles are all the same. In spite of our efforts to demonstrate competency, Black professors are challenged more on our intellectual authority than our White counterparts. In most of these challenges, students question our knowledge directly or indirectly in a way that is inappropriate or disrespectful. These challenges might include arguments on basic points of the discipline. For example, students might argue that the sociological imagination is not defined as I defined it. They might question the

---

[7] See Citizens Commission on Human Rights (1995).

validity of lecture material or use more indirect forms of resistance. For instance, this particular White student simply thought he knew everything and that he certainly couldn't learn anything from me. He went so far as to say, when I was trying to explain something, "That's wrong, that's just wrong, that's not true." This is very, very difficult because you can't go off on him because you've got to be respectful and you've got to be this professional person, but it's very, very hurtful, particularly from someone who was not an excellent student.

The young reporter nodded as if she heard something familiar in the statement. I continued reading the examples. "Here's a Black female developmental psychologist who had been experiencing tension backaches and elevated blood pressure and spoke about constant microaggressions in the classroom. She said,

> Our White colleagues do not understand how our classroom experiences qualitatively differ from theirs. White students expect the traditional hierarchy of society to prevail in the class. That is, White male on the top, and Black woman on the bottom. And they can't get ready for the fact that a Black woman is teaching this class! And that the White males are not in charge. ... I think that if I were White, that I wouldn't have to go through those sorts of things in my classroom ... but at every turn I have to remind students that I am the professor. I'm not just the instructor ... I have a Ph.D. ... I have to tell students, "Look. I graduated summa cum laude; I got two master's degrees and my PhD. ... I published these books and these articles, blah, blah, blah," to let them know that I may be Black, but what you think about in terms of what it means to be Black is not necessarily what I am, if it's a negative perception ... being uneducated and being illiterate and not able to think and basically being an affirmative action kind of a person. So those are the kinds of things that I think make my job more difficult. Much more difficult than White professors. And it's unfortunate that the so-called standardized evaluation process that we have been using in colleges and universities does not take these things into consideration. In fact, if you raise the subject, the college will look at you like you're crazy because they don't deal with that. And they're actually being honest because they don't understand the sheer level of complexity on the part of the professor and the student in dealing with these kinds of issues. So I'm not blaming my colleagues. I'm just saying they're really very ignorant. Ignorant about what goes on in my classes and the extent to which I have to use measures above and beyond what they have to use to even survive in the classroom.

The reporter continued to nod in agreement and I read one more example of classroom experiences with microaggressions. "This next one is a Black female chemistry professor. This very accomplished woman had little confidence in her university and maintained even less confidence in herself. She shared a pretty blatant example with us."

I found my place in the transcript and began to read remembering vividly the pained expression on this woman's face as she shared this incident with us. "She said,

> The first time I walked as an instructor into a classroom in a large research university, I immediately experienced such a racially stressful event. I wrote my name on the board, turned around, and, to my utter dismay, a White male student was staring at me with contempt and holding up his middle finger to me. "Can this be happening to me?" I asked myself. I began my lecture, but I was having an out-of-body experience as the young man continued to stare at me in contempt, still "shooting a bird" until, finally, I could no longer pretend that this was not happening. So I walked slowly toward him and deliberately stared him straight in the eye as I lectured. It was the longest walk … but it would be one that I would repeat many times in the years to come, in different circumstances.

I flipped through the next few pages of the transcription to make sure I was staying on track. I continued, "A few of the professors also shared their experiences that follow in with the theme of a subtle yet stunning and cumulative nature of racial microaggressions. And these here certainly suggest that the cumulative effect of microaggressions is racial battle fatigue. For example, a Black male psychiatry professor who admitted to having sleep broken by haunting conflict-specific dreams said,

> What is it like to be a Black person in White America today? One step from suicide! The psychological warfare games that we have to play everyday just to survive. We have to be one way in our communities and one way in the workplace or in the business sector. We can never be ourselves all around. I think that may be a given for all people, but us particularly; it's really a mental health problem. It's a wonder we haven't all gone out and killed somebody or killed ourselves.

I shared one last example of the overall cumulative effect of racial microaggressions with the reporter. "A Black male psychiatry professor reporting insomnia and rapid breathing in anticipation of conflict, explained,

> If you can think of the mind as having 100 ergs of energy, and the average man uses 50% of this energy dealing with the everyday problems of the world—just general kinds of things—then he has 50% more to do creative kinds of things that he wants to do. That's a White person. Now, a Black person also has 100 ergs. He uses 50% the same way a White man does, dealing with what the White man has to deal with, so he has 50% left. But he uses 25% fighting being Black, with all the problems of being Black in America and what it means.

"And then I told the faculty, 'So that's what brings us to you today, to ask humbly if you would share with us some of your stories so we can add your voices to the testimony we give next month. We would like for these folks to hear your story about the racial attacks—or what we call racial microaggressions—you may have had to endure just trying to be a Black professor on a White campus." I paused from reading the transcript and shared with the reporter the inspiring scene that followed. "One after another, each professor in the room stood up to share stories of the racial microaggressions they faced on and around historically White campuses. We could see as we had read the examples out loud that these professors were realizing they were no longer struggling with incidents and symptoms of racial battle fatigue in isolation, now they had a name for their pain. Although some were hesitant to share their psychophysiological symptoms in that large group setting, they noted that our dataset reflected their own experiences and remarked that our thematic analysis had reached saturation. Even Golightly conceded to experiencing racial microaggressions. Although he tried to dismiss their effect on his personhood, I noticed he tended to yawn and demonstrate extreme fatigue after drinking multiple cups of Black coffee."

I smiled at the ever-patient reporter and said, "So there it is. The meeting adjourned and each person stayed until they shared their experiences. Chet was frustrated at the multiple experiences of racism his colleagues had been subjected to, but he didn't let too much of this anger show. Instead, he assured them that their voices would be heard at the meeting Monday the 6th. Many expressed doubt as we headed off campus whether folks from the organizations and universities would really listen, but they thanked me for organizing the meeting and they thanked Chet in advance for bringing their stories and this research to such a forum.

Will Institutions Listen to and Learn From Effects of Racism? Waiting for an Update: April 7, 1972

So I left a message for Chet the morning of Friday, April 7th, to let him know I had arrived safely from my red-eye flight from California and that I'd see him at the association meeting shortly. I was anxious to hear about any recent reports stemming from the meeting. I didn't tell the reporter that it was strange that he hadn't called to give me an update earlier, but I didn't think much of it because I knew he believed his university phone and perhaps his home phone had been wiretapped. I also knew Chet usually volunteered at the hospital a few days a month and also visited the prison hospital on occasion, so I figured he may have been busy. He would often remind me of how he would much rather be involved in clinical work, challenging racism as a kind of street therapist who helped young Black youth learn to recognize and respond to racial microaggressions before racism took its toll on their mental and physical health.[8]

I described to the reporter that the association meeting was scheduled for every first Friday of the month while school was in session. "So since we hadn't had our usual meeting in March, everyone was in attendance for that April 7th meeting. Most of us assumed Chet would be on time in one of his customary three-piece Brooks Brothers suits and his camel brown Allen-Edmonds' shoes, with his calming and reassuring smile despite how grave the circumstances. By the time I got to Mather Hall at 11:50 a.m., the room was packed. Since no one had heard from Chet since last Wednesday, members thought that he had been planning something special in response to what was rumored to be disappointing news. At noon, the Sergeant at Arms called the meeting to order but Chet did not show."

The reporter asked me to pause briefly so she could start a new tape. I took the opportunity to drink some tea as I noted to myself that recounting the story today was the first time that a lump in my throat had not developed. My emotions had grown numb over the years thinking about the racial microaggressions that I have continuously experienced. But I have always gotten exceptionally angry when I think about how Chet was treated.

Once the new tape was recording, I continued, "After waiting for 20 minutes we decided to check his office. Several colleagues volunteered to join me and walk across campus to check on him. As we approached his building, the Cambridge police met us in the hallway. They were looking for Chet's office. One of the Harvard faculty members said that we were on our way to get him for a meeting and inquired what was wrong. An officer indicated that a missing person's report had been filed and they were sent to investigate Dr. Toboa's whereabouts. By this time there's almost a mob of folks heading up to Chet's office. And of course there was no elevator in that building, so we were

---

[8] See Pierce (1970).

all crammed together going up the stairs to the third floor! When we got there, the door was wide open. On his desk was an opened envelope, with a return address labeled "Committee on Campus and Community Culture and Climate." We learned this letter was delivered via certified mail Tuesday, April 4th, but there was no letter to be found. Instead, there was a note written on the back of the envelope, in what looked to be Chet's writing. It referred to Supreme Court Justice Brown's opinion in the *Plessy v. Ferguson* case of 1896 and simply read: 'It is only in Black people's minds that racial conditions in America are oppressive.'"[9]

I excused myself momentarily to refill my mug with hot water and searched through my kava kava bag for another herb tea as the young reporter looked at the writing on the empty envelope, still sealed in the police protective covering. I brushed away a few tears and I stirred some honey into my tea, lost in my thoughts for a moment before I sat back at the table and continued, "Not much is really known about what happened to Chet. The department secretary reportedly saw him when he picked up his mail earlier that day. No one saw him leave his office or the building, even though folks were there until late in the evening."

"Noticing that there were various awards and certificates strewn all over the floor, the police asked us not to touch anything, and I think that's what caused us to finally start getting scared that something may have happened to Chet. So we were pretty much silent, almost frozen with fear and concern, but you know, right then in the silence of the moment, we heard Chet's little transistor radio playing on the shelf." I closed my eyes and began to sing softly the song that was playing: "People get ready there's a train a comin' Don't need no baggage, you just get on board" I opened my eyes and saw a blank stare from the young reporter, so I explained that Curtis Mayfield and the Impressions recorded "People Get Ready" in 1965. The song symbolically described how people felt in the midst of the civil rights movement, that there was a train coming, that history was moving with a sense of inevitability. I continued singing:

> "People get ready for the train to Jordan
> Picking up passengers coast to coast

---

[9] We paraphrase Justice Brown's majority opinion of the court in *Plessy v. Ferguson*, 163 U.S. 537, 538 (1896

Faith is the key, open the doors and board 'em
There's hope for all those that love Him most"

I paused again to explain that the song goes on from there to issue a warning, and I sang this part to the young reporter as well:

"There ain't no room for the hopeless sinner
Who would hurt all mankind just to save his own
Have pity on those whose chances grow thinner
For there's no hiding place from the Kingdom's throne."

I smiled thinking that since this interview was being recorded; someday my singing might become part of an FBI file, as seemed to be the trend in the last few years with many of my politically active friends. Realizing the reporter was waiting for me to continue, I explained, "Well, as you might imagine, the police quickly regained their composure and finished digging around his office, asking each of us to 'stay in touch.' I walked with the other faculty back to Mather Hall and broke the news to the larger group that Chet had gone missing, and many of us were brought in for questioning over the next few weeks."

The reporter thanked me for my time and confirmed my summer contact information for possible follow-up questions. She noted that this would probably be a series of articles. She hadn't connected the date Chet received the certified letter, April 4th, with the anniversary of the assassination of Martin Luther King, Jr., and I was sure that would be a future follow-up question. Both Dr. King and Dr. Toboa were about nonviolent, peaceful resolutions. Both had visions of a better condition for *all* people. Each tried to break down the same system, which took an ultimate toll on each of their lives. I had learned not to worry too much about such ironies, but deep down, I knew it was no coincidence.

Alice's Epilogue

I walked to a small campus cafeteria to grab a quick bite before heading to the airport. The interview had gone longer than I anticipated. Out of the corner of my eye I saw a familiar face across the yard. It was the janitor I had met in Chet's building. I thought back to when the university decided to move another professor into Chet's office and asked me to prepare his work for the archives. It had been such a short time since Chet's disappearance, yet the office was almost all cleaned out by the time I got there.

The janitor was sweeping up Chet's office as I arrived. He smiled and tipped his cap. Maybe he recognized my picture from one of Chet's family photos he used to have in his office, I don't know, but he knew who I was immediately. Before leaving me to go through the stack of Chet's papers, the janitor handed me a small book that he said I might find useful. Given the huge task before me, I didn't even open the book until a few hours later. I realized it was Chet's personal journal and I wondered how the janitor came across it and why the police never mentioned it. I flipped through it briefly, stopping at one of the pages titled "I almost killed a White man today." Chet sketched out a scene, which apparently took place at an airport, where a White man verbally accosted him. He had just returned from a trip to McCurdo Base in the Antarctic, where he was studying how military personnel and scientists adapted and survived the stressors of extreme climates after a year of residency. Chet had mentioned some of this early work to me, and how he was comparing the extreme climates of Antarctica with the extreme climates of racism that Blacks had been trying to survive for centuries in the Americas.[10] I sighed, thinking of how Chet must have looked in his full-grown beard, snow shoes in his bag, facing an extreme climate of hostility in the Boston airport terminal. Certainly there have been multiple incidents he described to me where he was belittled in front of colleagues with comments like "When I was talking about those Blacks, I didn't mean you, you're different," or nonverbal exchanges such as being followed at the supermarket or not served at a restaurant. One night he was detained while walking to his apartment near Harvard. Police insisted that he "assume the position" because he "fit the description" of a burglar. I turned the pages to read a more recent journal entry. It was apparently inspired by the poem "Whitey on the moon," by Gil Scott-Heron.[11] Most of the lines had been edited from the original poem.

> Whitey needs more room
>
> Those rats done sent us all to hell, 'cause Whitey needs more room
> Bit my sister then wished her well, 'cause Whitey needs more room
> Can't live in those precious hills, 'cause Whitey needs more room
> Ten years from now still taking pills, 'cause Whitey needs more room

---

[10] See Carroll (1998).
[11] For the original poem, see Scott-Heron (2001).

No relief from the front-line, Black
One step forward 10 steps back
Feel my blood pressure going up
And as if all that crap wasn't enough

Those rats done sent us all to hell, 'cause Whitey needs more room
Bit my sister then wished her well, 'cause Whitey needs more room
Never got our 40 acres and a mule, 'cause Whitey needs more room!
Need national guards just to go to school? Hmm ... only Whitey's in the room!

You know I've just about had my fill of Whitey needing room
I think I'd like to take my shot and send Whitey—Pow! Bang! Zoom!—to the moon.

Thinking back now about that creative entry, I marveled at Chet's multiple hidden talents. For me, the journal was a gentle reminder that things are never quite what they seem. I waved at the janitor, hoping he might have a moment and walk over. The janitor smiled and tipped his cap, but headed in the opposite direction. My questions would have to wait because I knew the plane would not. As I hailed a taxi to the airport, I realized that something in the janitor's smile back when he gave me Chet's journal and again today gave me an unexplainable sense of calm. The gloomy feelings I had from recounting so many memories of Chet began to ease, like the Boston sky, where the sun had finally broken through the cloud cover only to begin its descent into the horizon.

Discussion

Through this counterstory, we introduce the concepts of microaggressions and racial battle fatigue as a way to examine some of the implications of racism on the health and lifespan of Faculty of Color in historically White colleges and universities.

Our counterstory characters confirm that a few or even one microaggression may cause serious emotional and physical stress. Yet as Carroll (1998) reminds us, in a society plagued by racism, People of Color endure a lifetime of mundane, extreme, environmental stress. In this context, People of Color expend a tremendous amount of psychological energy managing and negotiating microaggressions.

The counterstory examines some of the effects of racial microaggressions on Faculty of Color by allowing brief entry into a moment in the lives of two composite character—Professors Canon and Toboa.

The composite characters analyze and personify data on racial battle fatigue. Indeed, as the Black faculty recount their individual experiences with racial microaggressions, their collective experiences begin to demonstrate how a lifetime of microaggressions and their corresponding, cumulative stress, leads to racial battle fatigue. The psychophysiological symptoms of racial battle fatigue may cause lowered self-esteem, social withdrawal from perceived racial stressors, and many negative health complications, which can diminish one's quality of life and even shorten one's lifespan. The research presented through the counterstory shows that Faculty of Color report various psychophysiological symptoms as a result of battling an accumulation of racial microaggressions on historically White college and university campuses. Clara Lomas (2003) explains that this tradition of listening to and recounting *testimonios* (life experiences) of subordinated groups is can transform both the storytellers and listeners/readers. She asserts that *"In making sense of the text as a whole the reader is forced to go outside the text itself and examine the real world in relation to the text"* (2003:2–3). In format and content, the counterstory told in this chapter attempts to build on the transformative capacity of narratives.

This chapter and counterstory show that People of Color experience racial microaggressions, but the cumulative effect of this seemingly innocuous form of racism—racial battle fatigue—remains underresearched. Without further research in this area, the racial battle fatigue symptoms experienced by People of Color will remain misdiagnosed or even dismissed. As historically White colleges and universities maintain structural barriers that deny access to students of color while perpetuating a discourse of tolerance and diversity, racial microaggressions and ensuing racial battle fatigue will continue to be an area in need of study. For example, research should address some of the coping mechanisms People of Color engage in response to racial microaggressions and racial battle fatigue.

CRT, with its epistemological insistence on recognizing the knowledges of People of Color and methodological flexibility in utilizing counternarratives, represents a useful framework for challenging both macro and micro-forms of racism in education. Counterstorytelling holds pedagogical potential in its accessible story format embedded with critical conceptual and theoretical content. CRT counterstories can foster community building among subordinated groups by recognizing shared experiences with racism, sexism, classism, and other forms of subordination. The evidence is clear: External stressors can permanently alter physiological functioning. For People of Color, racism increases the degree of stress that one endures and this directly correlates to the physiological arousal that is an indicator of stress-related diseases (Smith 2004a). It is our humble hope that this counter-story and the painful realities of racial battle fatigue shared herein can help strengthen traditions of social, political, and cultural survival and resistance.

References

Aguirre Jr, Adalberto. 2000. "Academic Storytelling: A Critical Race Theory Story of Affirmative Action." *Sociological Perspectives* 43:319–339.
Allen, Walter and Daniel Solórzano. 2001. "Affirmative Action, Educational Equity, and Campus Racial Climate: A Case Study of the University of Michigan Law School." *Berkeley La Raza Law Journal* 12:237–363.
Arriola, Elvia R. 1997. "LatCrit Theory, International Human Rights, Popular Culture, and the Faces of Despair in INS Raids." *Inter-American Law Review* 28:245–262.
Bell, Derrick. 1987. *And We Are Not Saved: The Elusive Quest for Racial Justice*. New York: Basic Books.
———. 1992. *Faces at the Bottom of the Well: The Permanence of Racism*. New York: Basic Books.
———. 1996. *Gospel Choirs: Psalms of Survival for an Alien Land Called Home*. New York Basic Books.
Bonilla-Silva, Eduardo and Tyrone A. Forman. 2000. ""I'm Not a Racist but …": Mapping White College Students Racial Ideology in the U.S.A." *Discourse and Society* 11:51–86.
Bowman, Phillip J. and William A. Smith. 2002. "Racial Ideology in the Campus Community: Emerging Cross-Ethnic Differences and Challenges." Pp. 103–120 in *The racial crisis in American higher education: Continuing challenges to the twenty-first century*, edited by W.A. Smith, P.G. Altbach, and K. Lomotey. Albany: Sate University of New York Press.
Carroll, Grace. 1998. *Environmental Stress and African Americans: The Other Side of the Moon*. Westport, CT: Praeger.
Citizens Commission on Human Rights. 1995. Creating Racism: Psychiatry's Betrayal. Citizens Commission on Human Rights, Los Angeles, CA.
Clark, Rodney, Norman B. Anderson, Vernessa R. Clark, and David R. Williams. 1999. "Racism as a Stressor for African Americans: A Biopsychosocial Model." *American Psychologist* 54:805–816.
Delgado, Richard. 1984. "The Imperial Scholar: Reflections on a Review of Civil Rights Literature." *University of Pennsylvania Law Review* 132:561–578.
———. 1992. "The Imperial Scholar Revisited: Reflections on a Review of Civil Rights Literature." *University of Pennsylvania Law Review* 140:1349–1372.
———. 1995a. "Critical Race Theory: The Cutting Edge." Philadelphia: Temple University Press.
———. 1995b. *The Rodrigo Chronicles: Conversations About America and Race*. New York: New York University Press.
———. 1996. *The Coming Race War?: And Other Apocalyptic Tales of American After Affirmative Action and Welfare*. New York: New York University Press.
———. 1999. *When Equality Ends: Stories About Race and Resistance*. Boulder, CO: Westview.

———. 2003a. "Crossroads and Blind Alleys: A Critical Examination of Recent Writings About Race." *Texas Law Review* 82:121–152.
———. 2003b. *Justice at War: Civil Liberties and Civil Rights During Times of Crisis*. New York: New York University Press.
Delgado Bernal, Dolores. 1998. "Using a Chicana Feminist Epistemology in Educational Research." *Harvard Educational Review* 68:555–582.
Du Bois, W. E. B. 1920. *Darkwater: Voices from Within the Veil*. New York: Harcourt, Brace.
Espinoza, Leslie G. 1998. "Latino/a Identity and Multi-Identity: Community and Culture." Pp. 17–23 in *The Latino/a condition: A critical reader*, edited by R. Delgado and J. Stefanic. New York: New York University Press.
Feagin, Joe R. 2000. *Racist America: Roots, Current Realities, and Future Reparations*. New York: Routledge.
Feagin, Joe R. and Melvin P. Sikes. 1994. *Living with Racism: The Black Middle-Class Experience*. Boston, MA: Beacon Press.
Freire, Paulo. 1973. *Education for Critical Consciousness*. New York: Seabury Press.
Harlow, Roxanna. 2003. "'Race Doesn't Matter, but…'": The Effect of Race on Professors' Experience and Emotion Management in the Undergraduate Classroom." *Social Psychology Quarterly* 66:348–363.
Izard, Carroll E. 1972. *Patterns of Emotions: A New Analysis of Anxiety and Depression*. New York: Academic Press.
———. 1977. *Human Emotions*. New York: Plenum Press.
Krieger, Nancy and Sstephen Sidney. 1996. "Racial Discrimination and Blood Pressure: The CARDIA Study of Young Black and White Adults." *American Journal of Public Health* 86:1370–1378.
Ladson-Billings, Gloria. 1996. "Silences as Weapons: Challenges of a Black Professor Teaching White Students." *Theory into Practice* 35:79–85.
Ladson-Billings, Gloria and William F. Tate. 1995. "Toward a Critical Race Theory of Education." *Teachers College Record* 97:47–68.
Lomas, Clara. 2003. "Latina Feminisms: Reflections on Theory, Practice, and Pedagogy Emerging in Telling to Live." in *16th Annual MALCS Summer Institute*. San Antonio, TX.
Lynn, Marvin, Tara J. Yosso, and Daniel G. Solórzano. 2002. "Critical Race Theory and Education: Qualitative Research in the New Millennium." *Qualitative Inquiry* 8:3–6.
Olivas, Michael A. 1990. "The Chronicles, My Grandfather's Stories, and Immigration Law: The Slave Traders Chronicle as Racial History." *Saint Louis University Law Journal* 34:425–441.
Pierce, Chester. 1970. "Offensive Mechanisms." Pp. 265–282 in *The Black Seventies*, edited by F. B. Barbour. Boston, MA: Porter Sargent.
———. 1974. "Psychiatric Problems of the Black Minority." Pp. 512–523 in *American Handbook of Psychiatry*, edited by G. Caplan and S. Arieti. New York: Basic Books.
———. 1975. "The Mundane Extreme Environment and Its Effect on Learning." Pp. 111–119 in *Learning Disabilities: Issues and Recommendations for Research*, edited by S. G. Brainard. Washington DC: National Institute of Education, Department of Health, Education, and Welfare.
———. 1980. "Social Trace Contaminants: Subtle Indicator of Racim in TV." Pp. 249–257 in *Television and Social Behavior: Beyond Violence and Children*, edited by S. B. Withey and R. P. Abeles. Hillsdale, NJ: Lawrence Erlbaum.
———. 1989. "Unity in Diversity: Thirty-Three Years of Stress." Pp. 296–312 in *Black Students: Psychosocial Issues and Academic Achievement* edited by G. L. Berry and J. K. Asamen. Newbury Park, CA: Sage.
———. 1995. "Stress Analogs of Racism and Sexism: Terrorism, Torture, and Disaster." Pp. 277–293 in *Mental Health, Racism and Sexism*, edited by C. Willie, P. Rieker, B. Kramer, and B. Brown. Pittsburgh: University of Pittsburg Press.

Prillerman, Shelly L., Hector F. Myers, and Brian D. Smedley. 1989. "Stress, Well-Being, and Academic Achievement in College." Pp. 198–217 in *Black Students: Psychosocial Issues and Academic Achievement*, edited by G. L. Berry and J. K. Asamen. Newbury Park, CA: Sage.

Scott-Heron, Gil. 2001. *Now and Then: The Poems of Gil Scott-Heron*. Edinburgh, Scotland: Payback Press.

Smith, William A. 1993–2003. "National African Americans Study." University of Illinois at Chicago and the University of Utah.

——. 2004a. "Battle Fatigue on the Front Lines of Race: Teaching About Race and Racism at Historically White Institutions."

——. 2004b. "Black Faculty Coping with Racial Battle Fatigue: The Campus Racial Climate in a Post-Civil Rights Era." Pp. 171–190 in *A Long Way To Go: Conversations About Race by African American Faculty and Graduate Students*, edited by D. Cleveland. New York Peter Lang.

——. 2004c. "The Impact of Racially Primed White Students on Black Faculty: Manifestations of Racial Battle Fatigue on Historically White Campuses."

Smith, William A., Philip G. Altbach, and Kofi Lomotey. 2002. "The Racial Crisis in American Higher Education: Continuing Challenges to the Twenty-First Century." Albany: State University of New York Press.

Solórzano, Daniel. 1997. "Images and Words that Wound: Critical Race Theory, Racial Stereotyping, and Teacher Education." *Teacher Education Quarterly* 24:5–19.

——. 1998. "Critical Race Theory, Race, Racial and Gender Microaggressions, and the Experiences of Chicana and Chicano Scholars." *International Journal of Qualitative Studies in Education* 11:121–136.

Solórzano, Daniel, Miguel Ceja, and Tara J. Yosso. 2000. "Critical Race Theory, Racial Microaggressions, and Campus Racial Climate: The Expereinces of African American College Students." *Journal of Negro Education* 69:60–73.

Solórzano, Daniel and Dolores Delgado Bernal. 2001. "Examining Transformational Resistance Through a Critical Race and LatCrit Theory Framework: Chicana and Chicano Students in an Urban Context." *Urban Education* 36:308–342.

Tate, William F. 1994. "From Inner City to Ivory Tower: Does My Voice Matter in the Academy." *Urban Education* 29:245–269.

——. 1997. "Critical Race Theory and Education: History, Theory, and Implications." *Review of Research in Education* 22:195–247.

Williams, David R., Harold W. Neighbors, and James S. Jackson. 2003. "Racial/Ethnic Discrimination and Health: Findings from Community Studies." *American Journal of Public Health* 93:200–208.

Williams, Patricia J. 1991. *The Alchemy of Race and Rights: Diary of a Law Professor*. Cambridge, MA: Harvard University Press.

Willie, Charles V. and Jayminn S. Sanford. 1995. "Turbulence on the College Campus and the Frustration-Aggression Hypothesis." Pp. 253–276 in *Mental health, racism, and sexism*, edited by C. V. Willie, P. Rieker, B. Kramer, and B. Brown. Pittsburgh, PA: University of Pittsburgh Press.

Yosso, Tara J. 2006. *Critical Race Counterstories Along the Chicana/Chicano Educational Pipeline*. New York: Routledge.

COVERT RACISM IN THE U.S. AND GLOBALLY[1]

Rodney D. Coates

> The feeling that relegation of the Negro to a subordinate status was in fact the covert end of legislation prescribing unequal treatment seems to have underlain the uniformity with which such laws have been struck down. (Columbia Law Review 1949, 636)

While race is unarguably a social construction, it is also a means of social control (Coates 2003). This particular form of social control differentially serves to restrict and regulate the behavior of specified racial groups to the advantage of other specified racial groups. Systems of inequality and oppression must be preserved and perpetuated by societal control mechanisms (Coates 2003). More specifically, race, as a socially constructed means of social control, serves to perpetuate economic, social, political, psychological, religious, ideological, and legal systems of inequality. If you could imagine a series of concentric circles, each labeled according to the above (not exhaustive) list, which serve to define, structure, and limit the varied racialized group experiences – then a more dynamic conceptualization of race can be realized.

As concentric circles, these constraints appear to be much like Frye's 'bird cage' (1983, 1–16). To the casual observer, each wire does not appear to be sufficient to retain the bird. But when viewed from either within or as a whole we see a finely constructed cage. The problem, from a pedagogical, policy, research, or activist perspective, is that we tend to concentrate on only one wire – or phenomenon – the removal of which leads to great anticipation that the war has been won. Unfortunately, in systems of racialized oppression, as one wire is removed from the cage, even more insidious wires are being constructed and still others are left intact. Elsewhere, I argue that:

> Race is neither an event nor a specific series of events. Race is a process of structured events which over time demonstrate a system whereby

---

[1] "Covert Racism in the U.S. and Globally" by Rodney Coates is a revised version of a paper of the same title originally published in Sociology Compass 2/1 (2008):208–231.

groups and individuals are racialized. Race, consequently, must be studied from a socio-historical frame of reference which provides the critical rubric by which and through which systems of racialism may be understood. Absent such an analysis one is more likely to confuse events which may have racial overtones with processes which are racialized. The mere fact that outcomes may be categorized within racial terms does not a priori lead to the conclusion that these outcomes are a result of racialization. (Coates 2006, 5)

Racist indictments have a long and sordid history in our world. One of the earliest of which can be found in the 14th century CE writings of the Tunisian Ibn Khaldun:

> The Negro nations are, as a rule, submissive to slavery, because [Negroes] have little that is [essentially] human and possess attributes that are quite similar to those of dumb animals. (Muqaddimah 2007, http://en.wikipedia.org/wiki/ Racism#_ref-bboxhill_0, last accessed July 17, 2007)

Al-Abshibi (1388–1446), during the same period in Egypt, wrote: 'It is said that when the [black] slave is sated, he fornicates, when he is hungry, he steals' (Bernard 2002).

Race is a multilayered, multidimensional beast that, although socially constructed, has a momentum and inertia of its own. The deeper we go, the more we see. The beast has a life of its own primarily because we (all of us) are indoctrinated from birth and enmeshed in this viscous interacting web of confusion. What makes race and its analysis so difficult is that often it is treated as a constant when in reality it is a variable. Any historical and/or cross-national examination of race and systems of race would reveal its variability (Branton and Jones 2005; Carlson, Armelegos and de Laubenfels 1971; Cartmill 1998; Coates 2002). Racial domination as a means of social control appears to be quite agile or adept at adjusting to changing social climates (Omi and Winant 1994). When under attack, it can be found deeply submerged in the societal psyche. To the extent that these psyches are obvious across several generations and institutions – we can talk not only about the social construction but also the cultural production of race and racialized systems. Thus, from the cultural production of race and racialized systems, we suggests that as social, political, economic, psychological, and/or situational conditions change – new pressures emerge that insist on sacrificial lambs, thus race reemerges – fresh, clean, and newly adorned (Bonilla-Silva 1997; Carr 1997). The most significant process in the cultural production of race is seen in the process of socialization (Van Ausdale and Feagin 2001).

Race is continually under construction through the various means of socialization. The chief agents of socialization are the family, government, school, church, peers and friendship networks, and of course the media. In this section I shall deal here with the family as it applies to the production, manipulation, alteration and perpetuation of racial social constructs. (Van Ausdale and Feagin 2001)

Children are born with neither a concept of race nor their identity within a racial matrix. Rather, these are learned and constantly manipulated throughout one's life. From infancy to the fourth year, children typically are unaware of their racial identity. After this period, they seem preoccupied with it as evidenced by their ability to label themselves and significant others by virtue of physically identifiable learned racial classifications (Corenblum et al. 1997; Stevenson et al. 2002; Van Ausdale and Feagin 2001). Implicitly, race, may be viewed as a rudimentary extension of family and community (Lipsitz 1995). Within these institutions typically the child bonds with, identifies with and learns to prefer this group above others. It is here that the infant first learns to differentiate between self and others. As this process is extended to those outside of the family racial categorization comes into being. In this process of differentiation, the child also learns the biases implicitly and explicitly projected by significant role models and socialization agents (Van Ausdale and Feagin 2001).

Racialization (i.e. the process by which groups are racially coded) must be continually reproduced if it is to survive social transformations (Hughes and Johnson 2001). Previous studies, based primarily in the USA, have documented the continued racially stratified (Carter et al. 1998), segregated (Massey and Denton 1988, 1989, 1993), and thus polarized society. The interaction of these characterizations with those presented (either implicitly or explicitly) through national culture, school, church, peers, and friendship networks, and the media serves to preserve and/or modify ones attitudes with reference to racial identity (Li 2004). National identity and culture serve as foils by which and through which race is perceived (Spencer and Markstrom-Adams 1990). Consequently, as national identity and culture change we would also expect a change in forms of racism (Omi and Winant 1994).

Forms of racism – covert and overt

While it seems that racism has changed to a more subtle form. In actuality, both overt and covert racism have long been recognized.

Indeed, as observed by Coughey and Coughey (1966), covert racism served to keep the schools of Los Angeles segregated even during a period of increasing pressure to desegregate. Carmichael and Hamilton a year later similarly conclude that:

> Racism is both obvert and covert. It takes two, closely related forms: individual whites acting against individual blacks, and acts by the total white community against the black community. We call these individual racism and institutional racism. The first consists of overt acts by individual, which cause death, injury or the violent destruction of property ... the second type is less overt, far more subtle, less identifiable in terms of specific individuals committing the acts. But it is no less destructive of human life. The second type originates in the operation of established and respected focus in the society, and thus receives far less public condemnation than the first type. (Carmichael and Hamilton 1967, 4)

With time scholars came to realize that overt racism operated at multiple levels and dimensions of society. Thus, both overt and covert racism may be understood to be multidimensional. What I am suggesting is a dynamic, as opposed to a static, process. Covert racism remains submerged, entangled in the centuries-old tentacles borne of exploitation, extortion, and hyper-oppression. As we will discuss below, manifestations of covert racism may be triggered by social, political, and social crises and unrest. Within the racial state, covert racism may be masked and appear under several guises ranging from color blindness to racial profiling. Among former imperial colonies (see, for example, Nkrumah 1965), one of its obvious manifestations are what some have termed 'odious debt' coupled with catastrophic institutional failures, economic inertia and/or decline, and the resulting political and social morass, fatalism, and nihilism (West 1994). Covert racism is what is left when 'capital flees' (Hartman 1962; Ndikumana and Boyce 1998). In such situations, liberal guilt and its band-aid proscriptions are poor balms for what ails society. Misdiagnosed, covert racism results in blaming the victim, defining the debilitating plight as a culture of poverty (Lewis 1966), or a poverty of will (Bodner 1973) – we speak of cultural deficits, deficient human capital, etc. Thus, the newly 'enfranchised', 'liberated', or the freed – appear to have fallen into situations even worse than the previous situations of exploitation, extortion, and hyperoppression. Unfortunately, this view of covert racism is not only naive, but dangerous as well. So rather than looking toward the structure for answers and to provide remedies, we turn to trying to reform, transform, and conform the victim. A more critical examination of covert racism reveals that it is much more than the symptomatic – it is systemic remains of a more overt, structurally embedded component of the systems of exploitation and oppression. Put simply, covert racism, twin born with overt racism, has just as long a lineage and, hence, its development has been just as pervasive.

The problem is that covert racism has existed, developed, matured beneath the social level of awareness (see Cross 1964; Littell 1965). It has only recently become quite visible with the formal removal of the more obvious overt racism. What then are the contours of covert racism?

Contours of covert racism

Covert racisms are subtle, subversive, and deliberate informal and formal mechanisms that allow differential access to rewards, prestige, sanctions, status, and privileges based on racial hierarchies. While covert racism does not carry the weight of law – tradition, norms, and customs typically uphold, justify, or obscure its operation. As a consequence, members of select racialized groups are 'expected' to (out) perform selected tasks, develop specific skills and excel in certain environments – as compared to other racialized groups. Thus, covert racism serves to explain obvious racial outcomes as 'natural'. Alternatively, and correspondingly any deficiencies, lack of achievement, or failure to perform by selected/specificracialized groups is similarly obscured, misdiagnosed, or misrepresented as individual or group failure, lack or deficiency. Thus, the insidiousness of covert racism is revealed – whether under the guise of the end of racism (D'Souza 1995), or the declining significance of race (Wilson 1980) – the presumption is that any resultant failure has nothing to do with race, racism, or any structural impediments (past, present, or perceived). Therefore, even as apartheid has been formally dissolved, and Jim Crow outlawed, or colonial rule abandoned – covert racism yet operates as its tentacles continues to remain deeply lodged in the social, economic, cultural, psychic, and political – fabric of societies. Yet, understanding the general natures of the tentacles affords little concreteness to the concept of covert racism.

Covert racism refers to those subtle and subversive institutional or societal practices, policies, and norms utilized to mask structural racial apparatus. Thereby masked, this racial apparatus serves to restrict, deny, or otherwise distort the opportunities available to the racialized nonelite. Multiple examples can be drawn from business, education, and politics – which demonstrate various mechanisms of covert racism. For example, recent Harvard studies document.

> '... as doctors' unconscious biases against blacks increased, their likelihood of giving [clot-busting] treatment decreased,' said the lead author of the study, Dr. Alexander R. Green of Massachusetts General Hospital. 'It's not a matter of you being a racist. It's really a matter of the way your brain processes information is influenced by things you've seen, things you've experienced, the way media has presented things.' (Smith 2007)

Racialized nonelites, particularly blacks and Latinos, are more likely to pay more to lease a car (Cohen 2003), to be targeted by subprime lenders (CRL 2006), and less likely to obtain key information regarding job interviews (Bonds 2002). While there may not be any identifiably blatant intent the systemically enhanced information, access, or assistance provided to racialized elites increase the likelihood of their success vis-à-vis nonelites. Alternatively, the selective enforcement of various laws, or the increased surveillance of certain laws in selected communities increase the likelihood that select racialized groups will experience greater levels of criminalization then others (Beckett et al. 2006). Disparities in educational funding, again with racial nonelites among the biggest losers, significantly increase the achievement gap (Condron and Roscigno 2003). All of these different practices, although patently legal, are examples of covert and very subtle forms of racism.

Consequently, covert racism often undetected, is often inherently inculcated with each generation of new members of any given social situation. The process, operating within both racial elite and nonelite groups, represents a kind of closed feedback loop. At the heart of covert racism one finds a deliberate policy of denial, omission, and obfuscation of black, brown, and yellow issues, persons, and groups. In this pseudo-color-blind universe, race appears nullified under the veneer of 'benign neglect' (Moynihan 1968, 8–9). Thus, 'anything but "race"' (Bonilla-Silva 2006, 62) becomes the clarion call to justify differences in outcomes as 'race declines in significance'. When such devices do not work, then we simply 'define race out of existence' (Henderson 2007, 340), make it seemingly insignificant as in 'the social construction of race' (Sanchez 1998), or reduce its effect as in the 'culture of poverty' (Leiter 1986), or 'cultural deficiency' (Blanton 2003).

In terms of action, covert racism may actually masquerade as racial liberalism, by misdirecting attention to the symbols of racism, but avoiding the structures of such (Guinier 2004). Thus, as Dyson recently observed:

> ... it should also be clear that although one may not have racial intent, one's actions may nonetheless have racial consequences ... Active malice and passive indifference are but flip sides of the same racial coin, different modalities of racial menace that flare according to the contexts and purposes at hand ... In a sense, if one conceives of racism as a cell phone, the active malice is the ring tone at its highest volume, while passive indifference is the ring tone on vibrate. In either case, whether loudly or silently, the consequence is the same: a call is transmitted, a racial meaning is communicated. (Dyson 2006, 20–21)

I am also reminded of Charles Mills's observations:

> ... the requirements of 'objective' cognition, factual and moral, in a racial polity are in a sense more demanding in that officially sanctioned reality is divergent from actual reality ... one has an agreement to misinterpret the world. One has to see the world wrongly, BUT with the assurance that this set of mistaken perceptions will be validated by White epistemic authority ... Thus, in effect, on matters related to race, the Racial Contract prescribes for its signatories an inverted epistemology, an epistemology of ignorance, a particular pattern of localized and global cognitive dysfunctions (which are psychologically and social functional), producing the ironic outcome that Whites will in general be unable to understand the world they themselves have made ... (Mills 1997, 18)

The term 'covert' – derived from military operations – suggests a quasi-legal, subversive, or hidden form of racism. In addition, the term covert racism suggests a more subtle, often subconscious or unconsciousness cognitive perceptual terrain and even may operate in such a way that both victims and perpetrators may not be aware of its operation. Thus, as Omi and Winant (1994) suggest regarding racial hegemony – it involves a sort of common sense notion of normative processes. Therefore, while no one significantly questions the correctness of a white man flying an airplane, some may automatically question the credentials of a black or Asian woman. Whereas a black man functioning as a football or basketball player is deemed common, it is also understandable and acceptable if that same player is not so good in academic pursuits. This is of course 'common sense', but is it really? The reality of this aspect of covert racism is that the mechanisms produce differential expectations for different racial groups. More specifically, these racial 'self-fulfilling prophecies' are exemplified by the expectation that Chinese students will do well in computer sciences, or that Jews will do well in business, or that Germans make better craftsmen. In reality, this form of covert racism, which would accept less then excellence by one set of racialized individuals, and not another is clearly in operation. Finally, who and what gets defined as legitimate representatives/representations of various racialized groups are an important dimension of covert racism, as it defines who is and can claim a racial identity. Hence, very subtle or covert racisms are in place that would attempt to force biracial or multiracial individuals to choose one or the other racial identity; furthermore regardless of which they choose there is disconnect as their legitimacy is constantly challenged by members of the particular racial elite within the racialized group (Rockquemore 2002). Thus, racial labels serve to determine who gets to claim normalcy or identity, as well as to logistically structure and/or limit access to other racialized rewards (Russell 2002).

Critical racial and ethnic studies attempt to understand the process by which systems of racialization are preserved, maintained, and perpetuated (Crenshaw 1995). The 'critical' designation implies that such studies recognize the multiple dimensions in which systems of oppression operate from the vantage point of the oppressed (Delgado 1995). These multiple dimensions, of which race and ethnicity are but two, operate interactively and systemically to produce and reproduce structures of exploitation. The social and cultural institutions provide the situational context in which these dimensions interact. Therefore (either implicitly or explicitly), courts and police, schools and churches, friendship and family networks, and various media outlets – all serve to preserve, perpetuate and/or modify racial attitudes, group formation and systems of racial oppression and exploitation. Finally, as economic, political, and cultural systems of production change we note similar changes in the various oppressive and exploitative systems. What I am suggesting is a dynamic, as opposed to a static, process underlying covert racism.

This dynamic process is, as indicated above, multifaceted, multidimensional, situationally, historically, economically, and geopolitically specific. Consequently, while we focus on singular dimensions of oppression, it is understood that they are embedded in pluralist systems of exploitation.

Such pluralist systems of exploitation, with global ramifications, increase the difficulty for those seeking solutions, remedies, and positive change.

Covert racism – USA and beyond

The basic idea of justice is that if damage has been done then remedies must be provided (Beetham et al. 2001). Within a democratic framework, I believe that justice must be racially sensitive to balance the racial reality of our past. The American reality pitted against this democratic ideal, produces a paradox. While democratic ideology suggests that justice is blind; in reality the USA has a historical legacy of racial sensitivity that has consistently favored racial elites at the expense of racial nonelites. The reason why our legal structure should be racially sensitivity has to do with our racial legacy of insensitivity (i.e. slavery, segregation, Jim Crow, *Plessey v. Ferguson*, *Dred Scott*, lynching, Japanese and Chinese Exclusionary Acts, the Internment of Japanese 1942, the Trail of Tears, current and past immigration policies, Tuskegee Syphilis Experiments, differential sentencing, etc.). It is strange that some the very same racial elites who benefited, sanctioned, and applauded such racially biased laws now lead the calls for a racially blind or neutral system to challenge remedies such as affirmative action (Bush 2003). The irony of such calls is that they hide a more insidious form of racism, that of covert racism.

From genteel racism to enlightened colonialism – The shifting racial terrain

'Suddenly one day I broke my silence and found myself advocating on behalf of black and mixed race children' after feeling she had become 'an unwilling partner in a type of genteel racism' in which subtle discrimination prevailed against such children in the Agency's adoption practices. 'For better or worse I had taken the plunge, had stepped on sacred ground and had finally articulated a taboo issue.' (Rambally 2002)

Both 'genteel racism' and 'enlightened colonialism' makes reference to the form of bigotry associated within Western culture and its racial elite or high society. These particular forms of bigotry have historically been identified to reflect a cultural norm that justified racial exclusion (Loewen 2005), presumed superiority and the notion that these were necessary to 'uplift' the darker races (Janiewski 2004). For both genteel racism and enlightened colonialism one finds a justification for what is often described as a more benign, beneficial, and often necessary forms of racism and exploitation. The necessity was a consequence of the

'White Man's Burden' to tend to and take care of the darker races of man. As I will show in the sections below, both genteel racism and enlightened colonialism are merely other forms of covert racism.

Genteel racism can be traced to some of the most prominent scholars in the academy. While many have noted Max Weber's apparent obsession with Protestantism and his attendant biases (Turner, 1974); others have suggested that this obsession actually masked a subtle form of racism. Specifically, Furuhashi (2003) argues that Weber's apparent obsession was actually a form of genteel racism, actually targeted Islam and Middle Easterners. Within the USA during this same period of time, politicians and intellectuals facing the blatant racism of fascism made a deliberate attempt to appease the blacks and other minorities. As observed by Lieberman:

> The massive anti-racist propaganda and the racist enemy undermined the strength of the racist groups in the United States that had been so vocal in the 1930s. Racism began to recede on the surface and to be replaced by an appearance of genteel tolerance as a public police ... (1968, 137)

Lewis concludes that 'the philanthropic-intellectual complex' whose vision was blurred by 'genteel racism' 'recoiled from the prospects of learning about Negroes from Negroes' (Lewis 2001, 433).

More recently, this sophisticated form of covert racism has been associated with The New Century Foundation and its publication – *American Renaissance* – which promotes a more 'genteel racism: pseudoscientific, questionably researched and argued articles that validate the genetic and moral inferiority of nonwhites and the need for racial "purity". Generally avoiding overt bigotry and stereotyping, many of North America's leading intellectual racists have written for the journal or have addressed the biannual American Renaissance conversances' (Anti-Defamation League 2005). In Canada, Purvis (2004) discusses how 'genteel racism' legitimated a system that tortured aboriginals while utilizing an educational system to basically strip them of their culture. In this system, the presumed superiority of all that was white ridiculed and delegitimized all that was native. (The same policy has long been documented in the USA and requires no further comment here.) Asians in England (Sivanandan 2005) suffered similar abuse. Blackness has long been the color of choice for 'genteel racist'; therefore it's not surprising at how many non-African groups become Africanized by scholars in another form of genteel racism. Such is the case when Endicott (1979) discusses the indigenous Malaysian Aslians and their 'Negrito religion'. Dentan (1981) argued that such classification ignores both genetics and Malaysian sensibilities, and relies on racial stereotypes and scientific racism.

Finally the term dates back to a genteel racist taxonomy that divided Aslian people into three neat linguistic-racial-cultural categories (Semang, Sakai, and Jakum) none of which stands up to close analysis. Scholars of that earlier time postulated an *Urkultar* (italics in original) and a totally unempirical dream psychotherapy on the basis of presumed equivalence of short, dark, kinky haired peoples worldwide. (422–23)

While a wide assortment of examples for this 'genteel racism' abound, I personally like the ones identified by John Hope Franklin. The scars of this form of racism endured long after he had reached intellectual and scholarly superstardom and became the first black to chair 'white' departments of history at both Brooklyn College and the University of Chicago. He regarded the almost paternalistic, self-emulating praise almost with disdain as he remarked: 'My colleagues at Brooklyn College and the University of Chicago were so full of self-congratulations for persuading their institutions to invite me to join them that I generally focused my efforts on other departments and other institutions, urging them to take their first steps in the experiment of diversifying their faculties' (cited by Smith 2005). Even superstardom, national and international acclaim were not sufficient to keep John Hope Franklin at the age of 80 from being the target of 'genteel racism'. In 1995, in Washington DC's exclusive club Cosmos, at a dinner party to celebrate reception of America's highest civilian award – the Medal of Freedom – and as he tells it: 'Some of my guests hadn't arrived and I went to find them. I went down the grand staircase – it is a grand staircase – and at the bottom this white woman saw me and said, "Here" and handed me her coat check, saying, "Go get my coat." I told her that if she presented that check to a uniformed attendant, and all the club's attendants were uniformed, perhaps she would get her coat. And I walked away' (Morris 2006).

At this point, I would like to differentiate 'genteel racism' from 'enlightened colonialism'. It appears that they refer to the same general tendencies, with 'genteel racism' being more applicable to individuals, groups, and regions and 'enlightened colonialism' referring to the institutionalization of 'genteel racism' on a national and international scale. Therefore, imperial countries have described or encouraged the belief that their actions of aggression and exploitation in colonial situations were aimed at extending civilization, good government, and morality that accrue to whiteness to the darker peoples of the world. Thus, under the guise of the 'White Man's Burden', the savages and heathens occupying India, Africa, and Asia were to be saved.

The Black races of Africa have not attained a complete and coherent civilization of their own nor do they possess the necessary foundation on which to build up a real system of education. The great contribution that we can make is precisely in the interweaving and blending of primitive civilization with our own universally applicable civilization which will have to justify its position of superiority by the manner in which it acquits itself of the responsibility it has assumed. (Charton 1930, 100 cited by White 1996, 15)

Enlightened colonialism allowed the French not only to discover their whiteness but also to justify their racism. Again, colonialism became the vehicle by which the French could enlighten, tame, and bring the 'high culture' that was French to the darker peoples of the world. This 'enlightenment' came with a cost – torture, exploitation, and destruction. Ignoring the apparent contradictions with the French notions of 'liberté, egalité, fraternité', colonial officials were determined to 'save' the savages (Groff 1999). Of interest is that those Africans able to acquire French qualities, not least among which were language and culture, were accorded the labile of *Afrique blanke*. The French in Algiers utilized this designation to distinguish the 'good' Kables from the 'bad' Arabs (Stovall 2003, 56).

Color-blind racism and invisibility

Color-blind racism is the central ideology of post-Civil Rights that subtly mask racial ambivalence, hostility, and allows whites to 'talk nasty about blacks' politely (Bonilla-Silva 2002). Color-blind racism can also serve to make racialized individuals appear invisible and their problems nonexistent or no longer viable (Walsh 2004). The problem with a color-blind standard is that it also tends to ignore past and contemporary forms of racial discrimination, and assumes a level playing field when there is indeed none. As Halstead (1988) concludes:

> ... color-blindness not only leads to undesirable outcomes (the disadvantaging of black people by ignoring or marginalizing their distinctive needs, experiences and identity), but may also involve racial injustice. When a color-blind approach is adopted to any social policy in this country, white people are usually able to dominate because the common

experiences are defined in terms which white people can more easily relate to than blacks and which tend to bolster the white self-image at the expense of the black. Color-blindness falls down because it is based on an idealistic principle (that all people are equal) which may be valid sub specie aeternitatis but which fails to take account of the contingent facts of racial inequality and disadvantage in our present society. (139–55)

Such reasoning fails to take into consideration the gross inequities that distinguish America's racial nonelites. Even with a college degree, African Americans are two times more likely to be unemployed as their white counterparts. Hispanics can expect to earn half as much as Asian Americans and whites. Both African Americans and Hispanics are significantly less likely than whites to get proper medical care after a heart attack (Lehrman 2007). Lurking in the shadows of this color-blind racism is what McIntosh (1988) called the 'invisible knapsack'. This invisible shield guarantees that whites will enjoy a presumption of innocence, competency, and legitimacy.

Racialized systems, that is, those that are constructed to generate racial outcomes, have long been recognized (Bonilla-Silva 2001). Those charged with gate-keeping perform a vital role in maintaining racialized systems (Pearce 1979). These systems, so imbedded in our cultural frames of reference), appear innocent, and rarely appear as racist (Roediger 1999). Unfortunately, even with their recognition, the remedies designed to correct the problems are often circumvented, nullified, or simply ignored. Feigned innocence, amnesia, or lack of culpability hence responsibility by the racial elite further serves to distort the racial landscape. This gets played out in many different forums, as noted by Morrison:

> In matters of race, silence and evasion have historically ruled literary discourse. Evasion has fostered another, substitute language in which the issues are encoded, foreclosing open debate. The situation is aggravated by the tremor that breaks into discourse on race. It is further complicated by the fact that the habit of ignoring race is understood to be a graceful, even generous, liberal gesture. To notice is to recognize an already discredited difference. To enforce its invisibility through silence is to allow the black body a shadowless participation in the dominant cultural body. (Morrison 1992, 129)

While most people are aware of the extreme racist views of such groups as neo-Nazis and skinheads, etc., few recognize that it is the 'shadowless participation' of blacks in cultural institutions that remain hidden. Shadowless participation is only now being documented in such areas the media (Entman and Rojecki 2000), calls for welfare reform and reproductive rights (Roberts 1997), human genome studies (Gannett 2001), and public policy debates and formulations (Kellstedt 2000). The opposite of racial invisibility or shadowless participation is racial profiling.

Racial profiling – By police, media, and others

Racial profiling, the systematic singling out of racial and ethnic nonelites for differentially negative sanctions, is alive and well throughout America. While most recent research and concern has been in terms of police and crime, a long history of racial profiling has and continues to be well documented. 'Racial profiling is a new term for an old practice known by other names: institutional racism and discrimination and owes its existence to prejudice that has existed in this country since slavery' (ACLU [American Civil Liberties Union] 2007).

Current efforts, led by the ACLU, have resulted in multiple lawsuits being initiated, a series of laws being passed, and a number of policies being changed. Unfortunately, as long as racial profiling is treated as a problem and not a symptom few actual remedies will be forthcoming (ACLU 2007). Racial profiling is part of a larger, more ingrained, problem in Western culture (Coates 2006).

In the raging debate over racial profiling, it should be understood that most Americans, both racial elites and nonelites, agree that racism is bad, that vestiges of racism yet remain, and that laws and their enforcement should be racially neutral. The degree to which groups and individuals assess such neutrality is dependent on which side of the racial divide they find themselves. Much like the 1997 O. J. Simpson trial, many racial elites view the criminal justice system as basically fair, while many racial nonelites view the same system as being basically unfair (Auther 1997). Most racial nonelites know with certainty that police, the courts and the laws unfairly target, systematically restrict, and regularly harm members of their groups. Alternatively, most racial elites know with certainty that their only protection from an increasingly hostile and criminal underclass is the police, the courts and the laws. Although several factors may account for these differences, the force of the news media cannot be ignored. Evidence seems to support the belief that the media frequently vilifies racial nonelites.

Specifically, blacks and Hispanics are more likely to be presented as criminals than as victims or more positively (Chiricos and Eschholz 2002). These types of perceptual biases have dire and negative consequences when racial nonelites confront the legal system (Berger 2002).

Police are more likely to use deadly force in cities where racial inequality is greatest (Jacobs and O'Brien 1998). When challenged, police typically defend their actions as the legitimate use of deadly force. There is some evidence that police respond to challenges to their use of deadly force by practicing a form of 'benign neglect'. Under this version, the police look the other way, or merely ignore crime. Police on the street, using such names as 'de-policing', 'selective disengagement', 'tactical detachment' argue that such is the logical reaction to being charged with being a racist. In Cincinnati, after a riot, boycott, and federal oversight – police held back, and crime began to soar. In 3 months after the shooting of the 15th unarmed black man and the ensuing riots, traffic and other arrests declined 50 percent. During this same period, there were 59 shootings, producing 77 victims. This compares to just 9 shootings and 11 victims during the same period just 1 year before (Prendergast 2002).

The news media, public officials, and police continue to represent urban/inner city crime as significantly more dangerous, violent, and threatening than the suburbs (Yanich 2001). This is particularly significant because these representations are not based in reality. The FBI has reported that various forms of crime have actually decreased in urban areas, while they have increased significantly in the suburbs (Johnson 2003). In a strange reversal, life (and racial profiling) may indeed be mimicking art. As demonstrated by Prosise (2004), much of our attitudes of crime, police, and race stem from our addiction to so-called 'crime-based reality' programs. Reality programs – such as *Law Enforcement, Crime on Cops* or *World's Wildest Police Videos* – actually suggest that racial profiling is not only the norm, but a necessary tool in the police crime fighting arsenal.

Covert racism and the media

I am constantly amazed at how consistently race is celebrated in US culture. What is so amazing is that many of these celebrations are rarely viewed as being complimentary by various racialized segments of our society. The commercialization of racial and ethnic nonelites often serves to reinforce negative stereotypes. For example, this past Black History Month celebration one noted the following features on commercial television 'Pootie Tang', 'Booty Call', 'Kingdom Come', and '12 Angry Men'. Pathological representations of black males are the central feature of all of these programs. As we go from TV to the press, the observation that these same individuals are more likely to be vilified and victimized, to be projected as being the problems or the source of the problems, and least likely to be projected in a positive light. A recent set of commercials advertising Viagra is an exemplar here – two different sets of commercials were produced. One set, featuring a white man in a loving caress with his partner, centers attention to his new found ability to perform his marital duties. Alternatively, the other, featuring a partnerless black man, centers attention on his ability to continue to pursue multiple sexual conquests. After her Jezebel role in *Monster's Ball* (2001), Halle Berry received an academy award. Such movies basically reaffirm a cultural devaluation and sexualization of black women. Various Internet 'stores' sell videos with titles like – *Black Chicks in Heat, Black Bitches, Hoochie Mamas, Video Sto' Ho, Black and Nasty, South Central Hookers,* and *Git Yo' Ass On Da Bus*! In the privacy of their homes or hotel rooms, Americans can watch Black actresses – Purple Passion, Jamaica, Toy, Chocolate Tye, Juicy, Jazz, Spontaneeus Xtasy, and others – 'validate' the belief that Black women are whores. (Pilgrim 2002)

While not often recognized as such, these are clearly evidence of a covert, more subtle form of racism targeting racial and ethnic nonelites.

Many Americans believe that race and racism, while bad, are basically relics of the past (Gallop and Gallop 2000). Some believe that those who still claim to be victims of racism are just being overly sensitive (McWorter 2000). And even when many people repeat such claims over a long span of time, such claims are still dismissed as nonfactual or even worse counter factual. The fact that such claims are not isolated, random, or restricted to one single group but appears to be continuous, targeted, and widespread – leads many, others to conclude that something else is going on. We do not live in a vacuum, nor are our experiences isolated. All too often, our existence, our experiences, and how we learn about others is linked to our collective representations of others (Fine et al. 1998). These collective representations, grouped along racial lines, serve to define racial identities. Racial identities, much like movie images, appear to be concrete, solitary objects but in reality are multidimensional and fluid (Howard 2000). What this means is that while our perceptions of racial identity suggests stagnation, the reality of racial identity is that it is constantly changing. What accounts for this apparent paradox? Often our perceptions of racial identity are a result of the media and the stereotypical representations that are not only projected but also preserved.

Correspondingly, these stereotypical representations account for not only the widespread transmittal of racial images, but also assure their uniformity across society (Balkaran 1999). As a consequence, the media as an instrument of covert racism serves to preserve the relative boundaries of racial identity. One of the primary vehicles by which and through which racial identities are preserved is through the mass media's manipulation of racial etiquette.

Racial etiquette, within zones of intimacy characterized by family and close friendship networks, proscribes different sets of behaviors for in-group versus out-group actions (Ritterhouse 2006). It is noted that within group settings overt racist practices may indeed be condoned and even encouraged (Killen 2004). Externally a veneer of political correctness may be observed, were racialized elites may assume a state of racelessness (Lewis 2004). Alternatively in what has been termed 'two-faced racism', within some racialized zones racial elite may participate in racial jokes, anecdotes, and derogatory opinions regarding the excluded racialized groups or couched as insider jokes to those currently present. Thus, often fearing ostracism racialized elites and nonelites through their silence essentially lend their support and reaffirm racial etiquette (Picca and Feagin 2007).

Santa Ana (2006), deconstructing this racial etiquette, demonstrates how seemingly innocent jokes about Hispanics frequently part of Jay Leno's opening dialogue, are actually skillfully crafted, racist diatribes. He notes:

> Most of Leno's viewers have come across the pitiful sight of someone struggling to move a broken-down car out of traffic. Such a figure gains our sympathy in an instant ... subtext of Leno's joke is that the value of an unauthorized immigrant is far lower than the family car ... Although his jokes are not overtly violent or crude, it's clear that Leno is a cheerful hatemonger. By laughing at his jokes, his audience claims superiority over an 'inferior other' – the proverbial butt of a joke. Leno's jokes reinforce social boundaries – at the expense of the nation's most vulnerable people. (Santa Ana 2006)

It should be observed that these types of observations are not limited to the USA; in fact, it seems to be universally associated with racial and ethnic discrimination. For example, research conducted in South Africa by Horwitz (1997) and Binnell (1997) document how racial elites inflate their own superiority by deflating that of racial nonelites. Consequently, while they perceive themselves as being superior they describe racial nonelites as greedy, lazy, sexually aggressive, deviant, disrespectful, irresponsible, dependent, greedy, and backward (cited in Burger Allen 2002). Furthermore, as seen in Russia, when racial elites also dominate the police, these types of attitudes can result in selective enforcement, extremism and ethnic intolerance (Punanov and Spirin 2002).

Globally, since 9/11, rising fears of immigrants have been utilized to justify anti-immigrant hostilities, racial profiling and intimidation. Xenophobic fears have surfaced in Denmark, the Netherlands, Belgium, England, France, and Italy, to name but a few.

How racial nonelites respond to racial profiling may be the difference between life and death. In cities across the nation, increased levels of incarceration, fear, and even death has resulted as these nonelite have found their opportunities for freedom and security impaired. Thus, repeated episodes of racial intimidation, profiling, and discrimination may produce increased levels of stress, hypertension, various forms of cancer and other related health conditions.

Back in 1977, Rainville and McCormic demonstrated that covert racism operated in most nationally broadcast games. They observed that announcers were more likely to be sympathetic and excuse poor performance of white players than blacks. Similar research by Hamamoto (1994, 58–61) has demonstrated that both electronic and print media tends to project a Japanese threat to American corporations. As noted by Adachi (2006), the narrow portrayal of Asian Americans as kung fu fighter, studious nerd, mercenary businessman, 'dragon lady', and prostitute covertly maintains the negative views held by many Americans.

Even food and drink can become a tool of covert racism. In France several right wing groups began serving the homeless pork in a deliberate attempt to force both Jews and Moslems from their doors (Smith 2006). In New Orleans, a 2005 study revealed within bars that covert racism took three forms:

> 1 Black 'testers', or patrons, were charged more than white testers for the same drink, often served by the same bartender minutes apart. This was

the most common form of discrimination and occurred in 40 percent of the audited locations.

2 Black patrons were advised of drink-minimum rules while white patrons were not. This occurred in 10 percent of the audited sites.

3 Black patrons were advised of dress codes while white patrons were not. This occurred in 7 percent of the audited sites (Perry 2005).

Racial codes

Racial codes are words, phrases, and/or ideas that may camouflage its true racist intent or purpose. 'Crime and welfare' are racial codes frequently utilized by whites to stigmatize blacks (Gilens 1996). Racial code words are exemplified in Richard Nixon use of the phrases 'law and order' and 'neighborhood schools' (McAndrews 1998, 197). Black politicians have long identified how opponents and the media utilize racially coded messages to their disadvantage (Kleppner 1985). As outlined by Piliawsky:

By the 1980s, white racism had evolved from its nastier blatant forms to respectable racism. No longer fashionable in polite conversation to explicitly race-bait, racism today is more subtly expressed in the code words of merit, competency based education, reverse discrimination, tax revolt, and tuition tax credits. Today's respectable racism is particularly dangerous because it attempts to deprive blacks of the validity of their grievances, thereby placing demands of blacks in the position of appearing to be outrageous. (Piliawsky 1984, 141)

In the south, racially coded words became the norm in political, religious, and social discourse. These subtle words typically are used to describe crime, welfare payments, drug abuse, or out of wedlock births (Kinder and Sanders 1996; Himelstein 1983). Neoconservatives and the new right frequently utilize racial code words in their attacks against affirmative action. (Ansell 1997, Omi and Winant 1994). Frequently, welfare and its reform are often argued in racially coded words where black women are vilified as 'welfare queens'.

> Over a period of about five years, Reagan told the story of the 'Chicago welfare queen' who had 80 names, 30 addresses, 12 Social Security cards, and collected benefits for 'four nonexisting deceased husbands', bilking the government out of 'over $150,000.' The real welfare recipient to whom Reagan referred was actually convicted for using two different aliases to collect $8000. Reagan continued to use his version of the story even after the press pointed out the actual facts of the case to him. (Washington Monthly 2003)

Racially coded words have served to classify many African women in Europe as sexual deviants. An analysis of black women in Europe by Mukami McCrum concludes that the dominant stereotype of black women's sexuality is affirmed and almost legitimized in advertisements in mail order bride magazines that present them as sex objects. Not only does this serve to diminish self-esteem, but also encourages the sexual abuse and exploitation of black women. Similar to what has been documented in the USA, the rape of a black woman, she concludes, is not seen as serious as that of a white woman. She continues that:

> [...] the Single European Act of 1992 banded all Black people together with criminals, terrorists, drug traffickers, and all of them are suspected of being illegal. Women coming to Europe on their own or living here as single parents are seen as economic migrants who work at the low and sinister end of the labour market such as prostitution. They are often condemned and despised by the system and by some Black people who see them as low status women with poor morals and who are a danger to society. (McCrum 1999)

Covert racism, within medicine, has long been documented. In 1990, the American Medical Association Council of Ethical and Judicial Affairs concluded that the association and its members had a long ways to go in 'eradiating racial discrimination'. Louis Sullivan, former secretary of health, stated that there was clear evidence that racial disparities existed in treatment. More recently a 1999 *New England Journal of Medicine* study concluded that heart patients, with similar insurance, 'were afforded inequitable and inferior health care' based solely on color and sex (Callender and Miles 2004, 178).

Racially coded words have also long been recognized within American Psychiatry. Often these words have appeared as 'legitimate' psychiatric or medical diagnoses. The fact that they are presented by so-called authorities merely adds to the veneer of respectability and legitimacy. Benjamin Rush, known as the father of American Psychiatry, articulated the view that the Negro suffered from a congenital form of 'leprosy' that 'appeared in so mild a form that excess pigmentation was its only symptom' (Szasz 1997, 138). Samuel Cartwright, during the same period, determined that slaves who habitually ran away suffered from what he termed as 'drapetomania'. Depending on severity, the cure for drapetomania ranged from frequent beatings and the amputation of the toes (Thomas and Sillen 1972, 128–29). As psychiatry has developed, societal racial biases have been infused into its core. Consequently, for decades

Higher black rates of schizophrenia and paranoid personality disorders, combined with lower black rates of affective disorders, were often explained in terms of innate racial differences. Critics of traditional diagnosis have argued that the prevailing diagnostic categories are largely a result of professional bias. As with sex biases, there is undoubtedly a combination of bias and real difference. (Brown 1990)

Currently, many fear that racial and ethnic nonelite children are more likely to be misdiagnosed as being either mentally ill or developmentally challenged. Therefore, these children are far more likely to be prescribed mind altering antipsychotic and antidepressant drugs. Alternatively, those with 'diagnosed' developmental problems are far more likely to be in so-called 'dummy' tracks. Either extreme leaves the child with little hope for an education, much less hope for the future. Currie (2005) argues that much of the achievement gap witnessed between white and black men has less to do with either psychological or developmental problems, and more to do with access to adequate health systems.

Conclusion: Covert racism and the future

Covert racism, born out of imperialist needs to maximize profit at the expense of racialized others, stands shielded by institutions, culture, stereotypical assumptions, and tradition. Whereas overt racism assumed blatant and insidious forms, covert racism hides behind the façade of 'politeness', politically correctness and expediency. Racially coded words and calls for racial blindness obfuscate the reality of this subtle, subversive, and often hidden form of racism. Covert racism, just like its twin overt racism, is neither innocent nor harmless. The scars of covert racism, often seen in terms of increased levels of disease, negative sanctions, inadequate information, and lost opportunities – serve to continually victimize racial nonelites. Unfortunately, when attention is brought to these subversive and subtle attacks there is a deliberate attempt to minimize, trivialize, or delegitimize the complaints. While this accounts for some of the virulence of covert racism, it leaves more to be addressed. One of the most subversive aspects of covert racism is its practitioners are quite astute and adept at adaptation. Therefore, as implied by Omi and Winant (1994), covert racism also rearticulates. The rearticulation of covert racism functions to produce, recycle, and redefine methods, procedures, and processes targeting racial nonelites to the benefit of racial elites.

Ignoring the problems caused by covert racism does not mean that they will wither away. Part of the reason for the permanence of any form of exploitation is that significant members of society benefit from its presence. One of the tasks of sociology and its' practitioners is to shine the light of reason into the darkness. More specifically, as implied by Baldus (2006, 578), the study of forms of inequality such as covert racism allows sociologists to investigate the 'regenerative and transformative aspects of inequality'. For is it not to this purpose that we as sociologists have answered the call of sociology?

References

American Civil Liberties Union2007, Racial Profiling. http://www.aclu.org/racialjustice/racial profling/index.html (Last accessed September 11, 2007).
Adachi, Jeff 2006. *The Slanted Screen*. Documentary. New York: AAM Productions.
Anti-Defamation League 2005. 'New Century Foundation (American Renaissance).' Extreme in America. http://www.adl.org//learn.ExtUS/Ameren.asp?aaxpicked=58& item=amren (Last accessed July 11,2007)
Ansell, Amy 1997. *New Right, New Racism: Race and Reaction in the United States and Britain*. New York: New York University Press.
Auther, Jennifer 1997. 'American Press reflects racial divide on Simpson Case.' *CNN News Interactive*. http://www.cnn.com/US/9701/20/simpson.press/index.html (last accessed September 12, 2007).
Baldus, Bernd 2006. '... to Race and Gender, Everyone? Some Thoughts on the Future of Research on Social Inequality.' *Canadian Journal of Sociology* 29: 577–82.
Balkaran, Stephen 1999. 'Mass Media and Racism.' *Yale Political Quarterly* 21 (1). http:// www.yale.edu/ypq/articles/oct99/oct99b.html (last accessed October 11, 2007).
Beckett, Katherine, Nyrop Kris and Lori Pfingst 2006. 'Race, Drugs, and Policing: Understanding Disparities in Drug Delivery Arrests.' *Criminology* 44: 105–37.
Beetham, Davis, Sarah Braking, Ian Kearton and Stuart Weir 2001. *International IDEA Handbook on Democracy*. Hague, The Netherlands: Kluwer Law International.
Berger, Vivian 2002. 'A Legacy of Racism.' *National Law Journal* 24 (55).
Bernard Lewis 2002. *Race and Slavery in the Middle East*. Oxford University Press, p. 93. http:// en.wikipedia.org/wiki/Racism#_ref-bboxhill_0 (last accessed July 16, 2007).
Binnell, B. 1997. *A Discourse Analysis of the Racial Talk and Identity Construction of a Group of Working Class Afrikaans Speakers*. Unpublished Dissertation. Johannesburg, South Africa: University of the Witwatersrand.
Blanton, Carlos Kevin 2003. 'From Intellectual Deficiency to Cultural Deficiency: Mexican Americans, Testing, and Public School Policy in the American southwest, 1920–1940.' *Pacific Historical Review* 72: 39–62.
Bodner, John E. 1973. *The Ethnic Experience in Pennsylvania*. Lewisburg, PA: Bucknell University Press.
Bonds, Michael 2002. 'Racial Disparities in Welfare Reform: The Wisconsin Works (W-2). Experience in America's Heartland.' *W. K. Kellogg Foundation*. http://wkkf.org/pubs/Devolution/Pub3703.pdf (last accessed October 20, 2007)
Bonilla-Silva, Eduardo 2006. *Racism without Racist: Color Blind Racism and the Persistence of Racial Discrimination in America*. Lanham, MD: Rowman and

Littlefield. Bonilla-Silva, Eduardo 1997. 'Rethinking Racism: Toward a Structural Interpretation.' *American Sociological Review* **62**: 465-80.

Bonilla-Silva, Eduardo 2001. *White Supremacy and Racism in a Post-Civil Rights Era*. Boulder, CO: Lynne Rynner. Bonilla-Silva, Eduardo 2002. 'The Linguistics of Color Blind Racism: How to Talk Nasty about Blacks without Sounding "Racist".' *Critical Sociology* **28**: 41-64.

Branton, Regina and Bradford S. Jones 2005. 'Reexamining Racial Attitudes; The Conditional Relationships between Diversity and Socioeconomic Environment.' *American Journal of Political Science* **49**: 359-72. http://en.wikipedia.org/wiki/Racial_liberalism_era (last accessed August 2, 2007).

Brown, Phil 1990. 'The Name Game: Toward a Sociology of Diagnosis.' *Journal of Mind And Behaviour* 11: 385 [139]-406 [160]. http://www.power-probe.co.uk/library/pb.htm (last accessed July 17, 2007).

Burger Allen, Danielle 2002. 'Race, Crime and Social Exclusion: A qualitative Study of White Women's Fear of Crime in Johannesburg.' *Urban Forum* **13**, 53.

Bush, George 2003. *President Bush Discusses Michigan Affirmative Action Case* http://www.whitehouse.gov/news/releases/2003/01/20030115-7.html (last accessed October 17, 2007).

Callender, Clive O. and Patrice V. Miles 2004. 'Institutionalized Racism and End-Stage Renal Disease: Is Its Impact Real or Illusionary?' *Seminars in Dialysis* **17**: 177-80.

Carlson, David S., George J. Armelagos and David J. de Laubenfels 1971. 'Problems of Racial Geography.' *Annals of the Association of American Geographers* **61**: 630-33.

Carmichael Stokely and Charles Hamilton 1967. *Black Power: The politics of Liberation in America*. New York, NY: Vintage Books.

Carr, Leslie 1997. *Color Blind Racism*. Thousand Oaks, CA: Sage.

Carter, William H., Michael Schill and Susan Wachter 1998. 'Polarization, Public Housing and Racial Minorities in U.S. Cities.' *Urban Studies* **35**: 1889-911.

Cartmill, Matt 1998. 'The Status of the Race Concept in Physical Anthropology.' *American Anthropologist* (New Series) **100**: 651-60.

Charton, Albert 1930. 'The Social Function of Education in French West Africa.' Pp. 120-1 in *Africans Learn to Be French*, edited by W. Bryant Mumford. London: Evans Brothers.

Chiricos, Theodore and Sarah Eschholz 2002. 'The Racial and Ethnic Typification of Crime and the Criminal Typification of Race and Ethnicity in Local Television News.' *Journal of Research in Crime & Delinquency* **39**: 400-20.

Coates, Rodney D. 2002. 'I Don't Sing, I Don't Dance, and I Don't Play Basketball! Is Sociology Declining in Significance, or Has It Just Returned to Business as Usual?' *Critical Sociology* **28**: 255-70.

Coates, Rodney D. 2006. 'Introduction.' Pp. 1-18 in *Race and Ethnicity: Across Time, Space and Discipline*, edited by Rodney D. Coates. Leiden, MA: Brill.

Coates, Rodney D. 2003. 'Law and the Cultural Production of Race and Racialized Systems of Oppression: Early American Court Cases.' *American Behavioral Scientist* **47**: 329-51.

Cohen, Mark A. 2003 Report on the Racial Impact of GMAC's Finance Charge Markup Policy in the matter of Addie T. Coleman, et al. v. General Motors Acceptance Corporation (GMAC). http:// www.njcitizenaction.org/craautofinancreport.html (last accessed October 20, 2007).

Columbia Law Review 1949. 'Is Racial Segregation Consistent with Equal Protection ofthe Laws? Plessey v. Ferguson Reexamined.' *Columbia Law Review* **49**: 629-639.

Condron, Dennis J. and Vincent J. Roscigno 2003. 'Disparities within: Unequal Spending and Achievement in an Urban School District.' *Sociology of Education* **76**: 18-36.

Corenblum, B., R. C. Annis and J. S. Tanaka 1997. 'Influence of Cognitive Development, Self-Competency, and Teacher Evaluations on the Development of Children's Racial Identity.' *International Journal of Behavioral Development* **20**: 269–86.

Coughey, John and Laree Coughey 1966. *School Segregation on Our Doorsteps: The Los Angeles Story*. Los Angeles, CA: Quail Books.

Crenshaw, Kimberlé (ed.) 1995. *Critical Race Theory: The Key Writings That Formed the Movement*. New York, NY: New Press.

CRL 2006. 'Racial Disparities with Sub-Prime Lenders.' Center for Responsible Lending. http://www.responsiblelending.org/pdfs/rr011exec-Unfair_Lending-0506.pdf (last accessed October 19, 2007).

Cross, Granville 1964. 'The Negro, Prejudice, and the Police.' *Journal of Criminal Law, Criminology, and Police Science* **55**: 405–11.

Currie, Janet 2005. 'Health Disparities and Gaps in School Readiness.' *The Future of Children* **15**: 117–38.

D'Souza, Dinesh 1995. *The End of Racism*. New York, NY: Free Press.

Delgado, Richard 1995. *Critical Race Theory: The Cutting Edge*. Philadelphia, PA: Temple University Press, 1995.

Dentan, Robert K. 1981. '*Batek Negrito Religion: The World View and Rituals of a Hunting and Gathering People of Peninsular Malaysia*. By Kirk Endicott – A Review.' *Journal of Asian Studies* **40**: 421–3.

Dyson, Michael 2006. *Come Hell or High Water: Hurricane Katrina and the Color of Disaster*. New York, NY: Basic Civitas.

Endicott, Kirk 1979. *Negrito Religion: The World-View and Rituals of a Hunting and Gathering People of Peninsula Malaysia*. New York, NY: Clarendon Press.

Entman, Robert M. and Andrew Rojecki 2000. *The Black Image in the White Mind: Media and Race in America*. Chicago, IL: University of Chicago Press.

Fine, Gary Alan, Beth Montemurro, Bbonnie Semora, Marybeth C. Stalp, Dana S. Claussen, and Zayda Sierra 1998. 'Social Order through a Prism: Color as Collective Representation.' *Sociological Inquiry* **68**: 443–457.

Frye, Marilyn 1983. *The Politics of Reality*. Trumansburg, NY: Crossing Press.

Furuhashi, Yoshie 2003. *Max Weber's Genteel Racism*. http://nuance.dhs.org/lbo-talk/0012/0497.html (last accessed July 11, 2007).

Gallop, Alex and George Gallop Jr. 2000. *The Gallop Poll: Public Opinion 1999*. Lanham, MD.: Rowman and Littlefield.

Gannett, Lisa 2001. 'Racism and Human Genome Diversity Research: The Ethical Limits of "Population Thinking".' *Philosophy of Science* **68**: S479–92. Proceedings of the 2000 Biennial Meeting of the Philosophy of Science Association. Part I: Contributed Papers. (September).

Gilens, Martin 1996. '"Race Coding" and White Opposition to Welfare.' *American Political Science Review* **90**: 593–604.

Groff, David H. 1999. A Mission to Civilize: The Republican Idea of Empire in France and West Africa, 1895–1930.' *Journal of World History* **10**: 488–91.

Guinier, Lani 2004. 'From Racial Liberalism to Racial Literacy: Brown v. Board of Education and the Interest-Divergence Dilemma.' *Journal of American History* **91**: 92–118.

Halstead, Mark 1988. *Education, Justice, and Cultural Diversity: An Examination of the Honeyford Affair, 1984–85*. London: Falmer Press.

Hamamoto, Darrell Y. 1994. *Monitored Peril: Asian Americans and the Politics of TV Representation*. Minneapolis, MN: University of Minnesota Press.

Hartman, Heinz 1962. *Enterprise and Politics in South Africa*. Princeton, NJ: Industrial Relations Section, Princeton University.

Henderson, Errol A. 2007. Navigating the Muddy Waters of the Mainstream: Tracing the Mystification of Racism in International Relations.' In *African American Perspectives on Political Science*, edited by Wilbur C. Rich. Philadelphia, PA: Temple University Press.

Himelstein, Jerry 1983. 'Rhetorical Continuities in the Politics of Race. The Closed Society Revisited.' *Southern Speech Communication Journal* **48**: 153–66.
Horwitz, Kevin 1997. *White South African Kinship and Identity*. Unpublished Dissertation. Johannesburg, South Africa: University of the Witwatersrand.
Howard, Judith A. 2000. 'Social Psychology of Identities.' *Annual Review of Sociology* **26**: 367–93.
Hughes, Diane and Deborah Johnson 2001. 'Correlates of Children's Experiences of Parents' Racial Socialization Behaviors.' *Journal of Marriage and the Family* **63**: 981–95.
Jacobs, David and Robert M. O'Brien 1998. 'The Determinants of Deadly Force: A Structural Analysis of Police Violence.' *American Journal of Sociology* **103**: 837–62.
Janiewski, Dolores E. 2004. 'Taking Land, Breaking Land: Women Colonizing the American West and Kenya (Review).' *Journal of Colonialism and Colonial History* **5**: 99–101.
Johnson, Kevin 2003. 'FBI Reports Small Drop in Crime Rates.' *USA Today*. http://www.usatoday.com/news/washington/2003-06-16-fbi-crime_x.htm (last assessed October 26, 2006).
Kellstedt, Paul M. 2000. 'Media Framing and the Dynamics of Racial Policy Preferences.' *American Journal of Political Science* **44**: 245–60.
Killen, Melanie 2004. 'Social Reasoning about Racial Exclusion in Intimate and Nonintimate Relationship.' *Youth and Society* **35**: 293–322.
Kinder, Donald and Lynne Sanders 1996. *Divided by Color. Racial Politics and Democratic Ideals*. Chicago, IL: University of Chicago Press.
Kleppner, Paul 1985. *Chicago Divided: The Making of a Black Mayor*. DeKalb, IL: Northern Illinois University Press.
Lehrman, Sally 2007. *Color-Blind Racism*. Maynard Institute. http://www.maynardije.org/news/features/040913_lehrman-part2/sidebar1/ (last accessed on October 21, 2007).
Leiter, Jeffrey 1986. 'Reactions to Subordination: Attitudes of Southern Textile Workers.' *Social Forces* **64**: 948–74.
Lewis, Amanda 2004. 'What Group: Studying Whites and Whiteness in an Era of "Color-Blindness".' *Sociological Theory* **22**: 623–46.
Lewis, David L. 2001. *W.E.B. Du Bois: The Fight for Equality and the American Century, 1919–1963*. New York, NY: Owl Books.
Lewis, Oscar 1996. 'The Culture of Poverty.' In *Urban Life*, edited by George Gmelch and Walter P. Zenner. Prospect Heights, IL: Waveland Press.
Li Leiwei, David 2004. 'On Ascriptive and Acquisitional Americanness: The Accidental Asian and the Illogic of Assimilation.' *Contemporary Literature* **45**: 106–34.
Lieberman, Leonard 1968. 'The Debate over Race: A Study in the Sociology of Knowledge.' *Phylon* (1960–) **28**: 127–41.
Lipsitz, George 1995. 'Toxic Racism.' *American Quarterly* **47**: 416–27.
Littell, Franklin H. 1965. 'From Persecution or Toleration to Liberty Theory into Practice.' *Our Religious Heritage and the Schools* **4**: 3–7.
Loewen, James W. 2005. *Sundown Towns: A Hidden Dimension of American Racism*. New York, NY: New Press.
Massey, Douglas and Nancy Denton 1988. 'The Dimensions of Residential Segregation.' *Social Forces* **67**: 281–315.
Massey, Douglas and Nancy Denton 1989. 'Hypersegregation in U.S. Metropolitan Areas: Black and Hispanic Segregation Along Five Dimensions.' *Demography* **26**: 373–91.
Massey, Douglas and Nancy Denton 1993. *American Apartheid: Segregation and the Making of the Underclass*. Cambridge, MA: Harvard University Press.
McAndrews, Lawrence J. 1998. 'The Politics of Principle: Richard Nixon and School Desegregation.' *Journal of Negro History* **83**: 187–200.

McCrum, Mukami 1999. '"Letter" Cited in WCC (World Council of Churches) 1999.' *Understanding Racism Today: A Dossier.* http://www.wcc-coe.org/wcc/what/jpc/doss-e.html (last accessed September 26, 2006).
McIntosh, Peggy 1988. 'White Privilege: Unpacking the Invisible Knapsack.' Wellesley College Center for Research on Women, Wellesley, MA.
McWorter, John 2000. *Losing the Race: Self-Sabotage in Black America.* Glencoe, IL: Free Press.
Mills, Charles 1997. *The Racial Contract.* Ithaca, NY: Cornell University Press.
Morris, Benny 2006. 'Power without Grace Is a Curse.' *The Guardian*, February 9, 2006. http:// www.guardian.co.uk/usa/story/0,,1705532,00.html (last accessed on line on July 18, 2007)
Morrison, Toni 1992. *Playing in the Dark: Whiteness and the Literary Imagination.* Cambridge, MA: Harvard University Press.
Moynihan, Daniel P. 1968. 'Toward a National Urban Policy.' *Public Interests* (**Fall**): 8–9.
Ndikumana, Leonce and James Boyce 1998. 'Congo's Odious Debt: External Borrowing and Capital Flight in Zaire.' *Development and Change* **29**: 195–217.
Nkrumah, Kwame 1965. *Neo-Colonialism, The Last Stage of Imperialism.* London: Thomas Nelson & Sons.
Omi, Michael and Howard Winant 1994. *Racial Formation in the United States: From 1960s to 1990s.* New York, NY: Routledge Press.
Pearce, Diana M. 1979. 'Gatekeepers and Home Seekers: Institutional Patterns in Racial Steering.' *Social Problems* **26**: 325–42.
Perry, James 2005. '*Bourbon Street Discrimination Audit*' conducted by the Greater New Orleans Fair Housing Center. http://www.gnofairhousing.org/index.html (last accessed October 12, 2006).
Picca, Leslie Houts and Joe R. Feagin 2007. *Two-Faced Racism: Whites in the Backstage and Frontstage.* UK: Taylor and Francis.
Pilgrim, David 2002. 'The Jezebel Stereotype.' *Jim Crow Museum*, http://www.ferris.edu/news/ jimcrow/menu.htm (last accessed July 10, 2007)
Piliawsky, Monte 1984. 'Racial Equality in the United States: From Institutionalized Racism to 'Respectable' Racism.' *Phylon* (1960–) **45**: 135–43. Prendergast, Jane 2002. 'Cincinnati Riots, One Year Later: Violence up, Arrest down.' *The Cincinnati Enquirer* (April 7). http://www.enquirer.com/oneyearlater/ (last assessed October 26, 2006).
Prosise, Theodore O. 2004. 'Law Enforcement and Crime on Cops and World's Wildest Police Videos: Anecdotal Form and the Justification of Racial Profiling.' *Western Journal of Communication (Winter). http://www.allbusiness.com/legal/laws/987095-1.html* (last assessed October 26, 2006).
Punanov, Grigory and Yury Spirin 2002. 'Police Didn't Notice Anything Wrong.' *Current Digest of the Post Soviet Press* **54**: 13.
Purvis, Michaek 2004. '"Genteel" Racism Still with Us, Speaker Says.' *Sault Star*, May 7, 2004. http://www.debwewin.ca/articles.htm#article3 (last accessed July 12, 2007).
Rainville, Raymond E. and Edward McCormick 1977. 'Extent of Covert Racial Prejudice in Pro Football Announcers' Speech.' *Journalism Quarterly* **54**: 20–26.
Rambally, Rae Tucker 2002. *Practice Imperfect Reflections on a Career in Social Work.* Ste-Anne-de-Bellevue, QC: Shoreline.
Ritterhouse, Jennifer 2006. *Growing up in Jim Crow: The Racial Socialization of White and Black Southern Children: 1890–1940.* Chapel Hill, NC: University of North Carolina Press.
Roberts, Dorothy E. 1997. *Killing the Black Body: Race, Reproduction, and the Meaning of Liberty.* New York, NY: Pantheon Books.
Rockquemore, Kerry Ann 2002. 'Negotiating the Color Line: The Gendered Process of Racial Identity Construction among Black/White Biracial Women.' *Gender and*

Society **16**: 485–503. African American Women: Gender Relations, Work and the Political Economy of the Twenty-First Century (August).
Roediger, David 1999. *The Wages of Whiteness*. London: Verso.
Russell, Steve 2002. 'Apples Are the Color of Blood.' *Critical Sociology* **28**: 65–76.
Sanchez, Marta E. 1998. 'La Malinche at the Intersection: Race and Gender in Down These Mean Streets.' *PMLA* **113**: 117–28.
Santa Ana, Otto 2006. 'The Racial Politics behind Anti-Immigration Jokes.' UCLA Today, Online. http://www.today.ucla.edu/voices/otto-santa-ana_jokes/ (last accessed June 12, 2007).
Sivanandan, A. 2005. 'Asian Youth Movements: Here to Stay, Here to Fight.' *Red Pepper*. http:// www.redpeper.org.uk/society/x-jun05-sivanandan.htm
Smith, Craig 2006. 'In France a Meal of Intolerance.' http://www.iht.com/articles/2006/02/ 27/news/journal.php (last assessed September 26, 2006).
Smith, John David 2005. 'A Historic Life: John Hope Franklin Recalls His Distinguished Life and the Times He Helped Change.' *The News and Observer*. http://www.newsobserver.com/ 208/369295.html (last accessed July 11, 2007).
Smith, Stephen 2007. 'Test of Trainees Finds Signs of Race Bias in Care.' The Boston Globe, July 20 edition. http://www.boston.com/news/local/articles/2007/07/20/tests_of_er_trainees_ find_signs_of_race_bias_in_care/ (last accessed October 17, 2007).
Spencer, Margaret B. and Carol Markstrom-Adams 1990. 'Identity Processes among Racial and Ethnic Minority Children in America.' *Child Development* **61**: 290–310.
Stevenson, Howard C., Rick Cameron, Teri Herrero-Taylor and Gwen Davis 2002. 'Development of the Teenager Experience of Racial Socialization Scale: Correlates of Race-Related Socialization Frequency from the Perspectives of Black Youth.' *Journal of Black Psychology* **28**: 84–106.
Stovall, Tyler 2003. 'National Identity and Shifting Imperial Frontiers: Whiteness and the Exclusion of Colonial Labor after World War I.' *Representations* **84**: 52–72.
Szasz, Thomas 1997. *The Manufacture of Madness A Comparative Study of the Inquisition & the Mental Health Movement*. Syracuse, NY: Syracuse University Press.
Thomas, Audrey and Samuel Sillen 1972. *Racism and Psychiatry*. New York, NY: Brunner/ Mazel.
Turner, Stephen 1974. *Weber and Islam: A Critical study*. London: Routledge & Kegan Paul.
Van Ausdale, Debra and Joe R. Feagin 2001. *The First R: How Children Learn Race and Racism*. Lanham, MD: Rowman and Littlefield.
Walsh, Keith 2004. 'Color-Blind Racism in Grutter and Gratz.' *Boston College Third World Law Journal* **24**: 443–67.
Washington Post 2003. 'The Mendacity Index.' http://www.washingtonmonthly.com/features/ 2003/0309.mendacity-index.html (last accessed October 20, 2007).
West, Cornell 1994. *Race Matters*. New York, NY: Vintage.
White, Bob W. 1996. 'Talk about School: Education and the Colonial Project in French and British Africa (1860–1960).' *Comparative Education* **32**: 9–25.
Wilson, William J. 1980. *The Declining Significance of Race: Blacks and Changing American Institutions* (2nd edn). Chicago, IL: University of Chicago Press.
Yanich, Danilo 2001. 'Location, Location, Location: Urban and Suburban Crime on Local TV News.' *Journal of Urban Affairs* **23**: 3–4.

PART III

COVERT RACISM AND THE INDIVIDUAL

THE INEFFABLE STRANGENESS OF RACE

Patricia J. Williams

"I mean, you got the first mainstream African-American who is articulate and bright and clean and a nice-looking guy ... I mean, that's a storybook, man."
-Senator Joseph Biden, in faint but unfettered praise of Senator Barack Obama

Introduction

A few years ago, the New York Historical Society curated a fascinating show about the legacy of slavery in New York. One of the commissioned pieces that accompanied the display was a short film by artists Bradley McCallum and Jacqueline Terry. It featured McCallum, who is white, and Terry, who is black, configured as a so-called "twinning doll"–a nineteenth century toy that had two heads and torsos that met in the middle. At the dolls' waists would be attached a long skirt or a cloak. Held vertically, the skirt falls and obscures the other end. Flipped one way, it becomes, a white doll. Turned upside down, the skirt flips and suddenly it is a black doll. In the film, McCallum and Tarry, joined at the waist by some feat of pixilated trickery and dressed in 19th century clothing, flip head over head down a long dark marble corridor, first a white head, then a black head, then a white man, then a black woman, first a Thomas Jefferson, then a Sally Hemmings. As their monograph describes it, "the races are joined head to toe…continuously revealing and concealing one another." Such an interesting metaphor for the state of our union.

If our public discourse too often assumes a neat bipolarity of race–black, white and never the twain overlap–the reality has always been more complicated, more slippery, more malleable, more hidden. Race, so frequently and reductively biologized, is more comprehensively and accurately analyzed as a form of narration. It is what we say it is. Sometimes it is a stigma, sometimes a line of descent, sometimes a taboo, sometimes a phenotype, a behavior, an association, an intimacy, a state of mind, an economic condition, a pseudo-science, almost always ways a line in the sand.

The narrative bounds of race pick a line among competing civic legacies: between due process and its deprivation; between integration and its opposite; between negative stereotype and assumptions of human dignity. Race is hard work. It is political work, of course, as we struggle to be human rather than sub-human, free as opposed to enslaved or imprisoned, enfranchised rather than disenfranchised. It is psychological work as we pursue happiness through a discourse of esteem, a search for the kind of bodily and mental integrity that allows us to rest in the home of our corporeality–without having to leap out of our selves, alter our noses, literally tear out our hair, or go out of our minds in order to live among others and to be welcome in the marketplace as employable actors. It is ethical work, in that ethics is the study of normatively-derived minimal standards of care in our treatment of each other; and stereotyping is an ugly inversion of those formulaic norms. And of course it is, perpetually, the hardest of legal work.

We live in a precarious moment, when the legacy of the civil rights movement is at a kind of crossroads. A new eugenics movement is on the rise, reinvigorated by a "market" for "Ivy League" eggs and adoptive babies, and assisted by rapid enhancements in reproductive technology, cosmetic surgery, and genetic engineering. There is a reemergence of profiling by race, ethnicity, religion and medical condition–and greatly expanded abilities to mine that data, both because of the powers granted to governments by the USA Patriot Act, and because of the speed with which computers can now sort trillions of bits of information. And, in a world where DNA can pinpoint inherent INequalities, the very cornerstone of our constitutional identity–the notion of equal personhood–is increasingly vexed by a cultural context where one's value is negotiable rather than assumed; and where the power to fix that value is driven by advertising, profit, relative supply and demand, and fashion in the most fleeting and momentary sense.

In the essay that follows, I will look at three narrative models of race that frame much of contemporary discourse: first, the concept of neo-interracialism, second, the biologizing of blackness, and, finally, race as economic choice. I will discuss some of the limitations of each, and suggest how each offers opportunities for coalition in a diasporic, globalized world that is evolving toward a society that looks different from the demographic that shaped the civil rights movement of the last century. I do not mean to suggest that these three are the only ways in which race is discussed–not by any stretch of the imagination. They are not even the models that dominate the traditional legal literature of civil rights. But I focus on them because they seem to me to be some of the most influential of the trends that are shaping the future of how we think about race. At the same time, I do not write with a great sense of certainty about what the future holds. It is my hope that these thoughts will stimulate further discussion and caution about a world that is unfolding at a hurtling, disordered pace, faster than our collective imagination might easily grasp.

Neo-Inter-Racialism

When I was coming of age in the late nineteen sixties and early nineteen seventies, the operative imagery of the hopeful integrationist was the iconic "grey baby." This was a predictable reductionism given that the headlines of the day were absorbed with "love-ins" and "race-mixing." *Loving v. Virginia*, the 1967 Supreme Court case that struck down anti-miscegenation law, was a recent and seismic cultural event. The extensive history of actual miscegenation was still a great big public secret, unacknowledged, hidden within the dual dungeons of "rape" and/or "passing."

Today, interracial relationships are a complicated badge of something like assimilationist pride–not yet not-a-big-deal. The flutters are small but familiar lore. When a black man and a white woman become a couple they cannot just be happy: they will be analyzed. Does the man hate black women, or is he just selfish in not preferring a black mate to propagate "the race" in a time of its diminishment? The woman will be analyzed for signs of flooziness and drug use and gold-diggery. Her parents will be rumored to have fainted when told; his parents will fear for his life. Landlords and private school admissions committees will love their offspring because it will be assumed that a black child (the child is always and anthropologically black) of a white mother will not grow up to be as sulky as Al Sharpton. No matter what their personal circumstance, they will be cast as Romeo and Juliet, beleaguered and over-determined by social anxiety.

Similarly, a white man and a black woman who make their lives together will have to endure the presumption of those who wonder what he sees in her; they must navigate the silently-performed but rarely-verbalized aesthetic norms that weigh down the assertion that "black is beautiful." The white man will be assessed for social status, and for the degree to which he makes public his commitment. He will be expected to fly a small plane over Yankee Stadium advertising his smitten status in order to overcome the worry that he is a race fetishist with a fine array of antique whips and chains lined up neatly in the bedroom closet.

In essence, these sentiments are not new. The configurations are contemporary, perhaps, the byproduct of social and legal shifts allowed in the wake of the civil rights movement. But I do not think that the purported surge in interracial marriages, for example, is really a "new" inter-racialism. I prefer the term "neo"-inter-racialism to signify a revival or continuation of older, semi-repressed but much more conservative attitudes that do not equate race-mixing as exactly the same thing as the erasure of race.

Consider the 1998 case of Bethany Godby v. Montgomery, Alabama School District, 996 F.Supp. 1390 (M.D.Ala. 1998). The plaintiff was a USDA-certifiable grade-A "grey baby." Her mother was black and her father white. Despite an official posture of integration and post-race-ness, her high school celebrated the rites of matriculation with a series of proms: there was a black prom queen; there was a white prom queen; and then there was a school-wide election for which of the two would be the all-school prom queen (who in any event would be required to have both a black and a white attendant.)

Ms. Godby's classmates elected her to be prom queen: the (ahem) white prom queen. The school administration then invalidated the vote. There was a factual dispute as to whether it was because of inaccuracies in the voting process, but the plaintiff asserted that the school attempted to persuade her to accept the (more appropriate? eye-of-the beholder?) title of black prom queen. Ms. Godby sued. For what was not immediately clear. Judge Harold Albriton issued a somewhat confused opinion on procedural grounds and the case never went to trial. But the confusion surely must have stemmed from whether Bethany Godby was suing to be allowed to declare herself white; or whether she was suing to do away with this racially layered prom segregation and all racial designations; or if she was suing for recognition of some third category, to whit, "biracial" prom queen?

The public discussion, including some choice internet interventions, was widely consumed with wondering why the school couldn't take into account her mixed blood, her intertextual status–why couldn't they be more embracing of what was, frankly, by any other name, a very old color-informed hierarchy or tiered system, still extant but unacknowledged as such. What a paradox of desired resolution: the tragic mulatta prom queen. The dyspeptic quadroon prom queen. The angst-filled octaroon....

Do we want to call this progress?

Let me try to complicate the picture further: The front page of the March 22, 2007 edition of *The New York Post* offered a fascinating study in the contradictions of our culture. The top half of the page was consumed by "a stunning mother-child portrait" of Angelina Jolie with little Pax, then her newest adopted child, or as the Post put it, her "Viet man." For details, see Page Six. The lower half of the page was given over to a more lurid headline ("Baby Bungle: White folks' black child") trumpeting "a Park Avenue fertility clinic's blunder" that "left a family devastated–after a black baby was born to a Hispanic woman and her white husband…" Further details, see Page Six.

I did want more details. I turned to page six. As it turns out, *The New York Post* has a separate numerical universe in which celebrities romp, whether idolized, idealized, demonized or drunk. And so the story about Jolie's magical mothering of her rainbow brood was on the trademarked Page Six–a gossipy parallel universe of make-believe–to wit, on what the rest of us plebes would call page seventeen.

The bungled baby story, meanwhile, was to be found on page six as determined by the ancient fingers-and-toes methodologies of flat earth. No rainbow magic in this cave: New Yorkers Nancy and Tom Andrews had trouble conceiving after the birth of their first daughter. They employed in vitro fertilization and baby Jessica was born. Jessica is darker-skinned than either of the Andrewses, a condition that their obstetrician initially called an "abnormality." She'll "lighten up" according to that good doctor. Subsequent paternity tests showed that Nancy Andrews' egg was fertilized by sperm other than that of Tom Andrews. The couple has sued the clinic for unspecified damages.

If this were all there were, the story might simply fall within the growing precedent of a number of other technological mix-ups resulting in so-called "wrongful birth" suits for lost eggs, failed vasectomies, botched amniocenteses, etc. However freighted this relatively new area of bioethics may be, there is a general and legally recognized expectation interest that a certain standard of care will be observed in the handling of genetic material. This, despite the fact that there are undisputed ethical difficulties with any of these cases, particularly in considering how damages are awarded. Just to start with, it's a bit of a conundrum to call the birth of a healthy child "wrongful." Therefore, courts tend to be conservative in how monetary awards are framed: awarding the costs of raising an unplanned child or one who has health problems resulting from medical malfeasance is obviously less troubling than awarding damages for "the pain and suffering" of parenting a child labeled "unwanted." How does one measure, in dollar or public policy terms, parental "disappointment" at the birth of a baby? Indeed, in the Andrews case, a judge has permitted the malpractice claim to go forward but has thrown out the claim for the mental distress of the parents.

The Andrews case, however, goes a step further than compensation measured by the loss of the father's procreative interest in generation. The Andrews' also (and also unsuccessfully) sought damages for Jessica's pain and suffering, apparently for having to live life marooned on an island of blackness and misery. The judge's opinion quotes the Andrews' concern that Jessica "may be subjected to physical and emotional illness as a result of not being the same race as her parents and siblings." They are "distraught" about what she will do to the family dynamic given that she is "not even the same race, nationality, color ... as they are." They describe Jessica's conception as a "mishap" so "unimaginable" that they have not told many of their relatives about "the situation." (Telling the tabloids all about it must have come easier.) "We fear that our daughter will be the object of scorn and ridicule by other children, both in school and as she grows up" because Jessica has " "characteristics more typical of African or African-American descent." So "while we love Baby Jessica as our own, we are reminded of this terrible mistake each and every time we look at her; it is simply impossible to ignore…We are reminded each and every time we appear in public with her…" (Venezia 2007)

There is much to be said about what this construction of affairs will do to Jessica, now two, when she is old enough to understand; or about the mindset of an attorney who would press a case in such terms; or about why the media could not reign itself in from printing Jessica's real name. But here's the really interesting part. After reading the story in *The Post*, I turned to other media accounts, and it turns out that *The New York Daily News* had a embellished the story with a picture of the family–from a 2006 greeting card no less. And Jessica looks exactly like her mother and elder sister. It is true that Jessica is slightly darker than her mother, and that her hair is somewhat curlier than her sister's, but all three females are pretty clearly African-descended. As one of my students put it, if anything, it is the paleness of the father's skin that marks him as the "different" one.

More than anything else, the picture underscores the embedded cultural oddities of this case, the invisibly shifting boundaries of how we see boundary, extend intimacy, name "difference." According to the *Post*, Mrs. Andrews is "Hispanic"; and apparently one Hispanic woman plus one "white" man equals "a white couple." In other accounts, the mother is "a light-skinned Dominican" which ranking seems to indicate that while she may not be "white," she's surely not "black." In either event, the narrative seems to imply that if the correct sperm had been used, the Andrewses would have somehow been guaranteed a lighter-skinned child. But, genetically, that's impossible to say, particularly given that most all Dominicans trace their heritage to some mixture of African slaves, indigenous islanders and European settlers, and that darkness of skin color is a dominant trait. It could be, in other words, that the true sperm donor is as "white" as her husband.

That possibility is entirely absent from the word boxes in which this child is contained. Not only is she viewed as being of a different color than either of her parents, but also of a race apart from either of them and, "even" of a different nationality–this latter the most startling for its pure-blood-line configuration of citizenship itself.

Who knows? Maybe my worry is disproportionate. Indeed, I might have consigned all of this to the sensationalized nature of grist for the tabloid mills had I not participated in a lawyerly fracas some weeks later, a strategizing seminar at which this case came up. Well-educated legal minds of all political stripes were arguing that there is nothing wrong in the parents' claim, that it is a private choice they made to have a family that looks "like" them; and why shouldn't they get some money for the girl's "trauma" because after all it is empirically harder to be black in this society. (I could not help noticing that more than a few of the people arguing this stance were the same ones who have argued against affirmative action because we are supposedly such a colorblind society.) More significantly, if this reasoning is any kind of reflection of the culture at large, then its logic seems to signal a privatization not merely of family choice, but of the entire civil rights movement. By such calculation, discrimination is no longer a social problem that implicates all of us and our institutions as unloving or less than inclusive. The stigma of difference is positioned as something beyond what we ought to tackle collectively–it's "their choice" after all. Instead, difference becomes destiny, biological defect, and eugenic misfortune.

It is ironic, these purportedly colorblind times. In Georgia, just last year, there was a bill in the state legislature to make April no less than Confederate Heritage Month. Not Southern Heritage Month, but Confederate. Whatever romance there may be in the collective memory, I think it's important to remember that the Confederate Constitution was almost identical to that of the United States. The only significantly different provision was one that said: "No bill of attainder, ex post facto law, or law denying or impairing the right of property in negro slaves shall be passed." (Clause 4, Section 9)

In an era when none of us are slaves but all of us are increasingly objects in the market place, it is sad and alarming that "Negro" features, however whimsically perceived or shiftily delineated, still lower the value of the human product, of human grace.

The split front page of the New York Post reflected the cultural doublespeak of neo-inter-racialism—the Vietnamese-born Pax and the Cambodian-born Maddox and the Ethiopian-born Zahara all enjoying the ethereally perfumed embrace of Angelina and Brad, versus the local, on-the-ground "disaster" of being born Jessica.

This doublespeak is, clearly, a political phenomenon as well. When Jessica Andrews was described by her parents as being of a different "nationality," it made me think of Republican strategist Richard Viguerie's characterization of the Democratic Party: "With the feminists, the homosexual groups, the other interest groups, you put it all together with the black interest groups, and it does not look like America." (Williams 2007) It is an interesting question at this moment in history, the little matter of what America looks like. If one pursues Mr. Viguerie's point to its logical end, "real" Americans must be male and straight and white and not especially interested in any "other" group. This division between supposedly authentic Americans and those "others" is, according to a report in the *New York Times*, the new-for-the 2008-elections but ever-so-old line to be "pounded" into the media by the Republican punditry, of whom Viguerie is a prime player. The Democratic Party is to be figured as a ghetto of women, wusses and macaca-lovers. Republicans are straight arrows whose manly brows glisten with the pale dew of impartiality.

At the same time, Mr. Viguerie insists that this is not about race or gender. He's just against "special interests." If you are so crass as to think it's about prejudice, well, that's just because you're one of those annoying people who see isms under every rock. This rhetorical spinmanship is ubiquitous right now. Everywhere, there are protestations of high-mindedness while embracing the de facto resegregation of this entire nation. It can be seen in the endlessly reductive discussions about the Michigan Civil Rights Initiative, an anti-affirmative action measure voters endorsed in the last election. Like the one passed in California some years ago, it eliminates not just affirmative action but all mention of race in most every publicly funded arena, for any purpose including remediation (except law enforcement–got to leave that window for police profiling). It even bars collection of demographic data involving housing, health and schools. Talk about killing the messenger. Ward Connerly, lead architect of the initiative, is a black man himself, and so, the argument goes, how on earth could the initiative be bad for black people? Don't you like black men? In addition, what an exceptional black man he is! When the Ku Klux Klan formally endorsed the initiative, Connerly returned the embrace: "If the Ku Klux Klan thinks that equality is right, God bless them. Thank them for finally reaching the point where logic and reason are being applied, instead of hate." (Associated Press 2006)

This is not logic, reason, equality, colorblindness, or integration. Plain and simple, it is hypocrisy of the highest order.

The Pseudo-Biology of Blackness

There has been, of late, a broad swathe of Americans forking out loads of cash to determine their genetic connection to fame, to fortune, and to name-brand-worthy ancestors. There has been a veritable surge of quasi-phrenological parlor games, so to speak. A typical article appeared in the *New York Times* not long ago, entitled "DNA Tells Students They Aren't Who They Thought." It described a sociology class at Pennsylvania State University, where DNA tests are regularly administered to students and analyzed for "genetic ancestry." Professor Mark Shriver is a partner in a company called DNAPrint Genomics, which claims to have devised a test that "compares DNA with that of four parent populations, western European, west African, east Asian and indigenous American." (Daly 2005) (The degree to which this so-called identification is based on sample sets averaging about one hundred people is a flaw so egregious that it deserves a separate essay. The work of Harvard anthropologist Duana Fullwiley (2008) is an excellent resource on this point. Moreover, the ethics of a professor with a commercial interest in the banking of DNA making its collection part of routine course work was not addressed in the Times' article.)

Nevertheless, that a test could indeed reveal ancestry based on broad migratory patterns over human history is not a surprise. Certain clusters of genetic mutations over millennia occur more frequently among specific populations. Melanin concentration, for example, can reveal how one's ancestors adapted to more or less sunny climes; evolutionary selection for sickle cell anemia was a response to malarial mosquitoes. However, there is no specific genetic marker that distinguishes one race from another. External differences—like hair, skin color and eye shape–are not linked to inner differences, no matter how strong the myths about skull size, extra leg muscles or musical aptitude. I should think that this would all be abundantly clear by this enlightened age, but none of it was laid out in the article in the *Times*. Instead, there was only lengthy discussion of the degree to which the Penn State students were revealed to be "white" or "black."

About half of the one hundred students tested in Professor Shriver's seminar were white "according to another instructor." "And every one of them said, 'Oh man I hope I'm part black,' because it would upset their parents...People want to identify with this pop multiracial culture. They don't want to live next to it, but they want to be part of it. It's cool."

It's odd, this insistence that there is no such thing as race even as we wouldn't want it moving in next door. There is, too, a remarkable persistence in re-inscribing race onto the narrative of biological inheritance. This science is always pursued for only the noblest of reasons: in Shriver's instance, "the potential importance of racial or ethnic background to drug trials." I will save for another essay my concern about the errors embedded in the commercial competition for "race-specific" medicines. For now, consider the description of one student who "discovered" she was "58 percent European and 42 percent African." Yet the "parent populations" tested for were described only as "western European" and "west African." The young woman "has always thought of herself as half black and half white because her mother is Irish-Lithuanian and her father West Indian." But Lithuania is generally considered a part of Eastern Europe, and therefore not technically part of the population tested for. And while "West Indian" is clearly used as a cipher for her African ancestry, one can be "white"–like Alexander Hamilton–while being West Indian. And the Irish were not considered white in colonial times. Similarly, East Asians have gone in and out of being considered white in our history. South Asians, many being the closest descendants of the original "Aryans," are generally not thought of as white in this country. Yet the incoherent use of Aryan is apparent in any dictionary, to wit, Webster's: "1. Indo-European... 2. Nordic... 3. Gentile...." (Merriam-Webster)

The measure by which these indivisible habits work despite us, or unintentionally, is perhaps evident in what the Irish-Lithuanian-West Indian student–the one who thought she was half and half–had to say about the test results: "I was surprised at how much European I was, because though my father's family knows there is a great-great-grandfather who was Scottish, no one remembered him.... I knew it was true, because I have dark relatives with blue eyes, but to bring it up a whole 8 percent, that was shocking to me." What is interesting is the flat conception of half-and-half ancestry–a kind of assumed "purity" of blackness and whiteness. One side had to be entirely African by her measure, one side entirely European. If she's 58 percent European, she assumes the embodied 8 percent must be on the "black" side. The discussion never moves into the more difficult recognition that most West Indians probably have more than 8 percent European ancestry (but that like so many American families, hers might "know" but "not remember" the complicated, often clandestine couplings of the Triangle Trade). It certainly does not seem to occur to anyone that her white parent might also have an African ancestor.

The jumble of who we are, particularly as residents of the New World, with its centuries of rapid, recent migrations, is not explored in the *Times* article. The single mention of migratory patterns is misleading: The students whose DNA revealed both African and European ancestors were described as "members of the fastest-growing ethnic grouping in the United States...mixed race." But to the extent that a DNA swipe shows "mixing," there is nothing "new" about it; our ancestors have been mixing it up since the first mothers left central Africa–in the long-ago, ancient sense, it is true that "we are all African." Moreover, genes show neither race nor the cultural practices we usually refer to as ethnicity. The absurdity is highlighted by one of the Penn State students, a warm-brown-colored young man pictured in cornrows, who says that even though he tested at "48 percent European" he values his blackness, since "both my parents are black." He goes on to muse: "Just because I found out I'm white, I'm not going to act white." The article ends with an observation that "whatever his genes say," the young man will likely always "be seen as black–at least by white Americans."

Consider the narratives herein: Genes "speak" race; whiteness is a biological inheritance that can be consciously "acted"; and blackness is defined by the eye of the white beholder.

If history has shown us anything, it's that race is contradictory and unstable. Yet our linguistically embedded notions of race seem to be on the verge of transposing themselves yet again into a context where supposed genetic percentages act as the ciphers for culture and status, as well as economic and political attributes. In another generation or two, the privileges of whiteness may indeed be extended to those who, like Ms. Godby, are not only "half" this or that, but 53.2 percent thereof. Let us not mistake it for anything like progress. We've been this way before.

I wonder too, what becomes of liberalism itself, at a moment when DNA can pinpoint not just how closely I may be related to Tom DeLay or not just whether I am susceptible to a variety of dieases, but can also pinpoint and establish beyond the shadow of a doubt individual biological, medical, and mental inequalities. This poses an interesting challenge to our presumptions of political equality, in that it is beginning to spur policies that will privilege certain groups of people over others, if not as a matter of overt state policy, then as popular "privatized" eugenic "choice." Coming soon: preemptive quarantine or sterilization of those more prone to contracting certain diseases; preemptive detention of those prone to aggression; preemptive hiring; preemptive genetic alteration in favor of desired (meaning marketable rather than loved) qualities. A world of all sorts of well-meaning hierarchical mischief: whether the treasured allelomorph for blond hair or "gotcha" IQ numbers in a world where no one covets his neighbor's wife anymore, but only his neighbor's child's stratospheric SAT scores.

All this is occurring, moreover, in a market context where there's a price on our heads. We are not "unalienable" if every last thought, deed, and body part has a price tag hanging from it–when we can be marked as "alien" so easily, so permanently, so beyond the community of survival and exchange.

One separate but no less pressing question is why one would want to use DNA to track one's family history rather than excavate ancestral life lessons by more traditional narrative means. I suppose one obvious answer is that for us who are the near-descendents of slaves, it is precisely the lack of other records than our bodies–the traumatically aborted family narrative–that inspires the frantic pursuit of knowledge, the hunger for certainty given generations of namelessness and rupture. At the same time, we must ponder: what are the limits of such biologized hindsight? How many graves must we dig up to complete ourselves? Is there not inevitable disappointment in the quest to know everything, to know absolutely?

Recently, the American television-viewing public has been busily enjoying Harvard Professor Henry Louis Gates's exploration of his roots and those of a handful of other prominent African-American figures, including comedians Chris Tucker and Whoopi Goldberg; scholar Sarah Lawrence-Lightfoot; and, of course, media mogul Oprah Winfrey. It has been a fascinating series of TV programs, particularly from the perspective of the discipline of history. It reveals the peculiar difficulties of tracking lines of descent through slavery, the sales of human beings that acknowledged no family ties, the absence of last names, the absence of first names in some cases and the necessity of consulting not just census records but also "the master's" property holdings for listings of possible relatives. The reconstruction of family history is like an archeological dig, part intergenerational storytelling, part study of migratory patterns, part recovery of commercial transactions and part science.

The science du jour is, of course, DNA testing, and here is where the programs run into some rather careless uses of that science. On the one hand, DNA testing can be quite useful in establishing certain kinds of family relation. But it is hardly infallible. Oprah Winfrey's first test purported to show that she was part Zulu, a conclusion that was later retracted after review of the sample sets.

On a more complicated level of ancestral "truth", Gates' own test results showed that he had an Ashkenazi foremother, and that he has no relation to Samuel Brady, the white patriarch he'd grown up "knowing" as the man who impregnated his great-great-grandmother. His family lore had never hinted at what the *Wall Street Journal* dubbed his "Yiddishe Mama." By the same token, nothing had prepared him for Brady's *not* being his direct ancestor. Indeed, one of Gates's cousins remains adamant that the test must be wrong. If the test is right, he insists, there are two truths. One is the story he grew up with, the other is what the DNA says.

Somewhere in between what the DNA says and what shaped the family account is a gap that is something like an historical lie. A secret passing from black to white? An act of assimilation or aspiration? A myth to hide some shame, some rape? A change of identity to escape to freedom? One hesitates, surely, to put this on the same moral level as the kind of "lie" those prisoners, politicians and morally incomplete nine-year-olds tell to escape accountability and save their guilty hides. Rather, there is something very human, very moving about the repetition of family stories until they become epic rather than literal, about the burying of family secrets, the posturing of ancestors, the reinventions of migrants, the accommodations of raw ambition, and the insulations from terrible shame. This is, I suppose, distantly related to escapist manipulations; it might also be related to, but of a different order than, the magical thinking of mental patients or character-disordered people.

There is something very commonplace about the kinds of family mysteries that Gates' inquiries reveal–particularly in the American context. It is part of how many, many of our ancestors, regardless of where they came from, reinvented themselves in the New World. NYU law school Professor Jessie Allen describes the "magic" of legal remediation as follows: "What ought to have been prevails over the past." Family stories ritualize the past in a very similar way. It is part of what Professor Robert Pollack, head of Columbia University's Center for the Study of Science and Religion, calls the "eschatology of repair."

If there is value to this kind of "emotional truth"–if I can be permitted that term–it is important not to confuse it with the sort of truth that DNA tells us. So while DNA can undoubtedly pinpoint certain aspects of our ancestry, it does not make literal sense to say, as Gates does to Oprah Winfrey: "You've got education in your genes." Of course, he was speaking metaphorically at that moment, using the human genome as a trope for a pattern of socialization, a family habit, a thirst for knowledge modeled by parents. But at other points in the program that metaphoric dimension is applied rather more carelessly–and more dangerously. "I'm 50 percent white," says Gates. But there is no more an allele for "whiteness" than there is for "education." "White" is a malleable social designation with a freighted history. Were his putative Ashkenazi ancestors to appear before us today, they might be called white, but as Eastern or Southern Europeans coming to America a hundred years ago, they probably would not have been considered so.

It behooves us to be a bit less romantic about what all this DNA swabbing reveals. I worry about the craving to "go back to Africa," or to "connect with our Yiddishness" or to feel like new doors have been opened if we have an Asian ancestor. The craving, the connection, the newness of those doors is in our heads, not in our mitochondria.

It is the process of superimposing the identities with which we were raised upon the culturally embedded, socially constructed imaginings about "the Other" we just almost might be. The fabulous nature of what is imagined can be liberating, invigorating–but it is fable. If we read that story into the eternity of our bloodlines, if we biologize our history, we will forever be less than we could be.

Race As Economic Choice

A couple of years ago, I was trying to count the number of African-American students in my son's class. "Let me see..." I said. "There's you and A and B and C..."

C's not black, he said.

I was surprised. I knew C, her parents and her grandparents; by most societal measures, they would be thought of as black. So I asked: "Why do you say that?"

She hangs out with the white kids.

"And you don't? What about your three best friends, X, Y and Z?"

They're black.

"All three of them are quite blond! What makes them black?"

They hang out with me.

"So why aren't you white for hanging out with them, like C?"

Because white kids go to Starbucks and order light frappuccinos.

"I go to Starbucks!"

And you're white. That's why I don't hang out with you.

"But you go to Starbucks!"

Only twice, and then I ordered a dark chocolate mocha latte.

My son was joshing; he's always running a Monty Python or a David Chappelle on me. But even as this conversation made me laugh, it also made me think. I was organizing his classmates by some combination of phenotype, family history and culture. My interest in keeping such a tally was motivated by a wish that my son not be tokenized. Being "the only one" sparks my own anxieties about having grown up as the lone "colored" kid throughout elementary school. In high school there were a few more dark dots in the mix, which was better because those in the majority couldn't generalize about you quite so easily. And if they did generalize, at least you had someone to roll your eyes with at the absurdity of being lumped together. We fought for inclusiveness in a world that too often hoards life's rewards by racial assignation.

In contrast, my son's social construction of race reminded me of how protean this all is. If it's amusing to think of Starbuck's as racial arbiter, it would have been less funny if the racial arbiter had been a brand of sneakers or a particular accent or whether one is well-educated or not–in other words, if the reference had been to either fixed or negative assumptions about phenotype or class.

Some years ago, when "identity politics" first raised its contentious, snappish little head, the furor seemed almost entirely focused on African-Americans. The true complexity and importance of that debate, deemed largely academic at first, is perhaps increasingly clear. In recent times the world has shuddered with violent realignments unleashed by global challenges to line up with "them" or with "us," or with "truth" or with "treason." Identity is battered by varied appeals to conformity: Say it! prove it! swear allegiance to this or that nation, party, religion, bloodline of the moment–good or bad, for or against, red or blue, blue or gray, black or white, or many shades of other.

A deep planetary insecurity has fostered a rush to build boundaries around ourselves–psychic green zones, mental walls, panic rooms, little protective groupings–no matter how irrational. There's a Boondocks cartoon that captures the absurd tension of this moment, where young Huey excitedly tells his grandfather that there's good news abroad in the land. African-Americans are now only the third most hated group in America, he says, right after Muslims and the French. It is a bizarre phenomenon, this free-floating sense of well-being that derives comfort from being less hated rather than more loved.

I began this essay with a reference to McCallum and Terry's filmic rendering of the twinning doll. I was so struck by the image that I sought them out. They told me that there was an old children's song about the dolls: "Turn you up/Turn you back/First you're white/Then you're black." I tried googling those words in hopes of finding an actual recording. Instead I turned up a satirical piece by rocker Lou Reed, "I Wanna Be Black," in which a (presumably hypothetical) "I" desires "to be black" as an escape from a neurosis of whiteness. Actually, the word "white" is never used in the song. It's alluded to in the chorus–obliquely but with crystal clarity nonetheless: "I don' wanna be a f***ed-up middle-class college student any mo'." According to these lyrics, whiteness is a dull preserve defined by respectable class status, college education and world-class angsts; black people have ever so much more fun, what with having "natural rhythm," a "stable of foxy whores," and "getting shot in the spring" "like Martin Luther King."

The jolly entertainment of switching identity from white to black and back again is not the exclusive province of frat boys slumming around as pretenders to ghetto life. "Jungle parties" are still good clean fun at country clubs, at Halloween parties down at the precinct, and in the unfortunate confusion that is Kevin Federline. But the inverse–switching from black to white and black again–is a considerably more freighted proposition. "Moving on up" the social ladder is a more dangerous proposition for those with dark skin than it is for whites. Blacks who present themselves as clean, articulate, sober, and important risk viewed as being false, elitist, or duplicitous to white audiences; to other black people they risk being seen as "acting white." (If there is any doubt about this dilemma, consider the fine line that Barack Obama has had to walk at every stage of his campaign.)

Whites in blackface, on the other hand–i.e., any coded semblance of down and dirty–tend to be read as cool, or maybe disaffected, or ridiculous or at worst, stuck in some stage of rebellious adolescence.

This odd set of expectations, so inflected by race and class. Have we so soon forgotten the unfortunately spectacular hearings that we remember as the Anita Hill-Clarence Thomas hearings? What I found most unforgivable about Senator Biden's characterization of Senator Obama was his utter failure to learn from a past in which he was intimately implicated. Biden was, after all, chair of the Judiciary Committee when our spectacularly inarticulate president's father nominated Clarence Thomas to the Supreme Court. As every last minority graduate of Yale–whew, ten or fifteen at least–came forward to weigh in about which one, Clarence or Anita, was more believable, media forces expressed shock and awe that there were–gasp–just so many black people who could string a whole sentence together! Astonishing sequences of subject-verb-object! A few years later, it was Colin Powell who was perceived as shockingly articulate; then Condoleeza Rice–not just clean but stylish, not just articulate but brilliant because she plays the piano and speaks three languages.

The persistence of this narrative is not limited to Biden. On MSNBC's "Hardball," there was a discussion of Senator Barack Obama's decision to run for President. "No history of Jim Crow, no history of anger, no history of slavery," opined host Chris Matthews. "All the bad stuff in our history ain't there with this guy." Not true, I thought... The "bad stuff in our history" rests heavily upon each and every one of us. It shapes us all–whether me, Matthews, Obama, Biden–or Amadou Diallo, the decent, hard-working Malian immigrant without any

American racial "history," who died in a hail of bullets fired by New York City police officers, because he looked like what the white officers—themselves groaning with racial "baggage"–imagined to be a criminal. Some parts of our racial experience are nothing more or less than particular to one's accidental location in the geography of a culture.

If, for example, I migrated to South Africa and were greeted as an exciting, exotic black American prophet of hope and prosperity, I'd be no less implicated in the complexities of their racial struggles. This, even if I were entirely ignorant of those struggles–and however relatively privileged I might turn out to be within that hierarchy. At a more complex level, however, there's a way in which American identity is defined by the experience of willing diaspora, the break by choice that is the heart of the immigrant myth. It is that aspect of chosen migration that has exiled most African-Americans from a substantial part of the American narrative–and it is precisely this part that makes Obama so attractive, so intriguing and yet so strange. Obama's family history is an assemblage of elements of the American dream. His late father migrated from Kenya to the United States; his mother was a farmer's daughter from Kansas. Before him, the archetypal narrative of immigrant odyssey had been an almost exclusively white and European one. I suspect that Obama's intrigue stems not just from the Tiger Wood-ish-ly fashionable taste for "biracialism" but from the fact that he's managed to fuse the immigrant myth of meteoric upward mobility onto the figure of a black man. The migration narrative, moreover, comes to him, "by rights": Just beneath the surface lies an epic thread about how Obama's African father, now smiling down from a convenient heavenly remove, found his white Kansan mother in something like a Conestoga wagon and rescued her from stampeding herds of rabid buffalo and endless toil in the wheat fields, and then she and her parents were mystically transported to the paradise of Hawaii, after which his father died of other than a rain of bullets.

Or something like that. Truth be damned–as it so often is when it comes to origin myths–not a lot of people of color can lay claim to the property of this kind of heroic script.

Back on "Hardball," Christine Tucker, a black woman who writes for the Atlanta Constitution, responded: "...[H]e truly does seem to transcend race because his mother, after all, let's not forget, was white." Chris Matthews agreed: "His grandmother he went to visit in

Hawaii was white. Yeah." This, to me, was a baffling exchange. Obama's mother's being white is supposedly what automatically transcend this thing called race? He looks black but he really isn't? Is blackness really only defined by Jim Crow, anger, slavery? If American-ness is defined by patronymic immigrant hope, is racial transcendence then to be defined by maternity, relation to whiteness, biology? Transcendence implies rising above something, cutting through, being liberated from. What would it reveal about the hidden valuations of race if one were to invert the equation by positing that Barack Obama "transcended" whiteness because his father was black?

Senator Obama has so many attractive attributes–he's smart, a gifted writer and unparalleled speaker, a skilled tactician, full of fresh vision, youthful with a good-looking Kennedy–esque appeal. Yet there are many people to whom his appeal rests not on what he is, but on what they imagine that he isn't. He's not a whiner; he's not angry. He doesn't hate white people. He doesn't wear his hair like Al Sharpton. He is not the list of negatives that people like Chris Matthews or Joe Biden or a whole generation of fucked up middle-class college students identify as "blackness." Indeed, part of the reason I have always been so anxious about the trustworthiness of polls regarding Obama's popularity– sorely tested, even before Republicans got their taste of haunch, by the unfortunate acrimony of the contest against Hillary Clinton–is this inverted appeal based on his ability to performs "unexpected" aspects of both whiteness and blackness.

I wonder, for example, whether Obama's appeal would be as great, all else being equal, if his mother had been black, and his father a white immigrant. If he'd been raised by a black rather than a white single mother.

This not just about the dualism of black and white of course, or of the ever-flipping references of hypodescent and hyperdescent. Obama's family raised him in diverse locales–Hawaii, Indonesia, the world. Does the perception of his identity change if we think of him as our first Hawaiian presidential candidate? To paraphrase, is he the first mainstream Hawaiian-American who is articulate and bright and clean and a nice-looking guy who wouldn't be caught dead in a grass skirt holding a ukelele…Or our first mainstream Indonesian-American who is articulate and bright and clean and a nice-looking guy who had the interesting experience of going to a Roman Catholic school in a largely Muslim country, which might provide lots of useful cultural insights for a President to have in this time and place.

Worse yet, a lot of the analysis of Biden's comment has not focused on the underestimation of Obama's substance or even his remarkable ability to discern that the fish knife is not a shoe horn–rather it focuses on whether the comments destroyed *Biden's* chances to run for president. Who, after all, even knew Biden had his hat in the ring?

But back to Obama, a presidential candidate of profound decency, extraordinary smarts and great eloquence. He was president of Harvard Law Review, a position that requires not just the highest grades in the entire universe, but also the unanimous acclaim of a band of viciously competitive students and a famously divided faculty. Those who make law review are immediately famous, and famously fast-tracked–those who have served on the law review include a stunning and stellar array of familiar names: Supreme Court Justices Felix Frankfurter, Ruth Bader Ginsburg, Antonin Scalia, Stephen Breyer and Chief Justice John G. Roberts, Jr.; Secretaries of State Dean Acheson, Charles Hamilton Houston, Alger Hiss, Archibald MacLeish; Judge Richard Posner; Maryland State Senator Jamie Raskin; Homeland Security Secretary Michael Chertoff; former New York governor Eliot Spitzer, Harvard Law Dean Elena Kagan, Yale Law Dean Harold Koh; former Harvard University president Derek Bok. It is, in the secretly assigned world of global power, an even greater ticket to the top than being sealed in a coffin at Skull and Bones. It was acknowledged as such when Jews first joined the Review; when Democratic political pundit Susan Estrich became the first woman president of the Law Review; and when Obama became its first black president. It is a position whose credentialing power has never been questioned as far anyone knows–at least until this election: The New York Times, for example, published an article in which some of Barack Obama's so-called friends within the Bush administration wondered if being president of the Harvard Law Review really and truly required the same skill set as being President of the United States. As a cabdriver recently expressed it to me: "Maybe the mirage in the desert is no more than a benchmark constantly being moved out of reach." (He was articulate, and quite poetic, that cabbie. Made me wonder what benchmarks had been moved beyond his reach to leave him ferrying me around at midnight.)

Of course, the crown of the law review presidency is not the only aspect of Senator Obama's "authenticity" that's being refigured as a mess of thorns. If no one doubts his blackness when it comes to the uniqueness of his accomplishments on law review, it's apparently not "enough" in other contexts–as in "Is he black enough?" a query posed in another article in the New York Times. Perpetual contrarians like

Stanley Crouch, Debra Dickerson and Carol Swain were quoted as questioning whether he truly was a brother. It is surely ironic that Obama–one of very few Americans of any stripe who has actual first-degree relatives in Africa–is being figured in some quarters as an imposter of African-American-ness.

If nothing else, Barack Obama's identity reveals the complexly blind slipperiness of American conceptions of race, culture and ethnicity.

Conclusion

There's a lovely quote from Saidiya Hartman's remarkable book *Lose The Mother* (2007) As she wends her way through Ghana on a Ford Foundation grant, she notes: "I was the stranger in the village, a wandering seed bereft of the possibility of taking root. Behind my back people whispered, *dua ho mmire*: a mushroom that grows on the tree has no deep soil. Everyone avoided the word "slave," but we all knew who was who. As a "slave baby," I represented what most chose to avoid: the catastrophe that was our past...And what was forbidden to discuss: the matter of someone's origins." As I read Hartman's words, I wondered how familiar that sentiment felt to me, or to so many African Americans whether they've never left our shores or traveled the world, so relentlessly in search of "home." I wondered how familiar that passage must feel to recent arrivals to our shores. Not long ago, I met a Swedish woman who is phenotypically "Asian." When she a student at the University of California, she went to the hospital for stomach pains–and was almost committed as insane before she ever got to see a doctor because the administrative gatekeepers simply could not reconcile her appearance and her assertion of Swedish citizenship.

In this moment of unprecedented diaspora, I think of the image of Barack Obama or Condoleeza Rice or Colin Powell or Bethany Godby or Henry Louis Gates or Howard law students or any of us members of the much vaunted "new black middle class"–all divided against ourselves, like twinning dolls, flipped endlessly down a hall of mirrored images of blackness and whiteness, no less celebrated than Frederick Douglass as those whose entire identity is mired in the exhausted exceptionalism of the "surprisingly" hyper-articulated African phenotype; yet simultaneously embraced as those who have transcended the embodiment of a troublesome past and emerged on the other side– purportedly "cleansed" of baggage, of roots, of the unacknowledged rupture that is, paradoxically, our greatest national bond.

References

Associated Press, 2006 "Michigan Voters Decide Today on Ward Connerly, KKK-backed Initiative." Accessed on August 12, 2009, at urn http://diverseeducation.com/artman/publish/article_6625.shtml).
Daly, Emily 2005. "DNA Tells Student They Aren't Who They Thought", *New York Times*, April 13, 2005.
Confederate Constitution, Clause 4, Section 9.
Fullwiley, Duana 2008. "The Biologistical Construction of Race: 'Admixture' Technology and the New Genetic Medicine." *Social Studies of Science* 38(5): 695–735.
Godby v. Montgomery County Bd. of Educ., 996 F. Supp. 1390 (M.D. Ala. 1998).
Hartman, Saidiya, 2007. *Lose Your Mother A Journey Along the Atlantic Slave Route.* Farrar, Straus & Giroux: New York.
Loving v. Virginia, 388 U.S. 1 (1967).
Merriam-Webster, Accessed on line at URL: http://www.merriam-webster.com/dictionary/indo%20aryan, on August 15, 2009.
Venezia, Todd. 2007. "Baby Bungle: White folks' black child" *The New York Post,* March 22, 2007.
Williams, Patricia 2007. "Being A Black Man". *The Washington Post*, January 7, 2007.

THE SOCIAL SITUATION OF THE BLACK EXECUTIVE: BLACK AND WHITE IDENTITIES IN THE CORPORATE WORLD[1]

Elijah Anderson

African Americans in executive-level positions in the United States today must deal with extremely complex social dynamics. As blacks they are identified first and foremost as members of a historically stigmatized group; as corporate executives they are identified as members of an elite and powerful class. This ethnographic case study examining their problems and efforts to deal with them will yield insights into the situation not only of black executives but also of marginalized minorities more generally.

In preparing to enter the field, I requested complete access to the workers in a major financial service corporation in central city Philadelphia. Such access would have afforded me the opportunity to follow and observe the subjects of the study in their daily activities and to question them at will. I would have liked to have engaged in intensive participant observation, an ideal situation for generating slice-of-life portrayals of the work setting and for gleaning important insights into the corporate culture generally and the social situation of minority employees of the company more particularly. The company rejected this plan. Instead, I was permitted to roam the premises and interview persons referred to me by the vice president for employee relations, who is himself black.

The representation here is therefore based both on observation of the social setting and on intensive ethnographic interviews with a small sample of executive-level minority employees including blacks, Jews, and women. The resulting observations are meant to be not representative but rather suggestive of the quality of experience within the company. Over the course of six months, I conducted interviews on

---

[1] "The Social Situation of the Black Executive," by Elijah Anderson, is a revised version of a paper of the same title published in The *Cultural Territories of Race: Black and White Boundaries,* edited by Michelle Lamont (Chicago, University of Chicago Press; New York, Russell Sage Foundation, 1999).

the work premises or at area restaurants during the workday, and they frequently extended to ninety minutes. (In order to build on this primary research, I have been informally interviewing a variety of black and white, male and female executives of organizations throughout the Philadelphia area over the past ten years.) The company provided office space as well as time for employees to be interviewed, and the interviewees were most helpful and candid in their discussion of the questions put to them. The interviews were open-ended and informal in an attempt to elicit information and insights into the personal lives of employees and their situation within the organization.

Historical Basis of Affirmative Action

An adequate assessment of the present-day situation of executives in this company, and in the American corporate world in general, requires some historical perspective on black mobility. Such a viewpoint is important since social change within this corporate environment is related to important changes in other major institutions of American society. Over the past half century, American society changed prof9undly in the area of race relations (see Myrdal 1944; Drake and Cayton 1962 [1945]; Cox 1948; Hacker 1995; Wilson 1980, 1987, 1996). Largely as a consequence of affirmative action programs, black Americans, long segregated in ghettos and treated as second-class citizens, began to participate in the wider society in ways previously restricted to privileged members of the white majority. This process of racial incorporation signaled the beginning of the still very slow decline of the American caste-like system of race relations, and it may be traced to certain general sociohistorical developments. The most dramatic changes were spurred by the civil rights movement, the subsequent major civil disorders, and the social and political responses to these new and provocative developments (see Kerner et al. 1968). Major policy responses included the civil rights legislation of 1964, 1965, and 1968. Perhaps most important for the subject of this chapter was the executive order issued and signed by President John F. Kennedy in 1961 and later revised by President Lyndon Johnson in 1964 prescribing "affirmative action" as an important remedy for racial discrimination, social injustice, and the resulting inequality. At the time, public support for these' remedial measures was widespread and overwhelming, but by no means unanimous. Some critics have argued that because of the overarching concern of government, business, and academia for social peace, these policies were simply desperate measures to "cool out the long hot summers," in particular, and to mollify alienated black Americans and their white allies, more generally.

Although there was desire on the part of policymakers to prevent further outbursts of violence and disorder in American cities, there also appeared to be a genuine national consensus on the need to make the socioeconomic system more equitable, particularly for members of the nation's black community. Also important was the provocative international specter of black Americans being whipped and beaten daily in their efforts to obtain the basic right to vote in the world's leading democracy. This image was simply too much of a contradiction for many Americans, including policymakers, to bear, particularly with the emergence of so many newly independent "colored" nations of Africa and other parts of the Third World, which were in the process of trying to decide, in the midst of the cold war, whether to follow in the orbit of the Soviet Union or the West.

Whatever the reasoning or intentions of policymakers, American social life has moved toward equality for blacks since that time. Moreover, to a significant degree, the events that have provided more mobility for blacks also have done so for other minority groups. Blacks, women, and members of other minority groups, including newly arrived immigrants, have become the beneficiaries of significant civil rights legislation, including affirmative action, which has been strictly enforced by successive federal administrations, with the exception of those of presidents Reagan and Bush. As a result, members of these groups, most notably white women, are now participating in the American occupational structure at levels inconceivable a few decades ago.

Consistent with these trends, the black middle class has expanded in both size and outlook and appears to be in the process of transforming from a class of small business operators and professionals serving the black community almost exclusively to one that is increasingly economically independent of that community (see Frazier 1957; Wilson 1980; Landry 1987; Collins 1997). With such developments, more and more middle-class blacks are involved in the corporate and business sectors of society at large. Even to the casual observer, black Americans appear to be included more fully in American life than ever before. Largely shut out from becoming bankers, stockbrokers, corporate executives, and responsible government agents before the social upheaval brought on by the civil rights movement (see Stryker 1953), blacks have become increasingly visible in such occupations, although very few move beyond the middle levels to areas of major influence.

Beginning in the 1960s, as part of the general movement toward greater black incorporation, an impressive number of African Americans began attending predominantly white colleges and universities from which they were previously excluded, at times by law; the number of black professors, particularly those teaching at predominantly white institutions, also increased. This general process of incorporation did not bypass the corporations, some of which gladly recruited blacks; others, though, needed to be pressured into establishing affirmative action programs to remedy past underrepresentation and discrimination.

However, as African Americans became ostensible beneficiaries of affirmative action, leading to a growing presence of middle-class blacks in major social positions, especially in corporate life, growing numbers of white Americans began to feel highly threatened. In an era of deindustrialization, corporate downsizing, and the resulting insecurities of the American workforce, policies that were once indulged and viewed as noble efforts against racial discrimination became increasingly viewed as so many "race preferences" for blacks. In these circumstances, efforts to include blacks worked to create a growing backlash and resentment among a number of those whites with whom individual black beneficiaries would share work settings. Indeed, many whites, and some blacks, have gone so far as to mount legal and ideological challenges to affirmative action programs, arguing "reverse discrimination" (see Glazer 1987 [1975], 1997; *Regents of the State of California v. Bakke,* 438 U.S.. 265, 1978; Skrentny 1996; Bearak 1997). All this has culminated in a growing nationwide movement to legally dismantle affirmative action programs through state initiatives. Proposition 209 outlawed affirmative action in California, foreshadowing what could happen throughout the United States.

Ironically, along with the apparent growth of black representation and participation in various areas of American life, but particularly in the workplace, fewer citizens see a need for affirmative action. With such visible black participation, as well as the growing presence of other minorities, including white women, in the workplace, it becomes increasingly difficult to make the argument that racism is the sole factor denying opportunities to blacks and that the system itself is racially exclusionary. In these circumstances, race is prematurely degraded as a powerful explanation for inequality. In essence, the power of the concept has been weakened by the proliferation of symbolic elements that contribute to the appearance of inclusiveness in the corporate workplace; by their presence and high visibility, successful blacks imply that the occupational structure is now open and egalitarian, if not entirely meritocratic.

Nevertheless, black executives often express their doubts. Although it is clear that social conditions have improved considerably for many middle-class blacks and that the resulting progress toward attaining social parity with middle-class whites has given many hope, racial inequality is endemic to American society, and tremendous numbers of blacks as well as other people of color are segregated in ghettos, are poor, and continue to be treated as second-class citizens (see Massey and Denton 1993; Feagin and Sikes 1994; Cose 1993). In fact, as improvements in the condition of the black middle class become more pronounced, a social and economic split between members of the black middle class and the black lower class becomes more discernible.

The affirmative action initiatives and policies had their most direct and immediate effect on blacks who were well prepared and poised to take advantage of any opportunity that arose in the occupational system. In this scenario, the lower class was largely ignored at a time when the jobs on which this class depended were disappearing due to automation, de-industrialization, and the rise of the global economy (see Wilson 1980, 1987, 1996; Anderson 1990; Rifkin 1995). This historical context is important for understanding aspects of the social life of the company on which this chapter is based.

After President Johnson issued his executive order prescribing affirmative action, the company I studied instituted programs to recruit and train blacks. Without such pressure and the initiatives that followed, the number of blacks working and being promoted within the company would have been significantly smaller. To be sure, affirmative action has produced conflicting results in this corporate setting. A few blacks have indeed been highly successful, occasionally reaching upper-level management positions. Many others are frustrated, feeling strongly that they are being detained and kept from rising by an invisible job ceiling. They believe that there are certain jobs that blacks will never obtain and others into which blacks are being channeled. They do not feel or act as if they are accepted as full participants in the organization (see Cose 1993).

Since skin color, particularly its social and political significance, appears to be a problematic issue for the personnel of the organization, it would be conceptually useful, following Goffman (1963), to consider its relationship to the concept of stigma, or spoiled identity. Goffman distinguishes three categories: the own, the wise, and the normal. The own represents the stigmatized group in society. This group consists of individuals with a similar negative difference. Within the group, there is a discrepancy between each person's virtual and actual social identities, which can be seen as the difference between his or her good, virtuous, and positive qualities and his or her negative attributes. Stigma thus is a matter of degree and perhaps best viewed as a product of social interaction; in effect, it is a transaction between those who are stigmatized and those who assign stigma (see Becker 1973 [1963]). For Goffman, those who assign stigma include the normals (those members of the organization who feel that corporate life is fair to them and to others and who have few complaints), the wise (normals who have the capacity for empathy toward outsiders and who tend to extend themselves to the own, assisting them and making them feel welcome within the organization), and members of the own themselves.

However, much has happened in the politics of difference since Goffman advanced his position. Today, Goffman's view of stigma appears rather absolutist insofar as he has a generally clear conception of what does and does not constitute stigma. In his view, the one person in our society without stigma is the young, married, white, urban, northern, heterosexual, Protestant father, who is college educated, fully employed, and of good complexion, weight, and height and who has a recent record in sports (Goffman 1963, 128). All others, we are to presume, are in some way compromised and would rather be "normal"; they would be more than ready to trade in their status and identity as stigmatized if that were possible.

With respect to the tribal stigma of race, such an analysis is weakened by the fact that, since the beginning of the civil rights and black (cultural) nationalist movements that have culminated in today's Afrocentrism, many black people, but not all, appear increasingly black and proud and would cringe at the thought of giving up their blackness for promises of racial inclusion or assimilation. Such positions have their parallels among feminists, gays, and various ethnic groups. In present-day America there seems to be an emerging concern with valuing one's differences, playing up one's particularity, be it ethnic, racial, or sexual, and attempting to compete effectively for place and position among so many others who make up our pluralistic society (see Rose 1990 [1973]; Schlesinger 1992; Feagin and Sikes 1994; Glazer 1997). Nevertheless, Goffman's typology, taken as conventional commentary on race and difference, provides us with a conceptually useful, if ideologically conservative, benchmark from which to approach the social situation of the black executive.

The Own

Within the organization I studied, the own may be characterized as a loosely knit collection of black employees. Such people may at first glance appear, especially to outsiders, to be a monolithic, tightly knit, self-interested group. The actual situation, however, is more complicated than that. Membership in the own is usually involuntary and persistent, because it is determined by skin color, although in reality its members at times may fade in and out of the association. To a certain degree, this is a matter of perception, and putative members become more or less closely affiliated with the own depending on the issue at hand and the attendant social circumstances. Moreover, individuals with observable phenotypical features identifiable by all Americans, but especially by blacks, as "black" or black African in origin are automatically eligible for membership. During social interaction and instances of sociability, fellow blacks in effect claim them, and whites readily associate them with the own.

Among some blacks in the organization, the sense of affiliation with the own can be situational, while for others it can be a full-time preoccupation. At the same time, however, their awareness of the job ceiling and other indications of negative differential treatment, mixed with hurt but often hidden feelings, may set them apart from others in the company, including other minorities. Many feel strongly that their experiences in the workplace are unique and that other minorities-women, Asians, Jews, and Hispanics-do not confront the same personal and social problems. They see their skin color and the social significance it has acquired over the centuries as their chief and lingering problem, not just in the workplace but in society in general (see Cose 1993). Hence, for a large number of blacks in the organization, skin color *is* the persistent issue, a conspicuous and observable characteristic that often makes them subject a priori to negative consideration and treatment. They tend to keep such views to themselves or to share them mainly with fellow blacks who they think are trustworthy or, rarely, with whites who have earned their confidence.

At the same time many of those blacks who are doing well in the organization have found it necessary to distance themselves from the own and to present themselves as individuals who have struggled despite great odds and have made it. Indeed, for them, it is generally considered bad form to define oneself as publicly preoccupied with race, as a "race man" or "race woman," or as one who promotes "the race" over others (see Drake and Cayton 1962; Goffman 1963; Anderson 1997). In this context, at times with deep ambivalence, some feel it prudent to tone down their enthusiasm for company policies that appear to favor "the race" (see Steele 1990; Carter 1991; Kennedy 1997). For instance, such people may feel that they must publicly distance themselves from the concept of affirmative action, even though without this policy and the accompanying governmental pressure many probably would not hold the positions they do.

Accordingly, it is not uncommon to hear some of these blacks voice complaints about the wisdom of affirmative action programs and quotas. These complaints often stem from a complex psychological need to identify publicly with a corporate culture that at times denies them full participation. In working to resolve this dilemma, many have internalized conceptions of the organization as a virtual meritocracy, while others are left embittered by what they see as a sham of equal opportunity.

Generally in their daily behavior at work, most find themselves enacting their versions of the corporate orientation, a clear commitment to organizational rules and values that their white counterparts and superiors readily sanction. To enact such a role effectively implies that the individual him or herself is a standing member of that system. But in terms of feeling fully included, most are left with reservations. At least some of this acceptance of the corporate orientation may have to do with the felt need to present oneself as a team player or the desire to benefit-or at least to cover oneself-by "going along to get along," while offering up the classic caveat about not selling out and "remembering where you came from."

It is conceptually useful to divide black executives into two groups: the core own and the peripheral own. The core own are those blacks who have recently emerged from traditional, segregated black communities or who maintain a strongly expressed or a racially particularistic sense of identity. The peripheral own are often the products of less racially isolated backgrounds and tend to be more universalistic in outlook (see Anderson 1990, 40–42). Generally speaking, the core own tends to be organized around the belief that American society is irredeemably racist and that relationships with whites are to be entered into with a certain amount of suspicion, if at all, and that such relationships are best understood as being primarily instrumental. Those taking this position tend to interact with whites only on a formal level, and their friendships are mainly with other blacks who are "black enough," meaning those who place race first and emphasize solidarity with the African American community.

The peripheral own tend toward a more cosmopolitan orientation, while regarding the problem of American race relations as difficult but hopeful. In deference to norms of racial caste, they tend to engage other blacks for close friendships but are open to friendships with whites and others. Imbued with values of social tolerance, such blacks tend to be comfortable in relationships with various kinds of people and tend to see them as individuals first and people of a certain race second. As a result of these differential identifications, the core and the peripheral own tend to have different corporate experiences.

Complicating the picture, however, is the fact that certain coworkers, black and white alike, lump all blacks together into a single group. For such people, the member's skin color and physical attributes help define the person's special relationship with the company. Members of the own, who are generally expected to acknowledge, befriend, and support one another on the basis of skin color, thus assume a common social and cultural history with respect to racial prejudice and discrimination toward blacks (see Hughes 1945; Blumer 1958; Wellman 1977; Pettigrew 1980; Feagin and Sikes 1994; Hacker 1995). These assumptions serve as an important organizing principle for the own.

When brought to the organization, the core own's identity and its related values are sharpened by the distinctions they draw between themselves, the peripheral own, and other coworkers, who tend to be white and of middle-class background. Therefore, a member of the core own whose sense of identity is threatened by the everyday vicissitudes of life within the organization, particularly by the extent to which he or she is required to interact closely with white$, often gravitates to others who are black and have similar social attitudes and values. These individuals then find racial solidarity as a valuable defense because of what they view as a generalized pattern of bad treatment at the hands of whites and, by extension, of white oppression of black communities.

In these circumstances, many of the black employees are reminded of the strong adversity their people traditionally have experienced in their everyday dealings with whites. When the experience is not personally remembered, it may be socially reconstructed. Collectively, the own, particularly those in the core, tend to define the present situation as a hostile one, making it ever more difficult for them to trust white coworkers and easiest; to trust fellow blacks. This oversimplified view further encourages association on the basis of color and as a result reifies a racial division of labor, while undermining comity and goodwill among blacks and whites in the workplace.

Among themselves, functionally backstage, members of the own commune and commiserate with one another. Here they may "talk black," both articulating the frustrations they experience in working among insensitive whites and identifying the work-related issues they believe are racially based. They may greet one another as "sister" and "brother," invoking feelings of familial solidarity. On these occasions, members of the own appear relatively relaxed, but they may not be so: many feel that they must be alert and aware of those who might turn on them, selling them out to those in authority.

Highly motivated to succeed, they feel competitive not only with their white coworkers but at times with their black colleagues as well. As the issue becomes survival, they learn to watch and protect their backs. Yet as they meet and talk, and to a degree collude, they learn to trust and find themselves socializing, often on the basis of racial unity. Not only do they make small talk, perhaps discussing what was on television last night, but they also discuss public issues of the day, particularly issues that affect the lives of blacks in corporate life. They pass around relevant news clippings and, through sociability, gain perspective on the corporate world. Equally important, they compare notes on experiences with their white colleagues, at times collectively distinguishing between enemies and friends, or the "wise," in the general organization and discussing issues pertinent to their jobs. Here also, some might complain about problematic supervisors or about an errant white secretary who shows too little respect for blacks, or they might even single out members of the peripheral own who have shown themselves to be outside the fold or to have blatantly violated the rules of the own.

As a group, the peripheral own tend to have a more cosmopolitan orientation and in general are better educated than the core own.

They tend to occupy a higher status in the organization. Such blacks have a strong need to believe that they are present in the organization not solely because of the color of their skin, but because of their own success in the business world. Furthermore, in cases where racial particularism among blacks might be invoked to favor a black or other minority individual, these individuals might hesitate to offer an endorsement. Rather, they sometimes bend over backward to judge an individual not on the basis of color, but with regard to the issue at hand and on their own perceptions of that person's merit.

A major reason for this hesitancy and the attempt to neutralize racial particularism in public has much to do with the standing power relationships within the organization, as well as with feelings of insecurity experienced by members of this group. One way of dealing with such feelings is by embracing the corporate culture, including the meritocratic norms of the organization, and by demonstrating their team loyalty and worthiness at every opportunity. Such norms may be strongly affirmed through close attention to presentational rituals in the areas of dress, speech, and manners. If such behavior promises the approval of corporate higher-ups, such rituals also may put off members of the core own, sharpening the division between the two groups.

Compared with others in the company-both whites and blacks-members of the peripheral own appear utterly polished. The men usually dress in stylish fashions, wearing expensive corporate outfits tending toward dark pinstriped suits; their appearance seems carefully chosen to conform to some handbook on dressing for success. The women often are glamorous, not limiting themselves to the dark and subdued colors worn by the white women of their corporate status. In general, the peripheral own tend to be impressive looking to their white coworkers, particularly for persons of their color-caste. Moreover, their use of language suggests that they have been well educated; over the phone they are at times mistaken for educated whites.

Not only do they seem to feel at ease in the company of whites, but their demeanor seems almost casual and certainly confident. During such interactions, they leave no doubt that they are the social and intellectual equals of their white coworkers. Moreover, they give the impression of having had personally satisfying interactions and positive experiences with whites, and they" are mostly willing to blame whatever bad experiences they may have had on errant individuals, not on whites generally.

In managing the various and sundry issues of the corporate world, members of the periphery like to appear to be color-blind, indicating that race plays a limited role in their understanding of the social world. However, they display some ambivalence in this regard, particularly as the conservative political establishment effectively assaults the very basis of their existence by actively questioning affirmative action and other policies they feel have provided blacks with opportunities in the corporate world. Such actions and news reports give them pause, causing them to reserve judgment and to hold on to a racial analysis of the social and corporate world. Such reservations, and the dynamic tensions they create, allow race to continue to play an important role in their work and personal lives. Such ambivalence may encourage some of these individuals to defer to the powers that be, at times playing along with what they think their white colleagues would like them to think.

In such circumstances these individuals experience most acutely the racial "twoness" of which Du Bois spoke almost a century ago (Du Bois 1995 [1905]). Some others, to be sure, less ambivalent but well schooled by the dominant system and its ideology of egalitarianism, individualism, and merit, embrace the corporate culture more fully. It is with these ambivalences and reservations that, on a social basis, the peripheral own tend to fraternize with both blacks and whites, often believing they are making little distinction on the basis of skin color, yet doing so all the while.

Within this context, this benchmark, they project a cosmopolitan ideal. Yet when it comes to most issues affecting them personally, they do make distinctions based on color. Moreover, because of their class position, and the sense of privilege flowing there from, the peripheral own are likely to pursue activities that the core own most often associate with whites: golf and tennis as well as occasional evenings at the symphony, the opera, or the theater, at times in the company of white coworkers and friends. During backstage sessions, the core own sometimes jokingly accuses them of selling out or of being co-opted by the system. These barbs sometimes hit home. According to one male black senior vice president with whom I discussed my analysis:

> In terms of their lifestyles, some do the opera thing and the art museum thing. But all black executives will also do the jazz. They also do the house party. They wouldn't do it with the core group, but it would be a high-class house party. You'd have some where you'd do some socializing and you'd bring a few whites into it. But the ones that were really serious

parties were kind of isolated. You'd have two different sets of agendas: one where you'd want to create some cohesion with some of the whites so they could see how nice you could socialize, but where you'd really want to let yourself go and get down and talk about issues, then it would be blacks only. The core would never do that [invite whites to a party]. And they play golf, play tennis. About ten, twelve years ago, my wife bought me some golf clubs for Christmas. I never thought about playing golf before that. She said, "You need these to be a part of the team." So I took up golf. I bought her golf clubs the following Christmas. And I play several times a year. Before that, whenever we would go on a company retreat, there was always some free time, and there would be some golf and some tennis and some volleyball. And I would be in the volleyball game because I didn't have the skills to play tennis-I wasn't too good at that-and I never touched a golf club. And those folks are into a different group. I think that whole thing's gonna change twenty years from now because of Tiger Woods. We'll still have exclusive clubs because of the money, but it will be less so. So it won't be as prestigious because everybody's out there doing it.

To members of the peripheral own, such experiences support their values of openness to new social experiences and to social relationships more general than those bounded by color and race. Bent on upward mobility, they usually have some plan for realizing success, and to a degree most have already experienced it within the firm. However, because of their ambivalent relationship with the own, they run a distinct risk of becoming the subject of ambiguity for some whites. This question of their place in the structure becomes especially acute when whites see that they are congregating or fraternizing closely with other blacks. Outsiders might interpret such close associations as a violation of organizational etiquette regarding the relationships between superiors and subordinates. Such members harbor a certain ambivalence with 'respect to the own because they are haunted by the concern that associating closely with the own may seriously impair their own chances of advancing in the organization. Yet they feel some obligation to engage in such association.

When blacks rise in the company, they tend to move away from the core own to the more loosely knit peripheral own. A person whose status changes may easily be accused of disavowing membership in the own, for his or her behavior, including styles of interacting with white associates, can suggest a certain distancing from more ordinary black employees. As this occurs, depending on his or her status and behavior, the individual may be subject to sanctions by the loosely knit group of the own; to deal with such an individual, members of the own may come together. Their sanctions may amount to expressions of hostility including angry looks and gossip-and the threat of ostracism. However, because of the professional nature of business occupations, these sanctions are usually mild and somewhat indefinite. Their real impact is negated by the possibility that the person being sanctioned at one moment may be needed for support at a later point in time.

Instead of forcing issues, some people simply "stew" and gossip when they observe one of the own violating group norms. When this happens, it usually occurs behind a person's back, not to his or her face. Thus the complaints often remain subtle and only marginally effective. In general, the own becomes and remains something of a shadow group, emerging when it or one of its members is being or is feeling threatened; seldom, if ever, does it strike out as a major force.

The basis for the club of the own has to do primarily with the insecurities of its members about their standing in the wider group. This standing is thought to be strongly affected by their blackness and its meaning within a predominantly white firm. The members of the own believe that skin color has a direct impact on the way they are regarded within the firm. Many have the recurring feeling of being persecuted or "on" when in the presence of whites, a sense that someone is always watching and "just waiting to get something on me." There is also a general belief that although individuals may be unsure of themselves, the members of the own may be able collectively to do something about their situation. There is a sense that they are strangers in hostile territory and that the formation of an informal club is partly a matter of self-defense. Hence, "unity" becomes an important social value, if not a major principle of social organization.

Some of the own, particularly those on the periphery, are not sure how much legitimacy the group deserves. Accordingly, those seriously attempting to negotiate the organizational ladder tend to be careful about the racial and political implications of their public associations, particularly when on the job. They are cognizant of the fact that they have to avoid compromising themselves in the eyes of the powerful members of the organization. This set of issues operates to confuse and frustrate certain members of the own, contributing to their worries about appearing "too black" in one set of circumstances and "too white" in another. Whites are inclined to see these ambivalent blacks in one way, and fellow blacks are inclined to see them in another. Many of the whites may become disturbed by what appears to be insincerity on the part of a trusted black friend and colleague. Often this "insincerity" is an outgrowth of the black person's attempts to manage7 the various and sometimes conflicting demands placed on him or her by color and by its social meanings within the organization. The own and the larger group of whites are deeply implicated in the black executive's mode of operation.

The members of the own appear to understand and to be somewhat tolerant of the black executive's excesses, appreciating this member's need to deal with his or her white colleagues. In the words of one executive, it is acceptable to be "white," but only to a degree. To venture beyond the acceptable degree of association-and thus of perceived identification-is to risk the sanctions of the own. It is important to understand that such limits on behavior are in reality a matter of social negotiation and, depending on the executive's social resources in the situation, he or she may be able to get away with more or fewer transgressions in the face of the own. The executive's behavior may be interpreted simply as competence on the job and not as a conscious attempt (without good reason) to approximate "white" ways.

However, when the person negotiates effectively with the own group, he or she runs the distinct risk of alienating white coworkers and superiors. Given the political realities of this situation, the black executive often resolves the conflict by risking his or her relationships with other members of the own, assuming that those other members lack real power and influence in comparison with supervisors and other higher-ups, who tend to be white. From this perspective, fellow blacks are politically expendable, whereas upper-level whites are not. Understanding this reality creates tolerance in members of the own for the "deviance" of their members. In the words of the senior vice president referred to earlier:

> The (peripheral) own was like a support group. At the same time, I went to great lengths to keep a good relationship with the core own. I couldn't do everything that they would do because some things I didn't think were correct or politically savvy in terms of progressing. One of the issues is (as a member of the peripheral own) you can go along with the core and do everything they do, but the end result is you have no influence with the company. So by doing that you hurt the core. So even though the more astute ones will say, "What he's doing is OK," some of the core folks say that if you don't act the way I act, you've sold out. But some of them give the peripherals slack, because they understand you have to do that to stay in the good graces and have some kind of minimal power, marginalized power, whatever it is. So they don't call it acting white necessarily; it varies by the individual.

Some folks who were black executives whom I saw in that vein, whom I saw identifying a lot less than I did with blacks-at the bottom line, I also found out that they were doing things, low-key things, that would improve the plight of the black employees, but they just weren't raising the banner about it. They were keeping a low profile. I think it's a rare black executive who has no conscience about reaching back and doing something for his people. Some will go out of their way to relate, mentor, and coach, etc. Others will keep a distance. But even with that distance they will do things as the opportunity arises. And the thing is that the further you stay away from the core, the more power you have to make things happen. You might meet with the core privately, but some of these folks didn't meet with the core at all, didn't want to be seen with them.

I could see those things being played out. For the most part, I got very positive feedback (from the core), but I'm sure there were some folks saying, "He sold out. He's not one of the brothers." So even with myself I think it was a negative reaction [at times], but those folks who got an even more negative reaction were the very same folks who had the ability to make change. Those people would never socialize with the core, [although] they would say hi. They would take the company position on issues. They would not assume that everything was racist. They [the peripheral own) would ask questions as if they were objective arbitrators versus somebody who's going to defend their race to the end. So they would do things that would come across as being conservative or not understanding. And I think they were going through the process of trying to appear to be super-objective even to the point of being overly so and making you prove your case. I think in their heart, in small settings among the club, you'd hear what was really happening. But they would behave as if the structure was correct. And that would give them coin [leverage) with the power structure.

I had a lot of positive feedback, but just reading it as a possibility that there were folks who thought I sold out was painful. [But) in your heart you know you're doing good things and you're trying to do the right thing and you're doing what you need to do to not assimilate but at least have people not be concerned about you in terms of wanting to cut you out of any kind of power, decision-making process. In terms of who's going to be downsized, you need to act in a certain civil manner, so they'll say, "This guy, he's part of the group." You're never really part of the group, but you're close enough that you can sit in the room. And the thing is that once you get on that management track, either you change right away and you start wearing different suits and different clothing, or you never rise any higher. They're never going to envision you as being a white male, but if you can dress the same and look a certain way and drive a conservative car and whatever else, they'll say, "This guy has a similar attitude, similar values. He's a team player." If you don't dress with the uniform, obviously you're on the wrong team. I've talked to young guys who are becoming managers about the dress, the style, and why it's important. The way I would always put it to them would be, "It's a choice. You don't have to do what they do, but let me tell you what you're giving up. You dress like this [in a flamboyant, stereotypically black way), you're not part of the team. It shouldn't be important, but these are the rules." And so they can make conscious choices.

At the same time, for the larger organization, the members of the peripheral own often serve (although sometimes their role is not acknowledged) as cultural brokers, working to bridge the social gap between members of the minority community and management (see Collins 1997); in fact, such peripheral blacks often informally see themselves as communication links between people of their own racial background and the predominantly white firm. In informal conversations, they sometimes attempt to edify and sensitize their white colleagues about black life. They are sometimes successful in this regard and are often highly valued by those of the enlightened management group who increasingly must come to terms with minority issues. Because of this communication function and because blacks are so poorly represented at the higher reaches of the organization, the black executive runs the further, often debilitating, risk of becoming all-consumed by this role.

Sensitive to the risks involved, many black executives strongly resist this feature of their positions, at least formally. They would much rather see and identify themselves as persons with more general roles (or with roles they view as more central to the mission of the organization) than that of managing the minority community. When they feel themselves being used simply as communication links and representatives of blacks, many feel themselves seriously compromised and complain that they are unable to do the work for which they have been trained. They worry that they will be seen as tokens, and they often begin to question the roles they play in the organization. For some, this perception leads to demoralization, cynicism, or deeper questions concerning their real value to the organization. This role can also create difficulties for them within the own. Although whites may view their role as mainly helping to expand the horizons and influence of blacks within the company and as being leaders and role models, members may enact it somewhat grudgingly.

In general, however, the members of the peripheral own tend to display a positive attitude about life in the company and may become spokespersons for the company. This outlook is enhanced by their perception of the individual as master of his or her own destiny. If they have complaints, they take them to those in authority, as individuals, not as members of the own, thereby creating fewer tensions with white leadership. Also, with their presentation of self, including their dress and demeanor and general social outlook, they are the ones who seem most able to seek and gain effective relationships with white mentors or with white political allies in the company.

For members of the general organization, however, the distinctions between the core own and the peripheral own are often invisible. Rather, "the blacks" signify a reference group, although whites and blacks see the significance and meaning of the group quite differently (see Shibutani 1961; Merton 1957). When whites think of blacks, they may find it conceptually convenient to consider the individual as part of the black group. Although some whites may pride themselves on seeing and treating blacks as individuals, blacks often remain unconvinced of their ability to do so.

The Wise

This brings us to the wise. The wise are people in the organization who are privileged in some respect (usually upper-middle class) but who, because of their upbringing, education, or general life experiences, have developed a deeply sympathetic or empathetic orientation toward people they define as unfortunate victims of social injustice. The members of the wise have an appreciation of the special background of the own and so bring a unique brand of social awareness to the corporate setting. This awareness, mixed with their own intelligence and their understanding of the corporate world, generates in them a rare ability to appreciate the contributions of minorities to the corporation and to society in general. Combining this sense of appreciation with a real sensitivity to life within their own caste and its relation to the minority caste, such persons have developed a certain wisdom mixed with a sense of tolerance in the area of human relations. Compared with others in the organization, executives in the wise are particularly strong in the field of human affairs.

The wise are often made up of Jews, women, successful blacks (members of the peripheral own), and other minority members who occupy high-status positions within the firm. Significantly, liberal Jews tend to be overrepresented in this category. Because of the Jews' long history as victims of prejudice and discrimination at the hands of the majority group, they are often in a position to observe and to appreciate the plight of blacks in American society in general and in the corporation in particular. Because of their own group and personal experience with prejudice and discrimination or simply because they have taken a liking to the member of the own with whom they work, the wise are often able to empathize with the dilemmas of the black executive, particularly if he or she is young and located low on the corporate ladder.

Occupying positions of authority and influence, as well as having a certain independence, these executives have a chance to do something to alleviate the problems they see. They often go on record to demonstrate their empathy for the plight of blacks and other minorities in the organization. Among the own, such persons may be identified and spoken of as allies. With an understanding of the ways of both whites and blacks, the wise are able to express their special identity in ways that other whites might not notice but that are unambiguous to many blacks. They may demonstrate this quality by assisting a black employee during a difficult period or by associating closely with blacks at certain corporate functions, by showing a real and sincere interest in issues important to minorities, by displaying a tolerant manner toward minorities, or by appreciating contributions of the own and other minorities in the company. Of all the whites of the organization, in the minds of members of the own, the wise are viewed as the most likable and trustworthy. Because of these abilities, the wise more readily appreciate contributions of the own and other minorities to the company.

Although members of the wise are usually privileged and white, they may be located almost any place within the organization. In addition, blacks on the corporate ladder sometimes report how they have been befriended by a black janitor or doorman. In their encounters with such individuals, they discover how much more they have to discuss with them than with white peers or superiors who are not members of the wise. At times, a lower level white person may serve a similar purpose. The main quality that all such persons have in common with the member of the own is their perception of him or her as alone, as needing social support, or simply as approachable. Key features of the wise are their ability to understand the situation and their general receptivity to members of the own.

Because of their openness, the well-connected members of the wise often provide valuable connections for the upwardly mobile members of the own, particularly people who tend to make up the peripheral own. By developing this connection into a social relationship, the member of the own can gain even more mobility as well as a rare and useful perspective on the hierarchy of the organization and on how it may or may not be negotiated. A protégé-mentor relationship often grows out of such connections. One male black executive had such an experience:

> My first mentor in the corporate world was a Jewish man, and he helped me quite a bit. This man helped me, and after he left our company, he still stayed in contact. When my brother lost his job, I reached out to him, and he hired my brother. My brother was desperate. But he had the power to bring people in. If he said it would happen, it would happen. So he said to my brother, "Based on my knowledge of your brother, I know you must have some of the same qualities. So you're hired."
>
> Normally you don't have that kind of leverage, that kind of ability to reach out and say, "Hey, would you mind so-and-so, and have somebody help?" He could really shut the door, but I had nurtured this relationship with him for several years at one company. Then when he left, he was there to help. And again, this was a Jewish man. I wouldn't call him racially sensitive, where he was on top of all the issues, but he was a fair-minded man.
>
> The relationship [between us] started when I was having a problem. I was, I guess, pretty much full of myself, and I knew I was good at what I did. If I was at a meeting and somebody wanted to do something that was bureaucratic or would slow me down or whatever, I would say that. And this person would not raise an issue at the meeting, but they would go behind my back and undermine what I was doing behind the scenes. So this Jewish guy came to me and told me what was happening: "You need to learn how to not wear your emotions on your sleeve." It was the first time I thought about that, but he was right. He played cards quite a bit. He was talking about, "It's like playing poker and you're gonna gain, and everybody else is holding their cards, and you can't see what they are, but your cards are lying face up on the table." And I was used to being straight out and honest-this is how I feel. A lot of people wouldn't come out with it, but if they had some agenda, they would go about taking care of it. And I learned that. He explained it to me, how you need to mellow out and not be face to face in terms of how you address issues and how you deal with people. I guess the expression he used was that you have enough enemies in the corporate world without creating new ones. And it may not even be obvious that they're going after you, they're gunning for you. But he said, "If you put somebody down, say something ugly at a meeting, and the person has the opportunity to hurt you, they will." My attitude at the time was, because I'm good at what I do and I know what I'm doing, I could just say what I felt like saying. But that was not really the case at all.

So we would socialize. I played golf with him. We played racquetball together several times. He had my wife and me over to his house. I had risen to middle-management just acting a certain way. So since that carried me that far, why change? He explained to me why change, because it would hinder you as you went forward. And I used that same logic in terms of choosing your battles with my children, family, friends, other employees, whatever. I explained to them I had the wisdom that I picked up and used and now I was passing it on to them.

At the same time, the member of the own has a chance to mentor the wise and even sometimes the normals. Michelle is a case in point. A black manager who considers herself a member of the peripheral own, she in fact transcends all three categories, while maintaining links to all of them. She has used her considerable understanding to get on in the corporation and, in the process, has herself become wise in its ways. She has become a strategic actor (see Goffman 1961) who can, in turn, edify and assist members of the various categories with their problems in the organization. As such, she reverses the model by mentoring normals in the ways of the own and in their sensitivities to race issues. In return, she can wield a certain amount of power by helping people perform better for the organization. Unlike the male executive quoted earlier, Michelle is not ambivalent about her intermediate position between the core own and the normals; she is not concerned about being seen by the core as selling out because she is convinced that her style of behavior benefits all blacks:

> First of all, when I joined the department, I was basically the only black professional. There was one other black person who was, as far as they were concerned, the typical ghetto Negro, because she came from there. She lived in North Philadelphia, made no bones about it, she looked as the stereotype, she behaved as the stereotype. And I wanted to create my own positive image, not just as a black person, but as a person who is committed to professionalism but who happens to be black. So that my blackness would not be the only thing that they're concerned about.
>
> I would always deal with people in a way that respected who they were so that I would get the respect that I was demanding by my behavior. I also reported to someone who was a bright, young, Catholic male, who went to a Jesuit school and recognized that we have something in common in that he was Catholic and I was Catholic. He was young. He came to the position, of course, because of his father. And he certainly recognized that, so he took pains to always tell me how hard he worked and how he worked from the mail room up to where he is, which was not

true-he spent maybe two minutes in the mail room of his entire career. And he was made in charge of the department very young, probably at the age of thirty something. And he was not in a sense filled with all the old traditional tapes of people who would think about black people in a certain way. To him it was something that you looked at sort of funny or joking or whatever, but he was not punitive. If he did it, it would not be what I consider malicious. He would have done it based on what I think most white people have a problem with, and that is not by commission but by omission, by not realizing what it means. If confronted with it, which I constantly did, he was always, "Oh, I didn't realize. Oh, I'm sorry." There was another manager who was there who was also Italian, that he tried to be buddy-buddy with, but this Italian person had been with me for a long time so he knew me. So he would also share with me what they shared in the bathroom that he didn't tell me. He told me, "Michelle, a lot of decisions are made in the bathroom." So he would tell me. So I had this other relationship with this other person that sort of helped me deal with the boss.

My boss let me hire one other professional person (a black man), and he also put me in charge of the word-processing pool, and I made sure that I hired people of color. So I changed the complexion of the pool.

Even today, I'll tell you something else: when our jobs [her job and that of the Italian manager] were downsized, I went and interviewed for a job at Merrill Lynch, and it was clear to me they didn't want a woman because how could a woman know anything about financial stuff? So he had a job he didn't like. So I called him and said, "Why don't you go and apply for the job?" He got the job and eventually became a vice president.

Now he's still at Merrill Lynch, and I call him frequently, and he still calls me for advice. And every once in a while I have lunch with him, and I make him pay for it, and I say, "You still owe me."

Ironically, members of the core own group, because of different styles of communication and the social distance that normally exists between the core own and whites, have relatively little opportunity to make positive impressions on members of the wise. Members of the core group, more sensitive to race than the colorblind peripheral own, are likely to perceive such a wise person as white first, making him or her ineligible for trust. In an important sense, the members of the core own are handicapped by their inability to make distinctions among whites, to trust whites, or to conceive of a white person being able to go out of his or her way for a black person. For the core own, all relationships with whites tend to be instrumental, whereas the peripheral own are able to establish and sustain expressive friendships and associations with white people.

The Normals

The last group, the normals, are people who make up and identity with the majority in the corporate culture. Handicapped by their close identification with the majority, they are generally oblivious to the special situation and plight of blacks and other minorities in the company. Even when they understand the special problems that minorities encounter, many tend to be unsympathetic to them; they often feel that the workplace has done enough for minorities. They may feel this way in part because they have been conditioned to perceive the minority person as a threat to their own interests. Many such people emerge from a situation without advantages, and they are inclined to look on a black person or another minority group member as a competitor within the organization, even when there is no basis for such thinking. Furthermore, many are of the opinion that the company has already done enough or too much. These people often believe that blacks and other minorities, assisted as they are by government programs to remedy past prejudice and discrimination, do not deserve to be employed by the company, particularly when there are so many well-qualified normals around.

This outlook is at times shared, perhaps to an increasing degree, by some of the minority employees of the corporation themselves, including a number of the blacks. Such beliefs reflect an ethos that emphasizes homogeneity in a culture where white skin color and male gender predominate. There exists a need for all members of the corporation to present themselves as and to pass as normals. Blacks, women, Jews, and other minorities with conspicuous and observable differences find passing difficult. Those who more readily approximate the dominant standards and values, including language, dress, and style of self-presentation, may find it easier to pass. This group includes white minorities, particularly when their members are almost indistinguishable from the white majority.

In such an environment, certain minorities in pursuit of status within the organization may assume the posture of the majority, including a degree of indifference to the special needs of minorities within the company. Some minority individuals may consciously sever all connections with their group. And given what has become an increasingly competitive context, striving minorities may find some reward-psychological or otherwise-in ignoring or de-emphasizing the importance of the special concerns of blacks and others.

Because of a certain dissonance that results from being caught between the poles of fully accepting this position and identity as members of the own, blacks are more sensitive to the shortcomings of this outlook. Thus most blacks find themselves working to reshape the corporate ideology and culture to allow their own incorporation. Such actions ultimately place them outside of the normal group. Those minority group members who are white may not suffer the same dissonance, and, because of their own group's divergent interests within the corporation, they may find it difficult to display a tolerance of blacks and others who may be viewed as outsiders within the corporation.

In their efforts to embrace the identity of the normal, such people may show their annoyance with the black presence by actively discrediting blacks whenever possible. They seldom facilitate the hiring of blacks in their immediate surroundings and recount sad tales of the last one who failed to work out, stories that the wise and the own must often suffer through. In their conversations on the subject, they like to emphasize "standards." Members of the own, being aware of such implicit charges against their competence and integrity, are then encouraged, if not required, to be more formal, distant, and guarded with whites in general. Such experiences, and the responses to them, help to solidify the own's generally negative working conception of life in the company. The prevalence of such experiences encourages an ambivalent stance by members of the peripheral own as they try to negotiate the organizational ladder of the company.

Conclusions

A major result of this country's civil rights movement of the 1960s was the incorporation of large numbers of blacks into the American occupational structure. Since then, through antidiscrimination legislation, including affirmative action, the black middle class has grown. It presently amounts to roughly a third of the black population. In addition, with the arrival of fair housing legislation, it has gravitated away from the inner-city black communities. Over the years, in effect, middle-class black people have begun to participate in the broader society in ways that would have astounded their predecessors.

However, a primary instrument of this process of incorporation-affirmative action-is now being seriously challenged and becoming increasingly untenable ideologically and politically. The process, at least in part, is being undermined by its seeming success: the apparent proliferation of blacks, and other minorities of color, in the professions, academia, business, and government, at a time when the workplace is becoming increasingly competitive. In effect, the advent of diversity seems to have been the political price required by affirmative action to survive. In addition, the appearance of such diversity serves as impressive evidence that the system is open, fair, and egalitarian, while restrictions of race become obscured. With such ostensible success, the former participants and their allies (the wise) in the civil rights movement recede, feeling that they have little left to fight for, especially when preferences are severely criticized as racially based in the current social and political context. Moreover, de-industrialization, corporate downsizing, and increased immigration have led to a highly competitive workplace, in which established but insecure workers tend to be much less generous in their support of social programs of almost any kind, but particularly those viewed as favoring one race over another. In these circumstances, many former liberals question their earlier support for remedial measures like affirmative action as a tool for achieving equal opportunity.

In this context, they simultaneously degrade racism as an explanation for a black person's inability to succeed, a position strongly held by powerful and well-organized conservatives. Moreover, conservative activists have been successful in challenging and outlawing affirmative action policies in California and are presently waging similar campaigns in other states. Their goal is to redefine affirmative action ideologically as a beatable menace that is inimical to the interests of whites and others who view their rights as threatened, if not abrogated, by such policies. If successful, such campaigns will have important implications and consequences not just for colleges and universities throughout the land, but for the American workplace as well. As the black presence in such settings seriously declines, the struggle for black equality is set back, further alienating many black people.

In the organization I studied, before affirmative action policies were initiated, almost no black people were present. In the average firm of thirty years ago, when present at all, blacks were found most often in the lowliest positions, including those of janitor, night watchman, doorman, elevator operator, secretary (at times required to work out of sight), or an occasional assistant director of personnel. With the arrival of affirmative action policies, the situation began to change, as the workplace became more inclusive. Accordingly, top executives and supervisors began to recruit blacks, providing them with a new kind of racial coin. This development enabled blacks to negotiate not only with their talents, including education and people skills, but also with their skin color. One of the important effects, if not a goal, of affirmative action was to place a premium on black skin color, negating its historical demerit.

Traditionally, the racial system provided preferences to those with white skin color, but now the tables are somewhat turned. For many corporate, political, and civic leaders, the social good of racial incorporation, at least for a time, outweighed the ambiguous, if sometimes arbitrary, invocations of meritocratic standards. During the tensions of the civil rights movement, and later the civil disorders occurring in many cities, business and government leaders encouraged racial peace and social progress, creating incentives that strongly motivated their organizations to absorb and use black workers. Many who were now being recruited as corporate employees had once been involved or sympathized with the college student and black power movements of their day. Now they were upwardly mobile, residing outside the ghetto, driving nice cars, sporting expensive dress, lunching in upscale restaurants with white colleagues, and at times discussing business strategy with high corporate officials.

In time, these direct beneficiaries of affirmative action, particularly members of the peripheral own described in this chapter, gravitated from group concerns long associated with liberating subjugated blacks to more individualistic concerns associated with personal economic well-being. In general, theirs was often a socially tense passage through a kind of nether world, fraught with risks, including taunts and criticisms of being an "Oreo," a "sellout," or an "Uncle Tom." Most dealt with their dilemmas with ambivalence, either by forging a strong relationship with the own or by actively distancing themselves from it. Regardless, such tensions and choices took their toll on black unity.

As suggested throughout this chapter, many executives occupied an ambiguous position, which was at times resolved superficially by code switching. Depending on the issue and the audience at hand, they might behave in a racially particularistic manner in private, while embracing more mainstream behavior in public. Most had the strong desire to be included as full participants in the organization and to meet the standards that everyone else was expected to meet. Yet, on their jobs, many experienced all manner of reaction to their presence in the organization-from effective mentoring and acceptance with open arms to cold stares and hostile receptions and persistent racial discrimination.

With the increasingly effective assaults on affirmative action policies, many black executives have become disillusioned and insecure. Over time, alienation takes a toll, and people become more isolated in the workplace, gravitating to what I call the core own. Here, in response to perceptions of an unreceptive work environment, they may keep to themselves, looking inward, while becoming racially energized to collaborate in the outright racial polarization that infuses so many work settings today (see Cose 1993).

Such behavior often exacts a social cost that compounds the initial problems at work. In the corporate setting, blacks who become so isolated often remain a group apart, inhabiting a social ghetto on the lower rungs of the corporate ladder. From this perspective, when the occasional black person achieves success, the promotion may be met with cynicism rather than unqualified praise; ambiguity often rules. Among those strongly associated with the own, depending on how they wear success, epithets like token or sellout may be whispered behind their backs. Although government pressures and policies have enabled many blacks to land executive positions in major corporations-and most perform their duties with real competence-many have been unable to attain the corresponding informal social power, along with relative feelings of security, that are taken for granted and enjoyed by many of their white counterparts in the workplace.

Moreover, in the changing economy and the increasingly competitive workplace, uncertainty often prevails, negating feelings of generosity and empathy with those who are most often marginalized and excluded. Accomplishing the unfinished business of equal opportunity, and the full incorporation of blacks, promises to be extremely difficult. The task at hand cannot be fully achieved without the support and active engagement of the wise-enlightened normals with the strong capacity for empathy with outsiders-who willingly go about the sometimes daunting social task of reaching out to blacks in the firm, recruiting, welcoming, befriending, and carefully mentoring them. In actively supporting the prevailing levels of black presence in the workplace, such socially liberal people were at times actively engaged as though they were on some kind of mission, and many were: their collective, if unstated, goal was to move our society forward by creating black access to meaningful positions in the workplace, furthering the process of incorporation and racial equality. Ironically, in the present socially and politically competitive context, enacting such roles may seem inappropriate, even quaint, a throwback to the do-gooder era of not so long ago. Such people who once reached out to blacks are much less visible in today's workplace.

For the laudable goal of equal opportunity, the real challenge is that of somehow edifying, encouraging, cultivating-in essence, growing-the wise, including blacks who have risen in the firm. All this, at a time when many feel the economic pie to be shrinking, when often ambiguous notions and tests of merit are invoked, and when blacks are at times portrayed as unworthy and undeserving of close mentoring or a hand up. Without the full engagement of such allies in the struggle for racial justice, blacks and other minorities will remain marginalized, creating ever more tension in the workplace. Thus a major task is that of growing the wise and bringing them together with the own in spite of unrelenting social forces that are hard at work to create fewer of their collective number.

References

Anderson, Elijah. 1990. *Streetwise: Race, Class, and Change in an Urban Community.* Chicago: University of Chicago Press.

———. 1997. "The Precarious Balance: Race Man or Sellout?" In *The Darden Dilemma: 12 Black Writers on justice, Race, and Conflicting Loyalties,* edited by Elis Cose. New York: HarperCollins.

Bearak, Barry. 1997. "Between Black and White." *New York Times,* July 27, sec. 1, p. 1.

Becker, Howard S. 1973 [1963]. *Outsiders: Studies in the Sociology of Deviance.* Glencoe, Ill.: Free Press.

Blumer, Herbert. 1958. "Race Prejudice as a Sense of Group Position." *Pacific Sociological Review* 1(1): 3–7.

Carter, Stephen L. 1991. *Rejections of an Affirmative Action Baby.* New York: Basic Books. Collins.

Cose, Ellis. 1993. *The Rage of a Privileged Class.* New York: HarperCollins.

Cox, Oliver. 1948. *Caste, Class, and Race.* New York: Doubleday.

Drake, St. Clair, and Horace Cayton. 1962 [1945]. *Black Metropolis: A Study of Negro Life in a Northern City.* New York: Harper and Row.

Du Bois, W. E. B. 1995 [1905]. *The Souls of Black Folk.* New York: Dutton. Feagin, Joe R., and

Frazier, E. Franklin. 1957. *The Black Bourgeoisie.* New York: Free Press.

Glazer, Nathan. 1987 [1975]. *Affirmative Discrimination.* Cambridge, Mass.: Harvard University Press.

———. 1997. *We Are All Multiculturalists Now.* Cambridge, Mass.: Harvard University Press.

Goffman, Erving. 1961. *Strategic Interaction.* Indianapolis: Bobbs-Merrill.

———. 1963. *Stigma: Notes on the Management of Spoiled Identity.* Englewood Cliffs, N.J.: Prentice-Hall.

Hacker, Andrew. 1995. *Two Nations: Separate, Hostile, Unequal.* New York: Ballantine.
Hughes, Everett C. 1945. "Dilemmas and Contradictions of Status." *American Journal of Sociology* 50(5): 353–59.
Kennedy, Randall. 1997. "My Race Problem, and Ours." *Atlantic* 279(5): 55–66.
Kerner,
Landry, Bart. 1987. *The New Black Middle Class.* Berkeley: University of California Press.
Massey, Douglas S., and Nancy A. Denton. 1993. *American Apartheid: Segregation and the Making of the Underclass.* Cambridge, Mass.: Harvard University Press.
Merton, Robert K. 1957. *Social Theory and Social Structure.* New York: Free Press.
Myrdal, Gunnar. 1944. *An American Dilemma: The Negro Problem and Modern Democracy.* New York: Harper and Row.
Otto, et al. 1968. *Report of the National Advisory Commission on Civil Disorders.* Washington, D.C.: Bantam.
Pettigrew, Thomas. 1980. *The Sociology of Race Relations.* New York: Free Press.
Rifkin, Jeremy. 1995. *The End of Work: The Decline of the Global Labor Force and the Dawn of the Post-Market Era.* New York: Putnam.
Rose, Peter 1. 1990 (1973). *They and We.* New York: Random House.
Schlesinger, Arthur M., Jr. 1992. *The Disuniting of America.* New York: Norton.
Sharon M. 1997. *Black Corporate Executives.* Philadelphia: Temple University Press.
Shibutani, Tamotsu. 1961. "Social Status in Reference Groups." In *Society and Personality: An Interactionist Approach to Social Psychology.* Englewood Cliffs, N.J.: Prentice-Hall.
Melvin P. Sikes. 1994. *Living with Racism:* The *Black Middle Class Experience.* Boston: Beacon.
Skrentny, John David. 1996. *The Ironies of Affirmative Action.* Chicago: University of Chicago Press.
Steele, Shelby. 1990. *The Content of Our Character: A New Vision of Race in America.* New York: St. Martin's.
Stryker, Perrin. 1953. "How Executives Get Jobs." *Fortune* 48(2): 117 ff.
Wellman, David T. 1977. *Portraits of White Racism.* New York: Cambridge University Press.
Wilson, William Julius. 1980. *The Declining Significance of Race: Blacks and Changing American Institutions.* Chicago: University of Chicago Press.
———. 1987. *The Truly Disadvantaged: The Inner City, the Underclass, and Public Policy.* Chicago: University of Chicago Press.
———. 1996. *When Work Disappears: The New World of the Urban Poor.* New York: Knopf.

NOW YOU DON'T SEE IT, NOW YOU DON'T: WHITE LIVES AS COVERT RACISM

David L. Brunsma

"Plain and simp' the system's a pimp, but I refuse to be a ho'"
-"Who Stole the Soul?" *Fear of a Black Planet,* Public Enemy

"Thus in effect, on matters of race, the racial contract prescribes for its signatories and inverted epistemology, an epistemology of ignorance, a particular pattern of localized and global cognitive dysfunctions (which are psychologically and socially functional), producing the ironic outcome that whites will in general be unable to understand the world they themselves have made" (Mills 1997: 18)

In this chapter*, I want to look briefly at my own life, a life of one who has dedicated himself to understanding the workings of race, racial identity, racialization, and racism in order to be more able to fight for social and racial justice, through an autoethnographic lens, to critically question my own current lived experience as it relates to racial stories and racist structures, and to utilize the master's tools to create new, inclusive, and just houses. Ultimately, moving somewhat afield of the problematic discourse of "white privilege," this chapter seeks to begin the difficult road for all of us in assessing the possibility that white lives, in their current form, in this current capitalistic, neoliberal society, *are* a central form of "covert racism." I will end the chapter with some preliminary suggestions for what can be done and call all who care about human rights, social and racial justice to think about this argument and to consider the various methodologies implied in the contours of this brief essay.

What's in a Life?

What is in a life? Lives are structures and stories. To conceive of lives as structures is to recognize a blueprint for human existence; one that varies, is reflexive, and is implicated in social power. Lives are compli-

---

* I originally wrote this autoethnographic piece in 2006. While much has changed – much has stayed the same.

cated structures in that they are patterned and patterning, built environments and builders of environments, created and creating, positioned and positioning. Thus, our lives as members of society are an endeavor in structured structuring. In addition, to conceive of our lives as stories is to understand the role of meaning in human existence; the variation in the tales we tell to and about other lives, these too are highly reflexive, and animate the lexicon of humanity in the matrix of cultural power. Lives are fantastically influential stories in that they are narrated and narrating, valued and reevaulative, plotted and plotters, formulaic and formulating, articulated and articulating. Thus, our lives in societies are simultaneously a project in storied storytelling. So, living is not solely of our own making, it is also made (classic agency and structure). To live a life is to concurrently navigate and internalize storied structures as well as structured stories.

Race is a story that has been told for over 500 years. The contours and focus of this meta-narrative have ebbed and flowed, usually in a unidirectional stream – from the oppressors to the oppressed – but always catching up all in the flow of these hegemonic waters; allowing the powerful flow to continue. We know of many stories that are older than race, but few of these have been as relevant (nor as detrimental) to human existence as this particular one (with some exceptions, e.g., gender, hierarchy, etc.). For such a story to continue molding itself, reshaping itself, etch itself into human affairs for so long gives light to the fact that there is a systemic need for such a narrative. Since this story of race is lived, the system may continue to churn easily for some (i.e., "whites") at the expense of others (i.e., "non-whites"). The system that embeds and connects our racially storied lives to societies, cultures, and institutions is racism.

Racism is a structure that has patterned our lives for almost as long as the story of race has been articulated – it needed time to fully enmesh itself in our social structures, while simultaneously creating new ones. Thus, our environments, our institutions, our social fabrics, our interactions are structured (and lived as structures) via racism. Racism is an exploitative, cognitive, epistemological, linguistic, and relentless social structure of domination. Race, as a story, and racism, as a well-storied house, as a structure, permeate our lives and we are both created by them as racialized and racist beings, as well as active creators in proliferating race's story and racism's structure.

Whites have been complicit in the writing of lives through race as well as in the construction and maintenance of societies through racism. Not only have whites *been* party to these crimes against humanity, they continue, everyday, through their very lives, to retell race and reconfigure racism. Far from "name calling", this is a serious exercise in "system calling." Since whites' storied and structured lives are seen as normative, central, unmarked, and, largely, "uninteresting," they are made invisible, unremarkable, hidden (especially to whites). As the halls of academia, the boardrooms of corporations, the offices of government, the ranks of the police force, the classrooms of our public schools, the laboratories of our medical establishments, indeed most of our institutions and organizations of power and influence are overrepresented with whites, and as we mask deep racial inequality with color-blind rhetoric and policy, there is an urgent need for progressive whites to begin addressing head-on their systemic and pervasive privilege and unmasking both the stories and structures that have proliferated for far too long.

White Lives as Covert Racism

We are all quite aware of our own lives (while whites actually benefit from ignoring others' storied and structured lives), in fact most of us are told throughout our socialization that we, "alone," can, and should, work to "change *our* lives," to make them better, to "be the person we want to be," and so on. However, many white folks, being in the center, the majority, the norm, hear such cultural dictums (*their* culture) and work towards individualistic ends with little to no clue or acknowledgement (ignorance is indeed bliss for whites) that their own lives are intimately intertwined with all other lives. In their bubbles of unearned privilege, whites fail to realize that their biographies, their life histories, their dreams of the futures, and their successes along life's paths, are part of an exploitative equation of structures, policies, spaces, and stories, that ultimately affect everyone else's possibilities for living. Because of the relentless structure of racism and the ever-articulated and evolving stories of race in the United States, white lives have been both structured and storied into privilege, into normativity, into "race-lessness," into invisibility, meanwhile, through such processes, white lives are situated and converted into privilege – the system has been and *is* designed for them and, ultimately, it works best for them at the expense of others. Thus, even a white life like my own, of one who vehemently opposes such structures both structurally and ideologically, is channeled into a white life, and therefore into an active reproduction of white privilege. I want to begin looking at the basic contours of my white life here in order to critically assess how my white life might reproduce the stories of race and the structures of racism.

Becoming White

The details of my early life (from birth) are consequential; however, for the sake of space, I will discuss only the pertinent experiences, as my early life was a case of "becoming white." My birth, in Des Moines, Iowa, in 1970, to a Puerto-Rican mother (who was adopted by Mennonite missionaries to Puerto Rico in the 1950's) and a largely unknown white father made me, in some sense, a "Puerto Rican American." But birth does not a racialized life make. Stories and structures do this, from early on. My mother's brothers and sisters (four children were adopted from Puerto Rico) were raised by my solidly white, privileged, Christian grandparents in mostly white neighborhoods (post World War II – on the white side of FHA programs, and their racialized realities; i.e., redlining, denying loans, etc.). Indeed, one of my uncles, who was older and more solidly acculturated to Puerto Rico, was institutionalized in the 1950's (largely because of his "deviant" language, accent, appearance, etc.) and has, ever since, been addicted to anti-psychotic medications. The desire to "secure" life for 1950's and 1960's whites by racializing and basically cutting off the potential if my Latino uncle's life was but an example of how the stories and structures of American society work for some and not for others. My grandparents were fully complicit in this endeavor.

Yet, I was raised white. I have come to embrace my Puerto-Rican identity (though it is never really validated in interaction), but I did not really know of this until the stories and structures of my life were already quite fully built – along white lines. Whiteness, was what I lived, where I lived, how I lived, secured by my own family's desire to live in the "right" (read: "white" neighborhoods), so that I could attend the "right" (again) schools, hang out with the "right" (ditto) friends, date the "right" women (not men), and the list goes on – their minds already having been colonized by stories of race, and structured via racism. I had "become" white, and this was based on a variety of factors, the stories I was told (including the very stories I was read, and read to), my phenotype (reddish hair, freckles, blue eyes – go to the middle of the island, in Puerto Rico, and you will see such visages for yourself – a legacy of slavery on the island), my dreams (the American one – I've long divorced that notion, or have I?), my neighborhood (safe, safe neighborhoods, I recall being able to be outside, anywhere in the neighborhood, virtually sunup to sundown until the 1990's), my largely white friends (except for a couple of friends, one Indian, one Black, both solidly middle-class), virtually everything was "normal" – "everyone was doing it."

Though my life was also sprinkled with my own largely initiated forays into critical literatures, music, and film outside the scope of public school and family, as well as a consistently developing critique of racism, sexism, capitalism, and global poverty (articulated in ways I understood differently at each step of the way), by and large, it was expected that I be white, that I talk white, dress white, and, ultimately, think and live white. It is this ultimate fate that, unfortunately, determined that I would also be destined to reproduce the structures of white privilege and racism (while being patted on the back for my "successes" along the way). The point being, despite the fact that I could see then, and can see even more strongly now, the structures of racism and the stories of race unfolding before me, my life, as a white American, preordained my structural complacency and tacit agreement (even while fully disagreeing) with the exploitative and devastating racial contract in white America.

"Knowledge" as (White) Power

I went to college ("it's the thing to do", "one must do it"). A supposedly "liberal" college, a Mennonite college, that preached a kind of liberation theology, where many go on to serve in missionary or "development" capacities all around the world – with good intentions, but, in the story and structure of race and racism, often times end up as colorblind extensions of American (or Jesus) imperialism. My college experience was expected of me, of course, and, because of my white life, I went in and came out – at the expense of other minority students' opportunities there. In fact, there were precious few people of color there. A great number of international students (many of whom were of color, from the Diaspora, but from a higher social class); however, the American opportunity structure, created by and sustained by and for whites, was evident there just as in many colleges and universities across the nation.

Graduate school was worse. I recall the "concern" over the lack of minorities in the department of sociology (and indeed in the university); however, concern was not usually followed by any concerted action – as the white administration bemoaned the lack of "diversity" in their hallowed halls while failing to recognize or attempt to critique the structures of racist domination that make it extremely unlikely that there would be a cohort of Black and/or Latino students who could: a) graduate from high school, to b) graduate from college, to c) even consider going to graduate school, to d) actually coming; this is a structural issue (racism) and the stories told to rhetorically gloss over the lack of "minority presence" is complicity with racist structures. I benefited from graduate school because I am white, a man, and because the spaces were open, and remain open, due to the lack of "students of color" being able to get to the front steps. Furthermore, the city wherein I attended graduate school was deeply entrenched in gentrification policies and "development" projects that further secured such outcomes.

Meanwhile, my critical, social justice lenses were becoming more and more pronounced, partially due to the epistemological stranglehold of the social scientific methodology, its incessant documentation of dystopia, its squelched critical imagination rooted in its dominant, white mode of academic production. I was and still am outraged, and, yet, I have a PhD, am white, and the structures still continue to channel my life, to the detriment of those who have been racialized in this society. Graduate school allowed me to reshape my toolkit ("knowledge is power") and develop much more strident critiques of structures of domination, but it failed to give me tools to restructure the societal conduits within which my white life was situated – in fact, it seems to have set me on an even more privileged white life than before – the training seems to have distanced its trainees from those who struggle.

The Housing that Race Built

My family and I now live in a mid-sized, Midwestern college town. This town is predominantly white (87%), as is its central university (90%), where I teach and write. Slavery etched its way across Missouri here from Kansas City to St. Louis. There were lynchings in this town, minstrel shows, rapes of black women, denying of opportunities to cohorts of Black and, now, Latino youth. This space is highly racialized – there is a "Black part of town" and the rest of the white areas are divided along class lines. When my family and I moved here in the fall of 2004, we desired to live in an area of town where our children could grow up with a vast array of children, from all racial, ethnic, and, if possible (though this is extremely rare) class backgrounds. We made two offers on houses in a particular area that fit such criteria (that I *could* choose is indicative of a structured white life), helped along by a white realtor, and neither of those offers ever "came to fruition" – I often wonder why. Now, we live in the most white, "liberal," and fairly affluent section of town, ten blocks from my office, eight blocks from my boys' school, and in a house we can barely afford. I desired to make decisions in line with my understanding of the structures and stories of race, and, yet, I ended up here. My living here, the mortgage rates I received, the safety I enjoy, the stories I get to hear, the life I live, and the resale value I will enjoy, come at an expense, I know, to the housing and neighborhoods of my Black and Latino brothers and sisters, their mortgage rates (if they can even get one), their feelings of safety, the stories they are forced to hear, and, in the end, their very lives. All structured in radically different ways than mine – by design.

The United States is supremely racially divided. The paragons of our racial attitudes, racist policies, and racialization of groups of people, are tied intimately to the degree of racial apartheid that has been structured into our society so clearly for over 200 years. White lives are central to the remaking of racist structures and the maintenance of such segregation. As our lives are so separate, structured away from each other, so is our ideological cartography, our "racial attitudes", and the stories we tell each other through the media, through our families, through our institutions. But, wait, I denounce these stories! I chose to chart another path, one of racial and social justice! Ah, yes, that may be true, but the white life *is* the structure, without the white life racism as a structure (as articulated particularly in this country) might cease to exist – racism relies on white structured lives. Without white stories (the dominant narratives), racial stories might cease to exist.

The Four R's: Reading, 'Riting, 'Rithmatic, and Racism

I have three children. One of my children, who is of schooling age goes to "one of the best public schools in Columbia" (I heard this from mostly white folks before moving), while my other son is attending a Montessori on campus ("it is the best place to develop a young child") – both places are *very* white (despite the arguments that they were both extremely "diverse"). Believe me, we visited these schools, and we did see some "diversity", however, in institutional education, organized into schools and preschools, one does not capture the true sense of "diversity" until experiencing the daily interactions, the ideological contours of the curriculum, and the hierarchies inherent (structured) into the doing of education. Indeed, despite our "alternative" socialization of our children, my boys' white lives are being actively and solidly constructed. My seven-year old has a solid sense of individualism (devastating to anti-racism), entitlement (me, me, me, at the expense of them, them, them – but never stated as such), a teacher/school-inspired notion that the "black kids are always going to the focus room" (i.e., getting in trouble), a disturbingly tight network of white friends with similar if unfettered notions of the same, and, he is beginning to understand that being male and white (not to mention homophobic) comes with certain privileges. On the playground, in the classroom, at functions, etc., the curriculum is so solidly ethnocentric, nationalistic, white supremacist, patriotic, and fully marginalizing to non-white groups, I am appalled. However, this is whiteness in the making, through structures and stories, courtesy of your local public school.

Meditations on White Mediations

Both my wife and I understand that media (of all forms) have been central in the creation of racial stories and part and parcel of the racist structures that inform and channel our lives at the expense of those whose voices, stories, and visions have been marginalized. So, in our household, we have rid our lives of television. We have not wanted the racist ideologies of the network news, the sitcom machinery, the "human interest" stories, the cartoons, the propaganda of white supremacy and capitalist patriarchy to do any damage to our children's bourgeoning sense of who is and who is not, right and wrong, reality and myth, etc. This approach has opened up a space for true stories, diverse stories, new ways of thinking (television doesn't ask one to think) to some extent. We rely on our "entertainment" from rented DVDs, where we get to "pick and choose" what our children watch, and, what we have found is that it is difficult to choose any form of media that is actually outside the scope of rearticulated racial stories. Oh sure, and of course, virtually all of these films do indeed attest to my *white* children's' existence (mostly white lives, American dream, fantasyland [of whites] kind of stuff) – but there is a significant void. When non-whites *are* presented, they are caricatured, stereotypical, marginalized, and stripped of subjectivity. White supremacy and neoliberal market forces select and choose for us, and the choices they make are white ones, for white lives, for structures of racism and stories of race; thus, in our choosing, we may choose, but we choose from an array of racial stories.

When I think about these issues, it is clear to me as well that while we talk about colonization, globalization, and, for those who like to call these what they are, imperialism, "colonization" is typically "over there", and globalization is a "period of capitalism"; however, both of these practices are heavily color coded *and* we have internally colonized groups of people of color here on U.S. soil (Blacks, Latinos, Native Americans, etc.) and that the effects of colonization on the minds of black youth, for instance, are severe. Institutions developed in a white supremacist country, *will* produce white supremacist education, health care, insurance, investment opportunities, family structures, media, governments. Since these are our institutional realities, since these are the social contours of our lives, then these also become the cultural and ideological contours of our values and cognitions. In other words, white minds are colonized as well. This is clear when one can work extremely hard to overcome the years of white supremacist, individualistic, patriarchal, capitalistic ideological material in our K-12 education (only to receive more in post secondary school, and yet even more in graduate or professional schooling) without any alteration of the structures that reproduce them in schools, in hospitals, in corporate offices, in the stock market, in our families, in the media, and in our national, state, and local governments. A storied life can be re-storied, but this is insufficient without altering the structures of that storied life – the two, racial stories and racist structures, are sides of the same coin.

The (White) World of (Academic) Work

In my academic job I hold a joint position in sociology and Black Studies. Academia, and in my experience, sociology in particular, should be a space where stories are challenged, by and large, where voices, long silenced, are part of the ongoing conversation and dialogue towards more inclusive, deep democracy. It should be a place where structures of racism, for instance, are reconfigured in anti-racist ways, away from white privilege, away from white, and male, dominance. This has not been my experience. As a white man who has studied and taught incognito among other whites (and, largely, I am referring to white men), I have found universities to be profoundly white spaces – not only the structures, but the ideologies, epistemologies, pedagogies and methodologies that guide what we do. For structural (racist) reasons, and via the racial stories of the past and present (and desired future), discussions of the lack of diversity among faculty, staff and students abound, but the predominantly white power structures articulate self-serving and structure-preserving arguments (i.e., "we want to hire minorities and women, but only if they are *good* and *qualified*").

Institutionally, the university is deeply rooted in liberalism (while also structured to reproduce class and white privilege), meritocracy (while also defending a credentialist system), and tradition (while espousing progressivism). Demographically, the university is predominantly white. By and large university faculty (and administrators) are predominantly white and male (especially, among faculty, the full professoriate). As important as this is the fact that the student body is also predominantly white, European-decent, and middle- to upper-class. Ideologically, universities' missions advocate a striving toward a place for critical searches for truth, self-exploration, diversity, multiculturalism; yet, the structure of the university offers a different interpretation – there is a mismatch. Many of the white students in these universities will become white, middle-class, heterosexual, citizens of the United States without ever having to acknowledge their privilege, question their structural positions, scrutinize their sense of entitlement – indeed, students often can graduate without having to be critical. The "walls" around white students are thick and heavily buttressed by the dominant social structure and "blissful ignorance" on the part of universities and their faculties will only serve to add further reinforcements to protect these students' white privilege – at the cost of not only the oppressed, but the oppressor as well, of society.

Now What?

This chapter has illuminated some serious realities and equally serious dilemmas facing our lives as both structures and stories, as both determined and agentic, as ideology and as relentless social architecture. I am a "race-traitor" – if you will – and have been called such before. To be honest, I think was sort of hoping that the results of my reflections about my own life would illustrate the potentiality of ideological anti-racism, would show the utility of my anti-racist pedagogy, through my work, teaching, and life. Yes, I have seriously restocked my toolkit, worked diligently to "decolonize" my mind (and those of others); both interactionally and theoretically challenged stories of race and structures of racism through my "words." However, it is clear to me that I (and we) have a long way to go to alter the foundations that allow a white life (like mine) to continually reproduce the structures, which reproduce the stories, which buttress the structures, and so on, that make white lives an insidious form of covert racism.

It is also clear to me, though I may be fooling myself, that it is not that I do not practice what I preach (I certainly *try* desperately hard to do so) or that we progressive, anti-racist whites do not live by our own teachings and writings on white privilege and racism (we certainly *try* desperately hard to do so). It is more to the point that these preachings (anti-racist, anti-capitalism, anti-essentialism) and the "utopian" structures that they portend *do not, in fact, now exist*. Because of this social fact, the majority of this white life and its subsequent actions have been structurally preordained in so many ways and that there are a series of other stories that serve to bolster the stories of race and the structure of racism, for instance: individualism, (his)tory, heterosexism, individual rights, liberalism, gender, capitalism, "social policies," choice, color-blindness, entitlement, nationalism, the American Dream, liberty, etc.

We must both focus on holding the structures up to the light and critically challenge them at *every turn*, this involves incessant study, critical study, rooted in a starting point of justice and human rights, in universal morality and international cooperation. Study alone will not do it – the walls and boundaries have been built to high and thick – but it is necessary. We must also understand the stories that have been told and continue to be told, albeit in new, color-blind ways (ways that are equally racist) – color-blindness is our "newest" serious challenge because of the insidious ways it enmeshes structures and stories. Who tells the stories? Hold them accountable. We must question the dominant stories we've heard (that cover up and bolster structures) and illuminate the *real* structures of *all* lives. We must tell stories (however individually damning these are, the collective damnation is already written on the wall) that truly reflect the structures of our lives and opens spaces for true stories of real structures to emerge. We must work hard to alter our structured lives so that false stories cannot sustain themselves. Theory cannot exist without praxis.

Race-traitoring is not an identity. To think so is a dangerous ruse. Rather we must seek *structural* anti-racisms that include critical theory, but do not stop there. Race-traitoring is to speak truth to power, to subvert stories, and to tirelessly work to alter structures in the matrix of domination and exploitation – without a praxis of structural anti-racism, we will live as both covert anti-racists *and* complicit in covert racism. Those of us who stand upon unearned mountaintops must utilize this vantage of privilege to simultaneously dismantle it. We should be looking into the white lives that have worked against these structures and stories. Let's also look at how the meta-story of race and the meta-structure of racism have rearticulated and often beaten into submission these anti-racist pioneers who have combined theory and praxis. Real stories to reflect real structures. An exposing of false stories and the ways in which they rearticulate false structures.

Since all lives are intertwined, since stories and structures are mutually reinforcing, the point is clarified that race and racism hurt everyone – this is a point that is not often enough made. Because of the intertwined nature of structures and stories, our social lives tend towards the reproduction of each. The point is, it takes more than just realizing, theorizing, and building critical knowedges within individual lives, we have to get out and do the work, face the structure, try desperately not to live it. I (and we) have been bamboozled in a way. Because I know how racism works, I thought I was perhaps better, not part of the problem, not living "as much" in privilege, but I am. I can use this vantage point. We have an imperative obligation to use this vantage point – the statute of limitations on white privilege has definitely run out (an argument that could be used in pursuance, for instance, of Black reparations). The bottom line is that the structure is immoral no matter how you look at it, but those of us who have been unjustifiably privileged in this system can use – indeed have a universal moral obligation to use – such positions to alter the structures of racism – anything less will not do.

References

Mills, Charles 1997. The Racial Contract, NY: Cornell University Press.

AREN'T THEY ALL DEAD?
COVERT RACISM AND NATIVE AMERICANS

Claudia A. Fox Tree

Oral Tradition

Before I share my personal experiences to illustrate how covert racism impacts Native Americans[1], it is important to consider the role of "the story" as a teaching tool. Every culture began with an oral tradition. The oral story was the way a group of people passed on to its next generation such things as its history of creation, rules for behavior, consequences for misbehavior, rites of passage, and ways to treat other people and animals. Eventually, some cultures developed writing and chose to move from oral to written versions of the stories in order to pass them on to the next generation. We know some previously oral stories by these names: *The Koran*, *The Bible*, and *The Torah*. Writing has been one of the greatest inventions[2] (Diamond 1999) in history, allowing knowledge to be transferred into the storage medium of millions of books in thousands of libraries. But now, how do we cull through all that written word? How do we know what is most important? For cultures that have thousands of years of oral tradition, important information is distilled and passed down in stories and songs, and the very most important knowledge is encoded into a ceremony

---

[1] The author would like to acknowledge the long-standing difficulty in selecting a group term to describe the Indigenous Peoples of North and South America. *American Indian* and *Indian* both have controversies related to the history of European colonization and imposition of names. *Native American* is problematic because all people who are born in the United States are native to the country. There are other terms, such as *First Nations People* that are used in countries like Canada, but they are less frequently used in the United States. I have chosen to use *Native American* because that is the term I use to identify myself unless specifically referring to my particular Nation and heritage (Arawak). It is also the term that, in my experience, is most commonly used and accepted in my region of the country.

[2] The book, *Guns, Germs, & Steel* by Jared Diamond contains more information about the history of writing and implications for cultures who were proficient in particular forms of writing, whether syllabry, phonetic, or pictures, relative to cultures who were evolving written language, had their books burned and destroyed, or had no known written language.

(Alvord 1999). The significance of oral tradition and its value among Native Americans cannot be underestimated (Alvord 1999; King 2003). The metaphors, teachings, and examples laid out in a story are an integral part of the indirect communication style of Native Americans (Roseberry-McKibbin 1995). That communication style also includes the process by which stories are told. Stories are relayed to individuals within families and communities (clans, nations); with and among other people with whom a relationship exists. Having said that, the role of the story or the "narrative" takes on a new dimension in modern times (Lee 2003). It is a way for Native Americans to speak that allows the opportunity for non-Native people to listen and hear our authentic experiences, which too frequently are hidden and missing from the world. In this chapter, I will relay personal stories that highlight covert racism and connect these stories to the issues of racial identity development, marginalization, stereotypes and media, national holidays, multiracialness, and cultural survival. Listening to stories from people who are experiencing the pain of racism is a step toward understanding the many ways covert racism occurs.

David Wellman (1993) defines racism as a system of advantage based on race. This system includes personal, social/cultural, and institutional/systemic forms of racism. In my experience of teaching multicultural courses[3], most people conceptualize racism as overt, individual acts of meanness and therefore do not see themselves as engaging in racist behavior. Once they understand how the multiple levels of racism work together to maintain power and privilege of the dominant white European American group, they begin to understand that their privilege, as well as their silence (Ayvazian 1995), reinforces the cycle of oppression.

Researchers have identified this "silence" is different ways. Kivel (1996) and Batts (1998) use terms like "modern forms of racism" and Sue calls them "microaggressions" (2007). What we can say is that covert racism is characterized by silence around labeling and understanding actions as racist due to not knowing, not being aware, ignoring,

---

[3] Multicultural education has been defined in many ways. I use it here to include both content and pedagogy. It includes making underrepresented groups visible, teaching in ways to reach all learners, and acknowledging all oppressions and their intersections. The ultimate goal of multicultural education is social justice for historically oppressed groups.

and not taking action. Even the liberal adage, "I treat everyone the same" is part of this silence. By ignoring racial differences, as well as differences based on sex, sexual orientation, ability, and the like, one can not notice the impact of these factors and therefore act upon them. Ultimately, both covert and overt behaviors support a system that perpetuates racist ideologies. Individuals, as part of systems, unknowingly continue to pass along misinformation, limit opportunities for people of color, and perpetuate psychological damage to all, even by not doing anything, which allows the racism to continue (Sue 2003; Clark 1947). Some of the psychological damage to those who are in the dominant group include feelings of superiority, misinformation about oppressed groups, resistance to diverse ideas in the work place, inability to understand or interact with people from other groups, and fear of saying or doing something "wrong" (Ely 2006; Tatum 1992). No one intends to be covertly racist, but the unintentional outcome is that racist behaviors and actions do occur and people of color are put down, discriminated against, oppressed, hurt and expected to endure.

When covert behaviors are made visible, one can begin to take personal action and challenge systems to reduce racism and create a more equitable environment. In the examples that I will share, white European American people, as well as people of color, have advantages relative to Native Americans. It should be noted that even though people of color may have relative privilege (Suyemoto 2006) to one another, they are still operating within the system of racism which ascribes these privileges and ultimately advantages white European American people. While both white European American people and people of color can and need to take actions to challenge the system, white European American people are in the position of having more power and privilege. As Eduardo says, "You are the one who owe us for the years of cruelty! And you must compensate us now" by learning about us and using the advantages received from the system of racism to work toward social justice.

Developing Identity (and Racism at the Individual Level)

Both of my sons have been teased and bullied during and after school. Once, I was at a football practice where the teams broke early in order to have the annual family barbecue. While my sons, ages ten and twelve at the time, were waiting for the line to slow down, they were hanging out on the sidelines. After the event was over, on the car ride home, they told me that a group of girls was asking them why they wore their hair long. The boys told the girls that their mother (me) wanted them to understand their Native American heritage before they thought about cutting it (not exactly what I have taught them, but close enough). The girls then teased them saying they should cut their hair because otherwise they were girls. As they shared their story, I was angry that my children had to face the impact of racism again. I was angry that no parent, teacher, or religious leader had taught these girls about different cultural traditions, like why Native Americans wear their hair long, or how to politely ask about differences without making judgments, or how teasing can hurt. I was also angry that my children were put into the position of needing to explain their cultural tradition, to be an informant, and that there was an expectation that everyone be and do like mainstream America. However, I also saw this moment as a place for education and learning, so I put my feelings aside. I knew my sons felt embarrassed and humiliated and, at that moment, wanted to cut their hair. Being young and thinking concretely, they did not like the idea of being misinterpreted as the "wrong" sex. They wanted to fit in and be like every other boy, meaning have short hair. And, they did not remember why their mother would "make them" keep it long.

In order to build confidence about their heritage, I reviewed the meaning of long hair as I will now for the reader. I expect that you are in college and have made it to this point in your life believing that you are respectful of people and not racist. You may even believe that hair is not such a big deal. This belief and the traditions around hair are both cultural. I am aware of the mainstream traditions of how and why people wear their hair in certain ways. I have had to learn them, because I have had to teach my children that they have different traditions in order to be prepared for inevitable questions and comments. I could not "not know" about hair. But you, the reader, could very well spend your entire life not knowing about Native American hair traditions. What does this tell you about your education? What does it tell you about your social circle? What about your observations or conversations? What does this tell you about how covert racism works? The group with advantage does not have to learn about the group that is disadvantaged. It is the not knowing that makes racism covert, but you have reached a point in your life and education where you have the skills to locate information, update your knowledge, and learn to expect differences.

In our Native American[4] culture, the longer the hair, the longer the braid. The more "cross-overs" during the plaiting process, the more prayers that can be made. Long hair is a gift for prayer and for nature because the loosened hairs are put outside for animals to use in dens and nests. The time to cut one's hair is when there has been a tremendous loss, usually a person, and cutting one's hair symbolizes this loss. Native Americans typically recognize this symbolic change and will respond to each other in a manner befitting someone who is mourning. The time of grieving is expected to end when one's hair grows back to its original length; a visual reminder that there will come a time to let go and move on. In addition to explaining the tradition, I also provided my boys with tools for dealing with this kind of insult. They could walk away, they could stop and educate, or they could make a smart remark back. We had a conversation about what they could have said back, including that the last time they looked, hair was not the part of anatomy that defined gender and that just because a girl wears her hair short, does not mean she is a boy.

In third grade, my second son asked for and received a much-wanted and much-loved Mohawk haircut, which he spiked and wore the last day of school before summer vacation. He had been teased all year about being gay, so this was an "I want my hair cut" compromise between him and me. On this particular day, when he was called gay, he responded by punching the bully in the nose and was promptly sent to the office. Subsequently, he refused to spike his hair, and let it lay flat for the remainder of the summer. I was greatly saddened at what I perceived to be a rejection of his culture because dealing with the teasing was just too much.

Pardon me for stating the obvious, but Native girls/woman with long hair do not face the same issues in the mainstream culture as Native boys/men with long hair. In mainstream American culture, there is a strong association between boys who behave or look feminine and being gay and long hair looks feminine. Over the years, I have purposefully initiated conversations with my long-haired brothers and

---

[4] The traditions I share are what I have been taught from my Arawak family, as well as teachings I have learned from growing up in New England in the context of Northeast Woodland traditions. I use the term "Native American" to capture the teachings that in my experience are common across many nations. If you are interested in knowing more specifics details of an individual nation, I suggest you research the specific group.

my long-haired Native American male friends in the presence of my sons that addressed questions such as, how long have you worn your hair long? Why do you choose to wear it this way? Did you ever cut it? Were you ever teased? How did you handle it? I wanted my boys to see that grown men make this choice, that they live through it, that they are proud of their decisions, their Native American identity, and that no matter what their sexual orientation, they are still men.

At home, I have tried to "normalize" conversations about sexuality, including my own bisexuality. "Normalizing" is a process I do by substituting in a different referent than what is expected in a "normative" situation. For example, when one of my sons would come home and say, "I *really* like someone at school." Instead of the typical assumption that this person was of the opposite sex, I would respond with, "Boy or girl?" Though I have taught my sons to understand that it does not really matter what someone's orientation is unless a romantic relationship is desired and normalized the conversation, they have also internalized the dominant value that being gay is less desirable and long hair on men is associated with this.

When I teach racial/ethnic identity development to educators, I have my students read aloud poetry written by people from diverse ethnic backgrounds. I then ask them to tell me themes, feelings, and topics that came out in the writings. I sort the responses into four boxes and then title the boxes: *pre-encounter, encounter, immersion/emersion,* and *internalization* using William Cross's research (1987; 1995) on African Americans. Each box represents a "status." Although this is only one model, it is frequently cited and does provide a clear structure and introduction to understanding the process that people of color go through in order to develop a healthy sense of their racial identity. There are strong societal forces working to keep people of color from feeling good about their ethnic identity and cultural values, and it takes time to work through feeling like you are just like everyone else (pre-encounter), to finding out others do not think of you as the same and experiencing racism (encounter), to learning about one's ethnicity/race and feeling proud of that identity (immersion), to being able to build coalitions with other people of color (internalization).

In the example of my sons, in the pre-encounter phase, they felt like they fit in with everyone else and wanted to be white, which meant they felt like "white European Americans," not as Native Americans. Then the "encounter" experiences of being teased began happening, reinforcing that their Native American way of doing things was not the mainstream way, strengthening a racist ideology that does not accept diversity and works at chipping away any cultural sense of identity that does not fit into the mainstream. Growing up within the Native American community is the beginning of an immersion time that continues into adulthood. It is difficult and challenging to construct a positive racial identity from a position of powerlessness, when surrounded with negative images and comments. Typically, at the college level, young people of color seek opportunities to learn more about their racial group by taking courses about their group and associating with other people of color. Feelings of competence, well-being, and identification with the collective experience of a particular racial group are outcomes of racial identity development (Carter 1991; Helms 1995; Phinney 1990). When individuals "emerge," they feel proud of their heritage alongside that of mainstream and other groups of color. They understand the dominant culture and respect their cross-cultural allies. They may also continue to work with oppressed groups and/or built coalitions to further social justice goals.

When my first son was thirteen, he cried himself to sleep every night. So, with my permission, and desire to not completely alienate his Native American heritage, he eventually cut off all his hair in an effort to be accepted by his peers. He was somewhat surprised that his life did not completely change. My second son kept his hair long and then identified with the skateboarding culture, a mainstream socially acceptable place where he can wear his hair long. He says his brother "wants to be white." Cross and Helms (1995; 1995) both recognize that one's racial identity "status" can spiral back and forth. An individual in a developmental status has a predominant way of viewing the world and is able to deal with racism more effectively as they move along the continuum, but because of the nature of racism, "encounter" experiences continue to happen which may require times for emersion. My boys have about two years to go before they enter college.

While all people of color enter the process of racial identity development, not all white European American people do. According to Janet Helms, it is only when white European American people begin to notice that having white skin means something in this society, that they enter the racial identity development process (1990; 1995). Before this, racial identity is not perceived as affecting them. Understanding covert, cultural, and institutional racism is a journey that takes time. Covert racism, sometimes termed "modern racism," has been broken down into many valid and different categories (Batts 1998; Kivel 1996).

In my teaching I use a basic division I learned from Beverly Daniel Tatum and she retells in one of her books (Tatum, 2003). I draw a box and divide it into four quadrants. The row headers are "active" and "covert[5]," while the column headers are "racist" and "anti-racist" yielding four combinations: active racist, covert racist, active anti-racist, and covert anti-racist. I ask students to brainstorm examples of behavior for each box. What they discover is that there is no such thing as "covert anti-racism." Anti-racism always requires action, from understanding issues to doing something about them. They can also visually see that the "racist" behavior column contains the covert actions of not noticing and taking no action. Racist behaviors include name-calling and joke telling; knowing it is racist, but listening to the joke anyway; being a bystander; and not saying anything. The silence of not noticing, understanding or knowing that something is racist would be in the covert box because the system of racism continues to be maintained whether one is actively participating in racist behaviors or covertly participating by not knowing the behavior is racist. The intent may be different, but the outcome is the same, racism as a system of advantage for white European Americans continues. The activity highlights the need to educate oneself and become aware in order to "move" from the covert racist box (not noticing) to the active anti-racist one (taking action). In my story about the principal's office, it is interesting to note that, while hitting is wrong, the school missed the "first punch" in this case by not noticing the previous teasing. There would need to be an awareness of the issue in order to observe the behavior and take action to intervene, moving from the covert/unaware box to the action/anti-racist box.

Marginalization (and Cultural Racism)

Around 1910, the well-known American author O. Henry wrote, "The Ransom of Red Chief." This short story was assigned to my daughter when she was thirteen as an example of irony: a kidnapped boy is so bad that his kidnappers eventually pay his father to take him back. This story is supposed to be funny because the child is so badly

---

[5] I use the term "passive" racism, instead of "covert" when I teach. This was the term I first learned from Dr. Beverly Daniel Tatum and the one with which I am more familiar.

behaved. Even though the last thing an eighth-grade girl wants is a parent in her business, she brought the story to me because she was "having trouble understanding it." It starts off by showing just how bad this little boy is. He is throwing rocks at a kitten. What other bad thing does he do? He plays "Indian" by imitating his perception of Native American behavior based on the stereotypically bad things that Native Americans are supposed to have done. My daughter's confusion was a reaction to the racism of the short story, but she did not have the words to discuss it. Her teacher had not previewed any of the racist vocabulary, nor followed up with a class discussion about its exaggerations and stereotypes (burning at the stake, scalping, and examples of "savagery"), all of which are a mockery of Native American culture. Native American children are negatively affected by school policies which allow these stories to be taught without adequate discussion, and those actions and policies negatively impact the academic experiences of other children as well. When a whole class reads a book such as *The Courage of Sarah Noble* by Alice Dalgliesh, which portrays Native Americans as savages to be feared and as unhygienic, among other things, without also being exposed to books that present ethnic cultures in a positive light, racist ideology becomes the norm and therefore not noticed.

Images, music, dance, and myths created by the dominant culture are taken as reality, preventing accurate understanding of Native Americans and the contemporary ways we enact our culture. Covert racism is evident in multiple ways, including an unconscious inability to see one's own privilege even while seeing that others are disadvantaged (McIntosh 1992). Invoking "political correctness" as something bad, blaming the victim for being a complainer or creating their own problem, and arguing that "traditions" need to be upheld are examples of justifications which result in continued oppressive acts. One anti-oppressive strategy is explained by James Banks (2002) in a process that follows these steps: *to know, to care, to act*. Covert racism is a result of not knowing. Once someone *knows* the truth and learns new information, then they must feel the emotions. Emotions show *caring* and can include anger at not being told the whole story, sadness about the result of oppression, or guilt over having benefited at the cost of another group. In order to change these negative emotions, we must take the final step, which is to *act*. Actions require us to find our voice and take steps to initiate change. In institutions, actions may include diversifying staff. The more diverse the people, the more diverse the thinking, and the more inclusive the polices, procedures, and practices (Nieto 1996) become at systemic, institutional levels.

A monocultural lens does not notice how images of other racial groups are hurtful, oppressive, and counterproductive to a global society. A monocultural lens marginalizes people from ethnically and racially diverse backgrounds and is covertly racist. Marginalization is not limited to schools. It happens in movies, television, sports, and advertisement that I will collectively refer to as "the media." Racism is "systematic advantage," which means it works in multiple venues, but particularly systemically within cultural institutions such as schools, the media, and publishers/books. All people are affected by literary and media depictions in that they 1) learn to feel better or worse about themselves, their culture, and other people who look like them and 2) are learning accurate and inaccurate information about other groups. Banks writes about the importance of how knowledge is constructed (1997). We all need to be able to identify negative images in books and media, how they are hurtful, and why those images need to be dispelled. These are some of the first steps to undoing the "not knowing" characteristic of covert racism.

When It Feels As If We Have No Control (Cultural and Institutional Racism)

One mid-November, I was in the local grocery store at the register paying by check when I felt a tug on my elbow. My second son, who was twelve, pointed to a place toward the ceiling above my head. At first I saw the mylar balloons with images of turkeys, autumn leaves, and cornucopias, and then I saw what he was pointing at. There, floated a large, yellow smiley face, the ones with the black eyes and smile that are so very common on stickers and t-shirts. Only this smiley face had a brown headband and a mylar feather sticking out on the side. My son said, "We don't look like that. Isn't that racist?" The image of a Native American with a headband at Thanksgiving time has been so normalized in our society that no one even notices that it is racist.

I applied my "normalization" techniques in reverse, asking myself, "If I substitute another group, would it still be seen as *normal*?" If it were Martin Luther King, Jr. Day and that balloon had been black, would that been seen as normal and acceptable? If it were Rosh Hashanah, and that balloon had the hair of a Hasidic Jew, would that have been acceptable? If it were Chinese New Year, and that balloon had buck-teeth, wore a queue, and donned a rice paddy hat, would it have been offensive? Once I did this exercise in extremes, it was obvious to me that the Native American balloon depiction was grossly racist. I did speak to the manager, expressing all my concerns and examples, and he said he would need to speak to the other managers. By the time I made it back to the store, all the decorations had been taken down, so there was no way I could assess whether it was due to my voice or the end of the holiday season.

From Columbus Day until Thanksgiving, Native Americans are particularly bombarded with images of who we are supposed to be, based somewhat on who we were in the past, with very little regard to who we are now. When these two holidays arrive each year, how many people are aware that Native Americans have no national holiday? In fact, we are immersed in the systemic honoring of events that were devastating to our own people. Besides being subjected to such things as displays in stores depicting Native Americans, television shows portraying this holiday and sometimes poking fun at Native Americans, and the closing of banks and industries, Native Americans also endure the constant discussion by well intentioned liberal thinking colleagues and friends related to, "What are you doing/did you do for Thanksgiving?"

Some things are bigger than an individual, community, town, or state. The United States national holidays are excellent examples of institutional racism. Most people are unaware of the true history behind certain holidays, misinformation is perpetuated, and there is investment in maintaining ignorance – it is difficult to be happy once one knows the truth. Let us take Columbus Day as an example. In 1492, on his third night in the Indies on board ship, Christopher Columbus wrote in his journal, "I could conquer the whole of them with fifty men and govern them as I pleased" (Las Casas 1989). On his second voyage in 1493, Columbus arrived with seventeen ships, 1,500 men (no women), farmers, masons, carpenters, ironworkers, foot soldiers, priests, and twenty purebred mastiffs and greyhounds (Pelta 1991; Loewen 1995). He brought seeds, plants, and other domestic animals like cattle, horses, sheep, and pigs that completely transformed the environment. His ships also carried chains, medallions, and branding irons. Columbus came with the intention of enslaving. He set the tone and example for later Conquistadors, one of genocide, cultural destruction, and environmental damage.

Now let us take a look at the Thanksgiving holiday. When was the *first* Thanksgiving? Who was involved? It depends on how one looks at it. Native Americans celebrated their *first* Thanksgiving thousands of years before the arrival of the Pilgrims. In 1637, Governor Winthrop proclaimed the *first* official day of Thanksgiving to celebrate the safe return of Massachusetts Bay Colony men from a military endeavor. These men were being honored for having massacred over 700 Pequot men, women, and children in what is known as Mystic, Connecticut. Then there is the 1621 myth of Pilgrims and Native Americans sitting down to a great feast which has been debated, debunked, analyzed, and synthesized down to "What we really know about that event" by many, including *Plimoth Plantation*, the original site of Pilgrim and Native American contact (Armstrong 2002; Grace 2001; Loewen 1995; Plimoth 2006). In summary, experts believe the event was most likely a diplomatic envoy of Wampanoag led by Massasoit who was checking in on the Pilgrims, saw they needed food, and then went hunting. Native Americans did not trust the Pilgrims enough to bring their women and children. Pilgrims would not have prayed in the presence of Native Americans, whom they perceived of as "heathens." It was probably not a planned harvest celebration or religious event.

When people are not aware of controversies surrounding Columbus Day and Thanksgiving, or choose to dismiss them, then covert racism is occurring at the cultural and institutional levels. Given all the Native American contributions to the world that resulted from Columbus's contact, including 60% of all the food now grown and over 200 plants used as medicine (Loewen 1995), it would be fitting to celebrate the achievements of Native Americans. It is less appropriate to celebrate a person who initiated attempts at Native American genocide. Seventeen states currently do not celebrate Columbus Day (Roznik 2005). Regarding Thanksgiving, it is good to be thankful for abundance in our lives; it is not good to perpetuate misinformation about European and Native American contact or downplay the slaughter of Native Americans and the attempted destruction of our culture. Acknowledgments of the long-standing controversy surrounding Thanksgiving may include alternatives, such as saying, "Have a nice long weekend," having turkey on Friday instead of Thursday, or attending a Native American demonstration[6] in lieu of celebrating the institutionalized national holiday.

---

[6] Every year since 1970 in Plymouth, Massachusetts, Native Americans have gathered at noon Thanksgiving Day on Cole's Hill to remember the genocide of Native

Breaking the Stereotype – Multiracialness (Institutional Racism)

One fall, I was driving home from a birthday party and had my second son, who was nine at the time, and six of his friends in the car. One of them asked me why my boys wore their hair long, and I briefly answered, "Because we're Native American." From the back, another boy in all seriousness asked, "Then why do you drive a truck?" One of the strongest and most perpetual stereotypes about Native Americans is that we have brown skin and long black hair, wear buckskin and feathers, ride horseback, chase buffalo, and live in a tipi.

A few years later when my daughter was sixteen and in high school, she went to meet a friend in a classroom where there was an unfamiliar teacher. The friend promptly told the teacher, "You know *she* doesn't celebrate Christmas, she celebrates Solstice." The teacher turned to my daughter and asked her if she was pagan. My daughter, who is light skinned and dark-haired, explained that she was Native American. Then he asked her how *much* "Indian" she was. She looked at him confused and he persisted, asking how much "Indian" her parent was. She responded by explaining that her mother is technically half, so that would make her one-fourth, but that she is really "whole" in a way he would not understand. He pressed on asking her if she knew how "to do anything." She said she knew her cultural songs, dances and traditions. Then he said he had taken an Indian technology course in high school where he built a *wigwam*, then corrected himself to say *long house*. He explained that he would sit around a fire and tell Indian stories. She asked if there were any Native Americans there. There were not. She continued to push the teacher, concluding that the stories then were not really "Indian." She asked him if he had ever been to a sweatlodge and he said he had not, and asked what it was. She was surprised to hear this because she had thought that if he were taking a Native American technology course, he would have learned about a sweatlodge. She explained that the lodge was a spiritual place where one offered their sweat and prayed. His response was that he sweats a lot, so he did not think he would be able to do a lodge, and that it would be too "gross." My daughter gave up after that and said goodbye to her friend, leaving quite frustrated. This story illustrates several points. Without understanding different cultures, communication is stilted,

---

People. Since 1973, Alcatraz Island in California has hosted a sunrise gathering on Thanksgiving to "honor the spirit of continued resistance."

if not impossible. Comments out of ignorance are not *intended* to be offensive, but the *outcome* is that they are. The person in the subordinate group is frequently put into the position of being the teacher or informant, which can be frustrating, instead of the person from the dominant group having learned or finding out the information on their own. There is also a stereotype about how Native Americans look and what they do. Native Americans are expected to prove their legitimacy through blood quantum, ancestry, and knowledge of cultural customs. There is a belief that if a non Native American participates in a Native tradition or "dresses up and acts Indian," that they have some legitimacy, even while, we, as Native Americans, fall into the pattern of justifying who we are, what we do, and why we do it from a very early age. I am reminded of a t-shirt which illustrates this "validity trap" by sporting, "I'm part white, but I can't prove it."

In fact, the majority of Native Americans in the United States are of mixed racial heritage. According to the 2000 census (2002), 1.6 million people believed that they had an identifiable Native American[7] ancestor in combination with one or more races. Seven out of ten Native Americans outmarry (do not marry other Native American's), 98% are tribally hyphenated, and the majority is racially hyphenated (Russell 2000). Because the 2000 census was the first year which allowed for a multiracial designation there were three types of results related to Native Americans: Native American alone, Native American in combination, and all those who reported as either Native American alone or in combination. The United States Census (2002) reports the total United States population as 281.4 million people, of which about 1.5% is Native American; 2.4 million (.9%) reported only Native American and 1.6 million (.6%) reported Native American in combination with at least one other race. This means that about 4 million people now identify as Native American alone or in combination with at least one other race. Within this group, the most common multiracial combinations were (2002): Native American and White (66%), Native American and Black or African American (11%), Native American and White and Black or African American (6.8%), and Native American and some other race (5.7%). The 2000 census also indicated that 79% of us know

---

[7] The author uses the term *Native American* for what the United States Census categorizes as *American Indian and Alaskan Native* (AIAN).

our Nation[8]. Within the United States, the distribution of Native Americans is as follows: 43% live in the West, 31% live in the South, 17% live in the Midwest, and 9% live in the Northeast. No New England state has more than 1.5% of the total population reporting as Native American. Native Americans are less than 1% of the total population in twenty-one states (including Massachusetts). Approximately 22% (538,000) live on reservations; 78% do not (Russell 2004). Native Americans are diverse in physical appearance, and the majority live off the reserve in the western or southern part of the United States.

Our Future Generations (Institutional Racism)

At least once a month, I am at an event [9] where someone strikes up a conversation with me that goes something like this: "It's nice to meet you, so you are Native American?" I answer in the affirmative. Then he or she asks, "What nation?" I am impressed, because most people use the word "tribe," therefore using the word "nation" frequently indicates education about or an awareness of Native American issues. I answer that I am Arawak[10]. Through their blank stare I can see this new acquaintance tick off Nations in their mind *Navajo, Cherokee, Blackfoot…* until he or she says, "Oh, they are from the Caribbean, aren't they?" Dumbfounded, they glibly ask, "Aren't they all dead?" Another teachable moment has presented itself. Obviously, since I am standing in front of this person and have just identified myself as Arawak, my nation and I are not "all dead." I live in Massachusetts, an area where people consider themselves liberal, fair, and not "racist." However, covert racist behaviors like this are prevalent; and covert racism is still racism.

After the "Aren't they all dead?" opener, I begin my teachable moment with the question, "Where did you learn that?" As an educator working toward social change, I take the time to do "the work" and educate in the moment when a real life example presents itself. I frequently bring levity to the situation by speaking to the amazing way we

---

[8] The author uses the term *Nation* for what the United States Census categorizes as *tribe*.

[9] In my various roles as K-12 teacher, college course instructor, public speaker, parent, board member, and activist, I am involved in several activities each week.

[10] The Arawak originally inhabited the islands of the Caribbean. They are among the people who first greeted Christopher Columbus in 1492. The term Arawak may represent the language group or cultural group (Nation).

know about Columbus, but can not even name the specific people he met by anything but the term "Indian" and how I love this question because it gives me the chance to talk about the many things we do *not* learn. Lack of knowledge keeps us unaware of information about other groups, in this case Native Americans, and is an example of what Peggy McIntosh (1992) terms *white privilege*. In her women's study work, McIntosh points out that men are not willing to see they are over-advantaged even though they are willing to say that women are disadvantaged. She observed this argument and looked at herself to understand her own privilege as a white woman. McIntosh visualizes this privilege as an invisible knapsack of unearned advantages white European American people carry with them in all aspects of life without realizing it. By maintaining this state of unawareness a person is able to avoid examining the "knapsack" and therefore gets to hold on to their privilege. The concept of *privilege*, however, is not exclusive to white European American people. We can draw the same parallel which McIntosh does in any area of our life where we are part of the advantaged group, such as being heterosexual, temporarily able-bodied, right-handed, etc. When we have the privilege of unawareness, of not noticing, of not having to speak up, or of being able to walk away from an injustice because it does not appear to directly affect us, then we have that invisible, unearned privilege. Since we have grown up in a country that values hard work, many people feel that everyone has equal opportunity, if they work hard, to achieve the same things. What they do not realize is that only some of us fit into that cultural norm and never have to think about being different. To be unaware of situations when one is advantaged and someone else is not means the status quo will continue to go unchallenged. We need to unwrap the knapsack.

Next Steps – Ally Behavior

When there is an issue about racism, friends seek me out as a person of color and an activist. Once, a white European American colleague was relating a conversation about a dinner party she had with another white European American woman. The woman asked if my colleague's white European American husband would have a "problem" if she brought her husband, a person of color. My colleague was terribly upset that someone would assume that her husband would not see him as "just another person to be nice and courteous toward." She proceeded to explain that both she and her husband "treat all people the same." I took this as a teachable moment. I asked her if she ever worries about being alone, at night, on a dark street. She acknowledged that this was definitely true. I asked her if her husband ever worried about being alone, at night, on a dark street. She responded that this was certainly not the case. I asked if he knew how she felt and whether he acted differently because of it. She thought barely a moment and explained that he was a man; she was a woman, and that made all the difference. He would make sure that he or another person was with her if the late night situation arose. I made the analogy that being a woman means something in this culture, and being a man married to a woman causes him act in certain ways. As far as her white European American friend goes, being *white* means something in this culture, and being white married to a person of color means she will act in certain ways. I went on to say that treating white European American people and people of color "the same" would be akin to treating men and women the same, when in reality, their experiences (of safety, in this case) are not at all the same. Similarly, being a Native American means something in this country that is different from being non Native.

Knowing one's own culture, history, and traditions, being taught them in school, and receiving validation in all forms of written and visual media and institutionalized holidays is a privilege for some in this country. Unawareness of accurate Native American culture, history, traditions, and people leads to unintentional comments and actions which constitute covert racism and perpetuate the cycle of oppression. It is difficult, but not impossible, to self reflect and be aware of all the places we have privilege. When I am with friends talking about jobs, education, and opportunity, I appreciate their reminders of my social class privilege (both my parents were college professors). In my job as a special education teacher, I am acutely aware of my own able-bodied privileges. I have researched African American history and understand my relative privilege. I can trace back my history and cultural traditions for thousands of years. I know about this land, the teachings of the animals who live here, the meanings of the songs to honor the Earth, and the symbolism behind the stories of creation and behavior. Many of the people stolen from Africa do not even know what language, village, country, or region their ancestors are from. This was stripped away and taken. Our history has created different experiences in some ways, and similar experiences of oppression in other ways. We each have a part to play in doing our own work and in educating others.

Ely (2006) successfully presents general strategies for reducing racism in the corporate world, but to be more specific, in my experience,

I have found the following to be the most important things to keep in mind about Native Americans in order to move from the "covert box" to the "active anti-racist box" and challenge personal, cultural, and institutional racism. 1) Remember that we are still here; we are still alive. 2) Know that we have evolved and are a contemporary people, even though many of us retain traditional ways. 3) Do not perpetuate stereotypes and myths. 4) Keep in mind that language has power. Pay attention to how and when words are chosen. 5) Know that if it happened in the *Americas*, then we were there. The history of America IS our history. This is the land of our ancestors, we are connected to it, and we continue to want to protect it. The Native American perspective needs to be included and considered each time we look at anything related to American history. 6) Become educated. Use any and all resources available, for example: read books, watch documentaries, connect with organizations, and attend events. Listen to people who are sharing their experiences of oppression. Learn and generalize to other oppressed groups, not just to Native Americans. 7) Understand your own privilege and how to use it to create equity for others. As awareness grows, so does understanding, and ultimately empowerment to be a better ally and to make positive change. And finally, 8) oppression is a large "pie," but we can really only control a small slice. It is by joining with other allies who are in control of their "slice" that we will be able to make a dent in the whole pie.

Author's note

I wish to thank Jane Benes, Jennifer Wolfrum, and Elli Stern for their helpful feedback and editing in the process of writing this chapter. Also, I wish to thank my children, Cheyenne, Sequoya, Dakota, Savannah, and Indigo for sharing the lives and stories with me. Correspondence concerning this article may be addressed to Claudia A. Fox Tree, M.Ed., Brooks Building, The Lincoln School, Ballfield Road, Lincoln, MA 01730.

References

Alvord, L. 1999. *The scalpel and the silver bear: The first Navajo woman surgeon combines western medicine and traditional healing.* New York, NY: Bantam Books.

Armstrong, E. 2002. *The first thanksgiving.* Retrieved September 5, 2006, from the Christian Science Monitor Website: http://www.csmonitor.com/2002/1127/p13s02-lign.html

Ayvazian, A. 1995 Interrupting the cycle of oppression: The role of allies as agents of change. *Fellowship, Jan./Feb.* 7-10.

Babco, E. 2005. The status of Native Americans in science and engineering. *Commission on professionals in science and technology workshop, March 15, 2005.* New York.

Banks, J. A. 1997. Multicultural education: Characteristics and goals. In J. A. Banks and C. A. M. Banks (Eds.), *Multicultural education: Issues and perspectives* 3rd ed., 385-407. Boston, MA: Allyn and Bacon.

Banks, J. A. 2002. *An introduction to multicultural education (3rd ed.).* Boston, MA: Allyn and Bacon.

Batts, V. 1998. *Modern racism: New melody for the same old tunes.* Episcopal Divinity School. Cambridge, MA.

Carter, K. 1991. Racial identity attitudes and psychological functioning. *Journal of Multicultural Counseling and Development,* 19:105-114.

Clark, K.B. and Clark, M.P. 1947. Racial identification and preference in Negro children. In T.M. Newcomb & E.L. Hartley (Eds.), *Reading in social psychology.* New York: Holt, Rinehart & Winston.

Cross, W. E. J. 1987. A two-factor theory of Black identity: Implications for the study of identity development in minority children. In J. S. Phinney & M. J. Rotherham (Eds.), *Children's ethnic socialization: Pluralism and development* 117-133. Newbury Park, CA: Sage.

Cross, W. E. 1995. The psychology of Nigrescence: Revising the Cross model. In J. G. Ponterotto, J. M. Casas, L. A. Suzuki, & C. M. Alexander (Eds.), *Handbook of multicultural counseling* 93-122. Thousand Oaks, CA: Sage.

Diamond, J. 1999. *Guns, germs, & steel.* New York, NY: W. W. Norton & Company.

Ely, R., Meyerson, D., Davidson, M. 2006. Rethinking political correctness. *Harvard business review,* 84(9): 78-87.

Grace, C., Bruchac, M. & Brimber, S. 2001. *1621: A new look at Thanksgiving.* Washington, D.C.: National Geographic Society.

Helms, J. E. (ed.) 1990. *Black and white racial identity: Theory, research and practice.* Westport, CT: Greenwood Press.

Helms, J. E. 1995. An update of Helms's White and People of Color racial identity model. In J. G. Ponterotto, J. M. Casas, L. A. Suzuki, & C. M. Alexander (Eds.), *Handbook of multicultural counseling* 181-198. Thousand Oaks, CA: Sage.

King, T. 2003. *The truth about stories: A native narrative.* Minneapolis, MN: University of Minnesota Press.

Kivel, P. 1996. *Uprooting racism: How white people can work for racial justice.* Gabriola Island, BC: New Society Publishers.

Las Casas, B. 1989. *The log of Christopher Columbus's first voyage to America in the year 1492.* Hamden, CT: Linnet Books.

Lee, C.D., Rosenfeld, E., Mendenhall, R., Rivers, A., Tynes, B. 2003. Cultural modeling as a frame for narrative analysis. In Colette Daiute & Cynthia Lightfoot (Eds), *Narrative analysis: Studying the development of individuals in society.* Thousand Oaks, CA: Sage Publications.

Loewen, J. 1995. *Lies my teacher told me.* New York, NY: Touchstone.

McIntosh, P. 1992. White privilege and male privilege: A personal account of coming to see correspondences through work in women's studies. In P. H. Collins and M. Andersen (Eds.), *Race, class and gender: An anthology.* 102-118. Belmont, CA: Wadsworth Pub.

Nieto, S. 1996. *Affirming diversity: The sociopolitical context of multicultural education.* (2nd Edition.) New York, NY: Longman Publishers.

Pelta, K. 1991. *Discovering Christopher Columbus: How history is invented.* Minneapolis, MN: Lerner Publications Company.

Phinney, J. S. 1990. Ethnic identity in adolescents and adults: Review of research. *Psychological Bulletin,* 108(3):499-514.

Pinderhughes, E. 1989. *Understanding race, ethnicity, and power: The key to efficacy in clinical practice*. New York, NY: Free Press.
Plimoth Plantation, 2006. *Wampanoag homesite*. Retrieved September 2, 2005, from Plimouth Plantation Website: http://www.plimoth.org/visit/what/hobbamock.asp
Roseberry-McKibbin, C. 1995. *Multicultural students with special language needs: Practical strategies for assessment and intervention*. Oceanside, CA: Academic Comm. Assoc.
Roznik, S. 2005. *Columbus controversial figure in continuing historical debate*. Retrieved March 1, 2006, from Fond du Lac Reporter Website: http://www.wisinfo.com/thereporter/news/archive/local_22863601.shtml
Russell, G. 2000. *Native American FAQ's handbook*. Phoenix, AZ: Russell Publications.
Russell, G. 2004. *American Indian facts of life*. Phoenix, AZ: Native Data Network.
Sue, Derald Wing. 2003. *Overcoming our racism: The journey to liberation*. San Francisco, CA: Jossey-Bass.
Sue, Derald Wing, Capodilupo, Christina M, Torino, Gina C. Bucceri, Jenifer, M. Holder, Aisha, M, Nadal, Kevin, and Marta Esquilin. 2007. "Racial microaggressions in everyday life: Implications for clinical practice." *American Psychologist*, 62(4): 271-286.
Suyemoto, K. and C. Fox Tree. 2006. Building bridges across differences to meet social action goals: Being and creating allies among People of Color. *American Journal of Community Psychology*, 37(3-4): 237-246.
Tatum, B. 2003. *Why are all the black kids sitting together in the cafeteria?* Basic Books.
Tatum, B. 1992. Talking about race, learning about racism: The application of racial identity development theory in the classroom. *Harvard educational review*. vol. 62(1):1-23.
United States Bureau of the Census. 2002. *The American Indian and Alaska Native population: 2000*. Available: www.census.gov/prod/2002pubs/c2kbr01-15.pdf
Wellman, D. 1993. *Portraits of White racism* (Second Edition). New York: Cambridge University Press.

SILENT RACISM

Barbara Trepagnier

A decade ago, most white Americans believed that racism was no longer a problem in the United States, that racism disappeared when legal segregation was abolished with the civil rights legislation of the 1960s (Blauner 1994). Today, the claim that racism is a thing of the past continues to have a strong hold on the white American psyche. Indeed, conservative writers like to point out that racism has declined precipitously since the mid-1960s and that people today are treated equally (see Thernstrom & Thernstrom 2003; McWhorter 2006). This view, however, is shortsighted in that it considers only blatant expressions of racism, and it presumes equal treatment for people who do not share equal footing. This view ignores the gap between black and white life chances that still stands, a gap that results largely from covert forms of racism, some of which is performed by well-meaning white people. The thinking expressed in this chapter extends to all racial and ethnic minority groups; however, because the research was limited to racism against African Americans, references are limited to that group.

This chapter has three threads. The first reveals the presence of silent racism—the negative thoughts, images, and assumptions about African Americans—that exists in the minds of well-meaning white people who see themselves, and would be seen by other white people, as "not racist" (Trepagnier 2006:3). Evidence of silent racism forces us to question the commonsense, categorical thinking used to think about racism today, namely, that people are either *racist* or *not racist*. The second thread shows how passivity in well-meaning white people works with silent racism in the production of institutional racism. Together, silent racism and passivity maintain the racial and ethnic inequality that persists in the U.S. despite laws intended to lessen it. And finally, the third thread in this chapter illustrates that increasing race awareness in well-meaning white people, a topic generally overlooked by race theorists, is more important than trying to eliminate racism. Together these three threads construct a new way of thinking about racism in the 21st century.

Silent Racism

Silent racism stems from the racist ideology that permeates U.S. society and inhabits the minds of all white people, making silent racism a cultural phenomenon. This does not imply that all whites are affected by silent racism in a similar way; however, it does imply that all whites are infected. Silent racism is not the same as prejudice, which refers to an individual's attitude about particular social groups. In contrast, silent racism is not an attitude; it is a cultural artifact of U.S. society. Silent racism refers to the shared images and assumptions of members of the dominant group about subordinate groups (Blumer 1958)—that is, the shared images and assumptions held by white Americans about black Americans and other people of color.

This line of thinking leads to scrutiny of an erroneous way of thinking about racism prevalent in the minds of many, including racial progressives: the idea that people are either *racist* or *not racist*. The study of silent racism sought out well-meaning white women willing to talk about their own racism. The approach required openness about a topic that is rarely discussed, and yet people were eager to join the study. Twenty-five women participated in eight focus groups, and kept their thoughts about racism in a journal for three weeks following their discussion. Their stories indicate that silent racism does exist in the minds of well-meaning white people. Participants either acknowledged their own silent racism or demonstrated it in the study, indicating that the *not racist* category is both inaccurate and deceptive (Trepagnier 2001 and 2006).

Categorical thinking regarding racism does not accurately portray racism held by white Americans today because the oppositional categories, while they highlight blatant racism, hide silent racism and other forms that are not explicit. And yet, these subtle forms of racism do more to maintain racial inequality than blatant forms of racism, which are not portrayed by the categories. Transforming the oppositional categories *racist* and *not racist* into a continuum labeled *more racist* at one end and *less racist* at the other would illustrate that racism is a matter of degree—some is egregious and some is subtle. Even more important, a racism continuum would illuminate the fact that no one is literally *not racist*, suggesting instead that some racism is routine, informing the conduct of people going about their everyday lives. Everyday racism refers to the routine actions taken by whites that have negative effects for blacks (Essed 1991).

The oppositional categories tell well-meaning white people that they are not racist. People know that they are not hateful, that they differ from avowed racists like Klansmen and others associated with blatant racism. They assume that they must be in the *other* category, the non-racist one, which causes them to deny their silent racism, both to themselves and to others. This leaves silent racism free to do its damage undisturbed.

Edward T. Hall's (1959) theory of culture is pivotal in explaining the pervasiveness of silent racism. Hall differentiates between formal and informal learning. Formal learning involves both teacher and student, with the teacher playing an active role in correcting the student when a mistake is made. Informal learning, on the other hand, occurs "out of awareness" with the learner modeling the teacher without either party being aware of it (Hall 1959:96). Children are taught formally that racism is wrong; however, they learn the negative thoughts, emotions, and attitudes that comprise silent racism by informally mimicking parents, teachers, peers, and the media. According to Hall, ideas that are not aware are not necessarily unconscious, and they are easily accessible.

There are two primary manifestations of silent racism: *stereotypical images* that set black Americans, as a group, apart from white Americans, and *paternalistic assumptions* that denote a sense of superiority in whites in comparison to blacks. Stereotypical images result from the misinformation and false messages learned informally by white Americans that distinguish blacks as different. An example of silent racism expressed in the study came from Vanessa, a psychologist. She said, "Maybe the black races are not as verbally developed, and they are more developed in other ways." This view of biological differences between blacks and whites is rarely voiced by a well-meaning white person. Vanessa mentioned in her journal that she "felt safe" in the group, and voiced ideas that she "wouldn't dare say" any place else. The point I want to make is that Vanessa's silent racism is part of her perspective, her world view.

The other form of silent racism, paternalistic assumptions, results from a sense of false responsibility toward black Americans that is characterized by a condescending attitude. Karen shared the following experience she had in when she was a teenager:

> In high school my friend Belle—who was black—and I would go places and I would try and do everything [for her], especially in establishments where it was all white. One time I asked her what she wanted, and

I ordered her ice cream for her. She looked at me and said, "I can order for myself." And at the time I felt that I had messed up or whatever.

Karen thought she was being nice by "doing everything" for her friend—taking care of Belle was an act of generosity from her perspective. Yet, even though she was not being hateful in any way, she insulted Belle, who was not in need of help from anyone. Karen's intention to help was perceived as offensive because it was patronizing and placed Belle in a subordinate position to Karen. This example, like Vanessa's, shows us how silent racism in the mind of well-meaning white people guides their decisions. Karen's example also illustrates that an actor's intention not to be racist has little to do with the consequences of an act.

The fundamental difference between the two forms of silent racism is that stereotypical images are ideas about a "conceptualized group" (Killian 1970:184), whereas paternalistic assumptions emerge in actual relationships between blacks and whites. Both aspects of silent racism are platforms on which everyday racism is performed. Sometimes the negative effect is hurt feelings, as in the case of Belle. However, if the everyday racism involves a decision that affects the life chances of an African American, the result is more serious in that it adds to the racial inequality that exists in the U.S. today.

The suggestion that the *racist* and *not racist* categories be changed to a continuum rests on the assumption that racism is a process in the sense that deviance is a process that changes over time (Pfuhl and Henry 1993). A process approach entails looking at historical meanings attached to the racism categories. Before the civil rights movement, most white people were overtly racist. The few who did not express racism overtly were ostracized, and treated by other whites with contempt. Those whites who stood with blacks against Jim Crow were ostracized, and in some cases, treated as badly as blacks were treated. The opposite is the case today. Most whites are perceived as non-racist, and the racist is ostracized, and therefore deviant. Labeling overt and blatant racism deviant produces the assumption that racism, by definition, is overt and blatant. This assumption obscures racism that is routine and that white people contribute to and benefit from daily, whether they are aware of it or not. The labeling system is allowing everyday racism to flourish under cover of the oppositional categories.

Advocating for a racism continuum is not meant to diminish the difference between well-meaning white people and those in organizations such as the Ku Klux Klan. Hateful and blatant racism is despicable, and should be punished. But racism performed by well-meaning white people should not be ignored. Silent racism and the everyday racism following from it are causing racial inequality that lowers the life chances of thousands of black Americans. Categorical thinking in terms of racism implies that white people who do *not* commit hostile acts against, or make maliciously racist statements about, black Americans be labeled *not racist*. In this way silent racism—and the routine acts of everyday racism resulting from it—are hidden despite the fact that they sustain the racist culture that produces them. The oppositional categories also hide symbolic racism and colorblind racism that are used to intentionally argue against policies of racial equality using non-racial language (see Bonilla-Silva 2003).

Passivity

In addition to hiding silent racism, the "not racist" category also generates passivity in white people regarding race issues. Racial passivity is related to studies showing that bystanders are often present in situations where someone is the target of negative effects, whether the victim is present at the time or not (Staub 2003). Passivity in bystanders appears to have multiple roots, including alienation from the victim, identification with the perpetrator, and fear of repercussions. And, although bystanders in a given situation are neither victim nor perpetrator, their reaction demonstrates how passive bystanders differ from "active bystanders" (Staub 2003:3). Passive bystanders do nothing in the face of injustice or discrimination; active bystanders interrupt it.

Bystanders are important because they have a good deal of influence in how a given situation will proceed (Staub 2003). For example, when people make racist statements or make racist decisions and bystanders are passive, the bystanders are perceived as colluding with the exposed racist point of view. This perception, right or wrong, empowers perpetrators to persist in their racist point of view and expression of racism. By contrast, when bystanders actively interrupt racist statements or decisions, the balance of power shifts away from the person making racist statement in support of the target of discrimination. This means that, despite the connotation of the terms "bystander" and "passivity", neutrality is not an option. Doing nothing creates an alliance with the perpetrator, regardless of the bystander's intention (Barnett 1999). In other words, bystanders, simply by virtue of being present, align either with the perpetrator by remaining passive or with the target of discrimination by interrupting racism, including when it is not blatant.

In the study of silent racism, I found that the *not racist* category causes the detachment associated with passivity in well-meaning whites by distancing them from racism. White people who see themselves as *not racist* feel no connection to race matters of any sort, including racism. As Sharon said, "Racism has no connection to my life" (Trepagnier 2006:50). Sharon's detachment from race issues makes her a passive bystander when confronted with others' racism. When I asked, "What do you do when someone makes a racist remark or tells a racist joke?" Sharon responded, "Nothing, usually" (Trepagnier 2006:50). Her indifference is akin in some ways to willful blindness, a term used to describe perpetrators of white-collar crime such as Ken Lay, past chairperson and CEO of Enron. Lay claimed no knowledge of criminal behavior from which he and others greatly profited. Well-meaning white people who are passive bystanders quietly watch as America grows more divided regarding race. Yet, these are not innocent bystanders. They profit from the racial divide, reaping the same advantages received by people performing intentionally and unintentionally racist acts.

Institutional Racism

Racial passivity, as well as silent racism and the everyday racism that follows from it, are forces behind much of the institutional racism that produces racial inequality. Whites bent on maintaining white privilege are responsible for *direct* institutional racism, which is produced intentionally; however, well-meaning white people who intend no harm perform *indirect* institutional racism daily (see Feagin and Feagin 1994). My focus here is on indirect institutional racism that is responsible in large part for the overrepresentation of African American children in child welfare, a system dedicated to protecting all children. Studies show that racial bias accounts for some of the disproportionate representation (Derezotes and Poertner 2005). Research on silent racism indicates that decisions resulting in racial disproportionality in child welfare are not intentionally racist; and yet, the decisions produce negative effects for young African Americans, especially black males (Trepagnier 2008). Both aspects of silent racism appear to be at play, stereotypical images and paternal assumptions.

Black children as a group have a higher risk for child abuse and neglect than white children as a group because they are more likely to be in families below the poverty line, a primary risk factor. However, contrary to popular opinion, black children are not abused more often than white children, and may actually experience less child abuse and neglect than white children (Sedlak and Schulz 2005). Protection mechanisms such as close extended family members (Allen and Farley 1986), resilience (Hill 1998), and flexibility (Hill et al. 1993) are possible rationales for this finding. Despite the lower rate of abuse, black children outnumber white children in the child welfare system in almost every state where data are available.

Johnson et al. (2007), using state data from Minnesota, found that decisions made within the Child Protective Agency cause black children to become less likely to move out of the system than white children. For example, at a decision-point within the system called "referral [in or out] of the home", if alcohol abuse is present, a white child stands a 46.5 percent chance of being removed from the home; a black child has a 57.8 percent chance of the same outcome. Decisions such as these, which are responsible for racial disproportionality, are not made by blatantly racist white people; well-meaning white professionals who dedicated their lives to helping all children are making them. Additional evidence that silent racism is behind overrepresentation of black children can be found in a nation-wide qualitative study conducted in child welfare agencies in eight states (California, Georgia, Illinois, Michigan, Minnesota, North Carolina, Texas and Virginia) exploring agency workers' perceptions of disproportionality (Chibnall and Dutch 2003). Black participants raised racial bias in their white colleagues as a problem. More specifically, black caseworkers felt that white workers have no context for understanding cultural differences, including disciplinary practices within the black community.

Racial disproportionality and other forms of indirect institutional racism are hidden by the categorical way white Americans think about racism. As it stands now, racial common sense holds silent racism in white people's perspectives in place, and allows it to influence commonsense interpretations of race matters. Because the oppositional categories effectively imply that *racists* are the problem and *non-racists* are not, well-meaning whites do not think to consider their own culpability. On the contrary, categorical thinking encourages them to defend against their having any responsibility in the situation. This view corresponds to what Alfred Schutz calls "natural attitudes" (see Wagner 1970:320), which are taken for granted and go unquestioned (McHugh 1968). Natural attitudes are comprised of what we know, or think we know, to be true. We assume that others share our definitions and we act in accordance with them as if they make up the structure of reality (Garfinkel 1967).

Categorical thinking produces the illusion that well-meaning white people bear no responsibility for institutional racism or for racial inequality. Yet, silent racism produces indirect institutional racism, including the disproportionate representation of blacks, especially children, in several sectors of society. In this way, the illusion that most white people are not racist virtually ensures the perpetuation of institutional racism. Although silent racism itself, by definition, is not spoken aloud, it would be a mistake to assume that it is of little importance or that the behavior following from it is "not racist." Silent racism, which is protected by the categories, is responsible for everyday racism and indirect institutional racism, both of which perpetuate the racial divide.

What, in addition to changing how we think about racism, can well-meaning white people do to lessen silent racism and the everyday and institutional racism that results from it? Increasing race aware is an essential part of the solution. Although it will not end silent racism, nothing will, increasing race awareness will decrease the probability that silent racism will continue to produce the negative effects of everyday racism and indirect institutional racism.

Race Awareness

Even though race awareness appears to be a critical factor in lessening everyday racism and racial passivity, it receives little attention in the literature on race. My research shows that whites, including those who are well meaning, are badly informed about race matters, largely because of feeling detached from the issue. Most people "stumble onto" information about racism (Ansley 1997:646), if they get any at all, rather than seeking it out deliberately.

The white people who shout the loudest about not being racist are the least aware about race matters. That does not mean that they are the most racist—just that they do not understand much about racism. Acquiring race awareness depends on understanding three facets of racism that are not evident to most white people, including the most well meaning. First, race awareness requires knowledge of the racism that has occurred throughout U.S. history, including the cultural practices and beliefs that supported slavery and segregation (see Feagin 2001). White people often lack historical facts about racism; in school, we learn more about ending slavery than about slavery itself. For example, few white people know that slaves were branded like cattle, and punishment for disobeying a master's command included beatings, torture, and in some cases, burning at the stake for women (Giddings 1984).

Second, race awareness requires recognition of how racism operates systemically, through white privilege (McIntosh 1988 [1992]; Wellman 1994) and racial disproportionality (Trepagnier 2008). White people have no trouble acknowledging that African Americans have been put at a disadvantage due to past (and present) discrimination. However, even the most well-meaning whites have trouble recognizing that the disadvantage of blacks implies over-advantage of whites. And third, race awareness requires insight concerning one's own silent racism and the actions that proceed from it (see Trepagnier 2006, chapter 6). Many whites deny that they have negative thoughts about blacks; and most who are aware of having negative thoughts believe that they never let them slip out.

Developing race awareness entails listening to people who have knowledge about racism (Frye 1983)—primarily black Americans and other people of color. Relationships with black acquaintances and friends are especially helpful if they are based on trust and if conversations about race occur. High race awareness diminishes the need for defenses against being—or appearing to be—racist. Defenses protect the illusion that one is *not* racist, an illusion that is not present in those who have high race awareness. For example, Martha was extremely forthright when her focus group was asked this question: Have you ever said or done something that you later realized was racist? Martha's response was, "Oh yeah, last week." She continued:

> I was tutoring a student and she pointed out that she was born in Uganda, [a fact that] made her very different—her perception of the world was international. I said, "Gosh, that's wonderful, because when other people see you they might just think African American but really you've got this other quality." And I didn't know whether to apologize or just take my foot out of my mouth and go on.

Martha's statement includes a devaluation of black Americans compared to Africans, exoticizing the latter. Both references—the discrediting one toward black Americans and the complimentary one toward Africans—are based in stereotypical images that comprise silent racism. My reason for including Martha's comment is to illustrate that people who are aware of racism, including their own, also have silent racism in their perspectives, evidence that silent racism is present in us all.

Well-meaning white people who have a high level of race awareness sense that they harbor racist stereotypes and assumptions likely to influence their behavior. Race aware white people are open—not defensive—in terms of receiving information about their own racism. They know they will occasionally make mistakes and, like Martha, do not feel compelled to deny them. Instead, they expect to learn from their mistakes, painful though that might be. Race aware white people are also engaged in race matters. Martha and other very race aware participants in the study interrupted racism when it occurred in their groups.

Conclusion

Changing the racial status quo in the U.S. today requires a shift in the minds of well-meaning white people regarding race matters. This shift will not occur in the minds of all white people, only those at the "less racist" end of the racism continuum. The change away from categorical thinking suggested here requires moving away from whether well-meaning white people are racist—we are all somewhat racist—to focus on people's race awareness (Trepagnier 2006). Rethinking racism in this way would also decrease the emphasis currently placed upon people's intentions, illuminating instead the *effects* of racist behavior—regardless of whether it is intended—because those effects constitute institutional racism, including the way black children are overrepresented in child welfare.

The shift from a categorical modern form of thought to a more fluid postmodern approach is consistent with a pragmatic tradition that encourages self-reflection. Oppositional categories were useful in the 1960s when overt racism was rampant in the U.S. and the civil rights movement was just a dream. At that time the category *not racist* was meaningful in that white people who saw themselves as *not racist* took a against segregation. Today, the *not racist* category all too often represents a passive endorsement of the unequal racial status quo with no commitment to changing it. Clearly, the construction of oppositional categories regarding racism, which was functional before the civil rights movement, has outgrown its usefulness. Even worse, today the outmoded catgegories are causing harm.

Some believe that white people giving up their racial advantage is not rational and therefore unlikely to occur. Cornel West, for example, said in a speech I attended in 1994 that white people would give up race privilege only if they viewed the country as a sinking ship and everyone on board would drown unless a solution were found. I disagree. In contrast to West, I maintain that some well-meaning white people would care about race matters if they understood that they, too, perpetuate the racial divide. Rethinking racism as proposed here would bring about that realization.

Doing the right thing was the rationale of white abolitionists who assisted in the under-ground railroad and the white civil rights activists who marched with Dr. Martin Luther King, Jr. Rather than holding on to a racial advantage—the so-called rational choice—if a shift occurred in their race awareness, many well-meaning white people today would recognize the institutional racism surrounding them and take a stand against. The first step in a shift toward race awareness is ending the categorical thinking regarding racism, and replacing it with a racism continuum.

References

Allen, Walter and Reynolds Farley. 1986. "The Shifting Social and Economic Tides of Black America, 1950–1980." *American Sociological Review* 12:277–306.
Ansley, Frances. 1997. "A Civil Rights Agenda for the Year 2000: Confessions of an Identity Politician." In R. Delgado and J. Stefancic (eds) *Critical White Studies: Looking Behind the Mirror*. Philadelphia, PA: Temple University Press.
Barnett, Victoria. 1999. *Bystanders: Conscience and Complicity during the Holocaust*. Westport, CT: Praeger.
Blauner, Robert. 1994. "Talking Past Each other: Black and White Languages of Race." In *Race and Ethnic Conflict: Contending Views on Prejudice, Discrimination, and Ethnoviolence*, edited by F. Pincus and H. Ehrlich. Boulder, CO: Westview.
Blumer, Herbert. 1958. "Race Prejudice as a Sense of Group Position." *Pacific Sociological Review* 1(1):3–7.
Bonilla-Silva, Eduardo. 2003. *Racism Without Racists: Color-Blind Racism and the Persistence of Racial Inequality in the United States*. Lanham, MD: Rowman and Littlefield.
Derezotes, Dennette and John Poertner. 2005. "Factors Contributing to the Overrepresentation of African American Children in the Child Welfare System." In *Race Matters in Child Welfare: The Overrepresentation of African American Children in the System*, edited by D. Derezotes, J. Poertner, and M. Testa. Washington, DC: Child Welfare League of America Press.
Essed, Philomena. 1991. *Understanding Everyday Racism: An Interdisciplinary Theory*. Newbury Park, CA: Sage.

Feagin, Joe. 2001. *Racist America: Roots, Current Realities, and Future Reparations.* New York: Routledge.

Feagin, Joe and Clarice Feagin. 1994. "Theoretical Perspectives in Race and Ethnic Relations." In *Race and Ethnic Conflict: Contending Views on Prejudice, Discrimination, and Ethnoviolence,* edited by F. Pincus and H. Ehrlich. Boulder, CO: Westview.

Frye, Marilyn. 1983. "On Being White." In *The Politics of Reality: Essays in Feminist Theory,* edited by M. Frye. Freedom, CA: Crossing Press.

Garfinkel, Harold. 1967. *Studies in Ethnomethodology.* Englewood Cliffs, NJ: Prentice Hall.

Giddings, Paula. 1984. *When and Where I Enter: The Impact of Black Women on Race and Sex in America.* New York: Bantam.

Hall, Edward T. 1959. *The Silent Language.* New York: Doubleday.

Hill, Robert. 1998. "Understanding Black Family Functioning: A Holistic Perspective." *Journal of Comparative Family Studies* 29(1):15–25.

Hill, Robert, Andrew Billingsley, Eleanor Engram, Michelene Malson, and Roger Stack. 1993. *Research on the African American Family: A Holistic Perspective.* Westport, CT: Auburn House.

Johnson, Erik, Sonja Clark, Matthew Donald, Rachel Pedersen, and Catherine Pinchotta. 2007. "Racial Disparity in Minnesota's Child Protection System." *Child Welfare* 86(4):5–20.

Killian, Lewis. 1990. "Race Relations and the Nineties: Where Are the Dreams of the Sixties?" *Social Forces* 69(1):1–3.

McHugh, Peter. 1968. *Defining the Situation: The Organization of Meaning in Social Interaction.* New York: Bobbs-Merrill.

McIntosh, Paggy. 1988 [1992]. "White Privilege and Male Privilege: A Personal Account of Coming to See Correspondences through Work in Women's Studies." In *Race, Class, and Gender: An Anthology,* edited by M. Andersen and P. H. Collins. Belmont, CA: Wadsworth.

McWhorter, John H. 2006. *Winning the Race: Beyond the Crisis in Black America.* New York: Gotham Books.

Pfuhl, Erdwin, and Stuart Henry. 1993. *The Deviance Process,* 3rd ed. New York: Aldine de Gruyter.

Sedlak, Andrea and Dana Schulz. 2005. "Race Differences in Risk of Maltreatment in the General Child Population." In *Race Matters in Child Welfare: The Overrepresentation of African American Children in the System,* edited by D. Derezotes, J. Poertner, and M. Testa. Washington, DC: CWLA Press.

Staub, Ervin. 2003. *The Psychology of Good and Evil: Why Children, Adults, and Groups Help and Harm Others.* New York: Cambridge University Press.

Thernstrom, Abigail and Stephan. 2003. *No Excuses: Closing the Racial Gap in Learning.* New York: Simon & Schuster.

Trepagnier, Barbara. 2001. "Deconstructing Categories: The Exposure of Silent Racism." Symbolic Interaction 24(2):141–163.

———2006. *Silent Racism: How Well-Meaning White People Perpetuate the Racial Divide.* Boulder, CO: Paradigm.

———2008. "Lessening Racial Disproportionality of Children by Recognizing Silent Racism." Paper in progress.

Wagner, Helmut. 1970. *Alfred Schutz: On Phenomenology and Social Relations.* Chicago: University of Chicago Press.

Wellman, David. 1994. *Portraits of White Racism,* 3rd ed. New York: Cambridge University Press.

"ONE STEP FROM SUICIDE": THE HOLISTIC EXPERIENCE OF BEING BLACK IN AMERICA

Leslie H. Picca, Joe R. Feagin and Tracy L. Johns

This article theorizes a holistic view of the lived experience of those facing white racism, as well as of their representations and interpretations of that racism. By racism, we mean systemic racism: discriminatory patterns and practices which involve more than the actions of a few individual attitudes, but rather the systemic practices of racism built into society's major institutions (Feagin 2006).

The data presented here come from one black woman's detailed experiences with everyday racism. Kathryn, a forty-something successful entrepreneur in a large U.S. city, gives a narrative account of her experiences as a black woman in America–providing us with her representation, and consequent understanding, of racism. In Kathryn's interview we see the personal and family losses that have resulted from decades of dealing with whites who conceptualize and practice racism. Consider Kathryn's reply to a question about what it is like living in a white world:

> What is it like to be a black person in white America today? One step from suicide… what I'm saying is that the psychological warfare games that we have to play everyday just to survive. We have to be one way in our communities and one way in the workplace or in the business sector. We can never be ourselves all around. I think that may be a given for all people, but us particularly, it's really a mental health problem. It's a wonder we haven't all gone out and killed somebody or killed ourselves. [By the] time we learn the rules of the game, we learn, you know: They say get an education, go out and be entrepreneurs, pull yourself up from your boot straps – what boot straps? Hell, we've got to first get the boot in order to have the straps. We try to do all these things, we learn the rules of the games, and by the time we have mastered them…then they change the rules of the game. The game becomes something else, because now you have learned how to play it. So, it changes constantly, constantly. It always keeps us on edge.

Kathryn presses us to understand the pain and tension created by having to conform to the norms of white society while at the same time trying to maintain her integrity and identity as a human being. Let us be clear: Our aim is not to generalize Kathryn's experiences to all black women, although her experiences are very similar to those reported by other black women in other research studies and personal accounts (see Benjamin 1997; Scott 1991; St. Jean and Feagin 1998).

A first step in moving toward a holistic framework for understanding the impact of white racism focuses on specific events as reported and constructed by Kathryn to a black female interviewer. Her accounts of everyday racism accent the spatial, temporal, and relational dimensions of the events that take place. She usually does not have control over *where, when,* and *with whom* the events occur, and thus she must be constantly prepared to deal with them crashing into her everyday life–a time-consuming preparation not required of white women or men.

Spatial Dimensions of Everyday Racism

Racial oppression often has a distinctive spatial dimension, and its character can vary as a black person travels from a private site, such as home, to more public spaces, such as restaurants, hotels, or parking lots. Racial-cultural biases define, often in subtle ways, certain specific areas as "white" locations. In Kathryn's interview we observe tactics which convey, often covertly, that her presence as a black woman is not welcome in these public spaces by whites. Kathryn describes four typologies of space, best conceptualized along a continuum (very public, less public, near private, and private), that offer varying levels of vulnerability and protection from discrimination by whites.

The "Foreign Country": Vulnerability in Public Spaces

Kathryn describes how, with the help of her friends and the community, she prepares herself to deal with what she calls "the foreign country":

> Well, I try to be as humanistic as possible, but there are times, trying times. I try to keep myself, you know you can't remove yourself from society, but I try to, before I go into, I call it 'the foreign country,' I try to figure out what it's all about, so I'll know how to deal with it just to save myself some energy, stress, and help my mental state. I'll call somebody and say, who is so-and-so, well, how are they, or whatever, and that will kind of help me kind of prepare myself, so that if they do say something, then I can be prepared to deal with it.

This spatial metaphor of "the foreign country" is striking and calls attention to the distinctive whiteness of many places blacks must traverse in everyday life, and to the extreme alienation blacks must face. Kathryn must actively prepare herself in advance in her private spatial surroundings to handle the public domain of a white society that, on the whole, is against her succeeding. It is common for African Americans to think through in advance the repertory of responses to incidents of everyday racism. This "foreign country" reference is not the only illustration of alienation that Kathryn describes (we return to this in the relational dimension discussion).

In her accounts of living racism, Kathryn describes numerous locations within the everyday world in which her presence as a black woman is not welcome. It is in these "white" spaces that she is most vulnerable to overt racism. She recounts an event at a convenience store parking lot in which blatant racist stereotypes evoke her emotions:

> We had a new car, and [my husband and I] stopped at [a convenience store], to get some snacks to take to the babysitter for my son. ... And we pulled up and my husband was inside [the store] at the time, and this person, this Anglo couple drove up and they hit our car. It was a brand new car. So, my husband came out, and the first thing they told us was that we got our car "on welfare." Here we are, able-bodied, he was a corporate executive ... and I had a decent job. But they looked at the car we were driving and they made the assumption that we got it from welfare. I completely snapped, I snapped, I physically abused that lady. I did. ... And when the police came they arrested them, they didn't arrest us, because there was an off-duty cop who had seen the whole incident and said she provoked it. I just completely snapped. And, I'm just saying that we're always on the fringes.

What should have been a quick trip to pick up snacks ended up in a major material cost for her, a damaged car. This quick trip also evolved into a painful experience of interacting with ignorant and cruel whites who not only assume the stereotype that a black couple with a new car must be on welfare but also act openly on the belief, apparently with no fear of reaction. In Kathryn's phrase "they didn't arrest us because there was an off-duty cop," we can speculate that she might have been arrested for "physically abusing" the white woman if there had not been a credible witness to the event. As Kathryn's narrative reveals, the spatial dimension of the parking lot convenience store can be interpreted as a white location in which Kathryn's presence is questioned with hostility. Using white privilege, the white couple here felt safe to make openly racist comments. Whites have the privilege of constantly imposing their construction onto other persons, with little fear of retribution as evident in this account. Whites are at the center, both physically and socially. When a black woman enters this white space–as she comments in the last line–she is socially "on the fringes" of whites central public space.

Kathryn's interview reveals not only striking accounts of "what" is said, but the manner in which she describes her accounts are noteworthy. She relies on powerful metaphors such as "I just completely snapped," and later in the interview she describes "I wanted to tear their necks off." Without contextualizing her experiences holistically, Kathryn might be mistaken for fitting the stereotype of the angry black woman (St. Jean and Feagin 1998). Yet in understanding her experiences with ignorant whites as an everyday, constant, and interconnected series of events, Kathryn usually has to internalize these accumulating painful emotions, and actively contends with the daily costs of racism. As Kathryn does not choose to face discrimination or even know ahead of time where or when she will encounter discrimination, she must consistently and actively "prepare" herself to deal with what she calls the "foreign country."

At Work

Besides the spatial terrain of a public parking lot, Kathryn describes another spatial location in which she is reminded of prejudice against blacks. Early in her interview she describes an incident that occurred at her work, one where she had to prove herself to be competitive in winning a business contract:

> It was a struggle. And, after the evaluation panel had made a decision that I had the highest points and the best management program, and the track record they recommended me, and they took it back to their department. And the director of the their department made a very racial statement, that they were very sick and tired of these "niggers" and these other minorities because what they think is that they can come in here and run a business, none of them are qualified to run a business, especially the "niggers." A white female heard this statement, and because they had had some confrontational problems–I think that's the only reason she told me. ... I had to really do some internalizing [of the situation] to keep myself from being very bitter. Because you know there are so many roadblocks out there, it's just stressful trying to do these kinds of things, but I really had to do that just to keep from going off the deep end. So I had to handle him very professionally.

The language employed by Kathryn is telling, for the metaphors of "the struggle" and "the game" are consistently used in this narrative as well as the opening account. Here, we see the racial barriers ("roadblocks") faced by African Americans in trying to get business contracts. Kathryn's account in the workplace, and the opening narrative, vividly conveys the sense of struggle that she, as a black woman, is constantly engaged in. The actions that describe her everyday life encounters are described much like battles: "a struggle," "psychological warfare," "killed somebody or killed ourselves" as she mentions earlier. She is at war, metaphorically, with the whites she encounters in daily social interaction.

In that same first account, we see that Kathryn also uses the metaphor of the game for these situations. For a black person in white America, the rules "change constantly": "we learn the rules of the games, and by the time we have mastered them…then they change the rules of the game." We can see that her analysis of the situation at hand, applying for a contract with the city government, shows clear elements of both metaphorical comparisons, the war and the game. There are rules–explicit and covert–to every game, and Kathryn astutely notes, that those who make the rules are most likely to succeed at the game (Vera and Feagin 1995). In public places, others (usually whites) often make the rules that facilities the social reproduction of the racial hierarchy benefiting other whites to the disadvantage of blacks. It is a *struggle* to win a game if you do not know the rules, and blacks are systematically denied full access to the rule book.

In this entrepreneur's account we see the racial barriers ("roadblocks") faced by African Americans in trying to get business contracts. Clearly, not all barriers are overt and obvious. Many are hidden and covert, as we see here in the white male director's comments made not to the respondent but behind the scene. Though present in the spatial terrain of work, Kathryn was not confronted directly with racial epithets. Yet the director had no qualms saying racial epithets within the company of some other whites. Similar to Kathryn's experience in the convenience store parking lot, in the public spaces it is safe for a white person to make openly racist comments. In the workplace experience, Kathryn can only acquire the information through a sympathetic white coworker, as she is purposively blocked from the space where certain key work decisions are made. This knowledge became known to Kathryn only through an employee who had some problems with the director. Note here that once again the perpetrators of discrimination are middle and upper-middle class white Americans. Further in her account she describes how she used this knowledge to counter what was going on behind the scenes, and finally to secure the contract for which she had made the highest rated bid.

Analyzing this passage holistically, this situation should not be interpreted as 'just' an isolated experience with an ignorant bigot. The injustice done to Kathryn is not just being referred to as a "nigger," one of the oldest and the most emotionally-loaded racial epithets. The injustice done by the white director to Kathryn also includes the covert process of having her contract blocked, and hence her livelihood threatened. The material reality of this event has consequences not only for herself, but for her family and community as well.

There are other occurrences in the workplace that may be consciously or half-consciously invoked against blacks that are harder to prove. When blacks do enter white spaces, they are often controlled with minute surveillance. In this account Kathryn speaks to these costs of everyday racism, specifically in the spatial terrain of work:

> They're subtle things that are very difficult for us to prove, just like little antagonistic things. Like record the time you walk in, from the time you sit at your desk, to the time you go to the restroom, and these are adult people, and I think that if they were about the business of doing their jobs they wouldn't know what time people come in, what time they go to the restroom.

Most employees get some monitoring by their supervisors, so in this respect, the black experience is not atypical. However, what is especially difficult is the extra layer of surveillance experienced by black workers. By keeping constant surveillance of black bodies and monitoring how time is spent within the work space, the message conveyed is that the work domain is a white location in which blacks must be carefully patrolled. It is critical to keep in mind the social context (i.e. a racist society) in which Kathryn's accounts take place. Without understanding the situation holistically, whites might merely interpret Kathryn's comments as "paranoia," or thoughts that she is being watched (Feagin and Sikes 1994: 25).

Less Public Space

Not all of Kathryn's experiences with white racism occur in these very public domains such as work and public parking lots. Some happen closer to home. Typically a person's home is symbolic of a refuge away from the harsh reactions of strangers, a space where people can kick off their shoes and relax. Finding a safe home space creates an extra dimension of problems for African Americans, as recent audit studies show high levels of discrimination (Feagin 2000). Even in the home setting, Kathryn is reminded that the color of her skin puts her at a disadvantage:

> When we first moved here, we moved into an apartment and had to put up... the deposit and first and last month's rent. After we had been there for six months, our next door neighbor, who happened to have been a white male, we were just talking out by the pool; somehow we got on a discussion, and we found out that none of the white tenants had to do that. He said that they were only using that when blacks would come there, because most blacks would not have that kind of money to pay first and last month's rent plus the deposit. And that was a way to keep them out. ...I got my money back though. And then an interracial couple, that happened to them, and they sued them, and they got a settlement.

For African Americans, the costs of racism are also evident in the higher rental costs and, in the case of another couple, the legal hassle and expense. Similar to Kathryn's experience working to win a government contract, here too the costs of racism amount to a substantial financial loss. Using specific measures of overcharging (two months' rent plus some "heavy deposits" that she reports in some instances were *double* the cost of one month's rent), the landowner consciously attempted to keep blacks out of the spatial domain of the apartment complex.

This event is more than the actions of a bigoted landlord; it illustrates both how residential segregation and institutional racism in housing are reproduced. These large-scale institutions are created and recreated by routine actions at the everyday level by individuals and individual actions. Additionally, Kathryn would not have been aware of the injustice against her if it were not for a random conversation with an informed white. It is likely that many such whites are aware of the injustices enacted upon blacks, yet remain silent.

Kathryn is not simply a victim of racist acts against her, but with determination, she actively resists and fights against these illegal actions. Both she and the interracial couple she mentions exert emotional energy, time, and money (for lawyers and court fees to sue) in order to fight back against institutionally sanctioned and individually enacted acts of racism. It is noteworthy that this energy is exerted on an unnecessary (and illegal) activity of fighting racism, taking away energy that could be exerted elsewhere such as in her business or with her family. In this near-private setting, where the spatial landscape is more ambiguous, but still noticeably white, acts of racism may be more insidious. While Kathryn guards herself for the struggle against white racism in public territory, she is less guarded in the near-private apartment setting. They were in the setting for six months before discovering the true situation.

Spatial Dimensions Analysis

Examining the events Kathryn describes, it is evident that racial interactions are influenced by spatial dimensions. Kathryn describes racist acts in very public, less public, and near private settings. Compared to the other three spatial dimensions, Kathryn is generally protected in the safe *private* space of her own home, and in "black spaces" such as black communities and churches. We are quick to note that even the private home space is not spared from unwelcome racist intrusions, as many African Americans have been confronted with burning crosses, and bricks thrown through their windows.

Although Kathryn experienced racist acts in very public, less public, and near private settings, she was much more vulnerable to hate speech and violent acts in the public street than she was at home, or even at work. At work and at home, Kathryn has resources which she can draw from. For example, at home, there are laws protecting her against illegal real estate practices, such as mandating heavy deposits for certain segments of the population while privileging other (white) groups. At work, Kathryn is able to draw upon her strong work record to back her up against the blocking practices of a white director. However, in the public parking lot, Kathryn is vulnerable to racist stereotypes and the misrecognition of being just "another black body." In this example, her nice car illustrates not her hard work enabling her to earn the money to afford a luxury as it might for a white couple, but for Kathryn the car becomes translated into a welfare good (rather than the product of hard work). Very public spaces are "dangerous terrains" for blacks and whites alike for a person has no control over with whom she or he will interact with. However, blacks have an extra layer of vulnerability and danger as they have no control over interactions with persons who judge them solely on the basis of their skin.

Temporal Dimensions of Everyday Racism

Just as racial oppression has a distinctive spatial dimension, so too is the sense of time and memory socially and racially colonized.

The dimension of time must be clear in that racism is not limited to an immediate moment, nor should it be conceptualized in ordinary linear time (Feagin, Vera and Imani 1996). The everyday experiences with racism are not momentarily experienced then forgotten, but serve as lessons learned for future accounts.

Historical Legacy

At one point in her interview, Kathryn is asked, "What do you think is the level of intimacy that you can have with a white person?" to which she responds:

> It would be hard for me to ever have any level of intimacy with them [whites] because of all the pain that has happened in the past, and all the pain that happens today. I could never trust them. I would have a hard time trying to trust them. Even…I guess, I couldn't allow myself to because all in the back of my mind would be so many things. You know, I'll have visions of the men that were hanged in my hometown, because somebody said they had raped them but they had been going with them for years but had got caught in a comprising situation so they said they were raped.

Note the complexity of the situation: When asked about intimacy with whites, Kathryn does not simply respond with "none," but tells a chilling account of brutal lynchings at the hands of whites against black men in *her* hometown. That she specifies the actions as occurring in her hometown suggests that Kathryn is not revealing an abstract memory, but a concretely located and spatially generated memory that blends to the present. The question of interracial intimacy triggers the pain of a series of past events including brutal lynchings of black men and systematic rapes of black women. The vivid memory of racism means that an experience with racist whites is contextualized within past events as experienced by the individual and as shared within the collective memory among other blacks. The racist act is not limited to the immediate moment, nor is it interpreted as such. Through the connectedness of time, the past is *in* the present–time is collapsed. Within the collective memory, accounts of events are not only shared, but in addition, the understandings and interpretations of the events are shared. The everyday experiences with racism are not momentarily forgotten, but serve as lessons learned for future accounts.

In the next account, Kathryn talks about another spatial location, a legislative building, in which the temporal dimension of racism is also illustrated. Kathryn reveals a specific example of interracial contact, one that is well recorded in her memory. This took place in a distinctive space, the public setting of the state Capitol building's steps:

> I'll never forget a state [representative], a white state rep. He didn't mean anything, we were just standing at the Capitol, and he walked up and placed his hands on my shoulders. "Hey that was an insult to me. Don't put your [white] hands on me, okay." It was like "don't become familiar with me." Even though he might have meant nothing about it, it's just that psychology of the thing. It would just be all the hurt and the pain. It would just be very hard for me to develop that kind of relationship.

Uninvited touching is something many women in all racial groups endure, yet there is an added layer of significance for black women. That this incident occurred on the steps of the Capitol, a representation of America's history and politics, is revealing. Kathryn shares in the collective memory of African American exploitation and oppression of slavery and legal segregation. Her memory of previous and similar events likely enables her to see the sexism and the racism in this incident. Indeed, this combination has been termed "gendered racism" (Essed 1991) and "systemic gendered racism" (Harvey 2008). The respondent here may be referencing a time when black women were the sexual property to white male enslavers. We see too that one of the costs of *gendered* racism is a deep distrust, grounded in a racialized sexual oppression, of white men. Several times in her interview, she references her lack of trust in whites that comes from her own experience and that of her predecessors. The shared knowledge of white males sexually oppressing black females is transgenerational and illustrates the temporal dimensions of everyday racism, something which Kathryn says "I'll never forget." Analyzing the experience holistically requires this accumulated knowledge, rather than to piecemeal the situation (as Kathryn suggests, then discredits) by simply stating "he might have meant nothing about it." Layering this experience within the collective memory reveals raw emotion and costs of racism, "all the hurt and the pain."

Looking to the Future

The temporal dimension of racism, and the collective memory requires a transmission of information between generations and within one generation, including accounts of actual experiences and–more importantly–shared understanding of the events. Kathryn explicitly describes how she communicates white racism to her son:

What I try to instill, I try to make sure that my son reads black publications, knows something about his history. When things happen I try to educate him on what is happening… we sit down and talked about it, even though he is twenty-two years old, I still do that. When he was little, I'd make him tell me, who are the council members, and who's the governor of the state … give me some background on them, you know educate him on that. I try to tell him the signs about what people will do to you. That same white boy you're sitting in class with, his father owns the bank. Irregardless of whether he makes good grades or not, he's gonna make it in life because his father owns the bank. Your father does not own a bank. Your father works for his father, so we are dependent on him for our livelihood, not the other way around, so you have to understand the context of that, so you can't bullshit in your classroom, you've got to get it. Because even when you get it, you still will not succeed higher than he is because of the nature of who you are. You could be bright or smart or whatever. But you got to be twice as smart as he is just to get where he may get. You've got to do that.

Kathryn's son is receiving a different education than his white peers. He is not told "you can be whatever you want to as long as you give it your best," but he's learning about the harsh realities for blacks. Kathryn is actively preparing her son to deal everyday with the "foreign country," and part of that education includes providing her son with resources such as educating him on local government, and teaching him to recognize the "the signs about what [white] people will do to you."

The historical legacy of racism lies in the critical recounting of history to younger generations. In this way, the legacy of racist events in the past intersects in the present time. The collective memory of racism predates any one individual; the shared experiences and shared interpretations of the accounts of past and present generations of community and family members live in the present within the individual. A critical component of a holistic analysis is understanding and analyzing the collective memory, which reminds us that racism is not just an individual experience, but involves the collective sharing of concrete events and interpretations of the events that causes physical or emotional pain and suffering.

Years of cumulative experience (experienced by Kathryn, as well as those within her generation as well as generations before her) provides Kathryn and other blacks with the ability to have what some of them call a "second eye" to recognize prejudice or discrimination, even subtly in a gesture or in a gaze such as constant surveillance at work (Feagin and Sikes 1994).

Her account accents the systemic nature of racism: The creation and recreation of white wealth are trangenerational, a reality that illustrates the temporal dimension of racism. Kathryn describes how whites have privileges to fall back on, such as economic resources accumulated by previous generations. At a very early age, her son is forced to recognize the racial context and the meanings of his actions, as well as the actions of how people will treat him.

Not only did Kathryn teach her son how to survive in a racist culture, but she also actively worked to ensure he would not fall victim to criminal activities. In the following passage, Kathryn describes how she arranged for her son to volunteer at a prestigious political office in order to reinforce his self-esteem and learn valuable skills:

> So, ...he didn't get a full-time [job] but he was able to get it [as a volunteer], and that helped his self-esteem. Because everyday I had to reinforce it. I would have him come in a half a day, just to provide him something to do, to try to teach him some skills for half a day. I couldn't afford to have him in here all day, just to keep the self-esteem and motivation because it's very crucial to our black males. Because the few that we have, all the rest are in prison. I used to go down to the prison, and I would cry when I would leave because I would talk to those men, bright men, but somehow, because of the environment, racism in this country, they gave up hope and then they turned to other things. And then, I don't agree with the criminal element in our society, especially black crime, I do not agree with that, but I understand why it happens. I understand about welfare and why it happens.

As the mother of a young black man, the high rate of black men in prison is emotionally painful to the respondent. Although she does not endorse criminal activities, she realizes the link between much black crime and white racism. The costs of racism are apparent in this passage, as "bright men" often resort to criminal activities because of their oppressive environments, like many oppressed men of all groups before them; instead of becoming talented and full productive members of society, some racially oppressed men become financial burdens on society.

Most parents have a strong desire for their children to succeed in life, and provide them with resources and tools in order to accomplish their goals. However, Kathryn is describing something more than a maternal wish for her child to succeed. She recognizes the larger context of why it is so critical for her son—and for other black men—to succeed. Later in the interview, Kathryn reveals:

> That is a crime, that is a waste of a natural resource in this country. ... Black men, hey, I am very—I'm very [scared] about what is happening to our black males. When they can't get a job to take care of their families, you know, it creates a lot of friction. Because even though the spouse may understand, the female may understand, but still the bottom line there is no food on the table, there is no money for rent, so that creates a confrontation between the family, you know, in the family. And some men walk away because they can't take the pressure anymore. And it all goes back to racism.

Alluding to the racist context, Kathryn here references a breakdown in the black community that stems deeper than a maternal concern for the welfare of her son. She recognizes the links between employment and other institutions such as the family and the larger community. That is, Kathryn knows that employment is much more than the rhetoric of "work hard enough and you'll succeed," but rather knowing *how* businesses really operates, such as informal networks and nepotism which collectively benefit whites and disadvantage blacks.

Relational Dimension of Everyday Racism: Relationships with White Actors

In examining racism holistically, it is important to keep in mind how different aspects of relations are reproduced in the larger system of white-on-black racial oppression. As we mentioned in the case of Kathryn's experience in housing and paying a higher-deposit, racism is deeply embedded within the fabric of all macro-level institutions. Yet the situations are routinely produced and reproduced at the micro-level by white actors. Individuals are caught up in a complex web of *alienating racist relations* (Feagin 2006). Just as whites are actively socialized to believe blacks are an inferior race, so too are blacks taught (overtly, as illustrated in Kathryn's discussions with her son) to be wary of whites. Based on actual past experiences and racialized socializations (within the collective memory), blacks learn to be cautious with whites, as part of an ongoing struggle between racial communities.

In her comments in the section on the temporal dimension of racism, Kathryn revealed that it would be distressing to engage in an intimate romantic relationship with a white person ("It would just be all the hurt and the pain"). Additionally, Kathryn is skeptical not only of intimate romantic relationship with whites, but also friendships.

Later in the interview, Kathryn uses these same words ("hurt" and "pain") to describe friendships with whites:

> See, I'll remember all the pain and the hurt, so it's just very hard. I'll remember the ones who try to pick your brain to get all your knowledge and use it to do things to improve themselves, you know, and then ignore you, and still think that you are inferior. Because see, I always think that white people always think that they are better than us. *They* think that, I don't think that. But they always think that in the context.

Kathryn is using the concept of misrecognition, in the sense that—she believes—whites are not appreciating her for the full-human being that she is, but that she is being dehumanized and used. Based on her experiences, she believes there is a failure on the part of whites to see who she actually is (Feagin, Vera, and Imani 1996). Here again we see her reference to the accumulated pain of past racism.

It is important to note that Kathryn does not reference any experiences she has had with members of the Ku Klux Klan or neo-Nazi skinheads–she does not need to. Instead, she is describing interactions with mainstream white Americans, most of whom are defined as middle-class or members of white elites such as senators and business executives. Thus her pain is not attributed to racist extremists, but to "normal" white Americans. This is a very important point about contemporary racism. Most of the damage done by racist actors is done by relatively well-off and well-educated whites. Kathryn speaks directly about her lack of trust for middle class white liberals:

> Because see they'll befriend you, they've got to have their black friends to show how liberal they are, and they understand the cause, and they understand shit, because they ain't been through it. ... And they have a limitation on how far they'll go with you. As long as they're all massed up together with their little liberals, then everything is fine. But when it's isolated and they really have to prove about their little liberalism and all their little affirmative bullshit, well, then they'll tell you, well, John or Mary, this is as far as I can go. You know, I know you're right, but see if I do that, I may lose my job, or I may lose this. So, they wake up in the morning just as conservative as any conservative person. So, I don't trust them. I don't trust them at all, period. All they want to say is they cultivated some black friendship, or to find out if you really do eat chittlings, or hell, like watermelon or fried chicken, or if you can teach them how to do the bop or whatever. Just to say, "I know the black experience." You don't know the black experience until you live it.

Instead of developing healthy relationships, Kathryn reveals an alienation and a lack of trust for liberal whites who she believes are using her as a black person for their own gains rather than viewing her as a full human being. From Kathryn's experience, whites use her to appear liberal and mask a conservative ideology. Kathryn also comments that whites use her to test racist stereotypes such as blacks liking to eat watermelon or fried chicken.

Kathryn's lack of trust for whites is specifically referenced in terms of white women and the feminist movement:

> You know, it pisses me off about white women talking about "comparable worth." Where in the hell is our comparable worth? We been out here in the damn job market all this time, they ain't talked about our dollar matching against white male. They ain't talked about our equal rights, and I will not join their movement to help them get where they're going until they help us, black women and men. And I'm not going to separate black men from us, because I think a lot of the friction we have comes from them. You know, not just white women, white people, they pit us against each other. They tell white males that the reason you don't have good paying jobs is because of the black female, they lie. We are hired more than they are, but we're in clerical positions. We are not in managerial or professional positions, so they keep us fighting all the time about things like that.

Within this narrative, one can speculate that Kathryn feels stronger ties along her racial identity, as opposed to her gendered identity—not an uncommon feeling among black women. Kathryn also underscores the myth of the double minority, wherein women of color are incorrectly viewed as having hiring advantages as they fit a two-minority status based on race and gender. Recognizing the intersectionality of oppression, she cites the precarious position women of color face, in that their identities are not based solely on gender nor on racial group.

Costs of Racism

In the preceding sections, we illustrate how Kathryn must live every day within a racist system. She interacts daily in alienating racist relations, never having significant control over racist incidents or knowing when she will be confronted with ignorant and cruel whites. Utilizing a holistic approach to examine the experiences of everyday racism, we have examined the three dimensions of space, time, and relations to make sense of Kathryn's life narrative as told in a single interview. Not one of the three dimensions of space, time, and relations stands alone.

Instead, in the holistic perspective the dimensions cut across each other.

Let us make one final point: One aspect of everyday racism that can be observed in almost every one of Kathryn's commentaries is its heavy costs. In Kathryn's interview these costs of racism encompass psychological, physical, and material losses. As she describes it, living every day with racism amounts to a psychological cost including an emotional toll such as bitterness, anger, and rage. Guarding her emotions is just one strategy to survive and thrive in the racist society that is constantly present throughout her interview. Kathryn reveals the pain of having to reject being bitter and angry in order "to keep from going off the deep end." After recounting this experience at work, Kathryn divulged some of her strategies for dealing with the constant "struggle" of racism:

> I come in here and scream! (laughs) I talk to my friends, I come in here and talk to [my friend]. She sits and listens to me, I scream and holler. She's even seen me cry because I'm so angry 'til I am to the point of violence, but I know that I have to really, really, be cognizant of what I'm doing, because why go to jail for nothing? And, I'm not going to eradicate racism just by knocking off one person. So, I just call my friends and get it off my chest with them, because they understand. And then after I do that I feel better. That's how I get it out. But I can't let it stay in, because if I let it stay in it just makes me angrier and angrier, and every time a little thing happened, it might not even be a racist thing I would take it for that, so that's how I have to let it out to keep that…you know, it's fine line between that insanity line.

This very successful entrepreneur gives us a window into her psychological experiences with and reactions to the stress and strain of everyday racism. She is typical in her reactions. Many if not most African Americans periodically feel great anger and rage at having to deal constantly with racism. Her emotions of wanting to "scream," "holler," "cry," and feeling "angry" signal how extreme and painful the experiences of racism are. Research suggests most whites and other outside observers are ignorant to the extreme impact of racism on its target (Grier and Cobbs 1968; Feagin, Early, and McKinney 2001). Kathryn mentions the support and shared experiences of her friends which help her to deal with the strains of racist experiences. Her friends have a shared experience with racism; the cumulative effects of racism thus criss-crossed not only an individual's life but also the community in which she lives. Kathryn is describing a social character of discrimination in the sense that blacks share in the systemic experiences.

Analyzing Kathryn's experiences holistically, we see that there is a strong emotional component that is often overlooked in the racial discrimination literature. Kathryn reveals raw emotions which she eloquently shares. Her experiences with whites cause her to cry, scream, to feel violent, pressure, and pain, all affecting her overall mental health. Although Kathryn does not discuss it here, she is experiencing these emotions both due to her encounters that directly deal with her, but also with experiences that happen to her friends and family members that they share with her. She not only experiences these intense emotions herself, but is on the receiving end to other blacks who are repeatedly dealing with systemic racist acts as well. In stating that racism will not be eradicated by "knocking off one person," Kathryn also highlights the macro-structure of racism, as opposed to a micro-everyday experience of dealing with one or two racist individuals.

The emotional toll Kathryn experiences also includes a feeling of being unprotected and vulnerable, particularly in the public spaces, and also not knowing when racism will blindside her. She describes a pleasant evening with her husband, picking up snacks at a convenient store for her son, and how she was hit with racial slurs from a complete stranger. The experience left her with the psychological pain of having to be on guard, even at moments when she least expects discrimination. This energy loss told by Kathryn, and experienced by other blacks is not paralleled in the experiences of whites, especially white men.

Kathryn also describes some of the interpersonal costs of everyday racism, such as limiting her physical contact and relationships with whites. A white state representative who "placed his hands on my shoulders" reveals "all the hurt and the pain." In addition to the psychological and interpersonal costs, Kathryn's account exposes the material costs of everyday racism. Within the setting of the near-private space of her apartment complex, Kathryn describes how the costs of racism included a substantial financial loss, which was only made known through a white sympathetic informant.

Conclusion

Methodologically and theoretically, Kathryn's interview is important to examine in detail for it reveals how one woman's experiences as an African American woman in a white-controlled society have penetrated virtually every domain of her life. Kathryn is a narrator, interpreter, and theorist of white-racist practices and worldviews. Theory is not an isolated construct of the ivory towers, as some academics would have us believe. Rather, theory is interpretation and reasoned generalization, activities that are practiced by most ordinary people as they make sense of the everyday world in which they live. Indeed, the use of "theory" as "method" by those untrained in formal sociology can be more revealing than that done by formally trained social theorists. We can expand our sociological understanding and analysis by investing in the understanding and analysis of those living the experience under study.

A deeper understanding of racism can best be gained by examining black lives in their entirety, as they describe them. Kathryn describes, or alludes to, dozens of racialized events in her life, thereby illustrating that a case study of one person's life is in fact a multiplicity of data points. We go beyond one or two incidents in a black person's life to look at multiple interactions with racism. It is looking at multiple incidents that we can begin to understand that incidents of racism are not additive, per se, but multiplicative.

In our analysis we too have pulled apart her life somewhat in order to understand some of its many dimensions, yet even our more holistic and comprehensive account does not show how she and other African Americans actually live their lives every day. Unfortunately, racism does not rain in on life one incident at a time, one pain at a time, or one countering response at a time. Instead, living racism means contending with multiple layered incidents, feelings, reactions, pains, and responses at any one time–and the accumulation of these layers over an individual's, family's, and community's lifetime. These layers form the foundation upon which collective memory, social reproduction, and the cumulative costs of racism are built. A holistic perspective of racism examines the intersections of these components, as experienced *every day* by African Americans. As is evident in her interview, Kathryn—like other African Americans—has little or no control over when, where, and with whom racism crashes into her life.

Kathryn is not just a victim, but her interview suggests active agency and reflective resistance strategies. Kathryn describes choosing whether or not to fight, counter, cope, or contend with racist attitudes and actions against her. Especially in the public spaces of the workplace, Kathryn must fight to learn and keep up with the ever-changing "rules of the game" in order remain competitive and not succumb to the material costs of doing business within a racist work environment. Kathryn must utilize an array of successful resistance strategies, such as confronting a racist employer or devising a countering plan. In addition, in the convenience store parking lot she chooses to confront racist slurs head on, whereas in the workplace she devised a strategy to counteract her being treated as a "nigger." Other resistant strategies that she utilizes include seeking legal recourse and simply withdrawing from a discriminatory situation. Withdrawing from a racist encounter should not be equated with succumbing to the racist ideology, but as a tactic to save the time and energy required to fight a bigger battle, when the next racist encounter comes "crashing in."

Kathryn recognizes that she and other black persons invest vast amounts of time and energy in dealing with racism, that merely "surviving" in a white dominated society is interpreted as a daily struggle and long-term accomplishment. As she mentioned in her opening narrative, she describes feeling literally "one step from suicide." There is a shared understanding among blacks of the meaning behind this survival: it entails existing beyond the multiple, accumulating events of everyday injustices. When Kathryn was asked by the interviewer, "What barriers have you encountered that might be linked to our white dominated society?," she poignantly stated:

> It's just trying to survive. I want to be able to…it's so terrible that every black person you talk to, you say "how are you doing?" they say "just trying 'to survive'." And that's the thing, just trying to survive. I would like to see where one day we can succeed, you know, succeed on a level where we want to succeed and not inhibited by the color of our skin.

References

Benjamin, Lois. 1997. *Black Women in the Academy: Promises and Perils.* Gainesville, FL: University Press of Florida.
Essed, Philomena. 1991. *Understanding Everyday Racism: An Interdisciplinary Theory.* Newbury Park: Sage Publications.
Feagin, Joe R. 2000. Racist America: Roots, Current Realities, and Future Reparations. New York: Routledge.
Feagin, Joe R. 2006. *Systemic Racism: A Theory of Oppression.* New York: Routledge.
Feagin, Joe R., Kevin E. Early, and Karyn D. McKinney. 2001. "The Many Costs of Discrimination: The Case of Middle-Class African Americans." *Indiana Law Review* 34 (4): 1313–60.
Feagin, Joe R., Hernan Vera, and Nikitah Imani. 1996. *The Agony of Education: Black Students At White Colleges And Universities.* New York: Routledge.
Feagin, Joe R., and Melvin P. Sikes. 1994. *Living with Racism: The Black Middle-Class Experience.* Boston: Beacon Press.
Grier, William H. and Price M. Cobbs. 1968. *Black Rage.* New York: Basic Books.
Gubrium, Jaber F. and James A. Holstein. 1998. "Narrative Practice and the Coherence of Personal Stories." *The Sociological Quarterly 39(1)*: 163–87.

Harvey, Adia. 2008. *Doing Business with Beauty*. Lanham, Maryland: Rowman & Littlefield.
Miles, Matthew B. and A. Michael Huberman. 1994. *Qualitative Data Analysis: An Expanded Sourcebook*. 2nd edition. Thousand Oaks: Sage Publications.
Riessman, Catherine Kohler. 1993. *Narrative Analysis*. Newbury Park: Sage Publications.
Scott, Kesho Yvonne. 1991. *The Habit of Surviving: Black Women's Strategies for Life*. New Brunswick: Rutgers University Press.
St. Jean, Yanick and Joe R. Feagin. 1998. *Double Burden: Black Women and Everyday Racism*. Armonk, N.Y.: M.E. Sharpe.
Vera, Hernán and Joe R. Feagin. 1995. "African Americans' Inflicted Anomie." Pp. 155–72 in *Race and Ethnicity in America: Meeting the Challenge in 21st Century*, edited by Gail E. Thomas. Washington DC: Taylor and Francis Publishers.

LIFESTYLES OF THE RICH AND RACIST

Corey Dolgon

> Since day one of the formation of the Coalition for Justice you have been a guiding force for us all. Your great efforts have been an energy that has been inspiring and strengthening. To care so much in an attempt to have us recognize as a coalition, as people, that these events not only affect us as individuals, but as a community, will last with us far into the future of this group. The genuine friendships are invaluable—we have all inspired each other. Our wishes go with you, but we know this is not goodbye—it's a reason to celebrate everything we've gained and everything we have to gain! –The Coalition for Justice

A yellowing piece of paper taped to white cardboard backing inside a smudged aluminum frame bears this note above. The paper itself was originally wrapped around a small wad of bills (over $200 in singles, fives, tens and a few twenties). It was given to me as a going away present from the Coalition when I left the Hamptons after having taught at Southampton College for three years. During my last year there, I worked with a group of janitors, students and community activists who protested the College's outsourcing of the custodial unit. My increasing displeasure with the institution and the administration's increasing displeasure with my political activities led me to seek a job elsewhere. Although the efforts to reverse the outsourcing continued (and I traveled from Boston to Southampton once a month over the next year for meetings or events), this note marked a shift in both my involvement and in the groups' own work.

This is probably a hokey way to start a piece on covert racism. Maybe it betrays a little bit of my own not-so-covert racism as I look like one of those white guys who really gets off on having people of color like him. I will reflect on this dynamic later in the piece, hopefully without too much self-absorption or aggrandizing. But part of this story is my own transformation, and my own transformation is part of the theoretical and sociological analysis that I want to discuss. Too often academics and their activist work disappear in their scholarship, even when political engagements strongly influenced their intellectual endeavors or the theoretical schools they inherit.

For example, I wrote some articles a few years ago (Dolgon 1992 & 1995), critical of the cultural studies movements in the humanities and social sciences. The 1980s and 90s witnessed the rapid growth of scholarship and institutes related to radical cultural studies (Barker and Beezer 1992; Hall 1992; Harris 1992). Yet, the role played by scholars' own political engagements in the development of the field appeared less prevalent. Despite the fact that cultural studies' evolution was steeped in direct political action (Mattelart & Siegelaub 1983; Archer, et al. 1989; Williams 1990), professional intellectuals began obsessing more about *analyzing* political culture than *engaging* in it. I remember one of the directors of the University of Michigan's Center for the Study of Social Transformation telling an eager group of my graduate student cohort that our role as intellectuals required us to spend more time building theory than building movements.

In response, I wrote that too many scholars were posing culture as a totality, and then positioning themselves above the field of struggle and remaining free from implicating themselves as *always* necessarily a part of the contest. This positioning lead to what Brennan (1991) called the "problem of constituencies" where "the new information class, ever adept at investigating the field, is invisible to itself." Stuart Hall and his colleagues from the British Cultural Studies group had cut their teeth, first in post WWII popular education programs and then in 1960s anti-racist and urban organizing efforts in London. Many North American writers had been influenced by the Latin American cultural studies work coming out of Chile, Cuba, and elsewhere in the 1960s and 1970s. In each case, practical political analysis, strategies and organizing influenced intellectual work on the role of culture in constructing and challenging power. But, as the movement grew and cultural studies became formalized and institutionalized, scholars grew increasingly disengaged from political action, more prone to focus on cultural and political analysis than on actually engaging and changing culture and politics.

These dynamics, the ways in which institutionalization and "professionalism" alienate engaged scholarship, as well as how one's own identity gets shaped and reshaped by commitments to different constituencies, continued to impact my work. When College custodians were outsourced by the Southampton administration, deciding to get involved was easy. Yet, aside from the personal and political decision involved, it also meant once again thinking about the relationship between identity and scholarship, theory and engagement. It meant addressing the variety of structural and covert ways that identity politics obscure what we see, what we think and how we act.

Once Upon a Time...

This story begins on February 14, 1997 when custodial services at Southampton College were contracted out to LARO Service Systems, a company that specialized in busting unions, thus reducing the costs of providing maintenance to large corporate facilities. Custodians suddenly found themselves forced to fill out new job applications for positions some had held for thirty years. LARO supervisors told workers that no one's job would be guaranteed and that changes in staffing, schedules and procedures would soon follow. Custodians lost access to College retirement accounts, emergency loans, tuition remission, and a variety of other institutional benefits. Trading in his green LIU uniform for Blue LARO overalls and an uncertain future, one worker explained, "We felt like dogs kicked onto the sidewalk."

One week later, a group of students, faculty, staff, some local residents, and a core group of custodians met to discuss the situation. One of my non-traditional students, a part African-part Native American woman who worked on campus employee, was active in community politics, and was also engaged to one of the custodians, took the lead in organizing the meeting. I had researched the process of corporatization within academic institutions and presented material about schools where students and faculty had challenged the ethics of outsourcing. (White 2000) But the custodians felt strongly that racial dynamics had played a primary role in the LARO contract. They explained that their unit was the only one on campus comprised of predominately people of color—twelve of the nineteen members were either African American or Native American. In the thirty years since the College's inception, no person of color had ever been promoted from the custodial unit to the next level within the Physical Plant Department. The unit's new shop steward, Michael Knight, an African American, had started pressuring the College to create a formal and clear "promotional pipeline." Custodians believed that administrators wanted to avoid this pressure (as well as a couple of complaints and potential lawsuits about racial discrimination), and they told the meeting that the Physical Plant manager had punctuated the outsourcing announcement by saying, "and now I wash my hands of all of you." But, for local workers of color, the story of the racialization of class formation in the Hamptons began a long time before February of 1997.

The area's first real working class was comprised mostly of Native Americans who had lost their land through a series of corrupt land deals, and the onset of a cash economy. The historical record is pretty clear: some land agreements used forged signatures, some treaties were out and out ignored or broken by Europeans, and others included provisions for land use that Native Americans misunderstood since their cultural practices did not distinguish between use and ownership; they often misconstrued the implications of "giving over" land to Europeans (Strong 1983 & 1999; Cronon 2003). Historian John Strong has written, "as more and more of their ancient hunting grounds were cleared for agricultural production, and their dependency on manufactured tools and other trade goods increased, the Indians were drawn into the European economic system." (1983: 17) The local Shinnecock and Montauket Indians became fence builders and livestock tenders, acted as guides for European hunters and fishermen, and became the core of the local paid labor force.

The rise of the whaling industry would seal Native Americans' working class fate. The earliest companies were owned by Europeans but relied heavily on Native American crews. The labor market for such crews was so favorable in fact, that Indian whalers could "name their price" in goods and wages. Eventually, the State of New York stepped in to fix compensation levels in favor of owners. Meanwhile, employers established a credit or "lay" system that eventually created a kind of debt peonage very similar to the "lien" system of sharecropping in the post emancipation South. The owner would determine the value of the goods given to whalers and then the value of the product brought in at the end of the season. This system enabled the owners to have the total income from seasons' hunt minus only the goods they gave out, which they initially sold to the Indians at a large profit in the first place. During good seasons, Native Americans broke even; in bad ones, their debt would be carried over into the next whaling season.

The whaling industry also shaped the working class formation of African Americans in the East End. Some European settlers in the early 1600s had purchased slaves and brought them to the area. By the turn of the 18th century, over 5% of East Hampton's population was African American. While most worked in agriculture, the whaling industry created a growing demand not only for crewmen, but also for a variety of skilled and unskilled workers including coopers, carpenters, clerks, shipbuilders and many others. By 1750, almost 25% of Suffolk County's population was African American (mostly slaves) and, according to Historian Grania Bolton Marcus (1988: 22), "the growth of slavery on Long Island occurred for the same reason it did in the South: an acute shortage of labor." By the end of the Century, however, the whaling industry diminished and as the need for labor decreased, population growth among African Americans did as well—remaining essentially the same between 1810-and the end of the Civil War.

The major change for African Americans during this period was the switch from slave labor to wage labor. State manumission laws in the early 1800s resulted in a phasing out of slave labor until 1823 when it was completely outlawed. Regardless of their status, however, African Americans were relegated to the lowest echelons of the regional labor force, often working for their previous owners at agricultural or skilled positions. But the withered labor market, little access to credit or education, and a variety of discriminatory hiring practices and racial prejudices all combined to keep African Americans in the lowest paying, most physically difficult jobs. The labor market wouldn't change until late in the 19th Century when artists and aristocrats from New York City "discovered" Long Island's East End and turned it into a summer paradise. But by then, new racial and economic dynamics had changed the social and economic landscape.

It's the Racialized Political Economy Stupid…

Long Island's East End (similar to the rest of the U.S.) hosted massive waves of Eastern European immigration at the end of the 19th Century. By 1910, 45 percent of the County's population was either immigrant or the children of immigrants. But this immigrant working class had experiences vastly different from their African and Native American predecessors, as well as from their fellow countrymen who filled the New York City sweatshops and Chicago stockyards. Although East End immigrants faced a variety of explicit and implicit forms of discrimination, the fact that they could 'become white" would ultimately prove to be an advantage as they sought to improve their position in a society that already privileged whiteness. To transform themselves from immigrants to white Americans required significant efforts, but these new immigrants were aided by three major historical forces: economic, social, and political.

Economic

Despite the obvious hard work exhibited by many immigrants, hard work did not distinguish them from Native and African American workers whose labor had cleared forests and built the whaling industry. The economic conditions immigrants found in the late 19th and early 20th Centuries were very different than those experienced by Indians and slaves. In agriculture, for example, mostly Polish and Italians were aided by the availability of relatively inexpensive land and particularly high crop yields and high prices. Through out the period, articles appeared in the *East Hampton Star* announcing, "Farms Still Cheap," "potatoes pay well," L.I. Spuds Soar to $4.50," and "never before could a man buy a good farm in this state and make it pay for itself as quickly as is possible today." Polish farmers were especially successful in pooling family resources and purchasing large tracts of land in Riverhead and Bridgehampton.

Italian farmers received significant help from a series of farms developed by Hal B. Fullerton of the Long island Rail Road. Fullerton wanted to prove that the vast lands along the eastern portion of the LIRR could be economically viable for agricultural production. But the land was poor and Fullerton had trouble finding suitable workers. Italian farmers, however, had experience with difficult soil and had already taken up residence in Suffolk County as laborers. After some bad experiences with "native" white workers, Fullerton exhorted, "The Islanders must be replaced by the manual mainstay of civilization; the sons of Sunny Italy must be secured." (LaGumina 1989) Eventually, Italians also purchased large tracts of farmland throughout the region, while others converted cash into opportunities to open restaurants and grocery stores.

While some Jewish immigrants bought farmland as well, many began as peddlers who eventually turned backpacks into horses, trucks, stands, and eventually their own small retail stores for produce and other goods. Those who worked in regional industrial sites like Sag Harbor's Fahys Bulova Watch Case Factory or other small manufacturers in textile and silverware found decent wages in the factories and ethnic support systems in the community. As reported in the *Brooklyn Eagle*, Fahys "brought large numbers of Poles and Russian Jews to the village to seek employment in that manufactory....In business, the Jews have pushed rapidly to the fore [controlling] the clothing and fruit trade, and upon the main business thoroughfares 15 large stores testify to their industry." Jewish families on the East End pooled resources to form the Jewish Association United Brethren, establish the Temple Adas Israel, buy land for a Jewish Cemetery, and sponsored a variety of cultural, social and educational programs. (Gerard 1981; Frank 1966)

Meanwhile, the popularity of the Hamptons as a seasonal paradise literally paved the way for burgeoning immigrant populations looking for skilled and unskilled labor. Mostly Italian, Polish and Irish workers comprised the construction crews that extended LIRR service from New York's Penn Station, as well as those building Vanderbilt Motor Parkway. And as the summer colony moved from renters to residents, they first needed builders and craftsmen, then more domestic help, landscapers, and a host of specialty retailers and other service providers. While Eastern European immigrants provided much of this labor, it is also important to note that the first generation of whites who had first absconded the land used this opportunity to profit even more handsomely. Many longtime farmers and landowners made significant sums by selling off property to wealthy urban migrants for building their "summer cottages." Meanwhile, many of the East End's oldest European-American families started businesses that catered to the service needs of the growing seasonal set. According to Everett Rattray, "the vacation industry raised the demand for architects, builders, carpenters, plumbers, stores, and services of every description." In local publications like the *Star*, *Southampton* Magazine and the *Long Island Magazine*, Yankee families such as Bishop and Ellston advertised their painting and decorating shop; Havens and Wilde announced their team of carpenters and builders; R.H. Corwith listed his electrician's business and Frank Corwith his Pharmacy. The economic situation for late 19th and early 20th century European Immigrants gave then a significantly different set of circumstances than 17th and 18th Century native and African Americans experienced. These inequalities became a crucial part of the economic landscape.

Social

The 19th and early 20th Century European immigrants quickly established formal networks and institutions that resulted in powerful sources of social and cultural capital. Like the Jews who founded their own Temple and Cemetery, Poles and Italians created religious-based institutions such as St. Isadores Catholic Church in Riverhead and Our

Lady of Poland in Southampton (Poles) and St. Mary's in Southampton (Italians). More notable was the plethora of civic organizations that these immigrants participated in. Social clubs and recreational activities allowed immigrants to demonstrate their commitments to local identities and customs while still maintaining a sense of ethnicity and tradition. A notable example of this process is the story of Boston Red Sox Hall-of-Famer, Carl "Yaz" Yastrzemski.

Yaz's father, a potato farmer, was also the star shortstop for the Bridgehampton White eagles, a team that began at the local Polish American social club. "We used to hire bands and run dances," recalled Tom Yastrzemski, Carl's uncle and godfather. "We put all the money we made into uniforms." As Carl himself explained, "Baseball was more than an outlet, it was a unifying force. It was a different environment then...we all lived within a few miles of each other. My uncles would come over after work and pitch to me." But athletics not only unified the Polish community, it integrated them into the larger white community of the East End. According to journalist Joe Gergen, Southampton "revolved around sports in the postwar years." Yaz's baseball prowess brought success and recognition to the area as his Babe Ruth baseball team won the state championship in 1953. At Bridgehampton High School, he led both baseball and basketball teams to Suffolk County Championships. Such local notoriety dovetailed with the development of local boosterism and civic pride, especially as displayed by commitments to schools and school-based sports. In the Hamptons, Polish immigrants became noted for their prowess on the baseball diamond while the sons of Italian and German immigrants triumphed on the Gridiron. From the early 1920s to the 1950s, eastern and southern European immigrants used sports and other forms of civic activities to move from ethnic enclave to an "assimilated" local identity.

It is important to note that, in comparison, Native and African Americans experienced a much different social and cultural landscape. Native Americans, for example, experienced the degradation of their cultural heritage. From the earliest encounters with Europeans, Native Americans found their customs and folkways disparaged and attacked. The European churches called Indians savages and heathens. Early municipal governments outlawed native sports like lacrosse and cultural rituals known as powwows. While the Shinnecock and Montaukets were able to maintain some semblance of heritage and culture, the majority of their language, religion, and leisure practices were dismantled and destroyed, while their day-to-day lives were further isolated within the confines of their small reservation territory. It wasn't until the resurgence in cultural awareness and native history in the early 1900s and the growth of cultural nationalism in the 1960s and 70s that Native Americans could draw significant social and political strength from their heritage.

For African Americans, much of their cultural heritage had been stripped by the institution of slavery, while the possibility of assimilating into mainstream white America was precluded by racism and discrimination. Thus, even when African American children were finally permitted to attend the same schools and even participate in athletic events, rarely did inclusion and success spill over into the wider community at large. Black Americans did develop formal networks and institutions such as the AME Zion Church and a variety of social clubs and local businesses. In fact, the Eastville neighborhood, one of the major Black enclaves on the East End, developed a modicum of middle class stability and was known as an important stop on the Underground Railroad. But Eastville, and even smaller enclaves in Greenport and Three Mile Harbor, remained highly segregated neighborhoods. While European immigrants were able to exploit the growing sense of civic community life in the early and mid twentieth century, eventually negotiating identities as "white" ethnics, Native and African Americans remained distinguished by their racial otherness—their ideological and geographical exclusion.

Political

Both social and economic conditions, however, were shaped and sometimes driven by political forces. On a smaller scale, Polish and Italian immigrants developed political groups (such as the Italian American Voters and Taxpayers Association of Sag Harbor) and key alliances with local political parties. In 1932, for example, Poles formed the Cutchogue Polish Democratic Club, supporting local Dems in return for their hiring a Polish police officer, Anthony Chituk. By gaining access to these positions, immigrants furthered their acceptance as "locals." But, on a larger scale, these negotiations were made possible by the burgeoning need for more civil sector workers and links to the massive Americanization movement after WWI.

Public schools and civil service sectors grew rapidly after the War, in part to meet the needs of a growing population fueled by immigration, industrialization, and economic growth. But all of this expansion was quickly harnessed by federal efforts to quell radical labor and progressive political movements that were often popular among immigrant farmers and factory workers. According to Historian Roger Daniels (1998), the Americanization Movement "was an organized campaign to insure political loyalty and cultural conformity and enjoyed the support of most state governments and three federal agencies: the Bureau of Education, the Bureau of naturalization, and the Committee on Public Information." (p. 90–91)

In the Hamptons, these assimilation efforts took shape in local support for New York State's "Americanization Sunday" program. In 1921, the state's Department of Education asked churches and other civic groups to recognize George Washington's Birthday as Americanization Sunday. Long Island's Americanization Director, Alfred Rejall explained,

> There is perhaps no more fitting time to urge all our citizens to participate in the campaign of Americanization, loyalty, and neighborliness.... There is no single problem facing our country at the present time of greater importance than that of the assimilation of the immigrant into our national life....There are many of your communities which have large numbers of foreign-born people. They work on your estates, on the LIRR, and on your farms and roads; many find employment in your industries, which are growing rapidly.

Rejall acknowledged that immigrant identities were, in part, shaped by economic opportunities, but he maintained that Americanization programs could bring immigrants into the cultural and political mainstream.

Americanization, however, did not capture all white native's imagination as the 1920 also witnessed the rise of Ku Klux Klan activities in the Northeast. In fact, Klan projects on Long Island and the East End in particular, jostled alongside Americanization efforts and immigrant self-activity as they tried to graft their own version of white supremacy onto the growing efforts of local boosters and civic pride. The KKK participated openly in civic associations sponsored student scholarships and fire department trophies; it bought flag poles for schools and municipalities and entered floats in Fourth of July parades. The Klan ran candidates for local office and tried to fuse its anti-immigrant, racist ideology into mainstream Americanism through its support for popular "law and order" campaigns, especially around prohibition. By the late 1920s and early 30s, though, Klan support waned and few KKK programs gained any popularity.

Still, while the Klan's more narrow identification of patriotism and racial supremacy and violence was spurned, their efforts to meld white and American identities gained a wider acceptance as the more liberal Americanization programs gave immigrants an opportunity to become both Americans and white. Through economic opportunities, commitments to public education and school activities, civic associations and growing local boosterism, and the desire to harness immigrant political power, the public discourse around Americanization created economic, social and political opportunities for the period's immigrants. By the mid-Twentieth Century, Polish, Italian, Jewish and other European immigrants eventually had become full-fledged citizens, locals, and white—identities that African and Native Americans could only share in partially at best.

Not Everything Racist is the Fault of Racists…

The Coalition for Justice began meeting regularly on Mondays in a dormitory basement. The group initiated a campaign of letter writing, leafleting, giving speeches around the community to local groups about the outsourcing issue. Each weekly meeting began with one of the senior custodians recounting the history of the conflict and explaining the coalition's strategy. In part, the opening narrative served as a ritual activity that both indoctrinated new visitors and solidified the evolving collective identity of returning members. In addition, with each repetition of the story, new issues would emerge as well, often relating to long standing tensions both between janitors and administration, as well as among the janitors themselves.

Although the outsourcing was a "trigger" event, custodians, especially those of color, were angry about they way they had been treated for years. Although administrators spoke of "great labor relations" and a "family environment," custodians of color had long employed traditional and informal means of resistance to conditions they found exploitative and oppressive and degrading. As one janitor explained, "we were used to being ignored by white employers or even talked down to and mostly [we] just let things roll off our backs." This wasn't true of all custodians as one woman, Mae Anderson, had been at the College since its inception and had a reputation for "speaking her mind" if she felt disrespected by students, staff or administrators. Other custodians, one African American and one Native American had unsuccessfully pursued legal action for racial discrimination and civil right violations.

Collective action among custodians was rare, however, as internal tensions created various camps and clicks. Historical conflicts between workers from the Shinnecock Reservation and those from the Black enclaves in Hillcrest and Bridgehampton carried over onto the job. As one custodian, Tony Smith explained, he had tried to organize the unit to "get rid of Local 424 [their union] because they never responded to members' complaints. But we could never get it together to bring in someone new." These tensions made workers even more vulnerable to administrative efforts to divide and manipulate them. Thus, administrators often referred to white custodians as "the good workers " who didn't make trouble and often gave them unofficial perks like overtime and the use of college vehicles and tools. Smith explained his experiences with such labeling:

> I had been at the College a few years when they hired a few white custodians in 1994 or 1995. All of a sudden these guys became recognized as the best workers. I mean guys who were here a year or two were put on a pedestal compared to guys who had been here almost thirty years. We were always being pitted against each other. White workers were called "natural leaders." I never heard that about myself. It caused conflict.

These tensions increased as the Coalition's campaign made race more of a salient issue in the community as well.

The group approached the Town's Anti-Bias Task Force to complain that the outsourcing was an act of discrimination. Some white custodians were apprehensive, either disagreeing that race was an issue or as one white custodian put it at a meeting, "I'm worried about pressing buttons, because American society is very sensitive about race." One worker in particular, a Serbian immigrant named Manny, was concerned about his own status as one of the "good workers," He had been told by supervisors that he "wasn't like the other lazy ones." He was upset by the outsourcing because he was using his tuition remission to get a degree in Business. He found himself angry over the administrative decision, but hesitant to jeopardize the status his supervisors had given him. His conflicted sentiments came out at a meeting where he argued that he, too, had been discriminated against because of his accent. One custodian, Percy Hughes replied, but Manny, you can *become* white; you may not be white yet, but you can become white."

At another meeting, Manny and Mae got into a verbal sparring match over an incident that had occurred earlier in the afternoon. While the actual event was never fully described, it was clear that both had used racial epithets in their fight. The other custodians intervened.

Percy exclaimed, "Manny, I've never said anything bad about you and I've always been with you, but we can't say things like that. We have to be able to disagree and argue without using that language...we have to fight like we're family, you know? We can't let arguments break us up.... if we don't stick together we'll all be working at K-Mart." Manny eventually stopped attending meetings, although he said he still supported most of the Coalition's efforts. But for those who continued to attend meetings, the issues of race took on new dimensions as the group openly discussed what it meant to be white and non-white. One white custodian, Wayne Hudson, remarked how unfair it was that custodians of color such as Mae Anderson and Frank Jones had never been approached about promotion although they had been at the College for almost thirty years.

Racial and other tensions never completely disappeared, but through the process of discussing them, Coalition meetings became a place that exposed and challenged previously fixed racial identities, allegiances, and divisions. The commitment of white workers, students and other Coalition members to accept the importance of race in the campaign convinced most custodians of color that they could trust the group's sincerity. Eventually, a new identity group formed among custodians and others based on their regular Coalition meeting attendance—they became "Coalition members." For custodians, this new level of solidarity allowed them to act more collectively and challenge Local 424 and its lack of representation. The Coalition's work had also inspired the Local 424 Business Agent to become a regular attendee at meetings.

Custodians believed Rudy, the Agent, was only there to "keep an eye on them," and they challenged him about what they saw as collusion between the union and the College because the Local had signed off on the outsourcing. Rudy was defensive about directives from his superiors and often said "his hands were tied," when it came to new directives. Eventually, though, he started contributing substantively to discussions and closed one meeting by comparing the group to his early union experiences. He recalled "roomfuls of workers joining hands and singing *Solidarity Forever*." Rudy volunteered to talk at the first CFJ campus rally and gave a rousing speech comparing the custodians struggle to that of his boyhood hero, Jackie Robinson. Rudy claimed Robinson had shown great dignity and humanity while fighting for justice and equality; it was his "integrity that exposed the viciousness and immorality of racism in baseball." "The custodians," according to Rudy, "were simply speaking truth to power, forcefully, but with dignity." Unfortunately, the custodians were probably right about Local 424's motives as Rudy was immediately reassigned after the rally. But the custodians were able to respond collectively and eventually terminated their contract with Local 424 and affiliated with Teamsters Local 898 by a vote of 18–0.

Students involved with the Coalition went through similar transformations as they not only learned about institutional power and discrimination, but explored their sense of privilege and commitment to social justice. As one student put it, "I was upset and disgusted" at the way the custodians had been treated by the College. But, "coupled with anger towards the College was a growing respect [for] the custodians and an understanding of their position." This student was surprised ay how grateful custodians were for student support because she considered it her "duty and responsibility" to get involved. She explained: "For it was not 'their problem' but our community's problem...and it was a microcosm of what has happened and is still happening throughout the country."

Most Coalition students were white, middle-upper class sons and daughters of professional parents from suburban communities around the country. Many became noticeably uncomfortable at meetings when heated discussions took place about campus racism and the privilege white workers and students enjoyed. In interviews following the Coalition's campaign, most of these students said their unease came from the fact that they never thought much about race and pretty much ignored it—they preferred to think of themselves as colorblind. Still, most students quickly came to respect custodians as Coalition leaders and faculty would often refer to the custodians as the most effective teachers on campus—giving the entire community lessons in courage and integrity as well as the workings of local race and class dynamics. Students "bought into" race as a defining feature of both the campus outsourcing, as well as larger issues through out the community. Campus demonstrations and community campaigns including letters to the local newspaper and meeting with groups like the Anti-Bias Task Force solidified the Coalition's resolve and also helped to establish a collective identity for *all* participants as "Coalition members."

These activities also paid off with some initial victories as the College's Provost asked to meet with Coalition members when the Coalition came out publicly against the College's efforts to partner with Southampton Town officials in building a pool and aquatics center on campus. The coalition appeared at a public hearing on the proposal and argued that the College had not acted as a responsible community institution when it outsourced local residents and workers in hopes of breaking their union and avoiding charges of racial discrimination. In a meeting with the Provost, he refused to grant the demand made by the Coalition to terminate the LARO contract, but he did agree to three conditions that included: 1) restoring tuition remission; 2) studying the promotional pipeline issue; and 3) allowing the Coalition to conduct an evaluation of LARO's performance.

The partial victory satisfied most of the custodians, but students were frustrated. As custodians settled into their new conditions and had decided to continue fighting but begin the process of looking for new union representation, students wanted to increase pressure and conduct more direct action. Eventually, the Coalition decided that students should form their own task force to organize direct action tactics that custodians had always felt might jeopardize their jobs and ultimately give the College what it wanted—their termination. But a new dynamic evolved as new students who came to the Coalition joined the student task force, but never attended full meetings with the custodians themselves. Some of these students began questioning the narratives or frames that the coalition had for the outsourcing and its influences. In particular, some students became dubious of the role of race in the College's decision.

A few students met with the Provost independently and, while those who had continued to meet with the larger Coalition complained about Bishop's intransigence, and his whining about what he considered a "bias" against him, other students were swayed by his contention that there was no racism involved in the outsourcing. As one student explained:

> After the meeting, I came to the conclusion that I no longer felt appropriate accusing the College of acting with racial bias. I feel that Tim was a good person who is not racist and who simply made a stupid and unfair decision…He will not discuss the issue at all if race is brought up. He says he is not a racist nor does he discriminate against people on the basis of race. He feels the coalition is not practicing what it preaches by creating prejudices against him.

Eventually it became clear that students who continued to attend large Coalition meetings with custodians and other activists were much more likely to see racial discrimination as the basis for the custodians' situation, while those who didn't were more likely to identify with the Provost and his disclaimers.

Participation in the larger meetings had created a collective identity defined in part by a historical and ethnographic sensibility about the conditions that rendered custodians' point of view both convincing and legitimate. These students were less likely to accept the Provost's claims, instead adopting the Coalition's analysis, that administrative decisions had for many years reflected and reproduced historically race-based dynamics of local class relations. These conditions had become so institutionalized that what seemed to be simple administrative decisions could in fact also be racist without anyone particular administrator actually appearing racist—even to himself. At a sit-in in the provost's office, one student explained the concept of institutionalized racism to the Provost. She noted that even though someone might not intend to be racist, one's actions could still be racist in impact if they accepted or reaffirmed institutional conditions and policies that have been historically racist. Unless the provost was to challenge those traditional practices, he was only reinforcing institutionalized racism.

Covert Racism, Overt Struggles and Revolutionary Dreams

In reflecting on their work with the coalition, students explained that they had learned lessons in how social conformities, barriers, and hierarchies could be broken down." Another student described the process:

> Through meeting with the custodians and those faculty and students who had taken an interest, I was beginning to feel what it was like to be a community. This was a feeling different than any that I had felt here before. We were discussing issues that, according to the usual run of the campus, should not have included us. However, even though the coalition of people came together with a common goal, stopping the custodians' outsourcing, we discussed things in the context of all of our lives."

The impact of the Coalition resonated throughout the campus and the community: On campus, the College did promote the first African American custodial to the position of Maintenance worker. The semester following the Custodians being rehired, students from the Campus's Women's Issues group held a demonstration in the Provost's Office concerning the lack of a sexual harassment policy and for students, in general, who might be victims of discrimination and violence. Two of the leaders of this group had been involved with the Coalition for over a year.

In the community, the Anti-Bias Task Force [ABTF] voted out a Conservative leadership and elected Bob Zellner, a community activist and a famous civil rights organizer. (Bob was the first white field secretary for SNCC and had attended numerous Coalition for Justice Meetings). In fact, the ABTF's willingness to take up the Custodians' outsourcing as a "race" issue resulted in a host of new ABTF members including the local NAACP Chair, Lucius Ware. Ware had been active in a variety of political issues over the years, but under his recent stewardship, the group had begun a campaign to push Southampton's Town Board to take Affirmative Action seriously. On a cold, windy day in January of 1999, Ware, Zellner, and a group of other activists nailed a proclamation to the door of Town Hall demanding that the town increase the hiring of non-white city officials, town employees, and schoolteachers. For Zellner, the Coalition's work had held the ABTF responsible for being anti-racist, not just promoting "tolerance" and celebrating a "boutique multiculturalism." Zellner and Ware gave credit to the Coalition for pushing organizations in more activist and more militant directions. Zellner concluded: "the Coalition and the custodians created a space for a new kind of civil rights activism that builds on the legacy of the movement that I first participated in during the 1960s"

In some ways, though, the most lasting impact was on the participants themselves and how they viewed their own position within society. Let me conclude with the words of yet another student:

> One could easily be tempted to get discouraged with the idea that one person or even one group of people could do anything worth doing to solve the world's problems. But it is not true. There is something we can do. We must take action and start in our own backyards. That means organizing where there needs to be organizing. When there is something wrong in your school, or in your job, or in your life that is when YOU the people directly affected by injustices must take up arms. The Coalition and the plight of the custodians is just one example of a group of people taking action and taking control over their own futures. As history tells us, self-organization is the only way people ever make a lasting improvement in their own plights. Maybe some day all people will realize that once we are united, none of us shall fail.

It might be easy to write this off as passionately naïve. As a teacher I can embrace the energy and some of the lessons gained from experiential education, but it is also tempting to shun such misguided utopianism wrapped in somewhat pedantic and proselytizing tone. In the end, however, I want to argue that such lessons inspire what Robin D.G. Kelley has called revolutionary dreams. This is what, at their best, social movements do by raising new questions and new theories.

Kelley claims that these movements: do what great poetry always does: transport us to another place, compel us to relieve horrors, and, more important, enable us to imagine a new society...the conditions and very existence of social movements enable participants to imagine something different to realize that things need not always be this way.... Revolutionary dreams erupt out of political engagement; collective social movements are incubators of new knowledge."

The history of the working class in the Hamptons is in part the story of how individuals and groups struggled to survive and thrive amid changing economic and social conditions, some more conducive to success than others. Most workers struggled individually or with their families to make a living and improve the lives of their children. Others worked collectively to build ethnically or racially homogenous communities where individuals could find the autonomy and power to resist discrimination and achieve success. Those that could did assimilate. But there are few examples of social movements in the Hamptons that actually inspired people with a radical vision of a society free from racial segregation, discrimination and economic exploitation.

The Coalition itself was not a major social movement. It did represent, however, a type of social movement organization as it picked up the loose and disparate strands of resistance that did exist in the area, not only challenging a powerful institution to change a racist policy decision, but also creating a vision of an alternative democratic structure that embraced historical, social and cultural diversity as part of a new collective identity. This identity was never pure or uncontested, just a the vision itself was never crystal clear. But the impact of the group's work continued to resonate throughout the community. The Coalition demonstrated that a historical consciousness informed by diverse histories and cultures, energy and commitment, could be a powerful force—not just for understanding the complexity of history and racism, but for fighting racism and making history as well.

For me, the Coalition shaped the way I approach both teaching and research, as well as social activism. In some ways, I am a lot less arrogant, especially when I enter into collaborations with community organizations where, sociologically, a neighborhood's needs may be clear, but the level of assets—history, knowledge and strength—may be less so. The inability to see and often measure these assets in traditional ways is a result of a history of covert racism and inequality. But the traditional ways of research and knowledge production within the academy is also steeped in forms of covert racism and inequality, privileging various forms of data collection and theory. We implicate ourselves as scholars when we ignore, not just the flesh and bone behind our data, but the significant ways in which the sweat and blood of those struggling for social change have provided the most important materials and ideas for our work. When we engage these struggles, our understanding of them and our theories about them become richer and more complex, more meaningful for the movements and for ourselves.

To accomplish these goals, scholars have to change the way they do business. While universities and scholars are charged with producing new knowledge, Kelley concludes by suggesting that those in search of new visions for radical social change are "sorely lacking" among progressive scholars and organizers, "especially when it comes to dealing with the problems of a predominantly nonwhite, urban working class relegated to low-wage service work, part-time work or outright joblessness." While he thought that universities could be a source for new radical visions, he suggested that it would require paying "less attention to the classroom and its attendant culture wars and more attention to the cafeteria and the workers there." The Coalition did just that, transforming both the campus and the community into a dynamic, living and breathing classroom where all involved learned important historical, political, and sociological lessons. But even more importantly, we developed revolutionary dreams about why we create new knowledge, and in the process recreated ourselves.

References

Archer, Robin, et al. 1989. *Out of Apathy: Voices of the New Left Thirty Years on.* London: Verso Press.
Barker, Anthony and Anne Beezer. 1992. *Reading into Cultural Studies.* New York: Routledge.
Brennan, Timothy. 1991. "From Texts to Institutions and Back Again." *Critical Studies* 3.
Cavioli, Frank. 1992. "The KKK Memorial Day Riot." *Long Island Forum*, Winter.
Cavioloi, Frank. 1986. "People, Places, and the Ku Klux Klan on Long Island." *Long Island Forum*, August.
Cavioli, Frank. 1984. "An Incident at Eastport." *Long Island Forum*, November.
Cavioli, Frank. 1979. "The Ku Klux Klan on Long Island," *Long Island Forum*, May.
Daniels, Roger. 1992. *Not Like Us: Immigrants and Minorities in America, 1890–1924.* Chicago: Ivan R. Dee.
Dolgon, Corey. 2005. *The End of the Hamptons: Scenes from the Class Struggle in America's Paradise.* New York: New York University Press.
Dolgon, Corey. 2001. "Building Community amid the Ruins: Strategies for Struggle from the Coalition for Justice at Southampton College." *Forging Radical Alliances*

across Difference: Coalition Politics for the New Millennium, edited by Jill Bystydzienski and Steven Schacht. New York: Rowman & Littlefield.

Dolgon, Corey. 1999. "Ann Arbor, The Cutting Edge of Discipline: Postfordism, Postmodernism, and the New Bourgeoisie" *Antipode*: 3.

Dolgon, Corey. 1998. "Rising from the Ashes: the Michigan Memorial Phoenix Project and the Corporatization of University-based Scientific Research." *Educational Studies*, 24, 1 April.

Dolgon, Corey. 1995. Challenging Cultural Studies: Not By Culture Alone. *Minnesota Review*, Numbers 43 & 44.

Frank, Abe. 1966. *Together But Apart: The Jewish Experience in the Hamptons*. New York: Shengold Publishers.

Gerard, Helene. 1981. "And We're Still Here: 100 Years of Small Town Jewish Life." *Long Island Forum*, October.

Gergen, Joe. 1998. "Three of a Kind: Brown, Erving, Yaz grew up on LI, then grew into legends," in *LI Our Story*. New York: Newsday.

Hall, Stuart. 1991. "Cultural Studies and its Theoretical Legacies." *Cultural Studies Reader*, edited by Cary Nelson, Lawrence Grossberg and Paula Treichler. New York: Routledge.

Harris, David. 1992. From Class Struggle to the Politics of Pleasure: The Effects of Gramscianism on Cultural Studies. New York: Routledge.

Kelley, Robin D.G. 2003. *Freedom Dreams: The Black Radical Imagination*. Boston: Beacon Press.

Kelley, Robin D.G. 1997. "The Proletariat Goes to College," in *Will Teach for Food: Academic Labor in Crisis*, ed. Cary Nelson. Minneapolis: U of Minnesota Press.

LaGumina, Salvatore. 1989. "Fullerton and the Italians: Experiment in Agriculture." *Long Island Forum* February.

LaGumina, Salvatore. 1985. "Long Island Italians and the Labor Movement." *Long Island Forum* January.

Marcus, Grania Bolton. 1983. *Discovering the African American Experience in Suffolk County, 1620–1860* Mattituck, NY: Amereon House.

Mattelart & Siegelaub. 1979. *Communication and Class Struggle: Capitalism, Imperialism*. London: International General Publishers.

Rattray, Everett. 1979. *The South Fork: The Land and People of Eastern Long Island*. New York: Random House.

Strong, John. 2001. *We Are Still Here: The Algonquian Peoples of Long Island Today*. Interlaken, NY: Empire State Books.

Strong, John. 1999. *The Montaukett Indians of Eastern Long Island*. Syracuse, Syracuse University Press.

Strong, John. 1997. *The Algonquin Peoples of Long Island from the Earliest Times to 1700*. Interlaken, NY: Empire Books.

Strong, John. 1986. "From Hunter to Servant: Patterns of Accommodation to Colonial Authority in eastern Long Island Indian Communities," in *To Know the Place: Teaching Local History*, ed. Joann Krieg. New York: Long Island Historical Institute.

Strong, John. 1983. "How the Land was Lost: An Introduction" in *The Shinnecock Indians: A Cultural History*, edited by Gaynell Stone. Lexington, MA: Ginn Custom Publishing.

Williams, Raymond. 1989. *The Politics of Modernism: Against the New Conformists*. London: Verso Press.

JOURNEY TO AWARENESS: LEARNING TO RECOGNIZE INVISIBLE RACISM

Janet Morrison

Ignorance and fear drive racism. Being willing to confront that ignorance is often uncomfortable, scary, and overwhelming. However, a lack of willingness to confront our ignorance often leads us to excuse ourselves for our unintentional and prejudiced comments, which are not only hurtful to people, but wrong. Covert racism is the inability to understand the part we play in a society that helps perpetuate our fears and discomfort around people who are different than us and denies us the ability or willingness to see ourselves as part of the racist system that has been created.

Though it may seem ludicrous that I, a 38-year old White woman, was not aware of the Civil Rights movement until college, I simply had no way to connect with the experience. My rural Missouri hometown, population 707, had no people of color living there. In fact, the entire county, I found out later, was 99.998% White. (The .002% Eskimo/Aleutian Indians always seemed curious to me.) I did not see a person of color until 7th grade, when my family took me to Kansas City on vacation.

I felt as if I was in a time warp when I realized that people who had survived the torture and abuse of the Civil Rights movement were still alive. The authentic black and white footage of *Eyes on the Prize* (Williams, 1992) put me face to face with a reality that shocked and appalled me. After watching short clips of the documentary in my multicultural class in college, interest moved me to seek more information about my newfound reality. I borrowed the *Eyes on the Prize* videos from my professor so I could view the entire series. The eight-hour documentary showed personal testimonies and actual videotaped footage. As I watched, I became increasingly incensed and outraged at the horror of each successive event. Realizing I had been denied a dark, yet important, part of my history, I wept uncontrollably. The pride on the twisted, angry faces of White people as they tormented Black people made my stomach turn. That moment in my college class launched me on a quest to seek understanding about my own history, which

I discovered meant I needed to understand the experiences of cultures other than my own.

Personal Background

Shortly after college, I began working for a non-profit, urban ministry. At the beginning of my tenure, a book called *Real Hope in Chicago* (Gordon, 1995) caught my attention. The author's choice to move into the inner city community where he worked inspired me. Not long after reading the book, I moved into the low-income, African-American and Hispanic neighborhood where I worked.

People tried to discourage me. They cited safety, sanity, and burnout as reasons I shouldn't live there. Very few, if any, offered positive encouragement. It troubled me that my decision to live in an inner city, African-American and Hispanic neighborhood caused great concern for me and my safety, but not for the residents who already lived there.

My initial interactions in the community were primarily with the children. Though I was new to the community, didn't look like anyone else in the community, and had never lived in a low-income neighborhood, I was convinced I knew the best way to relate to the children and help them out of their situation. I did not think of myself as a savior, but looking back, my journal seems to illustrate my disregard for what already existed in the community and my immediate knowledge of how I could help them change. As you can see below, I wrote many comments about what I thought I could do for the children, my assumptions about what they *didn't* have, and what I thought they needed:

> *I feel like I will eventually move into [the apartments where the kids live]. I'm not sure why I haven't just yet. I miss those kids when I don't see them. … There's so many things I feel I could do there. Those kids have nothing to do over there. They need some outlet. They're kids. They need to be able to play. If I was over there, I could at least provide an apartment for them to hang out at. Tonight I went over and we all ended up hanging out at Big Mama's [apartment] brainstorming what we can do to raise money. They were coming up with all sorts of things. They need to realize they can dream their dreams and fulfill their vision. (Personal journal entry, 9-27-95)*

My terminology of "those kids" throughout that short paragraph makes me cringe. I realize now how much that language separated me from the community and allowed me to think of myself as someone who had all of the answers.

Beginning the Journey

Being White provides a sense of power. The power exists in everyday settings where White people are in the majority. However, White power even exists in places where White people are in the minority—inner city schools, urban ministry environments, and places of business. Though the power is pervasive, it is often unrecognized and unacknowledged by White people.

Before I moved to Dallas and began working in the inner city, I was unaware of the power that being White provided me. Living in an all-White town, I never thought about being in the majority. When I went on mission trips into areas that were predominantly Black or Hispanic or poor, I was there to help someone else, which kept me in a position of power in my mind. After moving to Dallas my choice to live, work, and shop in an African-American and Hispanic community 24-hours a day created a heightened sense of awareness about my place in society:

> I went to the new [grocery store] down the road. That was an experience. Yeah, I live in an all-black [apartment] complex. But walking into this [grocery store] was a whole new thing for me. I guess being white and working at the [food] pantry and living here; maybe I still am somewhat a majority figure. This [grocery store] was crowded and I saw 2 other white people. I wasn't afraid or anything, but uncomfortable would definitely be an appropriate word. It gave me a whole new perspective on what 2 or 3 black people feel like in all white places. (Personal journal entry, 11-6-95)

Living in the community challenged me. Though my social work degree had introduced me to the thought that our history was made up of a diversity of cultures and a tainted past, it did not prepare me to be a minority in a community. I did not know how to interact with the adults in my new community on a horizontal, peer relationship level. To create my own comfort zone, I continued interacting with the children and worked toward helping them.

Each evening when I returned home from work, the children in the apartment complex came to hang out at my apartment. My apartment became a default after school program. My interaction with them led me to volunteer in the elementary school across the street from our apartments. The more I watched and learned from the children, the more I felt I needed to know about the education system.

I returned to school to work toward a Master's degree in education. I wanted to understand the disparity I was beginning to notice in the learning levels of the children who visited me each afternoon versus the learning levels of other children I knew who lived in the suburbs and in middle or upper class families. To educate myself, while in graduate school I chose articles that would help me understand the community and cultures around me. I learned about Jonathan Kozol's research (1991) and work in the public schools. The work of Lisa Delpit (1995) and Shirley Brice Heath (1983) helped me begin to understand why Black students often end up marginalized in the classroom. Beverly Daniel Tatum's research (1997) discussed the psychology behind the need for Black children to affirm their identity and challenged me to recognize my own White identity.

Graduate school helped me gain information on cultural issues in a way that kept me comfortably distant from the problems I was beginning to encounter. I absorbed knowledge about the issues from articles and teachers who taught in urban schools. I learned what research said about the experiences of people of color. Insulated within the four walls of academia, my all-White and female classes discussed urban, Black and Hispanic issues as they related to the children we taught. The voices of people of color and direct contact with the students were conspicuously absent. The discussions led us to believe the inner city community was the problem instead of a part of the solution.

Instead of recognizing the urban communities surrounding our schools as having people we could learn from and potential resources to tap into, students and families in urban communities had already been labeled. Assumptions that parents didn't care about their child's education and children didn't want to learn were already unconsciously in place. As a result, my graduate classes often discussed doing a better job of teaching our values to the community in a more effective way, without taking into consideration the broader, systemic issues that factored into a child's inability to learn and a parent's inability or unwillingness to attend parent meetings.

To continue developing thoughts and exploring theories, I sought out academic research, but I also challenged myself to take steps outside of my comfort zone. I often felt uncomfortable and unsure of how to act. The absence of White people at these events was obvious. I saw how much de facto segregation played a part in keeping us afraid of and uncomfortable with one another. Going to events in the community helped me begin to realize my discomfort was often rooted more in assumptions of people based on my own fears of the unknown.

Becoming more engaged and involved in a predominantly Hispanic and African-American community had the unintended effect of causing me to question my identity. I knew I needed to be myself, but I felt that in order to truly be accepted, I needed to be able to relate. I realized it didn't matter how long I lived in the community, though, I would never experience racism, poverty, and life in general as the people who had lived their entire life in the community. My majority status, despite being a minority in this particular community, would always keep me in a position of power that kept me from those realities.

Over the years, I have begun to hear frustrations from people of color with the White community. A middle-class African-American friend explained that for the first two months after he moved to an upscale, predominantly White neighborhood, a police car would follow him home and park in front of his house. A Hispanic couple talked about manicuring their own lawn, only to have a neighbor walk up and ask how much they charged for their services. An African-American man relayed the story of dating a White woman and being stared down by a White man who then shook his head in disapproval. A Hispanic college student talked about how people abbreviate her mother's name from Margarita to Maggie when she cleans their houses. On the other hand, I have become more aware of conversations in all-White settings that demonstrate "white racial bonding." Sleeter (1994) explains these as subtle comments made in order to solicit agreement and understanding from the others around them.

One of these comments occurred during a get-together with friends when one person sarcastically commented to the group about me, "She won't date any of my friends because they're not Black." Though she did not know anything about my dating history, I can only suppose she drew conclusions from where I worked and my opinions about certain issues. On another occasion, a White friend explained to me her discomfort at a friend's wedding where the bride was White and the groom was Black. She explained, "I just wish she [the bride's mother] had told us he was Black! I was shocked and didn't know what to say." I wondered why it should make a difference, knowing that she didn't expect anyone to explain to her ahead of time if the groom was White. Though the racism is often subtle, there are times when racism is expressed overtly without any shame. In this day and time, overt and blatant racism often catches me off guard, especially in the politically correct world we live in.

My friend blatantly exposed his prejudices and stereotypes while recounting another friend's misfortune, as described in my journal:

> [Sam] started talking about how Michael [a friend of ours] had been robbed in Newport. As I inquired about it, Sam said Michael lost everything. He said they even stole his underwear! Then Sam had to go on and tell me that Michael had said, "It must've been a n—— cause only a n—— would steal someone's underwear." Then Sam laughed. He thought it was funny and couldn't figure out why that would bother me. (Personal journal entry, 11-27-03)

I was caught off guard by his flippant use of "n——." I was appalled that he made no effort to even try to restrain his racism and prejudices. On top of that, he had the audacity to chuckle when I asked him to stop! Although I did address his apparent disregard toward people of color, he showed no remorse. Later, I was upset with myself for not walking out immediately. What message did I communicate to him? Was it strong enough? Should I have left the minute I heard that word come out of his mouth?

As racism continues to perpetuate itself through underlying messages in the media, in our communities, and in our families, people are bound to take in the covert messages. For the most part, movies and media primarily show African-Americans selling drugs, portraying criminals, and being arrested on the nightly news. My friend's grandmother explained to me that although she liked Black people, she hoped I didn't bring one home to marry. That same day, a waitress at the restaurant asked my friend's grandma how she had "n—— rigged" something. I sat completely dumbfounded that neither statement seemed to even register as something that might have been wrong to say.

The more I heard derogatory statements toward and about people of color, the more I began to distance myself from the White people who said them. This also affected my identity. Often the people making the statements were people I had grown up with and still considered close friends. I no longer felt that they understood my reality or cared to.

Trying to figure out how negotiate and fit in to both cultures, I often found myself stuck in the middle with no one to turn to on either side. It bothered me that in many situations I was outspoken and very opinionated, yet my courage and voice failed as I struggled to figure out where I fit in.

When I started my journey, I searched long and hard for White people who had been on a path of anti-racism. I found very few leaders in this area. Fifteen years after I began my search, those writings are still rare. Though I have become comfortable in my skin, there are still times where I would like to read about and hear about other White people who have struggled with a bicultural identity despite being fundamentally White. Instead, I seek out writings by biracial people who seem to have experienced similar feelings.

Exploring Systemic Oppression

We live in a system that perpetuates our biases and it is my responsibility to figure out how I contribute to that system. The more awareness I have of my own advantages, the more I can fight against the system that has been created.

Growing up in an all-White community, it never occurred to me to notice the lack of representation or *mis*representation of certain groups of people in our history books. I became more conscious of these omitted pieces of our history when I ran across an article about the White-led Wilmington Race Riots in North Carolina (Staples, 2006). Despite the significance of this event and its effect on the entire political system in North Carolina, the race riot incident remains an appalling, though obscure, part of our history. The race riots that happened in Rosewood, Florida (Florida A & M University, Florida State, and the University of Florida, 1993) and Tulsa, Oklahoma (Johnson, 1998; Tulsa Historical Society, n.d.) join the ranks of the little known, yet powerful and disturbing events of our past. The absence of these major events presents a skewed view of our history. When the events are presented, the writer's perspective often leads us to believe people of color made no contribution to stopping the event and have always been victims instead of proactive leaders. White people are often given more credit for events that originated in communities of color.

In the history books, President Lincoln is usually the one recognized for signing the Emancipation Proclamation and ending slavery, rather than the text books acknowledging the people of color who rebelled and forged their own way to freedom, which ultimately brought about several of those changes. Lyndon B. Johnson is another president who is often recognized for his role in the civil rights movement. Though he signed the Civil Rights Act of 1968 and did much to stop discrimination,

Dr. Martin Luther King, Jr. and numerous other people of color were integral in leading the effort to create awareness and put pressure on the president to sign the bill (Zinn, 2003). By minimizing or removing these efforts completely from the history books, people of all ethnicities begin to believe that people of color have not contributed to our great nation.

Because people of color are not frequently presented in our history books, learning about heroes of color requires an individual effort. It is important for all children to know that Garrett Morgan invented the stoplight, Diane Nash was a major organizer for the Civil Rights movement, Charles Drew made blood transfusions possible, Madame C. J. Walker discovered the right chemical balances to make hair products for Black people, Gordon Parks was a famous photographer, and Shirley Chisholm ran for President in 1972. Each person just mentioned were pioneers in their field and each person mentioned was African-American.

Information on Hispanic heroes and events has always been more challenging to gather. An individual, personal search can find Sal Castro, a teacher who organized students during the Chicano Civil Rights Movement in California, Dolores Huerta, who coordinated the United Farm Workers grape boycott, and Plyler v. Doe, a lawsuit that ruled in 1982 that illegal immigrant children could not be denied a public education. Unfortunately, the few icons and events that we are informed of even remain somewhat distorted.

Every January Dr. King's deep voice pronounces across media outlets, "I have a dream!" and his legacy is celebrated with parades, musicals, film screenings, volunteering, and other events. Our society points to legalized integration as a fulfillment of King's hope that, *"one day right there in Alabama little black boys and black girls will be able to join hands with little white boys and white girls as sisters and brothers"* (Washington, 1986, p. 219), despite the fact that de facto segregation remains.

We have taken one single sentence from King's plethora of speeches to demonstrate that his dream has been fulfilled. Yet, if we looked at the rest of his speeches, we would see that Dr. King rallied people for much more than integration between African-Americans and White people. Dr. King had a Ph.D. in Systematic Theology and understood the broader context that oppressed people in poverty, African-Americans, and Hispanic people.

Dr. King fought for justice and equality for all oppressed people. Yet King is presented as a charismatic person who fought for African-American rights. His opposition to the Vietnam War and his efforts to improve working conditions for underpaid sanitation workers has been curiously left out of most discussions. King's profound comments are relevant and applicable to our political system today. Still, we have boiled Dr. King's message down to a four-word sound bite that limits a prominent African-American man in our history to being relevant only for a brief moment in time.

Contributions of people of color are invisible. While attending a conference in Atlanta, Georgia I was excited to be able to explore the roots of the Civil Rights movement and the historical significance of the city. As I settled into my room, I eagerly flipped through the glossy coffee table visitor's book wondering where to start. As I looked at page after page of the large book, I could find nothing that referenced Martin Luther King, Jr., the Civil Rights movement, or the Historically Black Colleges and Universities (HBCUs) situated right in the heart of Atlanta.

Convinced that I had missed something, I flipped back to the beginning of the book, scrutinizing each page. Not a single reference. Confused, I moved on to look at the visitor's map I had received. As I looked at the suggestions for "four days of sightseeing" that were placed in the margins of the map I, once again, found nothing related to Black culture. The rich civil rights history of Atlanta had been completely disregarded and ignored. Though the Coca-Cola museum, CNN studios, and Six Flags over Georgia seemed important and worth mentioning, it seemed insulting that a paper making museum, a patriotism museum, and a patio located in an historic district was more important and more worth mentioning than a major movement in our history.

Racism is not only the presence of certain verbal and physical acts. Racism is demonstrated in the absence of words and by making important historical events invisible. When significant people and events are left out of our history books and unrepresented by the visitor's guides, a strong message is sent that is often not even noticed by the mainstream culture. The absence of these people and events sends a pervasive message that people of color, the things they say and do, and the events they were a part of are not important. Even young children absorb that message.

As I drove home from church one Sunday, a 7-year old African American girl rode home with me. "I love you Miss Janet," she unexpectedly stated. "Why thank you. I love you, too," I responded. She went on to tell me, "I'm supposed to say that." Perplexed, I asked her why. She quickly explained, "Because you're White and Jesus is White. I'm supposed to love Jesus so I'm supposed to love you." A little taken aback by the entire conversation, I asked her how she knew Jesus was White. "Because that's what he looks like in all of the pictures!" she explained incredulously. Despite my efforts to challenge her view of what Jesus looked like, it didn't matter. She had seen Jesus a million times and every time he was a White man with long brown hair who looked nothing like her. Covert messages are absorbed by children.

Segregated and Poor Neighborhoods Perpetuate Injustice

We live in a system where communities, schools, and churches continue to be segregated. Segregation keeps us from getting to know each other. In the small town where I grew up, there was only one school. People in the community didn't have the option to live in the rich or poor part of town; there weren't separate parts of town. Unfortunately, larger cities have more options for people to move around and move away from lower-income neighborhoods and neighborhoods where people look different than themselves. In 2005, schools were more segregated than they were before bussing and other court-ordered measures were initiated in 1970 (Kozol, 2005; Orfield & Frankenberg, 2004).

Though ethnicity and poverty are not inevitably linked, the two characteristics are often connected. Low tax bases of poor neighborhoods create financial disparities that impact the schools, the economic development of the area, and the services provided to that area. Despite the desire to have access to resources and opportunities for themselves and their children, people in poverty are often limited by financial restraints. People without cars must live in affordable housing that is located on a bus line. Jobs are limited based on the quality of education they received, which is often from an under-resourced school system.

With little income, people are forced to depend on public transportation, public schools, and easily accessible jobs. Using public transportation makes parental involvement at school, preventative health care, and purchasing groceries more challenging. Parents are often unable to attend school events, purchase cheaper products in bulk at the grocery store, choose a higher paying job that is not on a bus line, fix dinner for their children, or be home during the critical after school hours. In addition, few grocery stores exist in the community. The ones that do are often overcrowded with low-quality and over-priced items. Because poverty and ethnicity are intricately linked, under-resourced neighborhoods often disproportionately affect people of color.

Poor neighborhoods are often under-resourced because of lower incomes resulting in lower tax bases. However, yet another factor impacting the income of people of color is simple discrimination. Studies show Black job applicants with no criminal background are less likely to receive call backs and acquire jobs than White applicants *with* criminal records (Pager, 2007). Job seekers with White sounding names are 50% more likely to get called for interviews (Bertrand & Mullainathan, 2004). Studies also show similar discrimination in housing and business transactions (Fix & Turner, 1998).

Despite the desire to do well, many systems are set up against people of color. It is important to acknowledge these systems of injustice. The majority of White people I know acknowledge that racism exists, yet very few admit or recognize that they are a part of a racist system and are acting within that system. Though individuals admit that it exists, each person assumes they are not a contributor to that system.

Covert racism is inherent in our system, but it does not have to be completely inevitable. Disabling a system that has been in operation for hundreds of years is not easy. However, awareness and gaining a firsthand perspective is an important first step.

Interact with people who are ethnically different
Friendships provide the opportunity and motivation to get to know more about each others' culture, traditions, religious beliefs, and interests. Interaction and friendship is more than observation from a distance. Interaction implies reciprocity. Reciprocity implies that we learn from each other. By listening to and learning about what is important to others make issues that may have been meaningless in the past suddenly become important.

Educate ourselves
Friendships provide the impetus for us to seek understanding on a deeper level. Listening to, learning from, and valuing the perspectives of people who don't look like us provides us the opportunity to become

educated about different perspectives. Going beyond personal opinions and seeking more information about how people who aren't in our history books played a role provides us with a deeper understanding of the contributions of people other than those typically presented. Seeking understanding about issues that are important to people who are ethnically and socioeconomically different than ourselves is important, even if it doesn't seem to directly impact us.

Inform others

Racism stems from an institution that was artificially created and continues to perpetuate itself. We must understand that if we are not consciously fighting against racism, we are flowing right along with it and contributing to it despite what we might think. Once we understand this, we can help others begin to learn, understand, and pass the information along as well.

We have great leaders in our past who have been our agents of change. We now have the opportunity to create that change. But to do that, we must become aware of the injustices that still exist and fight against those injustices on a systemic level. We must do what we can to change our own way of thinking and help educate other people within our sphere of influence. We must be courageous enough to start on the journey. No matter how far I think I've come, no matter how much I want to believe race relations have improved over the years, the journey is not over. Recognizing and dealing with covert racism is a process. It will not happen without a concentrated effort. The fight is not over. It is our turn to stand up and challenge the systems that continue to keep us separate and unequal.

References

Bertrand, M. & Mullainathan, S. 2004. Are Emily and Greg more employable than Lakisha and Jamal? A field experiment on labor market discrimination. *American Economic Review,* 94(4), pp. 991–1013.

Delpit, L. 1995. *Other people's children: Cultural conflict in the classroom.* New York: The New Press.

Fix, M. and Turner, M. A. (eds.). 1998. *A National report card on discrimination in America: The role of testing.* Washington D.C.: Urban Institute.

Florida A & M University, Florida State, and the University of Florida. 1993. *Submitted to the Florida Board of Regents, A documented history of the incident which occurred at Rosewood, Florida, in January 1923.* Retrieved February 5, 2006, from http://www.tfn.net/doc/rosewood.txt

Gordon, W. 1995. *Real hope in Chicago: The incredible story of how the gospel is transforming a Chicago neighborhood.* Grand Rapids, MI: Zondervan.

Heath, S. B. 1983. *Ways with words: Language, life and work in communities and classrooms.* University of Cambridge.

Johnson, H. B. 1998. *Black Wall Street: From riot to renaissance in Tulsa's historic greenwood district.* Austin, TX: Eakin Press.

Kozol, J. 1991. *Savage inequalities: Children in America's schools.* New York: Crown.

Kozol, J. 2005. *The shame of the nation: The restoration of apartheid schooling in America.* New York: Crown.

Orfield, G., & Frankenberg, E. 2004. Where are we now? *Teaching Tolerance, (Spring)*:57–59.

Pager, D. 2007. *Marked: Race, crime, and finding work in an era of mass incarceration.* Chicago: University of Chicago Press.

Sleeter, C. 1994. White racism. *Multicultural Education*, 1(4), 5–8, 39.

Staples, B. 2005. When Democracy Died in Wilmington, N.C. *New York Times*, January 8. (Accessed online on February 5, 2006 from http://www.nytimes.com/2006/01/08/opinion/08sun3.html.

Tatum, B. D. 1997. *"Why are all the black kids sitting together in the cafeteria?" And other conversations about race.* New York: Basic Books.

Tulsa Historical Society. (n.d.). *The Tulsa Race Riot.* Retrieved February 5, 2006, from http://www.tulsahistory.org/learn/riot.htm

Washington, J. M. (ed.) 1986. *A testament of hope: The essential writings and speeches of Martin Luther King, Jr.* New York: Harper Collins.

Williams, J. (ed.). 1992. *Eyes on the prize* [Television series]. PBS Production.

Zinn, H. 2003. *A people's history of the United States: 1492 – present.* New York: Harper Collins.

PART IV

EPILOGUE

POST-RACIAL MYTHS: DISRUPTING COVERT RACISM AND THE RACIAL MATRIX

Rodney D. Coates

Five years ago, when this volume was first being conceived, there were many who doubted that such a thing as 'covert racism' actually existed. Publishers and reviewers, academics and policy analysts, activists and moderates expressed such doubts. Fortunately, both David Fasenfest (Creator of this Series in Critical Sociology) and a stellar group of scholars and social observers, here assembled, have not only demonstrated but have documented the efficacy, utility and reality of covert racism. More recently (as the papers in this volume were being finalized) the election of Barrack Obama suggested that we just might have turned the racial corner in America. This election, with its promise and appeal, raised the hopes of millions that finally we might, just might, demonstrate that we can put aside our racial angst, heal the racial rifts, and actually live out the American creed of 'life, liberty, and the pursuit of happiness". Put simply, since the election of the first African American President, some would argue that we are witnessing the dawn of a Post-Racial America. While such hopes are indeed laudable –the reality is that we are witnessing the development of what might best be described as a "post-racial myth". And this particular myth, like many others, not only obscures but also distorts the racial landscape making both detection and remedies more than problematical. Hence, the purpose of this epilogue is to explore these post-racial myths. Concurrently, this exploration will also highlight ways by which we can effective disrupt covert racism and the racial matrix.

As I began thinking about this epilogue, I thought I would do a simple internet search Google news, blog, and face book on the following key words –covert racist and covert racism. Not surprisingly, thousands of hits were obtained. Scanning these produced some interesting results that will serve to examine the notion of a post-racial America. Let's start with a query:

> What do Porch Monkeys, Chinks, Homie Rollerz, religious conservatives, VA Governor Bob McDonnell, Mainstream Television, Genetic

Engineering, good ole boys, slick talker, clean and articulate, and Arizona have in common?

Answer: Two words –Covert Racism.

Randal Graves: Hey, what can I get for you, you little *porch monkey*? … (Clerks II)

Porch Monkeys (i.e. a lazy person who sits on the porch all day), long considered to a racially coded racial slur, finds its way back into mainstream America in the Movie Clerks II (2006). Now in the clip, when apprised that this is a racial slur, the actor commented that he was 'taking it back' or reclaiming it and using it in a racially neutral way. Therefore, like so many other racially coded words, they reflect the subtlety and deniability associated with covert racism.

> As you can imagine, the personal connection between computers and their users is unlikely to diminish anytime soon, so as the bad guys find the *chinks* on the virtualisation approach, the security community will strive to evolve fresh ways to protect the devices we need and love. (ITWire, 2010)

Chinks has frequently been used to diminish, racialized and marginalize persons of Chinese decent. Again, plausible deniability makes this a perfect covert term as one may merely say that they were making reference finding the slit or cracks. We, however have a long history whereby racial puns have been utilized quite effectively to denigrate and humiliate others. The utility of racial puns is that they are remarkably ambiguous and therefore work perfectly as covert instruments. Perhaps the most ambiguous and highly commercial racial pun is reflected in the 2008 release *Homie Rollerz (produced by Destineer for Nintendo DS systems)*. This video game, rated E for everybody, targets Hispanics and links them to dimwitted criminal gang leaders and "their generously tattooed ghetto chicas" who drive burrito like big wheels. (Bennett 2008)

A recent study published by "*Social Psychological and Personality Science*, found that people subliminally "primed" with Christian words reported more negative attitudes about African-Americans than those primed with neutral words". The responses to this study appearing in an Associated Baptist Press article are especially revealing.

> … God divided people at the Tower of Babel and there is good reason to believe that when people throughout the world unite once again, they will rebel against God as they did in Nimrod's time. That time of unity is

when the Anti-Christ ascends to lead a world-wide empire that is set against God.

On a more down-to-earth level, there are reasons that different cultural-ethnic-linguistic groups developed. One reason is to foster loyalty to one's group that then allows people to interact more spontaneously and in a trusting manner with one another. As studies by Harvard sociologist Robert Putnam and others have shown, when people are situated in more racially homogeneous settings, they interact more freely and comfortably. When people are forced, and usually they have to be forced, to live and work with those who are racially different, especially as nominal equals, then they withdraw from one another socially and psychologically.

Also, people evolve different ways of life that are best suited to their natural, political, and social environment. There is a reason that various peoples develop different speech patterns, values, and habits that shape everyday life that are unique to their biology, climate, terrain, geo-political positioning, etc. Why disrupt these naturally formed patterns? (Allen 2010)

So essentially, because God not only created racial divisions but also sanctioned them, racial prejudice is only natural and we should not "disrupt these naturally formed patterns". Such pseudo scientific, kneejerk responses are often used to not only dismiss charges of racial prejudice but also to condone it. The covert nature of these religiously and politically conservative beliefs is that they are then used to justify racial inequalities, segregation, and prejudices. "Students primed with religious terms scored higher both in terms of "*covert*" racism – where individuals evaluated whether conclusions were supported by certain arguments rather than whether they agreed with those arguments or conclusions themselves – and "overt" racism – negative attitudes expressed in responses to questions like how afraid they are of African Americans as a group or whether or not they like them." (Allen 2010)

Remarkably in 2010 two republican governors, Bob McDonnell (Virginia) and Sonny Perdue (Georgia) issued proclamations Declaring April Confederate History Month. While other southern Governors endorsed similar proclamations, what made these two distinctly different was the absence of any acknowledgement of slavery, racism, or the sacrifices of blacks during this same period. National and local outrage, negative media commentaries –forced both Governors to alter their initial proclamations. Both Governors suggested that they did not 'understand' why this was such a big deal. Their feigned ignorance, belied by previous controversies and actions of their predecessors, only highlights the attempted covert racial subterfuge. "It is the height of white male privilege for politicians like McDonnell or Georgia's Governor Sonny Purdue to use symbols of the Civil War, slavery, the Confederacy, and racism without regard to how painful that is for so many of our people – not just African-Americans." (Acoff, S. 2010) These Governors, however seem tame, when one considers the extreme positions being hailed as 'mainstream'.

Everyday Americans – we are told, representing the mainstream of values and common sense – are increasingly frustrated and angered by what they term the radical, leftist agenda of President Obama. These mainstream Americans, whose organizational efforts are expressed in movements ranging from the Tea Parties to the Militias, reflect an interesting phenomenon. This unique form of covert racism is also directly associated with who gets to be called an American. Thus when we think of African American, Hispanic American, Asian Americans, etc. the presence of a hyphen denotes difference. Specifically these hyphenated groups, by definition, suggest that such qualifications suggest not only difference, but also inferior departures from the norm.

Arizona, taking this notion to the extreme, even argues that we can essentially tell if a person is a real American by sight. Specifically, Arizona's Immigration Bill requires immigrants to carry their alien registration papers at all times and requires police to "question" those who they reasonably suspect are illegally in America. Contrary to Arizona's governor and other supporters of this bill, the obvious problem with this law is that it opens the door to racial profiling. The least obvious, and the covert aspects of this law, is that it also allows for a whole slew of subtle, easily hidden forms of racial processes ranging from simple harassment to extremely complex systems of discrimination, exploitation, and intimidation.

Simple harassment, associated with this new law, can take many forms. First, it is obvious that anyone who 'looks white, Asian, or African American' will not be troubled with proving that they have a right to be here. But, what is obviously white, Asian, and African American or for that matter Hispanic? What is obvious is that such categories are social constructions that vary depending upon a whole slew of criteria from situation and geography, history and social climate, economic and political realities. What this means, is that as these criterion change so also do our cognitive perceptions of racial categories. Specifically, here in Ohio we have seen where the perceptions of who 'belonged' and who did not was totally dependent upon the economic and political realities associated with the housing market, local economies, and labor pools. Therefore, during the height of the housing boom (2001–2007) the local economy was expanding quite robustly. This robust growth resulted in a significant labor shortage particularly in the building trades. To address these shortages many subcontractors explicitly recruited undocumented Latino immigrants. There were no official challenges to the presence of these workers until the housing bubble began to burst.

As the housing market became increasingly competitive, many home builders sought to improve their product marketability by trimming costs. Labor was one of the most obvious costs that could be contained. Therefore, local builders put increased demands upon the subcontractors. The response of the subcontractors was to displace their more expensive, domestic workers, for the less expensive undocumented immigrants. The results were predictable. A series of calls by displaced workers to the local sheriffs resulted in the enhanced targeting, surveillance, and detainment of suspected undocumented immigrants. During this same period – "Russian, Eastern European, Canadian and African immigrants in Greater Cincinnati, many of whom overstay their work or tourist visas, are not profiled because they blend into a larger population of whites and blacks …The dehumanizing concept of the 'illegal alien' here is the stereotypical Mexican with dark skin…" (Curnutte 2010)

As the housing market burst Hispanics, disproportionately concentrated in construction, were hit hardest. Many banks and other lenders responded more aggressively among obviously Hispanic clients. A recent lawsuit challenging the U.S. Department of Agriculture loan programs successfully demonstrated that many Hispanic and female farmers loans were either unduly delayed or denied while similarly credit worthy whites were fast paced through the system. (Harker 2010) During this same period there has been more heightened awareness of the 'illegal alien' among us. Some owners of bars and stores began declaring and posting English only.

Other forms of covert racism have also surfaced throughout the globe. In 2007, the highly popular British series *Celebrity Big Brother* was forced off the air for covertly racist remarks. The racist comments were made by several contestants directed at the Indian actress Shilpa Shetty. Shetty was variously described as the Indian, cunt, and Paka. Other contestants mocked Shetty's ascent stating that she should "fuck off home" because "she can't even speak English properly".

As demeaning as these statements were, it was not until over 47,000 viewers complained, the program was suspended, and most of the major sponsors cancelled their support – was there an official apology from the contestants and Directors of the Program. As horrendous as these may be, they are only horrendous because they were 'publically' aired. The same snide remarks –in reference to employment applications and interviews, by the scholarship and awards committees, the teachers and the supervisors –often go unchecked, unacknowledged, and therefore unreported. These covert racist acts, remaining under our collective radar, comprise just a small portion of those more systematic processes of discrimination, intimidation, and exploitation.

Covert racism, much like cockroaches and other vermin, thrives best in the dark. The most significant defense against covert racism is the light of publicity, information, and sanctions deliberately applied. While we cannot stop individuals, groups and institutions from purposefully devising covert racist systems and structures; we can deny such individuals their invisibility. Shining the light means insisting upon responsibility and accountability. Shining the light means being ever vigilant to the rearticulating, redefinition, and reemergence of racism –both covert and overt. In the process we shall witness the continual progress toward racial justice.

References

Acoff, Steward 2010. "Governor Bob McDonnel Is a Racist." *The Huffington Post*, April 12, 2010. (Accessed on June 2, 2010, online at URL: http://www.huffingtonpost.com/stewart-acuff/governor-bob-mcdonnell-is_b_534997.html.)

Allen, Bob 2010. "Study Links religion to racial prejudice." *Associated Baptist Press*, April 7, 2010. (Accessed on April 20, 2010, online at URL: http://www.abpnews.com/content/view/5044/43/.)

Bennett, Calotte 2008. "Homie Rollerz DS: polish up your rims and hydraulics". *Destroid*, Feb. 29, 2008. (Accessed on June 1, 2010 at URL: http://www.destructoid.com/homie-rollerz-ds-polish-up-your-rims-and-get-the-hydraulics-ready-72895.phtml.)

Curnutte, Mark 2010. "Is Arizona's Law Right for Ohio"? *The Sunday Enquirer*, June 6, 2010. (Accessed on June 7, 2010, online at URL: http://news.cincinnati.com/article/20100607/EDIT03/6060387/Is-Arizona-s-Law-Right-For-Ohio-)

Harker, Julie 2010. "Settlement offer in Hispanic discrimination suit". *Brownfield: Ag News for America*, May 28, 2010. (Accessed on June 3, 2010, online at URL: http://brownfieldagnews.com/2010/05/28/settlement-offer-in-hispanic-discrimination-suit/)

ITWire, 2010. "How to let Staff Use Their Personal Technology Securely". *ITWire*, April 12, 2010. (Accessed on April 28, 2010, online at URL: http://www.itwire.com/sponsored-announcements/38210-how-to-let-staff-use-their-personal-technology-securely.)

BIBLIOGRAPHY

Acoff, Steward 2010. "Governor Bob McDonnel Is a Racist." *The Huffington Post*, April 12, 2010. (Accessed on June 2, 2010, online at URL: http://www.huffingtonpost.com/stewart-acuff/governor-bob-mcdonnell-is_b_534997.html.)

Adachi, Jeff. 2006. *The Slanted Screen*, Documentary, AAM Productions.

Adarand Construction, Inc. v. Pena,, 515 U.S. 200 (1995).

Aguirre Jr, Adalberto. 2000. "Academic Storytelling: A Critical Race Theory Story of Affirmative Action." *Sociological Perspectives* 43:319–339.

Allen, Bob 2010. "Study Links religion to racial prejudice." *Associated Baptist Press*, April 7, 2010. (Accessed on April 20, 2010, online at URL: http://www.abpnews.com/content/view/5044/43/.)

Allen, Walter and Daniel Solórzano. 2001. "Affirmative Action, Educational Equity, and Campus Racial Climate: A Case Study of the University of Michigan Law School." *Berkeley La Raza Law Journal* 12:237–363.

——— and Reynolds Farley. 1986. "The Shifting Social and Economic Tides of Black America, 1950–1980." *American Sociological Review* 12:277–306.

Alvord, L. 1999. *The scalpel and the silver bear: The first Navajo woman surgeon combines western medicine and traditional healing*. New York, NY: Bantam Books.

American Staffing Association, *Annual Analysis 2004*, available at http://www.staffingtoday.net/staffstats/annualanalysis04.htm.

American Staffing Association, *American Staffing 2007: Annual Economic Analysis*, available at http://www.americanstaffing.net/statistics/economic2007.cfm#14r.

Anderson, Elijah. 1990. *Streetwise: Race, Class, and Change in an Urban Community*. Chicago: University of Chicago Press.

———. 1997. "The Precarious Balance: Race Man or Sellout?" In *The Darden Dilemma: 12 Black Writers on justice, Race, and Conflicting Loyalties*, edited by Elis Cose. New York: HarperCollins.

Anderson, Martin. 1964. *The Federal Bulldozer: A Critical Analysis of Urban Renewal, 1949–1962*. Cambridge: MIT Press.

Ashraf, Javed. 1994. "Differences in Returns to Education: An Analysis By Race." *American Journal of Economics and Sociology* 53: 281–290.

Alexander, Michelle. 2010. *The New Jim Crow: Mass Incarceration in the Age of Colorblindness*. New York: The New Press.

American-Arab Anti-Discrimination Committee 2003. *Report on Hate Crimes and Discrimination Against Arab Americans: The Post September 11 Backlash, September 11, 2001 - October 11, 2002*. Washington, D.C.: American-Arab Anti-Discrimination Committee Research Institute.

American Civil Liberties Union 2007, Racial Profiling. http://www.aclu.org/racialjustice/racial profiling/index.html (Last accessed September 11, 2007).

Ansell, Amy. 1997. *New Right, New Racism: Race and Reaction in the United States and Britain*. New York: New York University Press.

Ansley, Frances. 1997. "A Civil Rights Agenda for the Year 2000: Confessions of an Identity Politician." In R. Delgado and J. Stefancic (eds) *Critical White Studies: Looking Behind the Mirror*. Philadelphia, PA: Temple University Press.

Archer, Robin, et. al. 1989. *Out of Apathy: Voices of the New Left Thirty Years on*. London: Verso Press.

Armstrong, E. 2002. *The first thanksgiving*. Retrieved September 5, 2006, from the Christian Science Monitor Website: http://www.csmonitor.com/2002/1127/p13s02-lign.html.

Arriola, Elvia R. 1997. "LatCrit Theory, International Human Rights, Popular Culture, and the Faces of Despair in INS Raids." *Inter-American Law Review* 28:245–262.

Associated Press, 2006 "Michigan Voters Decide Today on Ward Connerly, KKK-backed Initiative" Accessed on August 12, 2009, at urn http://diverseeducation.com/artman/publish/article_6625.shtml).

Auther, Jennifer. 1997. 'American Press reflects racial divide on Simpson Case.' *CNN News Interactive*. http://www.cnn.com/US/9701/20/simpson.press/index.html (last accessed September 12, 2007).

Autor, David and Susan Houseman. 2002. "The Role of Temporary Employment Agencies in Welfare to Work: Part of the Problem or Part of the Solution?" *Focus*, v. 22, n. 1, Special Issue.

Ayvazian, A. 1995. Interrupting the cycle of oppression: The role of allies as agents of change. *Fellowship, Jan./Feb.* 7–10.

Babco, E. 2005. The status of Native Americans in science and engineering. *Commission on professionals in science and technology workshop, March 15, 2005*. New York.

Badgett, M. V. Lee. 1994. "Rising Black Unemployment: Changes in Job Stability or in Employability." *Review of Black Political Economy* 22: 55–75.

Bakke, Regents of the Univ. of Cal. v, 438 U.S. 265 (1978)

Baldi, Stepahne and Debra Branch McBrier. 1997. "Do the Determinants of Promotion Differ for Blacks and Whites?" *Work and Occupations* 24: 478–497.

Baldus, Bernd. 2006. '… to Race and Gender, Everyone? Some Thoughts on the Future of Research on Social Inequality.' *Canadian Journal of Sociology* 29: 577–82.

Balkaran, Stephen. 1999. 'Mass Media and Racism.' *Yale Political Quarterly* 21 (1). http://www.yale.edu/ypq/articles/oct99/oct99b.html (last accessed October 11, 2007).

Banks, J. A.. 1997. Multicultural education: Characteristics and goals. In J. A. Banks and C. A. M. Banks (Eds.), *Multicultural education: Issues and perspectives* 3rd ed., 385–407. Boston, MA: Allyn and Bacon.

—— 2002. *An introduction to multicultural education (3rd ed.)*. Boston, MA: Allyn and Bacon.

Banks, Taunya. 2000. "Colorism: A Darker Shade of Pale," 47 *UCLA Law Review* 1705.

Barker, Anthony and Anne Beezer. 1992. Reading into Cultural Studies. New York: Routledge.

Barnes, Jessica and Claudette Bennett. 2002. *The Asian Population: 2000: Census 2000 Brief*.

Barnett, Victoria. 1999. *Bystanders: Conscience and Complicity during the Holocaust*. Westport, CT: Praeger.

Barrett, James R., and David Roediger. 2002. "Inbetween Peoples: Race, Nationality and the 'New immigrant' Working Class." Pp. 138–168 in *Colored White: Transcending the Racial Past*, edited by David Roediger. CA: University of California Press.

Bartelt, David W. 1993. "Housing the 'Underclass'" in *The "Underclass" Debate: Views from History*, ed. Michael B. Katz, pp. 118–57. Princeton: Princeton University Press.

Batts, V. 1998. *Modern racism: New melody for the same old tunes*. Episcopal Divinity School. Cambridge, MA.

Bauman, John F., Norman P. Hummon and Edward K. Muller. 1991. "Public Housing, Isolation and the Urban Underclass." *Journal of Urban History* 17:264–92.

Bauman, John F., Roger Biles and Kristin Szylvian, eds. 2000. *From Tenements to Taylor Homes: In Search of an Urban Housing Policy in Twentieth-Century America*. University Park, Pennsylvania: State University Press.

Baxandall, Rosalyn and Elizabeth Ewen. 1999. *Picture Windows: How the Suburbs Happened*. New York: Basic Books.

Bayor, Ronald H. 1988. "Roads to Racial Segregation: Atlanta in the Twentieth Century." *Journal of Urban History* 15:3–21.

Bearak, Barry. 1997. "Between Black and White." *New York Times*, July 27, sec. 1, p. 1.
Becker, Howard S. 1973 [1963]. *Outsiders: Studies in the Sociology of Deviance*. Glencoe, Ill.: Free Press.
Beckett, Katherine, Nyrop Kris and Lori Pfingst 2006. 'Race, Drugs, and Policing: Beetham, Davis, Sarah Braking, Ian Kearton and Stuart Weir 2001. *International IDEA Handbook on Democracy*. Hague, The Netherlands: Kluwer Law International. Understanding Disparities in Drug Delivery Arrests.' *Criminology* 44: 105–37.
Bell, Derrick. 1987. *And We Are Not Saved: The Elusive Quest for Racial Justice*. New York: Basic Books.
———. 1992. *Faces at the Bottom of the Well: The Permanence of Racism*. New York: Basic Books.
———. 1996. *Gospel Choirs: Psalms of Survival for an Alien Land Called Home*. New York Basic Books.
Bendick, Marc Jr., Charles Jackson, Victor Reinoso, and Laura Hodges. 1991. "Discrimination Against Latino Job Applicants: A Controlled Experiment." *Human Resource Management* 30: 469–484.
Benjamin, Lois. 1997. *Black Women in the Academy: Promises and Perils*. Gainesville, FL: University Press of Florida.
Bennett, Calotte 2008. "Homie Rollerz DS: polish up your rims and hydraulics". *Destroid*, Feb. 29, 2008. (Accessed on June 1, 2010 at URL: http://www.destructoid.com/homie-rollerz-ds-polish-up-your-rims-and-get-the-hydraulics-ready-72895.phtml.)
Berger, Vivian. 2002. 'A Legacy of Racism.' *National Law Journal* 24 (55).
Bernard Lewis. 2002. *Race and Slavery in the Middle East*. New York: Oxford University Press.
Bertrand, M. & Mullainathan, S. 2004. Are Emily and Greg more employable than Lakisha and Jamal? A field experiment on labor market discrimination. *American Economic Review*, 94(4): 991–1013.
Bielby, William T. 2000. "How to Minimize Workplace Gender and Racial Bias." *Contemporary Sociology* 29(1):190–209.
Binnell, B. 1997. *A Discourse Analysis of the Racial Talk and Identity Construction of a Group of Working Class Afrikaans Speakers*. Unpublished Dissertation. Johannesburg, South Africa: University of the Witwatersrand. 93. http:// en.wikipedia.org/wiki/Racism#_ref-bboxhill_0 (last accessed July 16, 2007).
Blanton, Carlos Kevin. 2003. 'From Intellectual Deficiency to Cultural Deficiency: Mexican Americans, Testing, and Public School Policy in the American southwest, 1920–1940.' *Pacific Historical Review* 72: 39–62.
Blauner, Robert. 1994. "Talking Past Each other: Black and White Languages of Race." In *Race and Ethnic Conflict: Contending Views on Prejudice, Discrimination, and Ethnoviolence*, edited by F. Pincus and H. Ehrlich. Boulder, CO: Westview.
Blumer, Herbert. 1958. "Race Prejudice as a Sense of Group Position." *Pacific Sociological Review* 1(1):3–7.
Bobo, Lawrence, et al. 1997. "Laissez Faire Racism," in *Racial Attitudes in the 1990s*, edited by Steven Tuch & Jack Martin. Westport, CT: Praeger Publisher.
Bobo, Lawrence, and Kluegel, James. 1997. "Status, Ideology, and Dimensions of Whites' Racial Beliefs and Attitudes: Progress and Stagnation," in *Racial Attitudes in the 1990s*, edited by Steven Tuch & Jack Martin. Westport, CT: Praeger Publisher.
Bodner, John E. 1973. *The Ethnic Experience in Pennsylvania*. Lewisburg, PA: Bucknell University Press.
Bonds, Michael. 2002. 'Racial Disparities in Welfare Reform: The Wisconsin Works (W-2). Experience in America's Heartland.' *W. K. Kellogg Foundation*. http://wkkf.org/pubs/Devolution/Pub3703.pdf (last accessed October 20, 2007)
Bonilla-Silva, Eduardo. 2001. *White Supremacy and Racism in a Post-Civil Rights Era*. Boulder, CO: Lynne Rynner.

——. 2002. 'The Linguistics of Color Blind Racism: How to Talk Nasty about Blacks without Sounding "Racist". *Critical Sociology* **28**: 41–64.
——. 2003. *Racism without Racists: Color-Blind Racism and the Persistence of Racial Inequality in the United States.* Lanham, Md: Rowman and Littlefield Publishers.
——. 2004. "From Bi-Racial to Tri-Racial: Towards a New System of Racial Stratification in the USA." *Ethnic and Racial Studies* 27:931–950.
Bonilla-Silva, Eduardo, and Tyrone Forman. 2000. "'I Am Not a Racist But...': Mapping White College Students' Racial Ideology in the USA." *Discourse and Society* 11:50–85.
Booker, Michael A., Alan B. Krueger, and Shari Wolkon. 1992. "Race and School Quality Since Brown v. Board of Education." *Brookings Papers on Economic Activity. Microeconomics* 1992: 269–338.
Boston, Thomas D. 1988. *Race, Class, and Conservatism*. Boston: Unwin Hyman.
Bowman, J.E. and R.F. Murray. 1990. *Genetic Variation and Disorders in Peoples of African Origin*. Baltimore: Johns Hopkins University Press.
Bowman, Phillip J. and William A. Smith. 2002. "Racial Ideology in the Campus Community: Emerging Cross-Ethnic Differences and Challenges." Pp. 103–120 in *The racial crisis in American higher education: Continuing challenges to the twenty-first century*, edited by W.A. Smith, P.G. Altbach, and K. Lomotey. Albany: Sate University of New York Press.
Bradbury, Katharine L. 2002. "Education and Wages in the 1980s and 1990s: Are All Groups Moving Up Together?." *New England Economic Review* 1:19–46.
Braddock, James H. and James M McPartland. 1987. "How Minorities Continue to be Excluded from Equal Employment Opportunities: Research on Labor Market and Institutional Barriers." *Journal of Social Issues* 43:5–39.
Branton, Regina and Bradford S. Jones 2005. 'Reexamining Racial Attitudes; The Conditional Relationships between Diversity and Socioeconomic Environment.' *American Journal of Political Science* 49: 359–72.
Brennan, Timothy. 1991. "From Texts to Institutions and Back Again." *Critical Studies* 3.
Brewer, Marilynn B. and Rupert J. Brown. 1998. "Intergroup Relations." Pp. 554–94 in *Handbook of Social Psychology*,
Briggs v. Elliot, 132 F. Supp. 776 (E.D.S.C. 1955).
Brodkin, Karen, 1998. *How Jews Became White Folks and What That Says About Race in America.* New Brunswick, NJ: Rutgers University Press.
Brooks, Roy L. 1990. *Rethinking the American Race Problem*. Berkeley: University of California Press.
Brown, Phil 1990. 'The Name Game: Toward a Sociology of Diagnosis.' Journal of Mind And Behaviour 11: 385 [139]–406 [160]. http://www.power-probe.co.uk/library/pb.htm (last accessed July 17, 2007).
Burger Allen, Danielle 2002. 'Race, Crime and Social Exclusion: A qualitative Study of White Women's Fear of Crime in Johannesburg.' *Urban Forum* **13**, 53.
Burkey, Richard M. 1971. *Racial Discrimination and Public Policy in the United States.* Lexington, MA: Heath Lexington Books.
Bureau of Labor Statistics, U.S. Department of Labor, The 2004–2005 Career Guide to Industries: Employment Services, available at http://www.bls.gov/news.release/ecopro.t03.htm
Bush, George 2003. *President Bush Discusses Michigan Affirmative Action Case* http://www.whitehouse.gov/news/releases/2003/01/20030115-7.html (last accessed October 17, 2007).
Caditz, Judith. 1976. *White Liberals in Transition: Current Dilemmas of Ethnic Integration*. New York: Spectrum Publications.

Callender, Clive O. and Patrice V. Miles. 2004. "Institutionalized Racism and End-Stage Renal Disease: Is Its Impact Real or Illusionary?" *Seminars in Dialysis* 17(3): 177–180.
Carbado, Devon and Gulati, Mitu 2000. "Working Identity". *Cornell Law Review 85*: 1259–1308.
Carlson, David S., George J. Armelagos and David J. de Laubenfels 1971. 'Problems of Racial Geography.' *Annals of the Association of American Geographers* 61: 630–33.
Carroll, Grace. 1998. *Environmental Stress and African Americans: The Other Side of the Moon*. Westport, CT: Praeger.
Carter, K. 1991. Racial identity attitudes and psychological functioning. *Journal of Multicultural Counseling and Development*, 19, 105–114.
Carter, Stephen L. 1991. *Rejections of an Affirmative Action Baby*. New York: Basic Books. Collins,
Cashin, Sheryll. 2004. *The Failures of Integration: How Race and Class are Undermining the American Dream*. New York: Public Affairs.
Caraley, Demetrios. 1992. "Washington Abandons the Cities." *Political Science Quarterly* 107 (Spring):1–30.
Carmichael Stokely and Charles Hamilton. 1967. *Black Power: The politics of Liberation in America*. New York, NY: Vintage Books.
Carr, Leslie. 1997. *Color Blind Racism*. Thousand Oaks, CA: Sage.
Carter, William H., Michael Schill and Susan Wachter 1998. 'Polarization, Public Housing and Racial Minorities in U.S. Cities.' *Urban Studies* **35**: 1889–911.
Cartmill, Matt 1998. 'The Status of the Race Concept in Physical Anthropology.' *American Anthropologist* (New Series) 100: 651–60.
Cavioli, Frank. 1992. "The KKK Memorial Day Riot." *Long Island Forum*, Winter.
——. 1986. "People, Places, and the Ku Klux Klan on Long Island." *Long Island Forum*, August.
——. 1984. "An Incident at Eastport." *Long Island Forum*, November.
——. 1979. "The Ku Klux Klan on Long Island," *Long Island Forum*, May.
Charton, Albert 1930. 'The Social Function of Education in French West Africa.' Pp. 120–1 in *Africans Learn to Be French*, edited by W. Bryant Mumford. London: Evans Brothers.
CBS. 2009. "Poll: Blacks See Improved Race Relations." April 27. Available from www.cbsnews.com.
Center for Community Change. 1989. *Mortgage Lending Discrimination Testing Project*. Washington, DC: CCC/U.S. Dept of Housing and Urban Development.
Chase, A. 1980. *The Legacy of Malthus: The Social Costs of the New Scientific Racism*. Urbana: University of Illinois Press.
Cherry, Robert. 1989. *Discrimination: Its Impact on Blacks, Women, and Jews*. Lexington, MA: Lexington Books.
Chideya, Farai. 1995. *Don't Believe the Hype: Fighting Cultural Misinformation About African-Americans*. New York: Penguin Books.
Chiricos, Theodore and Sarah Eschholz. 2002. 'The Racial and Ethnic Typification of Crime and the Criminal Typification of Race and Ethnicity in Local Television News.' *Journal of Research in Crime & Delinquency* 39: 400–20.
Christian, Virgil, and Admentios Pepelasis. 1978. "Rural Problems." In *Employment of Blacks in the South: A Perspective on the 1960s*, edited by Virgil Christian and Admentios Pepelasi. Austin: University of Texas Press.
Ciecko, Anne. 2001. "Superhit Hunk Heroes for Sale: Globalization and Bollywood's Gender Politics." *Asian Journal of Communication* 11:121–143.
Citizens Commission on Human Rights. 1995. Creating Racism: Psychiatry's Betrayal. Citizens Commission on Human Rights, Los Angeles, CA.

City of Richmond v. Croson, 488 U.S. 469 (1989).
Clark, Rodney, Norman B. Anderson, Vernessa R. Clark, and David R. Williams. 1999. "Racism as a Stressor for African Americans: A Biopsychosocial Model." *American Psychologist* 54:805-816.
Clark, K.B. and M.P. Clark. 1947. Racial identification and preference in Negro children. In T.M. Newcomb & E.L. Hartley (Eds.), *Reading in social psychology*. New York: Holt, Rinehart & Winston.
Cleveland, Robert. 2005. *US Bureau of the Census: Alternative Income Estimates in the United States: 2003: Current Population Reports* (June).
Cloud, Cathy and George Galster. 1993. "What Do We Know About Racial Discrimination in Mortgage Markets?" *The Review of Black Political Economy* 21: 101-120.
Coates, Rodney D. 2002. 'I Don't Sing, I Don't Dance, and I Don't Play Basketball! Is Sociology Declining in Significance, or Has It Just Returned to Business as Usual?' *Critical Sociology* **28**: 255-70.
——. 2003. 'Law and the Cultural Production of Race and Racialized Systems of Oppression: Early American Court Cases.' *American Behavioral Scientist* 47: 329-51.
——. 2006. 'Introduction' Pp. 1-18 in *Race and Ethnicity: Across Time, Space and Discipline*, edited by Rodney D. Coates. Leiden, MA: Brill.
——. 2007. "Covert Racism in the USA and Globally." *Sociology Compass* 1:1-24.
Cohen, Adam, and Elizabeth Taylor. 2000. *American Pharaoh: Mayor Richard J. Daley—His Battle for Chicago and Nation*. Boston: Little, Brown.
Cohen, Mark A. 2003 Report on the Racial Impact of GMAC's Finance Charge Markup Policy in the matter of *Addie T. Coleman, et al. v. General Motors Acceptance Corporation (GMAC)*. http:// www.njcitizenaction.org/craautofinancreport.html (last accessed October 20, 2007).
Collins, Claiborne. 2006. *Listening Sessions Report* (2006). (Assessed on line on October 26, 2006 at URL http://www.interculturalorganizing.org/listeningsessionsreport .pdf.
Collins, Patricia Hill. 2000. *Black Feminist Thought: Knowledge, Consciousness, and the Politics of Empowerment*. NY: Routledge.
Collins, Patricia Hill. 2004. *Black Sexual Politics: African Americans, Gender, and the New Racism*. New York: Routledge.
Collins, Sharon M. 1989. "The Marginalization of Black Executives." *Social Problems* 36: 317-31. 1989.
Collins, Sharon M. 1997a. *Black Corporate Executives*. Philadelphia, PA: Temple University Press.1997b. "Black Mobility in White Corporations: Up the Corporate Ladder but out on a Limb." *Social Problems* 44(1)55-67.
Columbia Law Review. 1949. 'Is Racial Segregation Consistent with Equal Protection of the Laws? Plessey v. Ferguson Reexamined.' *Columbia Law Review* 49: 629-639.
Comte, Auguste. 1903. *A Discourse on the Positive Spirit* London: William Reeves.
Condon, Mark. 1991. "Public Housing, Crime and the Urban Labor Market: A Study of Black Youths in Chicago." Working paper series, no. H-91-3. Malcolm Wiener Center for Social Policy, John F. Kennedy School of Government, Harvard University.
Condron, Dennis J. and Vincent J. Roscigno. 2003. 'Disparities within: Unequal Spending and Achievement in an Urban School District.' *Sociology of Education* 76: 18-36.
Confederate Constitution, Clause 4, Section 9.
Connerly, Charles E. 1992. "From Racial Zoning to Community Empowerment: The Interstate Highway System and the African American Community in Birmingham, Alabama." *Journal of Planning Education and Research* 22:99-114.
Corenblum, B., R. C. Annis and J. S. Tanaka. 1997. 'Influence of Cognitive Development, Self-Competency, and Teacher Evaluations on the Development of Children's Racial Identity.' *International Journal of Behavioral Development* 20: 269-86.

Cose, Ellis. 1993. *The Rage of a Privileged Class: Why Are Middle Class Blacks Angry? Why Should America Care?* New York: Harper Collins.
Cotton, Jeremiah. 1989. "Opening the Gap: The Decline in Black Economic Indicators in the 1980s." *Social Science Quarterly* 70: 803–19.
Coughey, John and Laree Coughey. 1966. *School Segregation on Our Doorsteps: The Los Angeles Story.* Los Angeles, CA: Quail Books.
Cox, Oliver. 1948. *Caste, Class, and Race.* New York: Doubleday.
Cramer, J.C. 1995. "Racial and Ethnic Differences in Birthweight: The Role of Income and Financial Assistance." *Demography* 32:231–47.
Crenshaw, Kimberlé (ed.) 1995. *Critical Race Theory: The Key Writings That Formed the Movement.* New York, NY: New Press.
CRL 2006. 'Racial Disparities with Sub-Prime Lenders.' Center for Responsible Lending. http://www.responsiblelending.org/pdfs/rr011exec-Unfair_Lending-0506.pdf (last accessed October 19, 2007).
Cross, H., G. Kenney, J. Mell, and W. Zimmermann. 1990. *Employer Hiring Practices.* Washington, D.C.: Urban Institute Press.
Cross, Granville. 1964. 'The Negro, Prejudice, and the Police.' *Journal of Criminal Law, Criminology, and Police Science* 55: 405–11.
Cross, W. E. J. 1987. A two-factor theory of Black identity: Implications for the study of identity development in minority children. In J. S. Phinney & M. J. Rotherham (Eds.), *Children's ethnic socialization: Pluralism and development* 117–133. Newbury Park, CA: Sage.
Cross, W. E. 1995. The psychology of Nigrescence: Revising the Cross model. In J. G. Ponterotto, J. M. Casas, L. A. Suzuki, & C. M. Alexander (Eds.), *Handbook of multicultural counseling* 93–122. Thousand Oaks, CA: Sage.
Cumming v. Board of Education, 175 U.S. 528 (1899).
Curnutte, Mark 2010. "Is Arizona's Law Right for Ohio"? *The Sunday Enquirer*, June 6, 2010. (Accessed on June 7, 2010, online at URL: http://news.cincinnati.com/article/20100607/EDIT03/6060387/Is-Arizona-s-Law-Right-For-Ohio-)
Currie, Janet. 2005. 'Health Disparities and Gaps in School Readiness.' *The Future of Children* 15: 117–38.
Dalaker, Joe. 2005. *US Bureau of the Census: Alternative Poverty Estimates in the United States: 2003: Current Population Reports* (June).
Daly, Emily 2005. "DNA Tells Student They Aren't Who They Thought", *New York Times*, April 13, 2005.
Daniels, Roger. 1992. *Not Like Us: Immigrants and Minorities in America, 1890–1924.* Chicago: Ivan R. Dee.
Danziger, Sheldon, Deborah Reed, and Tony N. Brown. 2005. "Poverty and Prosperity: Prospects for Reducing Racial/Ethnic Economic Disparities in the United States." In *Racism and Public Policy,* edited by Yusuf Bangura and Rodolfo Stavenhagen. New York: Palgrave Macmillan.
Darity, William A., Jr., and Patrick L. Mason. 1998. "Evidence on Discrimination in Employment: Codes of Color, Codes of Gender." *The Journal of Economic Perspectives* 12: 63–90.
Darity, William A., Jr., and Samuel L. Myers. 1980. "Changes in the Black-White Income Inequality, 1968–1978: A Decade of Progress?" *The Review of Black Political Economy* 10: 365–392.
Darity, William, Jr., Jeremiah Cotton, and Herbert Hill. 1993. "Race and Inequality in the Managerial Age." In *African Americans: Essential Perspectives,* edited by Wornie L. Reed. Portsmouth, NH: Greenwood Publishing Group.
Davis, Adrienne. 1996. "Identity Notes Part One: Playing in the Light," 45 *Am. U. L. Rev.* 695.
Davis, Dernoral. 1991. "Toward a Socio-Historical and Demographic Portrait of Twentieth-Century African Americans." In *Black Exodus: The Great Migration from the American South,* edited by Alferdteen Harrison. Jackson, MS: University of Mississippi Press.

Day, Jennifer Cheeseman, and Eric Newburger. 2002. *The Big Payoff: Educational Attainment and Synthetic Estimates of Work-Life Earnings.* Washington, D.C.: U.S. Census Bureau.

Delgado, Richard. 1984. "The Imperial Scholar: Reflections on a Review of Civil Rights Literature." *University of Pennsylvania Law Review* 132:561-578.

———. 1992. "The Imperial Scholar Revisited: Reflections on a Review of Civil Rights Literature." *University of Pennsylvania Law Review* 140:1349-1372.

———. 1995a. "Critical Race Theory: The Cutting Edge." Philadelphia: Temple University Press.

———. 1995b. *The Rodrigo Chronicles: Conversations About America and Race.* New York: New York University Press.

———. 1996. *The Coming Race War?: And Other Apocalyptic Tales of American After Affirmative Action and Welfare.* New York: New York University Press.

———. 1999. *When Equality Ends: Stories About Race and Resistance.* Boulder, CO: Westview.

———. 2003a. "Crossroads and Blind Alleys: A Critical Examination of Recent Writings About Race." *Texas Law Review* 82:121-152.

———. 2003b. *Justice at War: Civil Liberties and Civil Rights During Times of Crisis.* New York: New York University Press.

Delgado Bernal, Dolores. 1998. "Using a Chicana Feminist Epistemology in Educational Research." *Harvard Educational Review* 68:555-582.

Delpit, L. 1995. *Other people's children: Cultural conflict in the classroom.* New York: The New Press.

DeNavas-Walt, Carmon, et al. 2004. *US Bureau of the Census: Income, Poverty, and Health Insurance Coverage in the United States: 2003: Current Population Reports* (August).

Dennick-Brecht, M. Kathryn. 1993. "Developing a More Inclusive Sociology Curriculum: Racial and Ethnic Group Coverage in Thirty Introductory Textbooks." *Teaching Sociology* 21:166-71.

Dentan, Robert K. 1981. '*Batek Negrito Religion: The World View and Rituals of a Hunting and Gathering People of Peninsular Malaysia.* By Kirk Endicott – A Review.' *Journal of Asian Studies* 40: 421-3.

Derezotes, Dennette and John Poertner. 2005. "Factors Contributing to the Overrepresentation of African American Children in the Child Welfare System." In *Race Matters in Child Welfare: The Overrepresentation of African American Children in the System*, edited by D. Derezotes, J. Poertner, and M. Testa. Washington, DC: Child Welfare League of America Press.

Desai, Jigna. 2005. "Planet Bollywood: Indian Cinema Abroad." In *East Main Street-Asian American Popular Culture*, edited by Dave, et. al. NY: New York University Press.

———. 2004. *Beyond Bollywood: The Cultural Politics of South Asian Diasporic Film.* New York and London: Routledge.

Diamond, J. 1999. *Guns, germs, & steel.* New York, NY: W. W. Norton & Company.

DiAngelo, Robin J. 2006. "The Production of Whiteness in Education: Asian International Students in a College Classroom." *Teachers College Record* 108 (10), 1983-2000.

DiMaggio, Paul J. and Walter W. Powell. 1982. "The Iron Cage Revisited: Institutional Isomorphism and Collective Rationality in Organizational Fields." *American Sociological Review* 48(2):147-160.

Doane, Ashley, Jr. 2003. "Rethinking Whiteness Studies." Pp. 3-18 in *White Out: The Continuing Significance of Racism*, edited by Eduardo Bonilla-Silva and Ashley Doane Jr. New York: Routledge.

Dobbin, Frank John R. Sutton, John W. Meyer, 1993. "Equal Opportunity Law and the Construction of Internal Labor Markets." *The American Journal of Sociology* 2:396-427.

Dolgon, Corey. 2005. The End of the Hamptons: Scenes from the Class Struggle in America's Paradise. New York: new York University Press.
——. 2001. "Building Community amid the Ruins: Strategies for Struggle from the Coalition for Justice at Southampton College." *Forging Radical Alliances across Difference: Coalition Politics for the New Millennium*, edited by Jill Bystydzienski and Steven Schacht. New York: Rowman & Littlefield.
——. 1999. "Ann Arbor, The Cutting Edge of Discipline: Postfordism, Postmodernism, and the New Bourgeoisie." *Antipode*: 3.
——. 1998. "Rising from the Ashes: the Michigan Memorial Phoenix Project and the Corporatization of University-based Scientific Research." *Educational Studies*, 24, 1 April.
——. 1995. Challenging Cultural Studies: Not By Culture Alone. *Minnesota Review*, Numbers 43 & 44.
Dovidio, J. F., and Gaertner, S. L. 2004. Aversive racism. In M. P. Zanna (Ed.), *Advances in experimental social psychology* (Vol. 36, pp. 1–51). San Diego, CA: Academic Press.
Dovidio, J. F., Gaertner, S. L., Penner, L. A., Pearson, A. R., and W.E. Norton. 2009. Aversive racism: How unconscious bias influences behavior: Implications for legal, employment, and health care contexts. In J. L. Chin (Ed.), *Diversity in mind and action* (pp. 37–54). Westport, CT: Praeger Press.
Dowd, Maureen. 2009. "Dark, Dark, Dark." *New York Times*. February 22.
Drake, St. Clair, and Horace Cayton. 1962 [1945]. *Black Metropolis: A Study of Negro Life in a Northern City*. New York: Harper and Row.
Du Bois, W.E.B. 1989. *The Souls of Black Folks*. New York: Bantam. (Originally published in 1903).
——. 1920. *Darkwater: Voices from Within the Veil*. New York: Harcourt, Brace.
——. 1935. *Black Reconstruction in America, 1860–1880*. NY: Free Press.
Duncan, Otis. 1968. "Patterns of Occupational Mobility Among Negro Men." *Demography* 5: 11–22.
Durham, G. 2001. "Displaced Persons: Symbols of South Asian Femininity and the Returned Gaze in U.S. Media Culture." *Communication Theory* 11:201–217.
Dyson, Michael. 2006. *Come Hell or High Water: Hurricane Katrina and the Color of Disaster*. New York: Basic Civitas.
D'Souza, Dinesh. 1995. *The End of Racism*. New York: Free Press.
Eakes, Martin D. 2003. "Wells Fargo's Application to Acquire Pacific Northwest Bankcorp: An Analysis of Its Implication for Consumers in Washington State." *Center for Responsible Lending*.
Edelman, Lauren B. 1992. "Legal Ambiguity and Symbolic Structures: Organizational Mediation of Civil Rights Law." *American Journal of Sociology* 97: 1531–76..... 1990. Legal Environments and Organizational Governance: The Expansion of Due Process in the Workplace. *American Journal of Sociology* 95:1401–1440.
Edelman, Lauren B. and Stephen Petterson. 1999. "Symbols and Substance in Organizational Response to Civil Rights Law." Research in Social Stratification and Mobility 17:107–136.
Elliot, Michael. 1999. "Telling the Difference: Nineteenth Century Legal Narratives of Racial Taxonomy," 24 *Law & Soc. Inquiry* 611.
Ely, R., Meyerson, D., and M. Davidson. 2006. Rethinking political correctness. *Harvard Business Review*, 84(9):78–87.
Endicott, Kirk 1979. *Negrito Religion: The World-View and Rituals of a Hunting and Gathering People of Peninsula Malaysia*. New York, NY: Clarendon Press.
Entman, Robert M. and Andrew Rojecki. 2000. *The Black Image in the White Mind: Media and Race in America*. Chicago, IL: University of Chicago Press.
Espinoza, Leslie G. 1998. "Latino/a Identity and Multi-Identity: Community and Culture." Pp. 17–23 in *The Latino/a condition: A critical reader*, edited by R. Delgado and J. Stefanic. New York: New York University Press.

Essed, Philomena. 1991. *Understanding Everyday Racism: An Interdisciplinary Approach.* London: Sage Publications.
Farley, Reynolds. 1984. *Blacks and Whites: Narrowing the Gap?* Cambridge, MA: Harvard University Press.
——. 1993. "The Common Destiny of Black and Whites: Observations about the Social and Economic Status of the Races." In *Race in America: The Struggle for Equality,* edited by Herbert Hill and James E. Jones, Jr. Madison, WI: The University of Wisconsin Press.
——. 2004. "Civil Rights and the Status of Black Americans in the 1960s and the 1990s." In *Race, Poverty, and Domestic Policy,* edited by Michael Henry. New Haven, CT: Yale University Press.
Farley, Reynolds, and Walter R. Allen. 1987. *The Color Line and the Quality of Life in America.* New York: Russell Sage Foundation.
Farley, Reynolds, and William H. Frey. 1994. "Changes in the Segregation of Whites from Blacks During the 1980s: Small Steps Toward a More Integrated Society." *American Sociological Review* 59: 23–45.
Farley, Reynolds, and Albert Hermalin. 1972. "The 1960s: A Decade of Progress for Blacks?" *Demography* 9: 353–370.
Feagin, Joe R. 2006. *Systemic Racism: A Theory of Oppression.* New York: Routledge.
Feagin, Joe R. 2000. *Racist America: Roots, Current Realities, and Future Reparations.* New York: Routledge.
Feagin, Joe and Clarice Feagin. 1994. "Theoretical Perspectives in Race and Ethnic Relations." In *Race and Ethnic Conflict: Contending Views on Prejudice, Discrimination, and Ethnoviolence,* edited by F. Pincus and H. Ehrlich. Boulder, CO: Westview.
Feagin, Joe R., Kevin E. Early, and Karyn D. McKinney. 2001. "The Many Costs of Discrimination: The Case of Middle-Class African Americans." *Indiana Law Review* 34 (4): 1313–60
Feagin, Joe R., Hernan Vera, and Nikitah Imani. 1996. *The Agony of Education: Black Students At White Colleges And Universities.* New York: Routledge.
Feagin, Joe R., and Karyn D. McKinney. 2003. *The Many Costs of Racism.* Boston: Rowman and Littlefield.
Feagin, Joe R., and Melvin P. Sikes. 1994. *Living With Racism: The Black Middle Class Experience.* Borton: Beacon Press.
Ferree, Myra Marx, and Elaine J. Hall. 1996. "Rethinking Stratification from a Feminist Perspective: Gender, Race and Class in Mainstream Textbooks." *American Sociological Review* 61:929–950.
Fields, Barbara Jeanne. 1990. "Slavery, Race and Ideology in the United States of America," 181 *New Left Review.* 95.
Fine, Gary Alan, Beth Montemurro, Bbonnie Semora, Marybeth C. Stalp, Dana S. Claussen, and Zayda Sierra 1998. 'Social Order through a Prism: Color as Collective Representation.' *Sociological Inquiry* 68: 443–457.
Fisher, Anne B. 1985. "Businessmen Like to Hire by the Numbers." *Fortune,* September 16, pp. 26–30.
Fiske, Susan T. 1998. "Stereotyping, Prejudice and Discrimination." Pp. 357–411 in *Handbook of Social Psychology,* edited by Daniel T. Gilbert, Susan T. Fiske, and Gardner Lindzey, New York: McGraw Hill.
Fix, M. and M.A. Turner (eds.). 1998. *A National report card on discrimination in America: The role of testing.* Washington D.C.: Urban Institute.
Florida A & M University, Florida State, and the University of Florida. 1993. *Submitted to the Florida Board of Regents, A documented history of the incident which occurred at Rosewood, Florida, in January 1923.* Retrieved February 5, 2006, from http://www.tfn.net/doc/rosewood.txt.

Foley, Neil. 1997. "Becoming Hispanic: Mexican Americans and the Faustian Pact with Whiteness," in *Reflexiones* edited by Neil Foley. Center for Mexican American Studies: The University of Texas Press.

Foner, S. Philip. 1981. *Organized Labor and the Black Worker, 1619–1981*. New York: International Publishers.

Fox, Radhika K., and Sarah Treuhaft. 2006. *Shared Prosperity, Stronger Regions: An Agenda for Rebuilding America's Older Core Cities*. Report prepared for PolicyLink, Oakland, CA.

Fram, Alan. 2005. "Bush to Seek $80B for Iraq, Afghan Wars." *Yahoo News*, January 24.

Frank, Abe. 1966. *Together But Apart: The Jewish Experience in the Hamptons*. New York: Shengold Publishers.

Frankenberg, Erika, Chungmei Lee, and Gary Orfield. 2003. *Multiracial Society with Segregated Schools: Are We Losing the Dream?* Cambridge, MA: Civil Rights Project, Harvard University.

Frazier, E. Franklin. 1957. The *Black Bourgeoisie*. New York: Free Press.

Fredrickson, George, M. 1981. *White Supremacy: A Comparative Study in American and South African History*. New York, NY: Oxford University Press.

Fredrickson, George, M. 2002. *Racism: A Short History*. Princeton, NJ: Princeton University Press.

Freeman, Richard B. 1978. "Black Economic Progress Since 1964." *The Public Interest*, Summer.

Freire, Paulo. 1973. *Education for Critical Consciousness*. New York: Seabury Press.

Frey, William H. 1996. "Immigration, Domestic Migration, and Demographic Balkanization in America: New Evidence from the 1990s," 22 *Population & Development Rev*. 741.

Frye, Marilyn 1983. *The Politics of Reality*. Trumansburg, NY: Crossing Press.

———. 1983. "On Being White." In *The Politics of Reality: Essays in Feminist Theory*, edited by M. Frye. Freedom, CA: Crossing Press.

Fullwiley, Duana 2008. "The Biologistical Construction of Race: 'Admixture' Technology and the New Genetic Medicine." *Social Studies of Science* 38(5): 695–735.

Fusfeld, Daniel R., and Timothy Bates. 1984. *The Political Economy of the Urban Ghetto*. Carbondale, IL: Southern Illinois University Press.

Furuhashi, Yoshie 2003. *Max Weber's Genteel Racism*. http://nuance.dhs.org/lbo-talk/0012/ 0497.html (last accessed July 11, 2007).

Gallop, Alex and George Gallop Jr. 2000. *The Gallop Poll: Public Opinion 1999*. Lanham, MD.: Rowman and Littlefield.

Gannett, Lisa 2001. 'Racism and Human Genome Diversity Research: The Ethical Limits of "Population Thinking"'. *Philosophy of Science* 68: S479–92. Proceedings of the 2000 Biennial Meeting of the Philosophy of Science Association. Part I: Contributed Papers. (September).

Gans, Herbert. 1998. "Best-Sellers by American Sociologists: An Exploratory Study." Pp. 19–30 in *Required Reading: Sociologists Most Influential Books*, edited by Dan Clawson. Boston: University of Massachusetts Press.

Garfinkel, Harold. 1967. *Studies in Ethnomethodology*. Englewood Cliffs, NJ: Prentice Hall.

Garfinkel, Irwin, Robert H. Haveman, and David Betson. 1977. *Earnings Capacity, Poverty, and Inequality*. New York: Academic Press.

Gerard, Helene. 1981. "And We're Still Here: 100 Years of Small Town Jewish Life." *Long Island Forum*, October.

Gergen, Joe. 1998. "Three of a Kind: Brown, Erving, Yaz grew up on LI, then grew into legends," in *LI Our Story*. New York: Newsday.

Giddings, Paula. 1984. *When and Where I Enter: The Impact of Black Women on Race and Sex in America*. New York: Bantam.
Gilens, Martin 1996. "Race Coding" and White Opposition to Welfare." *American Political Science Review* 90: 593-604.
Gittleman, Maury, and Edward N. Wolff. 2004. "Racial Differences in Patterns of Wealth Accumulation." *Journal of Human Resources* 39: 193-227.
Giuliano, Laura, Levine, David I. and Leonard, Jonathan. 2005. "Race, Gender, and Hiring Patterns: Evidence from a Large Service-Sector Employer". Unpublished manuscript assessed online on September 23, 2005 at URL http://gsbwww.uchicago.edu/labor/Giuliano_Levine_Leonard.pdf.
Glaeser, Edward L., and Jacob L. Vigdor. 2004. "Racial Segregation: Promising News." In *Redefining Urban and Suburban America: Evidence from Census 2000, Volume One* edited by Bruce Katz and Robert E. Lang. Washington, D.C.: Brookings Institution Press.
Glazer, Nathan. 1987 [1975]. *Affirmative Discrimination*. Cambridge, Mass.: Harvard University Press.
——. 1998. *We Are All Multiculturalists Now*. Cambridge, MA: Harvard University Press.
——. 2001. "The Future of Race in the United States," in *Race in 21st Century America* edited by Curtis Stokes, Theresa Melendez, and Gernice Rhodes-Reed. East Lansing, MI: Michigan State University Press.
Godby v. Montgomery County Bd. of Educ., 996 F. Supp. 1390 (M.D. Ala. 1998).
Goffman, Erving. 1961. *Strategic Interaction*. Indianapolis: Bobbs-Merrill.
——. 1963. *Stigma: Notes on the Management of Spoiled Identity*. Englewood Cliffs, N.J.: Prentice-Hall.
Golden, Marita. 2005. *Don't Play in the Sun: One Woman's Journey Through the Color Complex*. NY: Anchor.
Gordon, W. 1995. *Real hope in Chicago: The incredible story of how the gospel is transforming a Chicago neighborhood*. Grand Rapids, MI: Zondervan.
Gossett, Thomas. 1963. *Race: The History of an Idea in America*. Dallas: Southern Methodist University Press.
Grace, C., Bruchac, M. and S. Brimber. 2001. *1621: A new look at Thanksgiving*. Washington, D.C.: National Geographic Society.
Graddy, Kathryn 1997. "Do Fast-Food Chains Price Discriminate on the Race and Income Characteristics of an Area?" *Journal of Business and Economic Statistics*, 15(4)391-401.
Graham, Hugh Davis. 2002. *Collision Course: The Strange Convergence of Affirmative Action and Immigration Policy in America*. New York: Oxford University Press.
Otis-Graham, Lawrence. 1995. *Member of the Club: Reflections On Life in a Racially Polarized World*. New York: Harper Collins.
Graves, Joseph L. Jr. 2001. *The emperor's new clothes: Biological theories of race at the millennium*. New Brunswick, NJ: Rutgers University Press.
——. 2004. *The Race Myth: Why we pretend race exists in America*. New York: Penguin Books
Greeley, Andrew M., and Paul B. Sheatsley. 1971. "Attitudes toward Racial Integration." *Scientific American* 225: 13-19.
Greene, Lorenzo, and Carter G. Woodson. 1930. *The Negro Wage Earner*. New York: Association for the Study of Negro Life and History.
Grieco, Elizabeth M. and Cassidy, Rachel C. 2001. *US Bureau of the Census: Overview of Race and Hispanic Origin, Census Brief 2000* (March).
Grier, William H. and Price M. Cobbs. 1968. *Black Rage*. New York: Basic Books.
Groff, David H. 1999. A Mission to Civilize: The Republican Idea of Empire in France and West Africa, 1895-1930." *Journal of World History* 10: 488-91.

Gross, Ariella, 1998. "Litigating Whiteness: Trials of Racial Determination in the Nineteenth Century South," 108 *Yale Law Journal* 109.
Gross, Ariella. 2001. "Beyond Black and White: Cultural Approaches to Race and Slavery," 101 *Columbia Law Review* 640.
Gubrium, Jaber F. and James A. Holstein. 1998. "Narrative Practice and the Coherence of Personal Stories." *The Sociological Quarterly 39(1)*: 163–87.
Guglielmo, Thomas. 2004. *White on Arrival: Italians, Race, Color, and Power in Chicago, 1890–1945.* NY: Oxford University Press.
Guinier, Lani 2004. 'From Racial Liberalism to Racial Literacy: Brown v. Board of Education and the Interest-Divergence Dilemma.' *Journal of American History* 91: 92–118.
Guzman, Betsy. 2001. *US Bureau of the Census: The Hispanic Population, Census Brief 2000* (May).
Hacker, Andrew. 1992. *Two Nations: Black and White, Separate, Hostile, Unequal.* New York: Ballantine Books.
Hall, Edward T. 1959. *The Silent Language.* New York: Doubleday.
Hall, Elaine. 1988. "One Week for Women? The Structure of Inclusion of Gender Issues in Introductory Textbooks." *Teaching Sociology* 12:431–42.
Hall, Stuart. 1991. "Cultural Studies and its Theoretical Legacies." *Cultural Studies Reader*, edited by Cary Nelson, Lawrence Grossberg and Paula Treichler. New York: Routledge.
Halstead, Mark 1988. *Education, Justice, and Cultural Diversity: An Examination of the Honeyford Affair, 1984–85.* London: Falmer Press.
Hamamoto, Darrell Y. 1994. *Monitored Peril: Asian Americans and the Politics of TV Representation.* Minneapolis and London: University of Minnesota Press.
Haney Laney López, Ian. 1994. "The Social Construction of Race," 29 *Harvard Civil Rights and Civil Liberties Review.* 1.
Haney Laney López, Ian. 1997. "Race, Ethnicity, Erasure: The Salience of Race to LatCrit Theory," 85 *California Law Review* 1143.
——. 2003. *Racism on Trial: The Chicano Fight for Justice* Cambridge, Mass: Harvard University Press.
——. 2005. "Race on the 2010 Census: Hispanics and the Shrinking White Majority," 134 *Daedalus* 42.
——. 2006. *White By Law: The Legal Construction of Race* (revised ed.). New York: New York University Press.
Hanson, Victor Davis. 2003. *Mexifornia: A State of Becoming.* San Francisco, CA.: Encounter Books.
Harker, Julie 2010. "Settlement offer in Hispanic discrimination suit". *Brownfield: Ag News for America*, May 28, 2010. (Accessed on June 3, 2010, online at URL: http://brownfieldagnews.com/2010/05/28/settlement-offer-in-hispanic-discrimination-suit/)
Harlow, Roxanna. 2003. " "Race Doesn't Matter, but…": The Effect of Race on Professors' Experience and Emotion Management in the Undergraduate Classroom." *Social Psychology Quarterly* 66:348–363.
Harris, David. 1992. From Class Struggle to the Politics of Pleasure: The Effects of Gramscianism on Cultural Studies. New York: Routledge.
Harrison, Afterdneen. 1991. *Black Exodus: The Great Migration from the American South.* Jackson. MS: University Press of Mississippi.
Hartman, Heinz 1962. *Enterprise and Politics in South Africa.* Princeton, NJ: Industrial Relations Section, Princeton University.
Hartman, Saidiya, 2007. *Lose Your Mother A Journey Along the Atlantic Slave Route.* Farrar, Straus & Giroux: New York.
Harvey, Adia. 2008. *Doing Business with Beauty.* Lanham, Maryland: Rowman & Littlefield.

Heath, S. B. 1983. *Ways with words: Language, life and work in communities and classrooms*. University of Cambridge.
Heckman, James J., and Brooks S. Payner. 1992. "Determining the Impact of the Federal Antidiscrimination Policy on the Economic Status of Blacks: A Study of South Carolina." *American Economic Review* 79: 138–72.
Heilman, Madeline E., Caryn J. Block, and Peter Stathatos. 1997. "The Affirmative Action Stigma of Incompetence: Effects of Performance Information Ambiguity." *Academy of Management Journal* 40:603–25.
Helms, J. E. (ed.) 1990. *Black and white racial identity: Theory, research and practice*. Westport, CT: Greenwood Press.
Helms, J. E. 1995. *An update of Helms's White and People of Color racial identity model*. In J. G. Ponterotto, J. M. Casas, L. A. Suzuki, & C. M. Alexander (Eds.), Handbook of multicultural counseling *181–198*. Thousand Oaks, CA: Sage.
Henderson, Errol A. 2007. Navigating the Muddy Waters of the Mainstream: Tracing the Mystification of Racism in International Relations.' In *African American Perspectives on Political Science*, edited by Wilbur C. Rich. Philadelphia, PA: Temple University Press.
Henri, Florette. 1975. *Black Migration: Movement North, 1900–1920*. New York: Anchor Press, Doubleday.
Hernandez, Jesus. 2009. "Relining Revisited: Mortgage Lending Patterns in Sacramento 1930–2004." *International Journal of Urban and Regional Research* 33: 291–313.
Hernández, Tanya Katerí. 2002. "Multiracial Matrix: The Role of Race Ideology in the Enforcement of Antidiscrimination Laws, A United States-Latin America Comparison," 87 *Cornell Law Review* 1093.
Hernandez v. New York, 500 U.S. 352 (1991)
Hill, Robert. 1998. "Understanding Black Family Functioning: A Holistic Perspective." *Journal of Comparative Family Studies* 29(1):15–25.
Hill, Robert, Andrew Billingsley, Eleanor Engram, Michelene Malson, and Roger Stack. 1993. *Research on the African American Family: A Holistic Perspective*. Westport, CT: Auburn House.
Himelstein, Jerry 1983. 'Rhetorical Continuities in the Politics of Race. The Closed Society Revisited.' *Southern Speech Communication Journal* 48: 153–66.
Hipple, Steven. 2001. "Contingent Work in the Late-1990s," *Monthly Labor Review*, (March):
Hirsch, Arnold R. 1983. *Making the Second Ghetto: Race and Housing in Chicago, 1940–1960*. Cambridge: Cambridge University Press.
Hobbs, Frank and Stoops, Nicole. 2002. *US Bureau of the Census: Demographic Trends in the 20th Century: Census 2000 Special Reports* (November).
Hochschild, Jennifer. 2003. "From Nominal to Ordinal to Interval: Reconceiving Racial and Ethnic Hierarchy in the United States," paper delivered as Wesson Lectures, Stanford University, May 5 and 6, 2003.
Hochschild, Jennifer. 2005. "Looking Ahead: Racial Trends in the United States," *Daedalus* 134(1):70–81.
Holden, Stephen. 2009. "Meltdown on Wall Street, and Homeowners Left in the Lurch on Main Street." *New York Times*, September 2.
Holland, P.W. 1986. "Statistics and Causal Inference." *Journal of the American Statistical Association* 81:945–70.
Hollinger, David A. 1995., *Post-Ethnic America: Beyond Multiculturalism*. New York: Basic Books.
Hollinger, David A. 2003. "Amalgamation and Hypodescent: The Question of Ethnoracial Mixture in the History of the United States," 108 (1) *American Historical Review*.
Holt, Thomas. 2000. *The Problem of Race in the 21st Century*. Cambridge, MA: Harvard University Press.

Holzer, Harry J. 1995. *What Employers Want: Job Prospects for Less- Educated Workers.* New York: Russell Sage.
Holzer, Harry J. and Michael A. Stoll (2003). "Employer Demand for Welfare Recipients by Race." *Journal of Labor Economics,* 21: 210–241.
Hooks, Bell. 1992. *Black Looks: Race and Representation.* Boston: South End Press.
Horwitz, Kevin 1997. *White South African Kinship and Identity.* Unpublished Dissertation. Johannesburg, South Africa: University of the Witwatersrand.
Hout, Michael. 1984. "Occupational Mobility of Black Men: 1962–1973." *American Sociological Review* 49: 308–322.
Howard, Judith A. 2000. 'Social Psychology of Identities.' *Annual Review of Sociology* 26: 367– 93.
HUD – U.S. Treasury Report on Predatory Lending, 2001. U.S. Department of Housing and Urban Development. URL accessed on line on October 13, 2006 at http://www.hud.gov/library/bookshelf12/pressrel/treasrpt.pdf.
Hughes, Diane and Deborah Johnson 2001. 'Correlates of Children's Experiences of Parents' Racial Socialization Behaviors.' *Journal of Marriage and the Family* 63: 981–95.
Hughes, Everett C. 1945. "Dilemmas and Contradictions of Status." *American Journal of Sociology* 50(5): 353–59.
Human Rights Watch, *Race and Incarceration in the United States,* http://www.hrw.org/backgrounder/usa/race
Human Rights Watch. 2000. *Punishment and Prejudice: Racial Disparities in the War on Drugs.*
Huntington, Samuel P. 2004. *Who Are We? The Challenges to America's National Identity.*
Hyman, Herbert H., and Paul B. Sheatsley. 1964. "Attitudes Toward Desegregation." *Scientific American* 211: 16–23.
Ibarra, Herminia 1993. Personal Networks of Women and Minorities in Management: A Conceptual Framework." *Academy of Management Review* 18:46–87. ......1995. "Race, Opportunity and Diversity of Social Circles in Managerial Networks." *Academy of Management Journal* 38:673–703.
Ifill, Gwen. 2009. *The Breakthrough.* New York: Doubleday.
Ignatiev, Noel. 1996. *How the Irish Became White.* New York: Routledge.
ITWire, 2010. "How to let Staff Use Their Personal Technology Securely". *ITWire,* April 12, 2010. (Accessed on April 28, 2010, online at URL: http://www.itwire.com/sponsored-announcements/38210-how-to-let-staff-use-their-personal-technology-securely.)
Izard, Carroll E. 1972. *Patterns of Emotions: A New Analysis of Anxiety and Depression.* New York: Academic Press.
———. 1977. *Human Emotions.* New York: Plenum Press.
Jackman, Mary R., and Marie Crane. 1986. "'Some of My Best Friends are Black…' Interracial Friendship and Whites' Racial Attitudes." *Public Opinion Quarterly* 50: 459–486.
Jackman, Mary and Robert Jackman. 1980. "Racial Inequality in Home Ownership." *Social Forces* 58:1221–54.
Jackman, Mary. 1994. *The Velvet Glove: Paternalism and Conflict in Gender, Class, and Race Relations.* Berkley: University of California Press.
Jackman, Mary and Michael Muha. 1984. "Education and Intergroup Attitudes: Moral Enlightenment, Superficial Democratic Commitment, or Ideological Refinement?" *American Sociological Review* 49:751–69.
Jackson, Kenneth T. 1985. *Crabgrass Frontier: The Suburbanization of the United States.* New York: Oxford University Press.
Jacobs, David and Robert M. O'Brien 1998. 'The Determinants of Deadly Force: A Structural Analysis of Police Violence.' *American Journal of Sociology* 103: 837–62.

Jacobson, Matthew Frye 1998. *Whiteness of a Different Color: European Immigrants and the Alchemy of Race*, Cambridge, MA: Harvard University Press.

Janiewski, Dolores E. 2004. 'Taking Land, Breaking Land: Women Colonizing the American West and Kenya (Review).' *Journal of Colonialism and Colonial History* 5: 99–101.

Jargowsky, Paul. 2003. *Stunning Progress, Hidden Problems: The Dramatic Decline of Concentrated Poverty in the 1990s*. Washington, DC: Brookings Institution.

Jaynes, Gerald. 1990. "The Labor Market Status of Black Americans: 1939–1985." *Journal of Economic Perspectives* 4: 9–24.

Jaynes, Gerald D., and Robin M. Williams, editors. 1989. *A Common Destiny: Blacks and American Society*. Washington, D.C.: National Academy Press.

Johnson, Erik, Sonja Clark, Matthew Donald, Rachel Pedersen, and Catherine Pinchotta. 2007. "Racial Disparity in Minnesota's Child Protection System." *Child Welfare* 86(4):5–20.

Johnson, Kevin. 2003. "FBI reports small drop in crime rates." *USA Today*, (assessed on line on October 26, 2006 at URL http://www.usatoday.com/news/washington/2003-06-16-fbi-crime_x.htm.

Johnson, H. B. 1998. *Black Wall Street: From riot to renaissance in Tulsa's historic greenwood district*. Austin, TX: Eakin Press.

Jones, Trina. 2000. "Shades of Brown: The Law of Skin Color," 49 *Duke Law Journal* 49: 1487–1557.

Joy, Bill. 2000. "Why the future doesn't need us." *Wired* (April):238–262.

Kaestner, Robert and Wendy Fleischer. 1992. "Income Inequality as an Indicator of Discrimination in Housing Markets." *The Review of Black Political Economy* 20: 55–77.

Kalev, Alexandra, Frank Dobbin and Erin Kelly. 2006. "Best Practices or Best Guesses? Assessing the Efficacy of Corporate Affirmative Action and Diversity Policies." *American Sociological Review* 71(4):589–617.

Kalmijn, Matthijs. 1993. "Trends in Black/White Intermarriage," *Social Forces* 72(1):119–146.

Kanter, Rosabeth Moss. 1977. *Men and Women of the Corporation*. New York, NY: Basic Books.

Katz, Judith H. and Karen R. Moore. 2004. "Racism in the Workplace: OD Practitioners' Role in Change." *OD Practitioner*, 36(4): 13–16.

Katz, Michael B. 1993. "Reframing the 'Underclass Debate.'" In *The "Underclass" Debate: Views from History*, ed. Michael B. Katz, pp. 440–78. Princeton: Princeton University Press.

Kaur, Ravinder. 2002. "Viewing the West through Bollywood: A Celluloid Occident in the Making." *Contemporary South Asia* 11:119–209.

Kelley, Robin D.G. 2003. *Freedom Dreams: The Black Radical Imagination*. Boston: Beacon Press.

——. 1993. "The Black Poor and the Politics of Opposition in a New South City, 1929–1970." In *The "Underclass" Debate: Views from History*, ed. Michael B. Katz, pp. 293–333. Princeton: Princeton University Press.

——. 1997. "The Proletariat Goes to College," in *Will Teach for Food: Academic Labor in Crisis*, ed. Cary Nelson. Minneapolis: U of Minnesota Press.

Kellstedt, Paul M. 2000. 'Media Framing and the Dynamics of Racial Policy Preferences.' *American Journal of Political Science* 44: 245–60.

Kendall, Diana. 1999. "Doing a Good Deed or Confounding the Problem? Peer Review and Sociology Textbooks." *Teaching Sociology*. 27:17–30.

Kennedy, Randall. 1997. "My Race Problem, and Ours." *Atlantic* 279(5): 55–66.

Kerner,

Kibria, Nazli. 2000. "Race, Ethnic Options, and Ethnic Binds: Identity Negotiations of Second-Generation Chinese and Korean Americans." *Sociological Perspectives* 43:77–95.

Killen, Melanie 2004. 'Social Reasoning about Racial Exclusion in Intimate and Nonintimate Relationship.' *Youth and Society* 35: 293-322.
Killian, Lewis. 1990. "Race Relations and the Nineties: Where Are the Dreams of the Sixties?" *Social Forces* 69(1):1-3.
Kim, Claire Jean, and Taeku Lee. 2001. "Interracial Politics: Asian Americans and Other Communities of Color." *Political Science and Politics* 34:631-637.
Kinder, D. R., and D. O. Sears. 1981. "Prejudice and Politics: Symbolic Racism Versus Racial Threats to the Good Life." *Journal of Personality and Social Psychology* 40:414-431.
Kinder, Donald and Lynne Sanders 1996. *Divided by Color. Racial Politics and Democratic Ideals*. Chicago, IL: University of Chicago Press.
King, T. 2003. *The truth about stories: A native narrative*. Minneapolis, MN: University of Minnesota Press.
Kirschenman, Joleen and Kathryn M. Neckerman. 1994. "'We'd Love To Hire Them, But…': The Meaning of Race for Employers." In *Race and Ethnic Conflict*, edited by Fred L. Pincus and Howard J. Erlich. Boulder: Westview Press.
Kivel, P. 1996. *Uprooting racism: How white people can work for racial justice*. Gabriola Island, BC: New Society Publishers.
Kleppner, Paul 1985. *Chicago Divided: The Making of a Black Mayor*. DeKalb, IL: Northern Illinois University Press.
Klor de Alva, Jorge. 1996 "Our Next Race Question," *Harper's*, (April): 55-63.
Kluegal, J.R. 1990. "Trends in Whites' Explanations of the Black-White Gap in Socioeconomic Status, 1977-1989." *American Sociological Review* 55:512-525.
Konrad, Alison. M. and Frank. Linnehan. 1995. "Formalized HRM Structures: Coordinating Equal-Employment Opportunity or Concealing Organizational Practices." *Academy of Management Journal* 38:787-820.
Kovarsky, Irving, and William Albrecht. 1970. *Black Employment: The Impact of Religion, Economic Theory, Politics, and Law*. Ames: The Iowa Satre University Press.
Kozol, Jonathan. 1991. *Savage Inequalities: Children in America's Schools*. New York: HarperCollins.
——. 2005. *The shame of the nation: The restoration of apartheid schooling in America*. New York: Crown.
Kraiger, Kurt, and J. Kevin Ford. 1990. "The Relation of Job Knowledge, Job Performance, and Supervisory Ratings as a Function of Ratee Race." *Human Performance*, 3(4): 269-279.
Krieger, Nancy and Sstephen Sidney. 1996. "Racial Discrimination and Blood Pressure: The CARDIA Study of Young Black and White Adults." *American Journal of Public Health* 86:1370-1378.
Kumar, Anup. 2005. Bollywood and the Diaspora: The Flip Side of Globalization and Hybridity in the Construction of Identities. PhD. Seminar, School of Journalism and Mass Communication, University of Iowa.
Ladson-Billings, Gloria. 1996. "Silences as Weapons: Challenges of a Black Professor Teaching White Students." *Theory into Practice* 35:79-85.
Ladson-Billings, Gloria and William F. Tate. 1995. "Toward a Critical Race Theory of Education." *Teachers College Record* 97:47-68.
LaGumina, Salvatore. 1989. "Fullerton and the Italians: Experiment in Agriculture." *Long Island Forum* (February).
——. 1985. "Long Island Italians and the Labor Movement." *Long Island Forum* (January).
Landry, Bert. 1987. *The New Black Middle Class*. Berkeley: The University of California Press.
Las Casas, B. 1989. *The log of Christopher Columbus's first voyage to America in the year 1492*. Hamden, CT: Linnet Books.

Lav, Iris J., and Andrew Brecher. 2004. *Passing Down the Deficit: Federal Policies Contribute to the Severity of the State Fiscal Crisis*. Center on Budget and Policy Priorities, Washington, DC, May 12.

Lee, C.D., Rosenfeld, E., Mendenhall, R., Rivers, A., and B. Tynes. 2003. Cultural modeling as a frame for narrative analysis. In Colette Daiute & Cynthia Lightfoot (Eds), Narrative *analysis: Studying the development of individuals in society*. Thousand Oaks, CA: Sage Publications.

Lehrman, Sally 2007. *Color-Blind Racism*. Maynard Institute. http://www.maynardije.org/news/ features/040913_lehrman-part2/sidebar1/ (last accessed on October 21, 2007).

Leiman, Melvin M. 1992. *Political Economy of Racism*. London: Pluto Press.

Leiter, Jeffrey 1986. 'Reactions to Subordination: Attitudes of Southern Textile Workers.' *Social Forces* 64: 948–74.

Leonard, Jonathan S 1989. "Women and Affirmative Action." *The Journal of Economic Perspectives* 3:61–75.

——. 1990. "The Impact of Affirmative Action Regulation and Equal Employment Law on Black Employment." *Journal of Economic Perspectives* 4: 47–63.

Lewis, Amanda. 2003. "Some are More Equal than Others: Lessons on Whiteness from School." Pp. 159–172 in *White Out: The Continuing Significance of Racism*, edited by Eduardo Bonilla-Silva and Ashley Doane Jr. New York: Routledge.

——. 2004. 'What Group: Studying Whites and Whiteness in an Era of "Color-Blindness"'. *Sociological Theory* 22: 623–46.

Lewis, David L. 2001. *W.E.B. Du Bois: The Fight for Equality and the American Century, 1919–1963*. New York, NY: Owl Books.

Lewis, Oscar 1996. 'The Culture of Poverty.' In *Urban Life*, edited by George Gmelch and Walter P. Zenner. Prospect Heights, IL: Waveland Press.

Li Leiwei, David 2004. 'On Ascriptive and Acquisitional Americanness: The Accidental Asian and the Illogic of Assimilation.' *Contemporary Literature* 45: 106–34.

Liazos, A. 1972. "The poverty of the sociology of deviance: Nuts, sluts and perverts." *Social Problems* 20(1): 103–120.

Liberman, Vadim. 2003. "Workplace Diversity: It's All in the Mix." *Across the Board* XL: 51–2.

Lichter, Daniel T. 2010. "U.S. Far From an Interracial Melting Pot." *CNN*, June 16. Available at http://www.cnn.com/2010/OPINION/06/14/lichter.interracial.marriage/index.html?iref=allsearch

Lieberson, Stanley, and Mary C. Watters. 1988. *From Many Strands: Ethnic and Racial Groups in Contemporary America*. New York: Russell Sage Foundation.

Lieberman, Leonard 1968. 'The Debate over Race: A Study in the Sociology of Knowledge.' *Phylon* (1960) 28: 127–41.

Lind, Michael. 1995. *The Next American Nation: The New Nationalism and the Fourth American Revolution*. New York: Free Press.

Lind, Michael. 1998. "The Beige and the Black," *N.Y. Times Magazine*, Aug. 16: 38–39.

Lipsitz, George 1995. 'Toxic Racism.' *American Quarterly* 47: 416–27.

——. 1998. *The Possessive Investment in Whiteness: How White People Profit from Identity Politics*. Philadelphia, PA: Temple University Press.

Littell, Franklin H. 1965. 'From Persecution or Toleration to Liberty Theory into Practice.' *Our Religious Heritage and the Schools* 4: 3–7.

Livingston, Robert. 2001. "What You See is What You Get: Systematic Variability in Perceptual-Based Social Judgment". *Personality and Social Psychology Bulletin*. 27(9): 1086–1096.

Loewen, J. 1995. *Lies my teacher told me*. New York, NY: Touchstone.

Loewen, James W. 2005. *Sundown Towns: A Hidden Dimension of American Racism*. New York, NY: New Press.

Logan, John R. 2003. "Ethnic Diversity Grows, Neighborhood Integration Lags." In *Redefining Urban and Suburban America: Evidence from Census 2000, Volume One*,

edited by Bruce Katz and Robert E. Lang. Washington, D.C.: Brookings Institution Press.
Lomas, Clara. 2003. "Latina Feminisms: Reflections on Theory, Practice, and Pedagogy Emerging in Telling to Live." in *16th Annual MALCS Summer Institute*. San Antonio, TX.
Lopez, Mark Hugh, Gretchen Livingston, and Rakesh Kochhar. 2009. *Hispanics and the Economic Downturn: Housing Woes and Remittance Cuts*. Washington, D.C.:Pew Hispanic Center. January 8.
Loving v. Virginia, 388 U.S. 1 (1967).
Lower-Basch 2001. "TANF "Leavers", Applicants, and Caseload Studies: Preliminary Analysis of Racial Differences in Caseload Trends and Leaver Outcomes". U.S. Department of Health and Human Services (Accessed at http://aspe.hhs.gov/hsp/leavers99/race.htm on Sept. 5, 2008.)
Lui Meizhu, Barbara J. Robles, Betsy Leondar-Wright, Rose M. Brewer, and Rebecca Adamson. 2006. *The Color of Wealth: The Story Behind the U.S. Racial Wealth Divide*. New York: The New Press.
Lusane, Clarence. 1994. *African Americans at the Crossroads: The Restructuring of Black Leadership and the 1992 Elections*. Boston: South End Press.
Lynn, Marvin, Tara J. Yosso, and Daniel G. Solórzano. 2002. "Critical Race Theory and Education: Qualitative Research in the New Millennium." *Qualitative Inquiry* 8:3–6.
Marable, Manning. 1983. *How Capitalism Underdeveloped Black America*. Boston: South End Press.
Marcus, Grania Bolton. 1983. *Discovering the African American Experience in Suffolk County, 1620–1860* Mattituck, NY: Amereon House.
Marks, Carole. 1991. "The Social and Economic Life of Southern Blacks During the Migration." In *Black Exodus: The Great Migration from the American South*, edited by Alferdteen Harrison. Jackson: University of Mississippi Press.
Marks, Jonathan. 1995. *Human Biodiversity: Genes, Race, and History*. (New York: Aldine De Gruyter).
——. 2002. *What it means to be 98% chimpanzee*. Berkeley: University of California Press.
Marquez, Stephanie Amedeo. 1994. "Distorting the Image of 'Hispanic' Women in Sociology: Problematic Strategies of Presentation in the Introductory Text." *Teaching Sociology* 22:231–36.
Martinez, Elizabeth. 1998. *De Colores Means All of Us*. MA: South End Press.
Massey, Douglas, and Nancy Denton. 1993. *American Apartheid: Segregation and the Making of the American Underclass*. Cambridge.: Harvard University Press.
Massey, Douglas, and Nancy Denton. 1988. 'The Dimensions of Residential Segregation.' *Social Forces* 67: 281–315.
Massey, Douglas, and Nancy Denton. 1989. 'Hypersegregation in U.S. Metropolitan Areas: Black and Hispanic Segregation Along Five Dimensions.' *Demography* 26: 373–91.
Mattelart, Armand and Siegelaub, Seth (eds.). 1979. *Communication and Class Struggle: Capitalism, Imperialism*. London: International General Publishers.
McAdam, Douglas. 1982. *Political Process and the Development of Black Insurgency, 1930–1970*. Chicago: The University of Chicago Press.
McAndrews, Lawrence J. 1998. 'The Politics of Principle: Richard Nixon and School Desegregation.' *Journal of Negro History* 83: 187–200.
McCrum, Mukami. 1999. "Letter" cited in WCC (World Council of Churches) 1999. "Understanding Racism Today: A Dossier" (Accessed on line September 28, 2006, at URL http://www.wcc-coe.org/wcc/what/jpc/doss-e.html).
MCCleskey v. Kemp, 481 U.S. 279 (1987)
McDaniel, Antonio. 1995. "The Dynamic Racial Composition of the United States," *Daedalus* 124(1):179–198

McGoey, Chris. 2006. "Racial Profiling: Retail Store Shoplifting". (URL accessed October 13, 2006 at http://www.crimedoctor.com/shoplifting5.htm.)
McHugh, Peter. 1968. *Defining the Situation: The Organization of Meaning in Social Interaction*. New York: Bobbs-Merrill.
McIntosh, Peggy. 1995. "White Privilege and Male Privilege: A Personal Account of Coming to See Correspondences through Work in Women's Studies." Pp. 76–87 in *Race, Class, and Gender: An Anthology*, edited by Margaret Andersen and Patricia Hill Collins. Belmont: Wadsworth.
McWorter, John 2000. *Losing the Race: Self-Sabotage in Black America*. Glencoe, IL: Free Press.
——. 2006. *Winning the Race: Beyond the Crisis in Black America*. New York: Gotham Books.
Mauer, Marc. 1999. *Race to Incarcerate*. New York: The Sentencing Project.
Maxwell, Bill. 2003. "Names of pride or labels for stereotypes?," *St. Petersburg Times*, (February 12). (Accessed on April 23, 2007 at url http://www.sptimes.com/2003/02/12/news_pf/Columns/Names_of_pride_or_lab.shtml).
Melendez, Miguel. 2003. *We Took the Streets: Fighting for Latinos with the Young Lords*. New York: St. Martin's Press.
Merriam-Webster, Accessed on line at URL: http://www.merriam-webster.com/dictionary/indo%20aryan, on August 15, 2009.
Merton, Robert K. 1957. *Social Theory and Social Structure*. New York: Free Press.
Meyer, John W. and Brian Rowan. 1977. "Institutionalized Organizations: Formal Structure as Myth and Ceremony." *The American Journal of Sociology* 83(2):340–363.
Mills, Charles. 1997. *The Racial Contract*. Ithaca: Cornell University Press.
Miles, Matthew B. and A. Michael Huberman. 1994. *Qualitative Data Analysis: An Expanded Sourcebook*. 2nd edition. Thousand Oaks: Sage Publications.
Mohl, Raymond. 2000. "Planned Destruction: The Interstates and Central City Housing." In John F. Bauman, Roger Biles and Kristin Szylvian, editors. *From Tenements to Taylor Homes: In Search of an Urban Housing Policy in Twentieth-Century America*. University Park, Pennsylvania: State University Press, pp. 226–245.
Morris, Aldon. 1984. *The Origins of the Civil Rights Movement: Black Communities Organizing for Change*. New York: Free Press.
Morris, Benny 2006. 'Power without Grace Is a Curse.' *The Guardian*, February 9, 2006. http://www.guardian.co.uk/usa/story/0,,1705532,00.html (last accessed on line on July 18, 2007).
Morrison, Toni 1992. *Playing in the Dark: Whiteness and the Literary Imagination*. Cambridge, MA: Harvard University Press.
Moss, Philip, and Chris Tilly. 2001. *Stories Employers Tell: Race, Skill, and Hiring in America*. New York: Russell Sage Foundation.
Moynihan, Daniel P. 1968. 'Toward a National Urban Policy.' *Public Interests* (**Fall**): 8–9.
Murdock, Steve H. and David R. Ellis. 1991. *Applied Demography: An Introduction to Basic Concepts, Methods, and Data*. Boulder: Westview Press.
Myrdal, Gunnar. [1944] 1964. *An American Dilemma*. New York: McGraw-Hill.
National Fair Housing Alliance (2006). "2006 Fair Housing Trends: Unequal Opportunity- Perpetuating Housing Segregation in America. (Accessed on Oct. 13, 2006 at Url http://www.nationalfairhousing.org/resources/newsArchive/resource_20628126054870386567.pdf.)
Nayar, Sheila. 2003. "Dreams, Dharma and Mrs. Doubtfire: Exploring Hindi Popular Cinema Via Its 'Chutneyed' Western Scripts." *Journal of Popular Film and Television* 31:73–82.
Ndikumana, Leonce and James Boyce 1998. 'Congo's Odious Debt: External Borrowing and Capital Flight in Zaire.' *Development and Change* 29: 195–217.

Neckerman, Kathryn M., and Joleen Kirschenman. 1991. "Hiring Strategies, Racial Bias, and Inner-City Workers." *Social Problems* 38 (November):433–47.

"New Latino Nation," *Newsweek*, May 30, 2005, pp. 28–29.

Newman, Kathe and Elvin K. Wyly. 2004. "Geographies of Mortgage Market Segmentation: The Case of Essex County, New Jersey." *Housing Studies* 19: 53–83.

Nieto, S. 1996. *Affirming diversity: The sociopolitical context of multicultural education.* (2nd ed.) New York, NY: Longman Publishers.

Nkrumah, Kwame 1965. *Neo-Colonialism, The Last Stage of Imperialism.* London: Thomas Nelson & Sons.

Norton, Mary Beth, David M. Katzman, David W. Blight, Howard P. Chudacoff, Fredrik Logevall, Beth Bailey, Thomas G. Paterson, William M. Tuttle, Jr. 1990. *A People and a Nation: A History of the United States.* Boston: Houghton Mifflin.

Oakes, Jeannie, Molly Selvin, Lynn Karoly and Gretchen Guiton. 1992. *Educational Matchmaking: Academic and Vocational Tracking in Comprehensive High Schools.* Santa Monica, CA: Rand.

Obama, Barak. 2004. *The Audacity of Hope: Thoughts on Reclaiming the American Dream.* New York: Crown Publishers.

———. 2007. "Selma Voting Rights Commemoration." Speech at Brown University Chapel, Selma, AL, March 4.

———. 2008. "A More Perfect Union." Speech in Philadelphia, March 18.

Orfield, G. and E. Frankenberg. 2004. Where are we now? *Teaching Tolerance*, (Spring) 25: 57–59.

O'Hare, William, Kelvin Pollard, Taynia Mann, and Mary Kent. 1991. "African Americans in the 1990s." *Population Bulletin* 46, no. 1.

Olivas, Michael A. 1990. "The Chronicles, My Grandfather's Stories, and Immigration Law: The Slave Traders Chronicle as Racial History." *Saint Louis University Law Journal* 34:425–441.

Oliver, Melvin, and Thomas M. Shapiro. 2001. "Wealth and Racial Stratification." In *America Becoming: Racial Trends and Their Consequences, Volume 2,* edited by N. J. Smelser, W. J. Wilson, and F. Mitchell. Washington, D.C.: National Academy Press.

———. 2006. *Black Wealth/White Wealth.* New York: Routledge.

Omi, Michael and Howard Winant 1994. *Racial Formation in the United States: From 1960s to 1990s.* New York, NY: Routledge Press.

Orfield, Gary. 1993. "School Desegregation after Two Generations: Race, Schools and Opportunity in Urban Society." In *Race in America*, edited by Herbert Hill and James E. Jones. Madison: University of Wisconsin Press.

———. 2001. *Schools More Separate: Consequences of a Decade of Resegregation.* Cambridge, MA: Harvard University, Civil Rights Project.

Orfield, Gary and Franklin Monfort. 1992. *Status of School Desegregation: The Next Generation.* Alexandria, Va: National School Boards Association.

Orfield, Gary, and Chungmei Lee. 2005. *Why Segregation Matters: Poverty and Educational Inequality.* Cambridge, MA: The Civil Rights Project, Harvard University.

Osada, Masako. 2002. *Sanctions and Honorary Whites: Diplomatic Policies and Economic Realities in Relations Between Japan and South Africa.* Westport, Ct: Greenwood Press.

Otto, et al. 1968. *Report of the National Advisory Commission on Civil Disorders.* Washington, D.C.: Bantam.

Pager, Devah. 2003. "The Mark of a Criminal Record." *American Journal of Sociology* 108: 937–975.

———. 2007. *Marked: Race, crime, and finding work in an era of mass incarceration.* Chicago: University of Chicago Press.

Pager, Devah and Hana Shepherd. 2008. "The Sociology of Discrimination: Racial Discrimination in Employment, Housing, Credit, and Consumer Markets." *Annual Review of Sociology* 34: 181–209.

Palmore, Erdman, and Frank J. Whittington. 1970. "Differential Trends Towards Equality Between Whites and Nonwhites." *Social Forces* 49: 108–117.
Passel, Jeffrey S., Wendy Wang, and Paul Taylor. 2010. *Marrying Out*. Washington, D.C.: Pew Research Center. June 15.
Patterson, Ernest. 1974. *City Politics*. New York: Dood, Mead, and Co.
Pearce, Diana M. 1979. 'Gatekeepers and Home Seekers: Institutional Patterns in Racial Steering.' *Social Problems* 26: 325–42.
Pearson, A. R., Dovidio, J. F., amd S.L. Gaertner. 2009. The nature of contemporary prejudice: Insights from aversive racism. *Social and Personality Psychology Compass*, 3, 314–338 (DOI.10-.1111/j.1751-9004.2009.00183-x).
Pelta, K. (1991). *Discovering Christopher Columbus: How history is invented*. Minneapolis, MN: Lerner Publications Company.
Penner, L. A., Dovidio, J. F., West, T. V., Gaertner, S. L., Albrecht, T. L., Dailey, R. K., and T. Markova, T. 2010. Aversive racism and medical interactions with Black patients: A field study. *Journal of Experimental Social Psychology*, 46, 436–440.
Perdue, Charles W., John F. Dovidio, Michael B. Guttman, and Richard B. Tyler. 1990. "'Us' and 'Them': Social Categorization and the Process of Intergroup Bias." *Journal of Personality and Social Psychology* 59:475–86.
Perry, James. 2005. "Bourbon Street Discrimination Audit" conducted by the Greater New Orleans Fair Housing Center. (URL assessed on Oct. 12, 2006 at http://www.gnofairhousing.org/index.html.)
Pescosolido, B.A., E. Grauerholz, and M.A. Milkie. 1997. "Culture and Conflict: The Portrayal of Blacks in U.S. Children's Picture Books Though the Mid- and Late-Twentieth Century." *American Sociological Review* 62:443–463.
Pettigrew, Thomas. 1980. *The Sociology of Race Relations*. New York: Free Press.
Pettigrew, Thomas F. 1994. "New Patterns of Prejudice: The Different Worlds of 1984 and 1964." In *Race and Ethnic Conflict*, edited by Fred L. Pincus and Howard J. Erlich. Boulder, CO: Westview Press.
Pettigrew, Thomas F., and Joanne Martin. 1987. "Shaping the Organizational Context for Black American Inclusion." *Journal of Social Issues* 43: 41–78.
PEW Hispanic Center. 2002. *2002 National Survey of Latinos, Summary of Findings*.
PEW Research Center. 2007. *Optimism about Black Progress Declines: Blacks See Growing Values Gap Between Poor and Middle Class*. Washington, DC, November 13.
Pfuhl, Erdwin, and Stuart Henry. 1993. *The Deviance Process*, 3rd ed. New York: Aldine de Gruyter.
Phinney, J. S. 1990. Ethnic identity in adolescents and adults: Review of research. *Psychological Bulletin*, 108(3), 499–514.
Picca, Leslie Houts and Joe R. Feagin 2007. *Two-Faced Racism: Whites in the Backstage and Frontstage*. UK: Taylor and Francis.
Picker, Miguel. 2001. *Mickey Mouse Monopoly: Disney, Childhood and Corporate Power*. Art Media.
Pierce, Chester. 1970. "Offensive Mechanisms." Pp. 265–282 in *The Black Seventies*, edited by F. B. Barbour. Boston, MA: Porter Sargent.
——. 1974. "Psychiatric Problems of the Black Minority." Pp. 512–523 in *American Handbook of Psychiatry*, edited by G. Caplan and S. Arieti. New York: Basic Books.
——. 1975. "The Mundane Extreme Environment and Its Effect on Learning." Pp. 111–119 in *Learning Disabilities: Issues and Recommendations for Research*, edited by S. G. Brainard. Washington DC: National Institute of Education, Department of Health, Education, and Welfare.
——. 1980. "Social Trace Contaminants: Subtle Indicator of Racim in TV." Pp. 249–257 in *Television and Social Behavior: Beyond Violence and Children*, edited by S. B. Withey and R. P. Abeles. Hillsdale, NJ: Lawrence Erlbaum.

——. 1989. "Unity in Diversity: Thirty-Three Years of Stress." Pp. 296–312 in *Black Students: Psychosocial Issues and Academic Achievement* edited by G. L. Berry and J. K. Asamen. Newbury Park, CA: Sage.
——. 1995. "Stress Analogs of Racism and Sexism: Terrorism, Torture, and Disaster." Pp. 277–293 in *Mental Health, Racism and Sexism*, edited by C. Willie, P. Rieker, B. Kramer, and B. Brown. Pittsburgh: University of Pittsburg Press.
Pilgrim, David 2002. 'The Jezebel Stereotype.' *Jim Crow Museum*, http://www.ferris.edu/news/jimcrow/menu.htm (last accessed July 10, 2010).
Piliawsky, Monte 1984. 'Racial Equality in the United States: From Institutionalized Racism to 'Respectable' Racism.' *Phylon* (1960–) 45: 135–43.
Pinderhughes, E. 1989. *Understanding race, ethnicity, and power: The key to efficacy in clinical practice*. New York, NY: Free Press.
Pine, G.J. and A. G. Hilliard, III. 1990. Rx for racism: Imperatives for America's Schools". *Phi Delta Kappan*, 71, 593–600.
Pinkney, Alphonso. 1984. *The Myth of Black Progress*. Cambridge, England: Cambridge University Press.
——. 1993. *Black Americans, Fourth Edition*. Englewood, NJ: Prentice Hall.
Piper, Adrian. 1996. "Passing for White, Passing for Black," in *Passing and the Fictions of Identity* edited by Elaine K. Ginsberg. Durham, NC: Duke University Press.
Plessy v. Ferguson, 163 U.S. 537 (1896).
Plimoth Plantation. 2006. *Wampanoag homesite*. Retrieved September 2, 2005, from url at http://www.plimoth.org/visit/what/hobbamock.asp.
Pomer, Marshall. 1986. "Labor Market Structure, Intragenerational Mobility, and Discrimination: Black Male Advancement Out of Low-paying Occupations, 1962–1973." *American Sociological Review* 51: 650–59.
Prendergast, Jane. 2002. "Cincinnati Riots, One Year Later: Violence up, arrest down". *The Cincinnati Enquirer* (April 7). (Assessed on line on October 26, 2006, at URL http://www.enquirer.com/oneyearlater/).
Prillerman, Shelly L., Hector F. Myers, and Brian D. Smedley. 1989. "Stress, Well-Being, and Academic Achievement in College." Pp. 198–217 in *Black Students: Psychosocial Issues and Academic Achievement*, edited by G. L. Berry and J. K. Asamen. Newbury Park, CA: Sage.
Prison Reform Trust. 2006.. Experiences of Minority Ethnic Employers in Prison. (Assessed on line on October 23, 2006 at URL http://www.prisonreformtrust.org.uk/subsection.asp?id=640)
Prosise, Theodore O. 2004. "Law Enforcement and Crime on Cops and World's Wildest Police Videos: Anecdotal Form and the Justification of Racial Profiling." *Western Journal of Communication*. (Winter). (Assessed on line October 26, 2006, at URL http://www.allbusiness.com/legal/laws/987095-1.html).
Punanov, Grigory and Yury Spirin 2002. 'Police Didn't Notice Anything Wrong.' *Current Digest of the Post Soviet Press* **54**: 13.
Purkayastha, Bandana. 2005. *Negotiating Ethnicity: Second-Generation South Asian Americans Traverse a Transnational World*. Rutgers University Press.
Purvis, Michaek 2004. ' "Genteel" Racism Still with Us, Speaker Says.' *Sault Star*, May 7, 2004. http://www.debwewin.ca/articles.htm#article3 (last accessed July 12, 2007).
Quillian, Lincoln. 1999. "Migration Patterns and the Growth of High-Poverty Neighborhoods, 1970–1990." *American Journal of Sociology* 105(1):1–37.
Rajagopal, Arvind. 2001. *Politics after Television: Hindu Nationalism and the Reshaping of the Public in India*. Cambridge University Press.
Rainville, R. E. and E. McCormick, E. 1977. Extent of covert racial prejudice in pro football announcers' speech. *Journalism Quarterly*, 54(1):20–26.
Rambally, Rae Tucker 2002. *Practice Imperfect Reflections on a Career in Social Work*. Ste-Anne-de-Bellevue, QC: Shoreline.

Rattray, Everett. 1979. *The South Fork: The Land and People of Eastern Long Island.* New York: Random House.
Reed, Wornie L., and Bertin M. Louis, Jr. 2009. "No More Excuses." *Journal of African American Studies* 13:97–109.
Reich, Michael. 1981. *Racial Inequality: A Political-Economic Analysis.* Princeton: Princeton University Press.
Reskin, Barbara F. 2003. "Including Mechanisms in Our Models of Ascriptive Inequality." *American Sociological Review.* 68:1–21.
———. 2000. "The Proximate Causes of Employment Discrimination." *Contemporary Sociology* 29(2):319–328.
———. 1998. *The Realities of Affirmative Action.* Washington D.C.: American Sociological Association.
Ricardson, Lisa and Fields, Robin. 2003. "Latinos Account for Majority of Births in California," *L.A. Times* (Feb. 6): A1.
Riessman, Catherine Kohler. 1993. *Narrative Analysis.* Newbury Park: Sage Publications.
Ritterhouse, Jennifer 2006. *Growing up in Jim Crow: The Racial Socialization of White and Black Southern Children: 1890–1940.* Chapel Hill, NC: University of North Carolina Press.
Rifkin, Jeremy. 1995. *The End of Work: The Decline of the Global Labor Force and the Dawn of the Post-Market Era.* New York: Putnam.
Rivken, Stephen. 1994. "Residential Segregation and School Integration." *Sociology of Education* 67: 279–92.
Rivlin, Gary. 2000. "Busting the Myth of the Meritocracy," *The Industry Standard,* (February).
Roberts, Dorothy E. 1997. *Killing the Black Body: Race, Reproduction, and the Meaning of Liberty.* New York, NY: Pantheon Books.
Rockquemore, Kerry Ann 2002. 'Negotiating the Color Line: The Gendered Process of Racial Identity Construction among Black/White Biracial Women.' *Gender and Society* **16**: 485–503. African American Women: Gender Relations, Work and the Political Economy of the Twenty-First Century (August).
Rodriguez, Gregory. 2003. "Mongrel America," *Atlantic Monthly* (Jan./Feb) Volume 291, No. 1: 95–97.
———. 2003, "Dining at the Ethnicity Café," *L.A. Times,* (May 18): M3.
Rodriguez, Rishard. 2002. *Brown, The Last Discovery of America.* New York: Penguin Books.
Roediger, David 1999. *The Wages of Whiteness.* London: Verso.
———. 2003. *Colored White: Transcending the Racial Past.* Berkley: University of California Press.
———. 2005. *Working Toward Whiteness: How America's Immigrants Became White.* NY: Basic Books.
Roscigno, Vincent. 1998. "Race and the Reproduction of Educational Disadvantage." *Social Forces* 76: 1033–1060.
Rose, Peter 1. 1990 (1973). *They and We.* New York: Random House.
Roseberry-McKibbin, C. 1995. *Multicultural students with special language needs: Practical strategies for assessment and intervention.* Oceanside, CA: Academic Comm. Assoc.
Royster, Deirdre A. 2003. *Race and the Invisible Hand: How White Networks Exclude Men from Blue-Collar Jobs.* Berkeley: University of California Press.
Roznik, S. 2005. *Columbus controversial figure in continuing historical debate.* Accessed on March 1, 2006, at url: http://www.wisinfo.com/thereporter/news/archive/local_22863601.shtml
Russell, G. 2000. *Native American FAQ's handbook.* Phoenix, AZ: Russell Publications.

——. 2004. *American Indian facts of life*. Phoenix, AZ: Native Data Network.
Russell, Steve. 2002. 'Apples Are the Color of Blood.' *Critical Sociology* 28: 65–76.
——. 2002. *Racism and Cultural Studies: Critiques of Multiculturalist Ideology and the Politics of Difference*. Durham: Duke University Press.
Sampson, Robert J., and William Julius Wilson. 1995. "Toward a Theory of Race, Crime, and Urban Inequality." In *Crime and Inequality*, eds. John Hagan and Ruth Peterson, pp. 37–54. Stanford: Stanford University Press.
San Juan Jr., E. 2001. "Problems in the Marxist Project of Theorizing Race." Pp. 225–236 in *Racism: Essential Readings*, edited by Ellis Cashmore and James Jennings. London: Sage Publications.
Sanchez, Marta E. 1998. 'La Malinche at the Intersection: Race and Gender in Down These Mean Streets.' *PMLA* **113**: 117–28.
Santa Ana, Otto 2006. 'The Racial Politics behind Anti-Immigration Jokes.' UCLA Today. Accessed on June 12, 2007 at url http://www.today.ucla.edu/voices/otto-santa-ana_jokes/.
Scheurich, James Joseph. 1993. "Toward a White Discourse on White Racism." *Educational Researcher*, 22(8):5–10.
Schlesinger, Arthur M., Jr. 1992. *The Disuniting of America*. New York: Norton.
Schuman, Howard, Charlotte Steeh, Lawrence Bobo. and Maria Krysan. 1997. *Racial Attitudes in America: Trends and Interpretations, Revised Edition*. Cambridge, MA: Harvard University Press.
Scott-Heron, Gil. 2001. *Now and Then: The Poems of Gil Scott-Heron*. Edinburgh, Scotland: Payback Press.
Scott, Kesho Yvonne. 1991. *The Habit of Surviving: Black Women's Strategies for Life*. New Brunswick: Rutgers University Press.
Sears, David O. 1988. "Symbolic Racism." In *Eliminating Racism: Profiles in Controversy*, edited by Phylis A. Katz and Dalmas A. Taylor. New York: Plenum Press.
Sedlak, Andrea and Dana Schulz. 2005. "Race Differences in Risk of Maltreatment in the General Child Population." In *Race Matters in Child Welfare: The Overrepresentation of African American Children in the System*, edited by D. Derezotes, J. Poertner, and M. Testa. Washington, DC: CWLA Press.
Shapiro, Thomas M. 2004. *The Hidden Cost of Being African-American*. Oxford: Oxford University Press.
Sharfstein, Daniel 2003. "The Secret History of Race in the United States," 112 *Yale Law Journal*, 112: 1473.
Shibutani, Tamotsu. 1961. "Social Status in Reference Groups." In *Society and Personality: An Interactionist Approach to Social Psychology*. Englewood Cliffs, N.].: Prentice-Hall.
Shipler, David K. 1998. "Blacks in the newsroom: Progress? Yes but…"*Columbia Journalism Review*.
Sikes, Melvin P. 1994. *Living with Racism: The Black Middle Class Experience*. Boston: Beacon.
Sipuel v. Bd. Of Regents of the Univ. of Okla., 332 U.S. 814 (1947).
Sivanandan, A. 2005. 'Asian Youth Movements: Here to Stay, Here to Fight.' *Red Pepper*. http:// www.redpeper.org.uk/society/x-jun05-sivanandan.htm
Skaggs, Sheryl. 2001. "Discrimination Litigation: Implications for Women and Minorities in Retail Supermarket Management." Ph.D. dissertation, Department of Sociology, North Carolina State University, Raleigh, NC.
Skidmore, Thomas. 1993. "Biracial USA vs. Multiracial Brazil: Is the Contrast Still Valid?" *Journal of Latin American Studies*, 25:373–386.
Skrentny, John David. 1996. *The Ironies of Affirmative Action*. Chicago: University of Chicago Press.
——. 2002. "Inventing Race," 46 *Public Interests* 46:96–113.
Sleeter, C. 1994. White racism. *Multicultural Education* v1 n4 p. 5–8,39.

Smedley, Audrey. 1999. *Race in North America: Origins and Evolution of a Worldview* Boulder, CO: Westvew Press.
Smith, Craig. 2006. "In France a meal of intolerance." (Assessed on line September 26, 2006, at URL http://www.iht.com/articles/2006/02/27/news/journal.php)
Smith, James P., and Finnis R. Welch. 1986. *Closing the Gap, Forty Years of Economic Progress for Blacks.* Santa Monica, CA: Rand Corporation.
Smith, John David 2005. 'A Historic Life: John Hope Franklin Recalls His Distinguished Life and the Times He Helped Change.' *The News and Observer.* http://www.newsobserver.com/ 208/369295.html (last accessed July 11, 2007).
Smith, Ryan A. 2002. "Race, Gender, and Authority in the Workplace: Theory and Re search." *Annual Review of Sociology* 28:509–542.
Smith, Robert C. 1995. *Racism in the Post-Civil Rights Era, Now You See It, Now You Don't.* New York: State University of New York Press.
Smith, Stephen 2007. 'Test of Trainees Finds Signs of Race Bias in Care.' The Boston Globe, July 20 edition. http://www.boston.com/news/local/articles/2007/07/20/tests_of_er_trainees_ find_signs_of_race_bias_in_care/ (last accessed October 17, 2007).
Smith, William A. 1993–2003. "National African Americans Study." University of Illinois at Chicago and the University of Utah.
———. 2004a. "Battle Fatigue on the Front Lines of Race: Teaching About Race and Racism at Historically White Institutions."
———. 2004b. "Black Faculty Coping with Racial Battle Fatigue: The Campus Racial Climate in a Post-Civil Rights Era." Pp. 171–190 in *A Long Way To Go: Conversations About Race by African American Faculty and Graduate Students,* edited by D. Cleveland. New York Peter Lang.
———. 2004c. "The Impact of Racially Primed White Students on Black Faculty: Manifestations of Racial Battle Fatigue on Historically White Campuses."
Smith, William A., Philip G. Altbach, and Kofi Lomotey. 2002. "The Racial Crisis in American Higher Education: Continuing Challenges to the Twenty-First Century." Albany: State University of New York Press.
Sniderman, Paul, and Thomas Piazza. 1993. *The Scar of Race.* Cambridge, MA: Harvard University Press.
Sobel, M.E. 1994. "Causal Inference in Latent Variable Models." Pp. 3–35 in *Latent Variables Analysis: Applications for Developmental Research,* edited by A. von Eye and C.C. Clogg. Thousand Oaks, CA: Sage.
———. 1995. "Causal Inference in the Social and Behavioral Sciences." Pp. 1–38 in *Handbook of Statistical Modeling for the Social and Behavioral Sciences,* edited by G. Arminger, C.C. Clogg, and M.E. Sobel. New York: Plenum.
Solórzano, Daniel. 1997. "Images and Words that Wound: Critical Race Theory, Racial Stereotyping, and Teacher Education." *Teacher Education Quarterly* 24:5–19.
———. 1998. "Critical Race Theory, Race, Racial and Gender Microaggressions, and the Experiences of Chicana and Chicano Scholars." *International Journal of Qualitative Studies in Education* 11:121–136.
Solórzano, Daniel, Miguel Ceja, and Tara J. Yosso. 2000. "Critical Race Theory, Racial Microaggressions, and Campus Racial Climate: The Expereinces of African American College Students." *Journal of Negro Education* 69:60–73.
Solórzano, Daniel and Dolores Delgado Bernal. 2001. "Examining Transformational Resistance Through a Critical Race and LatCrit Theory Framework: Chicana and Chicano Students in an Urban Context." *Urban Education* 36:308–342.
Sowell, Thomas. 1984. *Civil Rights: Rhetoric of Reality?* New York: Morrow.
Spencer, Margaret B. and Carol Markstrom-Adams 1990. 'Identity Processes among Racial and Ethnic Minority Children in America.' *Child Development* 61: 290–310.

Staub, Ervin. 2003. *The Psychology of Good and Evil: Why Children, Adults, and Groups Help and Harm Others*. New York: Cambridge University Press.
Staples, B. 2005. When Democracy Died in Wilmington, N.C. *New York Times*, January 8. (Accessed online on February 5, 2006 from http://www.nytimes.com/2006/01/08/opinion/08sun3.html.
Steele, Shelby. 1990. *The Content of Our Character: A New Vision of Race in America*. New York: St. Martin's.
Steinberg, Stephen. 2001. *Turning Back: The Retreat from Racial Justice in American Thought and Policy*. Boston: Beacon Press.
Steinberg, Stephen. 2001. *The Ethnic Myth: Race, Ethnicity, and Class in America*. Boston: Beacon Press.
Stevenson, Howard C., Rick Cameron, Teri Herrero-Taylor and Gwen Davis 2002. 'Development of the Teenager Experience of Racial Socialization Scale: Correlates of Race-Related Socialization Frequency from the Perspectives of Black Youth.' *Journal of Black Psychology* 28: 84–106.
St. Jean, Yanick and Joe R. Feagin. 1998. *Double Burden: Black Women and Everyday Racism*. Armonk, N.Y.: M.E. Sharpe.
Stone, Pamela. 1996. "Ghettoized and Marginalized: The Coverage of Racial and Ethnic Groups in Introductory Sociology Texts." *Teaching Sociology* 24:356–63.
Stovall, Tyler 2003. 'National Identity and Shifting Imperial Frontiers: Whiteness and the Exclusion of Colonial Labor after World War I.' *Representations* 84: 52–72.
Street, Paul. 2009. *Barack Obama and the Future of American Politics*. Boulder: Paradigm.
Strong, John. *2001. We Are Still Here: The Algonquian Peoples of Long Island Today*. Interlaken, NY: Empire State Books.
——. 1999. *The Montaukett Indians of Eastern Long Island*. Syracuse, Syracuse University Press.
——. 1997. *The Algonquin Peoples of Long Island from the Earliest Times to 1700*. Interlaken, NY: Empire Books.
——. 1986. "From Hunter to Servant: Patterns of Accommodation to Colonial Authority in eastern Long Island Indian Communities," in *To Know the Place: Teaching Local History*, ed. Joann Krieg. New York: Long Island Historical Institute.
——. 1983. "How the Land was Lost: An Introduction" in *The Shinnecock Indians: A Cultural History*, edited by Gaynell Stone. Lexington, MA: Ginn Custom Publishing.
Stroobants, Jean-Pierre and Antoine Jacob. 2006. "The Netherlands Wants to Prohibit Burqua-Wearing." *Le Monde*, (Assessed on line October 23, 2006 at URL http://www.truthout.org/docs_2006/102306H.shtml)
Struyk, R. J., and M. A. Turner. 1986. "Exploring the Effects of Preferences on Urban Housing Markets." *Journal of Urban Economics* 119: 131–147.
Stryker, Perrin. 1953. "How Executives Get Jobs." *Fortune* 48(2): 117ff.
Sue, Derald Wing. 2003. *Overcoming our racism: The journey to liberation*. San Francisco, CA: Jossey-Bass.
Sue, Derald Wing, Capodilupo, Christina M, Torino, Gina C. Bucceri, Jenifer, M. Holder, Aisha, M, Nadal, Kevin, and Marta Esquilin. 2007. "Racial microaggressions in everyday life: Implications for clinical practice." *American Psychologist*, 62(4): 271–286.
Sugrue, Thomas J. 1993. "The Structures of Urban Poverty: The Reorganization of Space and Work in Three Periods of American History." In *The "Underclass" Debate: Views from History*, ed. Michael B. Katz, pp. 85–117. Princeton: Princeton University Press.
Suro, Roberto. 1999. "Mixed Doubles," *American Demographics*, (Nov) 21:56–62.

Suyemoto, K. and C. Fox Tree. 2006. Building bridges across differences to meet social action goals: Being and creating allies among People of Color. *American Journal of Community Psychology*, 37 (3-4): 237-246.

Szasz, Thomas 1997. *The Manufacture of Madness A Comparative Study of the Inquisition & the Mental Health Movement*. Syracuse, NY: Syracuse University Press.

Tate, William F. 1994. "From Inner City to Ivory Tower: Does My Voice Matter in the Academy." *Urban Education* 29:245-269.

——. 1997. "Critical Race Theory and Education: History, Theory, and Implications." *Review of Research in Education* 22:195-247.

Tatum, B. 2003. *Why are all the black kids sitting together in the cafeteria?* New York: Basic Books.

——. 1992. Talking about race, learning about racism: The application of racial identity development theory in the classroom. *Harvard Educational Review*, 62(1): 1-23.

Taylor, Charles, and Barbara B. Stern. 1997. "Asian-Americans: Television Advertising and the 'Model Minority' Stereotype." *Journal of Advertising* 26:47-61.

Taylor, Charles, Ju Yung Lee, and Barbara B. Stern. 1995. "Portrayals of African, Hispanic, and Asian Americans in Magazine Advertising." *American Behavioral Scientist* 38:608-621.

Taylor, Marylee. 1995. "White Backlash to Workplace Affirmative Action: Peril or Myth." *Social Forces* 73:1385-414.

Tehranian, John/ 2000. "Performing Whiteness: Naturalization Litigation and the Construction of Racial Identity in America," *Yale Law Journal* 109(4): 817-827.

The Himalayan Times Online. 2004. "Rimi Sen Calls Black Africans Ugly." Retrieved January 14, 2008 (www.thehimalayantimes.com).

Therborn, Goran. 1980. *The Ideology of Power and the Power of Ideology*. London: Verso.

Thernstrom, Abigail and Stephan. 2003. *No Excuses: Closing the Racial Gap in Learning*. New York: Simon & Schuster.

——.2006. *Silent Racism: How Well-Meaning White People Perpetuate the Racial Divide*. Boulder, CO: Paradigm.

——.20010. "Lessening Racial Disproportionality of Children by Recognizing Silent Racism." Paper in progress.

Thomas, Audrey and Samuel Sillen 1972. *Racism and Psychiatry*. New York, NY: Brunner/ Mazel.

Thurow, Lester C. 1975. *Generating Inequality*. New York: Basic Books.

——. 1969. *Poverty and Discrimination*. Washington, D.C.: The Brookings Institute.

Tolnay, Stewart, and E. M. Beck. 1991. "Rethinking the Role of Racial Violence in the Great Migration." In *Black Exodus: The Great Migration from the American South*, edited by Alferdteen Harrison. Jackson, MS: University of Mississippi Press.

Tomaskovic-Devey, Donald 1993. *Gender & Racial Inequality at Work: The Sources and Consequences of Job Segregation*. Ithaca, NY: Cornell ILR Press.

Travis, Dempsey J. 1991. *Racism-American Style: A Corporate Gift*. Chicago: Urban Research Press Inc.

Trepagnier, Barbara. 2001. "Deconstructing Categories: The Exposure of Silent Racism." *Symbolic Interaction* 24(2):141-163.

Tuan, Mia. 2001. *Forever Foreigners or Honorary Whites? The Asian Ethnic Experience Today*. New Brunswick, NJ: Rutgers University Press.

Tucker, W.H. 1994. *The Science and Politics of Racial Research*. Urbana: University of Illinois Press.

Tulsa Historical Society. (n.d.). *The Tulsa Race Riot*. Retrieved February 5, 2006, from http://www.tulsahistory.org/learn/riot.htm.

Turner, Margery A., Raymond Struyk, and John Yinger. 1991. *The Housing Discrimination Study*. Washington D. C.: The Urban Institute.

Turner, Margery A., and Felicity Skidmore. 1999. *Mortgage Lending Discrimination: A Review of Existing Evidence*. Washington, D.C.: Urban Institute.

Turner, Margery A., Stephen L. Ross, George Galster, and John Yinger. 2002. *Discrimination in Metropolitan Housing Markets*. Washington, D.C.: Urban Institute.

Turner, Stephen 1974. *Weber and Islam: A Critical study*. London: Routledge & Kegan Paul.

Tuttle, William M., Jr. 1970. "Labor Conflict and Racial Violence: The Black Worker in Chicago, 1894–1919." In *Black Labor in America*, edited by Milton Cantor. Westport, CN: Negro Universities Press.

United States Bureau of the Census. 2002. *The American Indian and Alaska Native population: 2000*. Accessed on line on September 23, 2009 at url: www.census.gov/prod/2002pubs/c2kbr01-15.pdf

US Bureau of the Census. 2004. *US Interim Projections by Age, Sex, Race, and Hispanic Origin*, http://www.census.gov/ipc/www/usinterimproj.

U.S. Census Bureau. 2000. *American Community Survey*. http://www.census.gov/acs/www/

U.S. Census Bureau. 2006. *Statistical Abstract of the United States: 2006*. Washington D.C.: U.S. Government Printing Office.

U. S. Equal Employment Opportunity Commission. 2003. "Muslim/ Arab Employment Discrimination Charges since September 11," Washington, D.C.: Government Printing Office (Accessed July 2, 2007 at url http://www.eeoc.gov/origin/z-stats.html)

U.S. Department of Housing and Urban Development. 1999. *The State of Cities*. Washington, DC: Government Printing Office. (Accessed on Feburary 13, 2008 at url http//www.dol.gov/esa/minwage/chart.pdf.)

U.S. Department of Labor. 2008. *Federal Minimum Wage Rates Under the Fair Labor Standards Act*. (Accessed on Feburary 13, 2008 at url http://www.dol.gov/esa/minwage/chart.pdf).

Van Ausdale, Debra and Joe R. Feagin 2001. *The First R: How Children Learn Race and Racism*. Lanham, MD: Rowman and Littlefield.

van den Oord, J.C.G. and D.C. Rowe. 2000. "Racial Differences in Birth Health Risk: A Quantitative Genetic Approach." *Demography* 37:285–98.

Van Dijk, Teun A. 1993. *Elite Discourse and Racism*. Newbury Park, CA: Sage Publications.

Venezia, Todd. 2007. "Baby Bungle: White folks' black child" *The New York Post*, March 22, 2007.

Vera, Hernán and Joe R. Feagin. 1995. "African Americans' Inflicted Anomie." Pp. 155–72 in *Race and Ethnicity in America: Meeting the Challenge in 21st Century*, edited by Gail E. Thomas. Washington DC: Taylor and Francis Publishers.

Virdi, Jyotika. 2003. *The Cinematic Imagination: Indian Popular Films as Social History*. NJ: Rutgers University Press.

Wagner, Helmut. 1970. *Alfred Schutz: On Phenomenology and Social Relations*. Chicago: University of Chicago Press.

Wallin, Bruce A. 2005. "Budgeting for Basics: The Changing Landscape of City Finances." Discussion paper prepared for the Brookings Institution Metropolitan Policy Program. Washington, DC: Brookings Institution, August.

Walsh, Keith 2004. 'Color-Blind Racism in Grutter and Gratz.' *Boston College Third World Law Journal* **24**: 443–67. Washington Post 2003. 'The Mendacity Index.' http://www.washingtonmonthly.com/features/ 2003/0309.mendacity-index.html (last accessed October 20, 2007)

Warren, Jonathan and Twine, France Winddance. 1997. "White Americans, the New Minority?" 28 *Journal Black Studies* 28(2): 200–218.

Washington, J. M. (ed.). 1986. *A testament of hope: The essential writings and speeches of Martin Luther King, Jr*. New York: Harper Collins.

Wellman, David.1993. *Portraits of White racism* (Second Edition). New York: Cambridge University Press.
Wellman, David T. 1977. *Portraits of White Racism*. New York: Cambridge University Press.
West, Cornell 1994. *Race Matters*. New York, NY: Vintage.
Westhues, Kenneth. 1991. "Transcending the Textbook World." *Teaching Sociology* 19:87-92.
White, Bob W. 1996. 'Talk about School: Education and the Colonial Project in French and British Africa (1860-1960).' *Comparative Education* **32**: 9-25.
Williams, David R., Harold W. Neighbors, and James S. Jackson. 2003. "Racial/Ethnic Discrimination and Health: Findings from Community Studies." *American Journal of Public Health* 93:200-208.
Williams, J. (ed.). 1992. *Eyes on the prize* [Television series]. PBS Production.
Williams, Kim, M. 2005. "Multiracialism and the Civil Rights Future," *Daedalus* 134(1) 53-60.
Williams, Kim, M. 2006. *Mark One or More: Civil Rights in Multiracial America*. Ann Arbor: The University of Michigan Press.
Williams, Patricia J. 1991. *The Alchemy of Race and Rights: Diary of a Law Professor*. Cambridge, MA: Harvard University Press.
———. 2007. "Being A Black Man". *The Washington Post*, January 7, 2007.
Williams, Raymond. 1989. *The Politics of Modernism: Against the New Conformists*. London: Verso Press
Williams, Richard, Reynold Nesiba, and Eileen Diaz McConnell. 2005. "The Changing Face of Inequality in Home Mortgage Lending." *Social Problems* 52: 181-208.
Willie, Charles V. 1989. *Caste and Class Controversy on Race and Poverty: Round Two of the Willie/Wilson Debate*. New York: General Hall Inc.
Willie, Charles V. and Jayminn S. Sanford. 1995. "Turbulence on the College Campus and the Frustration-Aggression Hypothesis." Pp. 253-276 in *Mental health, racism, and sexism*, edited by C. V. Willie, P. Rieker, B. Kramer, and B. Brown. Pittsburgh, PA: University of Pittsburgh Press.
Wilson, E.O. 1998. *Consilience: The Unity of Knowledge*. New York: Knopf.
Wilson, George. 1997. "Pathways to Power: Racial Differences in the Determinants of Job Authority." *Social Problems* 44:38-54
Wilson, George, Ian Sakura-Lemessy, and Jonathan P. West. 1999. "Reaching the Top: Racial Differences in Mobility Paths to Upper-Tier Occupations." *Work and Occupations* 26: 165-186.
Wilson, William J. 1978. *The Declining Significance of Race*. Chicago: The University of Chicago Press.
———. 1987. *The Truly Disadvantaged*. Chicago: The University of Chicago Press.
———.1996. *When Work Disappears: The New World of the Urban Poor*. New York: Knopf.
Winant, Howard. 1994. *Racial Conditions: Politics, Theory, Comparisons*. Minneapolis: University of Minnesota Press.
Woodward, C. Vann. 1966. *The Strange Career of Jim Crow, Second Revised Edition*. New York: Oxford University Press.
Wynn, Neil A. 1993. *The Afro-American and the Second World War, Revised Edition*. New York: Holmes and Meir.
Yancey, George. 2003. *Who is White? Latinos, Asians, and the New Black/Nonblack Divide*. Boulder, CO: Lynne Rienner Publishers.
Yanich, Danilo. 2001. "Location, Location, Location: Urban and Suburban Crime on Local TV News." *Journal of Urban Affairs*, 23(3-4).
Yinger, John. 1986. "Measuring Discrimination with Fair Housing Audits: Caught in the Act." *American Economic Review* 76: 881-893.
———.1995. *Closed Doors, Opportunities Lost: The Continuing Costs of Housing Discrimination*. New York: Russell Sage Foundation.

———. 2001. "Housing Discrimination and Residential Segregation as Causes of Poverty." In *Understanding Poverty*, edited by Sheldon H. Danziger and Robert H. Haveman. New York: Russell Sage.
Yosso, Tara J. 2006. *Critical Race Counterstories Along the Chicana/Chicano Educational Pipeline*. New York: Routledge.
Zackodnik, Teresa. 2001. "Fixing the Color Line: The Mulatto, Southern Courts, and Racial Identity," *American Quarterly* 53(3):420–451.
———. 2001. *Thicker Than Blood: An Essay on How Racial Statistics Lie*. Minneapolis: University of Minnesota Press.
——— and Eduardo Bonilla-Silva. 2008. *White Logic, White Methods: Racism and Methodology*. New York: Rowman and Littlefield, Inc.
Zhou, Min. 2004. "Are Asian Americans Becoming 'White'?" *Context* 3:29–37.
Zinn, H. 2003. *A people's history of the United States: 1492 – present*. New York: Harper Collins.
Zuberi, T. 2000. "Deracializing Social Statistics: Problems in the Quantification of Race." *Annals of the American Academy of Political and Social Science* 568:172–85.
Zweignhaft, Richard L. and Domhoff, G. William. 1998. *Diversity in the Power Elite: Have Women and Minorities Reached the Top?* New Haven, CT: Yale University Press.

INDEX

active bystanders 357
Affirmative Action 5, 13, 52, 53, 55, 88, 97, 102–104, 143, 145–147, 152, 247, 257, 275, 277, 292–295, 298, 302, 314–319, 325, 401
American Dream 9, 156, 158, 161, 163, 164, 286, 328, 331
autoethnographic lens 321
Aaversive racism 111–119, 195

benign neglect 121, 123, 124, 137, 244, 253
bias 21, 24, 30, 31, 33, 51, 58, 80, 81, 88, 104, 111–119, 123, 131, 134, 137, 143, 144, 146, 149, 151, 152, 175, 180, 183, 185–187, 222, 241, 244, 247, 248, 253, 258, 259, 358, 359, 366, 396, 398–400, 411
biologizing of blackness 12, 270
Bi-racial 156, 171
black ghetto 24, 28
blaming the victim 7, 242, 341
Bollywood 8, 9, 156, 158–161, 165–171
boundary heightening 8, 144, 148, 151

Civil Rights Movement 5, 13, 65, 86, 92, 101, 103, 105, 219, 230, 270, 272, 275, 292, 294, 314–316, 356, 362, 363, 405, 411–413
Color blind 2, 11, 121, 197, 214, 242, 244, 250, 251
  White Dominance 5, 90, 106
colorism 155, 156, 161, 169
conceptualized group 356
conspiracy of silence 125
contemporary racism 6, 113, 119, 378
counter storytelling 215–217, 233–235
covert Racism 1–3, 5–17, 121–127, 129, 130, 133, 136, 157, 193, 196, 239, 241–248, 253, 255, 256, 258–260, 321, 323, 331–334, 336, 339, 341, 342, 344, 347, 349, 385, 400, 402, 405, 415, 416, 421, 422, 424–426
  individual level covert racism 7, 11, 122
  informal covert racism 7, 122, 124, 127, 355
  group level covert racism 7, 122

critical race theory 8, 211
cultural studies 8, 386

decoupling 148
diversity 8, 65, 118, 127, 143–152, 156, 234, 315, 325, 327, 329, 330, 339, 402, 407
driving while black 4, 72, 367

emotional segregation 156, 161, 166
enlightened colonialism 247–250
ethnography
everyday racism 14, 354, 356–358, 360, 365–367, 370, 372, 374, 377, 379–381
exceptionalism 7, 87, 88, 127, 289
exotic other 127, 128

formal covert racism 133

genteel racism 247–249, 262, 437
Great migration 25, 26, 37, 44

holistic experiences 14, 365, 366, 368, 370, 374, 379, 381, 382
honorary whites 94–96, 98

identity politics 14, 284, 387
imperialism 199, 325, 329
Indians 8, 9, 156, 157, 158, 161–163, 165–171, 279, 388, 390, 392, 405
indirect institutional racism 358–360
inequality 4, 14, 23, 36, 37, 42, 52, 59–61, 75, 80, 85, 86, 89, 92, 99–101, 113, 143, 147, 150, 189–191, 194, 196, 201, 203, 204, 206, 239, 251, 253, 260, 292, 295, 323, 353, 354, 356–358, 360, 402
Institutional racism 118, 242, 252, 339, 342, 343, 345, 347, 350, 353, 358–360, 362, 363, 371
intercentricity 214
invidious 123
invisible racism 405

Jim Crow 4, 42–45, 47, 51, 55, 60, 100–104, 201, 243, 247, 285, 287, 356

Latin Americanization 87–90, 99
Levittown 23

marginalize 2, 9, 10, 124, 136, 162, 166, 198, 291, 305, 317, 318, 328, 342, 408, 422
model minority 94, 123, 127, 155, 170, 201
modern racism 195, 339
multi-racial coalition 171
multiracialists 89

Native Americans 13, 93, 155, 158, 201, 329, 333–338, 341, 343–348, 350, 388, 392, 393, 395
neo-interracialism 12
non-racial structures 3, 21, 23, 28, 31, 37, 45, 60

oppositional categories 354, 355, 356, 357, 359, 362
oral tradition 333, 334
overt racism 10, 112, 133, 196, 204, 242, 243, 259, 362, 367, 423

pariah 123, 127
passive bystanders 119, 357, 358
passive racism 13
paternalistic assumptions 355, 356
plausible deniability 2, 10, 422
political action 3, 20, 37, 386
post-civil rights 3, 13, 42, 51, 61, 155, 250
postmodern 362
post-racial 15, 59, 421
   post-racial narrative 15
production of racism 9, 189–191

Race
   awareness 353, 360–363
   related stress 211, 220
   relations 4, 13, 41–43, 45, 85, 90, 96, 99, 119, 143, 199, 203, 292, 299, 416
   racelessness 12, 255, 323
Racial
   attitudes 3, 4, 6, 19, 117, 119, 152, 246, 327
   battle fatigue 10, 212, 213, 215, 217, 220, 222, 227, 228, 233–235
   blindness 10, 259
   boundaries 15, 149
   codes 2, 10, 15, 123, 127, 128, 130, 257
   conservatives 102

discourse 4, 42, 45, 189, 197, 198
discrimination 6, 20, 33, 38, 45, 88, 102, 132, 136, 158, 162, 187, 213, 250, 258, 292, 294, 317, 381, 387, 395, 399
disproportionality 358, 359, 361
divide 96, 252, 358, 360, 363
domination 19, 90, 103, 240
dynamic 5, 54, 59, 90, 92, 106, 127, 131, 132, 133, 387
essentialism 123, 128
etiquette 126, 255
futures 87
genetics 69, 73
hierarchy 8, 86–88, 91–93, 99, 100, 155–157, 162, 198–200, 204, 369
ideology 41, 43, 91, 100, 106, 190
language 5, 357
matrix 1, 2, 11, 13, 15, 16, 241, 421
meanings 15
micro-aggression 10, 11, 212–214, 216, 217, 219, 220, 222, 225, 227–229, 233, 334
myth 15, 421
narratives 12
norms 94, 118, 195, 243, 299, 365
other 6, 7, 10, 156, 393
outcomes 3–5, 10, 243, 251
patterns 7
policies 23
pride movements 95
profiling 123
reasoning 4, 5, 12, 69, 72, 73, 79–82
results 5, 57, 242
shunning 7, 124, 125
statistics 69, 71, 73, 74, 76, 78, 81, 82
status quo 6, 14, 15, 86, 92, 101, 102, 189, 203, 362
structures 3, 10
superiority 86, 90, 105
supremacy 5, 395
values 4, 8
views 15, 196
racialization 6, 94, 95, 201, 240, 241, 246, 321, 327, 388
racialized 6, 8–10, 12, 14, 51, 58, 94, 124, 126–129, 143, 145, 146, 148, 150, 175, 192, 194, 195, 197–206, 211, 215, 216, 218, 225, 239, 240, 243, 244, 246, 250, 251, 253, 255, 259, 322, 324, 326, 374, 377, 382, 389, 422
elites 124, 126, 244, 255
non-elites 10, 124, 126, 127
situations 9, 124

INDEX

racism continuum 354, 356, 362, 363
reactionary colorblindness 102, 106
rearticulation 4, 42, 259
red-lining 135
reproducing racism 60, 157
reproduction of racism 9, 189–191

scapegoat 106
segmentation 51, 54, 65, 79
self-fulfilling prophecies 245
shadowless participation 251, 252
silent racism 14, 353–362
social justice 215, 326, 327, 334, 335, 339, 398
social representation 189
spatial dimensions 366, 372
statistical causation 70
stereotype 8, 58, 105, 123, 129, 130, 135, 136, 144, 149, 150, 152, 165, 166, 180, 185, 187, 197, 201, 249, 254, 258, 270, 311, 334, 341, 345, 346, 350, 362, 367, 368, 372, 379, 410
systemic 7, 8, 10, 13, 34, 37, 122, 135, 243, 244, 246, 322, 323, 334, 342, 343, 361, 365, 374, 376, 380, 381, 408, 411, 416

Token Minority 127
twoness 302
typology 7, 122, 297

White
  dominance 5, 85, 90–93, 97, 100, 102, 106
  lives 11, 321, 323, 327, 328, 331, 332
  meditations 328
  privilege 11, 12, 13, 56, 91, 190, 203, 223, 321, 324, 325, 329, 330, 331, 332, 348, 358, 361, 367
  racism 104, 105, 106, 195, 257, 365, 366, 370, 372, 374, 376
whiteness 8, 9, 11, 12, 15, 87, 92–99, 133, 134, 156, 161, 162, 165, 166, 169–171, 197, 198, 204, 205, 250, 279, 280, 282, 284, 287, 289, 324, 328, 366, 389

xenophobia 88, 94